CANNABIS

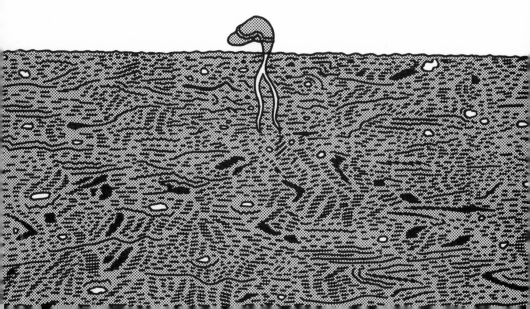

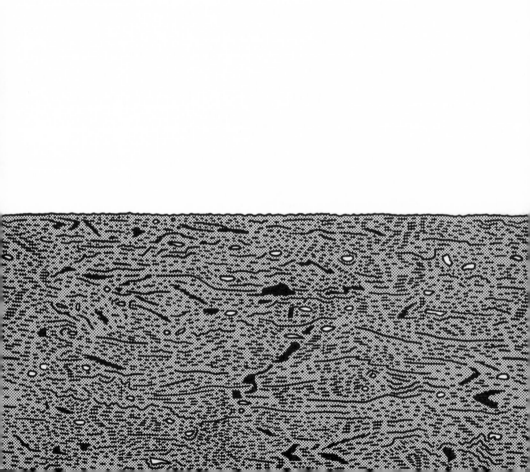

BOX BROWN

CANNABIS

The
Illegalization
of Weed
in America

:01

First Second
NEW YORK

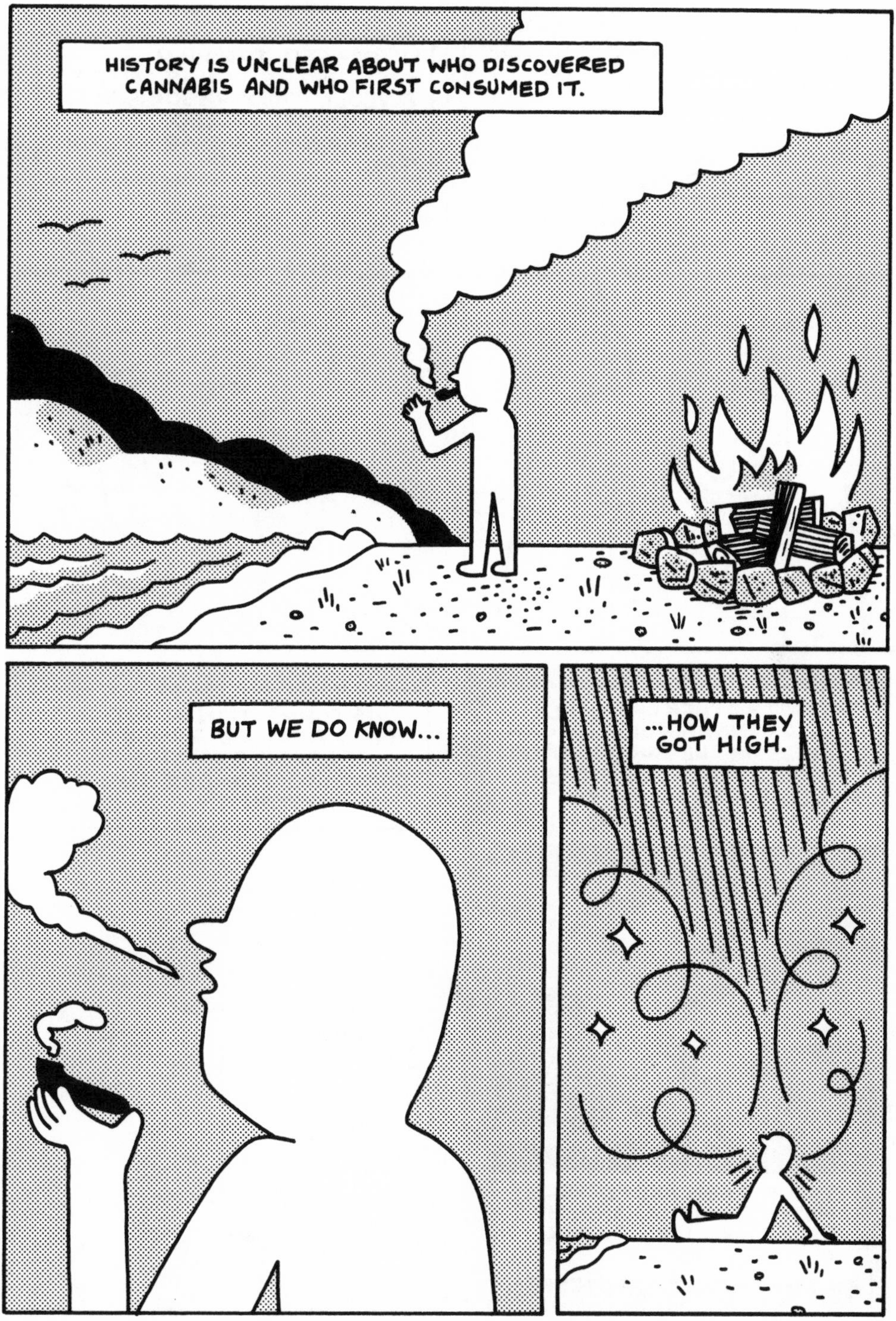
HISTORY IS UNCLEAR ABOUT WHO DISCOVERED CANNABIS AND WHO FIRST CONSUMED IT.
BUT WE DO KNOW...
...HOW THEY GOT HIGH.

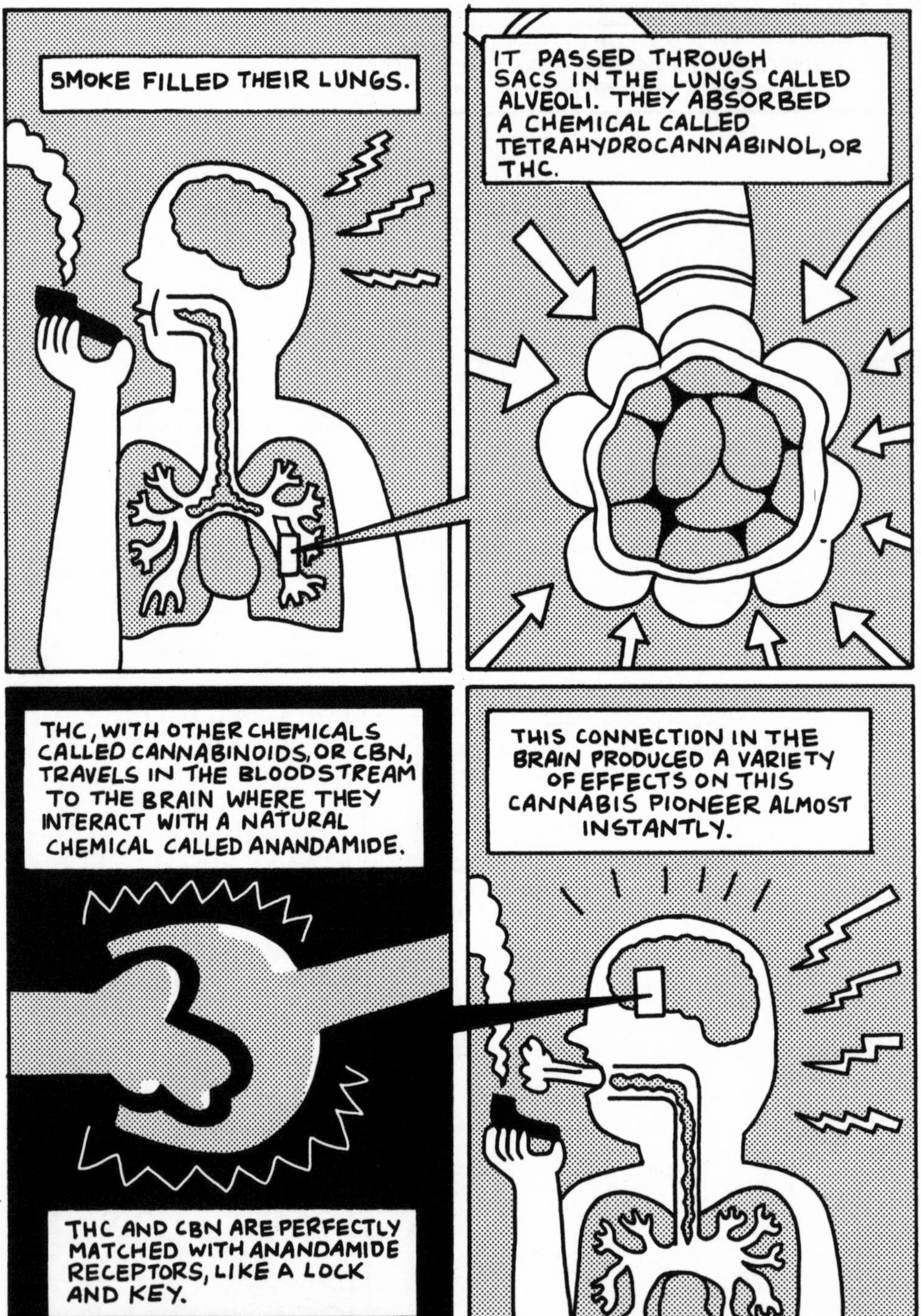
SMOKE FILLED THEIR LUNGS.
IT PASSED THROUGH SACS IN THE LUNGS CALLED ALVEOLI. THEY ABSORBED A CHEMICAL CALLED TETRAHYDROCANNABINOL, OR THC.
THC, WITH OTHER CHEMICALS CALLED CANNABINOIDS, OR CBN, TRAVELS IN THE BLOODSTREAM TO THE BRAIN WHERE THEY INTERACT WITH A NATURAL CHEMICAL CALLED ANANDAMIDE.
THC AND CBN ARE PERFECTLY MATCHED WITH ANANDAMIDE RECEPTORS, LIKE A LOCK AND KEY.
THIS CONNECTION IN THE BRAIN PRODUCED A VARIETY OF EFFECTS ON THIS CANNABIS PIONEER ALMOST INSTANTLY.

THE RECEPTORS ARE FOUND IN THE BRAIN AND NERVOUS SYSTEM BUT ALSO IN THE IMMUNE SYSTEM.

THIS REDUCED ANY INFLAMMATION IN THEIR BODY.

THEIR NAUSEA WAS ALLEVIATED

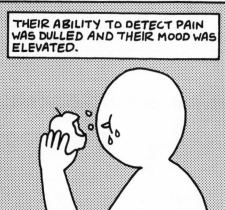

THEIR ABILITY TO DETECT PAIN WAS DULLED AND THEIR MOOD WAS ELEVATED.

AND THEIR SENSE OF CREATIVITY WAS STIMULATED.

SOME USERS CAN BECOME PARANOID.

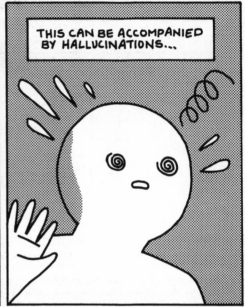

THIS CAN BE ACCOMPANIED BY HALLUCINATIONS...

...AND OTHER UNWANTED EFFECTS SUCH AS DISORIENTATION, SHORT-TERM MEMORY IMPAIRMENT, AND EVEN HEIGHTENED SENSITIVITY TO PAIN.

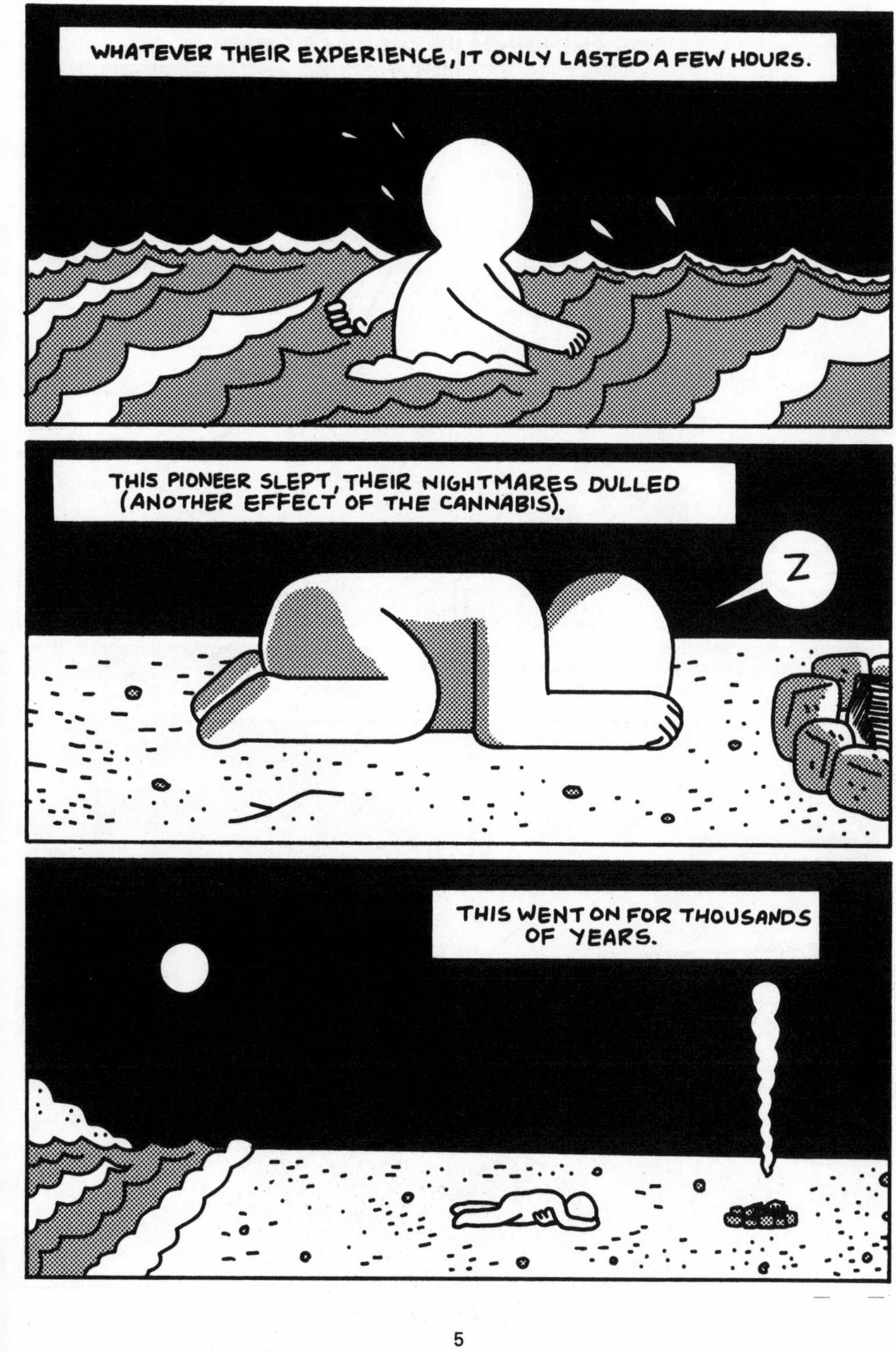
WHATEVER THEIR EXPERIENCE, IT ONLY LASTED A FEW HOURS.
THIS PIONEER SLEPT, THEIR NIGHTMARES DULLED (ANOTHER EFFECT OF THE CANNABIS).
Z
THIS WENT ON FOR THOUSANDS OF YEARS.

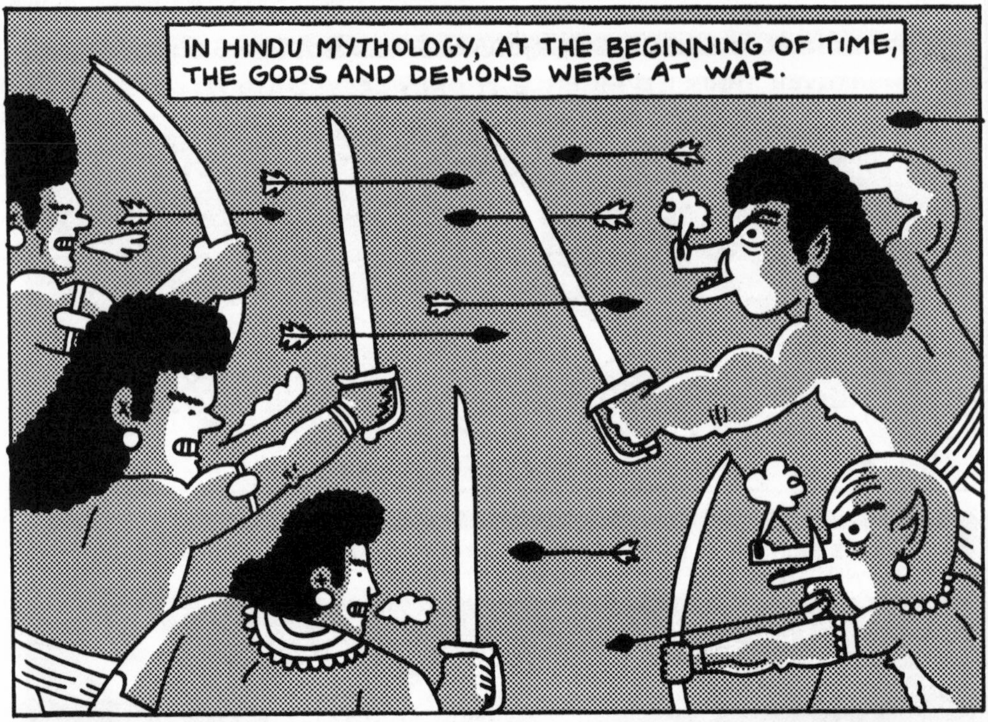
IN HINDU MYTHOLOGY, AT THE BEGINNING OF TIME, THE GODS AND DEMONS WERE AT WAR.

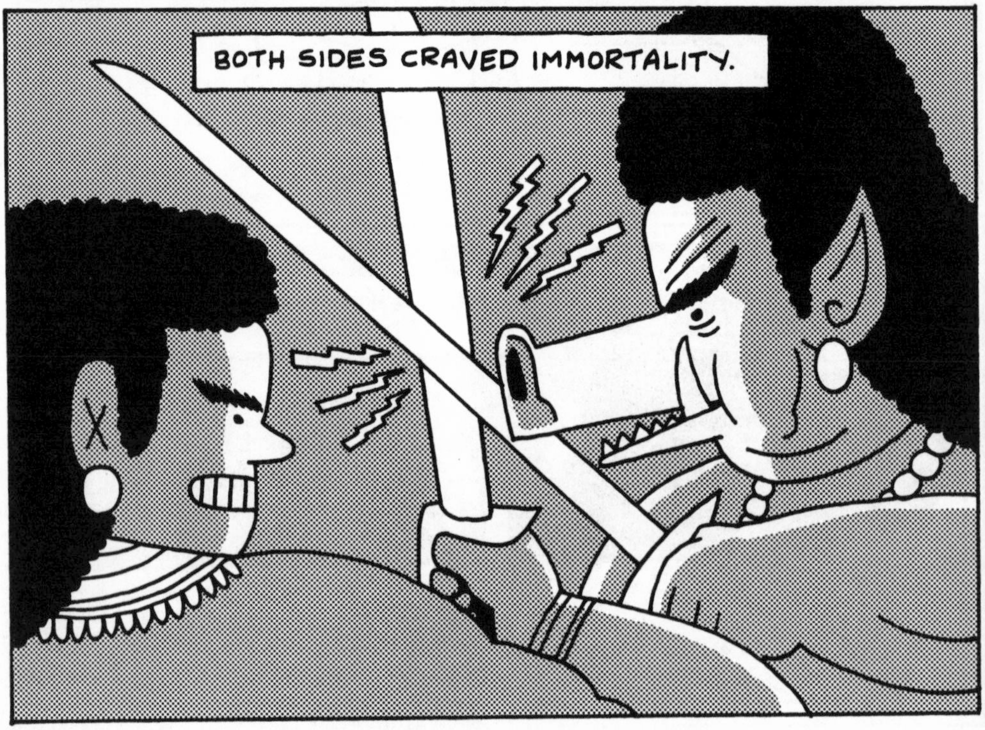
BOTH SIDES CRAVED IMMORTALITY.

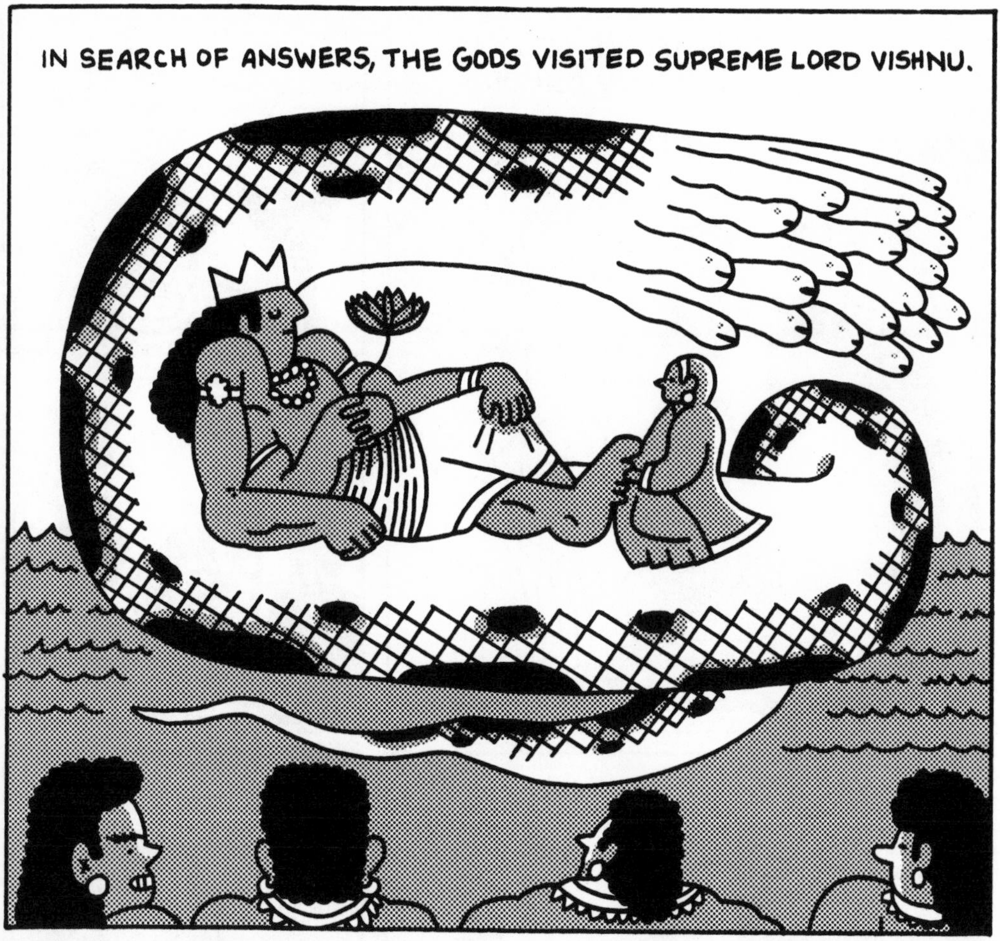
IN SEARCH OF ANSWERS, THE GODS VISITED SUPREME LORD VISHNU.

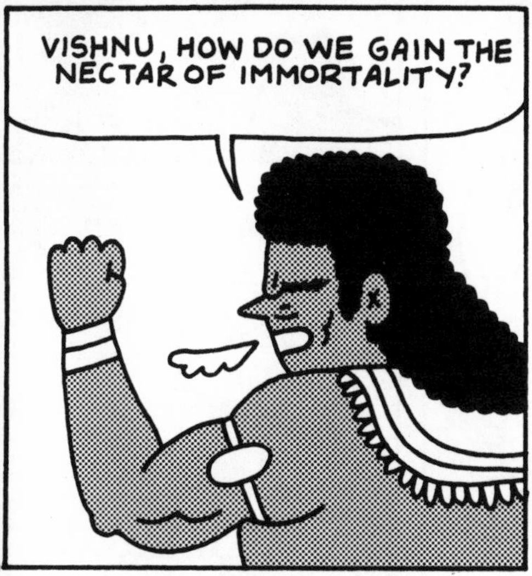
VISHNU, HOW DO WE GAIN THE NECTAR OF IMMORTALITY?

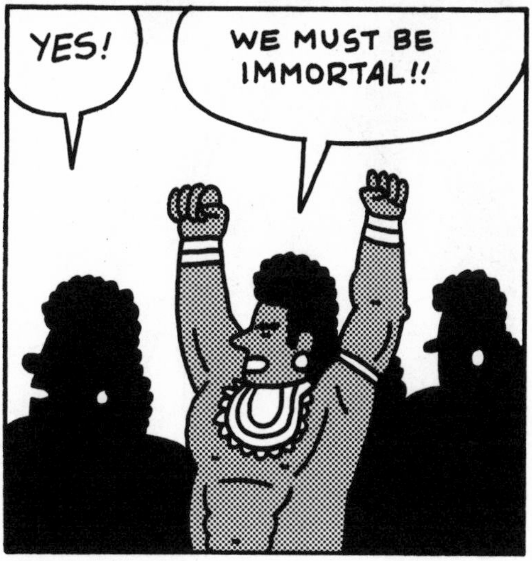
YES!
WE MUST BE IMMORTAL!!

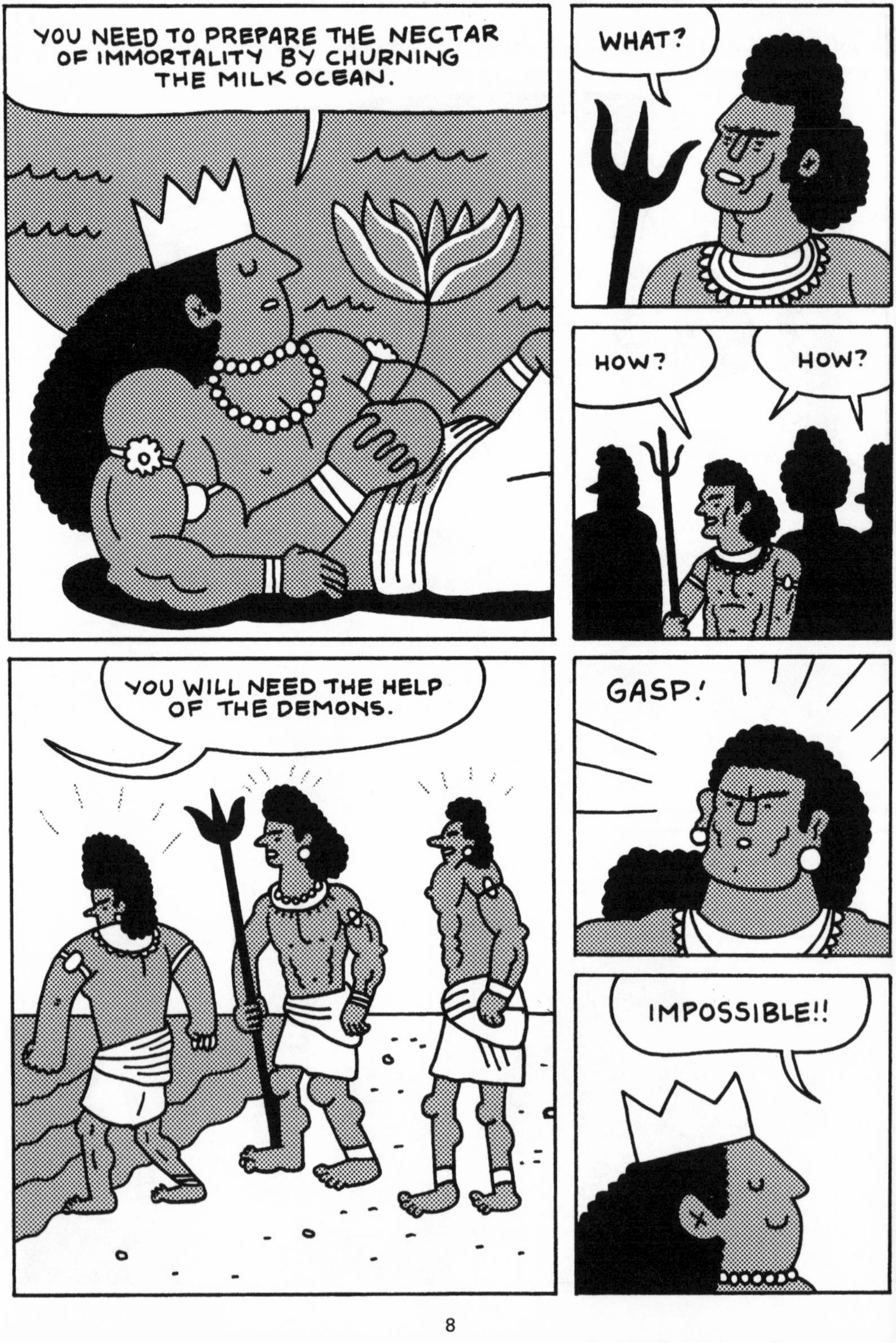
YOU NEED TO PREPARE THE NECTAR OF IMMORTALITY BY CHURNING THE MILK OCEAN.
WHAT?
HOW?
HOW?
YOU WILL NEED THE HELP OF THE DEMONS.
GASP!
IMPOSSIBLE!!

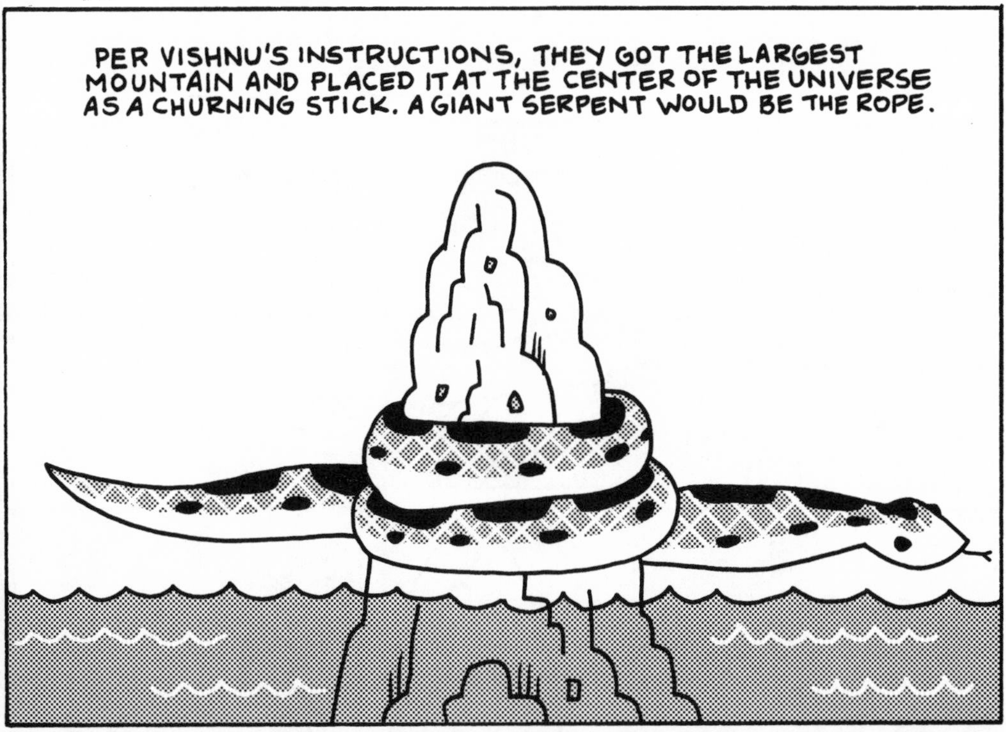
PER VISHNU'S INSTRUCTIONS, THEY GOT THE LARGEST MOUNTAIN AND PLACED IT AT THE CENTER OF THE UNIVERSE AS A CHURNING STICK. A GIANT SERPENT WOULD BE THE ROPE.

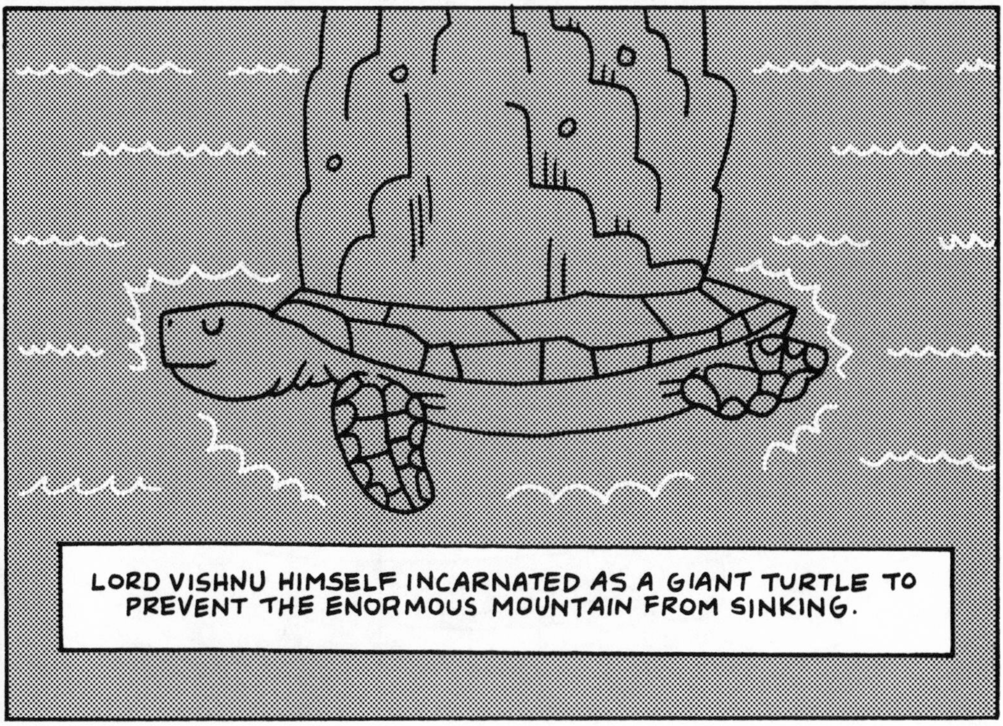
LORD VISHNU HIMSELF INCARNATED AS A GIANT TURTLE TO PREVENT THE ENORMOUS MOUNTAIN FROM SINKING.

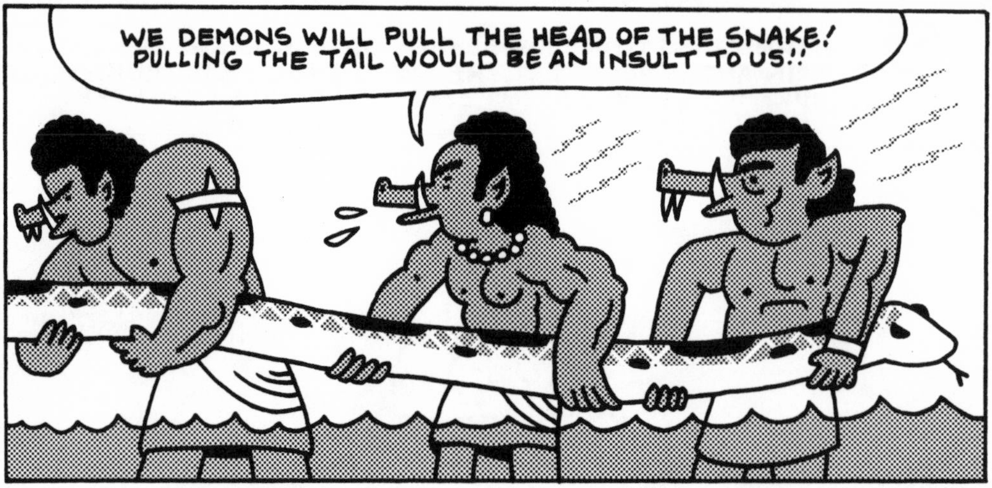
WE DEMONS WILL PULL THE HEAD OF THE SNAKE!
PULLING THE TAIL WOULD BE AN INSULT TO US!!

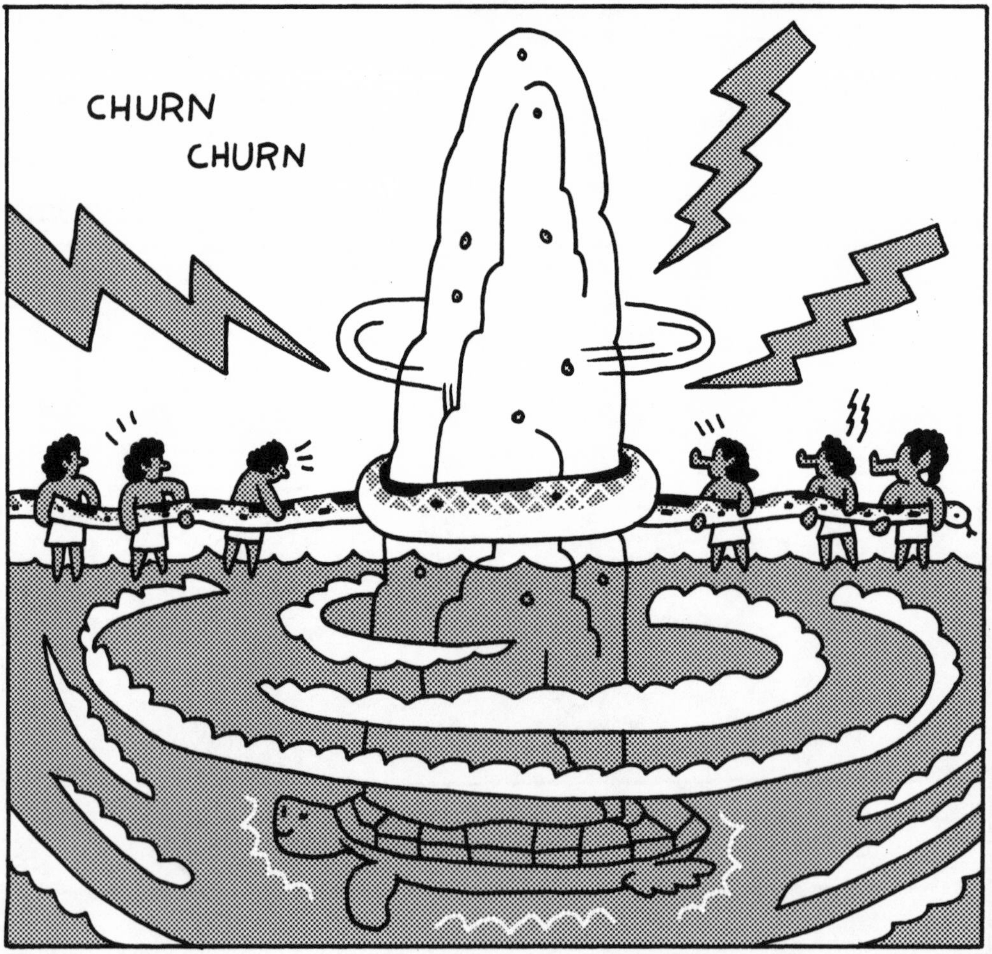
CHURN
CHURN

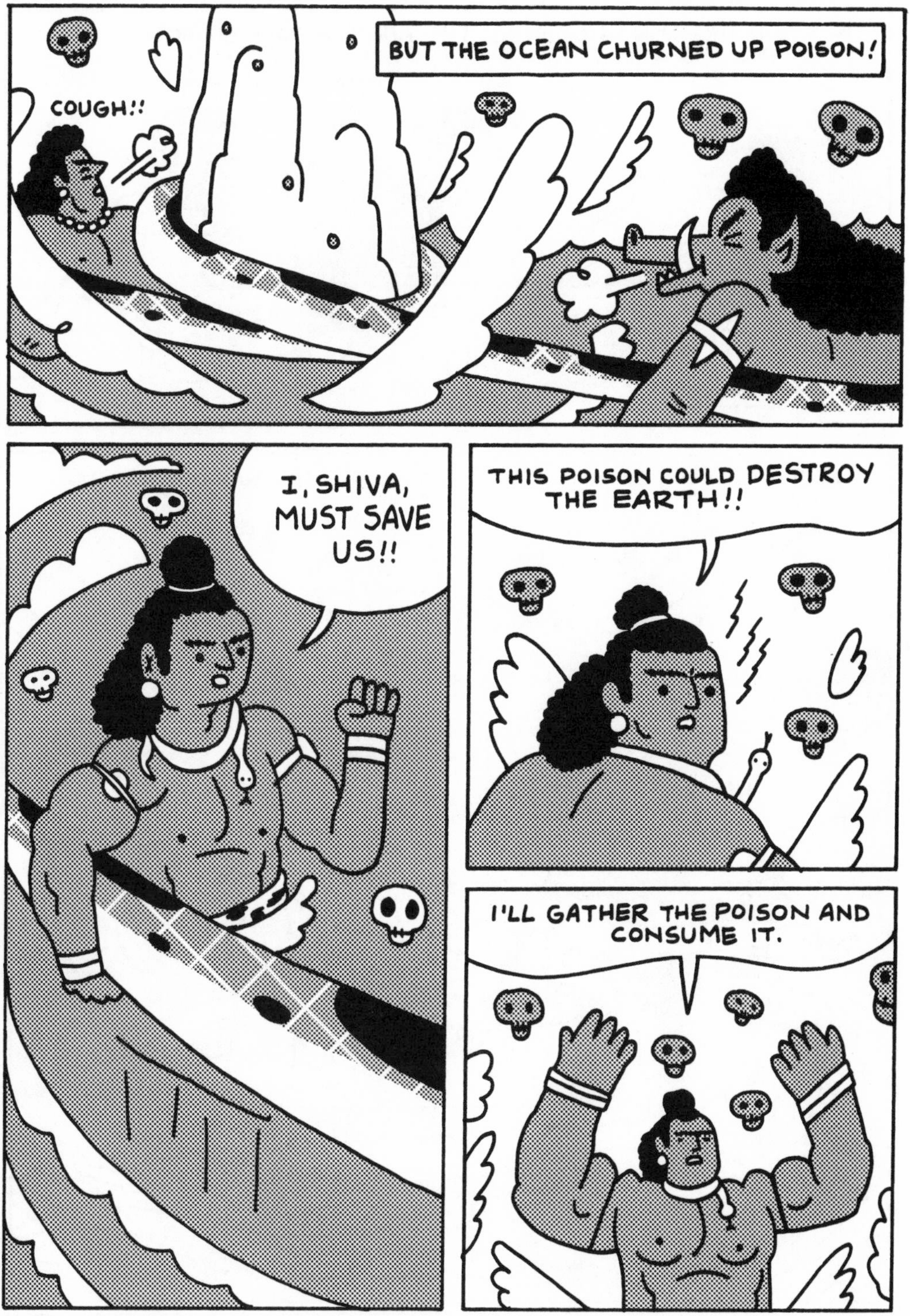
BUT THE OCEAN CHURNED UP POISON!
COUGH!!
I, SHIVA, MUST SAVE US!!
THIS POISON COULD DESTROY THE EARTH!!
I'LL GATHER THE POISON AND CONSUME IT.

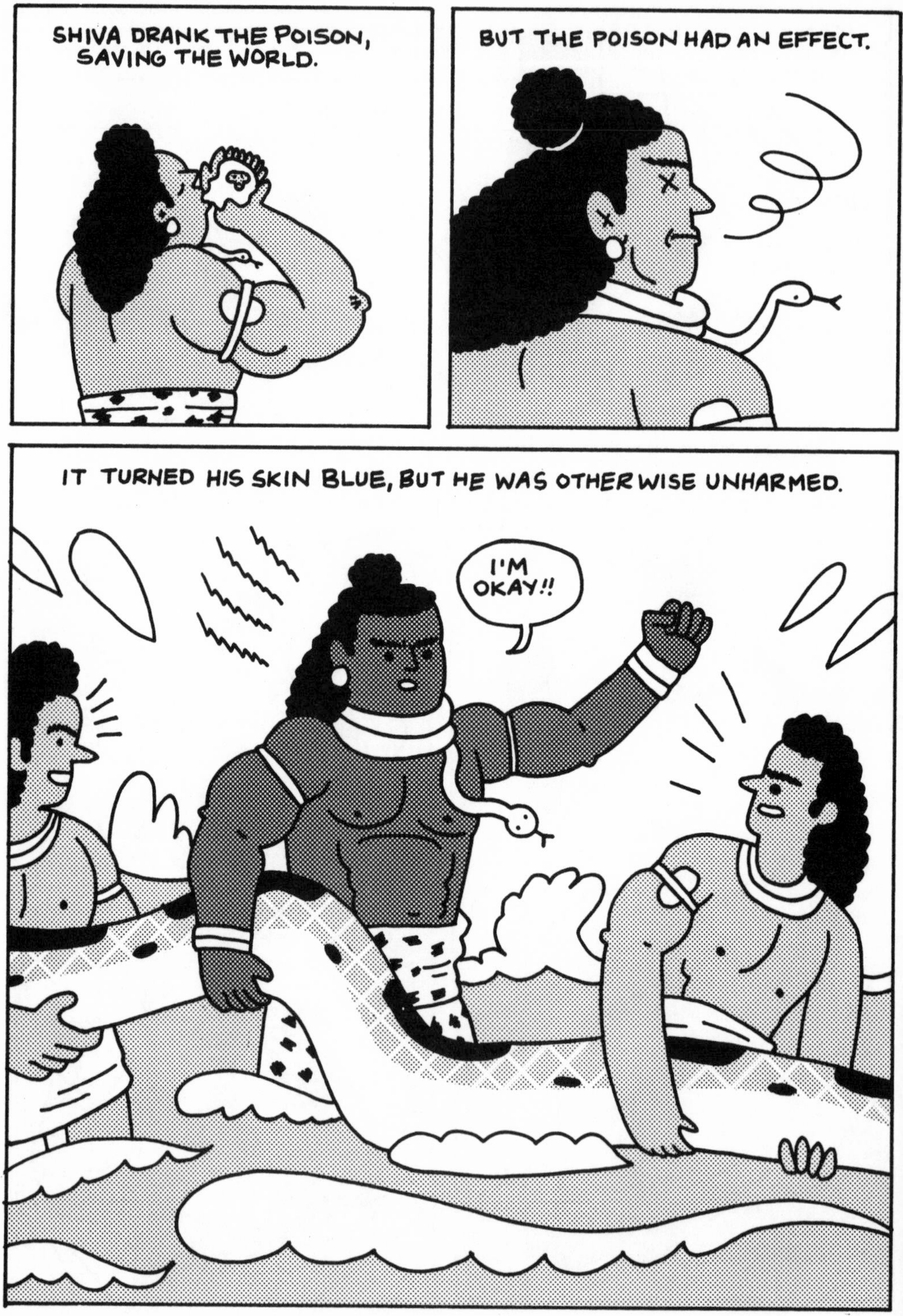
SHIVA DRANK THE POISON, SAVING THE WORLD.
BUT THE POISON HAD AN EFFECT.
IT TURNED HIS SKIN BLUE, BUT HE WAS OTHERWISE UNHARMED.
I'M OKAY!!

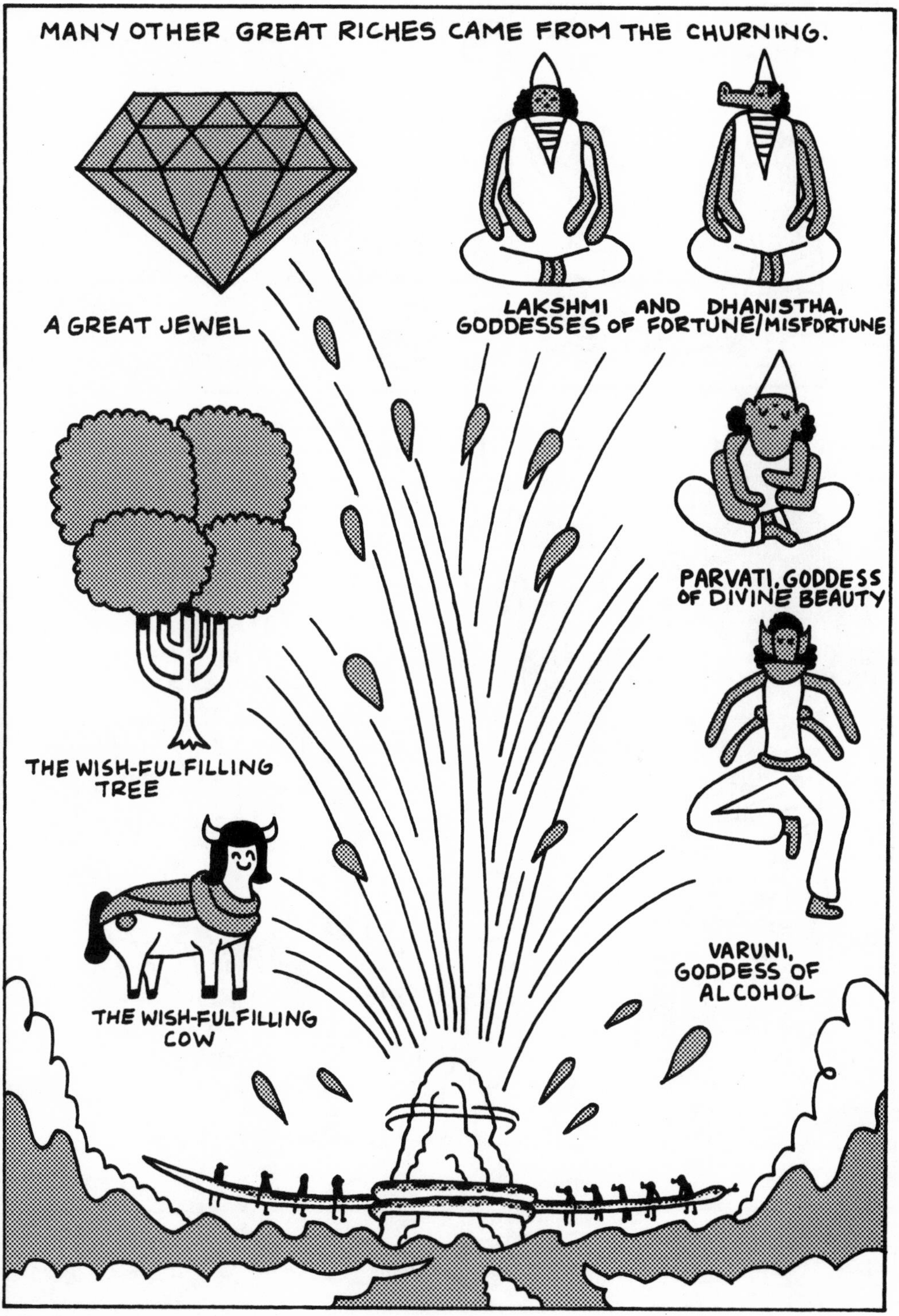
MANY OTHER GREAT RICHES CAME FROM THE CHURNING.
A GREAT JEWEL
LAKSHMI AND DHANISTHA, GODDESSES OF FORTUNE/MISFORTUNE
THE WISH-FULFILLING TREE
PARVATI, GODDESS OF DIVINE BEAUTY
VARUNI, GODDESS OF ALCOHOL
THE WISH-FULFILLING COW

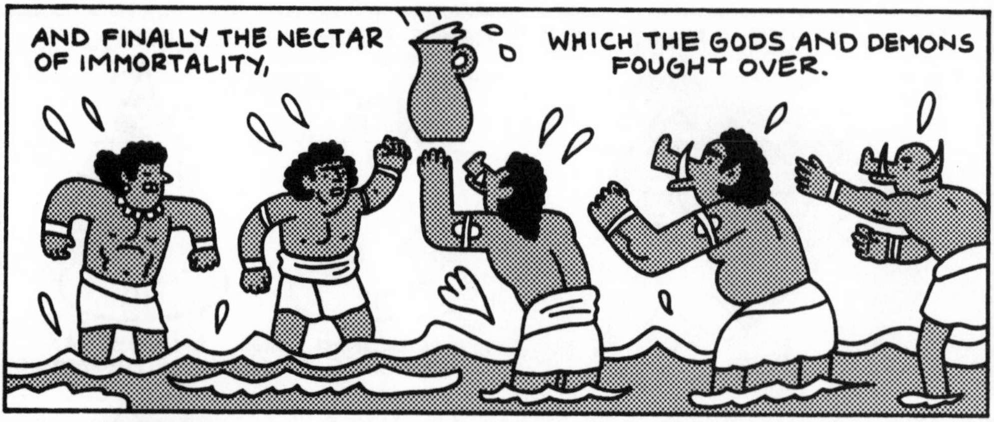
AND FINALLY THE NECTAR OF IMMORTALITY,
WHICH THE GODS AND DEMONS FOUGHT OVER.

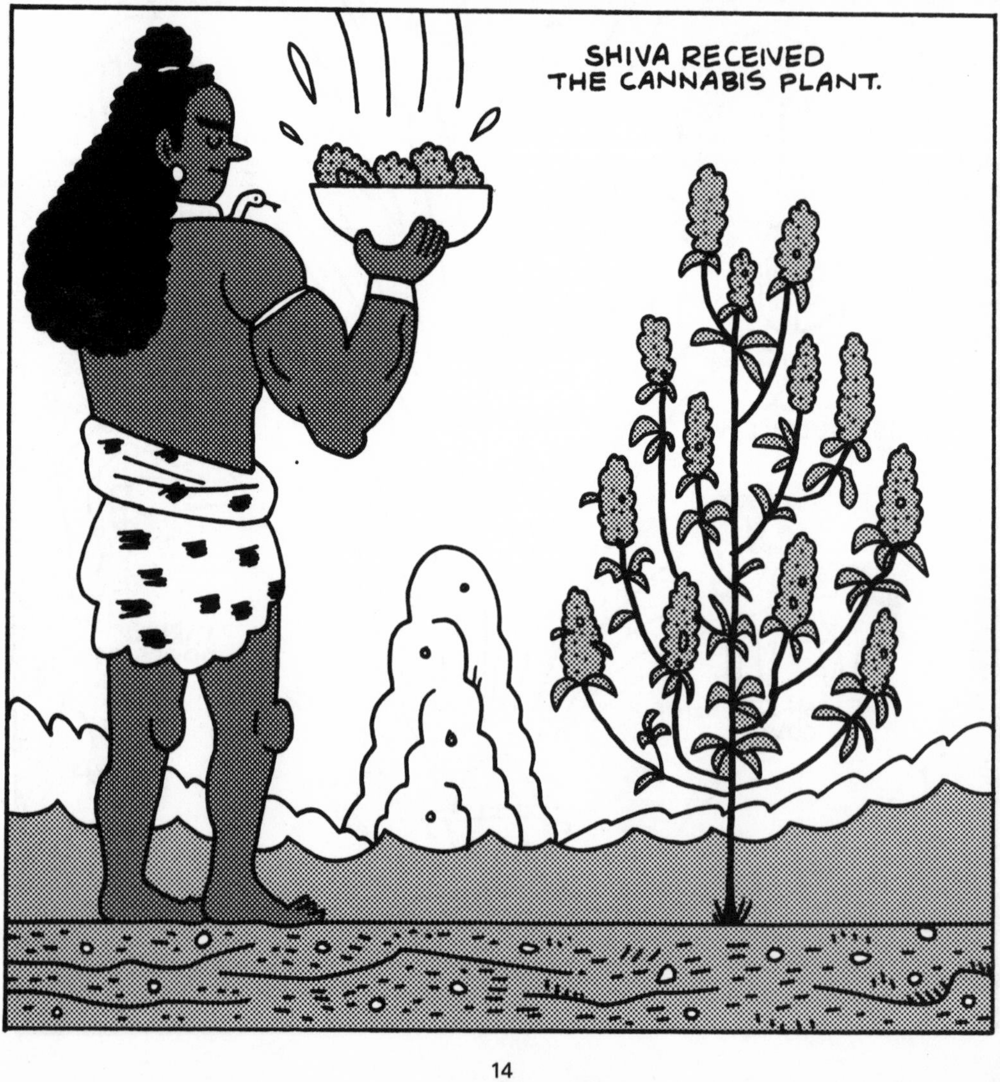
SHIVA RECEIVED THE CANNABIS PLANT.

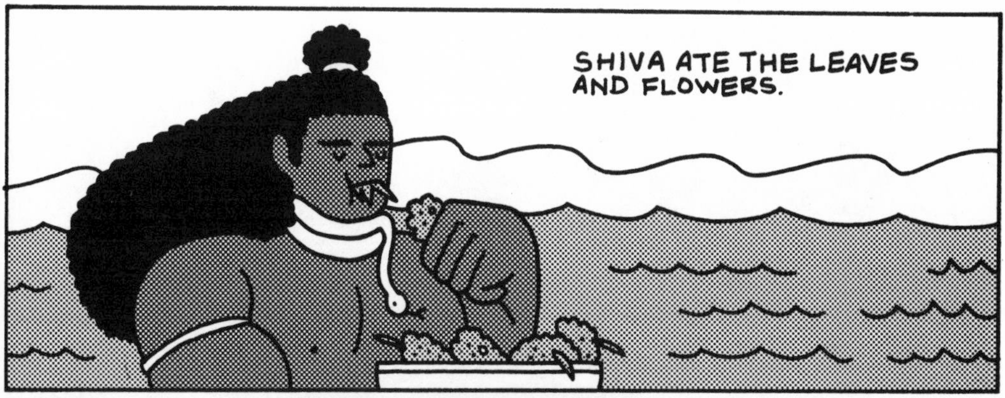
SHIVA ATE THE LEAVES AND FLOWERS.

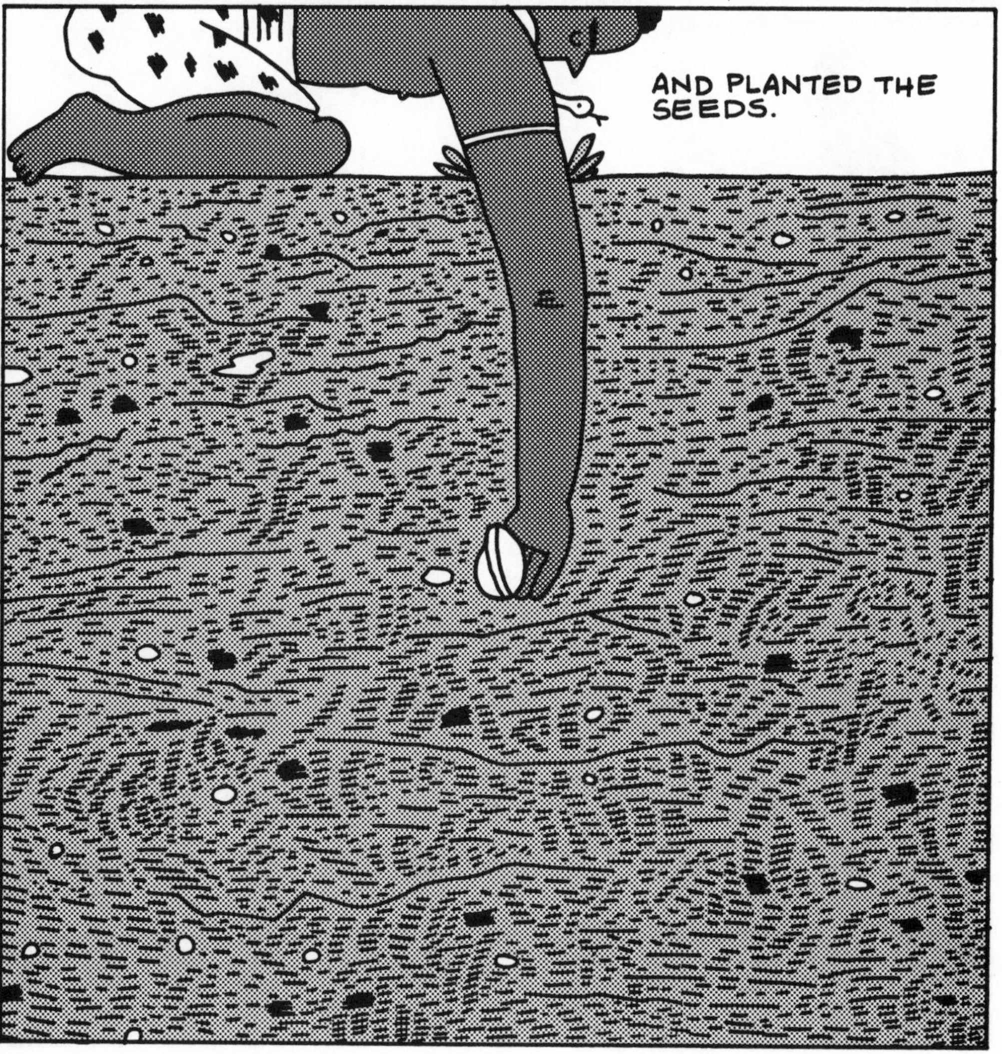
AND PLANTED THE SEEDS.

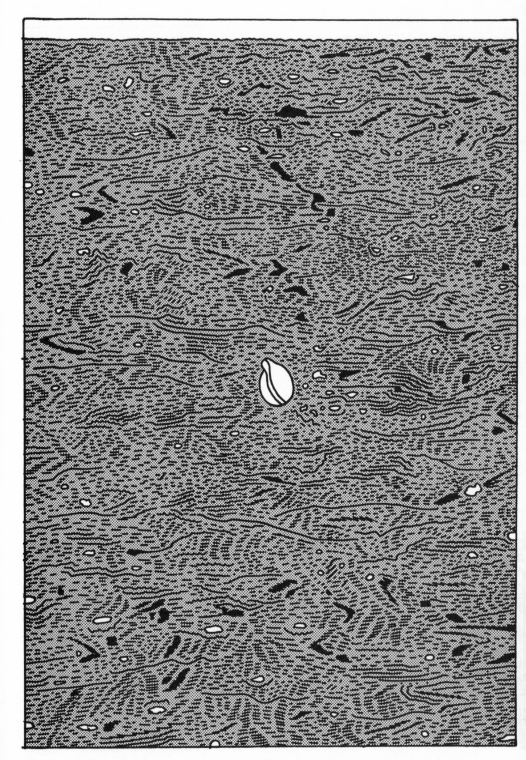

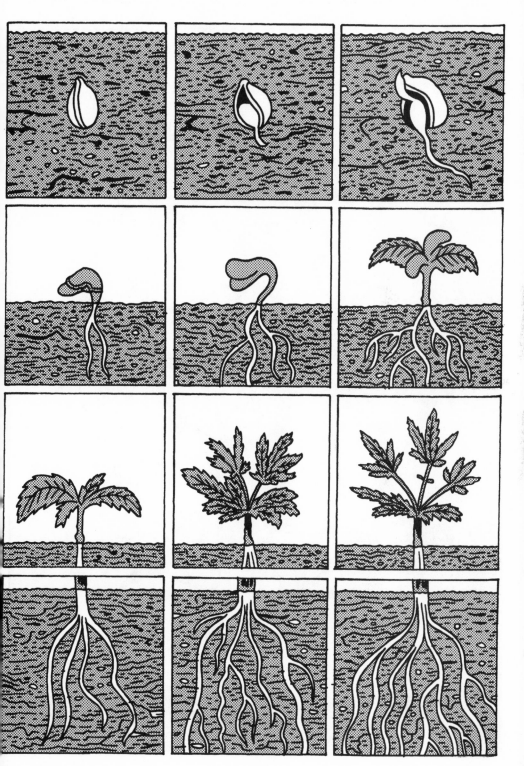

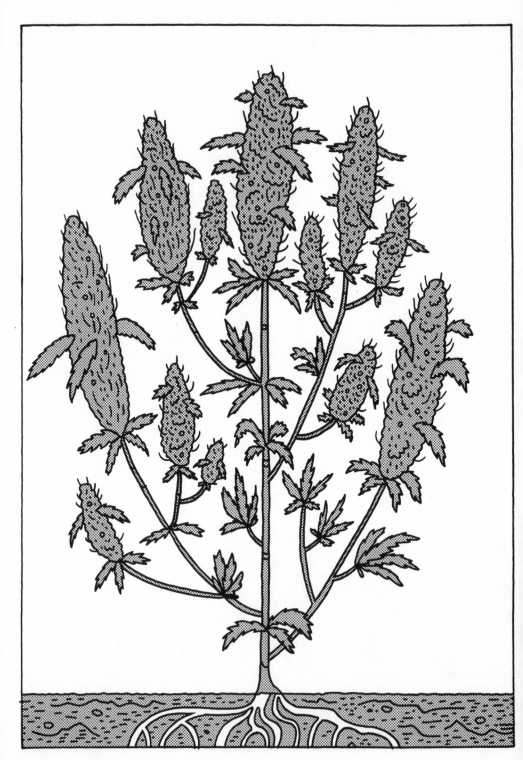

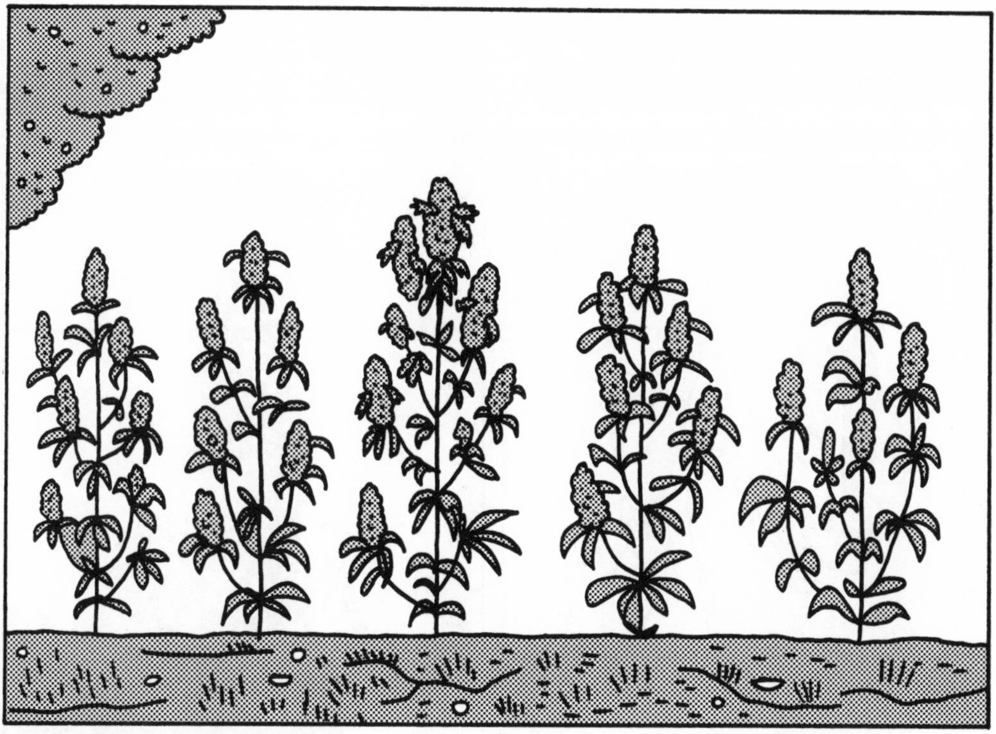

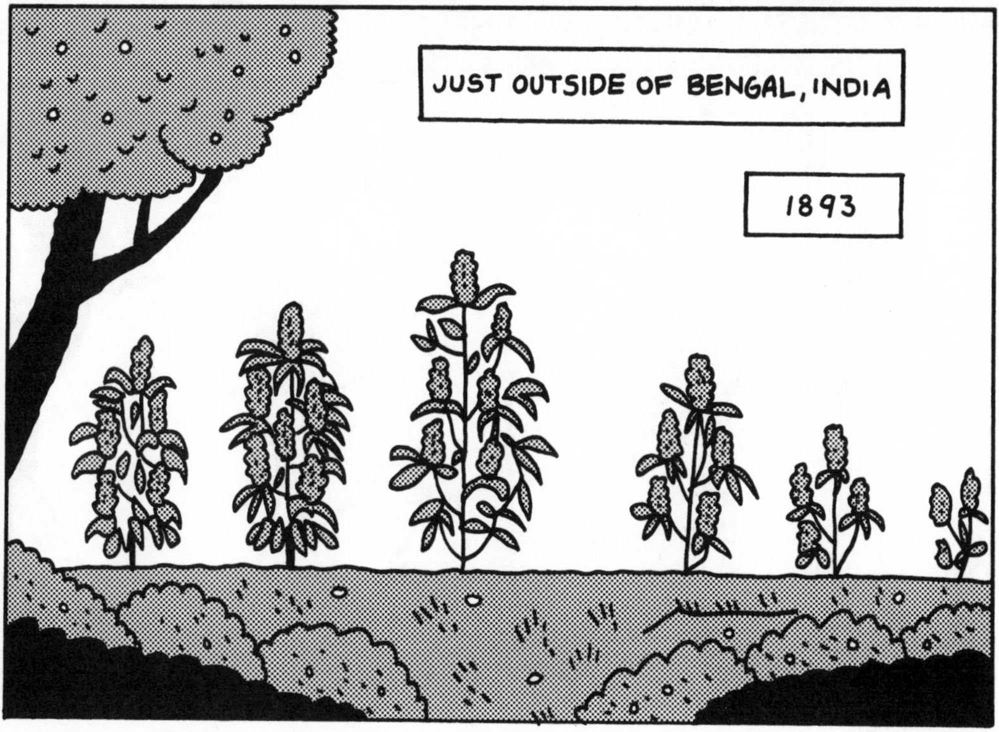
JUST OUTSIDE OF BENGAL, INDIA
1893

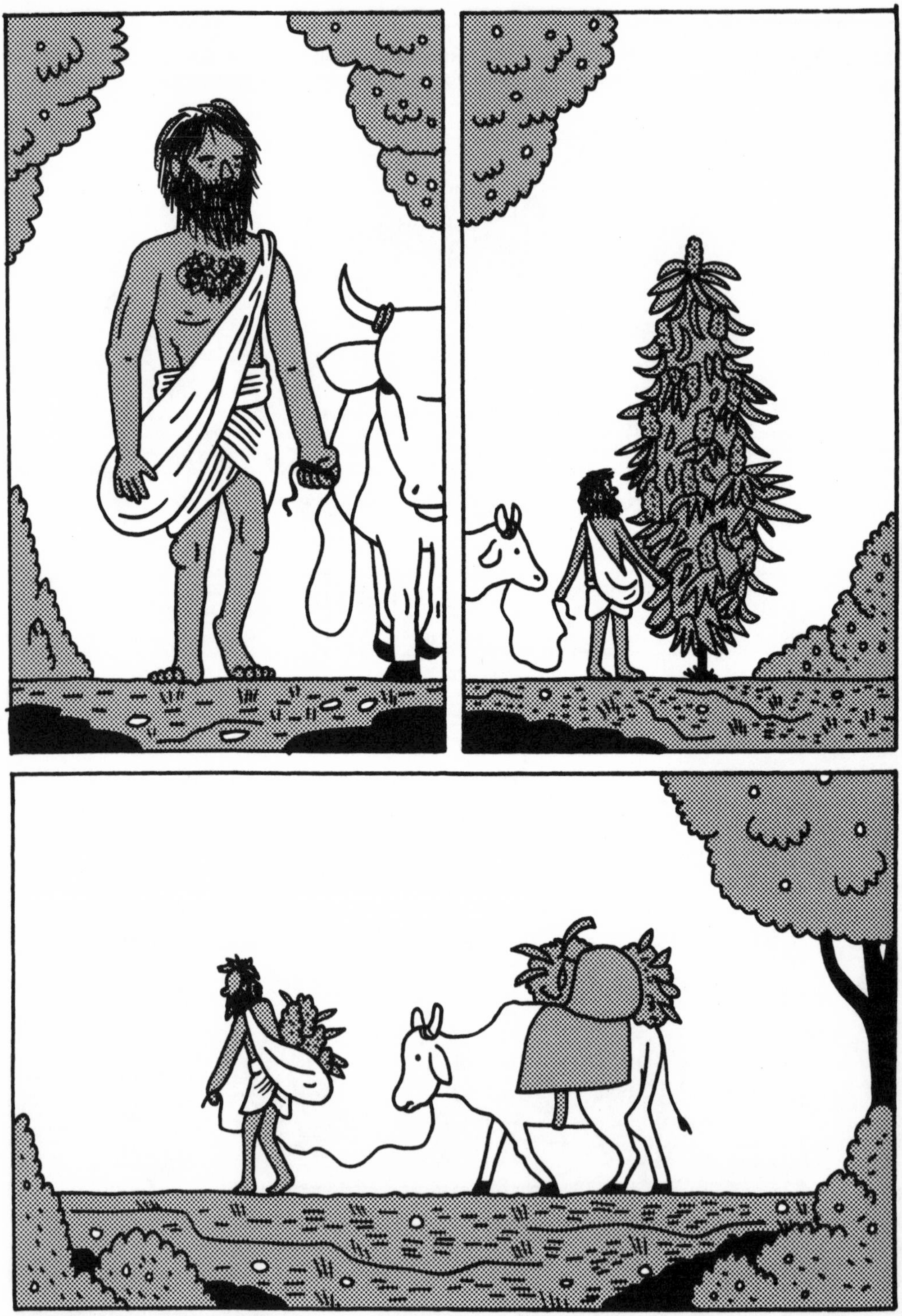

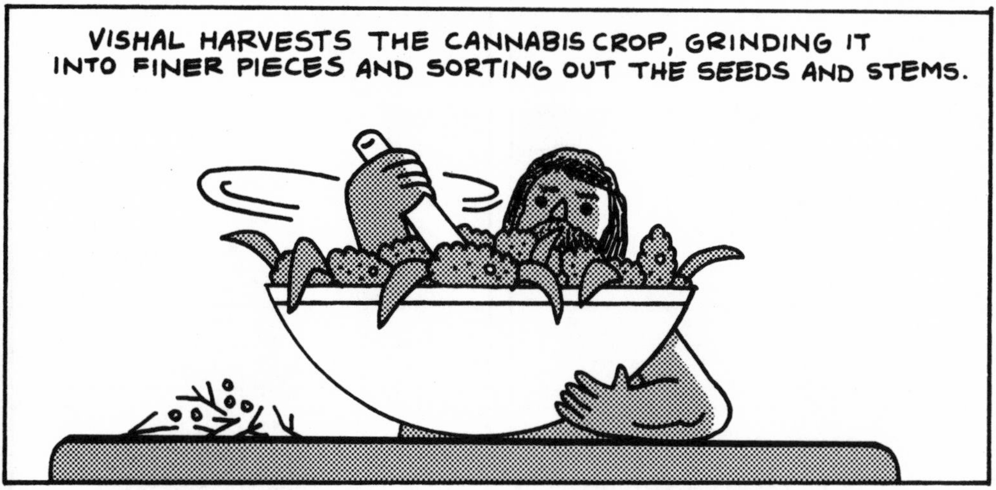
VISHAL HARVESTS THE CANNABIS CROP, GRINDING IT INTO FINER PIECES AND SORTING OUT THE SEEDS AND STEMS.

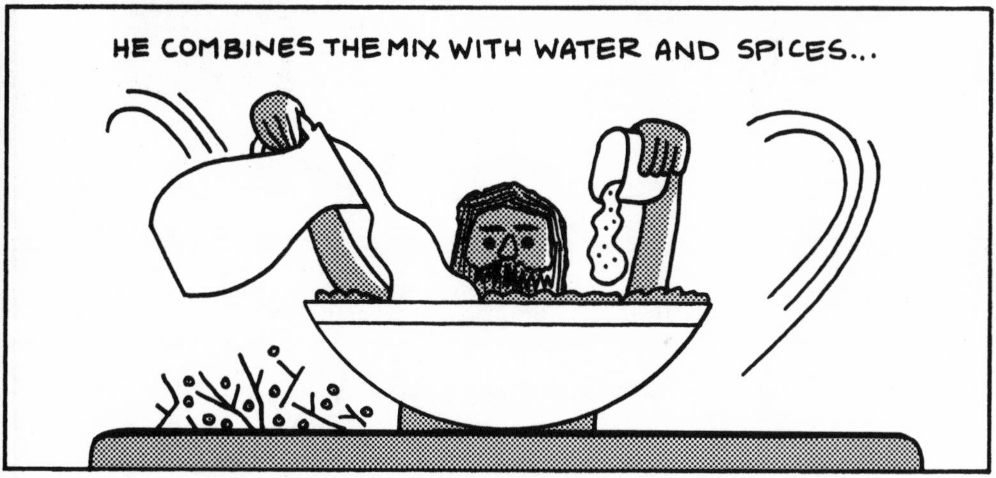
HE COMBINES THE MIX WITH WATER AND SPICES...

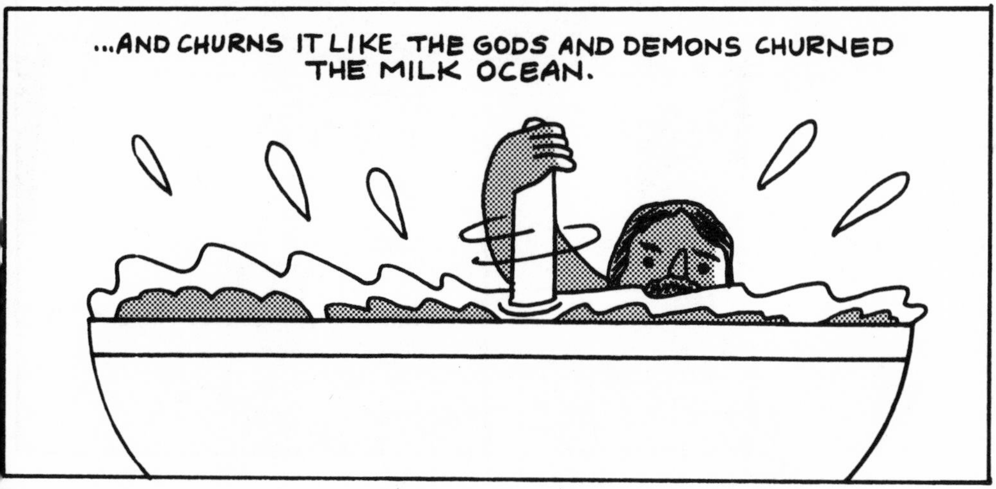
...AND CHURNS IT LIKE THE GODS AND DEMONS CHURNED THE MILK OCEAN.

VISHAL WORKS IT INTO A PASTE.

THEN ROLLS IT INTO BALLS CALLED BHANG.

THE BHANG IS RUBBED WITH FRUIT, YOGURT, AND SPICES OVER A SIEVE. WATER IS FILTERED THROUGH THIS MIX.

RUB RUB RUB

WATER

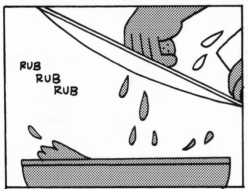

RUB
RUB
RUB

THIS CREATES A DRINK.

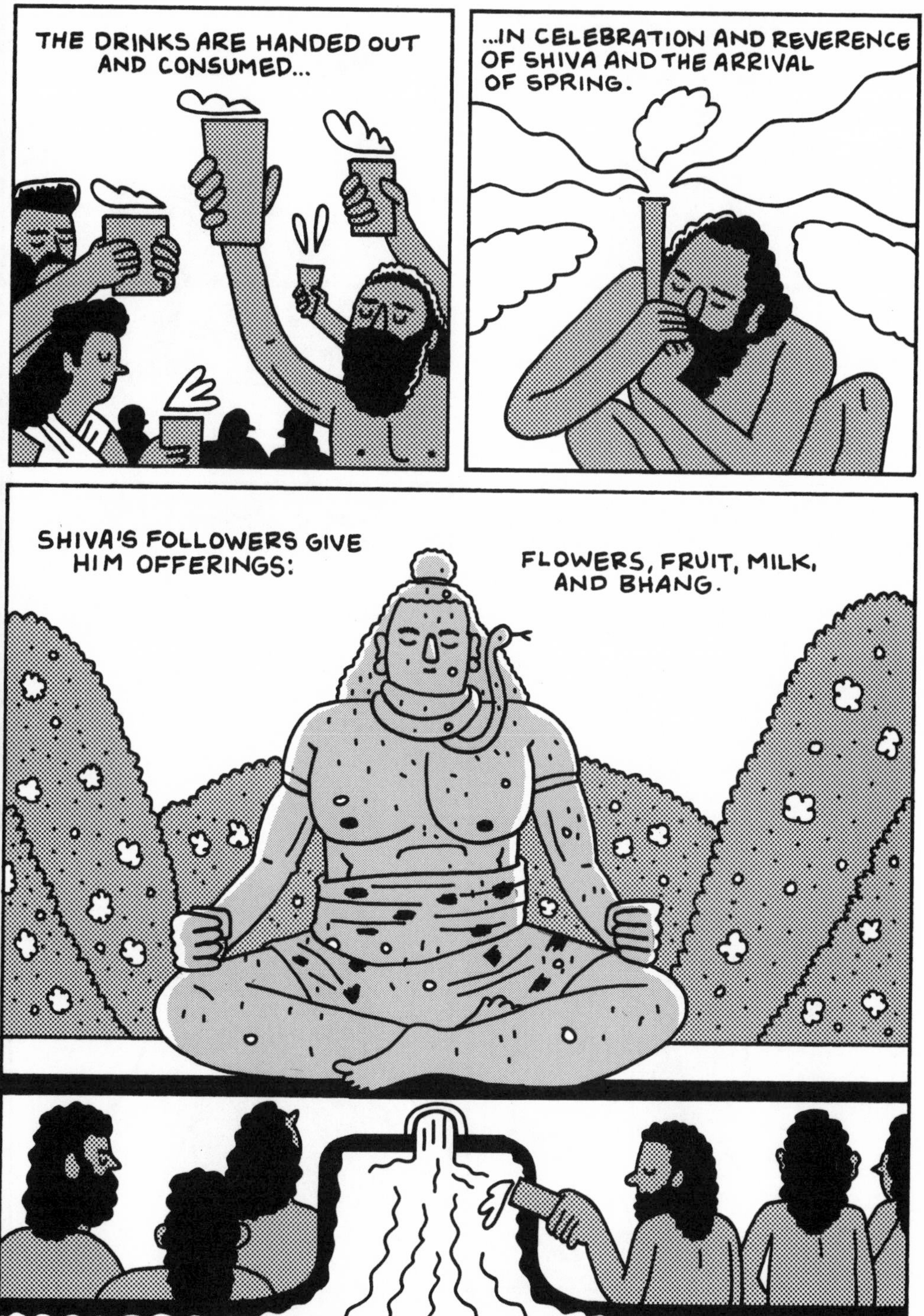
THE DRINKS ARE HANDED OUT AND CONSUMED...
...IN CELEBRATION AND REVERENCE OF SHIVA AND THE ARRIVAL OF SPRING.
SHIVA'S FOLLOWERS GIVE HIM OFFERINGS:
FLOWERS, FRUIT, MILK, AND BHANG.

SOME FOLLOWERS DEDICATE THEIR LIVES TO SHIVA.

SADHUS RENOUNCE ALL EARTHLY POSSESSIONS.

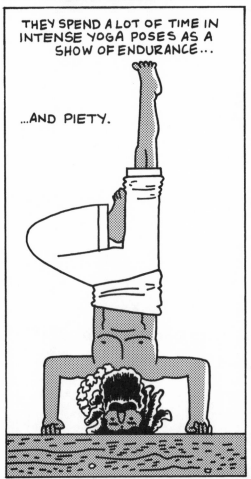

THEY SPEND A LOT OF TIME IN INTENSE YOGA POSES AS A SHOW OF ENDURANCE...

...AND PIETY.

CANNABIS AIDS IN THEIR MEDITATION.

SADHUS FIRST PREPARE THE CANNABIS FOR SMOKING BY CHOPPING IT UP FINELY.

SLICE
SLICE

THIS ALLOWS FOR A CONTINUOUS BURN USING A SINGLE MATCH.

RUB
RUB

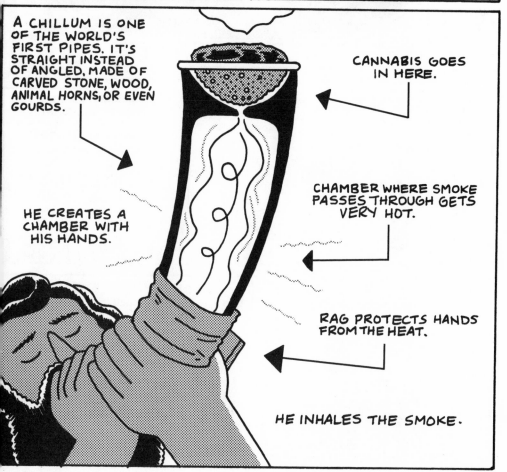

A CHILLUM IS ONE OF THE WORLD'S FIRST PIPES. IT'S STRAIGHT INSTEAD OF ANGLED, MADE OF CARVED STONE, WOOD, ANIMAL HORNS, OR EVEN GOURDS.

HE CREATES A CHAMBER WITH HIS HANDS.

CANNABIS GOES IN HERE.

CHAMBER WHERE SMOKE PASSES THROUGH GETS VERY HOT.

RAG PROTECTS HANDS FROM THE HEAT.

HE INHALES THE SMOKE.

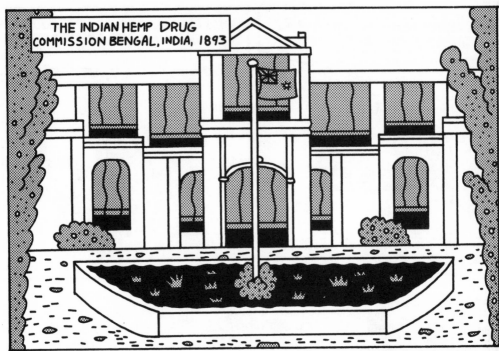

THE INDIAN HEMP DRUG COMMISSION BENGAL, INDIA, 1893

MR. H.T. OMMANEY, COLLECTOR, PANCH MAHALS...

MR. A.H.L. FRASIER, COMMISSIONER, CENTRAL PROVINCES

SURGEON-MAJOR C.J.H. WARDEN, OFFICIATING MEDICAL STOREKEEPER TO THE GOVERNMENT

THE HONORABLE W. MACKWORTH YOUNG, FINANCIAL MINISTER, PUNJAB

AHEM...

SO, GENTLEMEN... THE HEMP ISSUE. LET'S TALK.

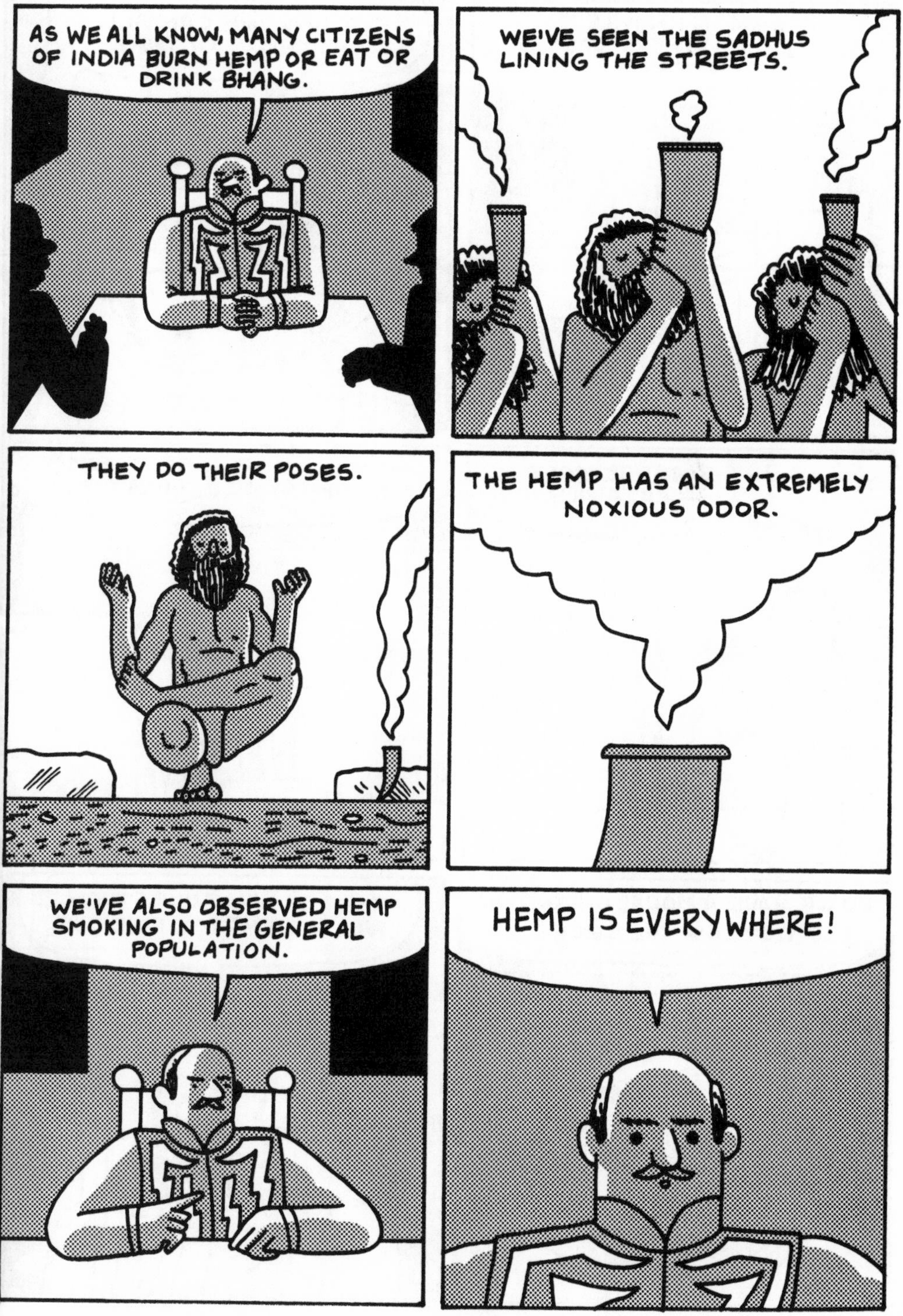
AS WE ALL KNOW, MANY CITIZENS OF INDIA BURN HEMP OR EAT OR DRINK BHANG.
WE'VE SEEN THE SADHUS LINING THE STREETS.
THEY DO THEIR POSES.
THE HEMP HAS AN EXTREMELY NOXIOUS ODOR.
WE'VE ALSO OBSERVED HEMP SMOKING IN THE GENERAL POPULATION.
HEMP IS EVERYWHERE!

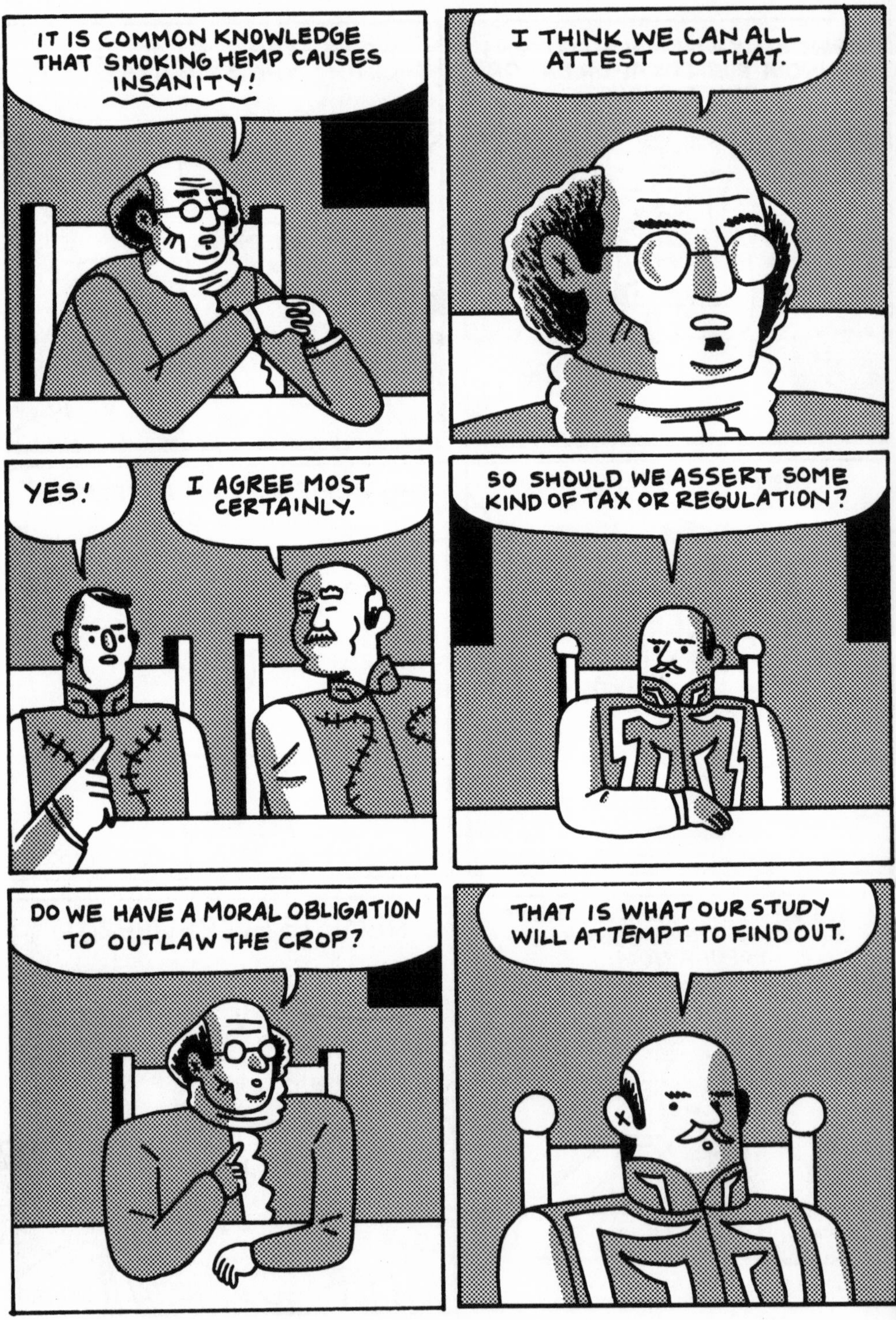
IT IS COMMON KNOWLEDGE THAT SMOKING HEMP CAUSES INSANITY!
I THINK WE CAN ALL ATTEST TO THAT.
YES!
I AGREE MOST CERTAINLY.
SO SHOULD WE ASSERT SOME KIND OF TAX OR REGULATION?
DO WE HAVE A MORAL OBLIGATION TO OUTLAW THE CROP?
THAT IS WHAT OUR STUDY WILL ATTEMPT TO FIND OUT.

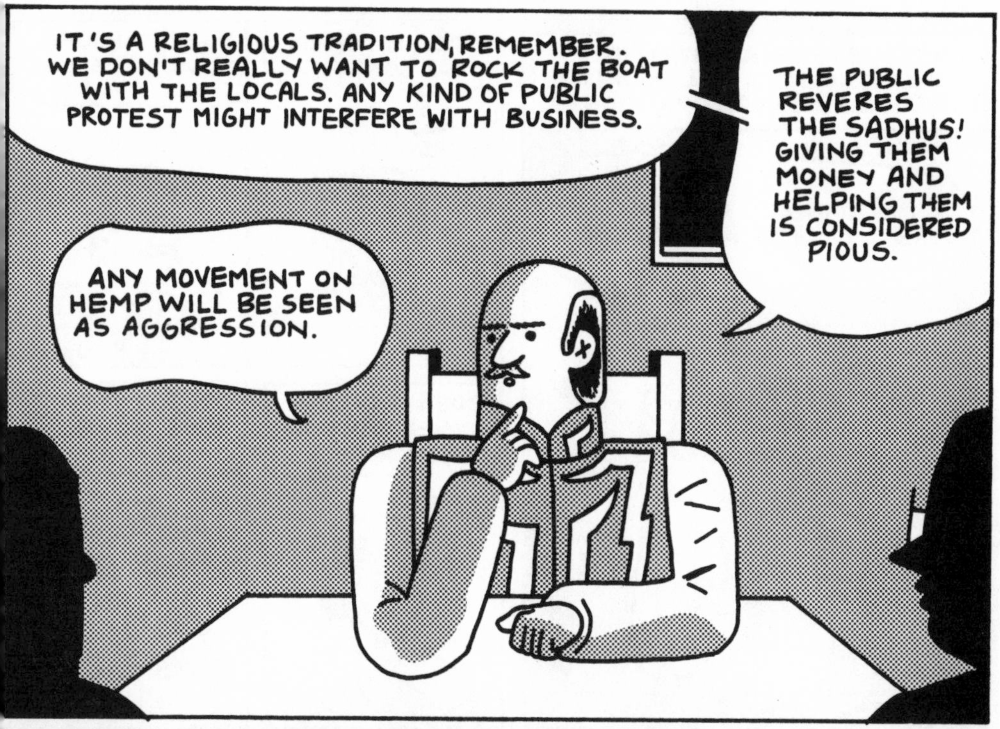
IT'S A RELIGIOUS TRADITION, REMEMBER. WE DON'T REALLY WANT TO ROCK THE BOAT WITH THE LOCALS. ANY KIND OF PUBLIC PROTEST MIGHT INTERFERE WITH BUSINESS.
THE PUBLIC REVERES THE SADHUS! GIVING THEM MONEY AND HELPING THEM IS CONSIDERED PIOUS.
ANY MOVEMENT ON HEMP WILL BE SEEN AS AGGRESSION.

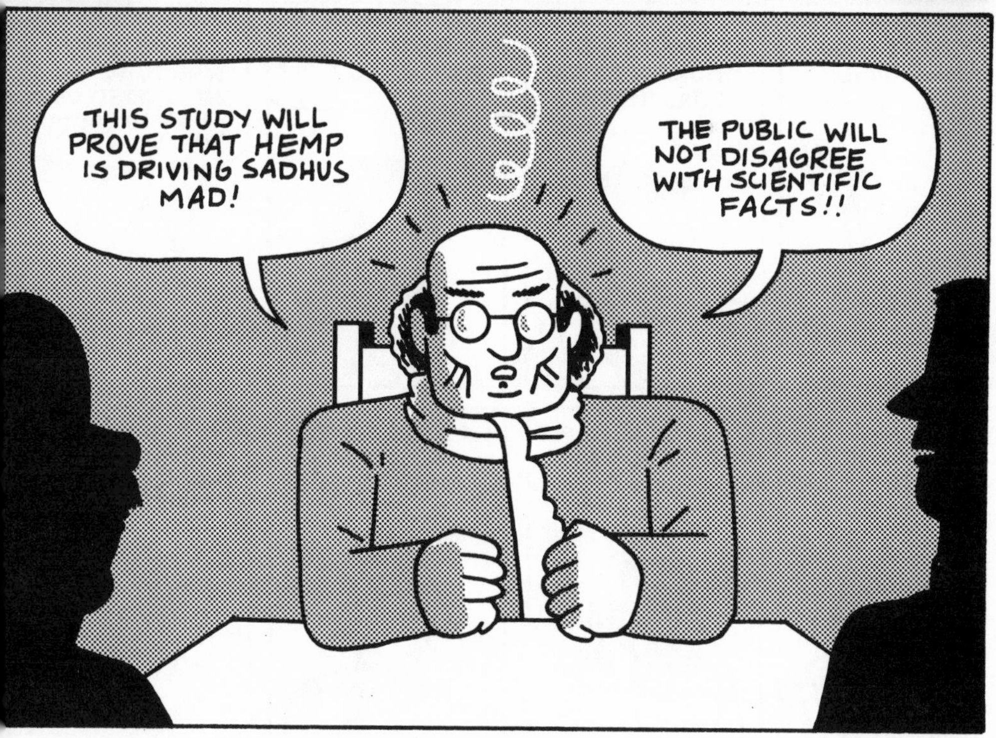
THIS STUDY WILL PROVE THAT HEMP IS DRIVING SADHUS MAD!
THE PUBLIC WILL NOT DISAGREE WITH SCIENTIFIC FACTS!!

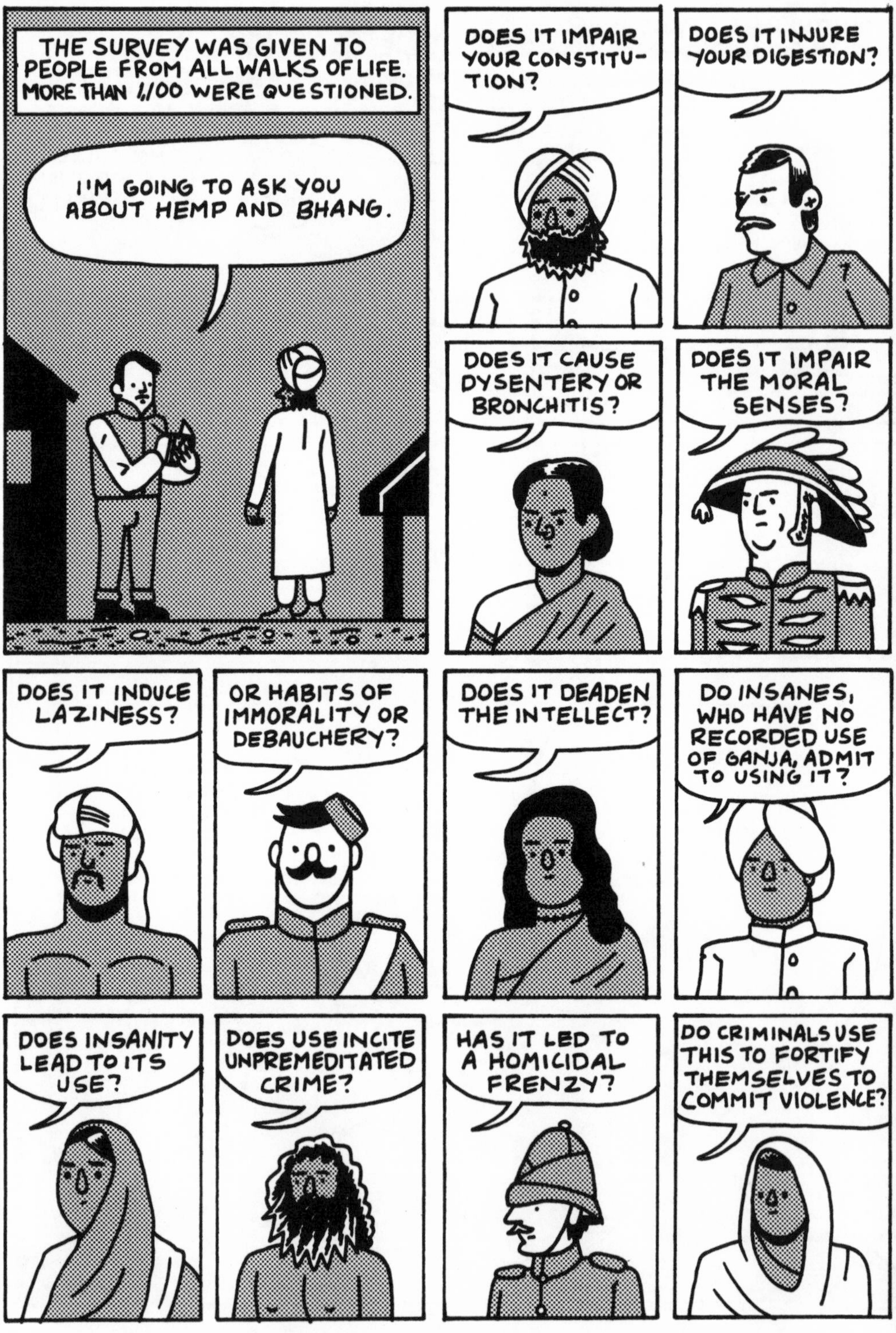
THE SURVEY WAS GIVEN TO PEOPLE FROM ALL WALKS OF LIFE. MORE THAN 1,100 WERE QUESTIONED.
I'M GOING TO ASK YOU ABOUT HEMP AND BHANG.
DOES IT IMPAIR YOUR CONSTITUTION?
DOES IT INJURE YOUR DIGESTION?
DOES IT CAUSE DYSENTERY OR BRONCHITIS?
DOES IT IMPAIR THE MORAL SENSES?
DOES IT INDUCE LAZINESS?
OR HABITS OF IMMORALITY OR DEBAUCHERY?
DOES IT DEADEN THE INTELLECT?
DO INSANES, WHO HAVE NO RECORDED USE OF GANJA, ADMIT TO USING IT?
DOES INSANITY LEAD TO ITS USE?
DOES USE INCITE UNPREMEDITATED CRIME?
HAS IT LED TO A HOMICIDAL FRENZY?
DO CRIMINALS USE THIS TO FORTIFY THEMSELVES TO COMMIT VIOLENCE?

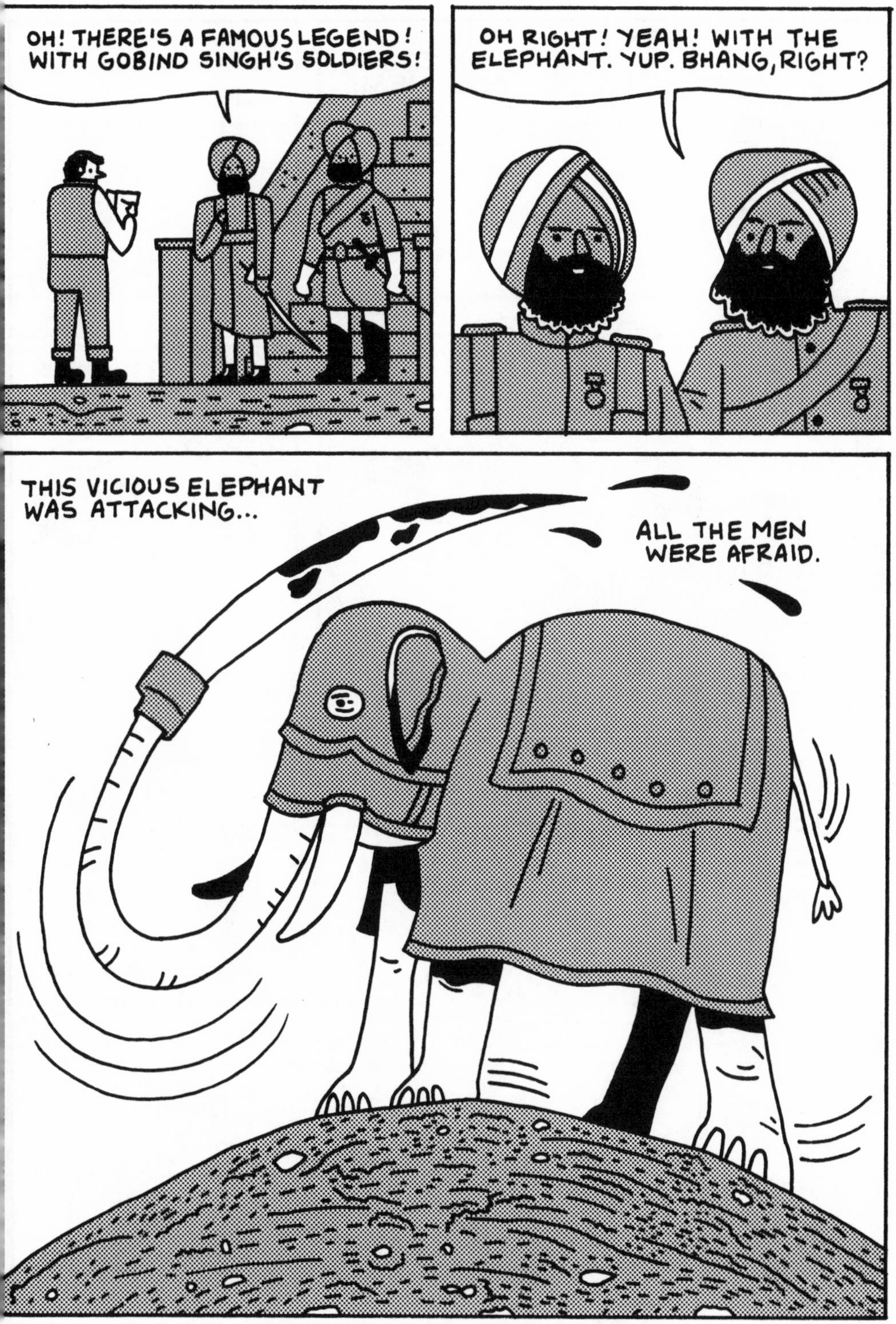
OH! THERE'S A FAMOUS LEGEND! WITH GOBIND SINGH'S SOLDIERS!
OH RIGHT! YEAH! WITH THE ELEPHANT. YUP. BHANG, RIGHT?
THIS VICIOUS ELEPHANT WAS ATTACKING...
ALL THE MEN WERE AFRAID.

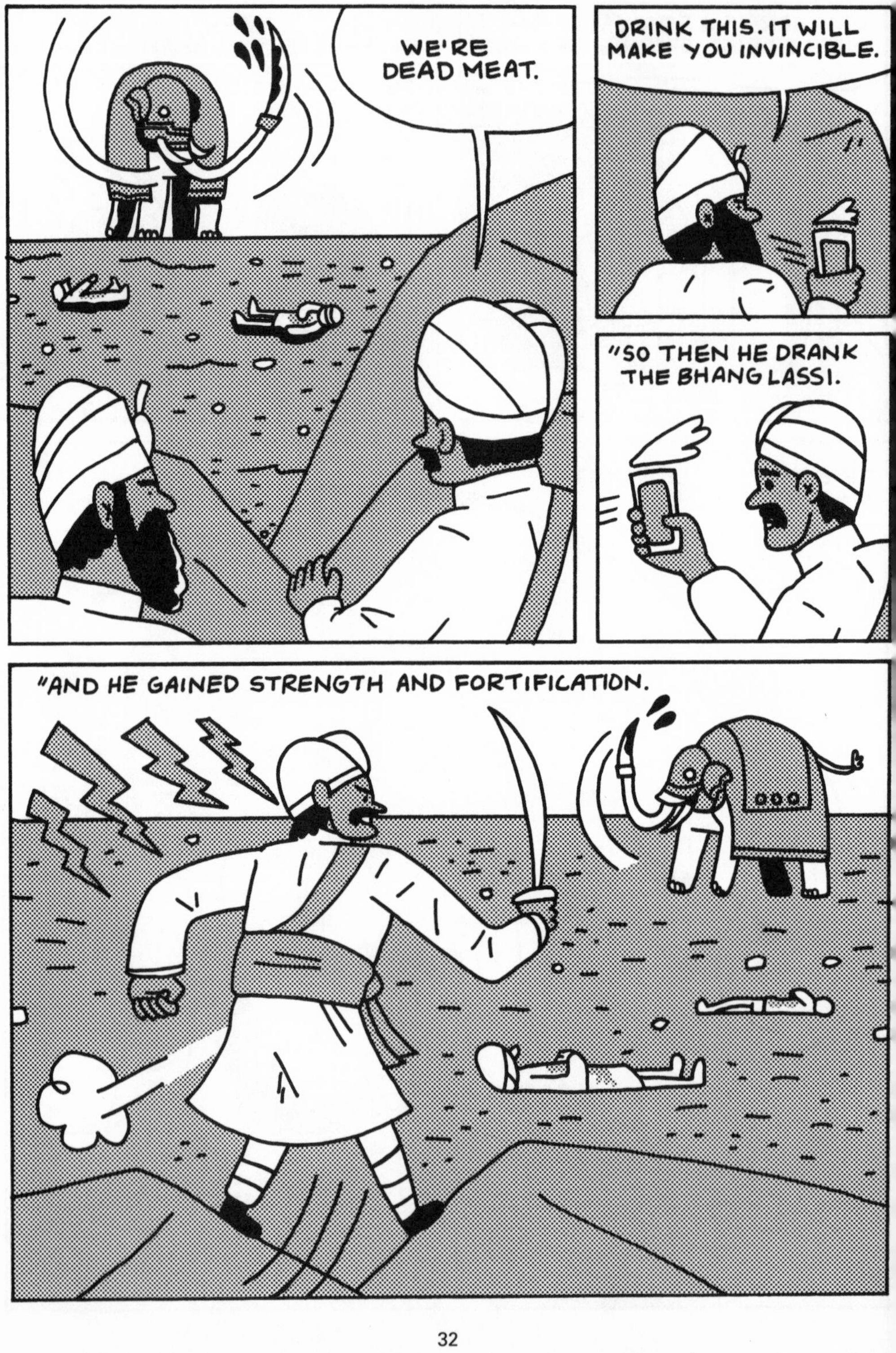
WE'RE DEAD MEAT.
DRINK THIS. IT WILL MAKE YOU INVINCIBLE.
"SO THEN HE DRANK THE BHANG LASSI.
"AND HE GAINED STRENGTH AND FORTIFICATION.

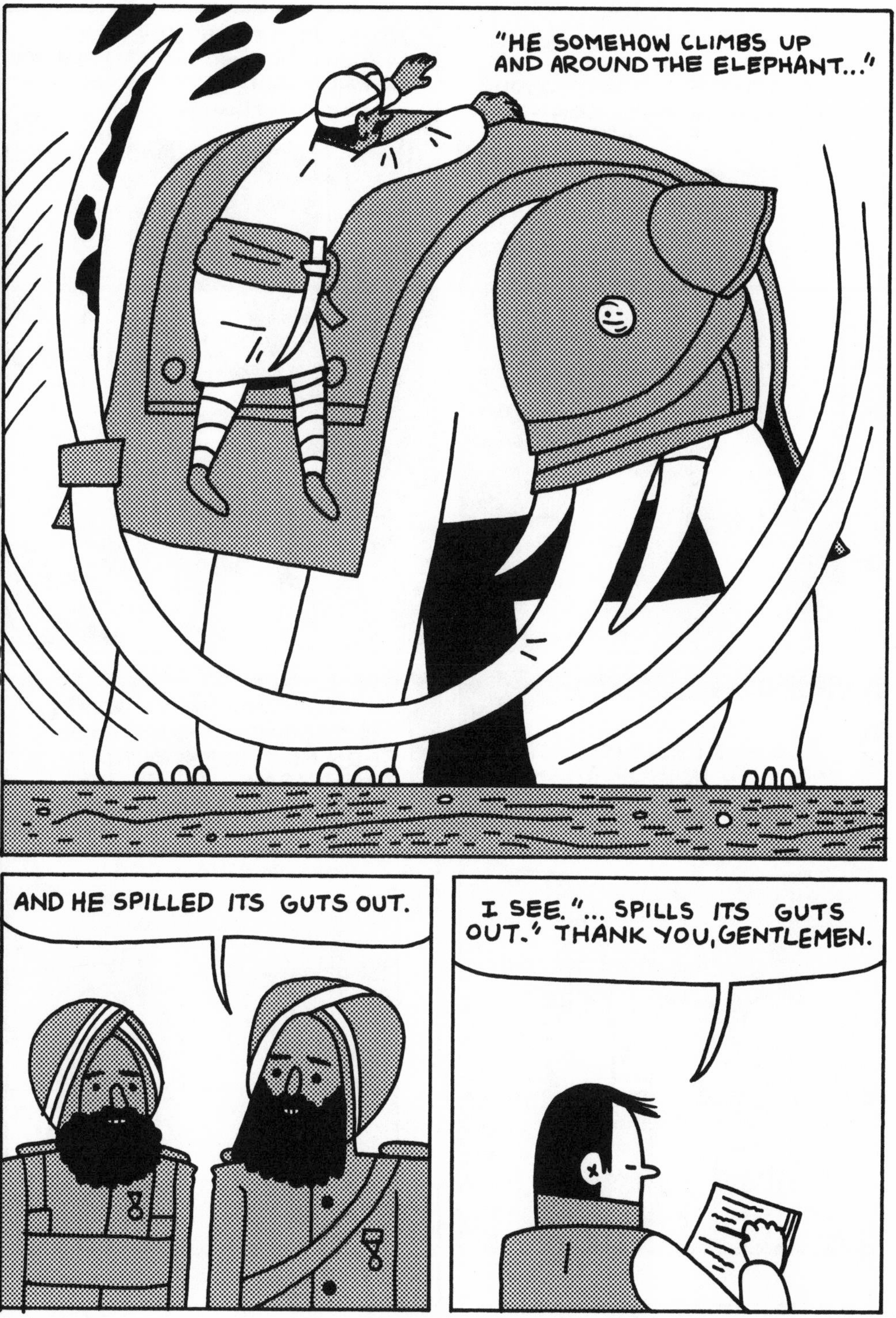
"HE SOMEHOW CLIMBS UP AND AROUND THE ELEPHANT..."
AND HE SPILLED ITS GUTS OUT.
I SEE. "... SPILLS ITS GUTS OUT." THANK YOU, GENTLEMEN.

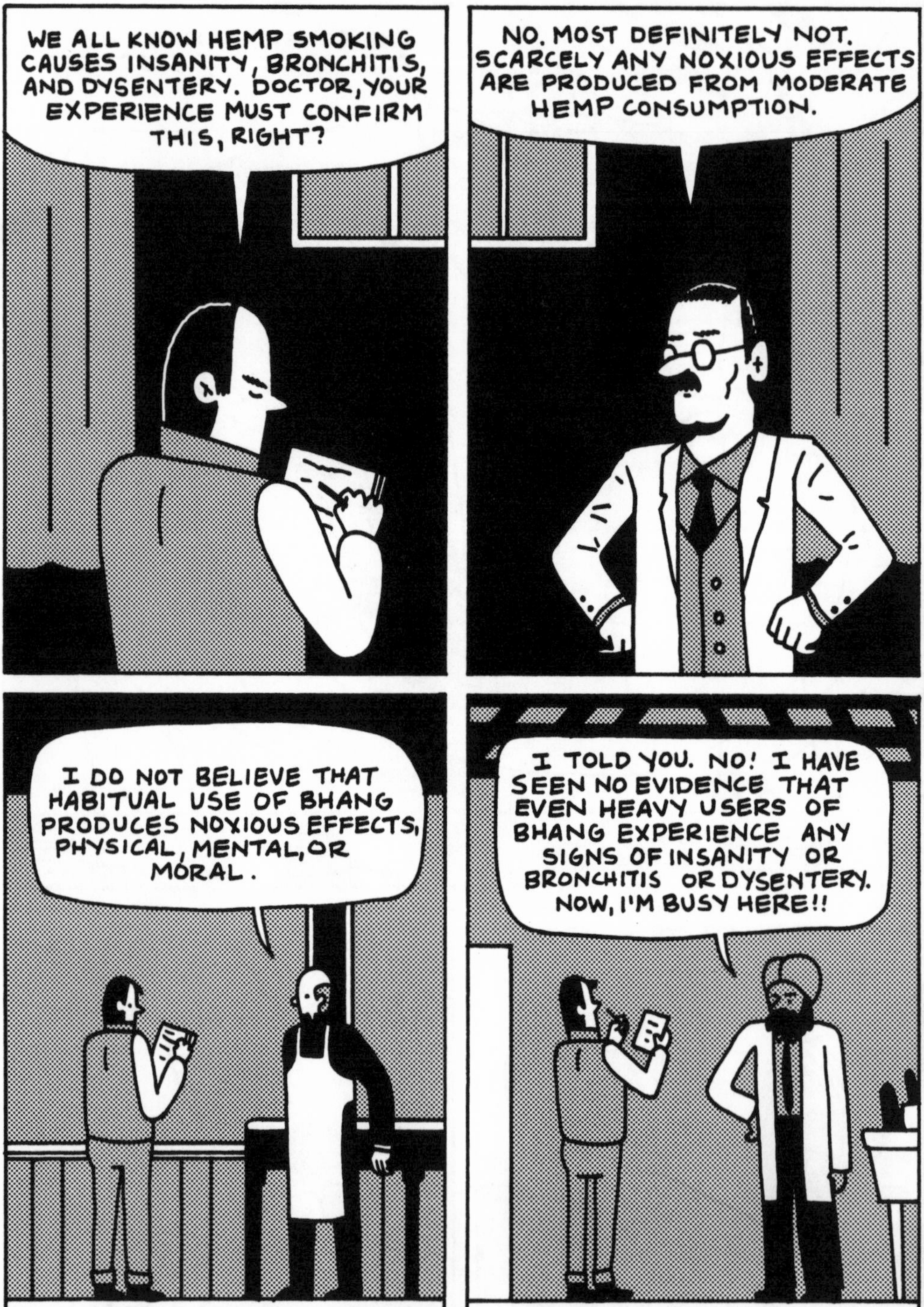
WE ALL KNOW HEMP SMOKING CAUSES INSANITY, BRONCHITIS, AND DYSENTERY. DOCTOR, YOUR EXPERIENCE MUST CONFIRM THIS, RIGHT?
NO. MOST DEFINITELY NOT. SCARCELY ANY NOXIOUS EFFECTS ARE PRODUCED FROM MODERATE HEMP CONSUMPTION.
I DO NOT BELIEVE THAT HABITUAL USE OF BHANG PRODUCES NOXIOUS EFFECTS, PHYSICAL, MENTAL, OR MORAL.
I TOLD YOU. NO! I HAVE SEEN NO EVIDENCE THAT EVEN HEAVY USERS OF BHANG EXPERIENCE ANY SIGNS OF INSANITY OR BRONCHITIS OR DYSENTERY. NOW, I'M BUSY HERE!!

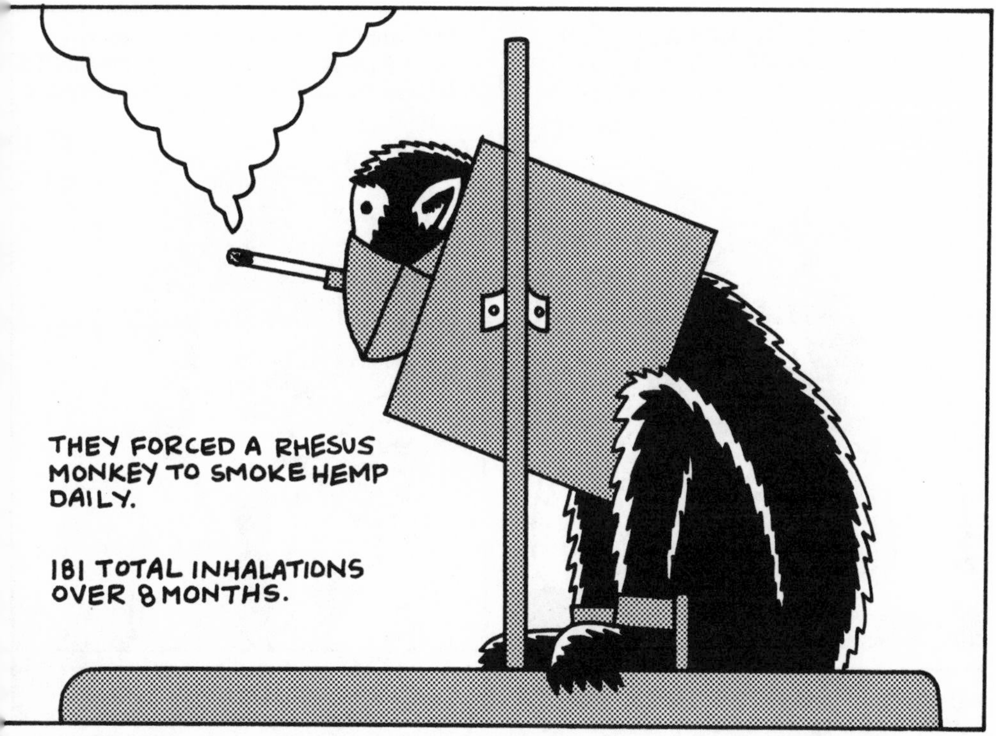
THEY FORCED A RHESUS MONKEY TO SMOKE HEMP DAILY.
181 TOTAL INHALATIONS OVER 8 MONTHS.

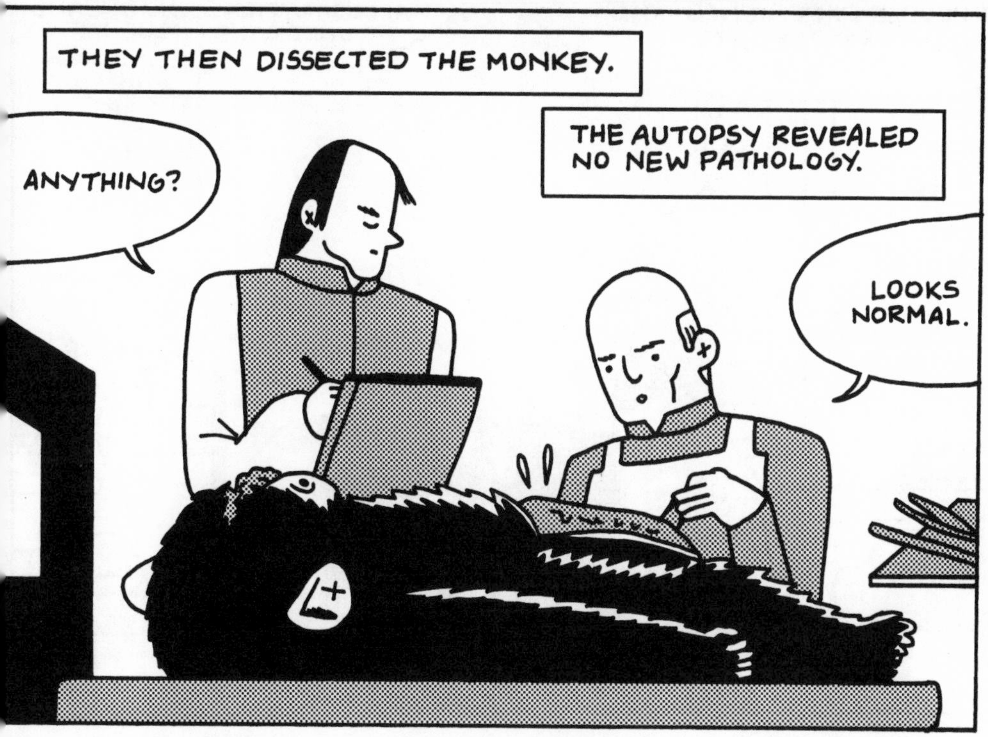
THEY THEN DISSECTED THE MONKEY.
ANYTHING?
THE AUTOPSY REVEALED NO NEW PATHOLOGY.
LOOKS NORMAL.

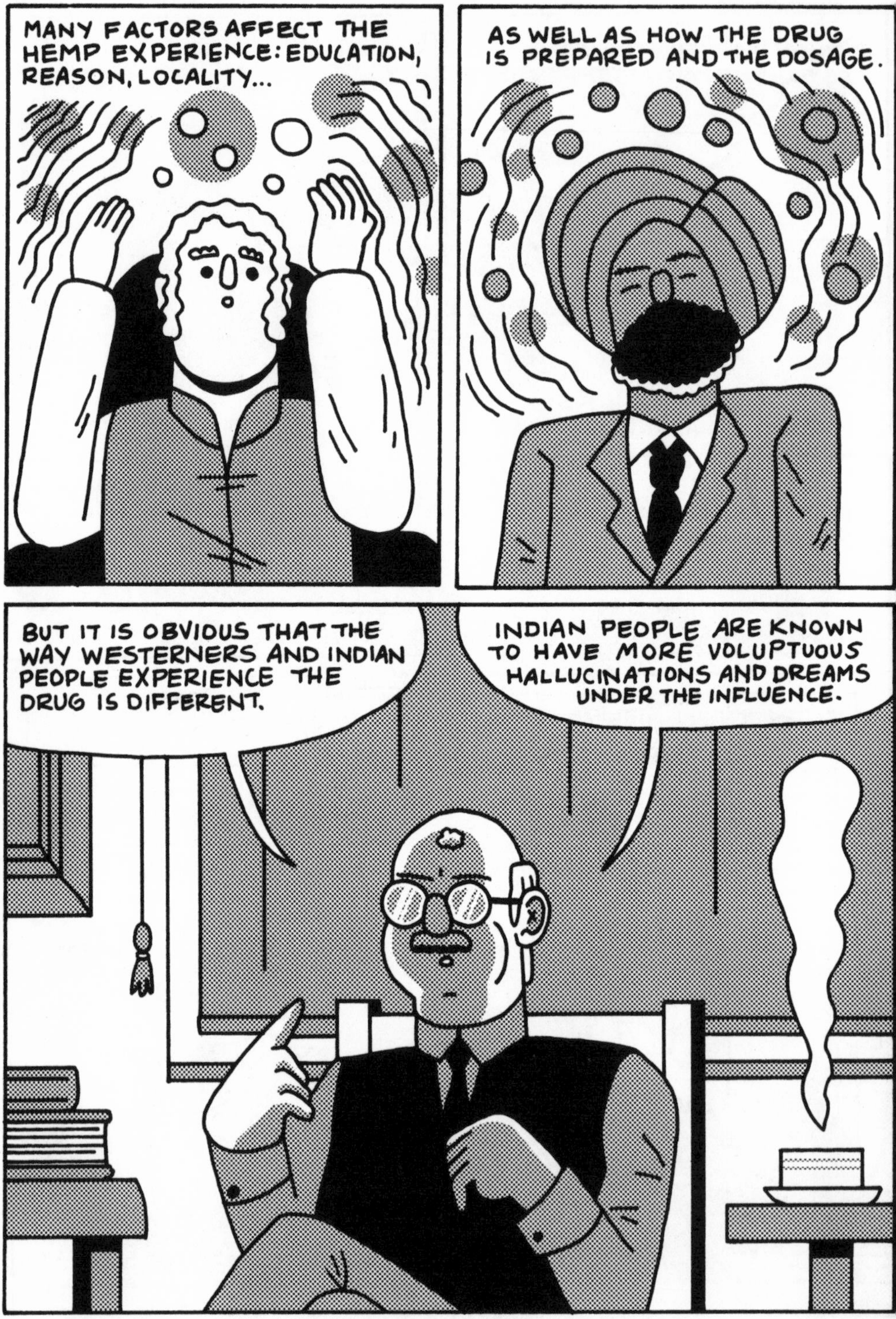
MANY FACTORS AFFECT THE HEMP EXPERIENCE: EDUCATION, REASON, LOCALITY...
AS WELL AS HOW THE DRUG IS PREPARED AND THE DOSAGE.
BUT IT IS OBVIOUS THAT THE WAY WESTERNERS AND INDIAN PEOPLE EXPERIENCE THE DRUG IS DIFFERENT.
INDIAN PEOPLE ARE KNOWN TO HAVE MORE VOLUPTUOUS HALLUCINATIONS AND DREAMS UNDER THE INFLUENCE.

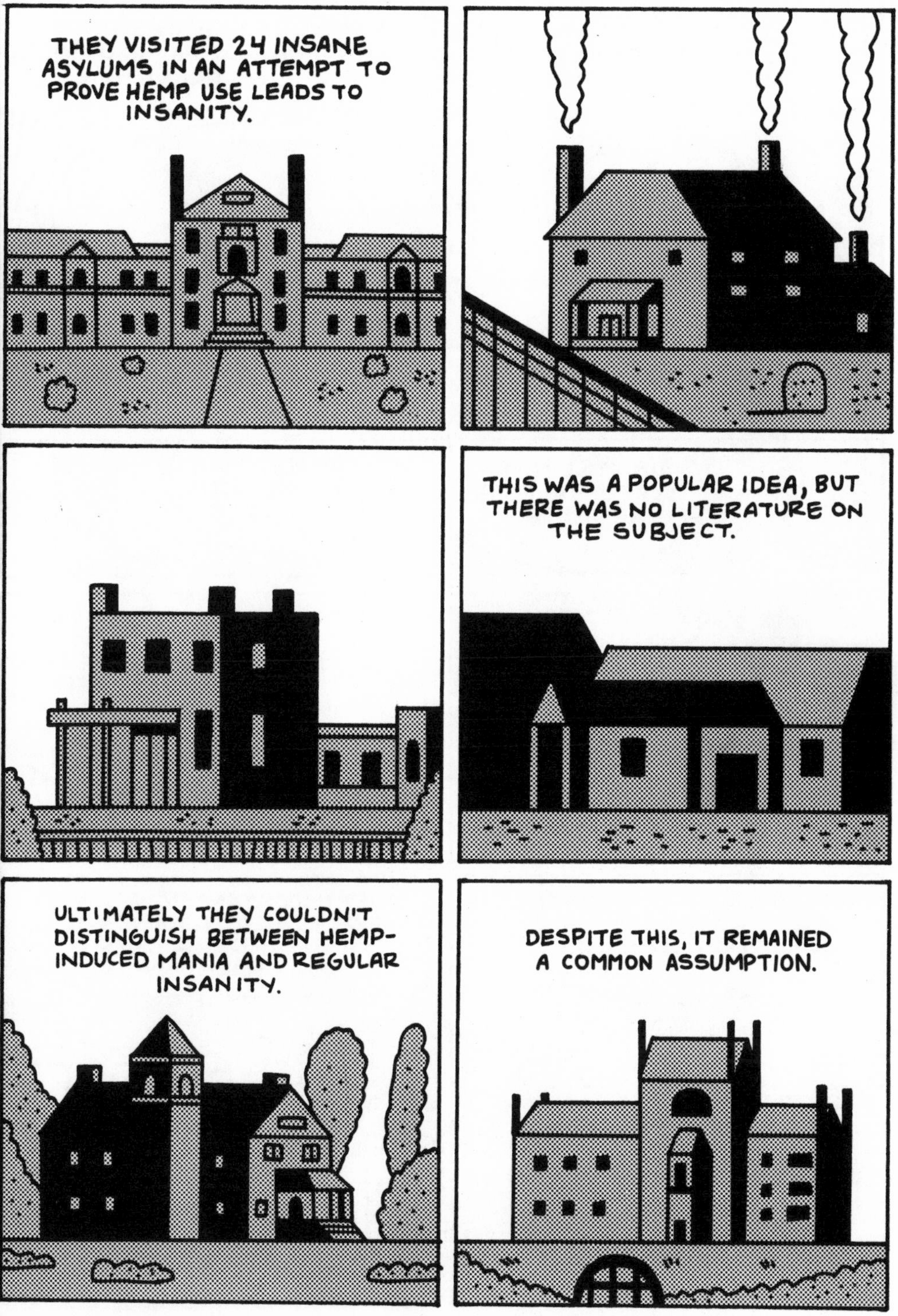
THEY VISITED 24 INSANE ASYLUMS IN AN ATTEMPT TO PROVE HEMP USE LEADS TO INSANITY.
THIS WAS A POPULAR IDEA, BUT THERE WAS NO LITERATURE ON THE SUBJECT.
ULTIMATELY THEY COULDN'T DISTINGUISH BETWEEN HEMP-INDUCED MANIA AND REGULAR INSANITY.
DESPITE THIS, IT REMAINED A COMMON ASSUMPTION.

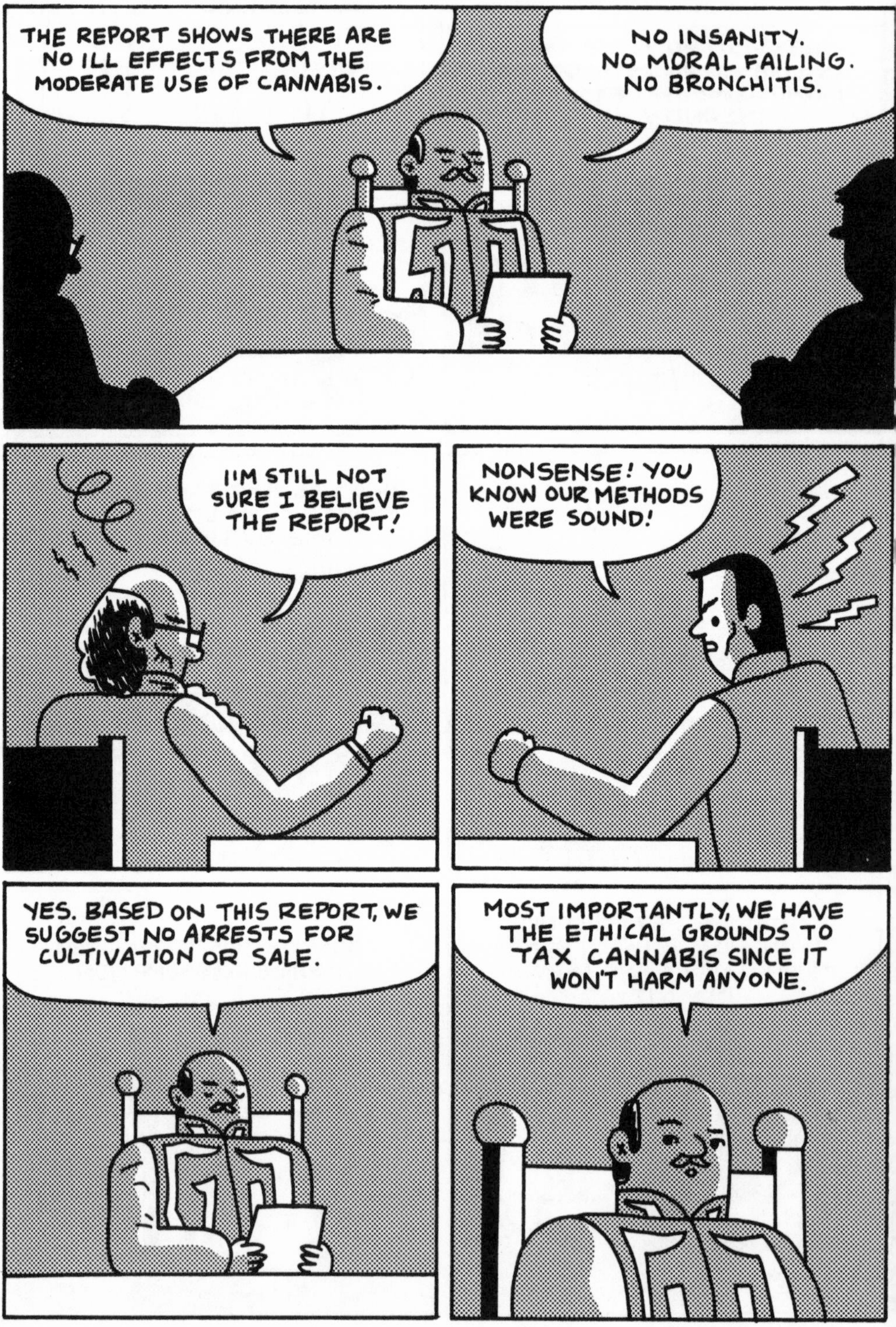
THE REPORT SHOWS THERE ARE NO ILL EFFECTS FROM THE MODERATE USE OF CANNABIS.
NO INSANITY. NO MORAL FAILING. NO BRONCHITIS.
I'M STILL NOT SURE I BELIEVE THE REPORT!
NONSENSE! YOU KNOW OUR METHODS WERE SOUND!
YES. BASED ON THIS REPORT, WE SUGGEST NO ARRESTS FOR CULTIVATION OR SALE.
MOST IMPORTANTLY, WE HAVE THE ETHICAL GROUNDS TO TAX CANNABIS SINCE IT WON'T HARM ANYONE.

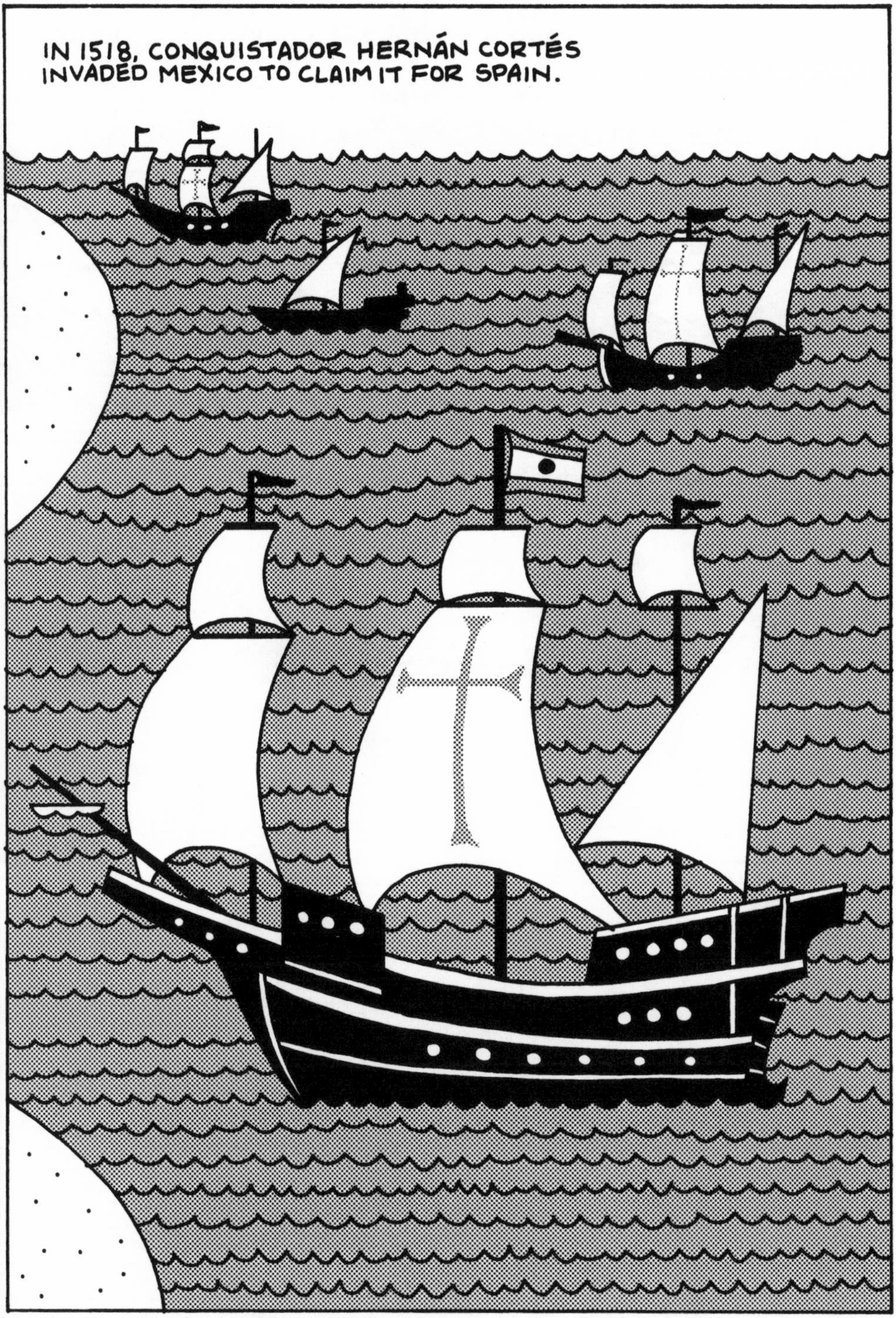
IN 1518, CONQUISTADOR HERNÁN CORTÉS INVADED MEXICO TO CLAIM IT FOR SPAIN.

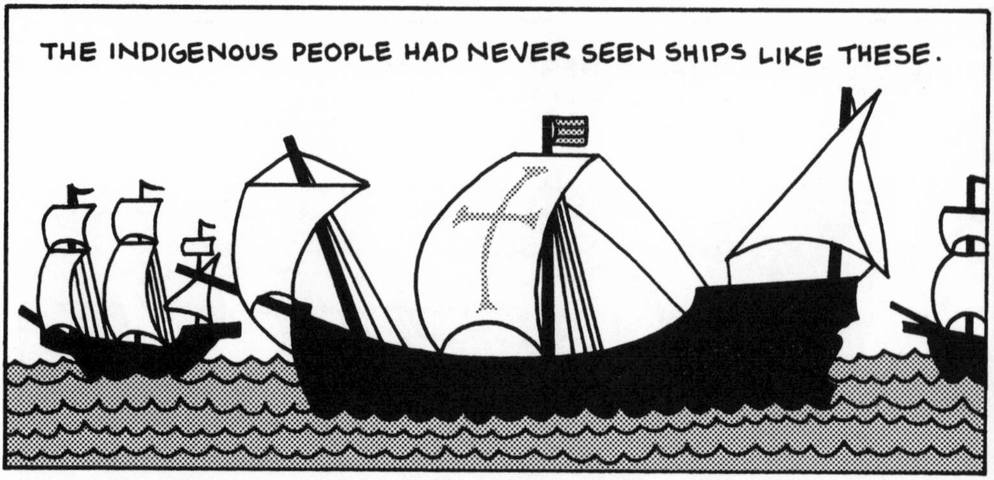
THE INDIGENOUS PEOPLE HAD NEVER SEEN SHIPS LIKE THESE.

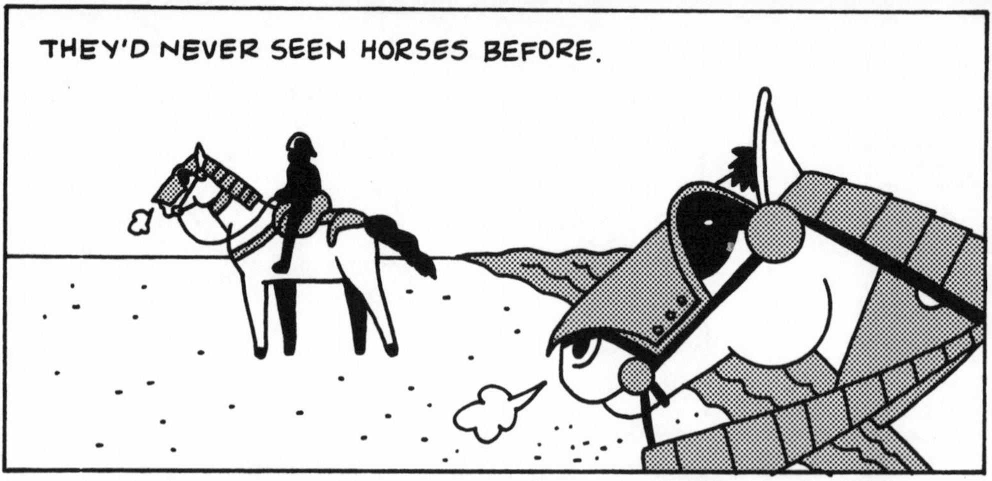
THEY'D NEVER SEEN HORSES BEFORE.

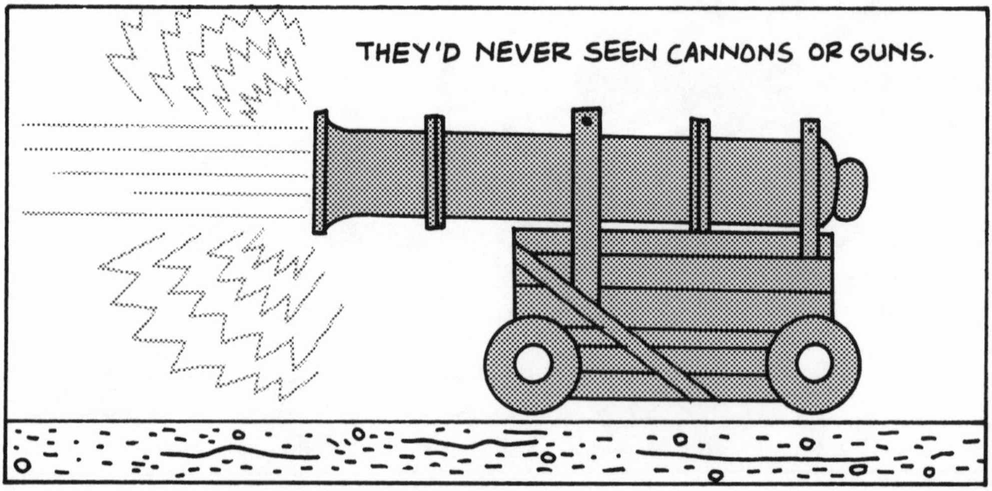
THEY'D NEVER SEEN CANNONS OR GUNS.

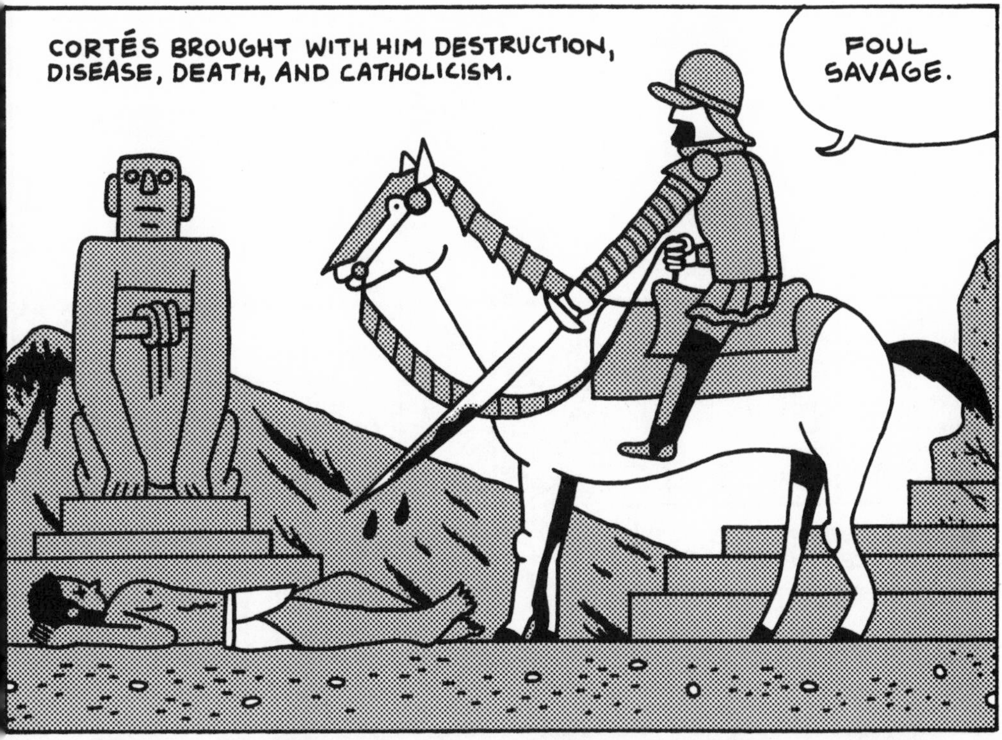
CORTÉS BROUGHT WITH HIM DESTRUCTION, DISEASE, DEATH, AND CATHOLICISM.
FOUL SAVAGE.

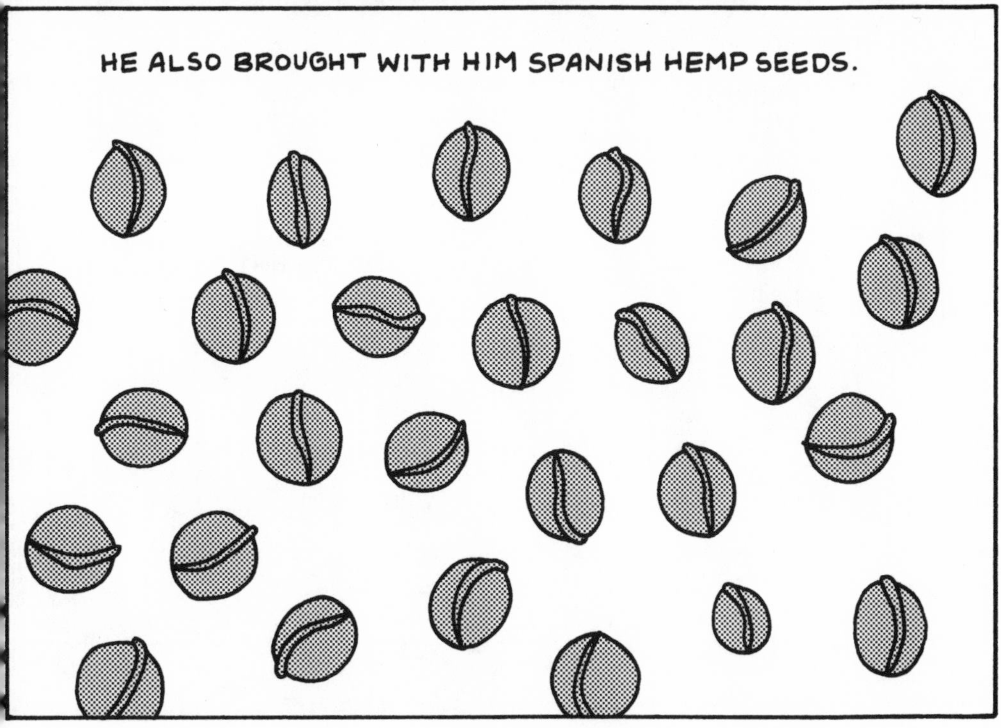
HE ALSO BROUGHT WITH HIM SPANISH HEMP SEEDS.

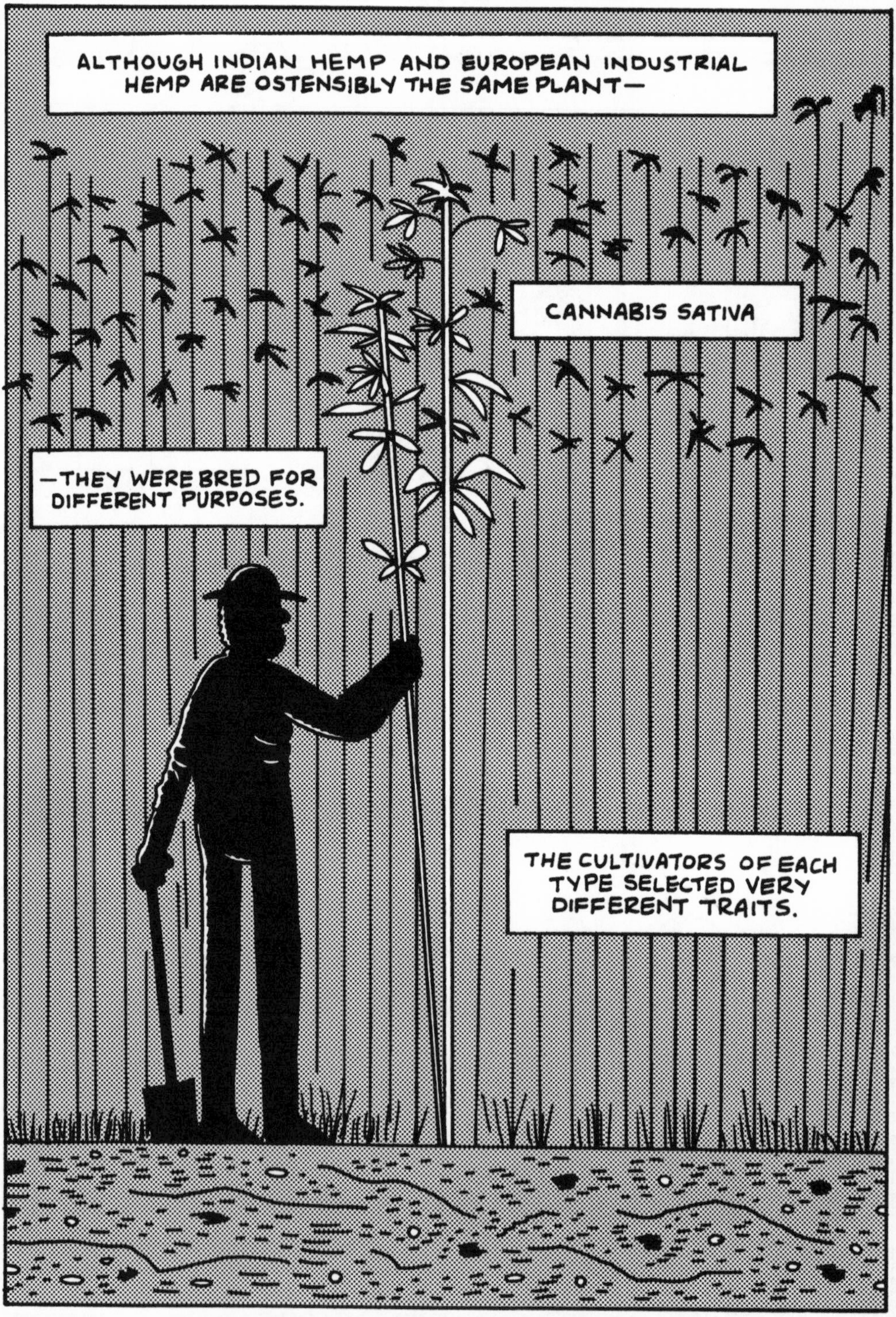
ALTHOUGH INDIAN HEMP AND EUROPEAN INDUSTRIAL HEMP ARE OSTENSIBLY THE SAME PLANT—
CANNABIS SATIVA
—THEY WERE BRED FOR DIFFERENT PURPOSES.
THE CULTIVATORS OF EACH TYPE SELECTED VERY DIFFERENT TRAITS.

INDUSTRIAL HEMP WAS SELECTED TO HAVE TALL AND STRONG FIBROUS STEMS.

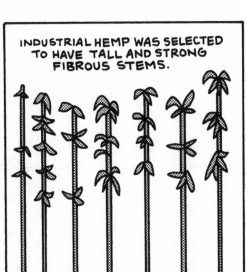

THESE FIBERS ARE WOVEN INTO RIGGING AND SAILS FOR SHIPS.

THEY'VE ALSO BEEN BRED TO PRODUCE SEEDS. HEMPSEED OIL WAS USED SIMILARLY TO LINSEED OIL.

HEMP WAS A CASH CROP.

PEOPLE IN SPAIN WEREN'T CONSUMING HEMP. THEY SMOKED TOBACCO, DRANK TEA AND LIQUOR.

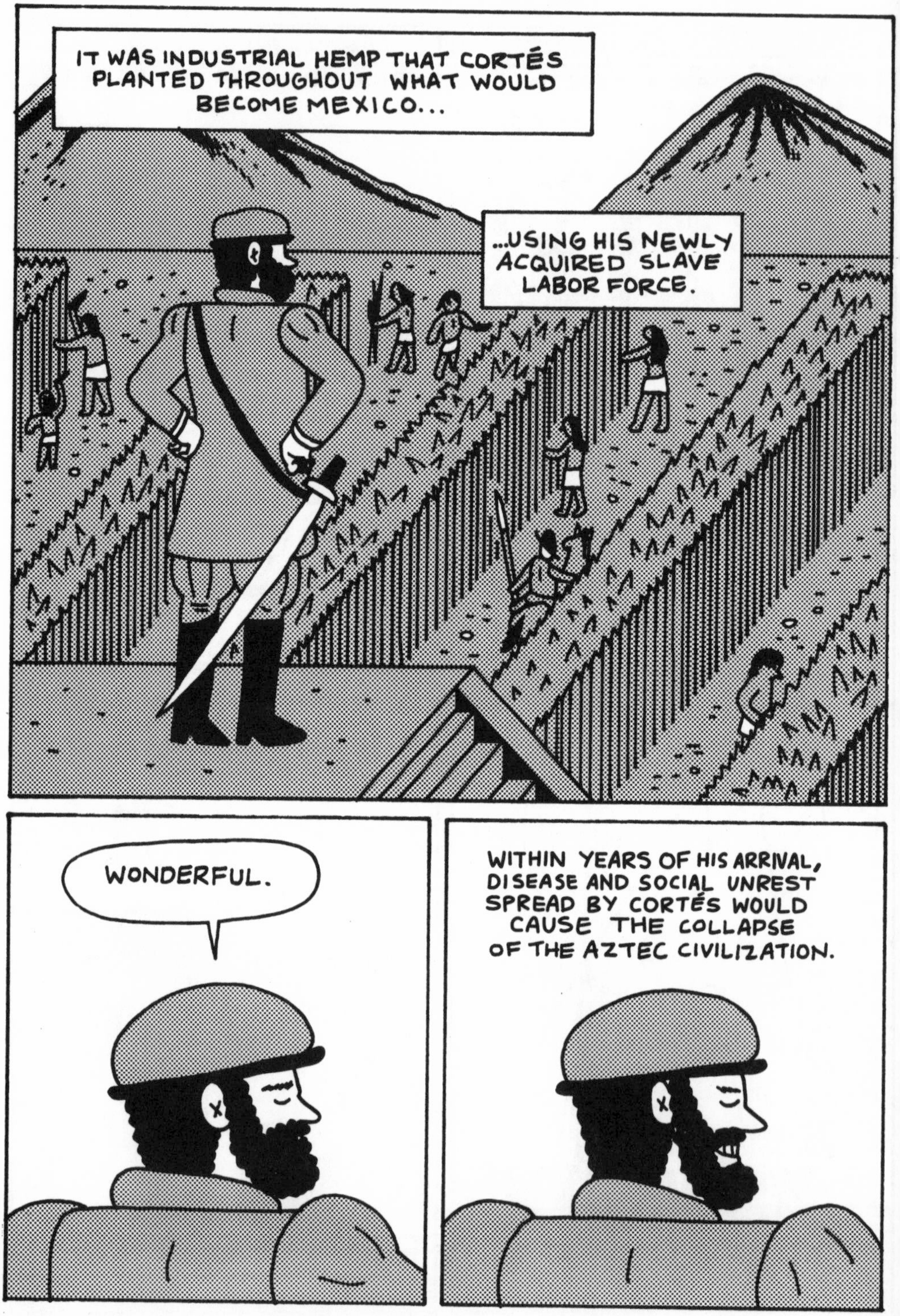
IT WAS INDUSTRIAL HEMP THAT CORTÉS PLANTED THROUGHOUT WHAT WOULD BECOME MEXICO...
...USING HIS NEWLY ACQUIRED SLAVE LABOR FORCE.
WONDERFUL.
WITHIN YEARS OF HIS ARRIVAL, DISEASE AND SOCIAL UNREST SPREAD BY CORTÉS WOULD CAUSE THE COLLAPSE OF THE AZTEC CIVILIZATION.

OVER THE NEXT FEW CENTURIES, CULTIVATORS OBSERVED SOME PLANTS GROWING FLOWERS OR BUDS.

AT SOME POINT, CULTIVATORS BEGAN TO CONSUME THE BUD.

AND FARMERS BEGAN CULTIVATING THE HEMP PLANT FOR CONSUMPTION, CHANGING THE CHARACTERISTICS OF THE PLANT. THEY BECAME SHORTER AND LESS FIBROUS, RESEMBLING THE CANNABIS PLANTS IN INDIA.

LESS FIBROUS STEMS

LARGER FLOWERS OR BUDS

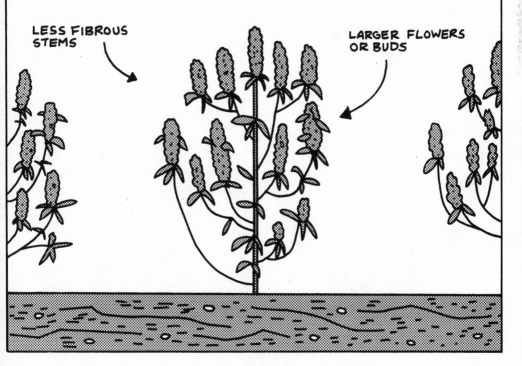

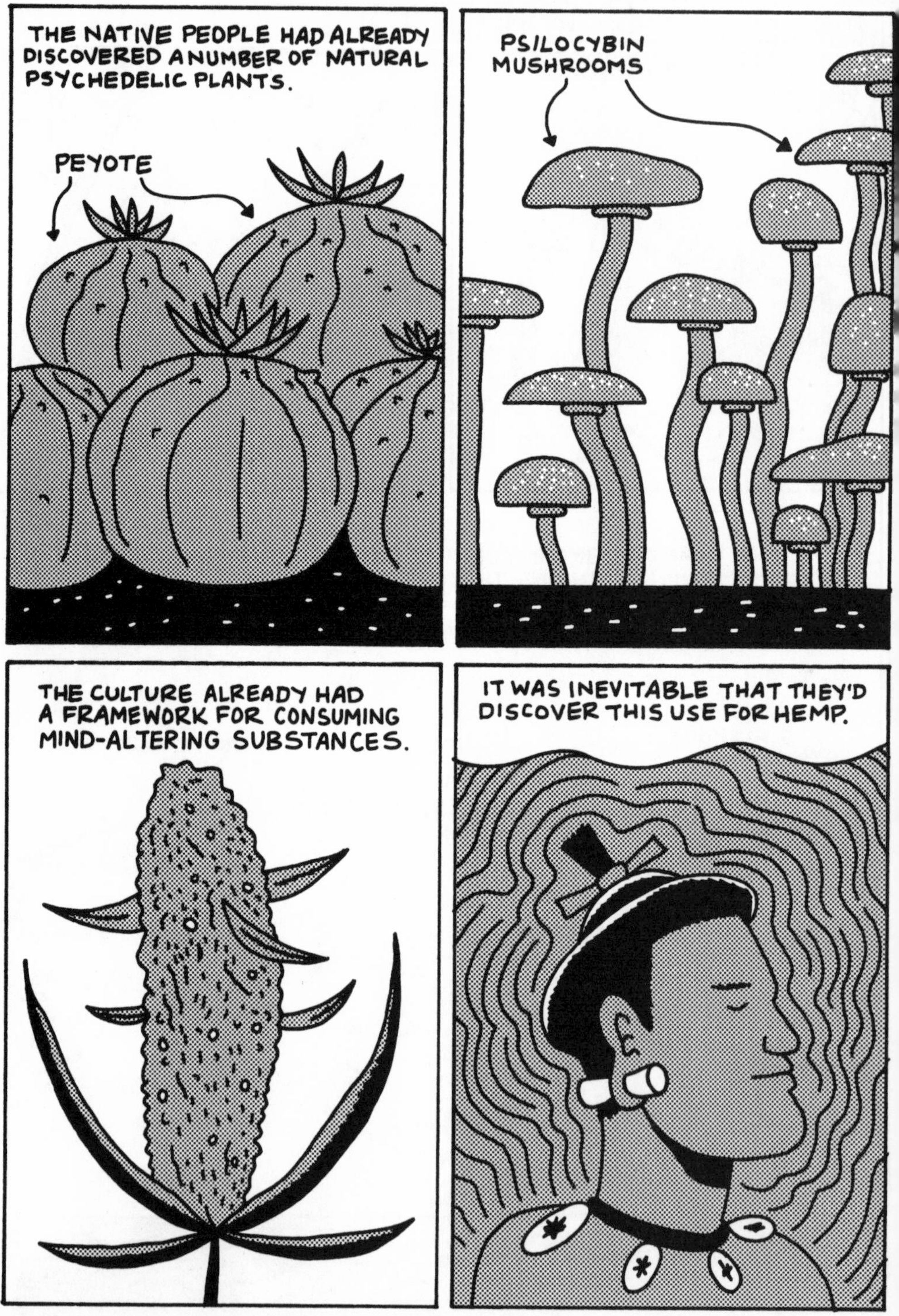
THE NATIVE PEOPLE HAD ALREADY DISCOVERED A NUMBER OF NATURAL PSYCHEDELIC PLANTS.
PEYOTE
PSILOCYBIN MUSHROOMS
THE CULTURE ALREADY HAD A FRAMEWORK FOR CONSUMING MIND-ALTERING SUBSTANCES.
IT WAS INEVITABLE THAT THEY'D DISCOVER THIS USE FOR HEMP.

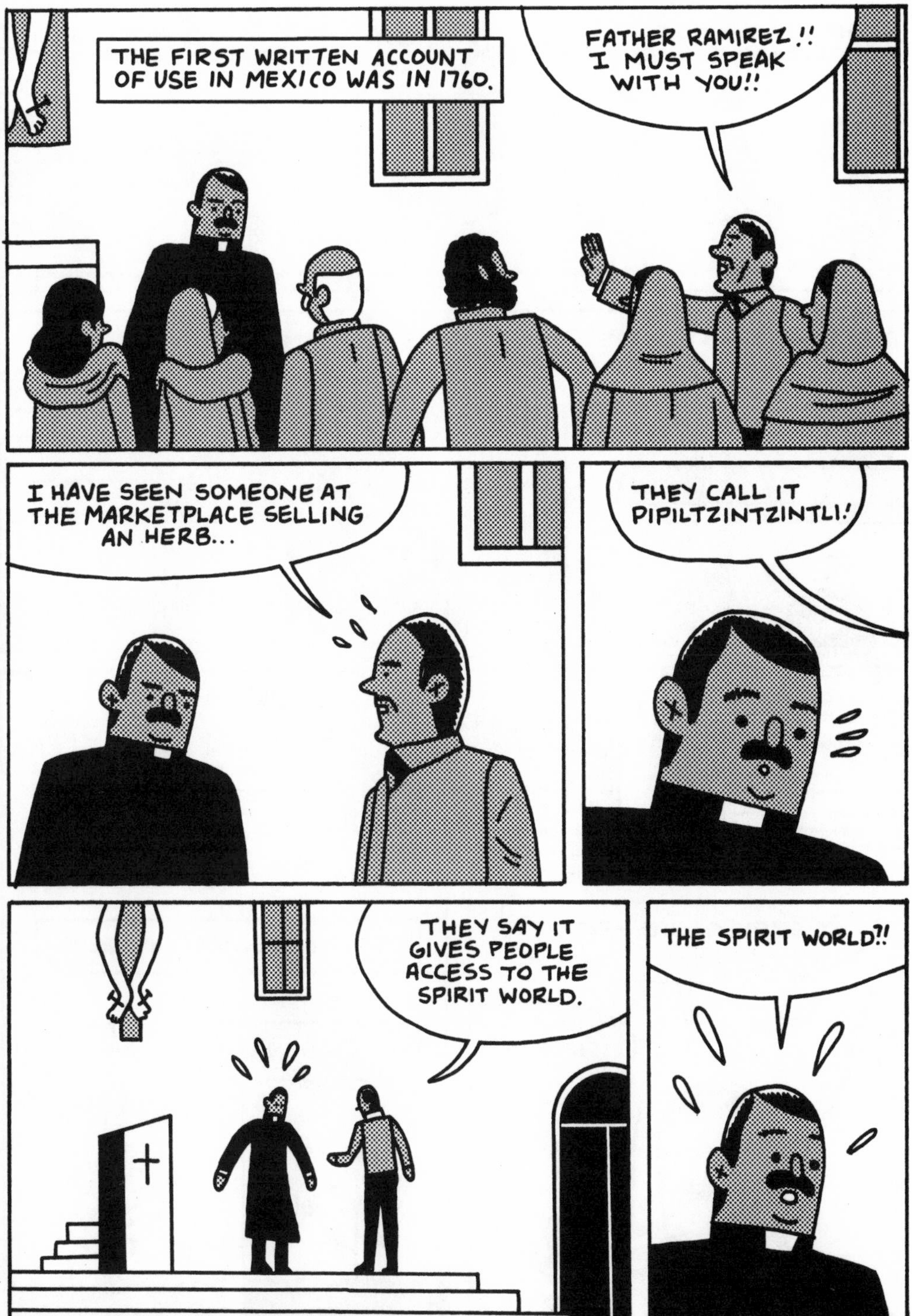
THE FIRST WRITTEN ACCOUNT OF USE IN MEXICO WAS IN 1760.
FATHER RAMIREZ!! I MUST SPEAK WITH YOU!!
I HAVE SEEN SOMEONE AT THE MARKETPLACE SELLING AN HERB...
THEY CALL IT PIPILTZINTZINTLI!
THEY SAY IT GIVES PEOPLE ACCESS TO THE SPIRIT WORLD.
THE SPIRIT WORLD?!

THE SPIRIT WORLD. THAT IS FRIGHTENING.

WHAT IS THIS HERB THAT WOULD ALLOW ITS USER TO BE CO-OPTED BY SATAN?

PIPILTZINTZINTLI? THIS? AND I MAKE A TEA OR CONSUME IT SOMEHOW?

IT SMELLS LIKE HEMP.

PUNGENT.

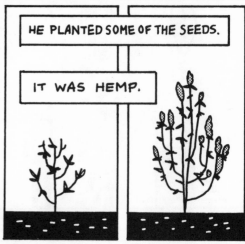

HE PLANTED SOME OF THE SEEDS.

IT WAS HEMP.

48

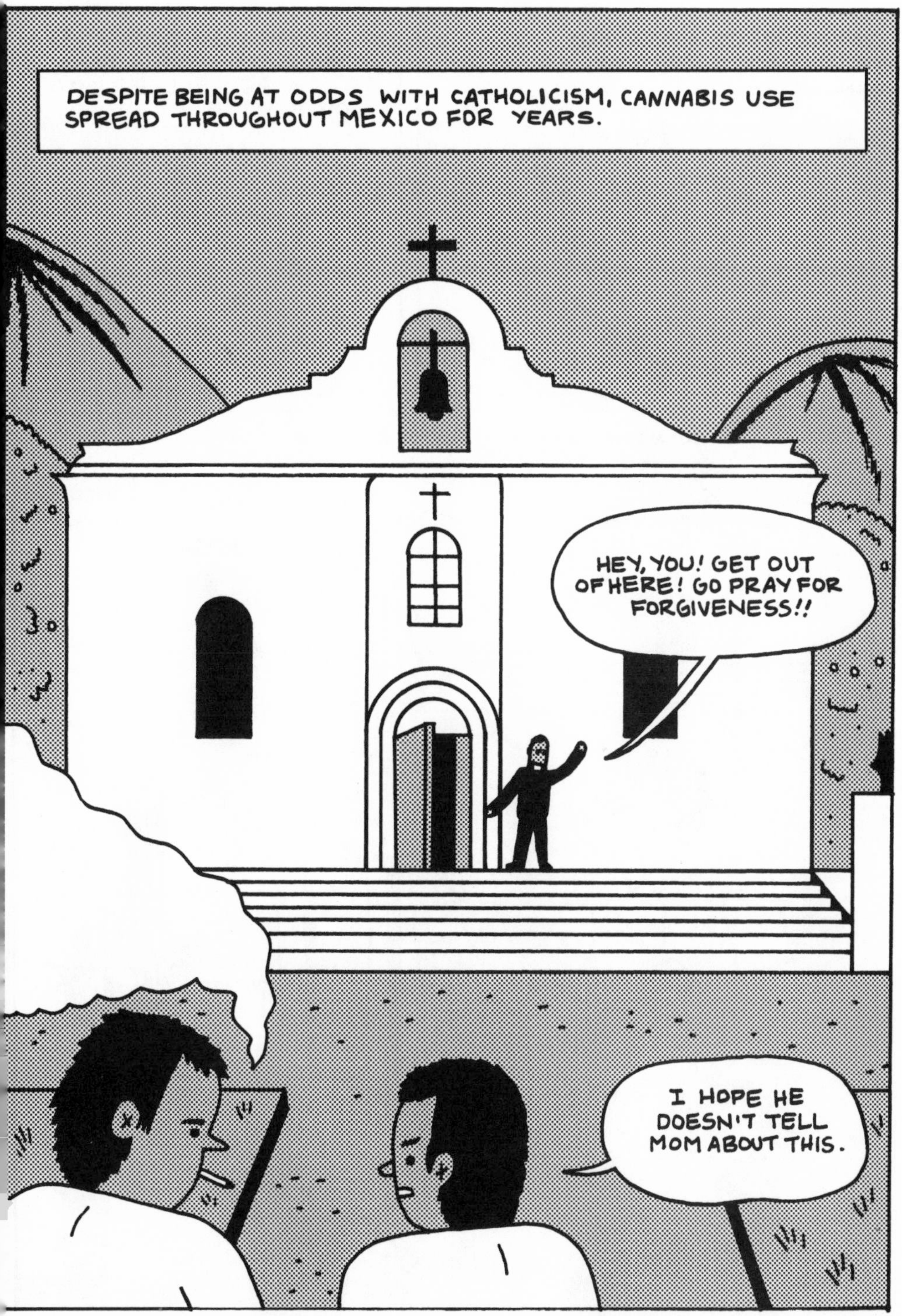
DESPITE BEING AT ODDS WITH CATHOLICISM, CANNABIS USE SPREAD THROUGHOUT MEXICO FOR YEARS.
HEY, YOU! GET OUT OF HERE! GO PRAY FOR FORGIVENESS!!
I HOPE HE DOESN'T TELL MOM ABOUT THIS.

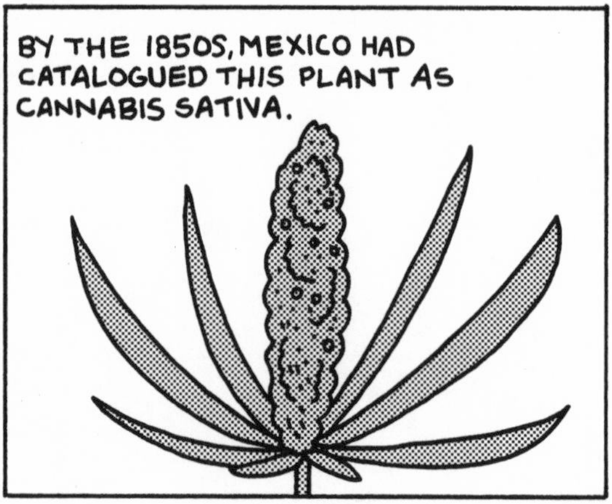
BY THE 1850S, MEXICO HAD CATALOGUED THIS PLANT AS CANNABIS SATIVA.

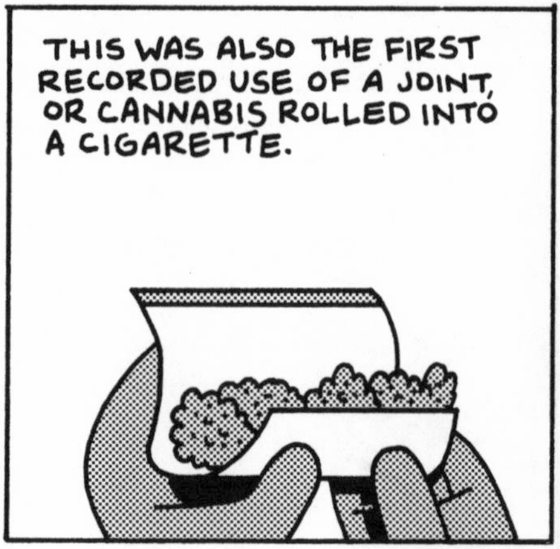
THIS WAS ALSO THE FIRST RECORDED USE OF A JOINT, OR CANNABIS ROLLED INTO A CIGARETTE.

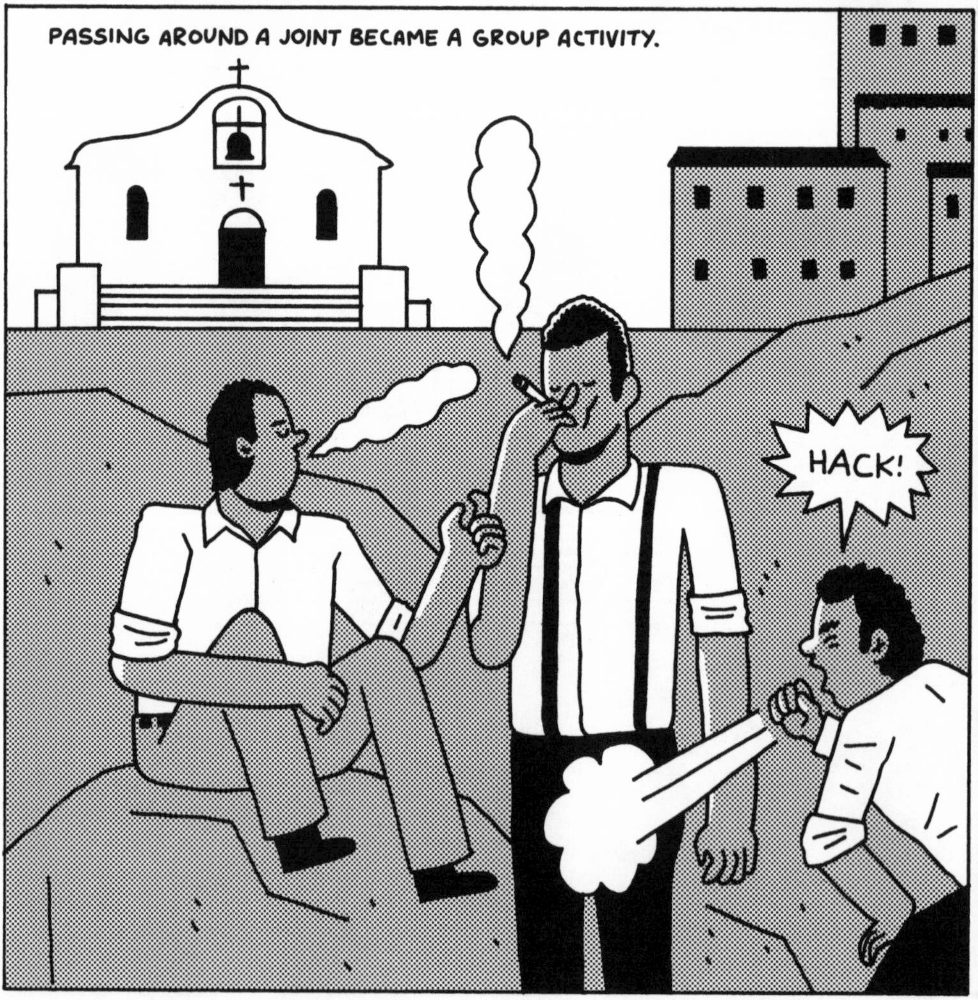
PASSING AROUND A JOINT BECAME A GROUP ACTIVITY.
HACK!

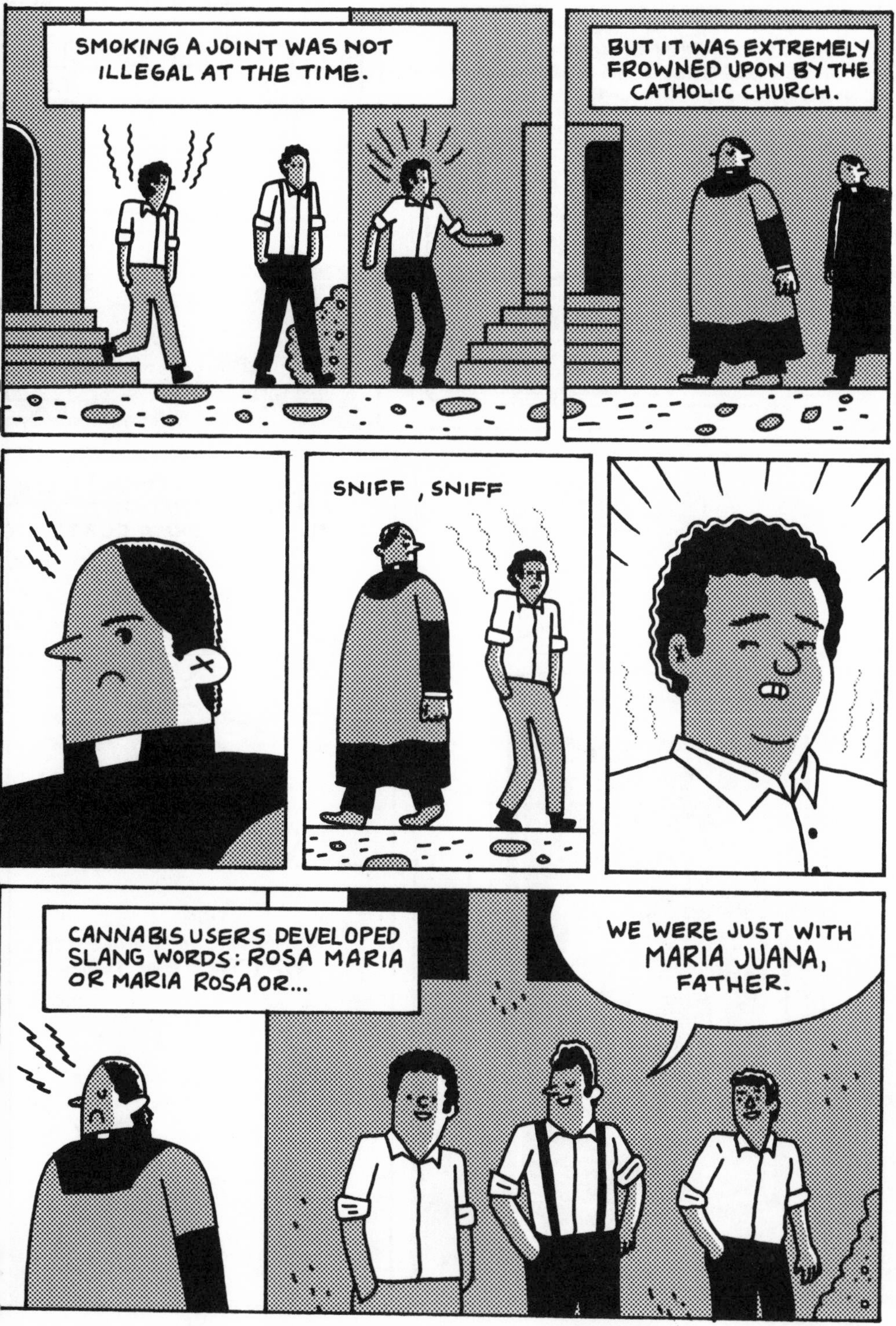
SMOKING A JOINT WAS NOT ILLEGAL AT THE TIME.
BUT IT WAS EXTREMELY FROWNED UPON BY THE CATHOLIC CHURCH.
SNIFF , SNIFF
CANNABIS USERS DEVELOPED SLANG WORDS: ROSA MARIA OR MARIA ROSA OR...
WE WERE JUST WITH MARIA JUANA, FATHER.

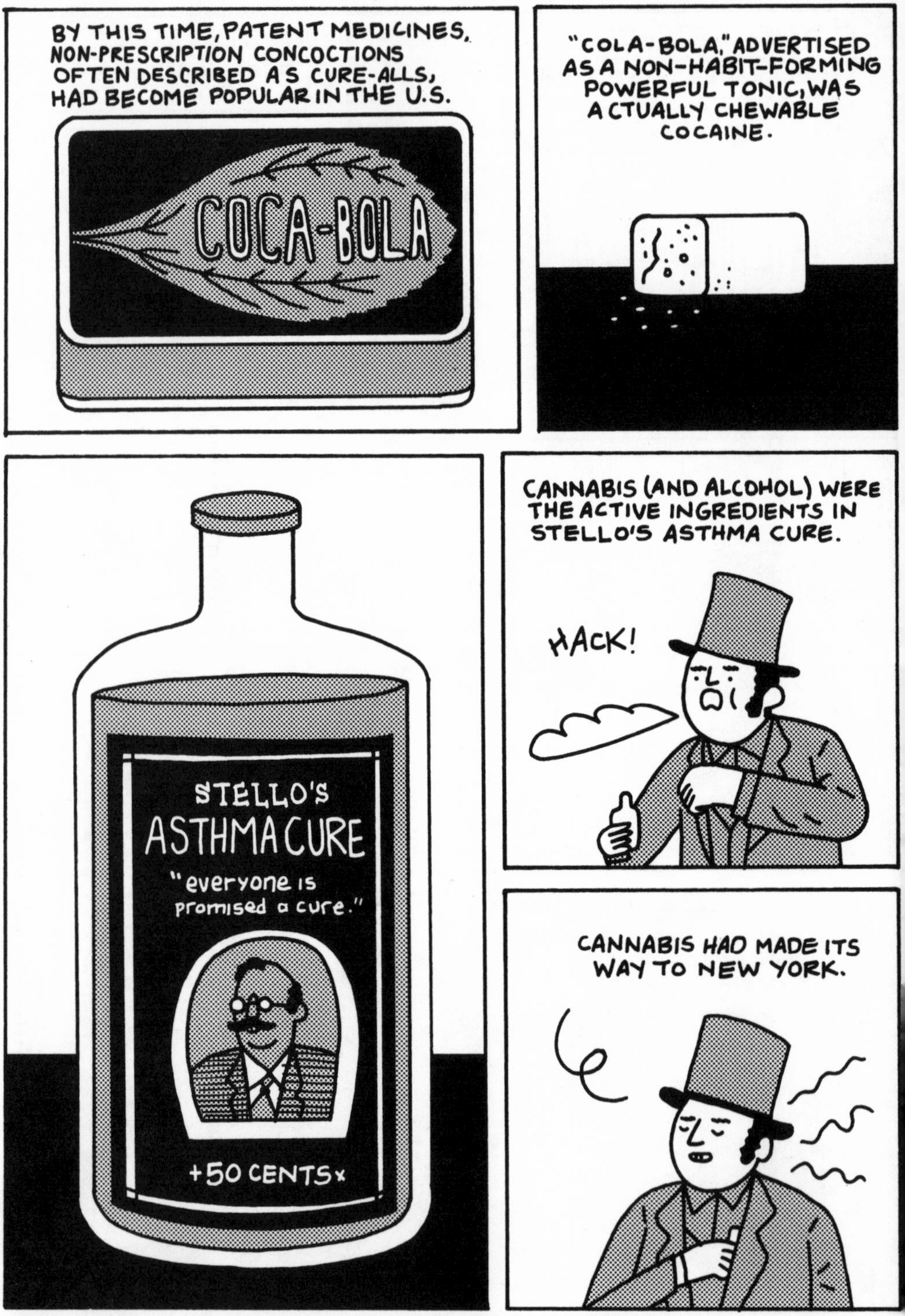
BY THIS TIME, PATENT MEDICINES, NON-PRESCRIPTION CONCOCTIONS OFTEN DESCRIBED AS CURE-ALLS, HAD BECOME POPULAR IN THE U.S.
COCA-BOLA
"COLA-BOLA," ADVERTISED AS A NON-HABIT-FORMING POWERFUL TONIC, WAS ACTUALLY CHEWABLE COCAINE.
STELLO'S
ASTHMA CURE
"everyone is promised a cure."
+50 CENTS×
CANNABIS (AND ALCOHOL) WERE THE ACTIVE INGREDIENTS IN STELLO'S ASTHMA CURE.
HACK!
CANNABIS HAD MADE ITS WAY TO NEW YORK.

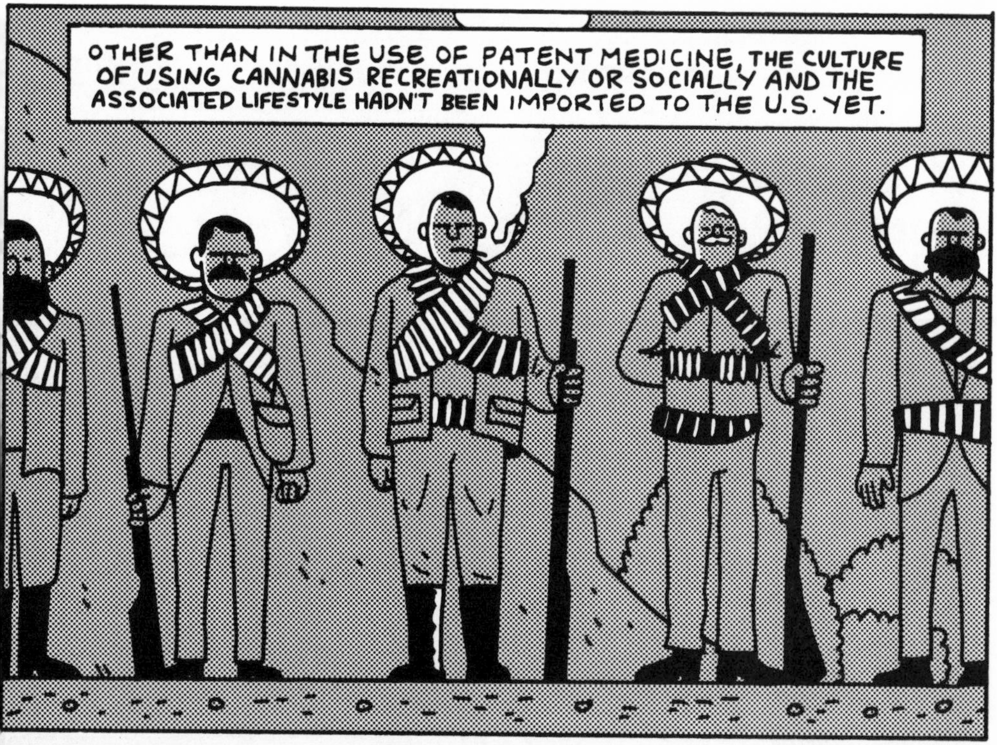
OTHER THAN IN THE USE OF PATENT MEDICINE, THE CULTURE OF USING CANNABIS RECREATIONALLY OR SOCIALLY AND THE ASSOCIATED LIFESTYLE HADN'T BEEN IMPORTED TO THE U.S. YET.

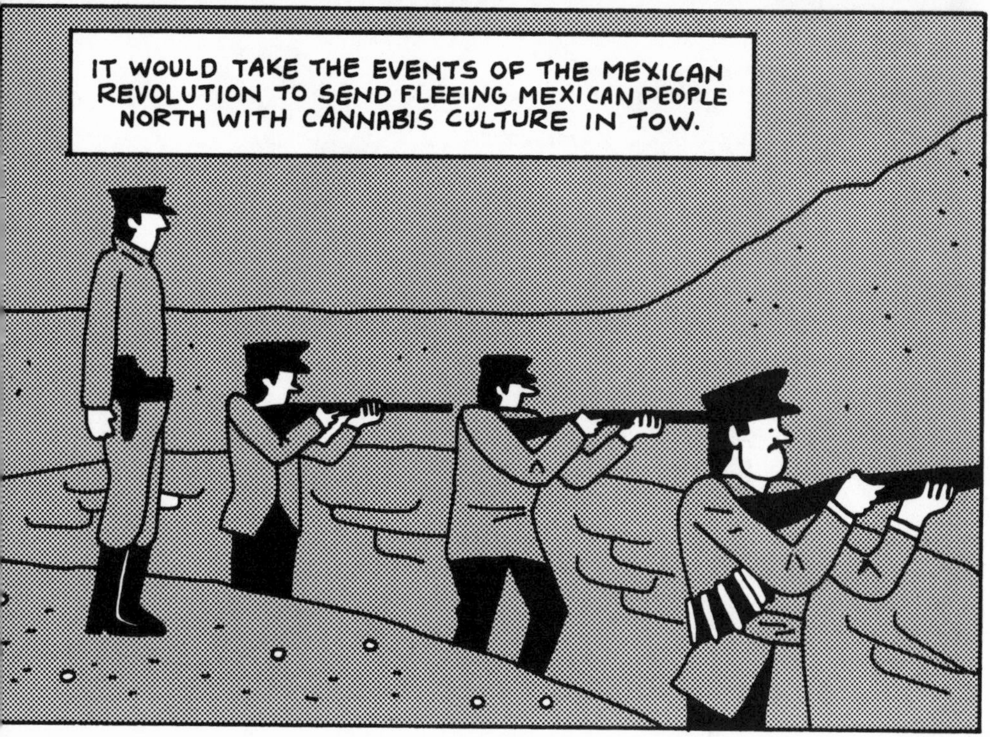
IT WOULD TAKE THE EVENTS OF THE MEXICAN REVOLUTION TO SEND FLEEING MEXICAN PEOPLE NORTH WITH CANNABIS CULTURE IN TOW.

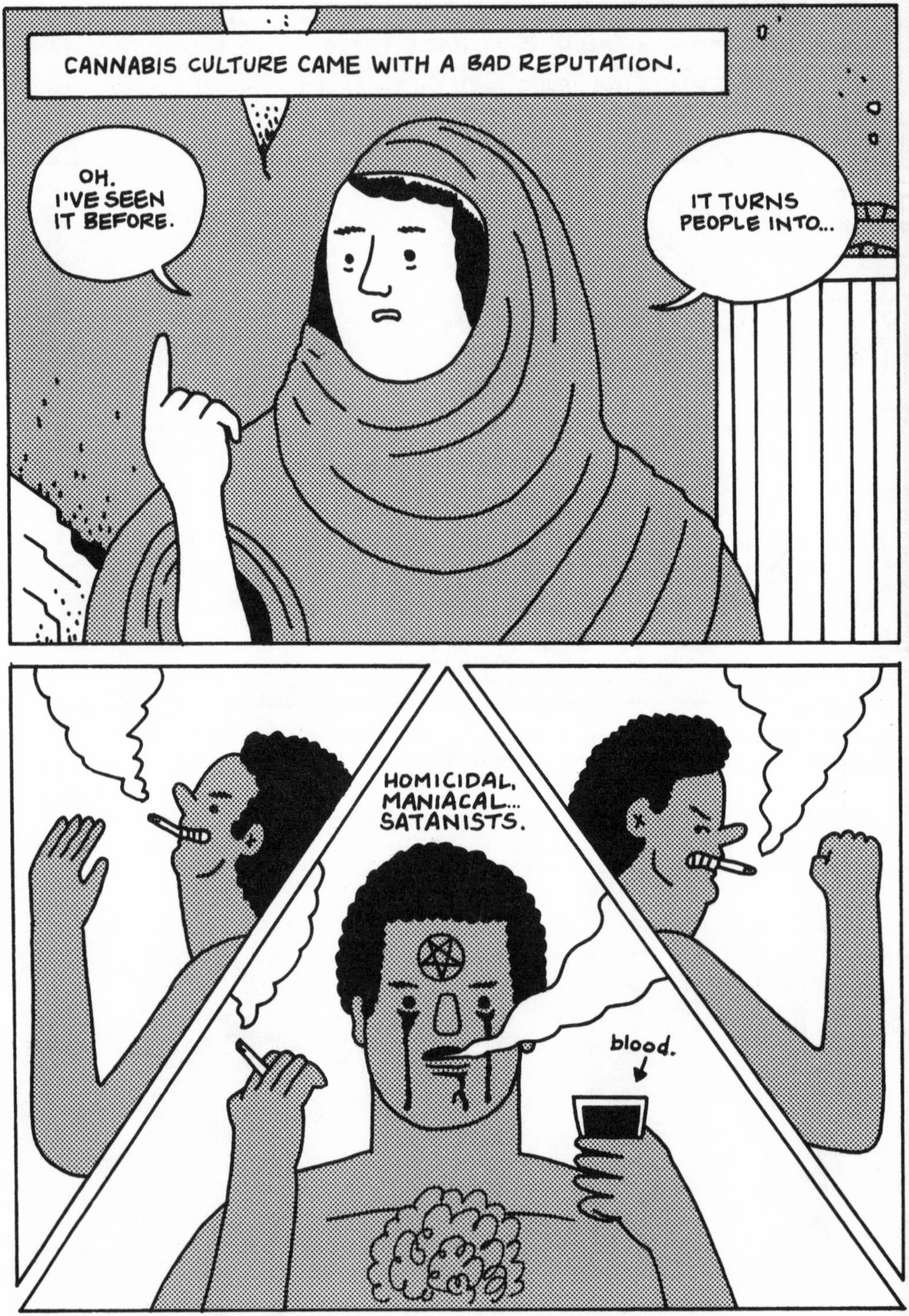
CANNABIS CULTURE CAME WITH A BAD REPUTATION.
OH. I'VE SEEN IT BEFORE.
IT TURNS PEOPLE INTO...
HOMICIDAL, MANIACAL... SATANISTS.
blood.

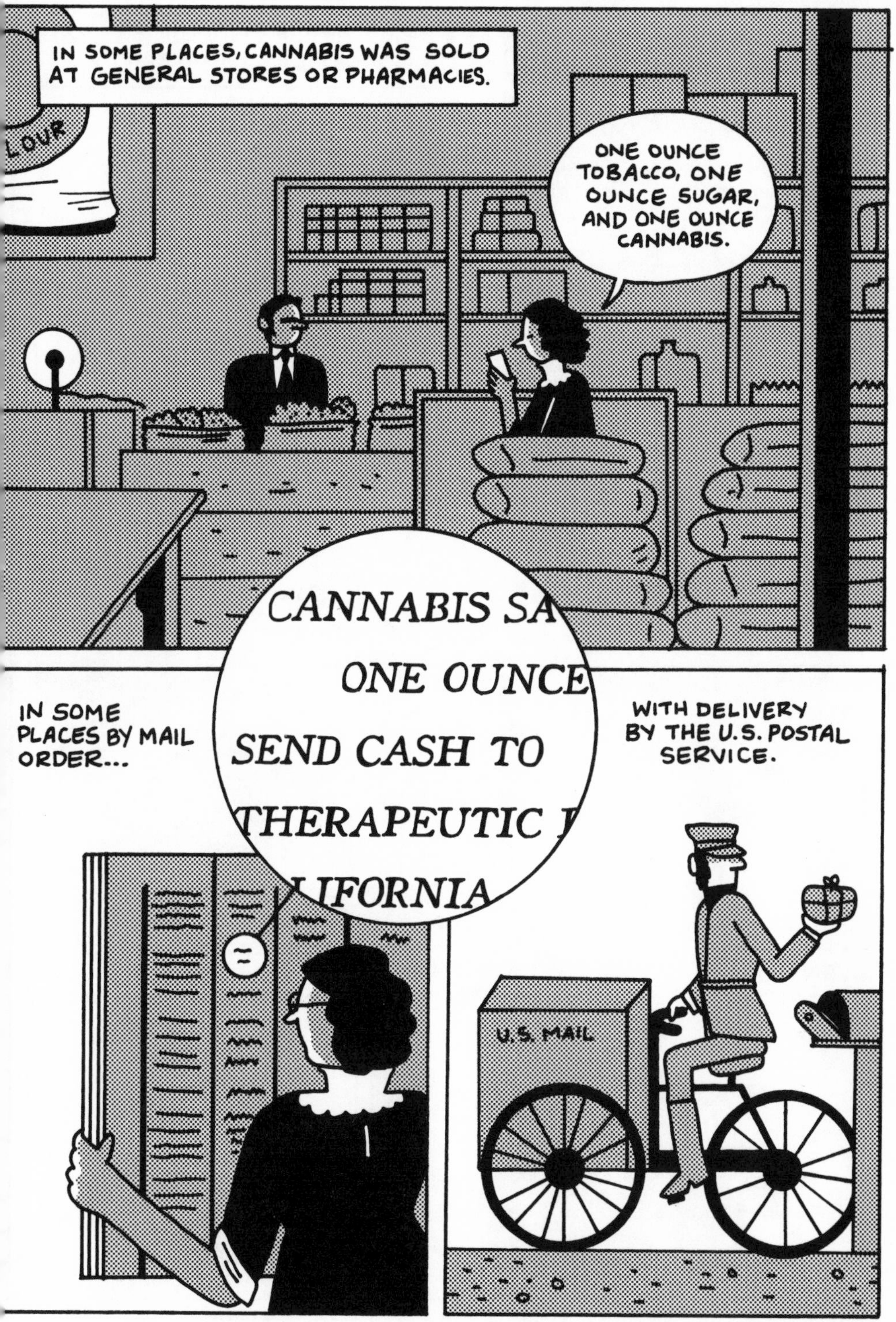
IN SOME PLACES, CANNABIS WAS SOLD AT GENERAL STORES OR PHARMACIES.
LOUR
ONE OUNCE TOBACCO, ONE OUNCE SUGAR, AND ONE OUNCE CANNABIS.
IN SOME PLACES BY MAIL ORDER...
CANNABIS SA
ONE OUNCE
SEND CASH TO
THERAPEUTIC
LIFORNIA
WITH DELIVERY BY THE U.S. POSTAL SERVICE.
U.S. MAIL

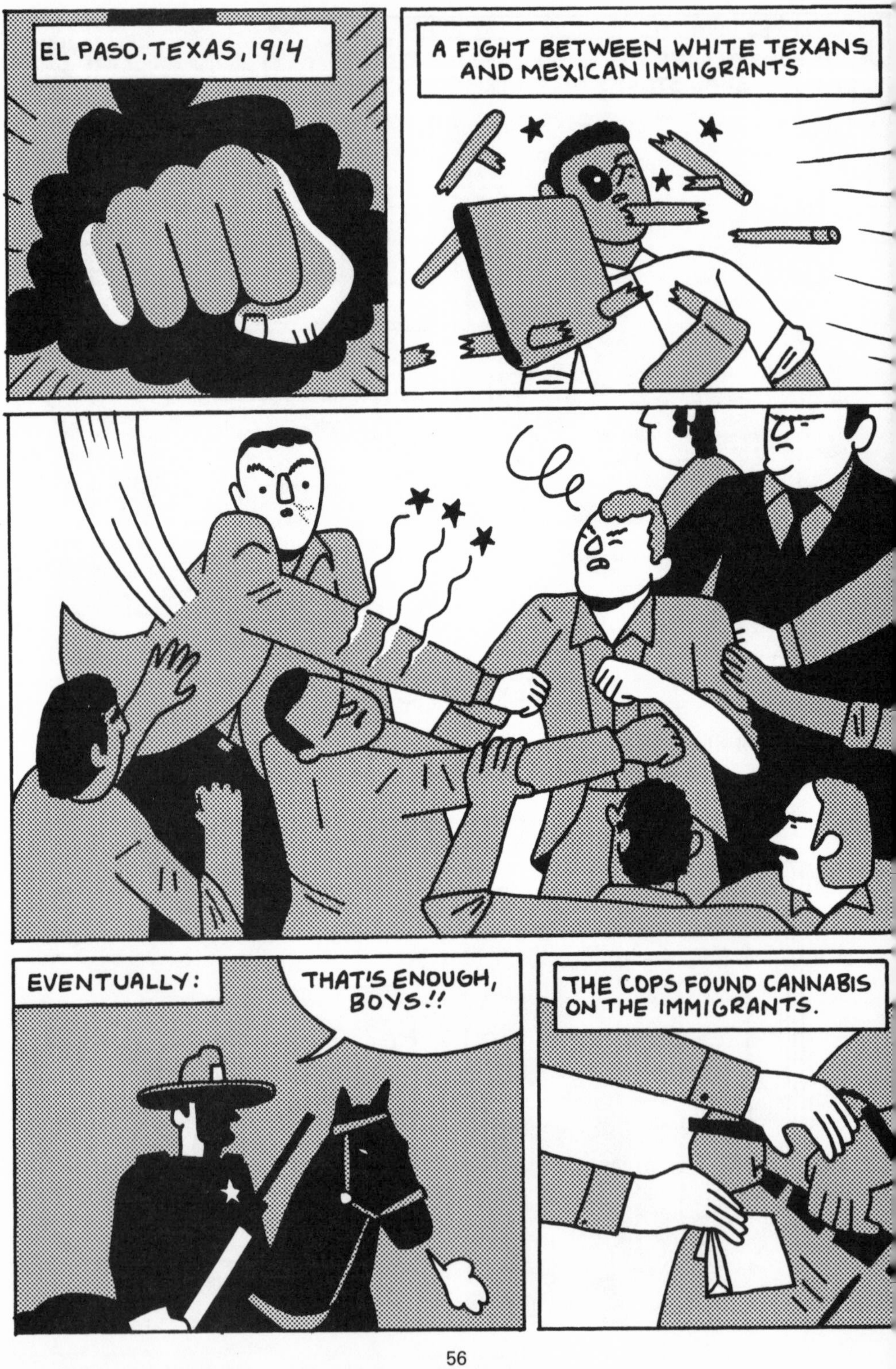
EL PASO, TEXAS, 1914
A FIGHT BETWEEN WHITE TEXANS AND MEXICAN IMMIGRANTS
EVENTUALLY:
THAT'S ENOUGH, BOYS!!
THE COPS FOUND CANNABIS ON THE IMMIGRANTS.

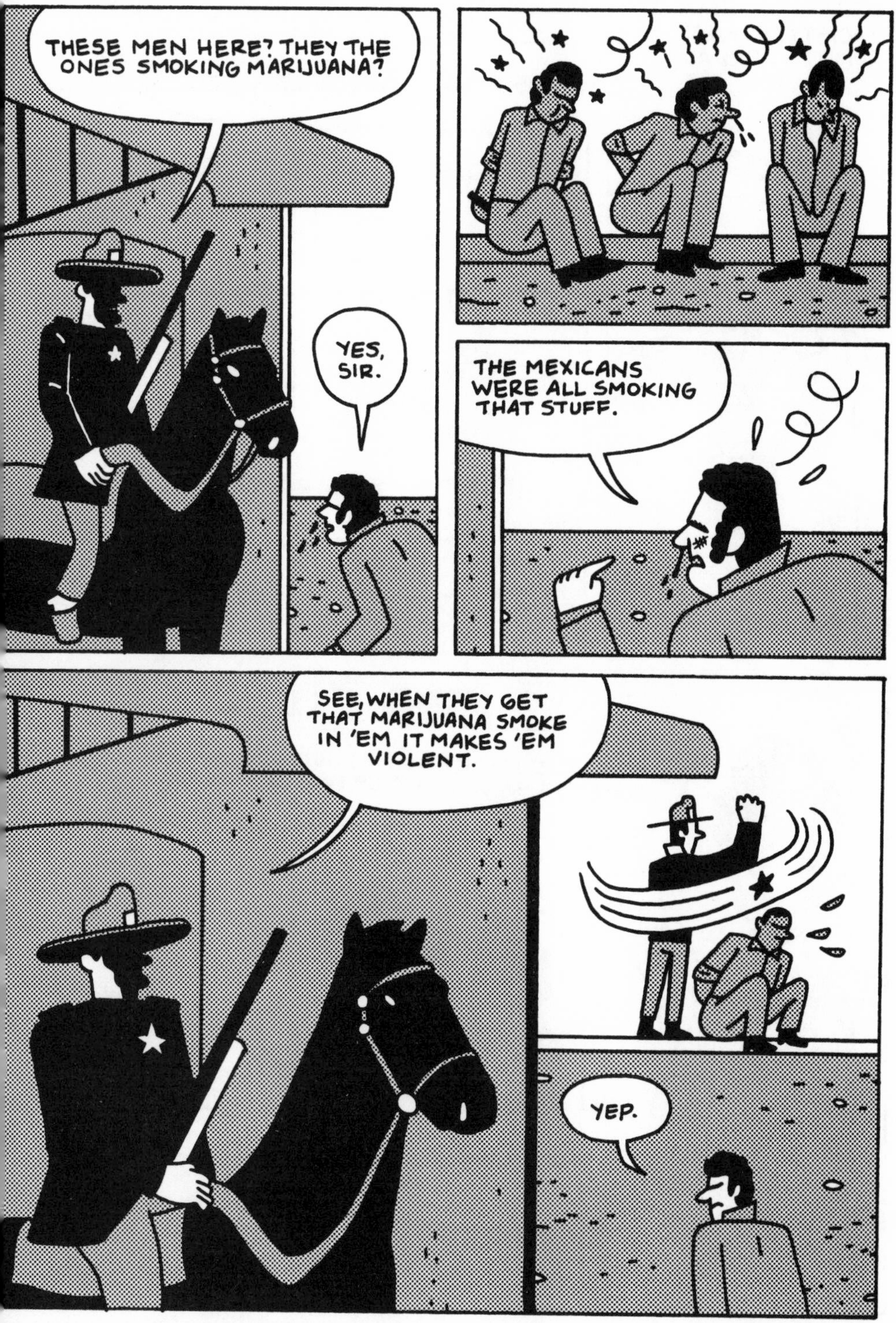
THESE MEN HERE? THEY THE ONES SMOKING MARIJUANA?
YES, SIR.
THE MEXICANS WERE ALL SMOKING THAT STUFF.
SEE, WHEN THEY GET THAT MARIJUANA SMOKE IN 'EM IT MAKES 'EM VIOLENT.
YEP.

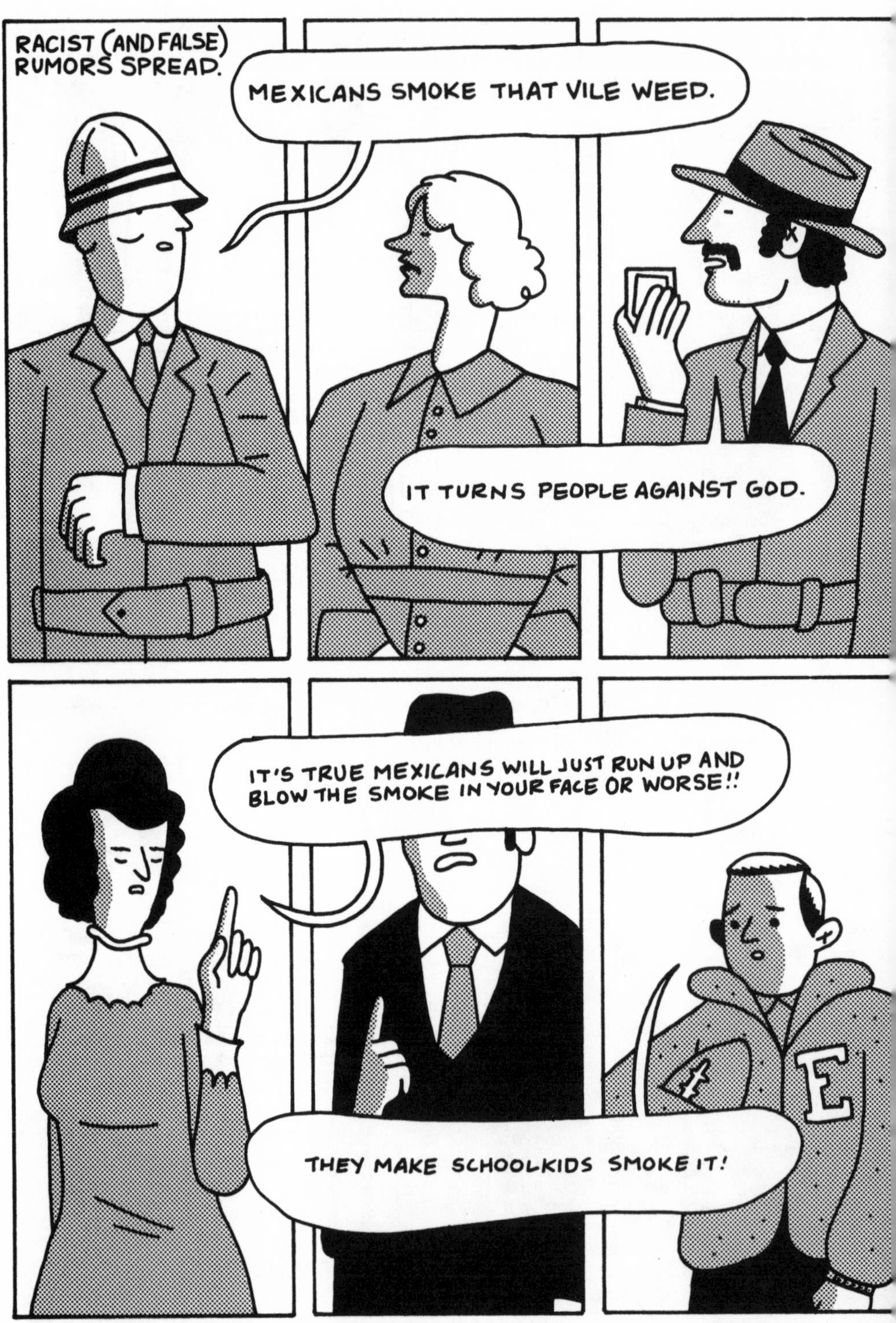
RACIST (AND FALSE) RUMORS SPREAD.
MEXICANS SMOKE THAT VILE WEED.
IT TURNS PEOPLE AGAINST GOD.
IT'S TRUE MEXICANS WILL JUST RUN UP AND BLOW THE SMOKE IN YOUR FACE OR WORSE!!
THEY MAKE SCHOOLKIDS SMOKE IT!
E

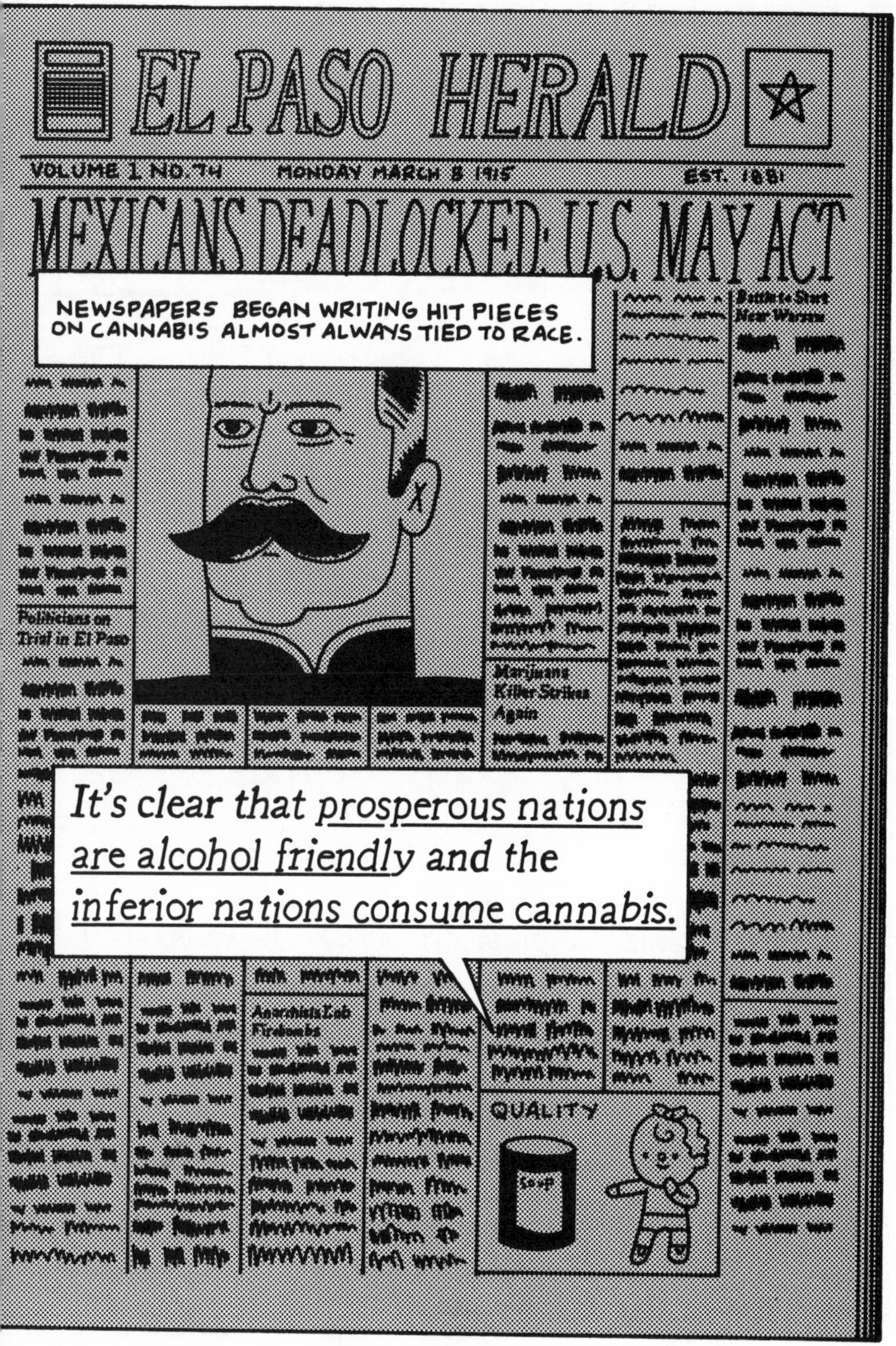
EL PASO HERALD
VOLUME 1 NO. 74
MONDAY MARCH 8 1915
EST. 1881
MEXICANS DEADLOCKED: U.S. MAY ACT
NEWSPAPERS BEGAN WRITING HIT PIECES ON CANNABIS ALMOST ALWAYS TIED TO RACE.
Battle to Start Near Warsaw
Politicians on Trial in El Paso
Marijuana Killer Strikes Again
It's clear that prosperous nations are alcohol friendly and the inferior nations consume cannabis.
Anarchists Lob Firebombs
QUALITY
SOUP

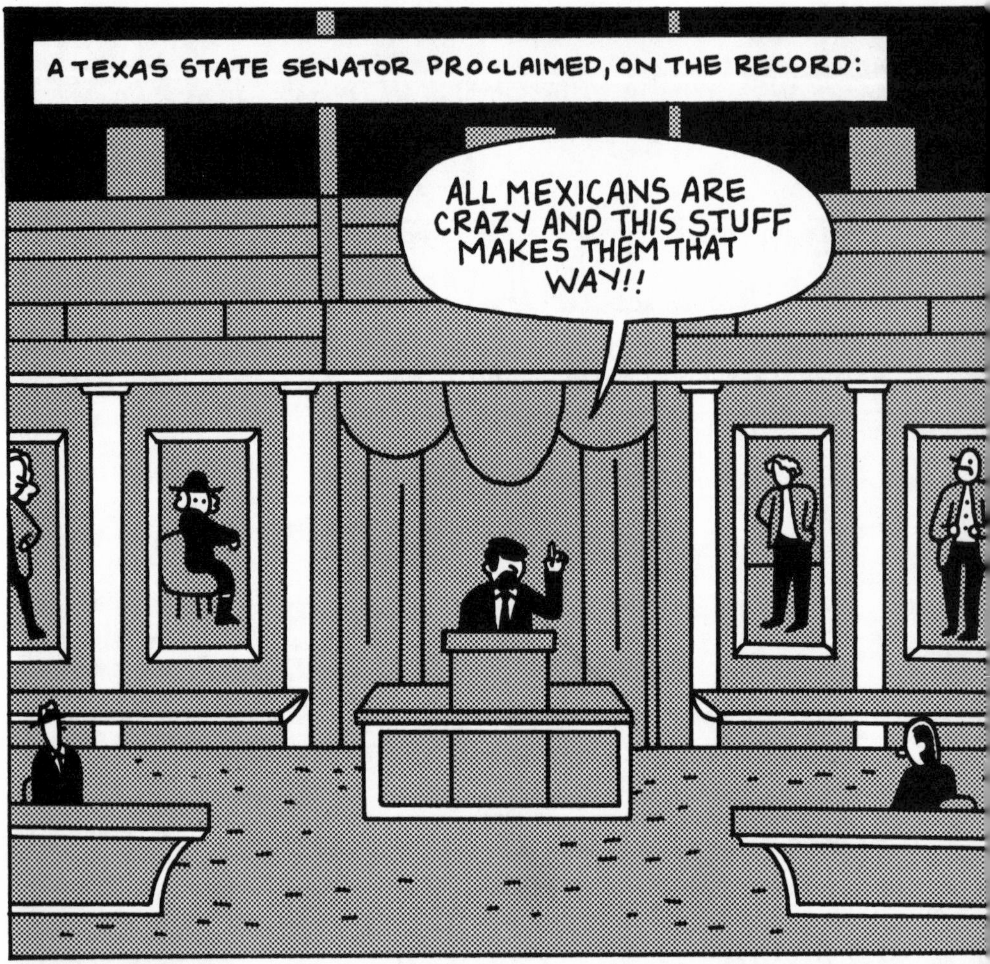
A TEXAS STATE SENATOR PROCLAIMED, ON THE RECORD:
ALL MEXICANS ARE CRAZY AND THIS STUFF MAKES THEM THAT WAY!!

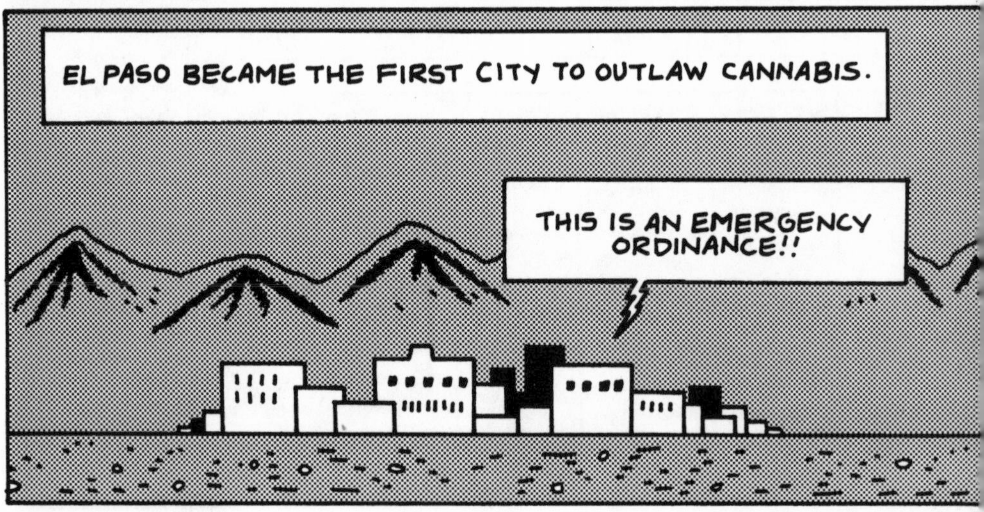
EL PASO BECAME THE FIRST CITY TO OUTLAW CANNABIS.
THIS IS AN EMERGENCY ORDINANCE!!

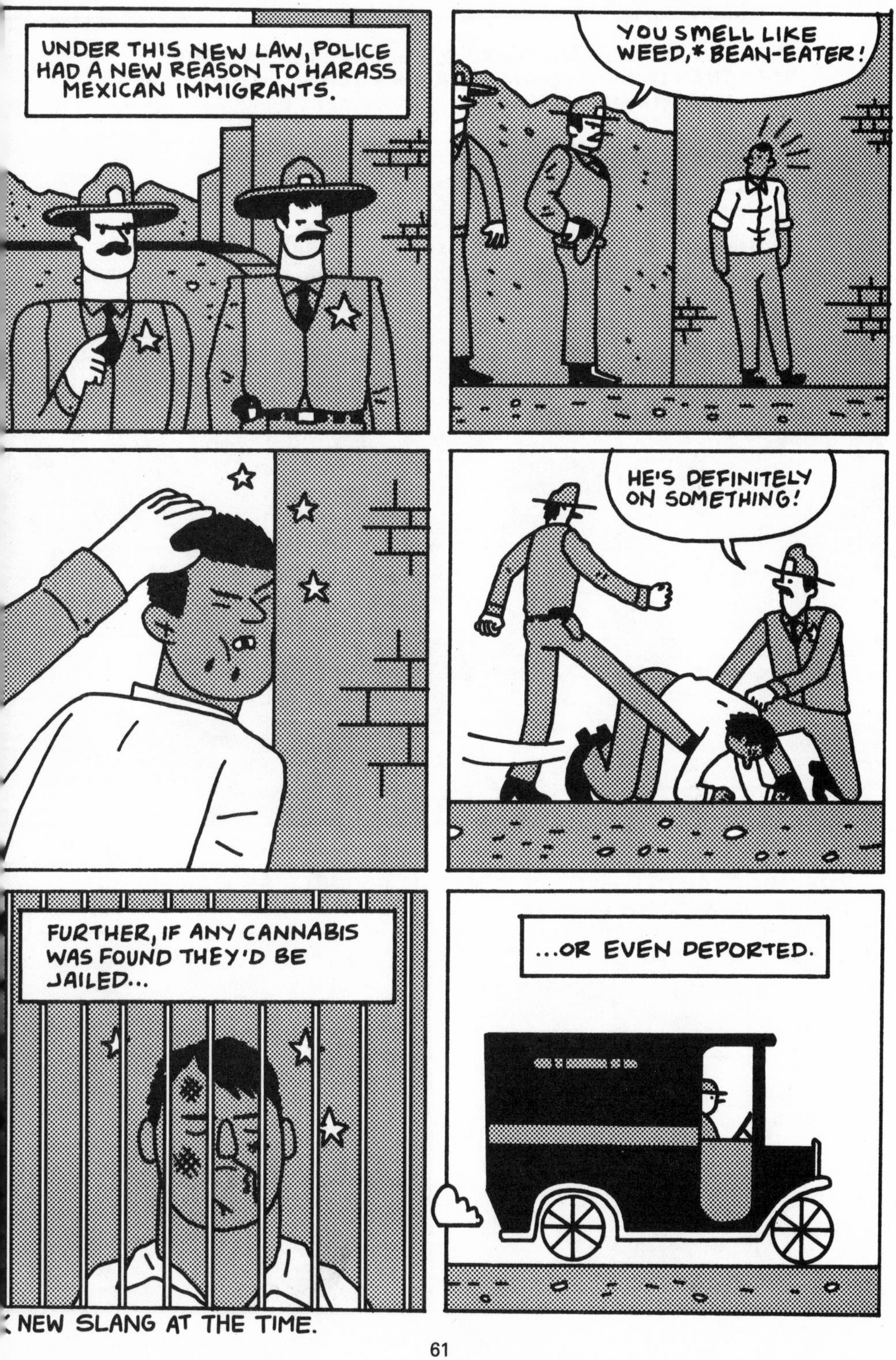
UNDER THIS NEW LAW, POLICE HAD A NEW REASON TO HARASS MEXICAN IMMIGRANTS.
YOU SMELL LIKE WEED,* BEAN-EATER!
HE'S DEFINITELY ON SOMETHING!
FURTHER, IF ANY CANNABIS WAS FOUND THEY'D BE JAILED...
...OR EVEN DEPORTED.

* NEW SLANG AT THE TIME.

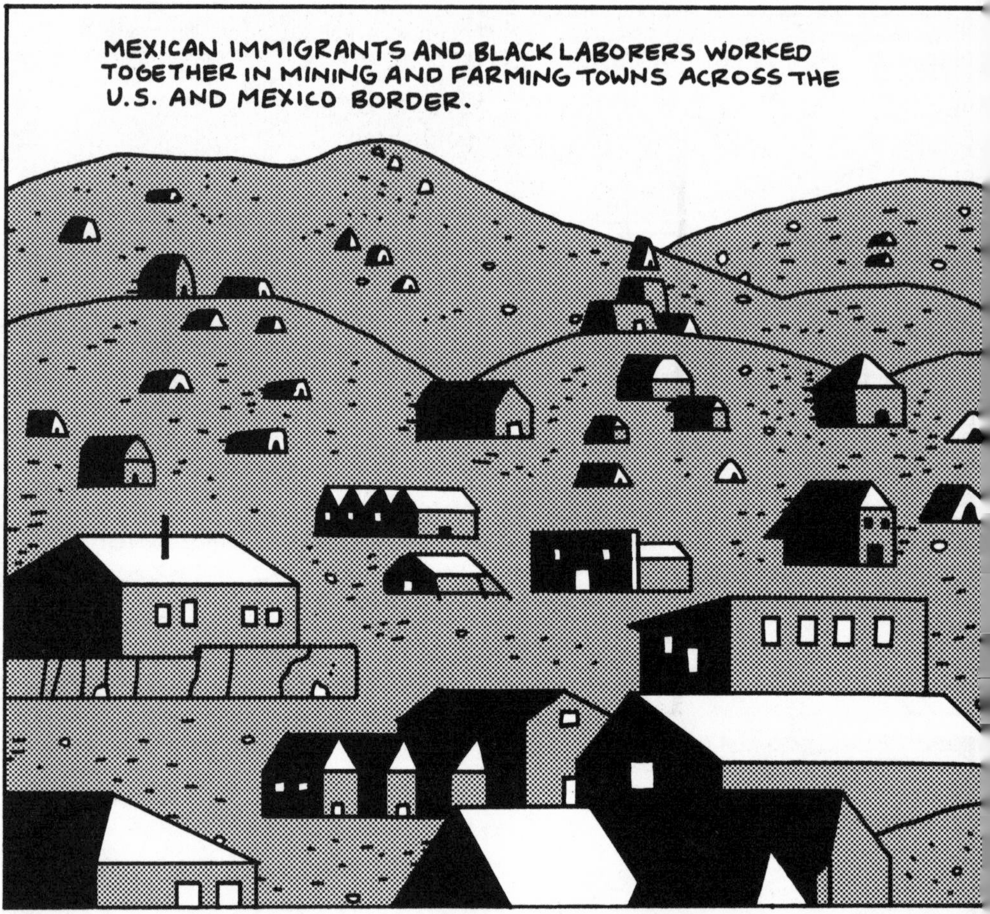
MEXICAN IMMIGRANTS AND BLACK LABORERS WORKED TOGETHER IN MINING AND FARMING TOWNS ACROSS THE U.S. AND MEXICO BORDER.

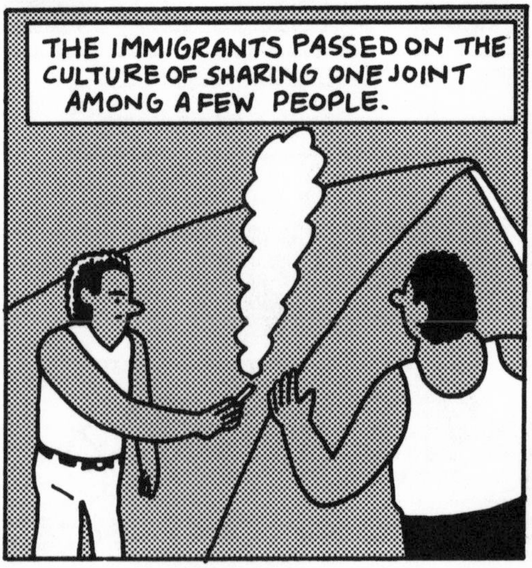
THE IMMIGRANTS PASSED ON THE CULTURE OF SHARING ONE JOINT AMONG A FEW PEOPLE.

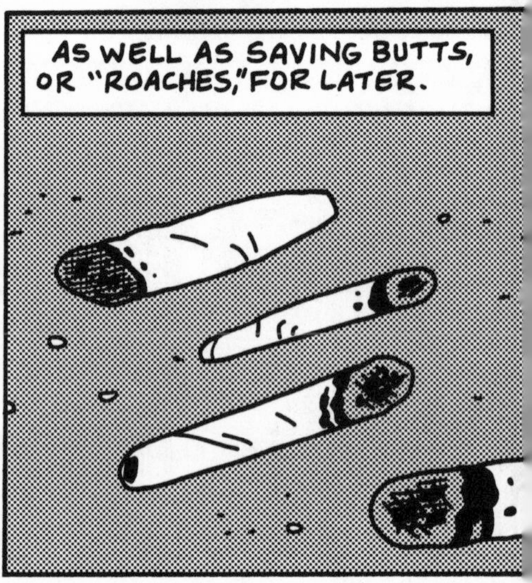
AS WELL AS SAVING BUTTS, OR "ROACHES," FOR LATER.

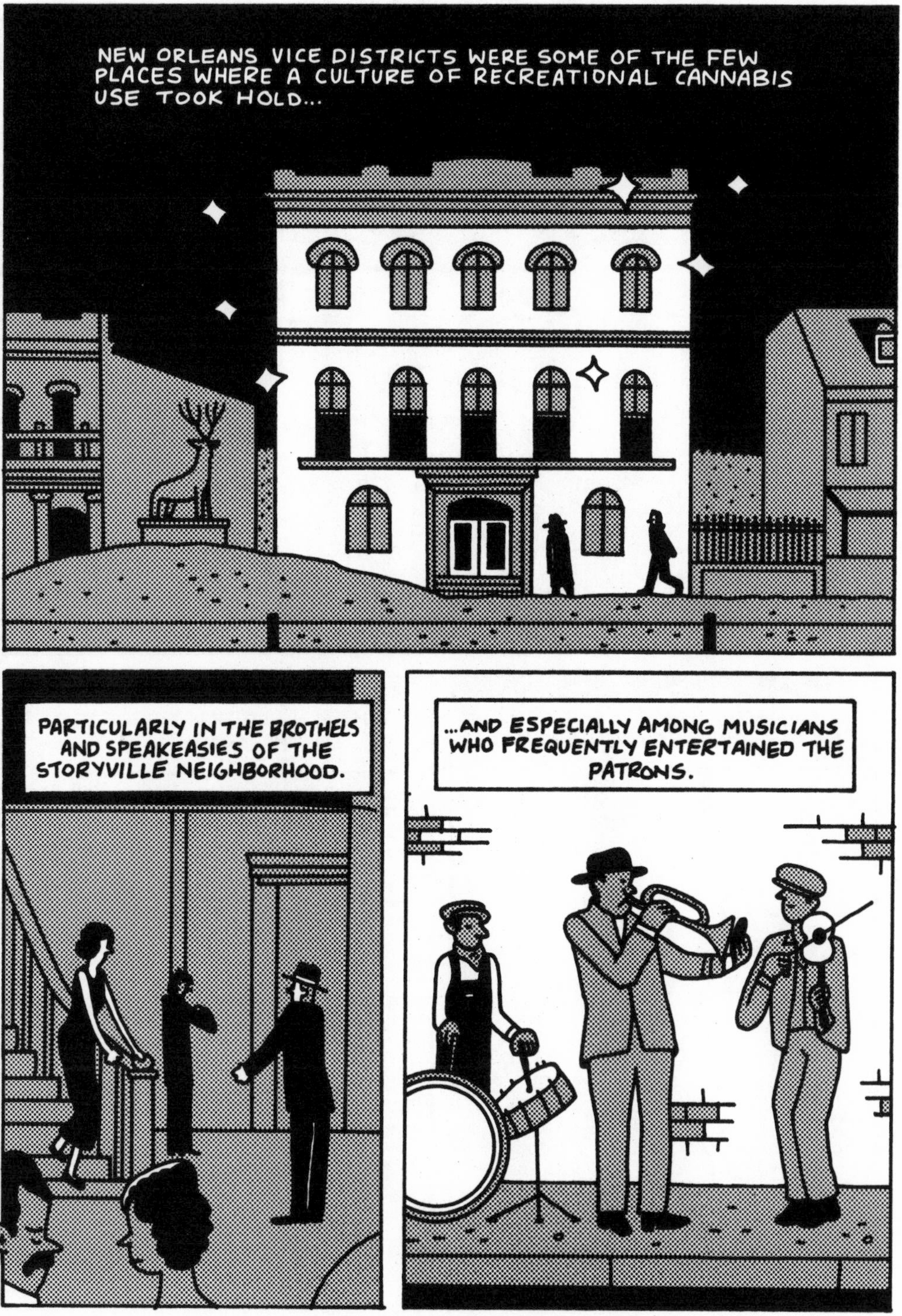
NEW ORLEANS VICE DISTRICTS WERE SOME OF THE FEW PLACES WHERE A CULTURE OF RECREATIONAL CANNABIS USE TOOK HOLD...
PARTICULARLY IN THE BROTHELS AND SPEAKEASIES OF THE STORYVILLE NEIGHBORHOOD.
...AND ESPECIALLY AMONG MUSICIANS WHO FREQUENTLY ENTERTAINED THE PATRONS.

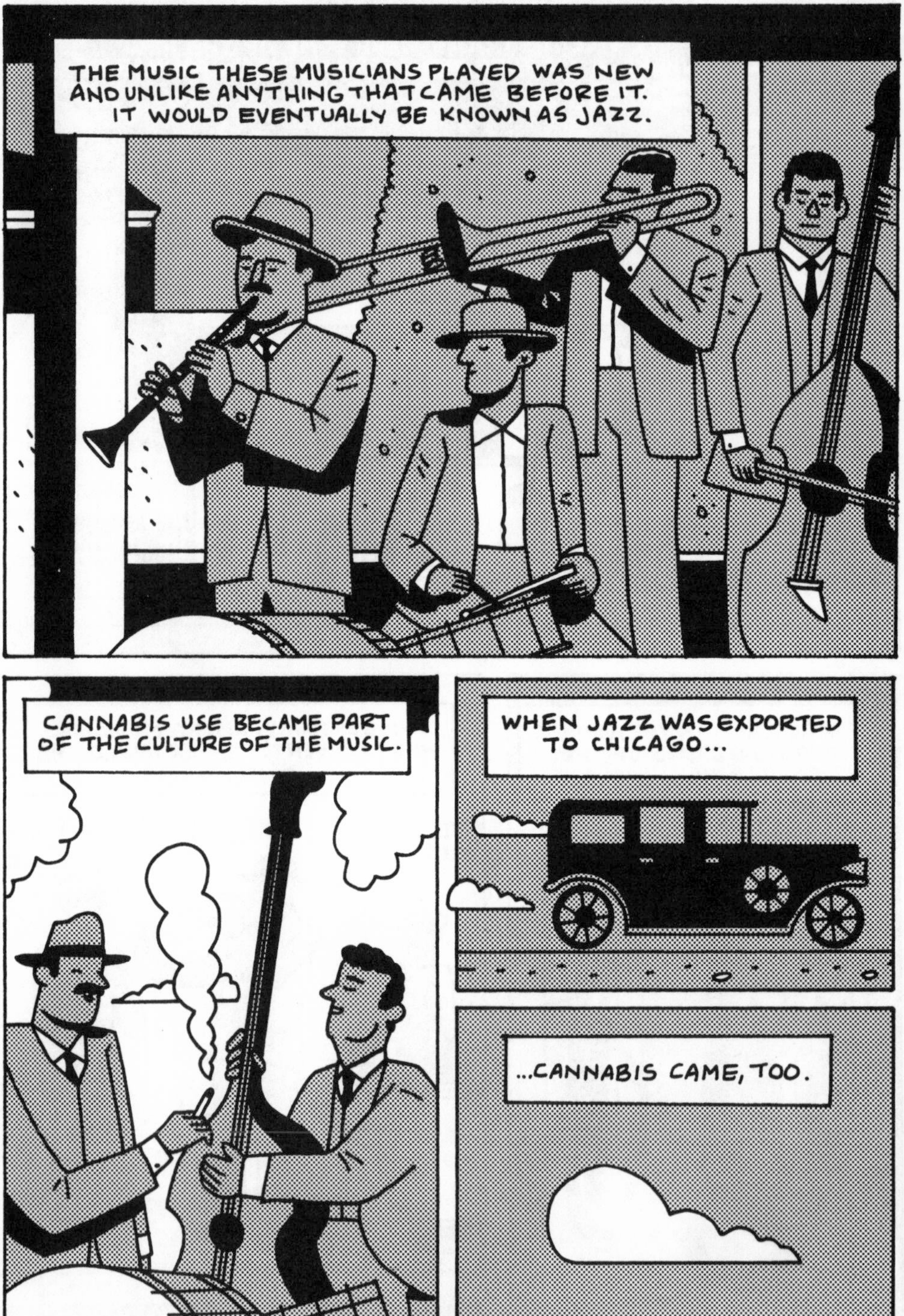
THE MUSIC THESE MUSICIANS PLAYED WAS NEW AND UNLIKE ANYTHING THAT CAME BEFORE IT. IT WOULD EVENTUALLY BE KNOWN AS JAZZ.
CANNABIS USE BECAME PART OF THE CULTURE OF THE MUSIC.
WHEN JAZZ WAS EXPORTED TO CHICAGO...
...CANNABIS CAME, TOO.

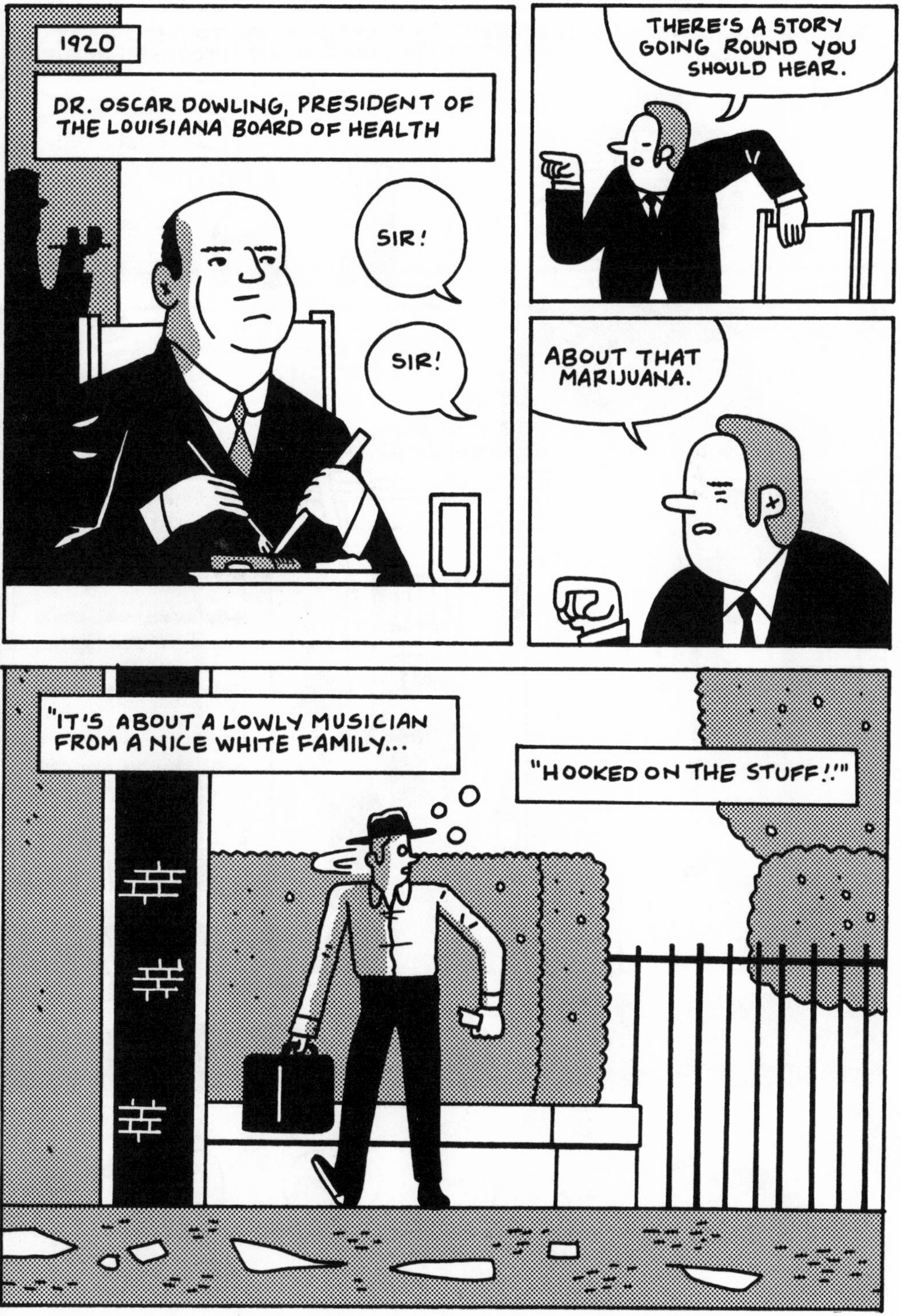
1920
DR. OSCAR DOWLING, PRESIDENT OF THE LOUISIANA BOARD OF HEALTH
SIR!
SIR!
THERE'S A STORY GOING ROUND YOU SHOULD HEAR.
ABOUT THAT MARIJUANA.
"IT'S ABOUT A LOWLY MUSICIAN FROM A NICE WHITE FAMILY...
"HOOKED ON THE STUFF!"

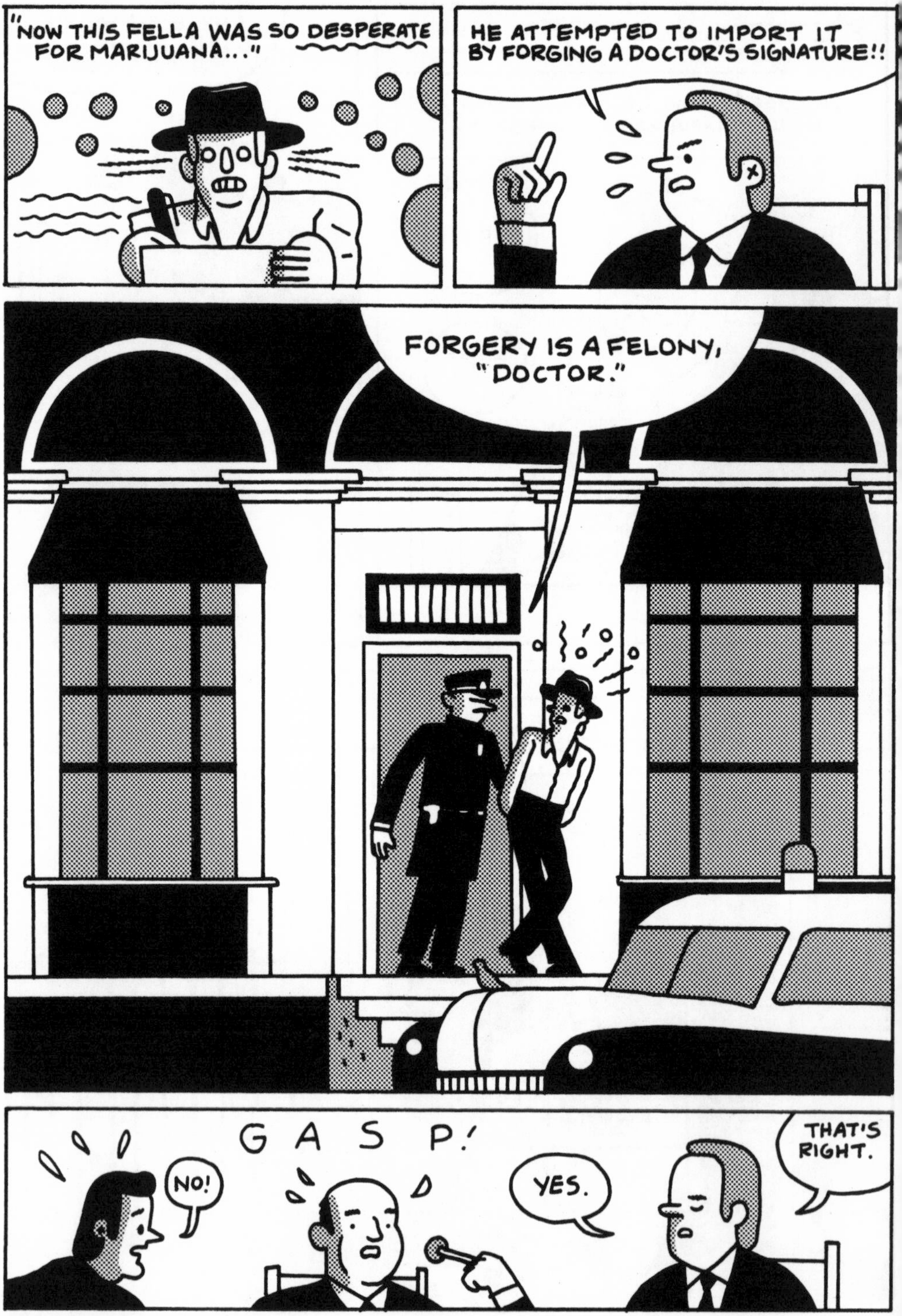
"NOW THIS FELLA WAS SO DESPERATE FOR MARIJUANA..."
HE ATTEMPTED TO IMPORT IT BY FORGING A DOCTOR'S SIGNATURE!!
FORGERY IS A FELONY, "DOCTOR."
GASP!
NO!
YES.
THAT'S RIGHT.

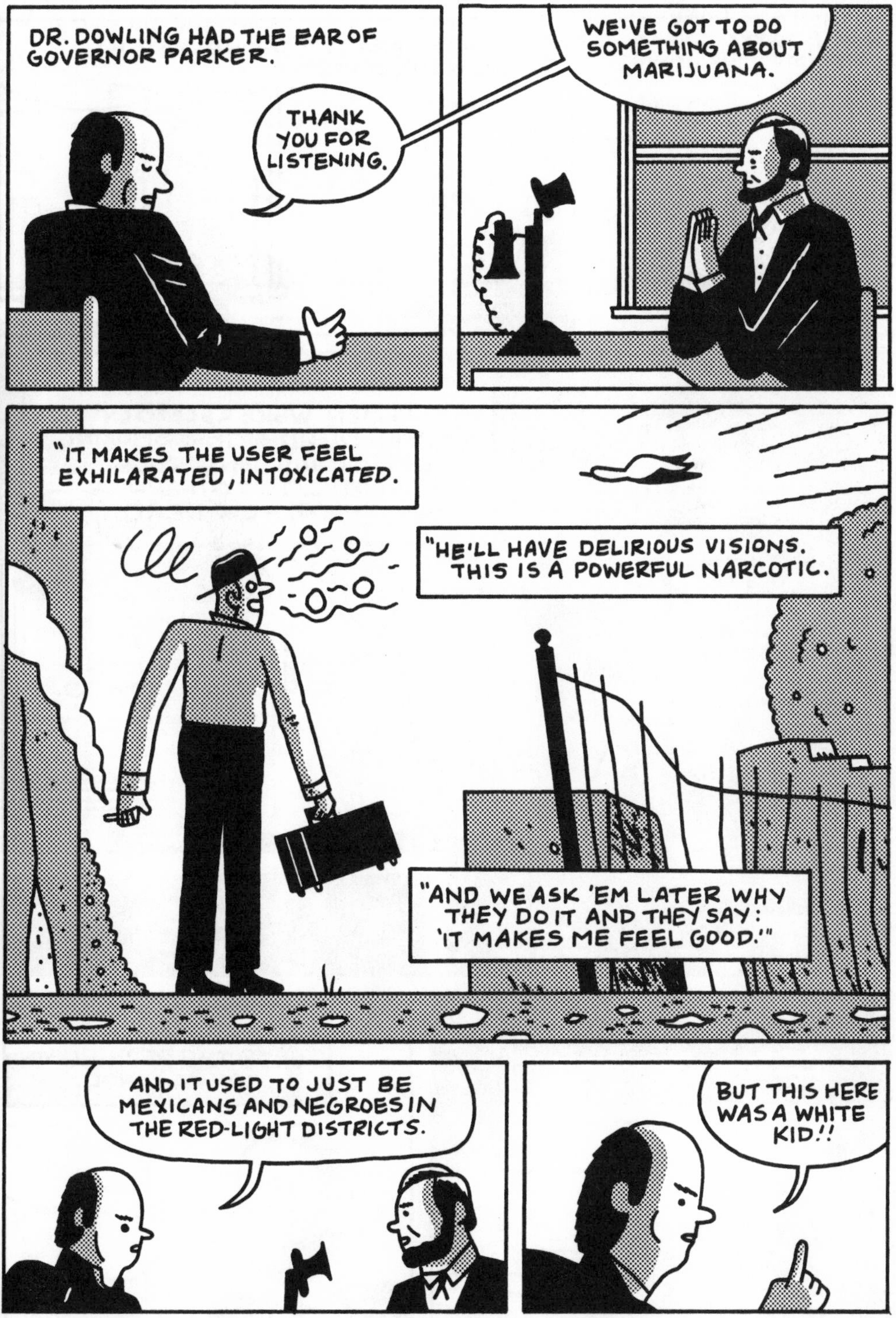
DR. DOWLING HAD THE EAR OF GOVERNOR PARKER.
THANK YOU FOR LISTENING.
WE'VE GOT TO DO SOMETHING ABOUT MARIJUANA.
"IT MAKES THE USER FEEL EXHILARATED, INTOXICATED.
"HE'LL HAVE DELIRIOUS VISIONS. THIS IS A POWERFUL NARCOTIC.
"AND WE ASK 'EM LATER WHY THEY DO IT AND THEY SAY: 'IT MAKES ME FEEL GOOD.'"
AND IT USED TO JUST BE MEXICANS AND NEGROES IN THE RED-LIGHT DISTRICTS.
BUT THIS HERE WAS A WHITE KID!!

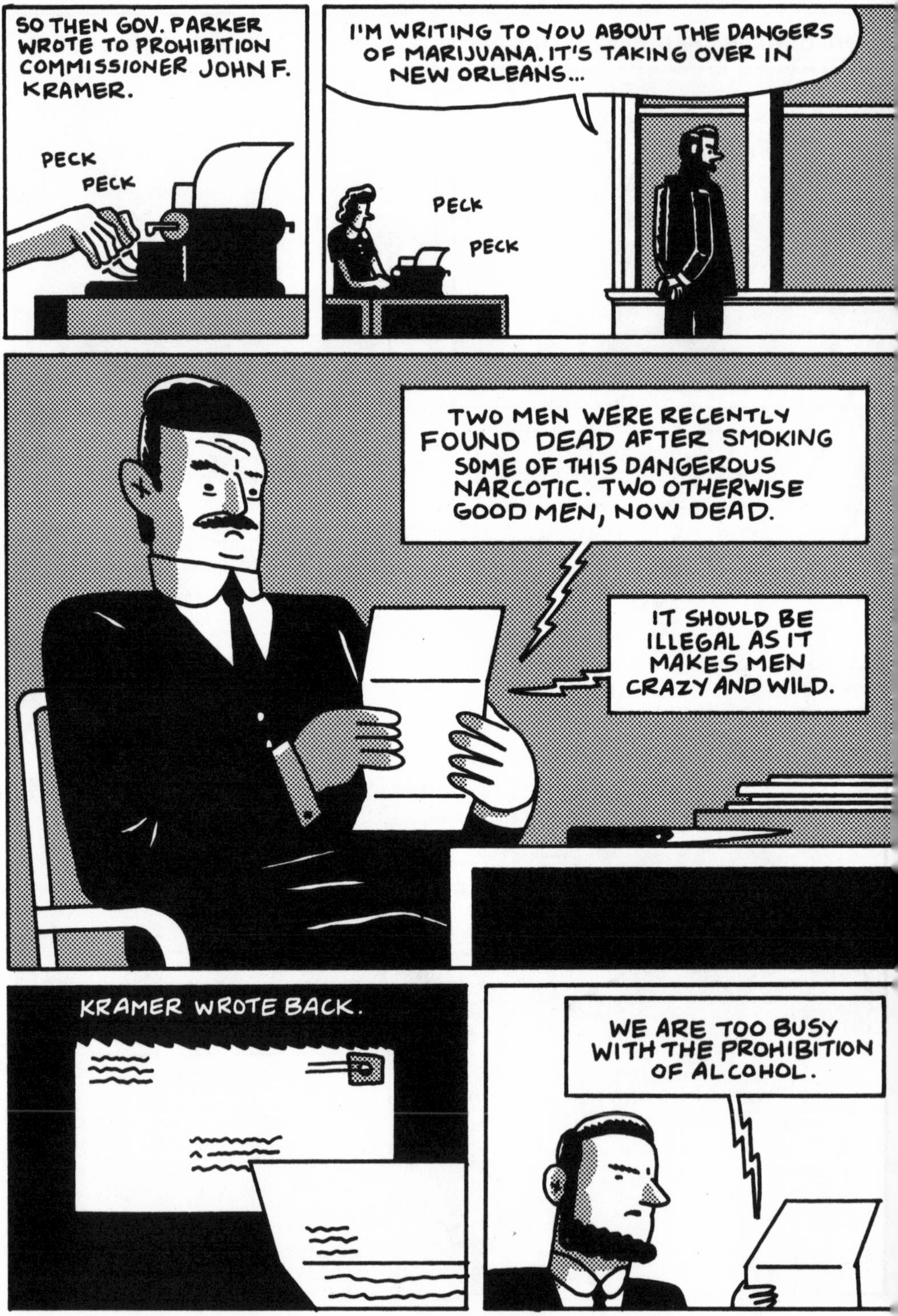
SO THEN GOV. PARKER WROTE TO PROHIBITION COMMISSIONER JOHN F. KRAMER.
PECK
PECK
I'M WRITING TO YOU ABOUT THE DANGERS OF MARIJUANA. IT'S TAKING OVER IN NEW ORLEANS...
PECK
PECK
TWO MEN WERE RECENTLY FOUND DEAD AFTER SMOKING SOME OF THIS DANGEROUS NARCOTIC. TWO OTHERWISE GOOD MEN, NOW DEAD.
IT SHOULD BE ILLEGAL AS IT MAKES MEN CRAZY AND WILD.
KRAMER WROTE BACK.
WE ARE TOO BUSY WITH THE PROHIBITION OF ALCOHOL.

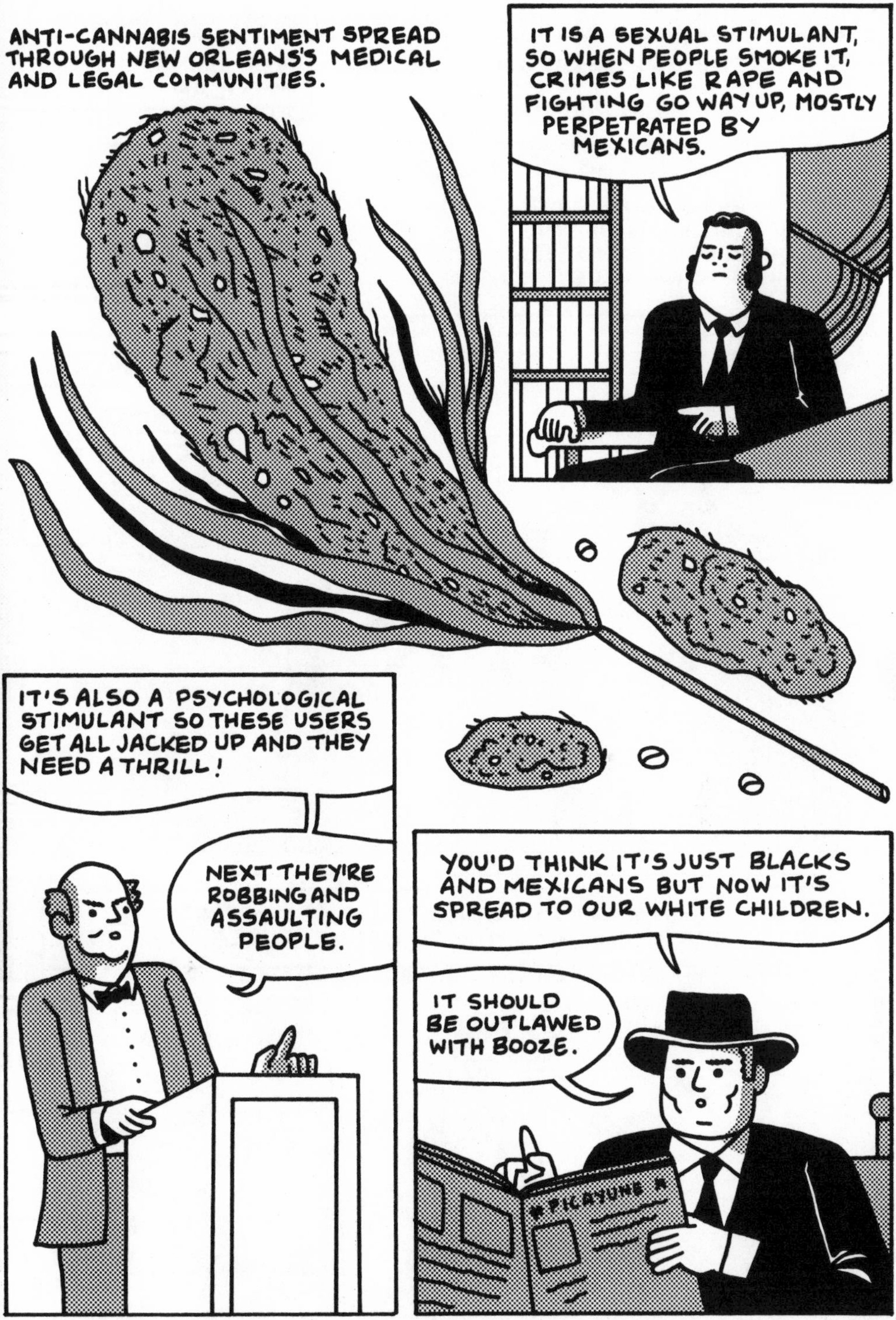
ANTI-CANNABIS SENTIMENT SPREAD THROUGH NEW ORLEANS'S MEDICAL AND LEGAL COMMUNITIES.
IT IS A SEXUAL STIMULANT, SO WHEN PEOPLE SMOKE IT, CRIMES LIKE RAPE AND FIGHTING GO WAY UP, MOSTLY PERPETRATED BY MEXICANS.
IT'S ALSO A PSYCHOLOGICAL STIMULANT SO THESE USERS GET ALL JACKED UP AND THEY NEED A THRILL!
NEXT THEY'RE ROBBING AND ASSAULTING PEOPLE.
YOU'D THINK IT'S JUST BLACKS AND MEXICANS BUT NOW IT'S SPREAD TO OUR WHITE CHILDREN.
IT SHOULD BE OUTLAWED WITH BOOZE.
PICAYUNE

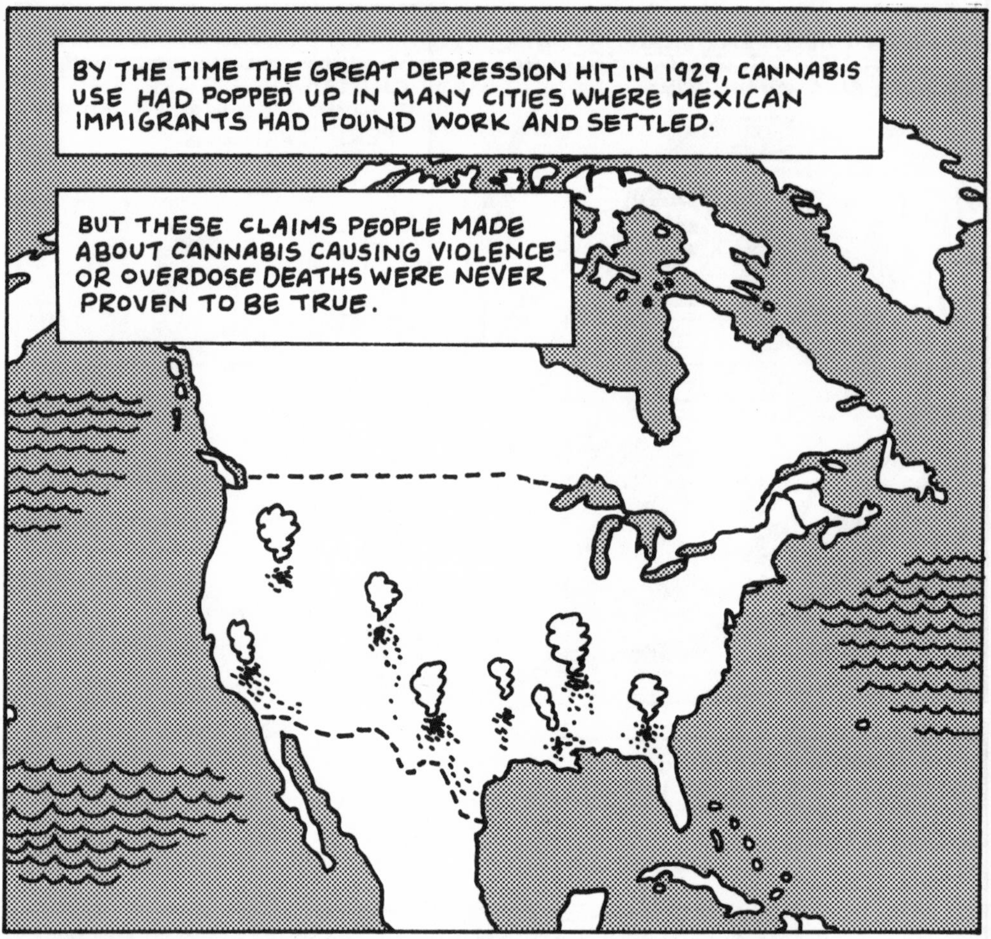
BY THE TIME THE GREAT DEPRESSION HIT IN 1929, CANNABIS USE HAD POPPED UP IN MANY CITIES WHERE MEXICAN IMMIGRANTS HAD FOUND WORK AND SETTLED.
BUT THESE CLAIMS PEOPLE MADE ABOUT CANNABIS CAUSING VIOLENCE OR OVERDOSE DEATHS WERE NEVER PROVEN TO BE TRUE.

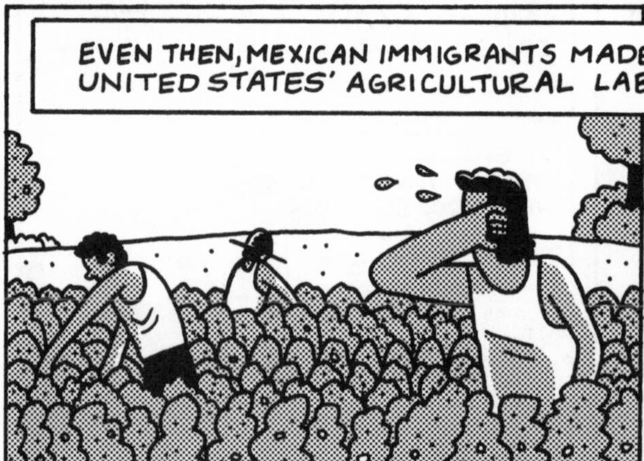
EVEN THEN, MEXICAN IMMIGRANTS MADE UP MOST OF THE UNITED STATES' AGRICULTURAL LABOR FORCE.

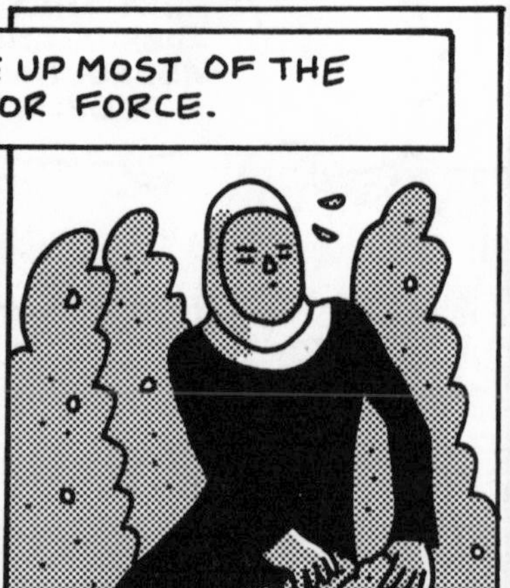

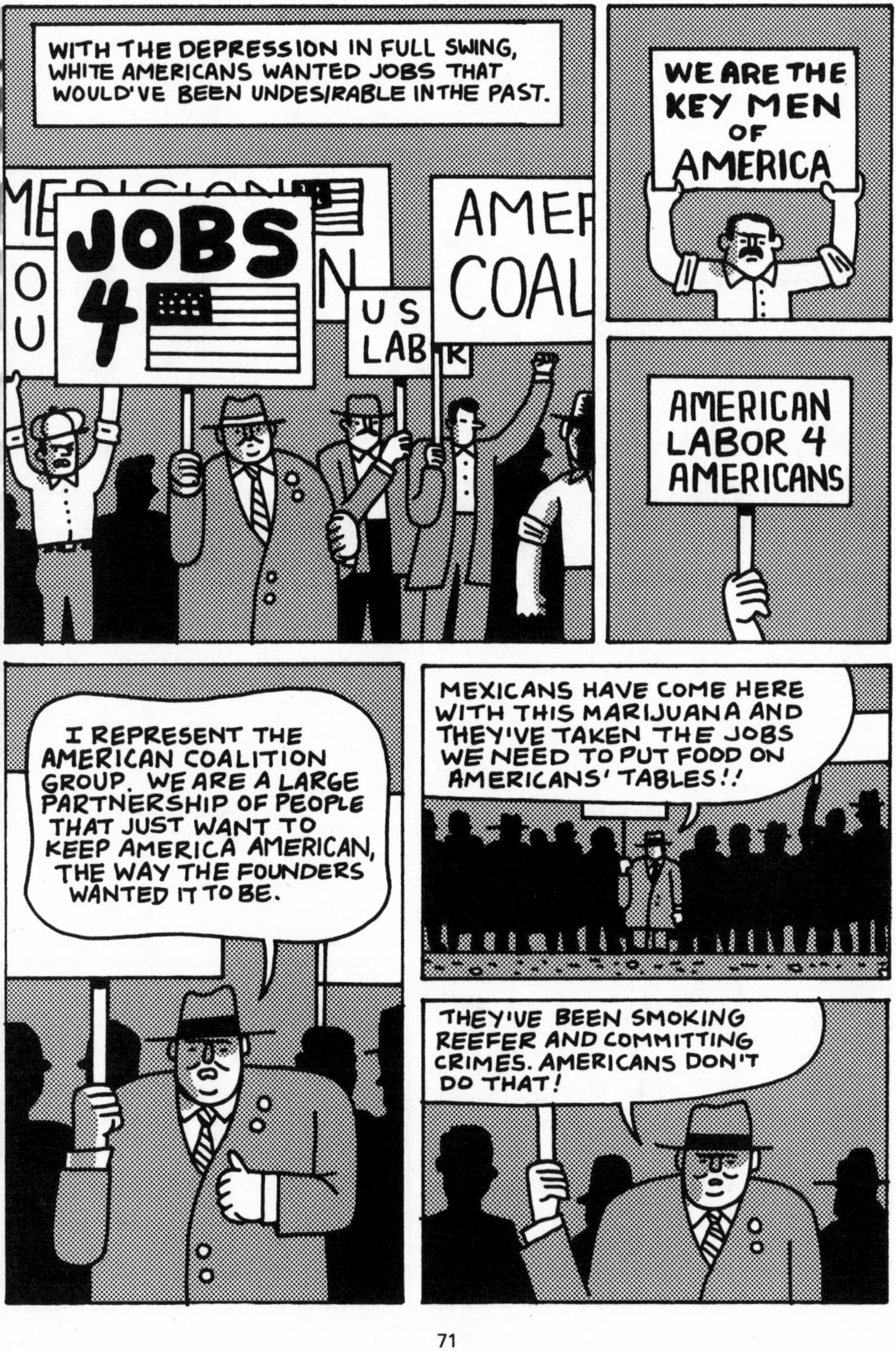

WITH THE DEPRESSION IN FULL SWING, WHITE AMERICANS WANTED JOBS THAT WOULD'VE BEEN UNDESIRABLE IN THE PAST.
JOBS 4
US LAB
AMER COAL
WE ARE THE KEY MEN OF AMERICA
AMERICAN LABOR 4 AMERICANS
I REPRESENT THE AMERICAN COALITION GROUP. WE ARE A LARGE PARTNERSHIP OF PEOPLE THAT JUST WANT TO KEEP AMERICA AMERICAN, THE WAY THE FOUNDERS WANTED IT TO BE.
MEXICANS HAVE COME HERE WITH THIS MARIJUANA AND THEY'VE TAKEN THE JOBS WE NEED TO PUT FOOD ON AMERICANS' TABLES!!
THEY'VE BEEN SMOKING REEFER AND COMMITTING CRIMES. AMERICANS DON'T DO THAT!

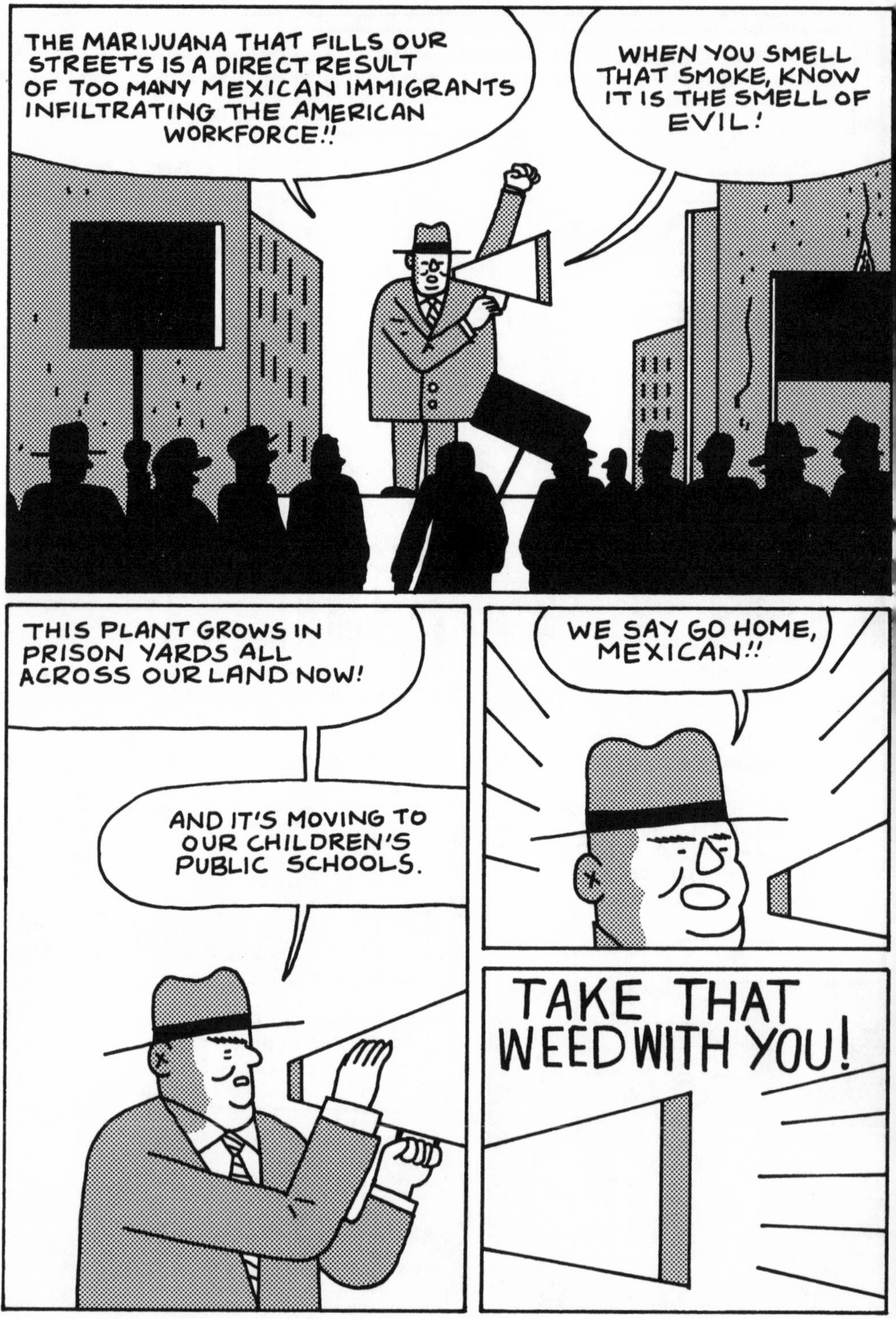
THE MARIJUANA THAT FILLS OUR STREETS IS A DIRECT RESULT OF TOO MANY MEXICAN IMMIGRANTS INFILTRATING THE AMERICAN WORKFORCE!!
WHEN YOU SMELL THAT SMOKE, KNOW IT IS THE SMELL OF EVIL!
THIS PLANT GROWS IN PRISON YARDS ALL ACROSS OUR LAND NOW!
AND IT'S MOVING TO OUR CHILDREN'S PUBLIC SCHOOLS.
WE SAY GO HOME, MEXICAN!!
TAKE THAT WEED WITH YOU!

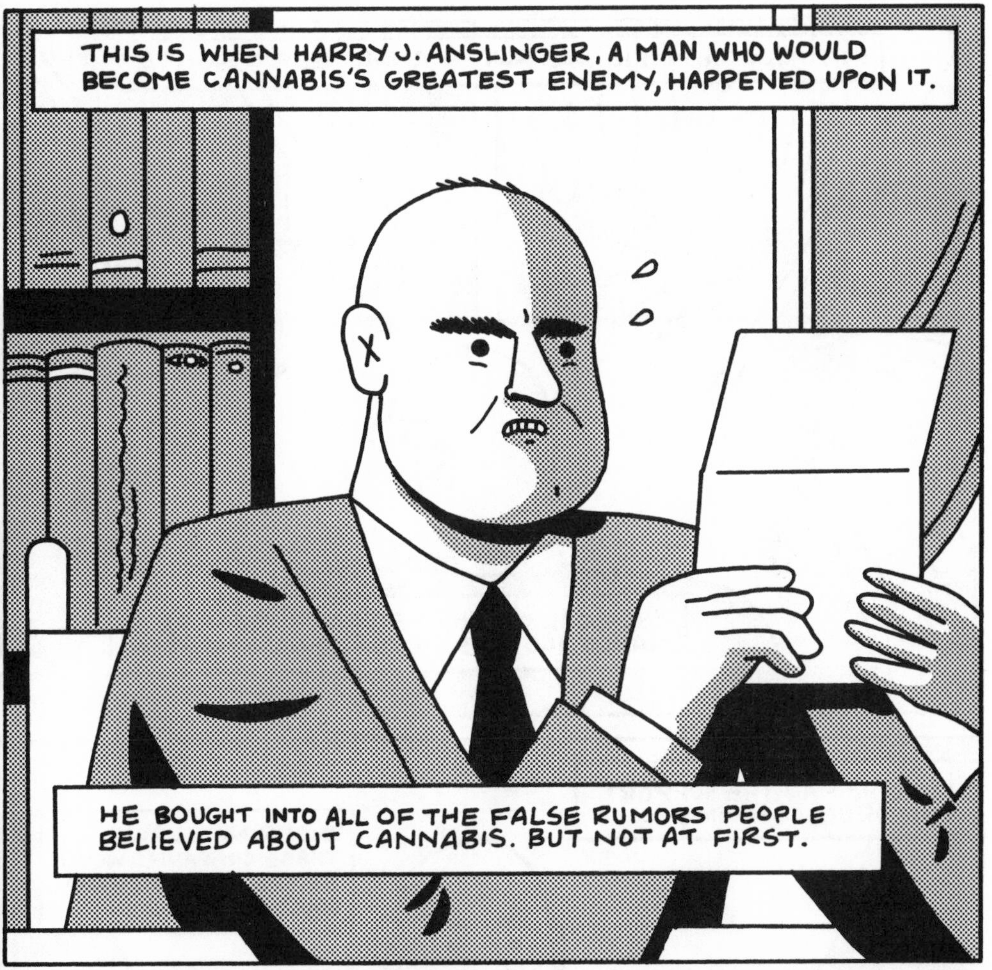
THIS IS WHEN HARRY J. ANSLINGER, A MAN WHO WOULD BECOME CANNABIS'S GREATEST ENEMY, HAPPENED UPON IT.
HE BOUGHT INTO ALL OF THE FALSE RUMORS PEOPLE BELIEVED ABOUT CANNABIS. BUT NOT AT FIRST.

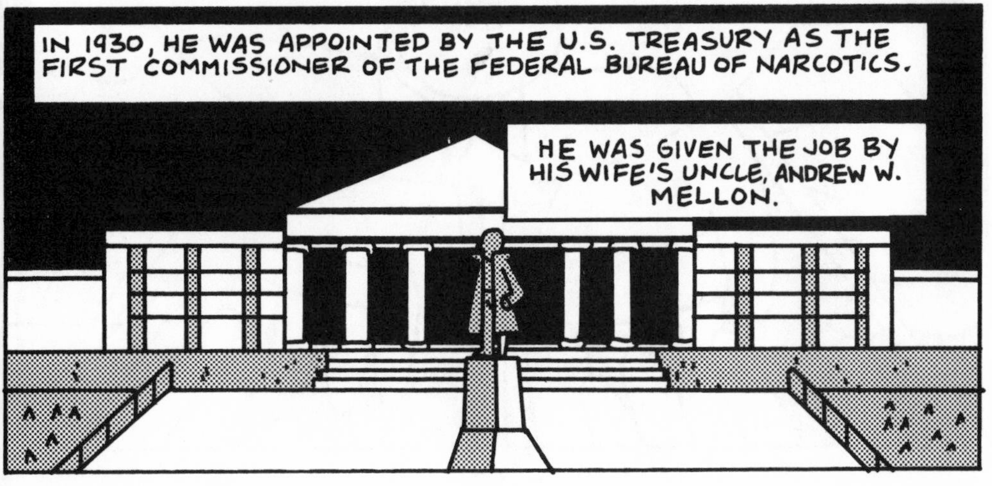
IN 1930, HE WAS APPOINTED BY THE U.S. TREASURY AS THE FIRST COMMISSIONER OF THE FEDERAL BUREAU OF NARCOTICS.
HE WAS GIVEN THE JOB BY HIS WIFE'S UNCLE, ANDREW W. MELLON.

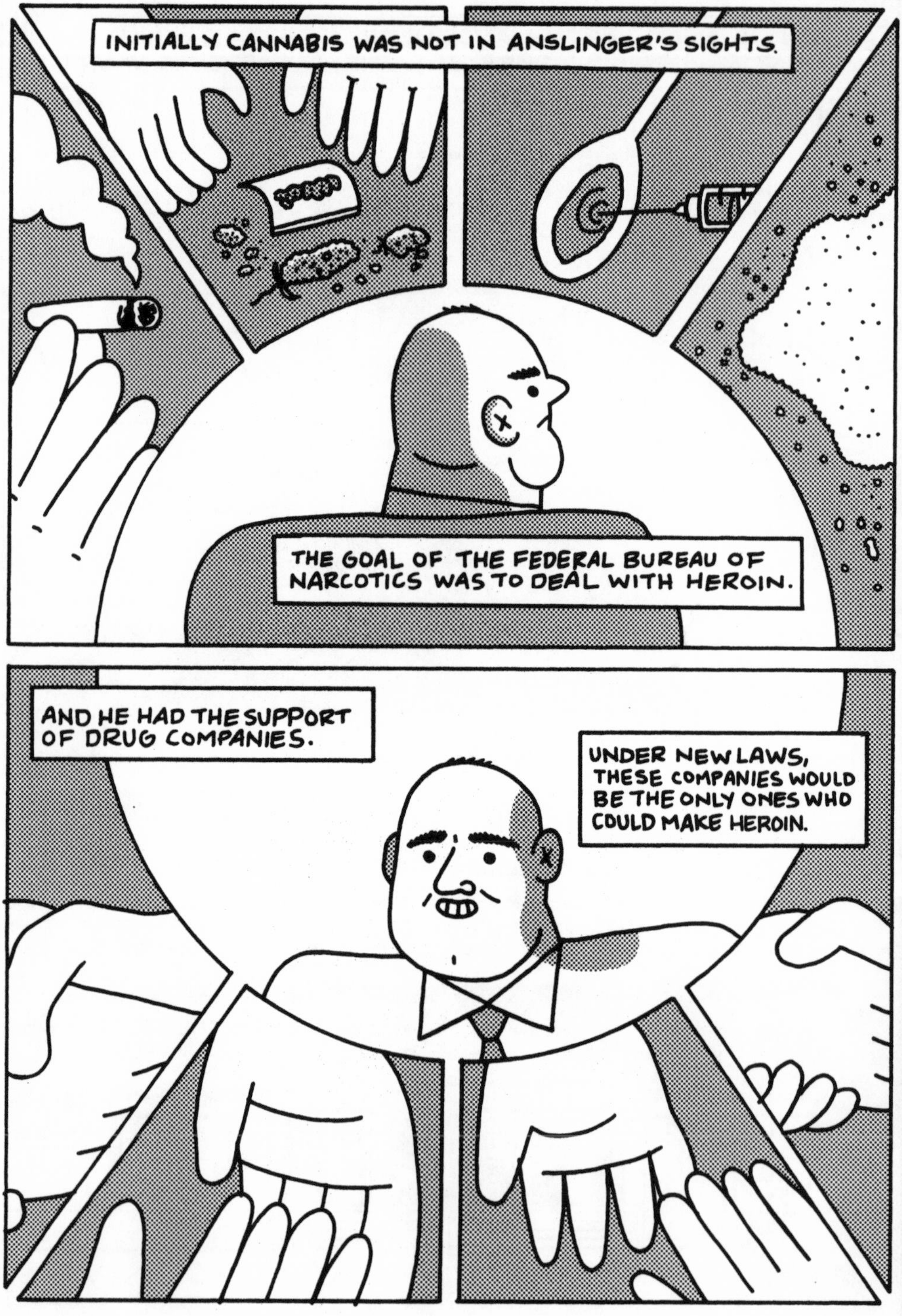
INITIALLY CANNABIS WAS NOT IN ANSLINGER'S SIGHTS.
THE GOAL OF THE FEDERAL BUREAU OF NARCOTICS WAS TO DEAL WITH HEROIN.
AND HE HAD THE SUPPORT OF DRUG COMPANIES.
UNDER NEW LAWS, THESE COMPANIES WOULD BE THE ONLY ONES WHO COULD MAKE HEROIN.

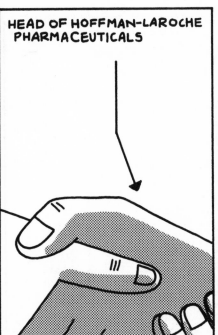

HEAD OF HOFFMAN-LAROCHE PHARMACEUTICALS

YOU'RE DOING THE LORD'S WORK, ANSLINGER.

RUNNING A TIGHT SHIP.

YOU BOYS PLAY A BIG ROLE HERE. IF REGULATION IS GONNA WORK WE NEED INDUSTRY SUPPORT. SOMEONE NEEDS TO PRODUCE THIS STUFF FOR THE PEOPLE THAT REALLY NEED IT.

WAR VETERANS...

...AND CRIPPLES AND WHAT HAVE YOU.

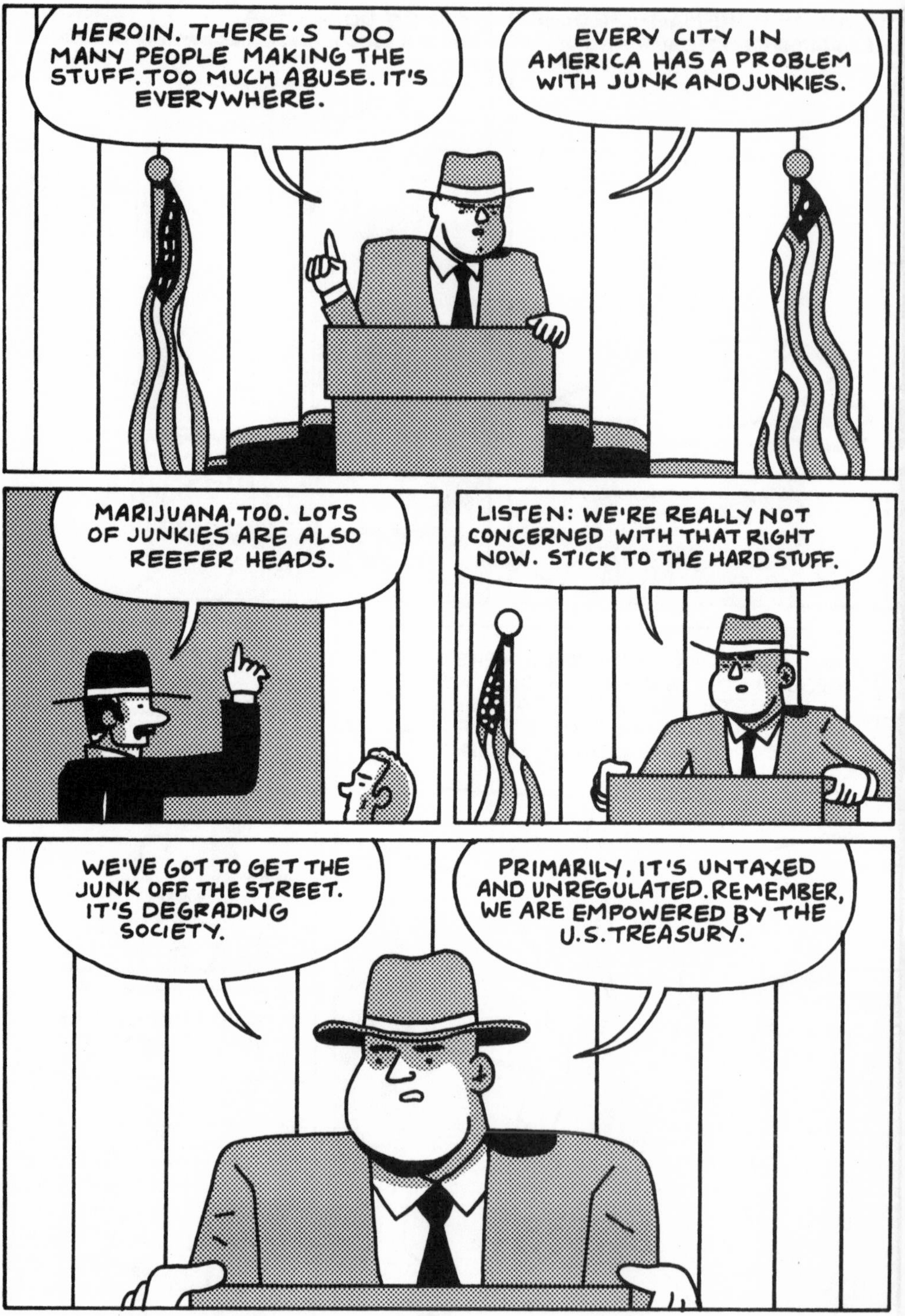
HEROIN. THERE'S TOO MANY PEOPLE MAKING THE STUFF. TOO MUCH ABUSE. IT'S EVERYWHERE.
EVERY CITY IN AMERICA HAS A PROBLEM WITH JUNK AND JUNKIES.
MARIJUANA, TOO. LOTS OF JUNKIES ARE ALSO REEFER HEADS.
LISTEN: WE'RE REALLY NOT CONCERNED WITH THAT RIGHT NOW. STICK TO THE HARD STUFF.
WE'VE GOT TO GET THE JUNK OFF THE STREET. IT'S DEGRADING SOCIETY.
PRIMARILY, IT'S UNTAXED AND UNREGULATED. REMEMBER, WE ARE EMPOWERED BY THE U.S. TREASURY.

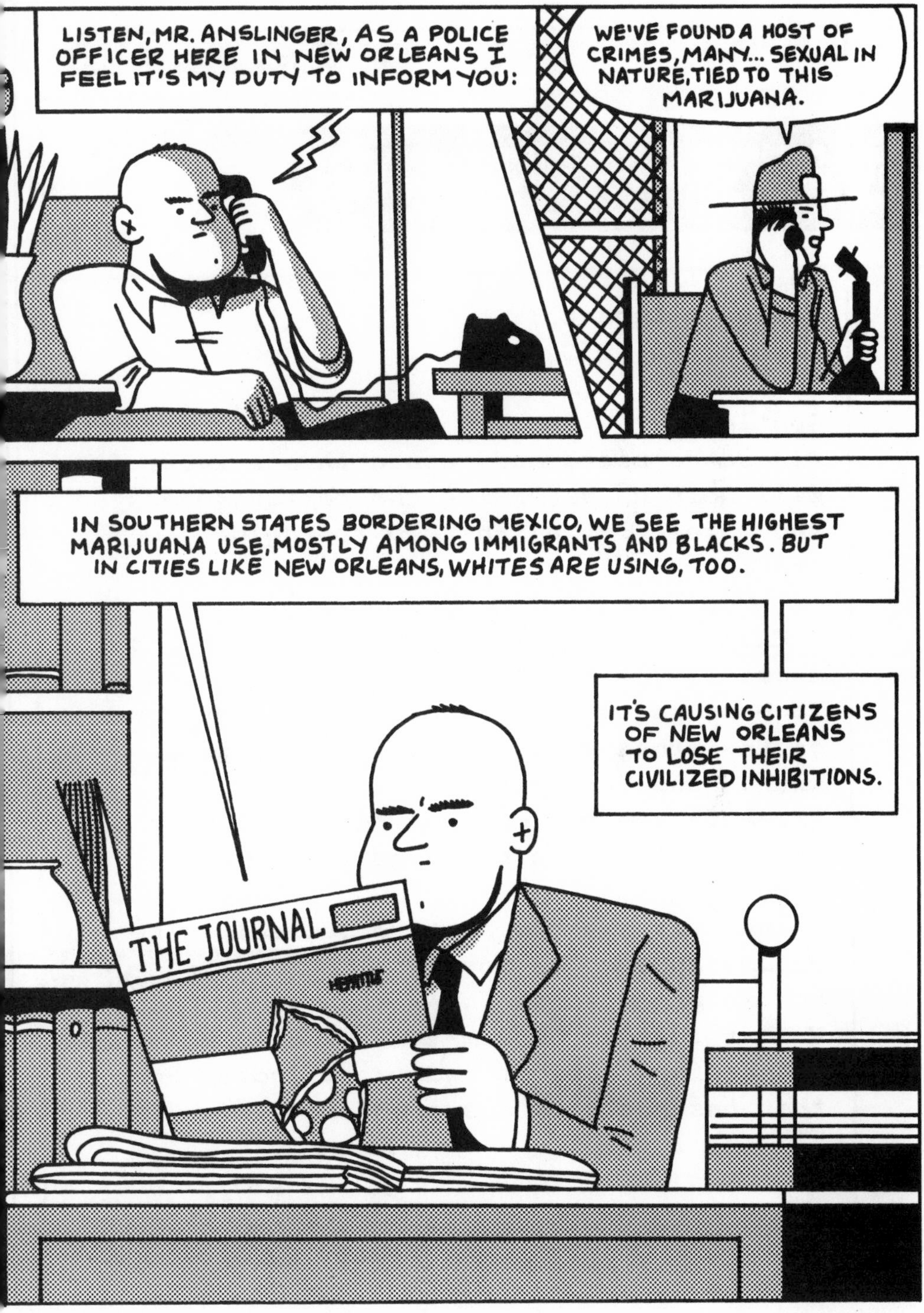
LISTEN, MR. ANSLINGER, AS A POLICE OFFICER HERE IN NEW ORLEANS I FEEL IT'S MY DUTY TO INFORM YOU:
WE'VE FOUND A HOST OF CRIMES, MANY... SEXUAL IN NATURE, TIED TO THIS MARIJUANA.
IN SOUTHERN STATES BORDERING MEXICO, WE SEE THE HIGHEST MARIJUANA USE, MOSTLY AMONG IMMIGRANTS AND BLACKS. BUT IN CITIES LIKE NEW ORLEANS, WHITES ARE USING, TOO.
IT'S CAUSING CITIZENS OF NEW ORLEANS TO LOSE THEIR CIVILIZED INHIBITIONS.
THE JOURNAL

42 Western 94th St.
New York, N.Y.
June 11, 1939

AMID PRESSURE TO REGULATE CANNABIS SALE AND USE AS A NARCOTIC, ANSLINGER SENT OUT A SURVEY:

Bureau of Narcotics,
Treasury Depart.,
Washington, D.C.

Gentlemen,
Please complete and return this survey. It will help us determine the pervasiveness and threat of Indian Hemp to the United States.

I.-What is the quality of Indian Hemp produced in the United States?
II.-What is the geographical distribution of the areas where Indian Hemp is grown within the United States?
III.-What are the medical needs and uses of the drug or drugs produced from Indian Hemp?
IV.-What is the comparative medical value of Indian Hemp as domes
and as produced in fore
V.-What further informa
concerning cannabis indica or Indian Hemp that has not been answered above.

THIS WOULD DETERMINE THE PERVASIVENESS AND THREAT OF CANNABIS IN THE U.S.

Yours,

Harry J. Anslinger

Harry J. Anslinger

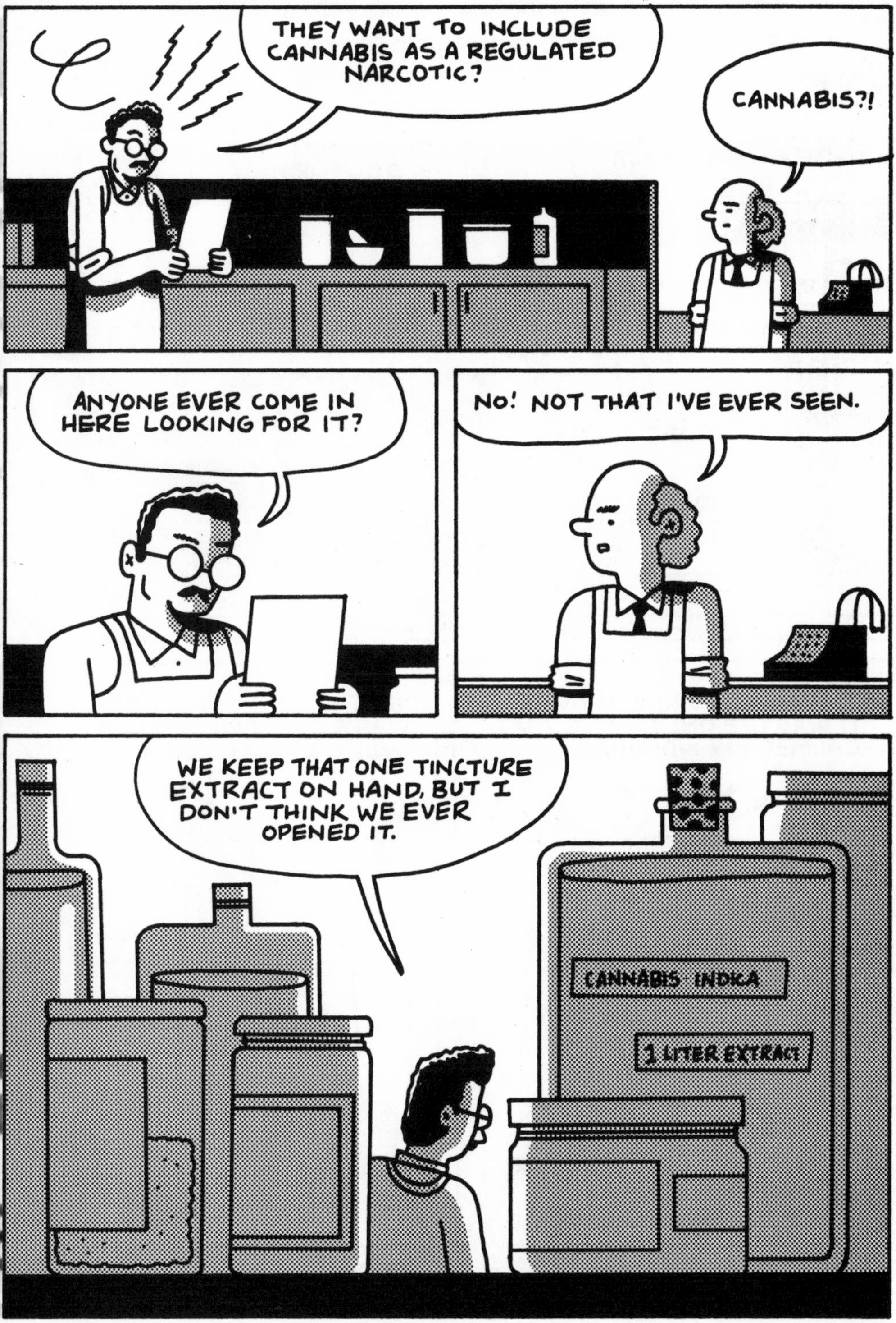
THEY WANT TO INCLUDE CANNABIS AS A REGULATED NARCOTIC?
CANNABIS?!
ANYONE EVER COME IN HERE LOOKING FOR IT?
NO! NOT THAT I'VE EVER SEEN.
WE KEEP THAT ONE TINCTURE EXTRACT ON HAND, BUT I DON'T THINK WE EVER OPENED IT.
CANNABIS INDICA
1 LITER EXTRACT

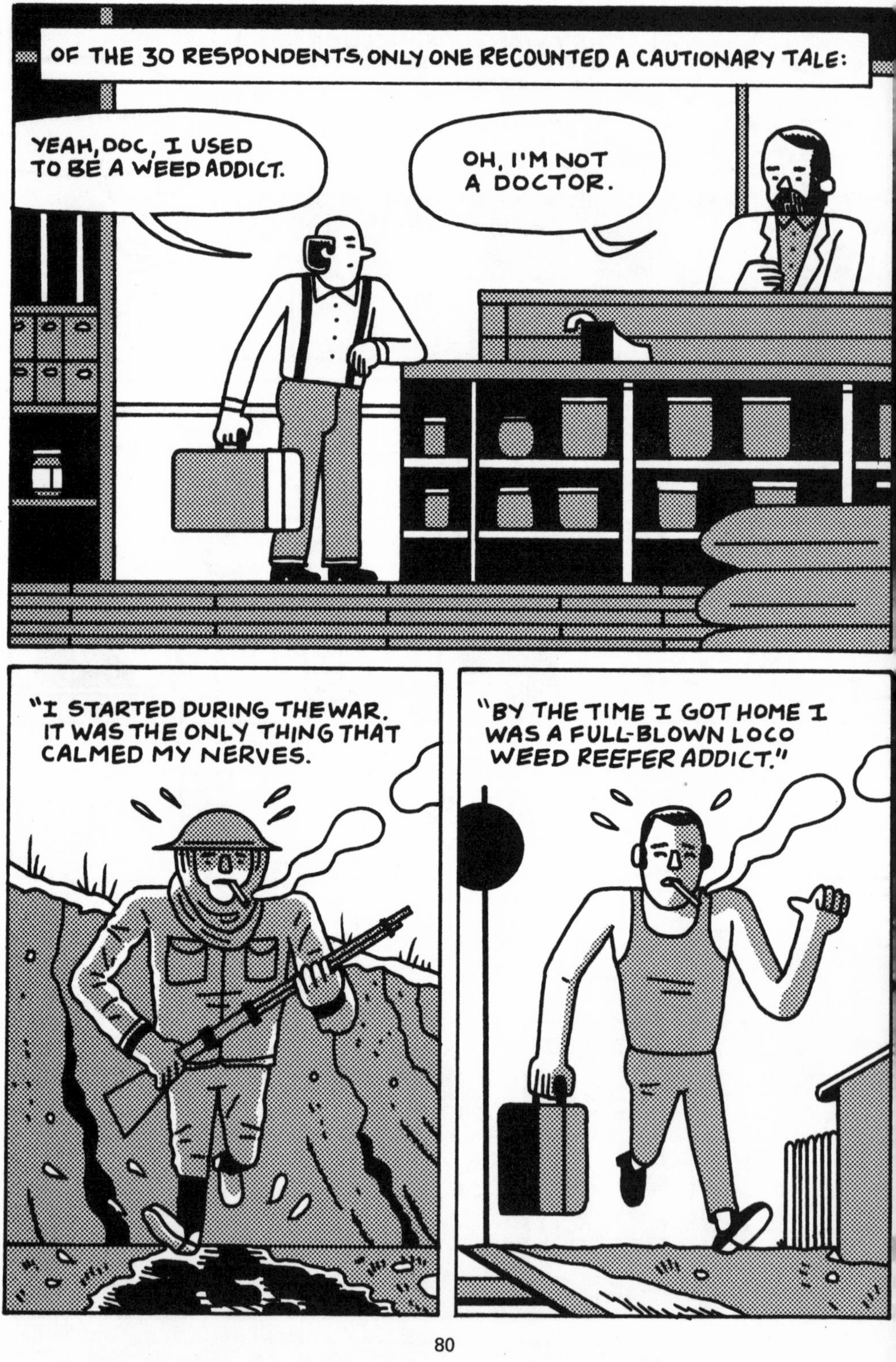
OF THE 30 RESPONDENTS, ONLY ONE RECOUNTED A CAUTIONARY TALE:
YEAH, DOC, I USED TO BE A WEED ADDICT.
OH, I'M NOT A DOCTOR.
"I STARTED DURING THE WAR. IT WAS THE ONLY THING THAT CALMED MY NERVES.
"BY THE TIME I GOT HOME I WAS A FULL-BLOWN LOCO WEED REEFER ADDICT."

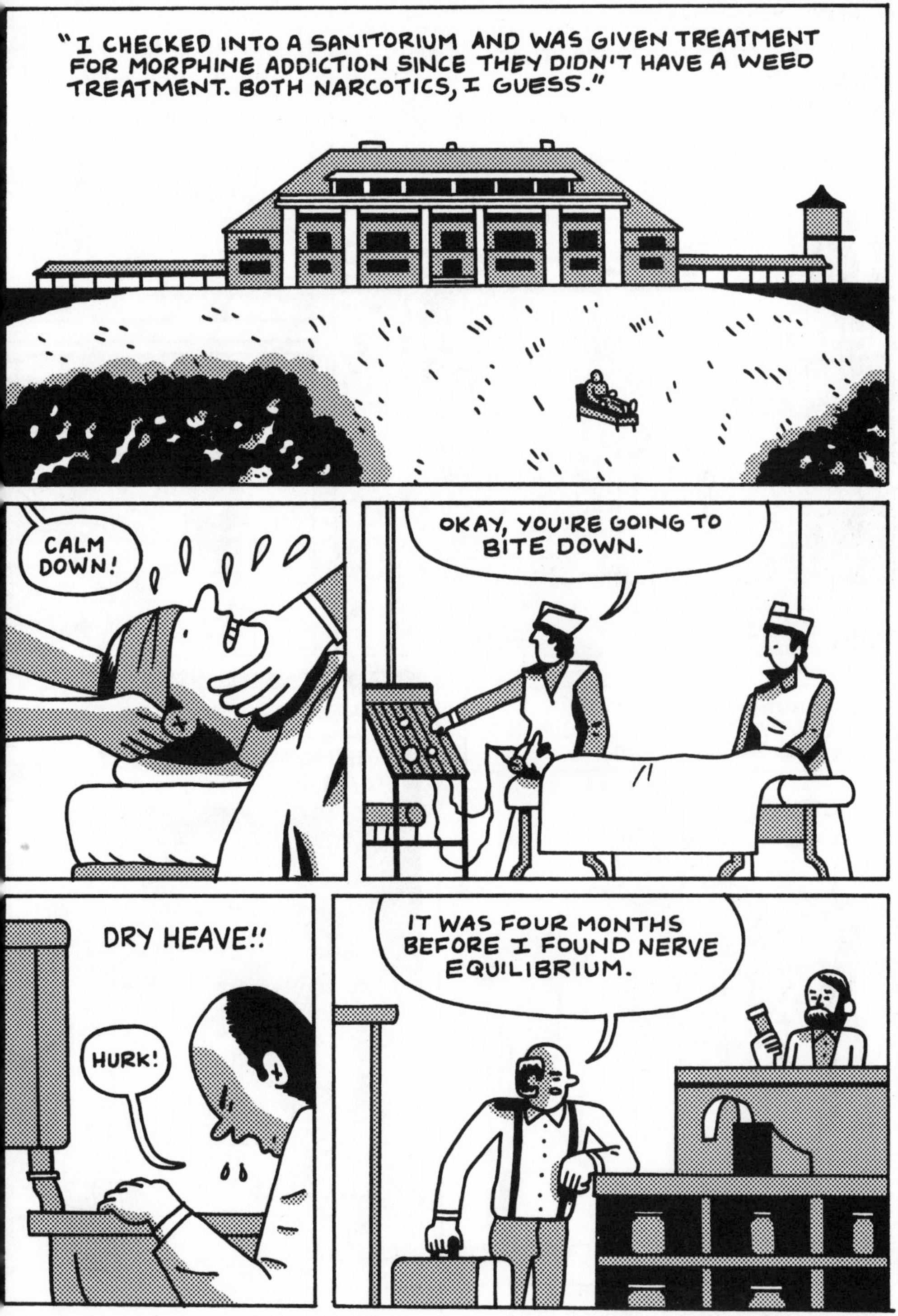
"I CHECKED INTO A SANITORIUM AND WAS GIVEN TREATMENT FOR MORPHINE ADDICTION SINCE THEY DIDN'T HAVE A WEED TREATMENT. BOTH NARCOTICS, I GUESS."
CALM DOWN!
OKAY, YOU'RE GOING TO BITE DOWN.
DRY HEAVE!!
HURK!
IT WAS FOUR MONTHS BEFORE I FOUND NERVE EQUILIBRIUM.

OF THE THIRTY RESPONDENTS, IT WAS THE SOLDIER'S STORY THAT STOOD OUT.

HE HAD SEEN THE HORRORS OF WORLD WAR I.

CANNABIS USE WAS LIKELY THERAPEUTIC IN THE FIELD...

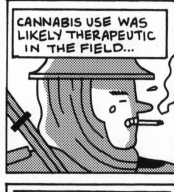

...AND IN DEALING WITH POST-TRAUMATIC STRESS.

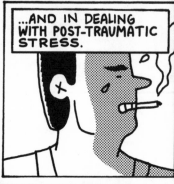

HE DIAGNOSED HIMSELF AS AN ADDICT AND WAS MISTREATED AT THE SANITORIUM.

ANSLINGER FOCUSED ON THIS ATYPICAL STORY AS AMMO TO USE AGAINST CANNABIS.

UNDERLINE

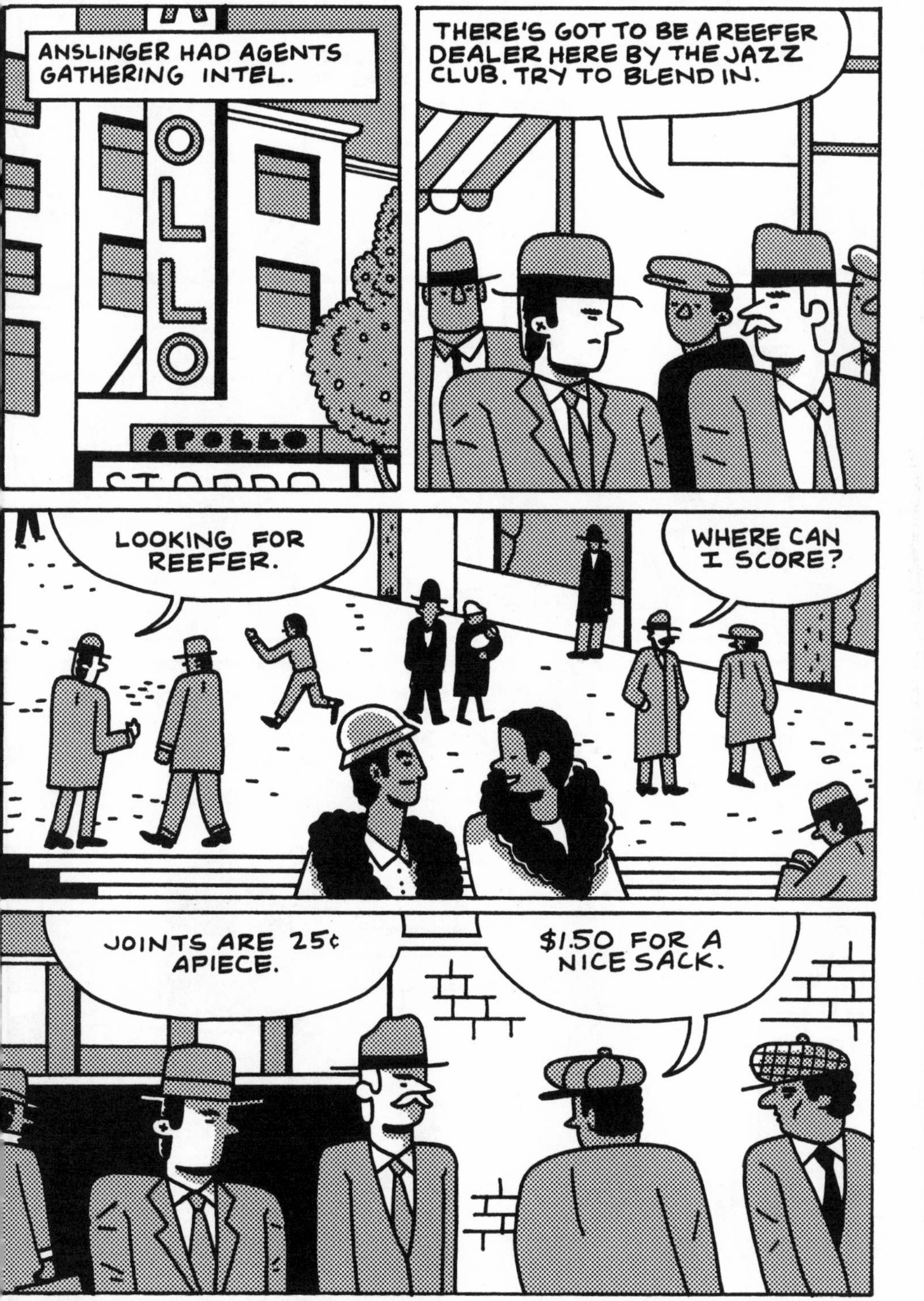
ANSLINGER HAD AGENTS GATHERING INTEL.
APOLLO
THERE'S GOT TO BE A REEFER DEALER HERE BY THE JAZZ CLUB. TRY TO BLEND IN.
LOOKING FOR REEFER.
WHERE CAN I SCORE?
JOINTS ARE 25¢ APIECE.
$1.50 FOR A NICE SACK.

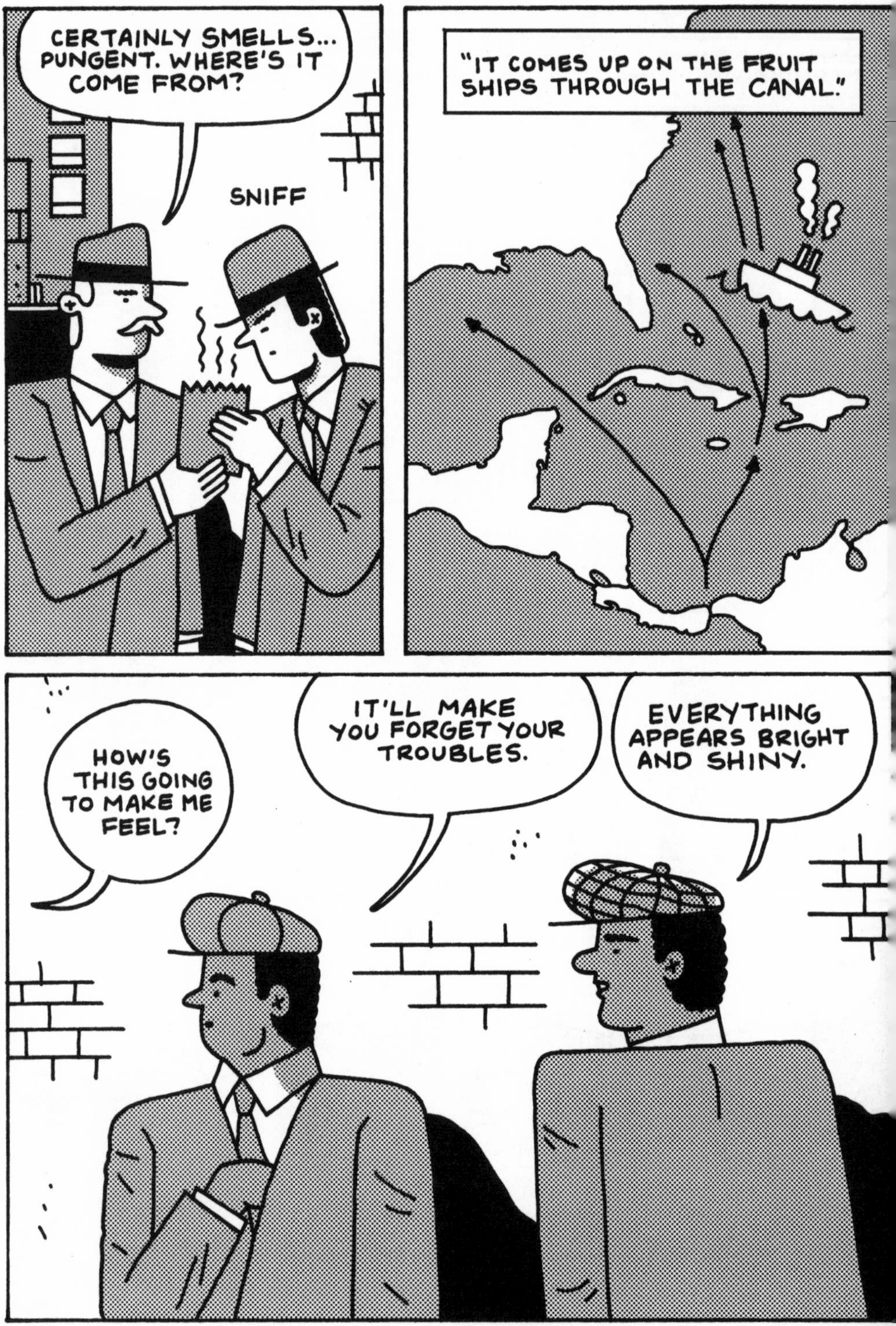
CERTAINLY SMELLS... PUNGENT. WHERE'S IT COME FROM?
SNIFF
"IT COMES UP ON THE FRUIT SHIPS THROUGH THE CANAL."
HOW'S THIS GOING TO MAKE ME FEEL?
IT'LL MAKE YOU FORGET YOUR TROUBLES.
EVERYTHING APPEARS BRIGHT AND SHINY.

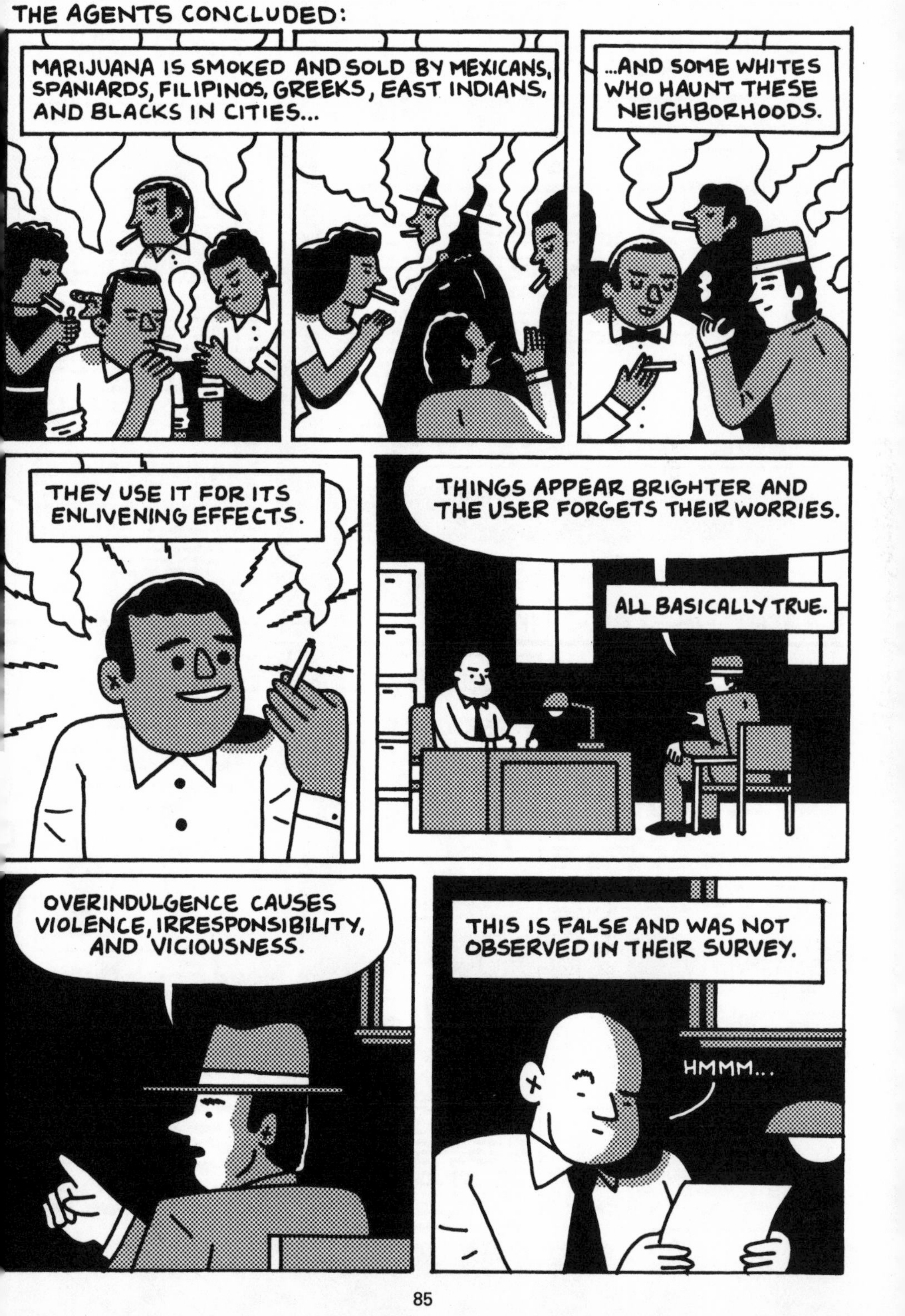
THE AGENTS CONCLUDED:
MARIJUANA IS SMOKED AND SOLD BY MEXICANS, SPANIARDS, FILIPINOS, GREEKS, EAST INDIANS, AND BLACKS IN CITIES...
...AND SOME WHITES WHO HAUNT THESE NEIGHBORHOODS.
THEY USE IT FOR ITS ENLIVENING EFFECTS.
THINGS APPEAR BRIGHTER AND THE USER FORGETS THEIR WORRIES.
ALL BASICALLY TRUE.
OVERINDULGENCE CAUSES VIOLENCE, IRRESPONSIBILITY, AND VICIOUSNESS.
THIS IS FALSE AND WAS NOT OBSERVED IN THEIR SURVEY.
HMMM...

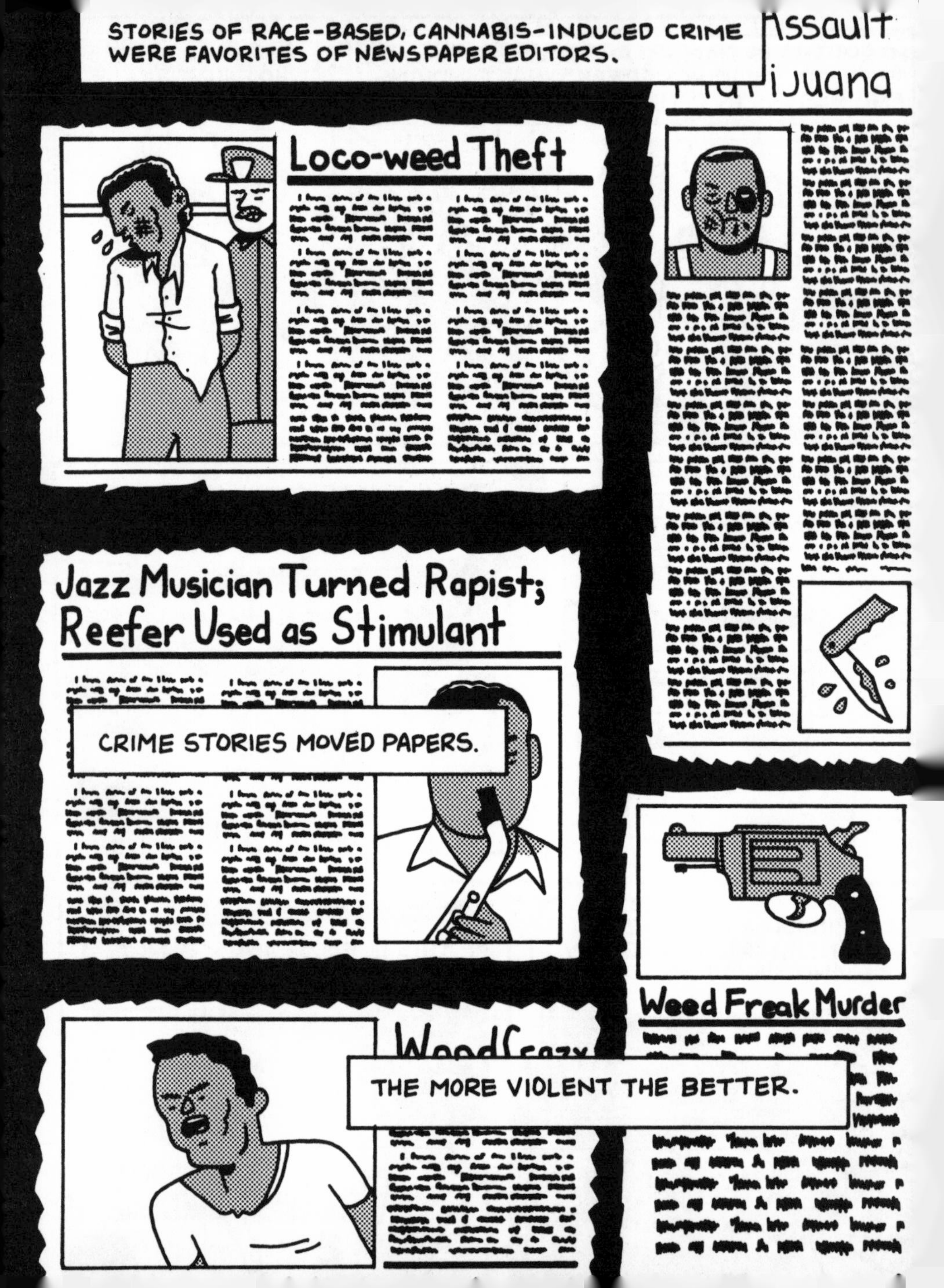

STORIES OF RACE-BASED, CANNABIS-INDUCED CRIME WERE FAVORITES OF NEWSPAPER EDITORS.
Assault
Loco-weed Theft
Jazz Musician Turned Rapist; Reefer Used as Stimulant
CRIME STORIES MOVED PAPERS.
Weed Freak Murder
THE MORE VIOLENT THE BETTER.

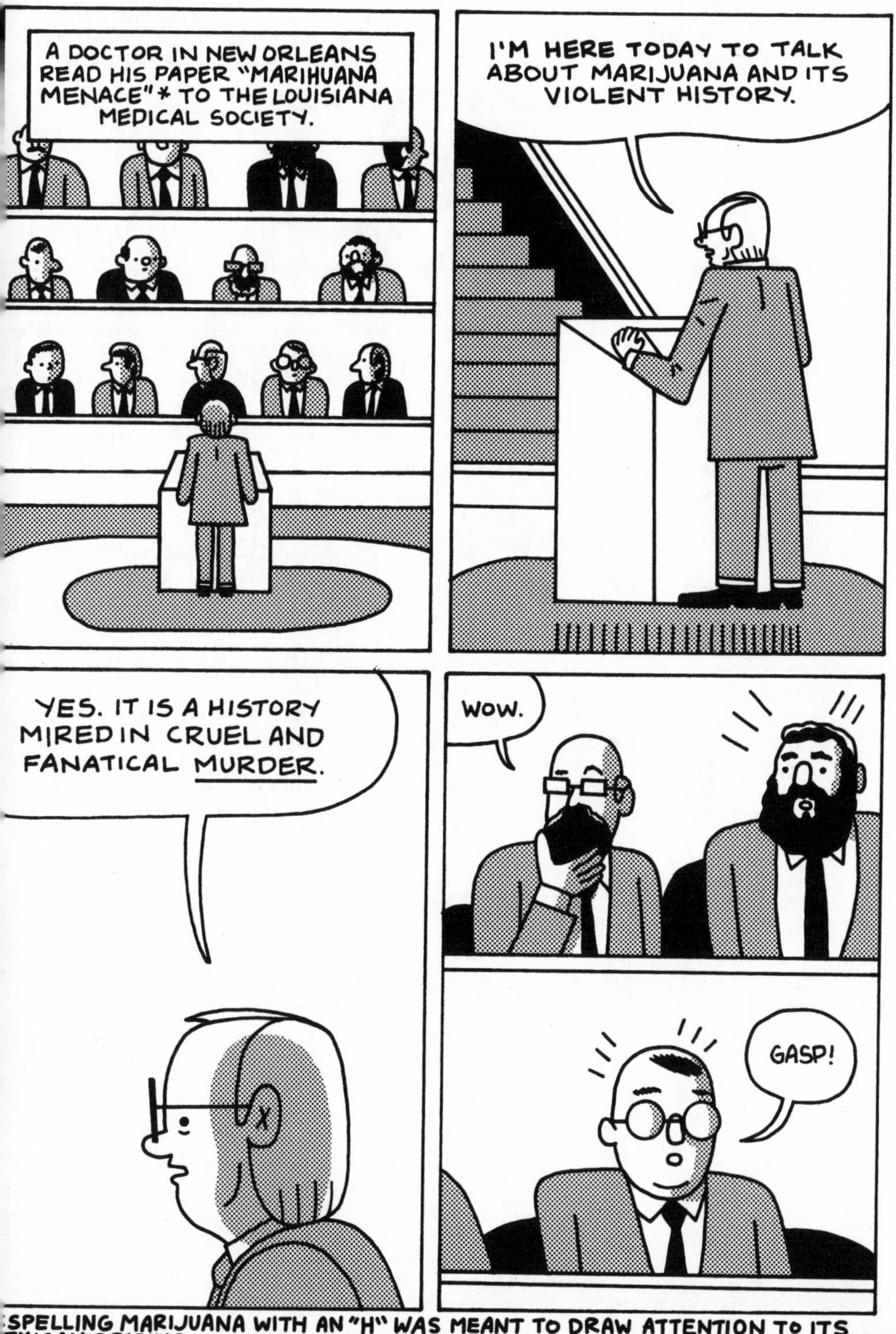
A DOCTOR IN NEW ORLEANS READ HIS PAPER "MARIHUANA MENACE"* TO THE LOUISIANA MEDICAL SOCIETY.
I'M HERE TODAY TO TALK ABOUT MARIJUANA AND ITS VIOLENT HISTORY.
YES. IT IS A HISTORY MIRED IN CRUEL AND FANATICAL MURDER.
WOW.
GASP!

SPELLING MARIJUANA WITH AN "H" WAS MEANT TO DRAW ATTENTION TO ITS EXICAN ORIGINS.

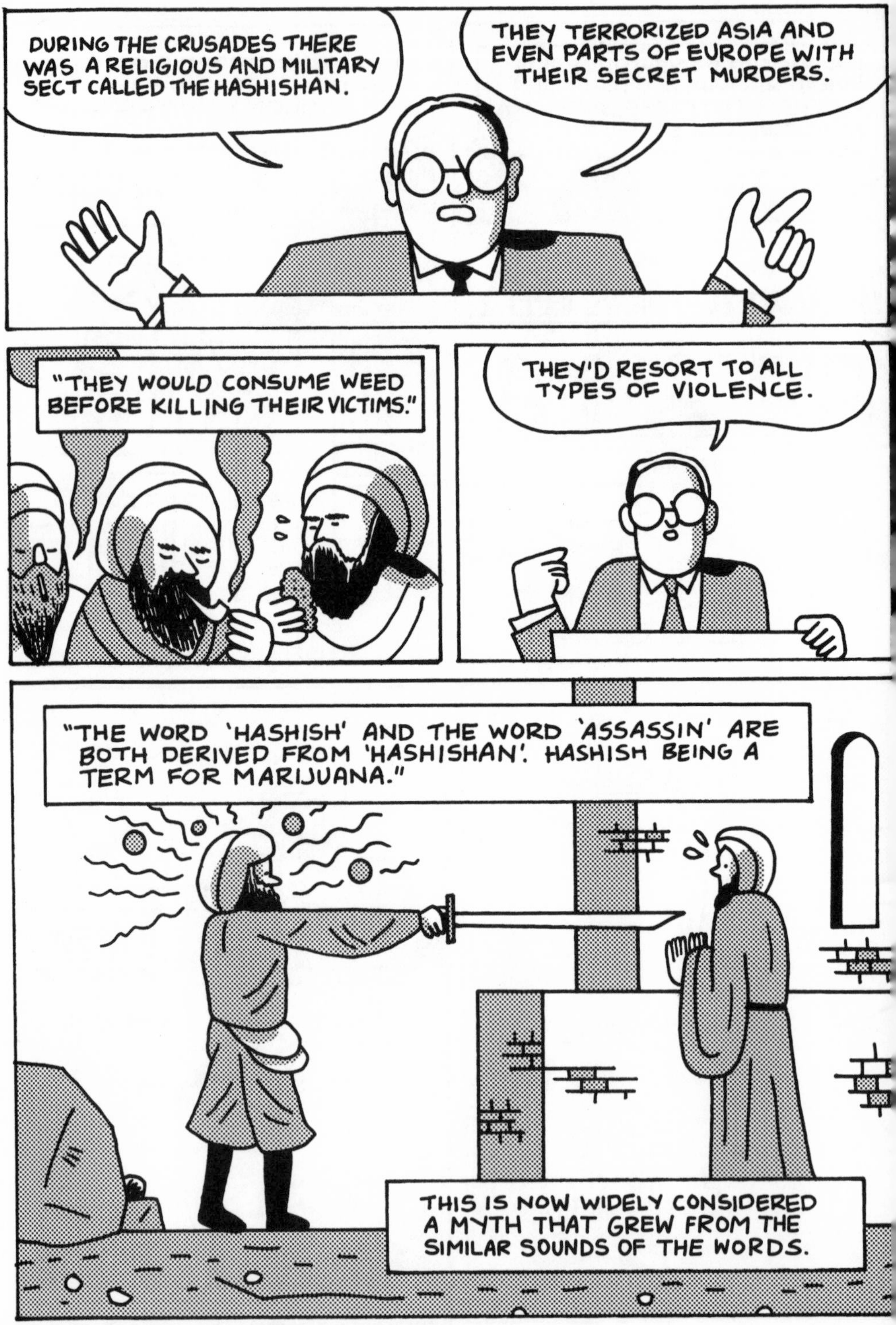
DURING THE CRUSADES THERE WAS A RELIGIOUS AND MILITARY SECT CALLED THE HASHISHAN.
THEY TERRORIZED ASIA AND EVEN PARTS OF EUROPE WITH THEIR SECRET MURDERS.
"THEY WOULD CONSUME WEED BEFORE KILLING THEIR VICTIMS."
THEY'D RESORT TO ALL TYPES OF VIOLENCE.
"THE WORD 'HASHISH' AND THE WORD 'ASSASSIN' ARE BOTH DERIVED FROM 'HASHISHAN'. HASHISH BEING A TERM FOR MARIJUANA."
THIS IS NOW WIDELY CONSIDERED A MYTH THAT GREW FROM THE SIMILAR SOUNDS OF THE WORDS.

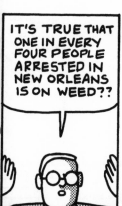
IT'S TRUE THAT ONE IN EVERY FOUR PEOPLE ARRESTED IN NEW ORLEANS IS ON WEED??

NOT TRUE.

YES!

MOST MURDERERS SMOKE MARIJUANA.

IT'S TRUE.

IT'S NOT.

IN PLACES LIKE INDIA AND EGYPT, ITS USE IS JUST AS COMMON AS ALCOHOL USE IN EUROPE.

WHILE THE EFFECTS ARE SIMILARLY INTOXICATING, IT'S CLEAR MARIJUANA IS THE MORE DANGEROUS SUBSTANCE.

THIS IS BECAUSE MARIJUANA CAUSES A MORAL FAILING. YES, ALCOHOL IS THE LESSER OF THE TWO EVILS.

AND THIS IS OBVIOUS BECAUSE THE DOMINANT RACE, WHITES, ARE AT THE HEIGHT OF CULTURE AND THOSE COUNTRIES THAT CONSUME MARIJUANA HAVE DETERIORATED.

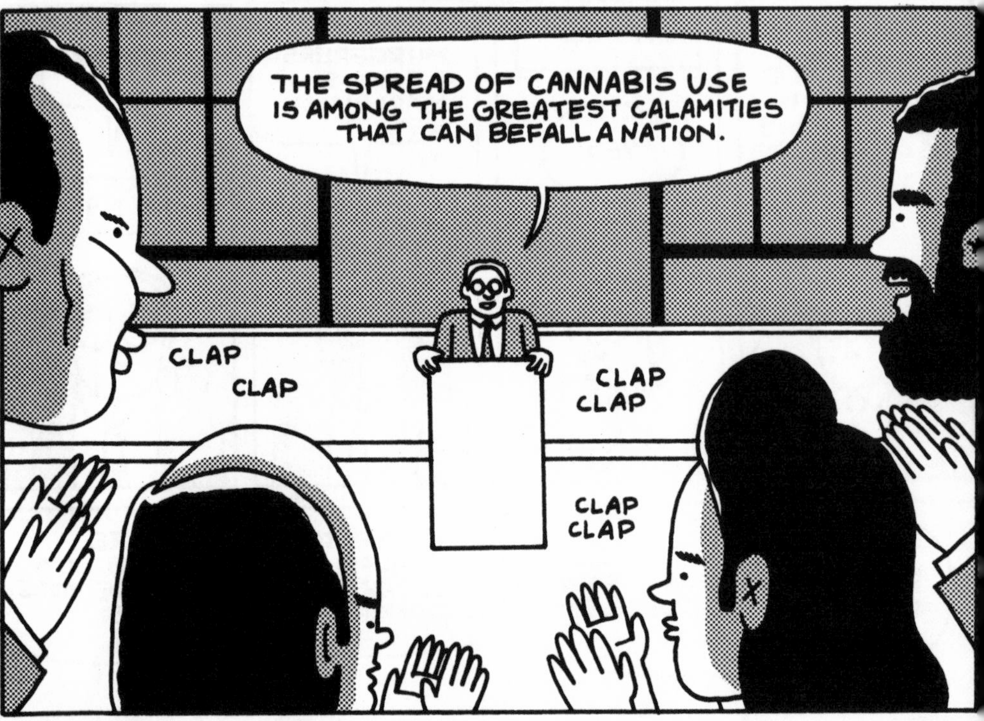
THE SPREAD OF CANNABIS USE IS AMONG THE GREATEST CALAMITIES THAT CAN BEFALL A NATION.
CLAP
CLAP
CLAP
CLAP
CLAP
CLAP

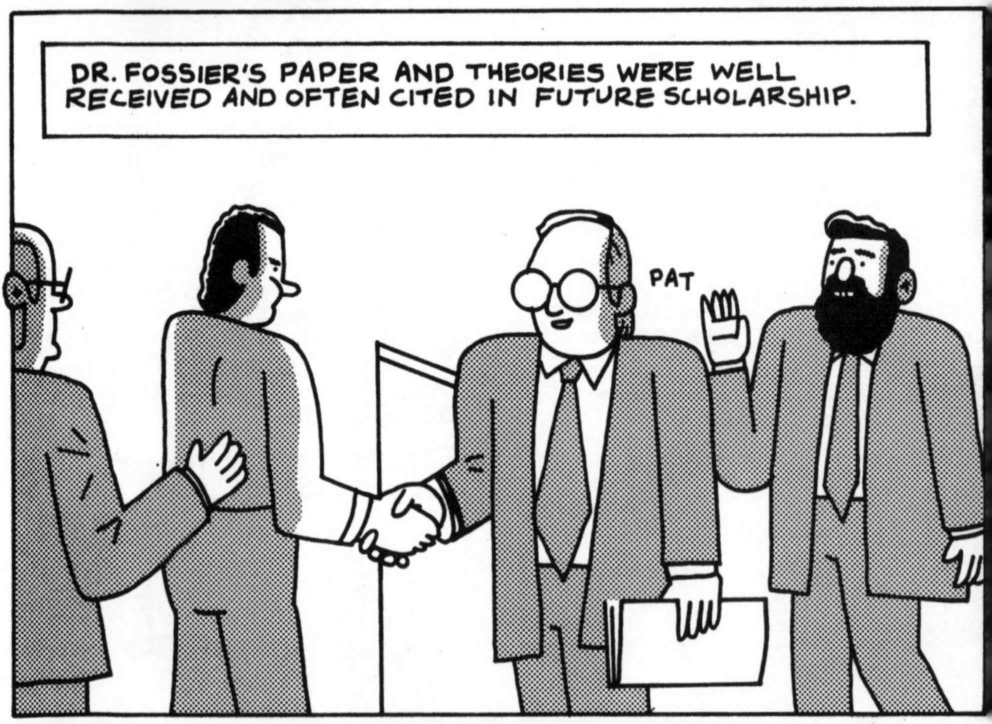
DR. FOSSIER'S PAPER AND THEORIES WERE WELL RECEIVED AND OFTEN CITED IN FUTURE SCHOLARSHIP.
PAT

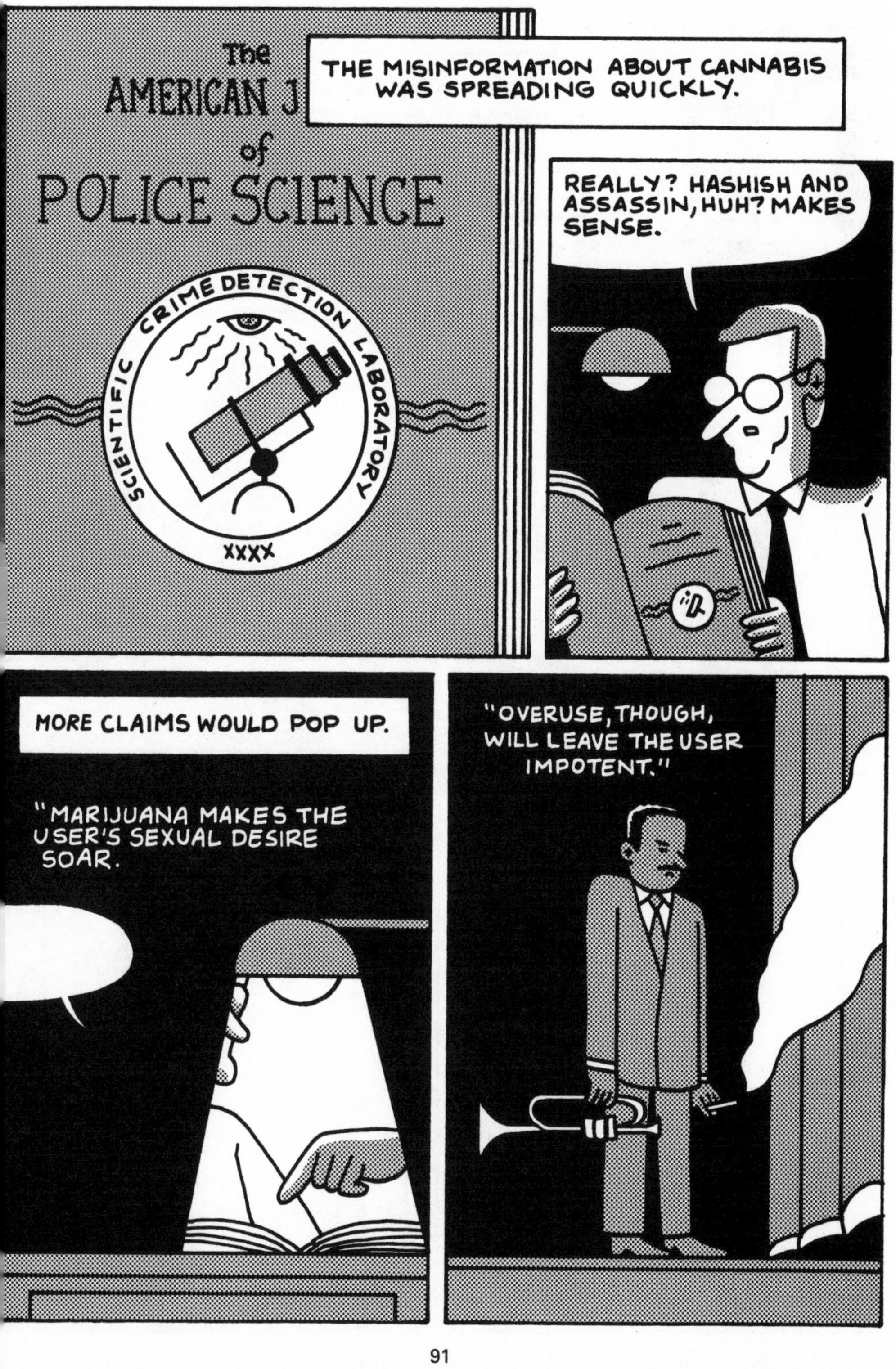

The AMERICAN J
of
POLICE SCIENCE
SCIENTIFIC CRIME DETECTION LABORATORY
XXXX
THE MISINFORMATION ABOUT CANNABIS WAS SPREADING QUICKLY.
REALLY? HASHISH AND ASSASSIN, HUH? MAKES SENSE.
MORE CLAIMS WOULD POP UP.
"MARIJUANA MAKES THE USER'S SEXUAL DESIRE SOAR.
"OVERUSE, THOUGH, WILL LEAVE THE USER IMPOTENT."

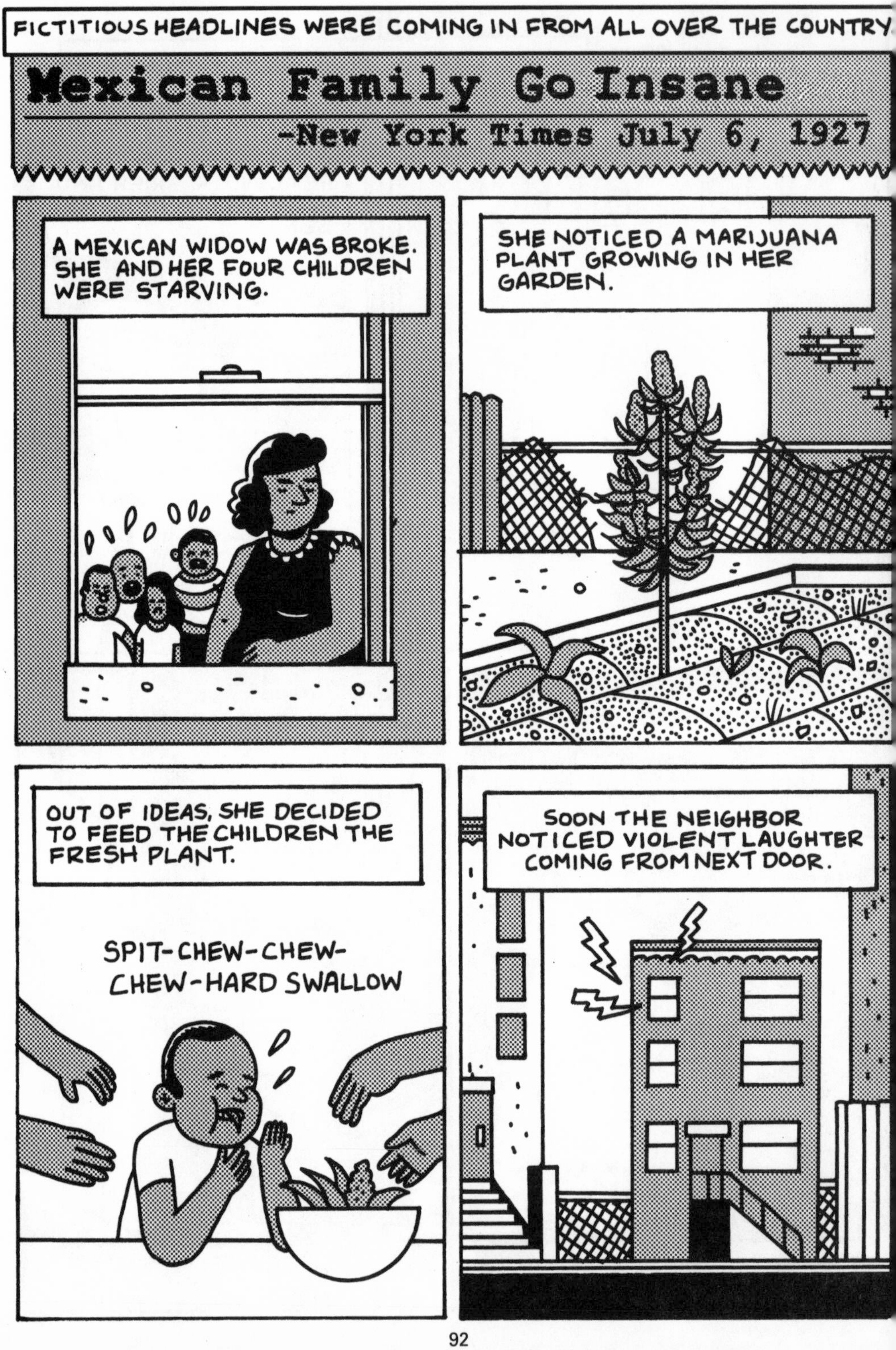

FICTITIOUS HEADLINES WERE COMING IN FROM ALL OVER THE COUNTRY.
Mexican Family Go Insane
-New York Times July 6, 1927
A MEXICAN WIDOW WAS BROKE. SHE AND HER FOUR CHILDREN WERE STARVING.
SHE NOTICED A MARIJUANA PLANT GROWING IN HER GARDEN.
OUT OF IDEAS, SHE DECIDED TO FEED THE CHILDREN THE FRESH PLANT.
SPIT-CHEW-CHEW-CHEW-HARD SWALLOW
SOON THE NEIGHBOR NOTICED VIOLENT LAUGHTER COMING FROM NEXT DOOR.

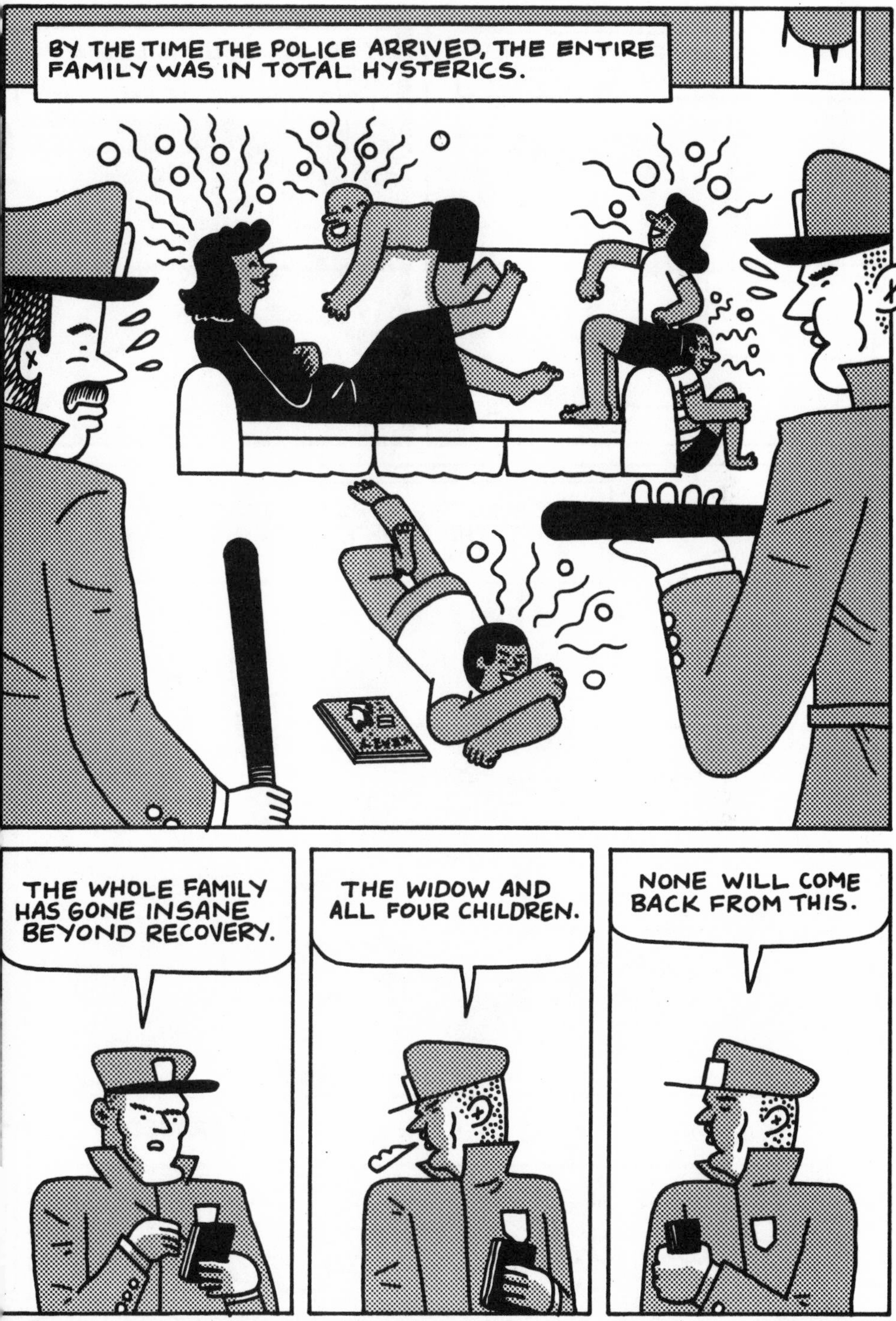
BY THE TIME THE POLICE ARRIVED, THE ENTIRE FAMILY WAS IN TOTAL HYSTERICS.
THE WHOLE FAMILY HAS GONE INSANE BEYOND RECOVERY.
THE WIDOW AND ALL FOUR CHILDREN.
NONE WILL COME BACK FROM THIS.

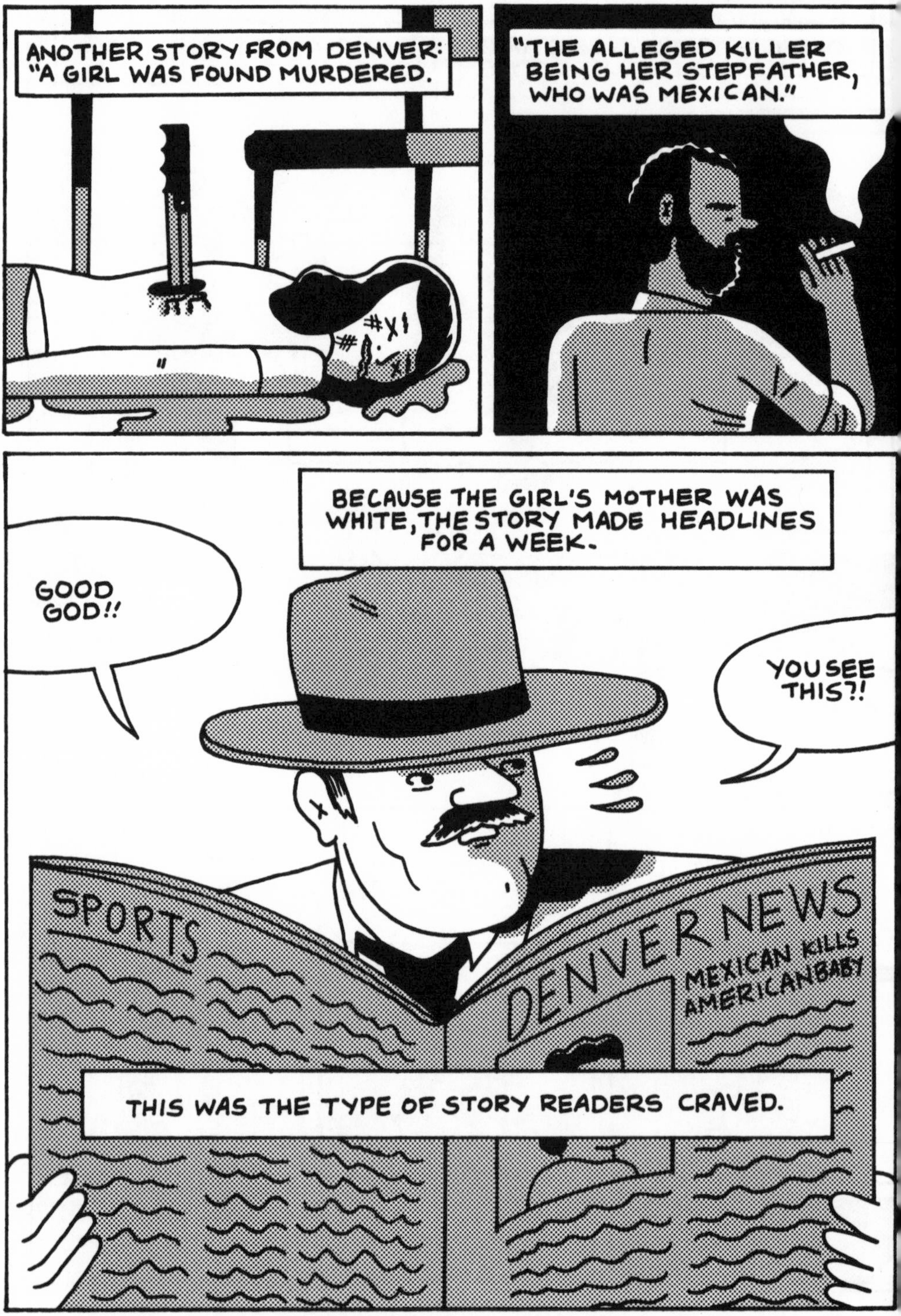
ANOTHER STORY FROM DENVER: "A GIRL WAS FOUND MURDERED.
"THE ALLEGED KILLER BEING HER STEPFATHER, WHO WAS MEXICAN."
BECAUSE THE GIRL'S MOTHER WAS WHITE, THE STORY MADE HEADLINES FOR A WEEK.
GOOD GOD!!
YOU SEE THIS?!
SPORTS
DENVER NEWS
MEXICAN KILLS AMERICAN BABY
THIS WAS THE TYPE OF STORY READERS CRAVED.

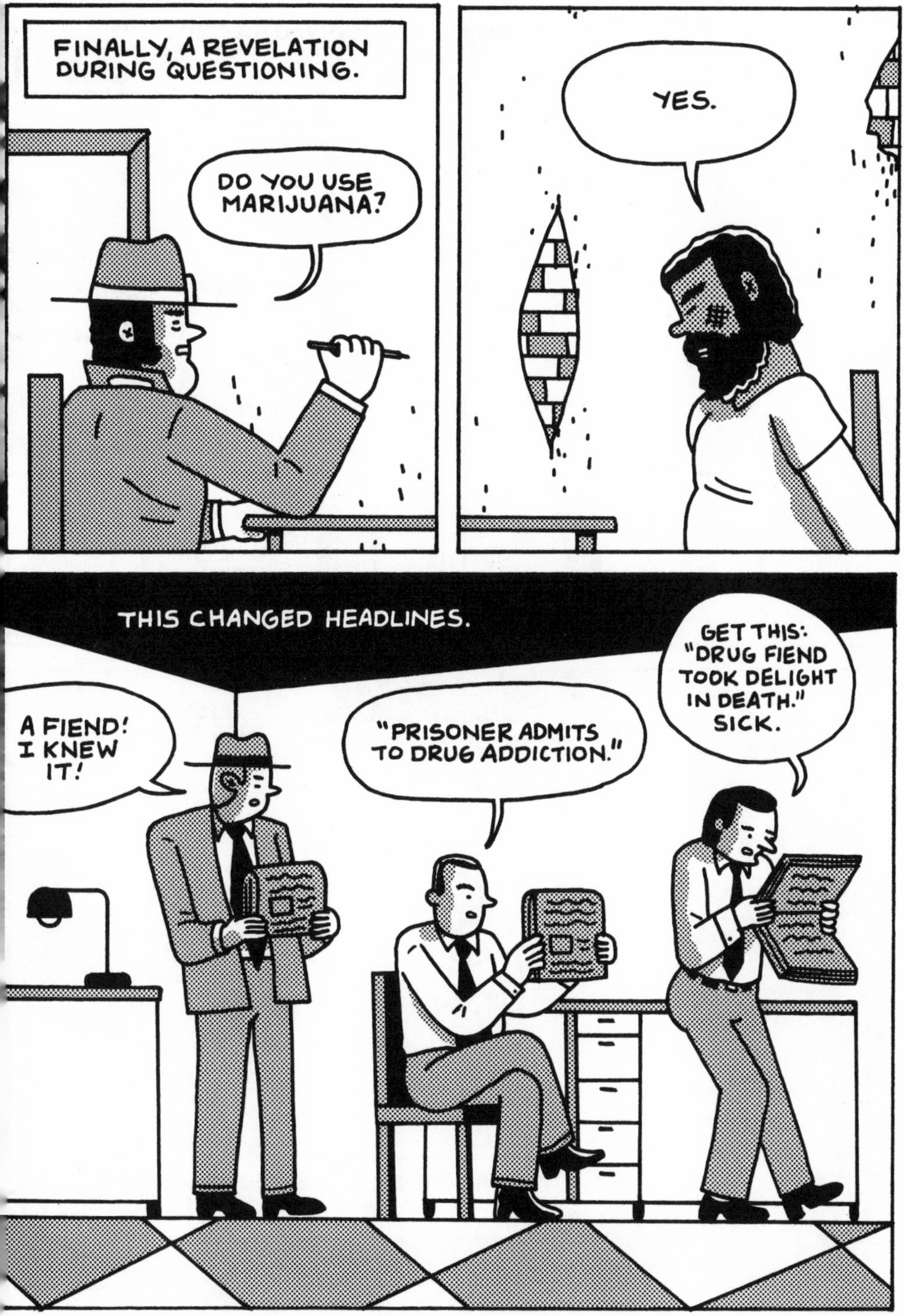
FINALLY, A REVELATION DURING QUESTIONING.
DO YOU USE MARIJUANA?
YES.
THIS CHANGED HEADLINES.
A FIEND! I KNEW IT!
"PRISONER ADMITS TO DRUG ADDICTION."
GET THIS: "DRUG FIEND TOOK DELIGHT IN DEATH." SICK.

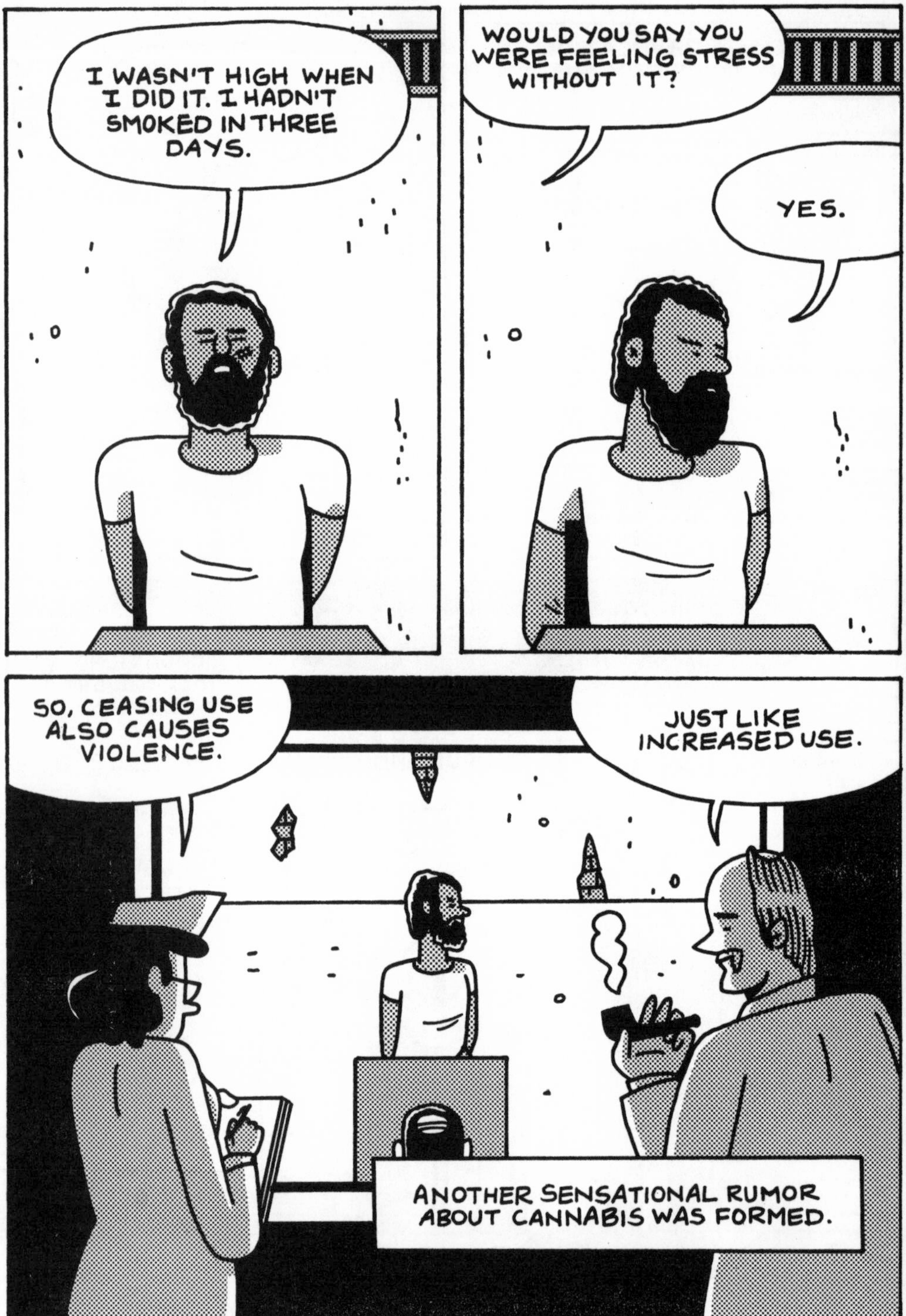
I WASN'T HIGH WHEN I DID IT. I HADN'T SMOKED IN THREE DAYS.
WOULD YOU SAY YOU WERE FEELING STRESS WITHOUT IT?
YES.
SO, CEASING USE ALSO CAUSES VIOLENCE.
JUST LIKE INCREASED USE.
ANOTHER SENSATIONAL RUMOR ABOUT CANNABIS WAS FORMED.

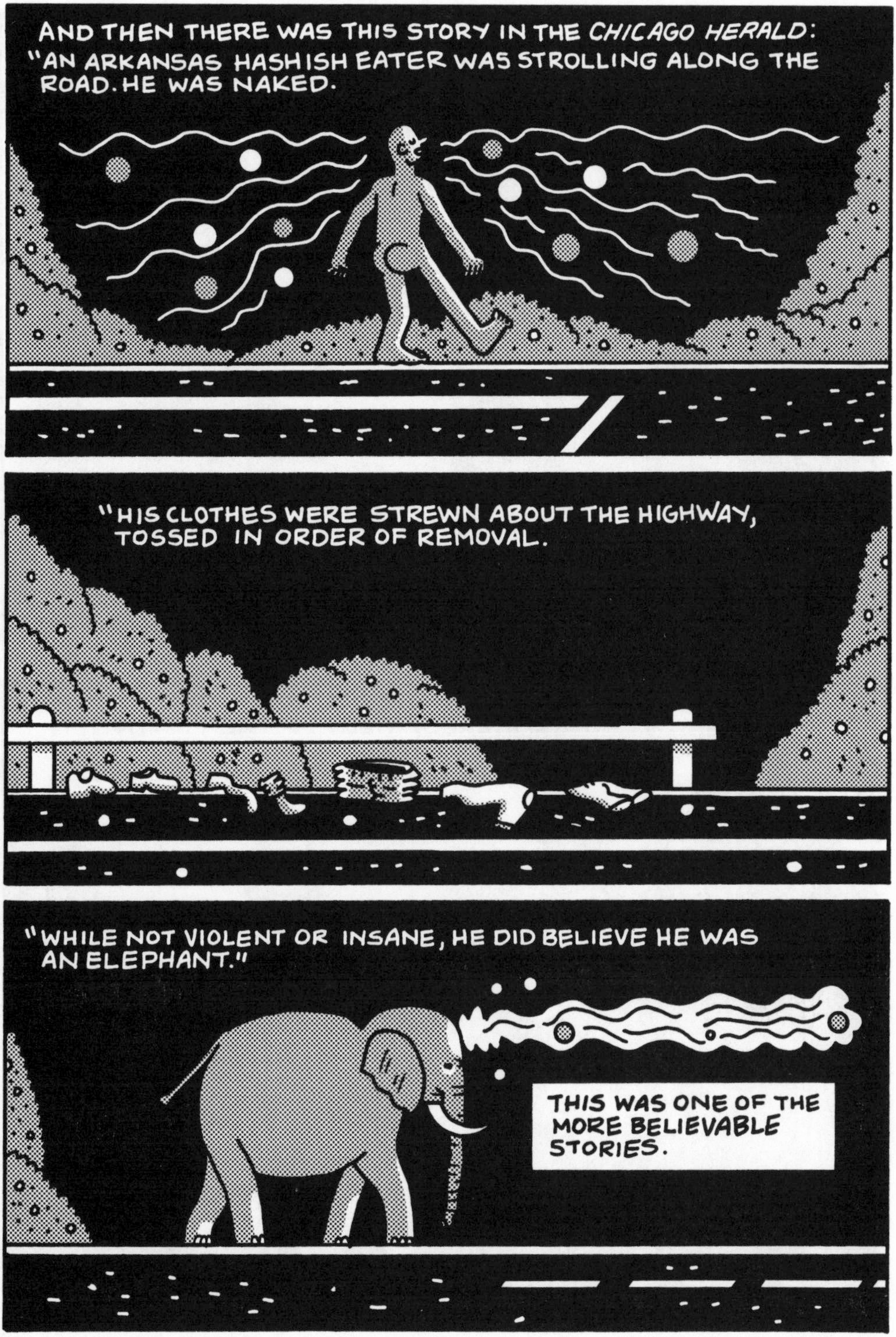
AND THEN THERE WAS THIS STORY IN THE *CHICAGO HERALD*:
"AN ARKANSAS HASHISH EATER WAS STROLLING ALONG THE ROAD. HE WAS NAKED.
"HIS CLOTHES WERE STREWN ABOUT THE HIGHWAY, TOSSED IN ORDER OF REMOVAL.
"WHILE NOT VIOLENT OR INSANE, HE DID BELIEVE HE WAS AN ELEPHANT."
THIS WAS ONE OF THE MORE BELIEVABLE STORIES.

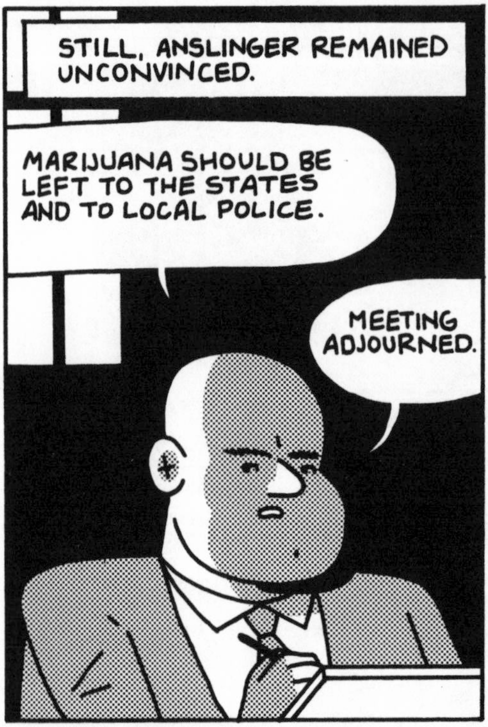
STILL, ANSLINGER REMAINED UNCONVINCED.
MARIJUANA SHOULD BE LEFT TO THE STATES AND TO LOCAL POLICE.
MEETING ADJOURNED.

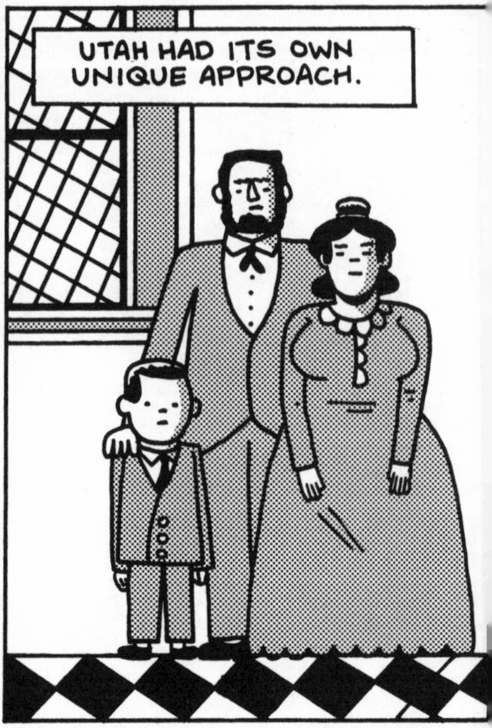
UTAH HAD ITS OWN UNIQUE APPROACH.

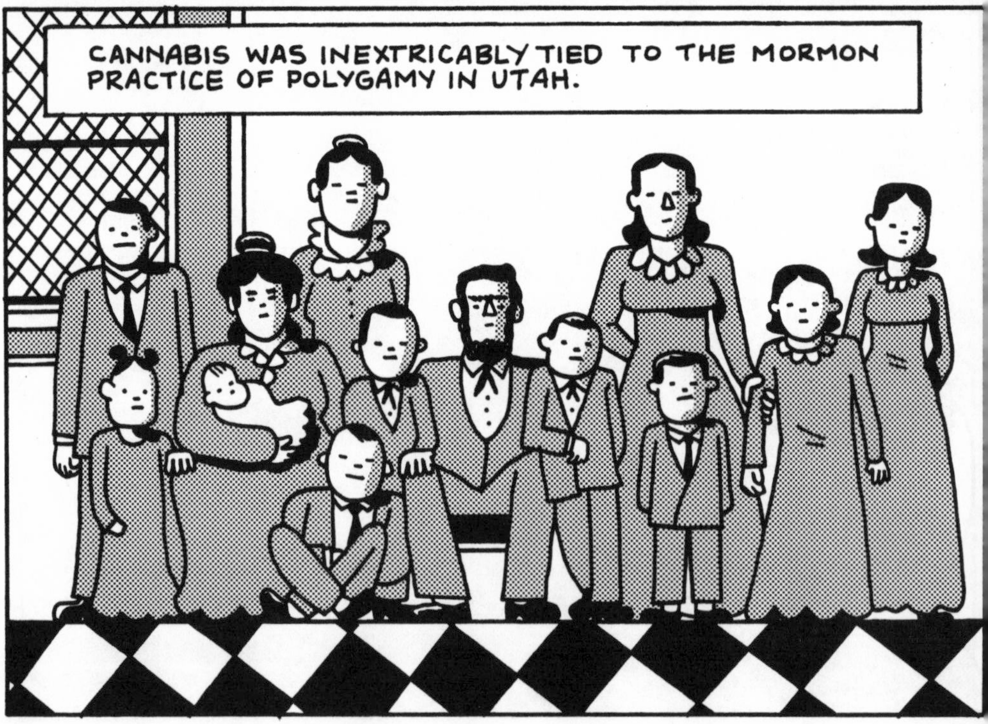
CANNABIS WAS INEXTRICABLY TIED TO THE MORMON PRACTICE OF POLYGAMY IN UTAH.

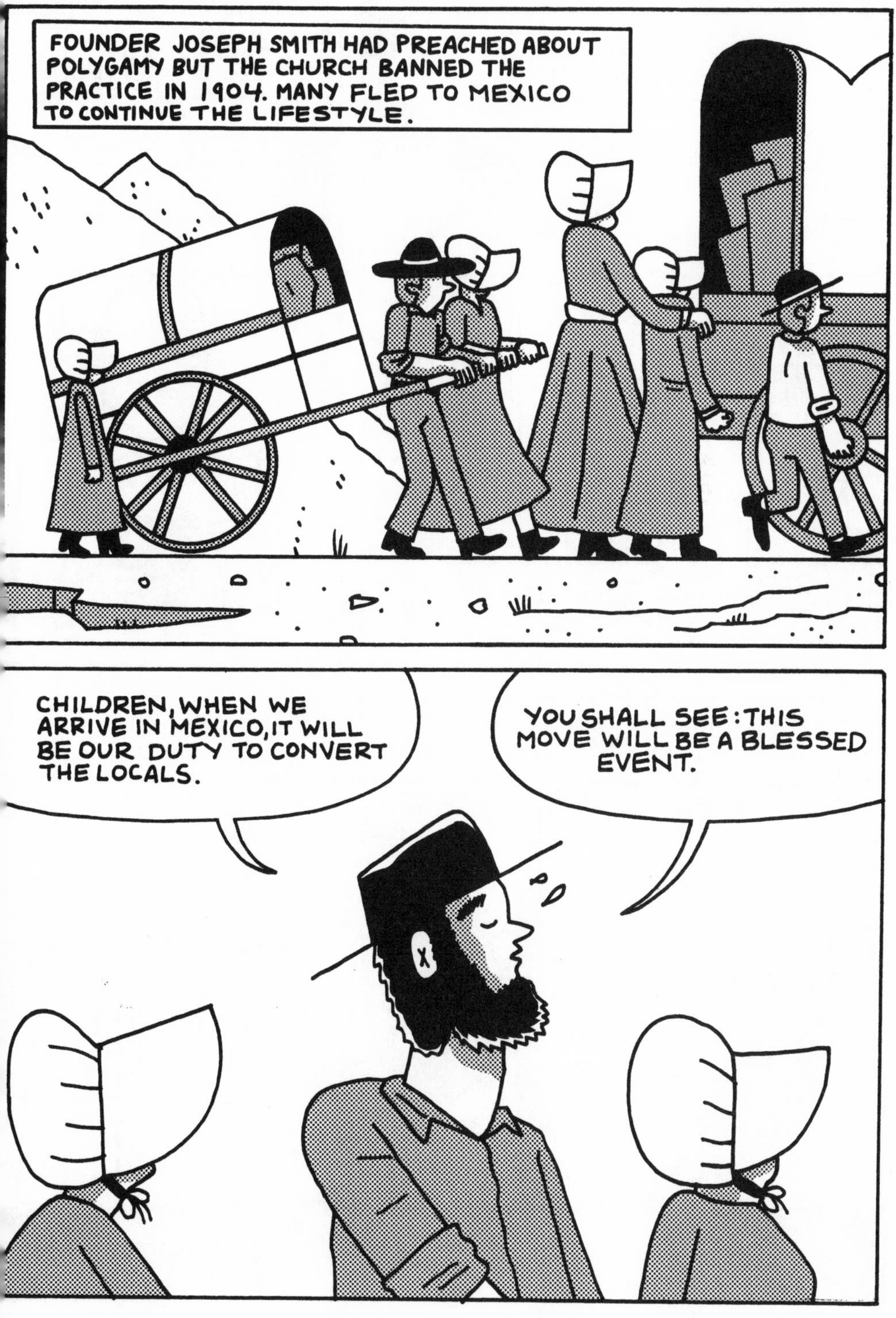
FOUNDER JOSEPH SMITH HAD PREACHED ABOUT POLYGAMY BUT THE CHURCH BANNED THE PRACTICE IN 1904. MANY FLED TO MEXICO TO CONTINUE THE LIFESTYLE.
CHILDREN, WHEN WE ARRIVE IN MEXICO, IT WILL BE OUR DUTY TO CONVERT THE LOCALS.
YOU SHALL SEE: THIS MOVE WILL BE A BLESSED EVENT.

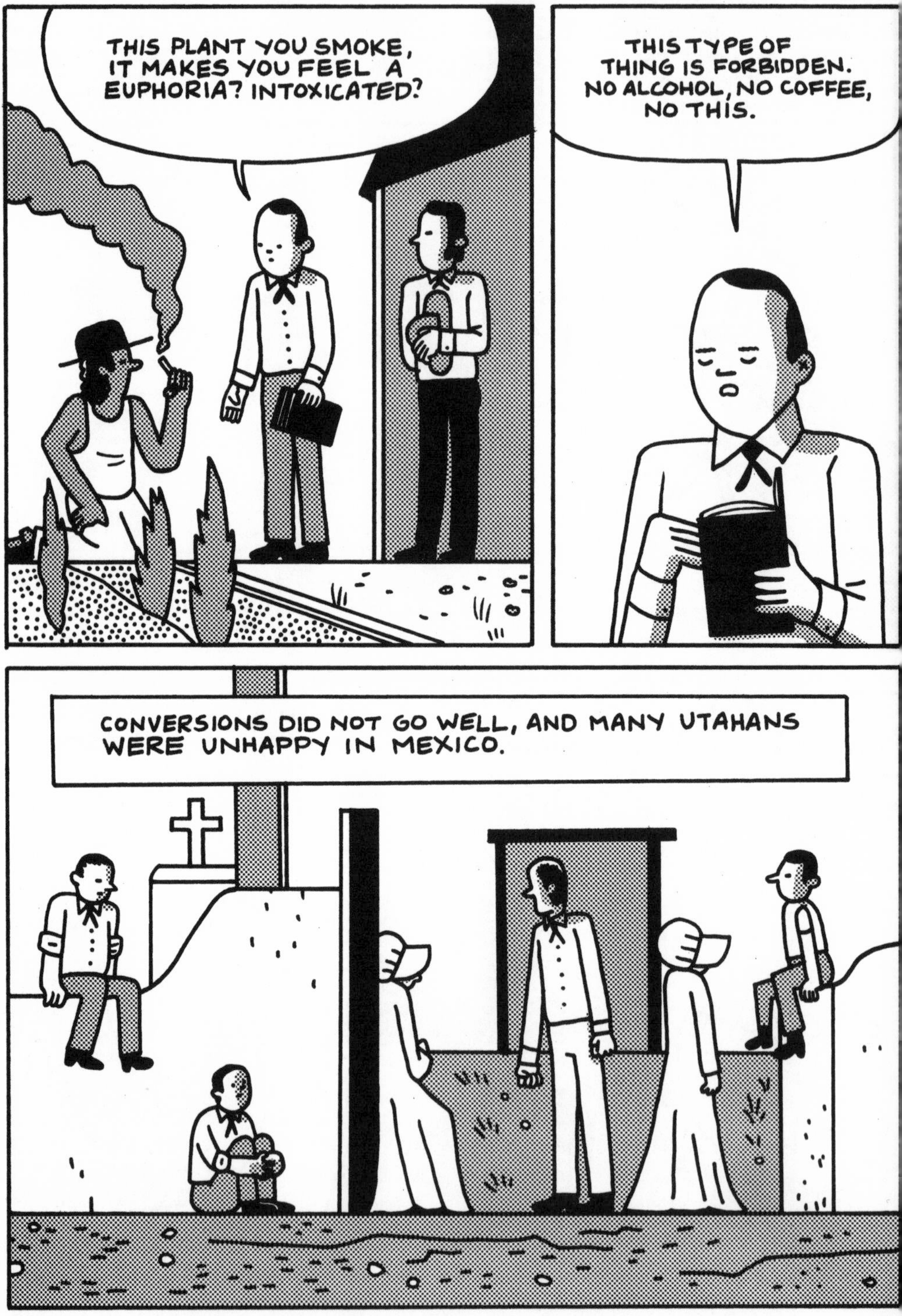
THIS PLANT YOU SMOKE, IT MAKES YOU FEEL A EUPHORIA? INTOXICATED?
THIS TYPE OF THING IS FORBIDDEN. NO ALCOHOL, NO COFFEE, NO THIS.
CONVERSIONS DID NOT GO WELL, AND MANY UTAHANS WERE UNHAPPY IN MEXICO.

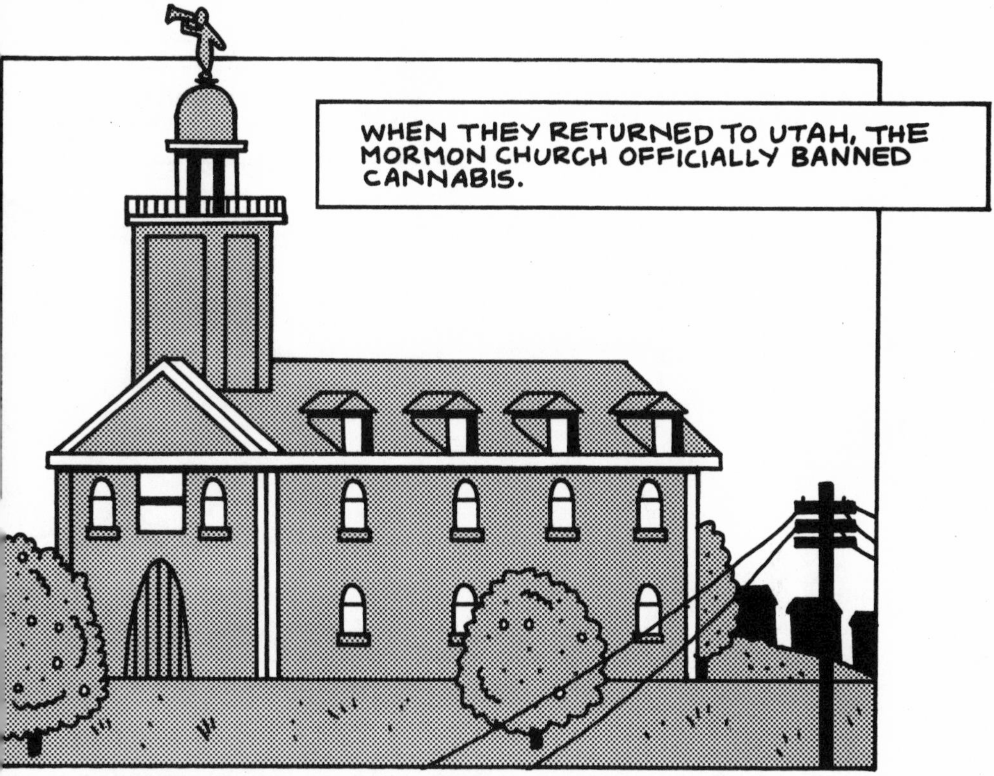
WHEN THEY RETURNED TO UTAH, THE MORMON CHURCH OFFICIALLY BANNED CANNABIS.

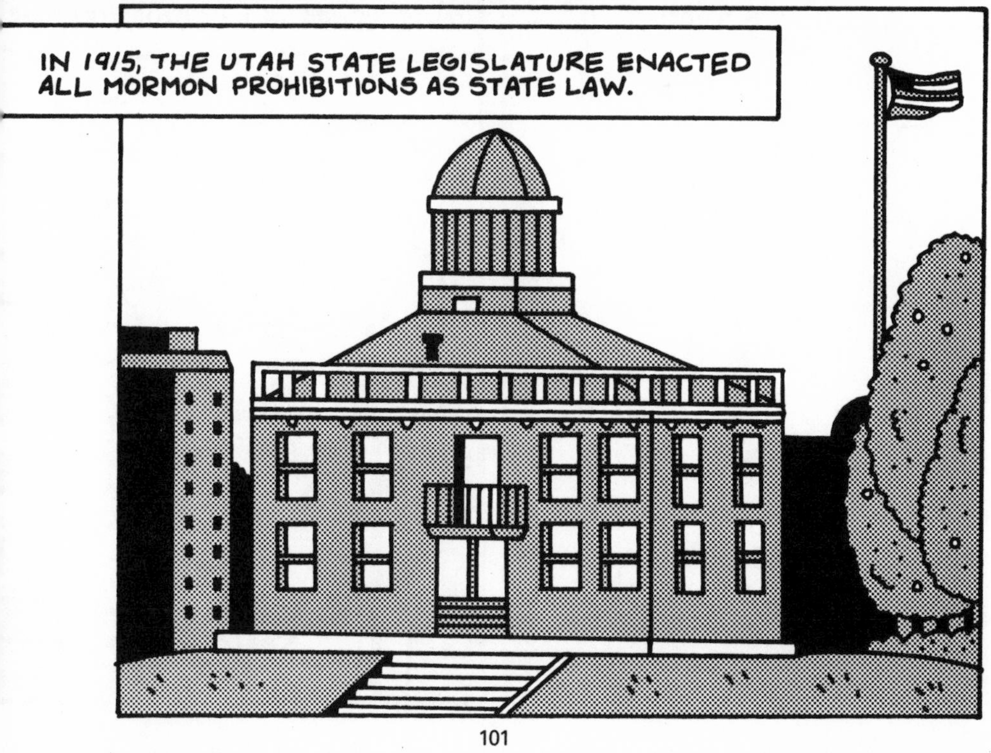
IN 1915, THE UTAH STATE LEGISLATURE ENACTED ALL MORMON PROHIBITIONS AS STATE LAW.

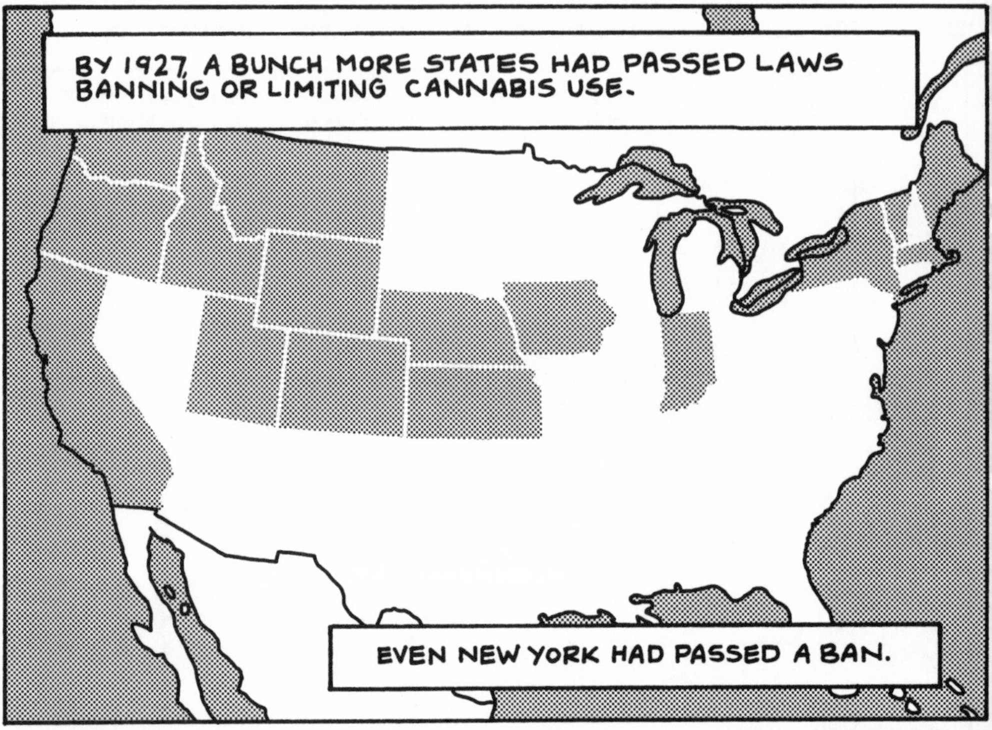
BY 1927, A BUNCH MORE STATES HAD PASSED LAWS BANNING OR LIMITING CANNABIS USE.
EVEN NEW YORK HAD PASSED A BAN.

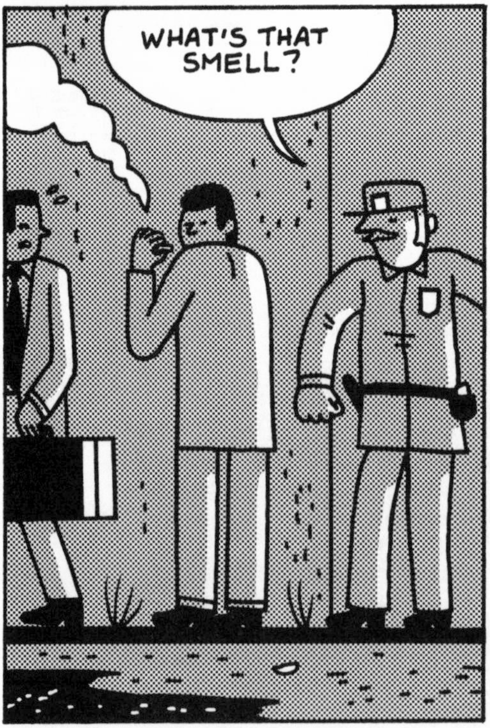
WHAT'S THAT SMELL?

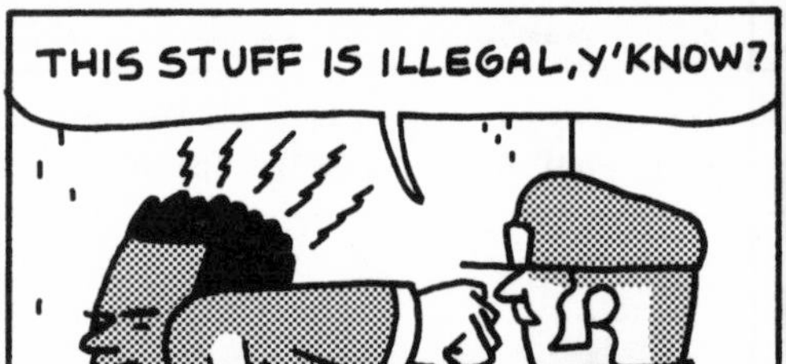
THIS STUFF IS ILLEGAL, Y'KNOW?

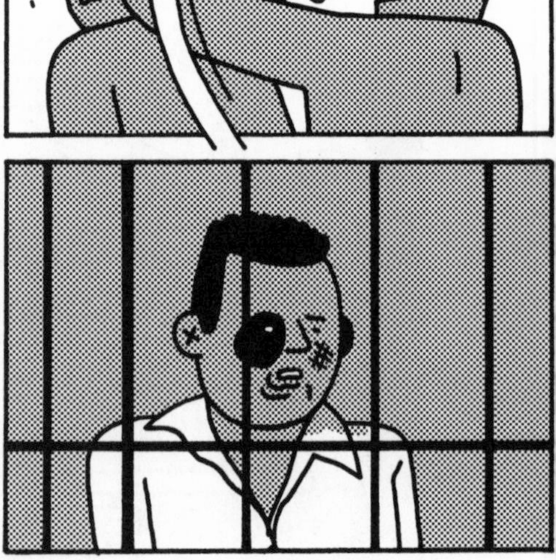

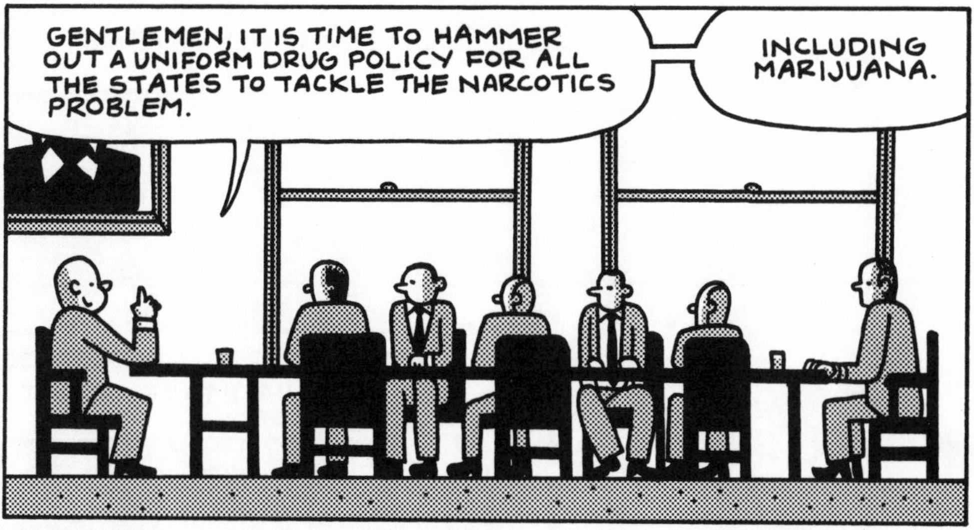
GENTLEMEN, IT IS TIME TO HAMMER OUT A UNIFORM DRUG POLICY FOR ALL THE STATES TO TACKLE THE NARCOTICS PROBLEM.
INCLUDING MARIJUANA.

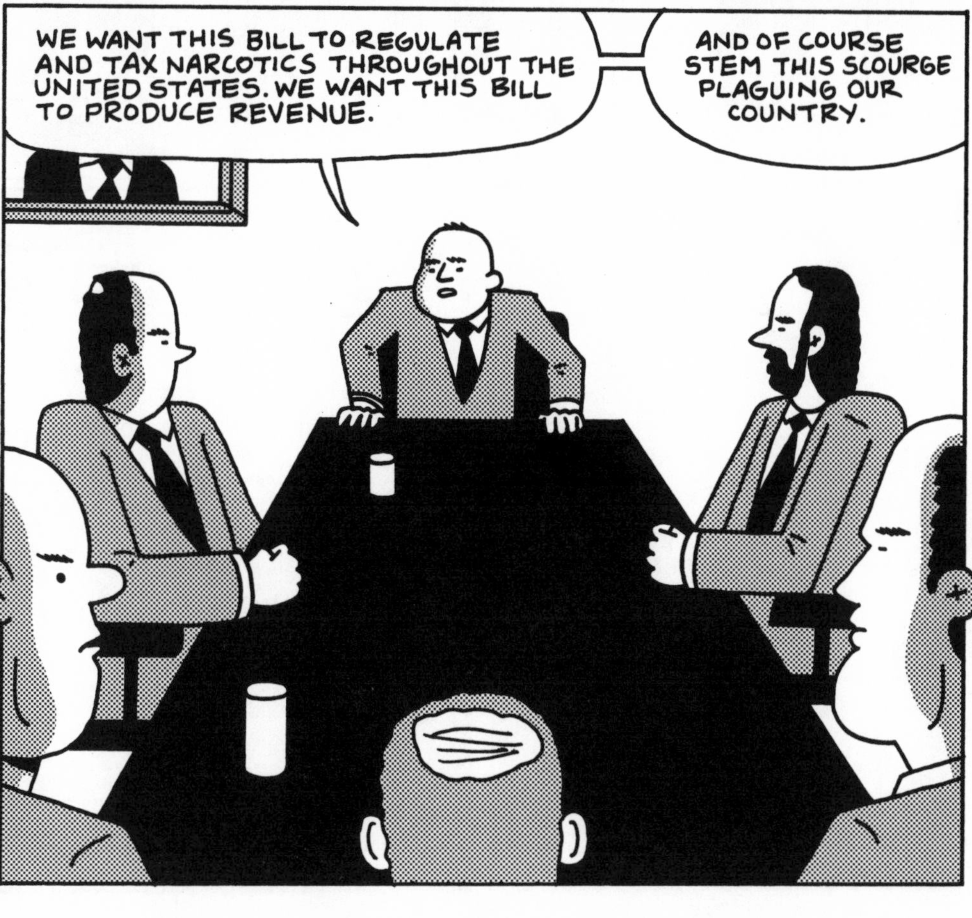
WE WANT THIS BILL TO REGULATE AND TAX NARCOTICS THROUGHOUT THE UNITED STATES. WE WANT THIS BILL TO PRODUCE REVENUE.
AND OF COURSE STEM THIS SCOURGE PLAGUING OUR COUNTRY.

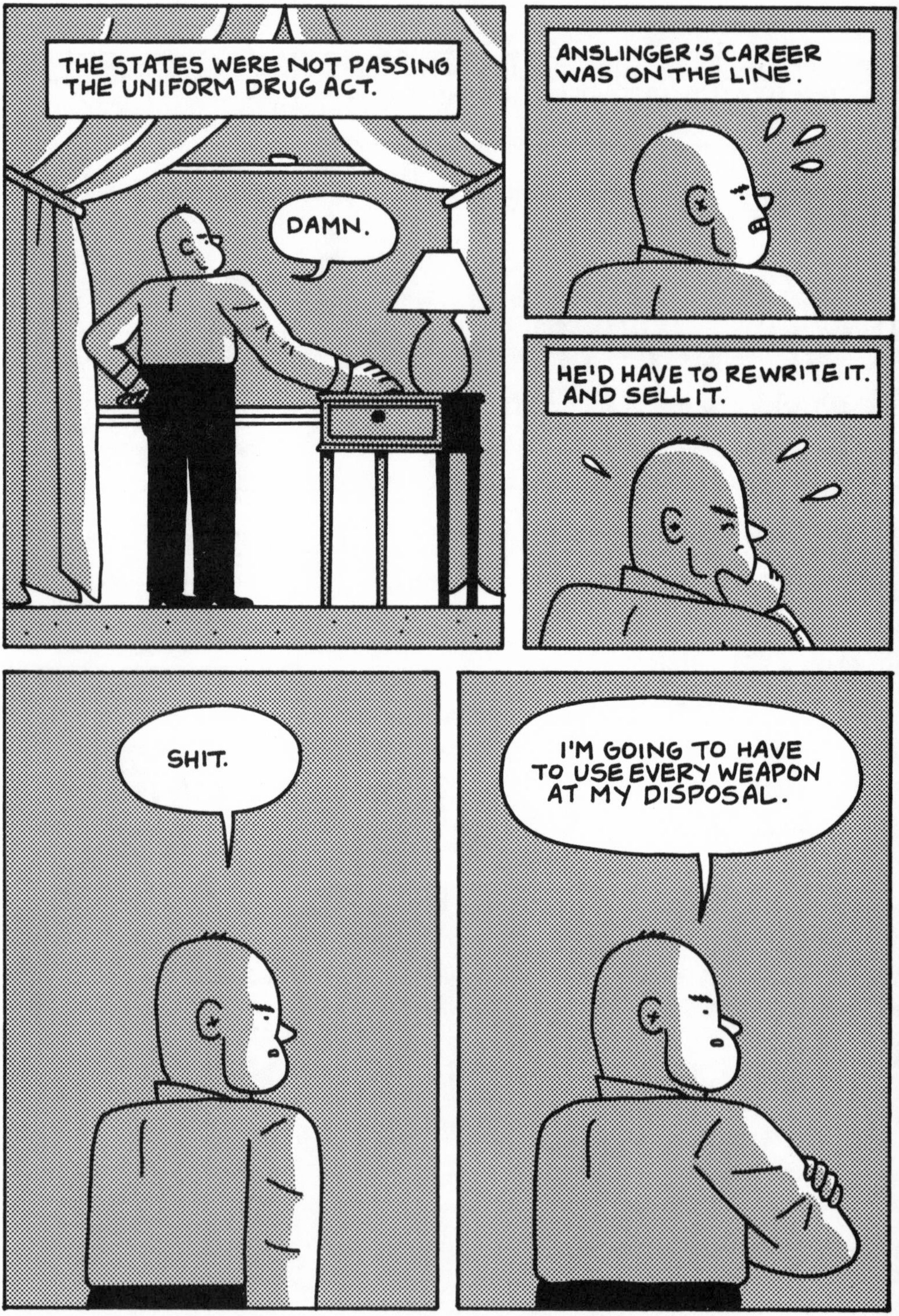
THE STATES WERE NOT PASSING THE UNIFORM DRUG ACT.
DAMN.
ANSLINGER'S CAREER WAS ON THE LINE.
HE'D HAVE TO REWRITE IT. AND SELL IT.
SHIT.
I'M GOING TO HAVE TO USE EVERY WEAPON AT MY DISPOSAL.

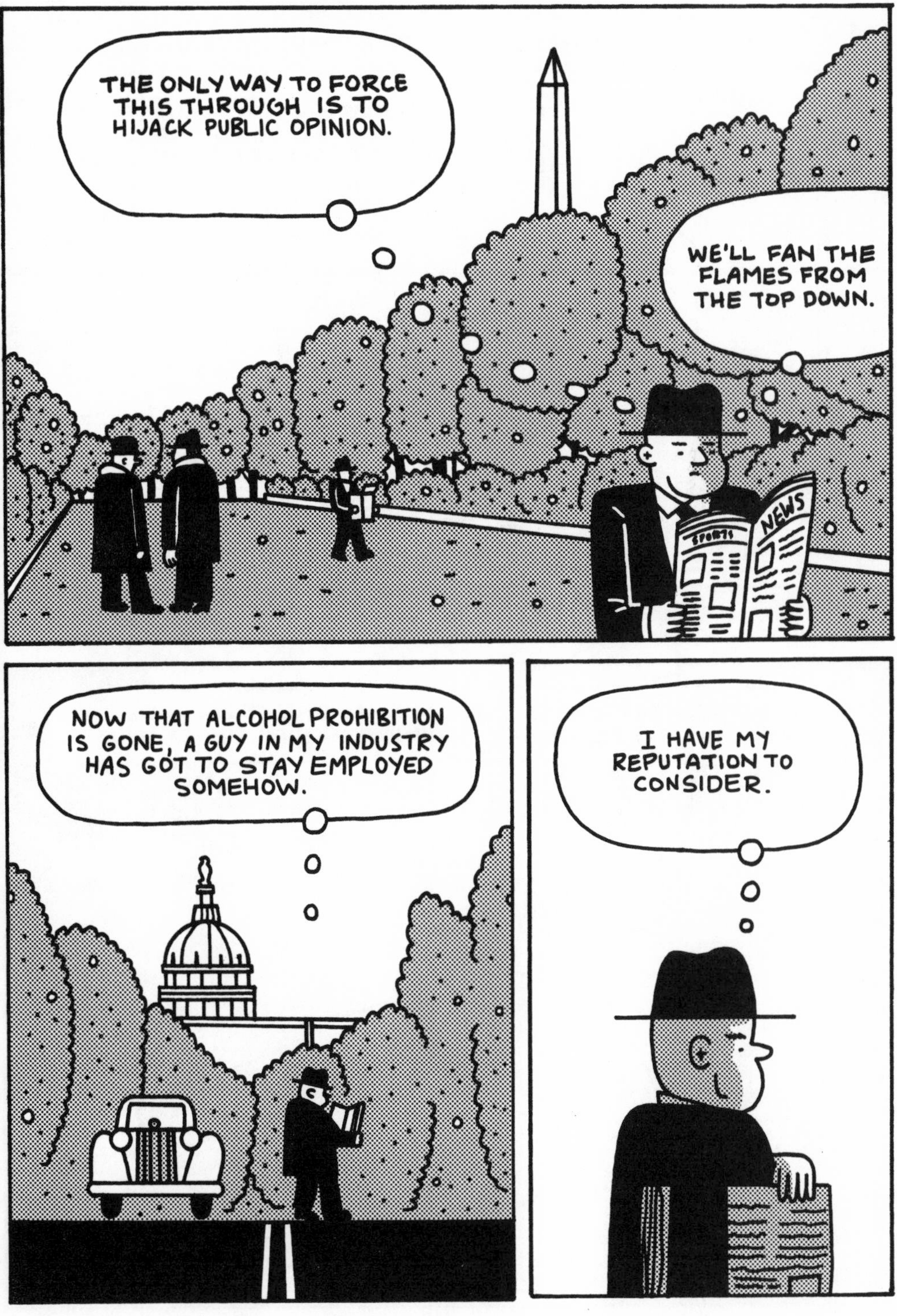
THE ONLY WAY TO FORCE THIS THROUGH IS TO HIJACK PUBLIC OPINION.
WE'LL FAN THE FLAMES FROM THE TOP DOWN.
NEWS
SPORTS
NOW THAT ALCOHOL PROHIBITION IS GONE, A GUY IN MY INDUSTRY HAS GOT TO STAY EMPLOYED SOMEHOW.
I HAVE MY REPUTATION TO CONSIDER.

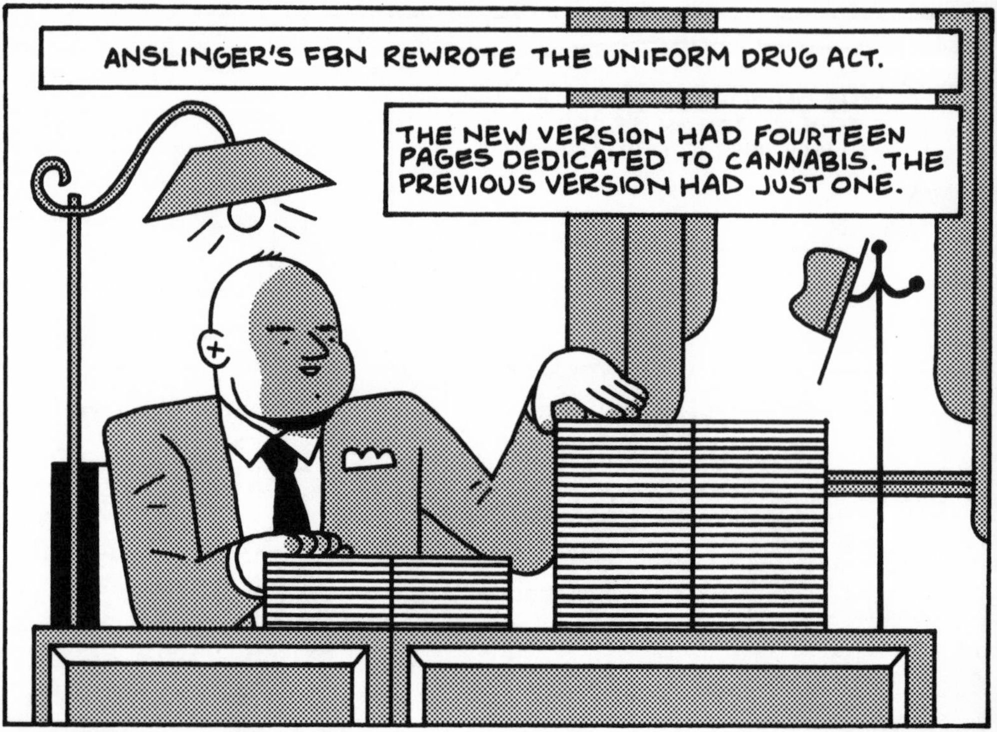
ANSLINGER'S FBN REWROTE THE UNIFORM DRUG ACT.
THE NEW VERSION HAD FOURTEEN PAGES DEDICATED TO CANNABIS. THE PREVIOUS VERSION HAD JUST ONE.

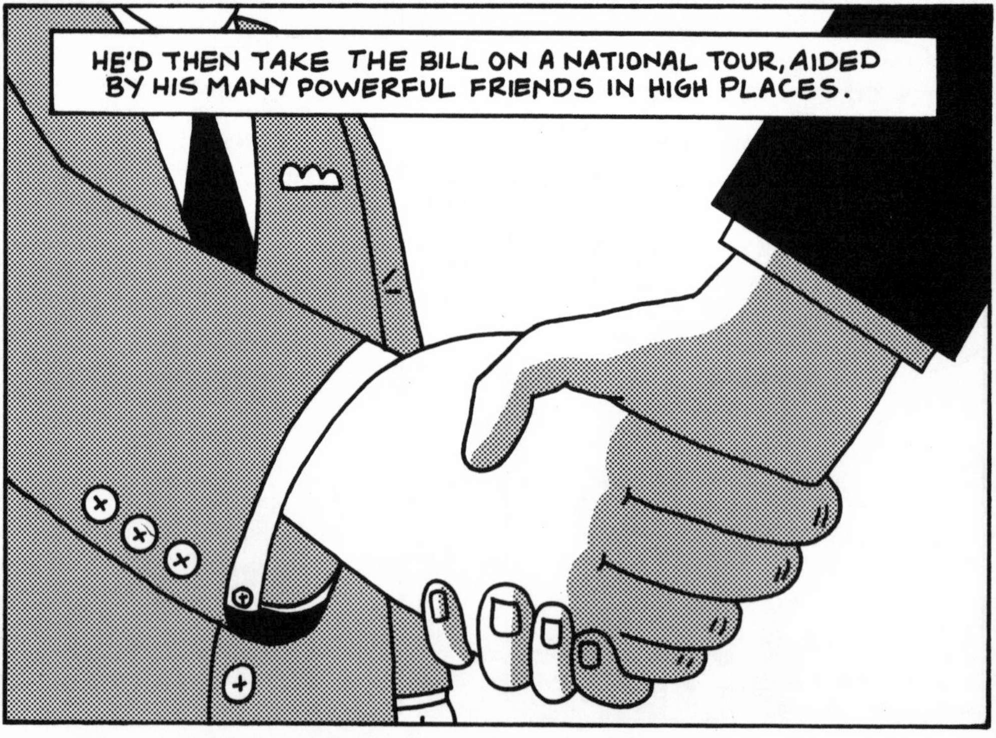
HE'D THEN TAKE THE BILL ON A NATIONAL TOUR, AIDED BY HIS MANY POWERFUL FRIENDS IN HIGH PLACES.

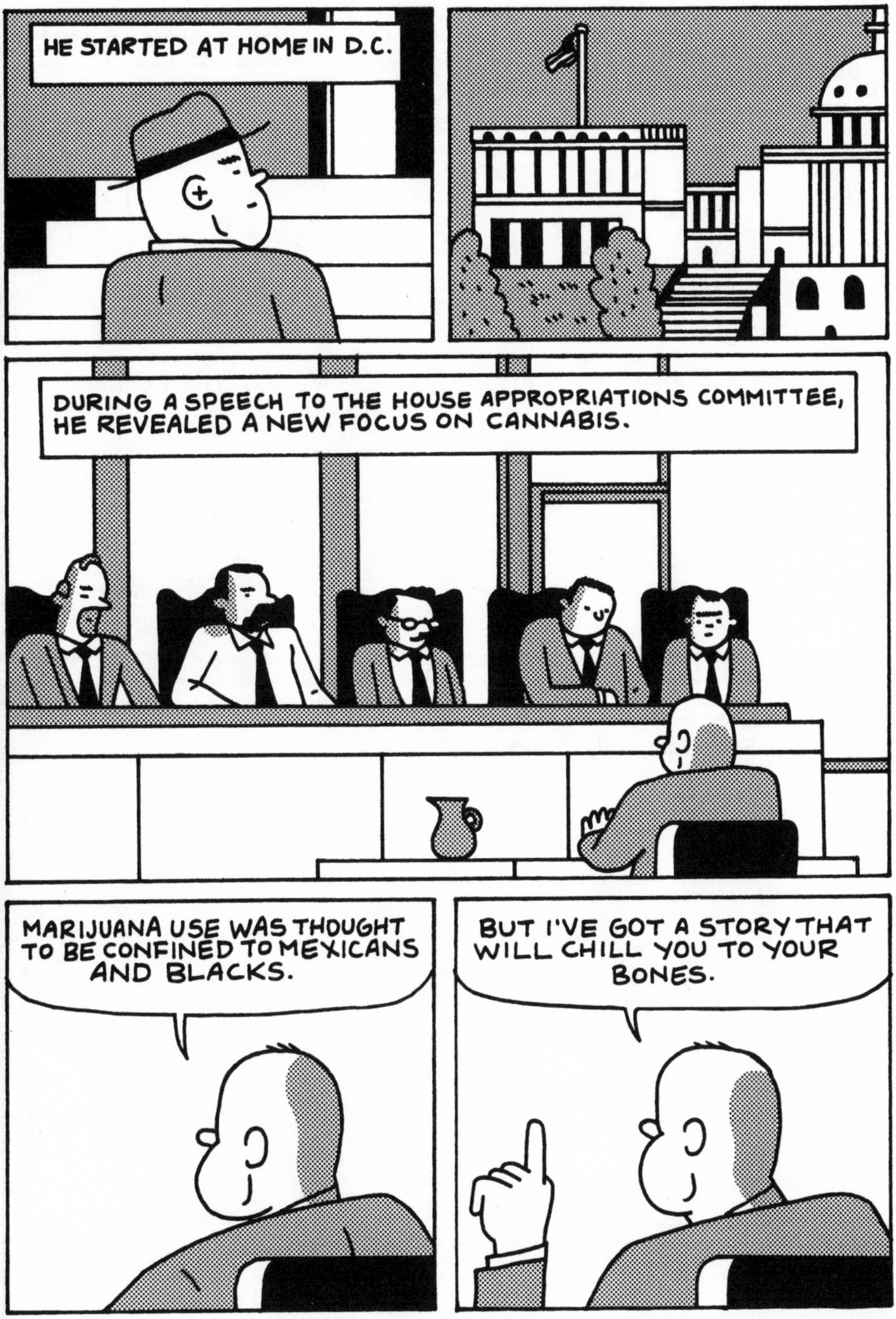
HE STARTED AT HOME IN D.C.
DURING A SPEECH TO THE HOUSE APPROPRIATIONS COMMITTEE, HE REVEALED A NEW FOCUS ON CANNABIS.
MARIJUANA USE WAS THOUGHT TO BE CONFINED TO MEXICANS AND BLACKS.
BUT I'VE GOT A STORY THAT WILL CHILL YOU TO YOUR BONES.

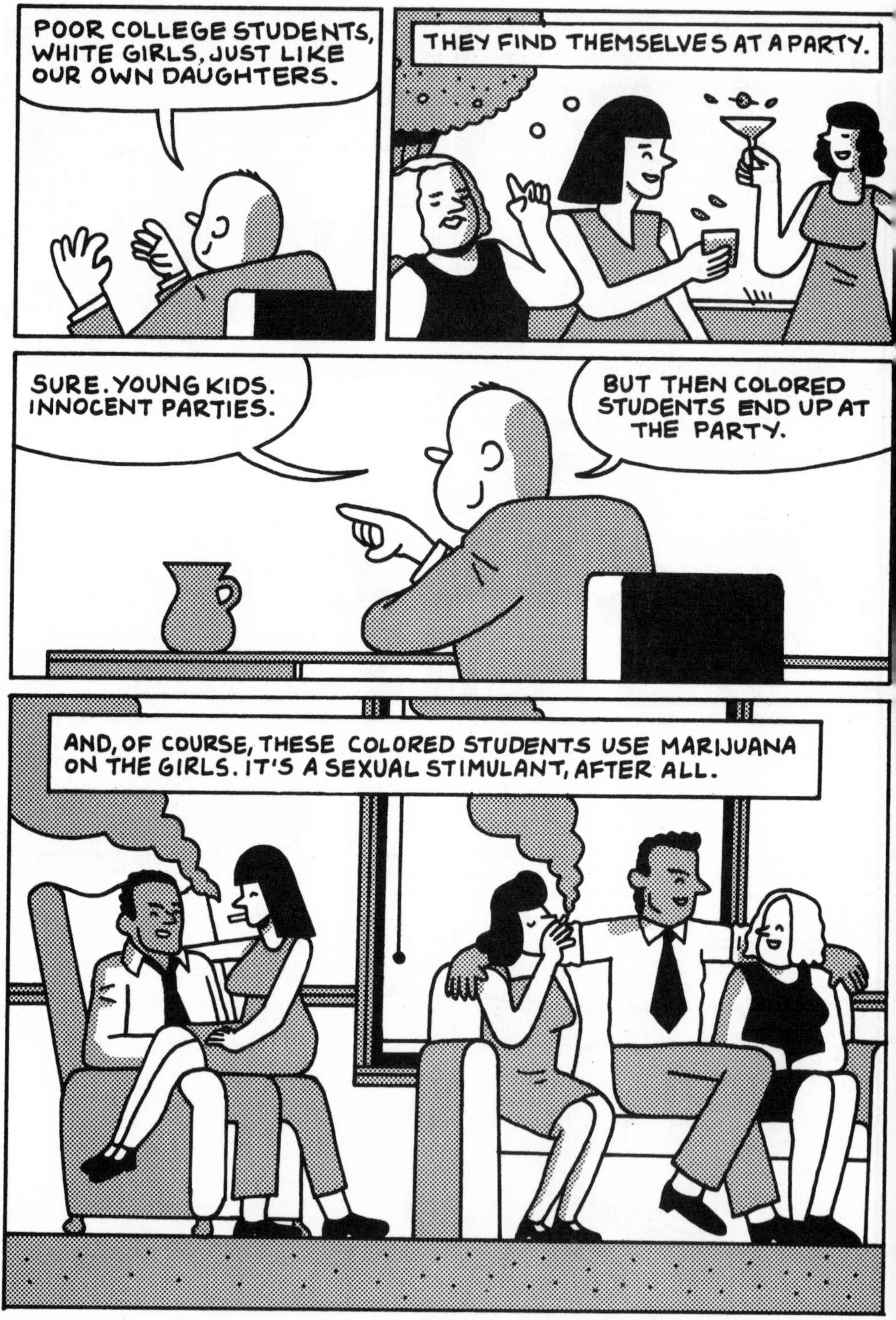
POOR COLLEGE STUDENTS, WHITE GIRLS, JUST LIKE OUR OWN DAUGHTERS.
THEY FIND THEMSELVES AT A PARTY.
SURE. YOUNG KIDS. INNOCENT PARTIES.
BUT THEN COLORED STUDENTS END UP AT THE PARTY.
AND, OF COURSE, THESE COLORED STUDENTS USE MARIJUANA ON THE GIRLS. IT'S A SEXUAL STIMULANT, AFTER ALL.

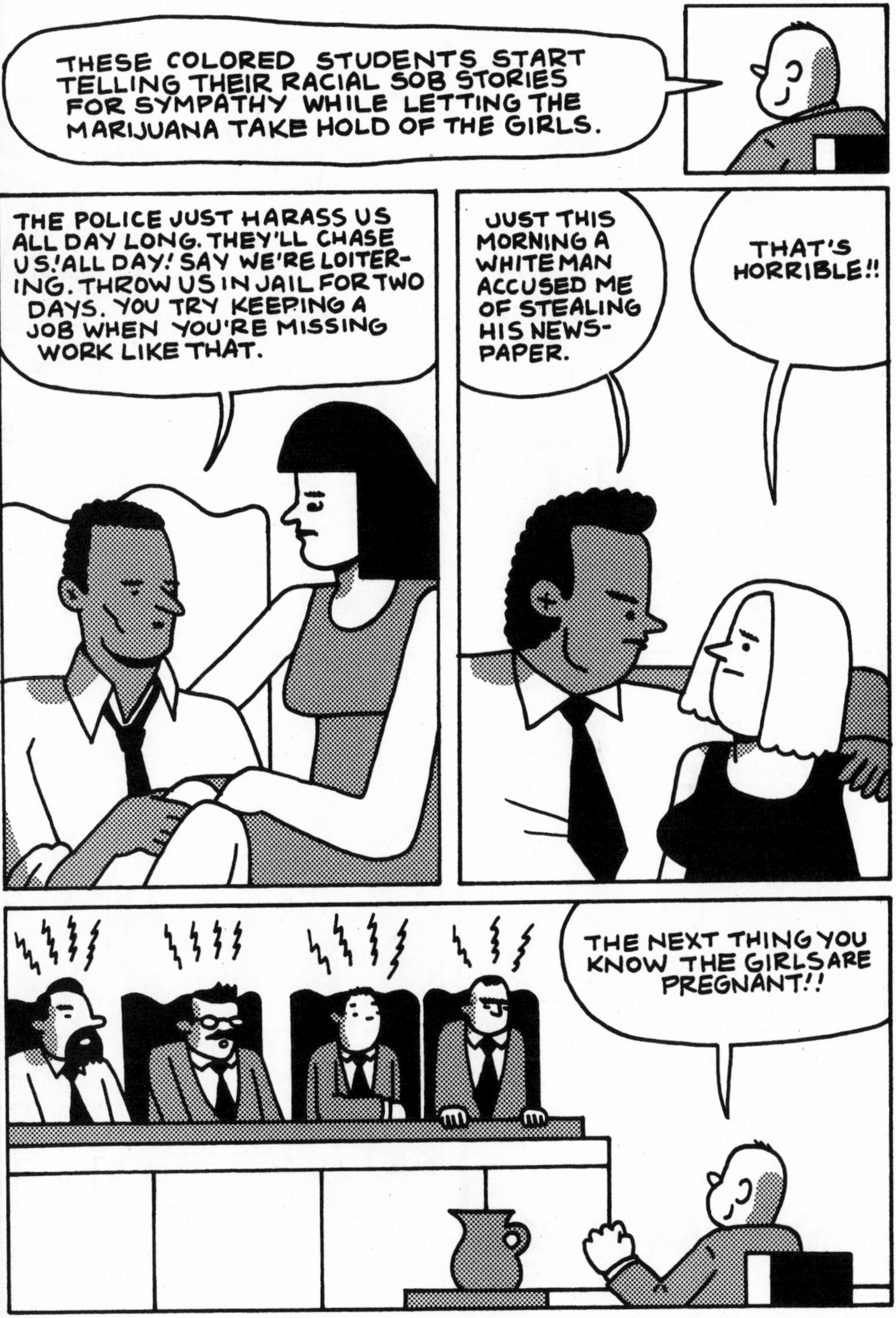
THESE COLORED STUDENTS START TELLING THEIR RACIAL SOB STORIES FOR SYMPATHY WHILE LETTING THE MARIJUANA TAKE HOLD OF THE GIRLS.
THE POLICE JUST HARASS US ALL DAY LONG. THEY'LL CHASE US! ALL DAY! SAY WE'RE LOITERING. THROW US IN JAIL FOR TWO DAYS. YOU TRY KEEPING A JOB WHEN YOU'RE MISSING WORK LIKE THAT.
JUST THIS MORNING A WHITE MAN ACCUSED ME OF STEALING HIS NEWSPAPER.
THAT'S HORRIBLE!!
THE NEXT THING YOU KNOW THE GIRLS ARE PREGNANT!!

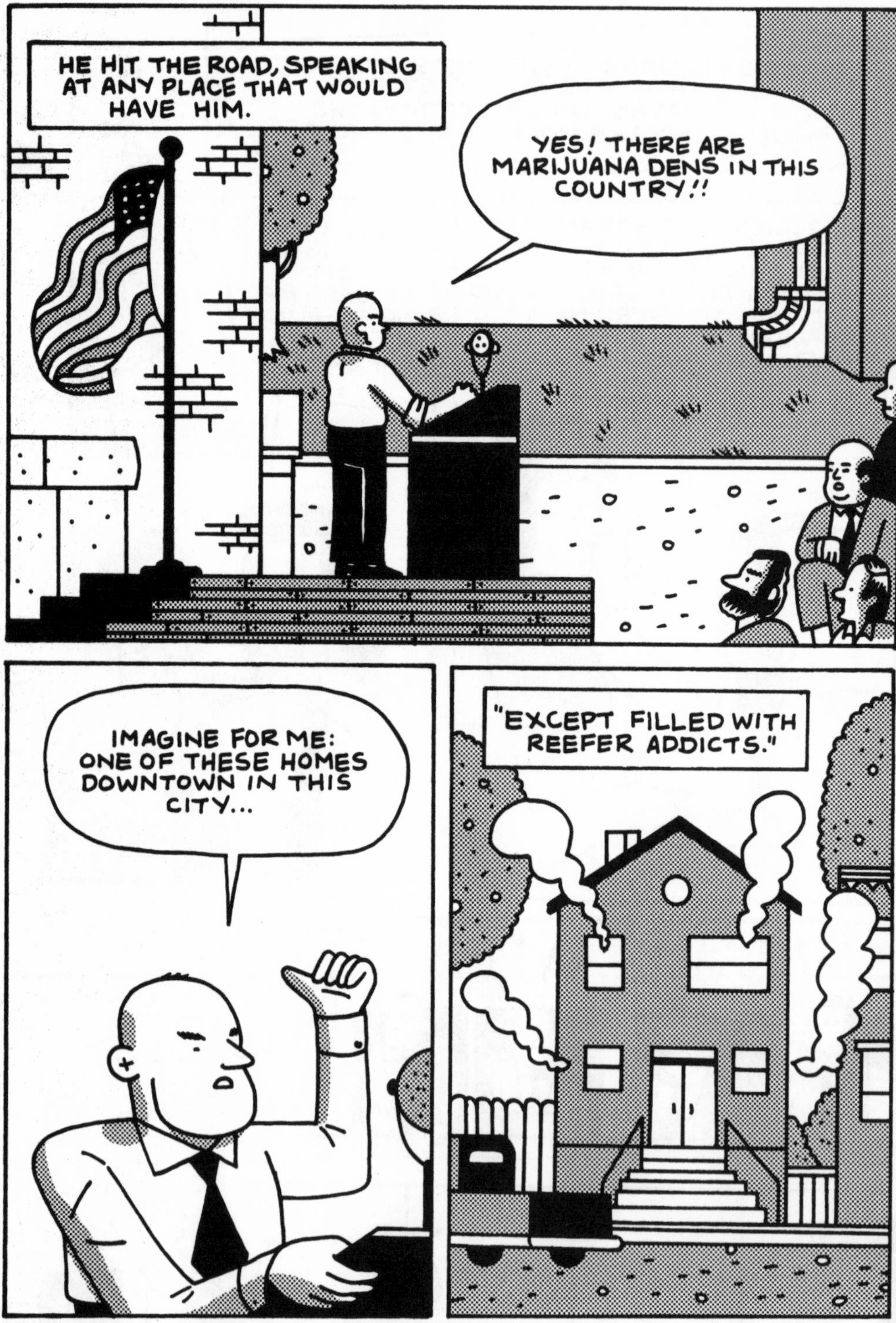
HE HIT THE ROAD, SPEAKING AT ANY PLACE THAT WOULD HAVE HIM.
YES! THERE ARE MARIJUANA DENS IN THIS COUNTRY!!
IMAGINE FOR ME: ONE OF THESE HOMES DOWNTOWN IN THIS CITY...
"EXCEPT FILLED WITH REEFER ADDICTS."

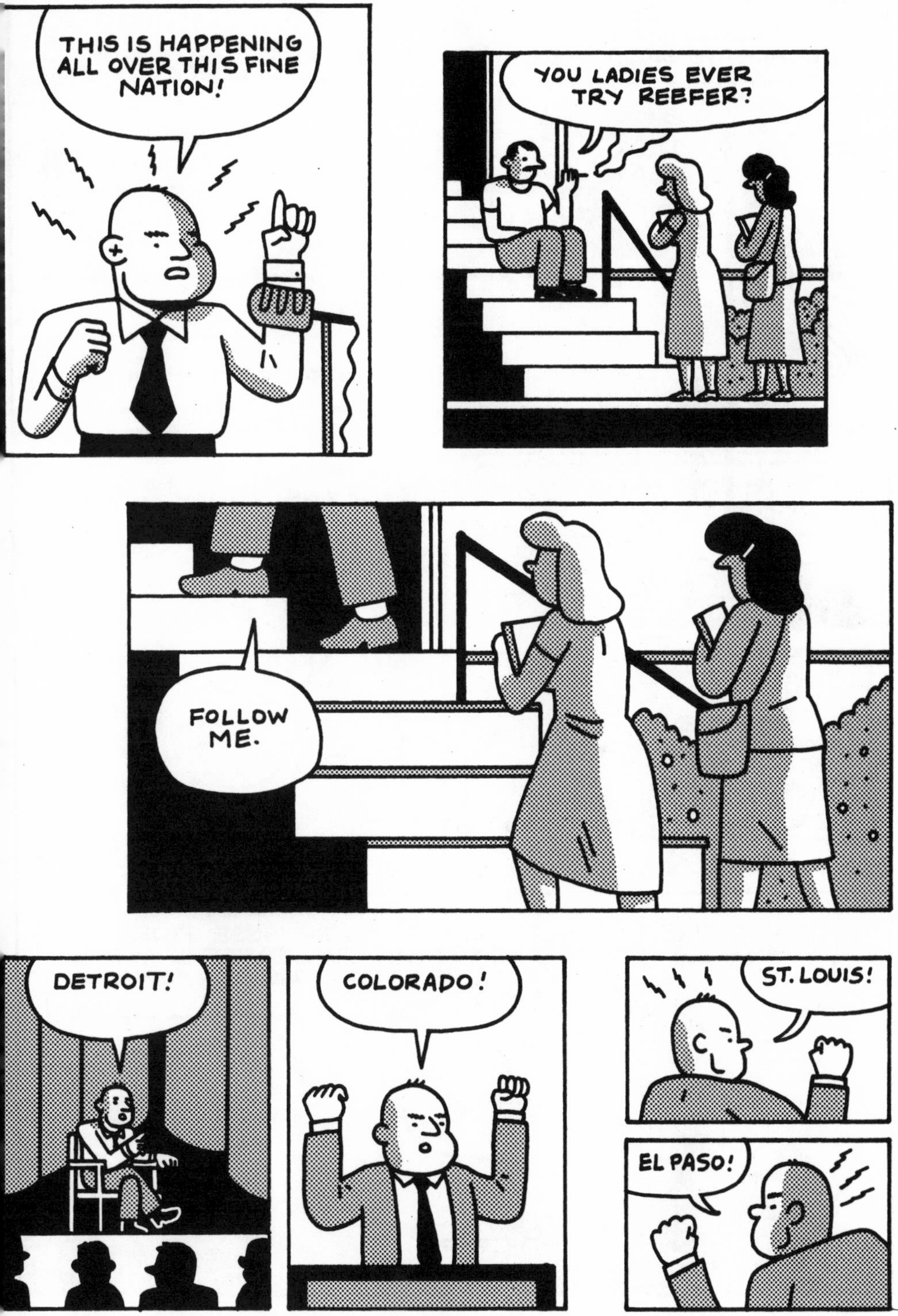
THIS IS HAPPENING ALL OVER THIS FINE NATION!
YOU LADIES EVER TRY REEFER?
FOLLOW ME.
DETROIT!
COLORADO!
ST. LOUIS!
EL PASO!

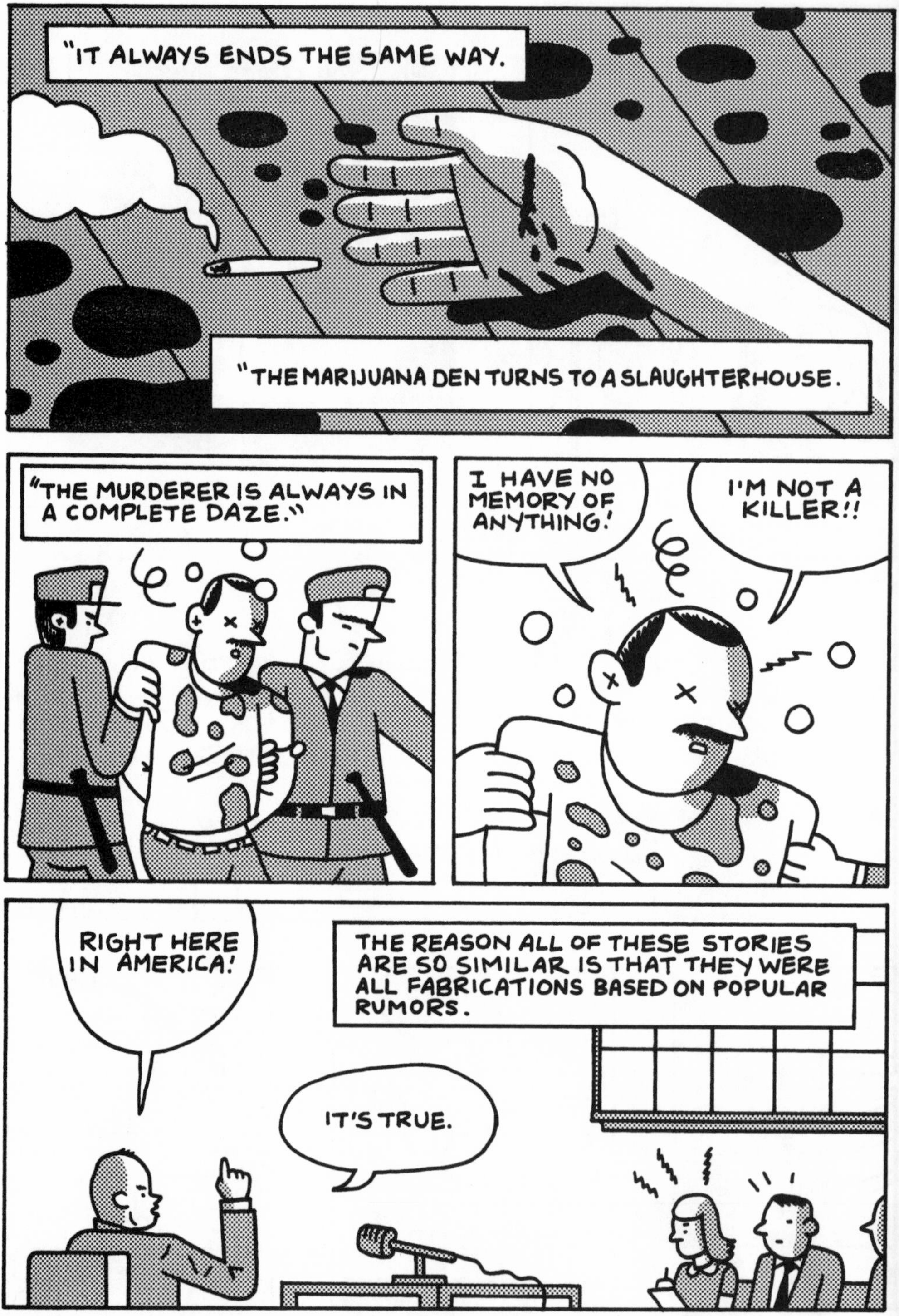
"IT ALWAYS ENDS THE SAME WAY.
"THE MARIJUANA DEN TURNS TO A SLAUGHTERHOUSE.
"THE MURDERER IS ALWAYS IN A COMPLETE DAZE."
I HAVE NO MEMORY OF ANYTHING!
I'M NOT A KILLER!!
RIGHT HERE IN AMERICA!
THE REASON ALL OF THESE STORIES ARE SO SIMILAR IS THAT THEY WERE ALL FABRICATIONS BASED ON POPULAR RUMORS.
IT'S TRUE.

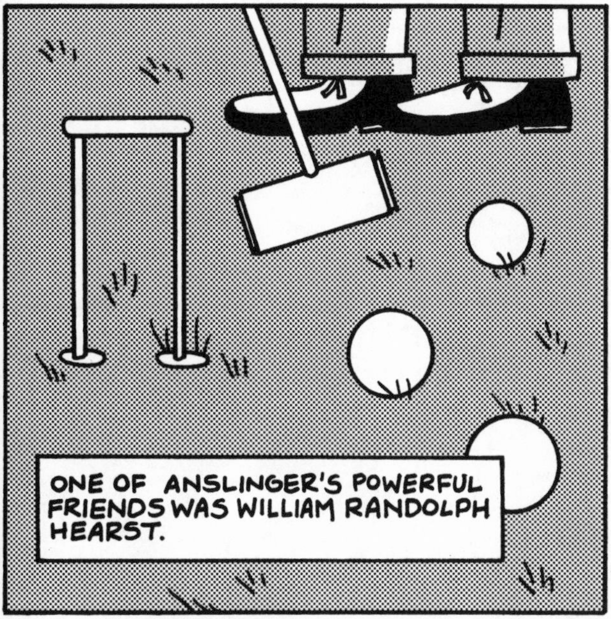
ONE OF ANSLINGER'S POWERFUL FRIENDS WAS WILLIAM RANDOLPH HEARST.

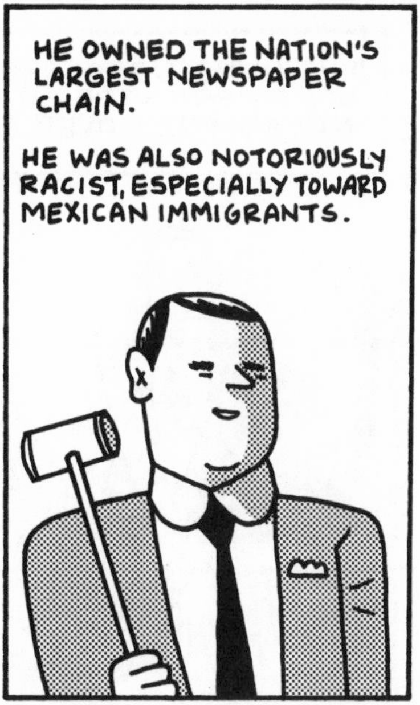
HE OWNED THE NATION'S LARGEST NEWSPAPER CHAIN.
HE WAS ALSO NOTORIOUSLY RACIST, ESPECIALLY TOWARD MEXICAN IMMIGRANTS.

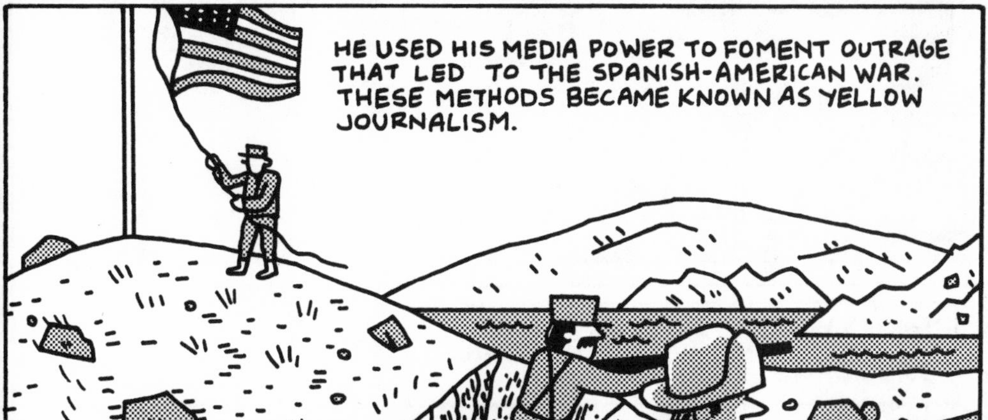
HE USED HIS MEDIA POWER TO FOMENT OUTRAGE THAT LED TO THE SPANISH-AMERICAN WAR. THESE METHODS BECAME KNOWN AS YELLOW JOURNALISM.

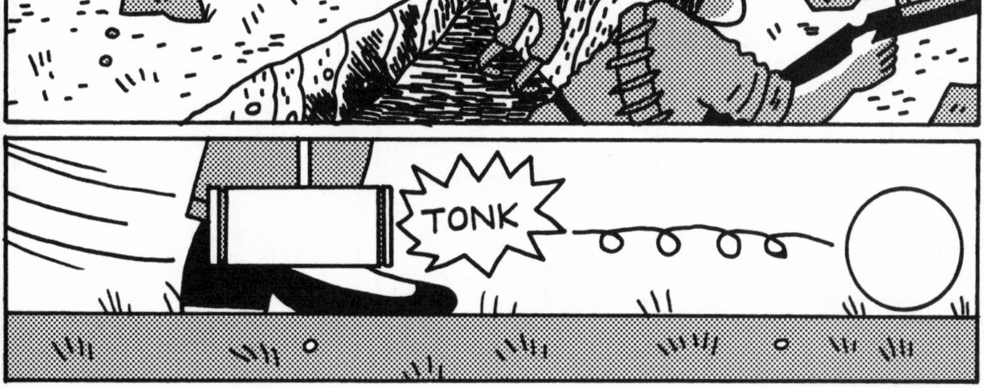
TONK

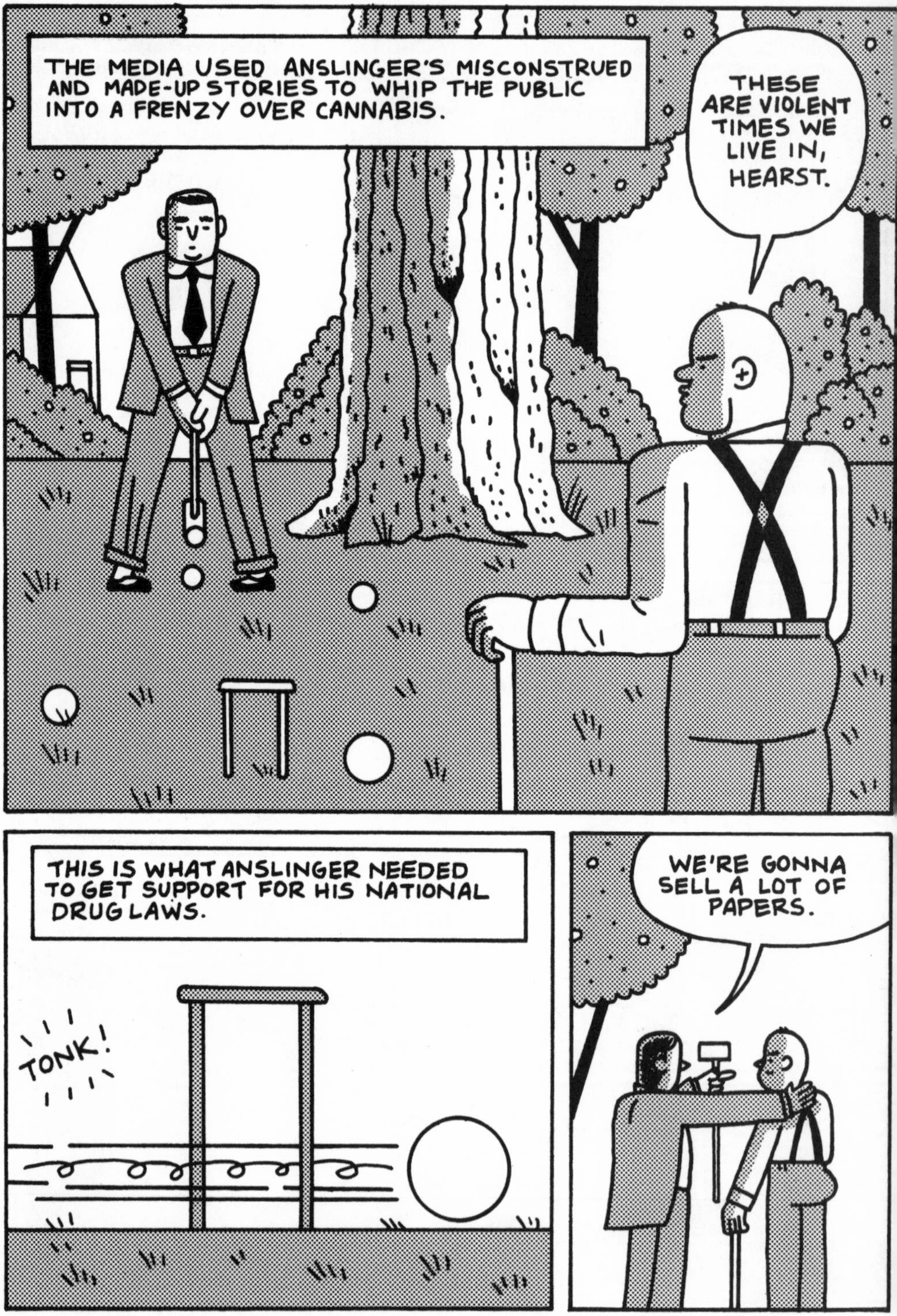
THE MEDIA USED ANSLINGER'S MISCONSTRUED AND MADE-UP STORIES TO WHIP THE PUBLIC INTO A FRENZY OVER CANNABIS.
THESE ARE VIOLENT TIMES WE LIVE IN, HEARST.
THIS IS WHAT ANSLINGER NEEDED TO GET SUPPORT FOR HIS NATIONAL DRUG LAWS.
TONK!
WE'RE GONNA SELL A LOT OF PAPERS.

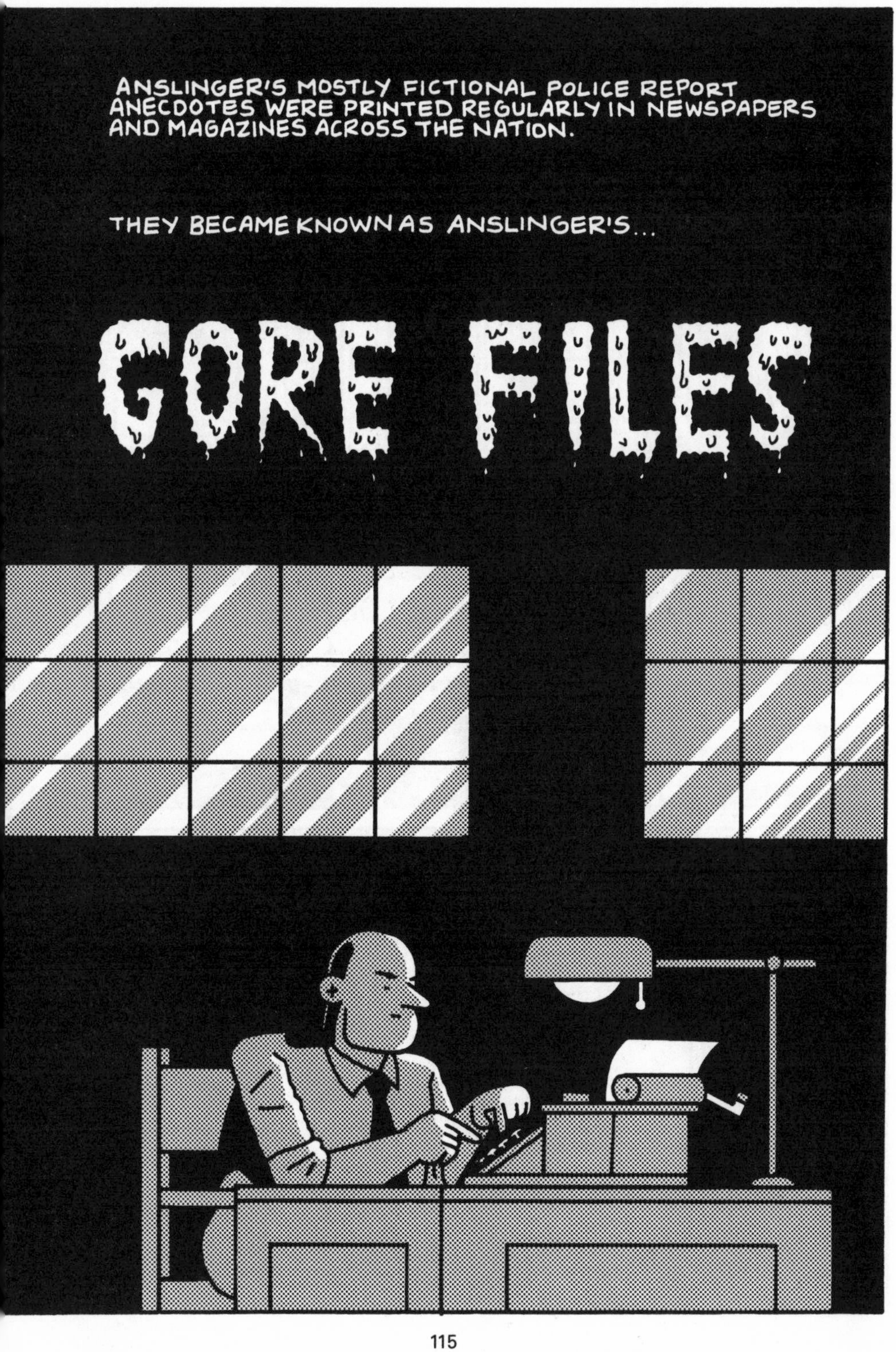
ANSLINGER'S MOSTLY FICTIONAL POLICE REPORT ANECDOTES WERE PRINTED REGULARLY IN NEWSPAPERS AND MAGAZINES ACROSS THE NATION.
THEY BECAME KNOWN AS ANSLINGER'S...
GORE FILES

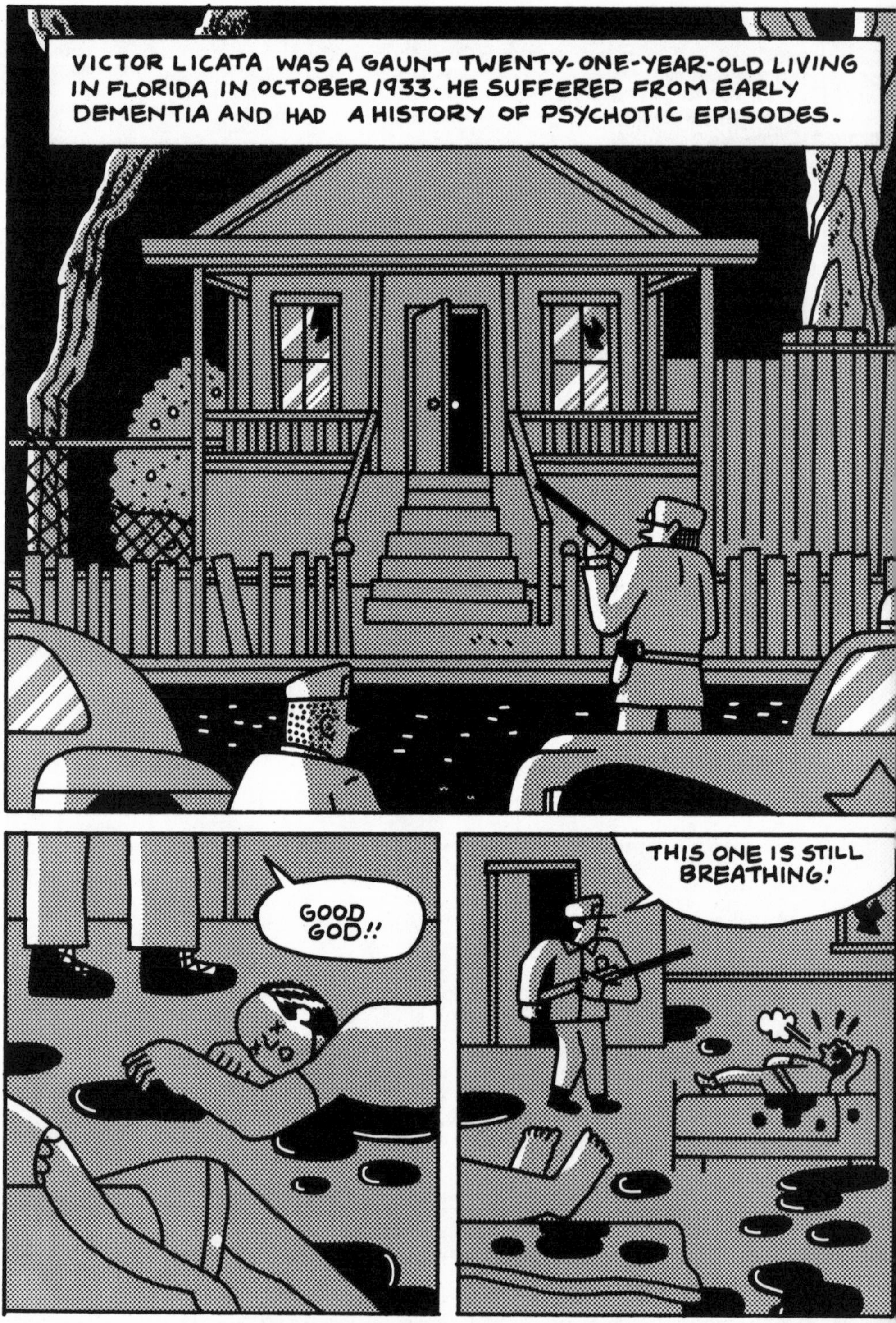
VICTOR LICATA WAS A GAUNT TWENTY-ONE-YEAR-OLD LIVING IN FLORIDA IN OCTOBER 1933. HE SUFFERED FROM EARLY DEMENTIA AND HAD A HISTORY OF PSYCHOTIC EPISODES.
GOOD GOD!!
THIS ONE IS STILL BREATHING!

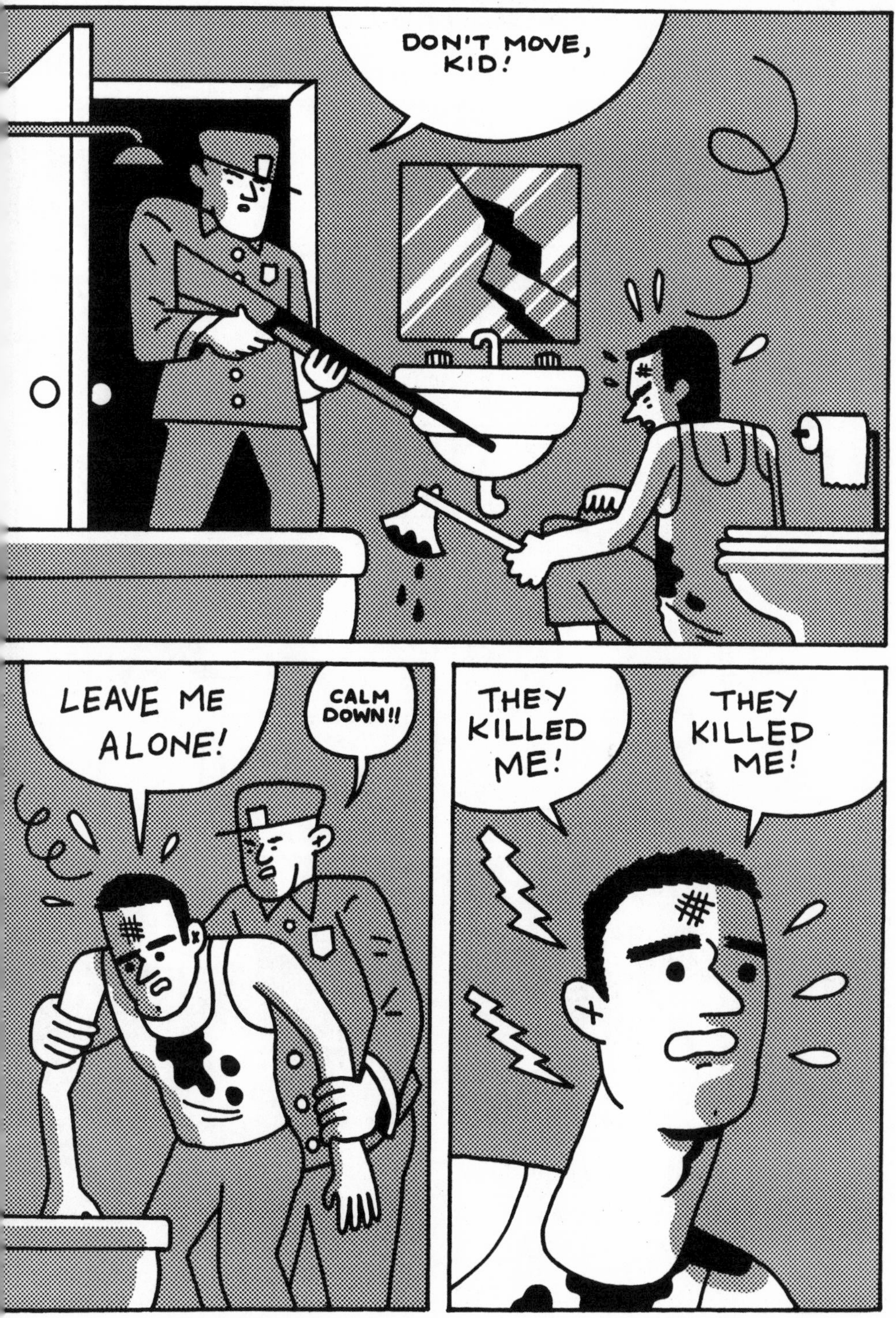
DON'T MOVE, KID!
LEAVE ME ALONE!
CALM DOWN!!
THEY KILLED ME!
THEY KILLED ME!

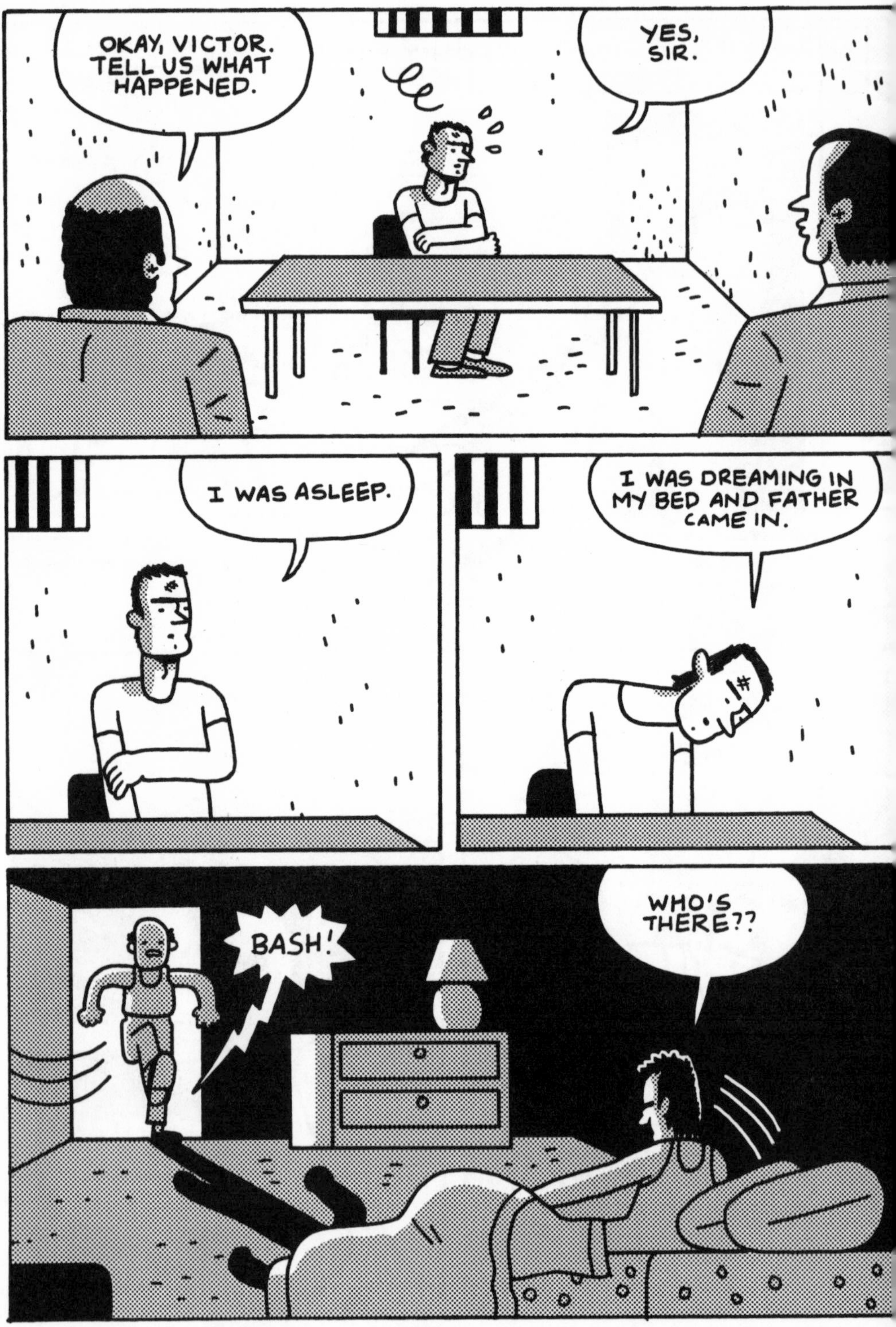
OKAY, VICTOR. TELL US WHAT HAPPENED.
YES, SIR.
I WAS ASLEEP.
I WAS DREAMING IN MY BED AND FATHER CAME IN.
BASH!
WHO'S THERE??

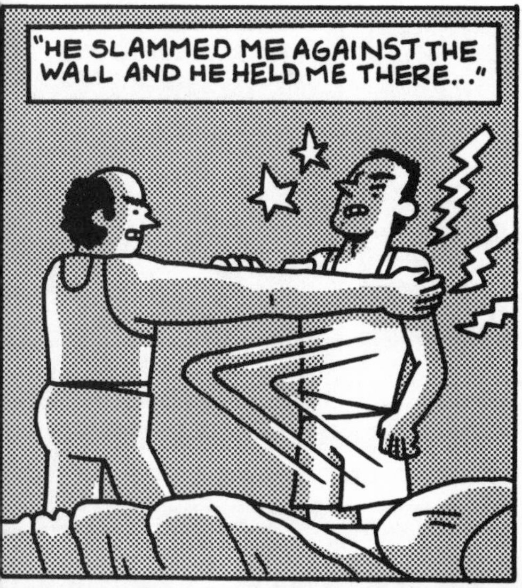
"HE SLAMMED ME AGAINST THE WALL AND HE HELD ME THERE..."

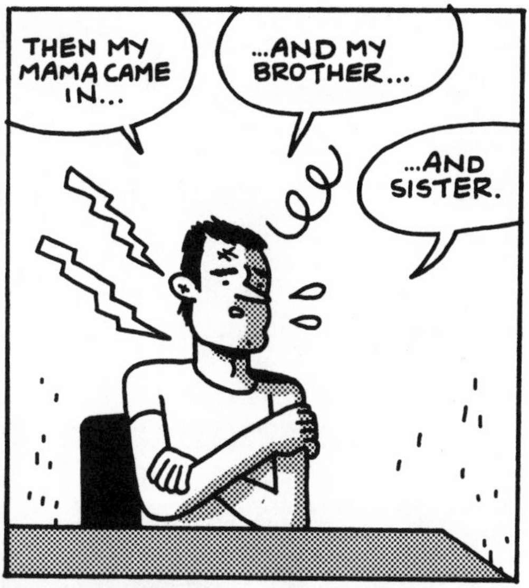
THEN MY MAMA CAME IN...
...AND MY BROTHER...
...AND SISTER.

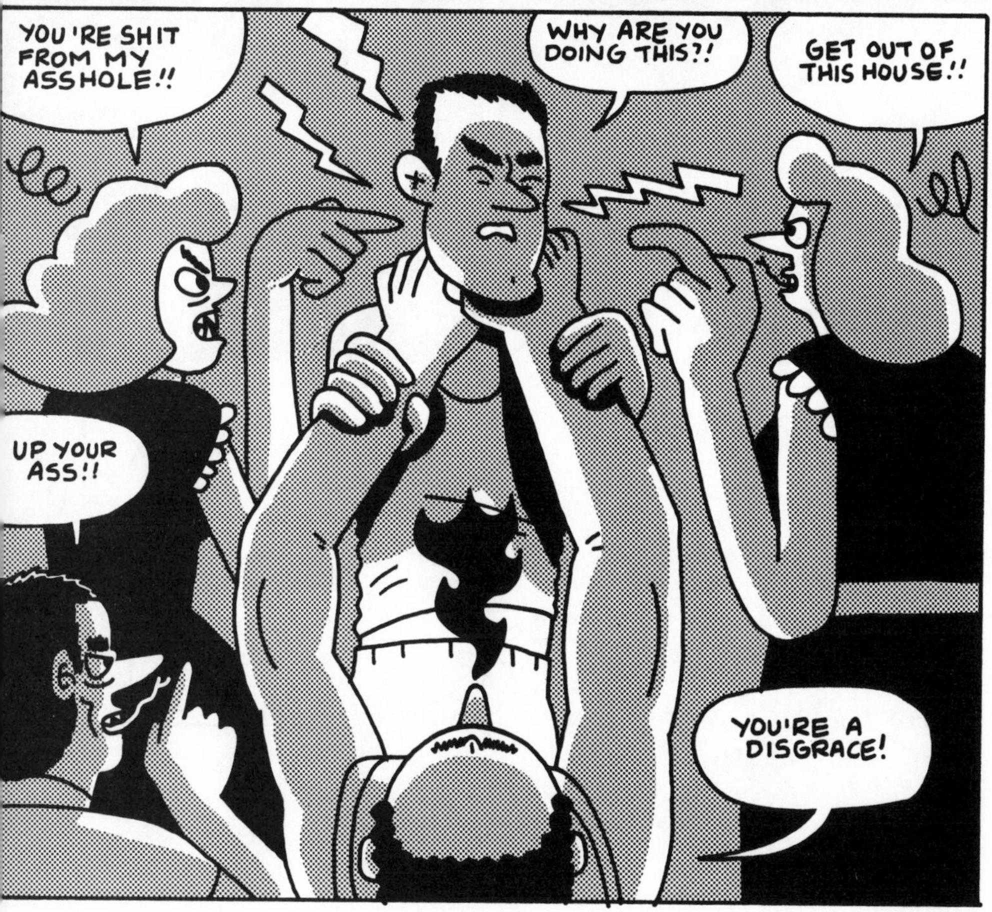
YOU'RE SHIT FROM MY ASSHOLE!!
WHY ARE YOU DOING THIS?!
GET OUT OF THIS HOUSE!!
UP YOUR ASS!!
YOU'RE A DISGRACE!

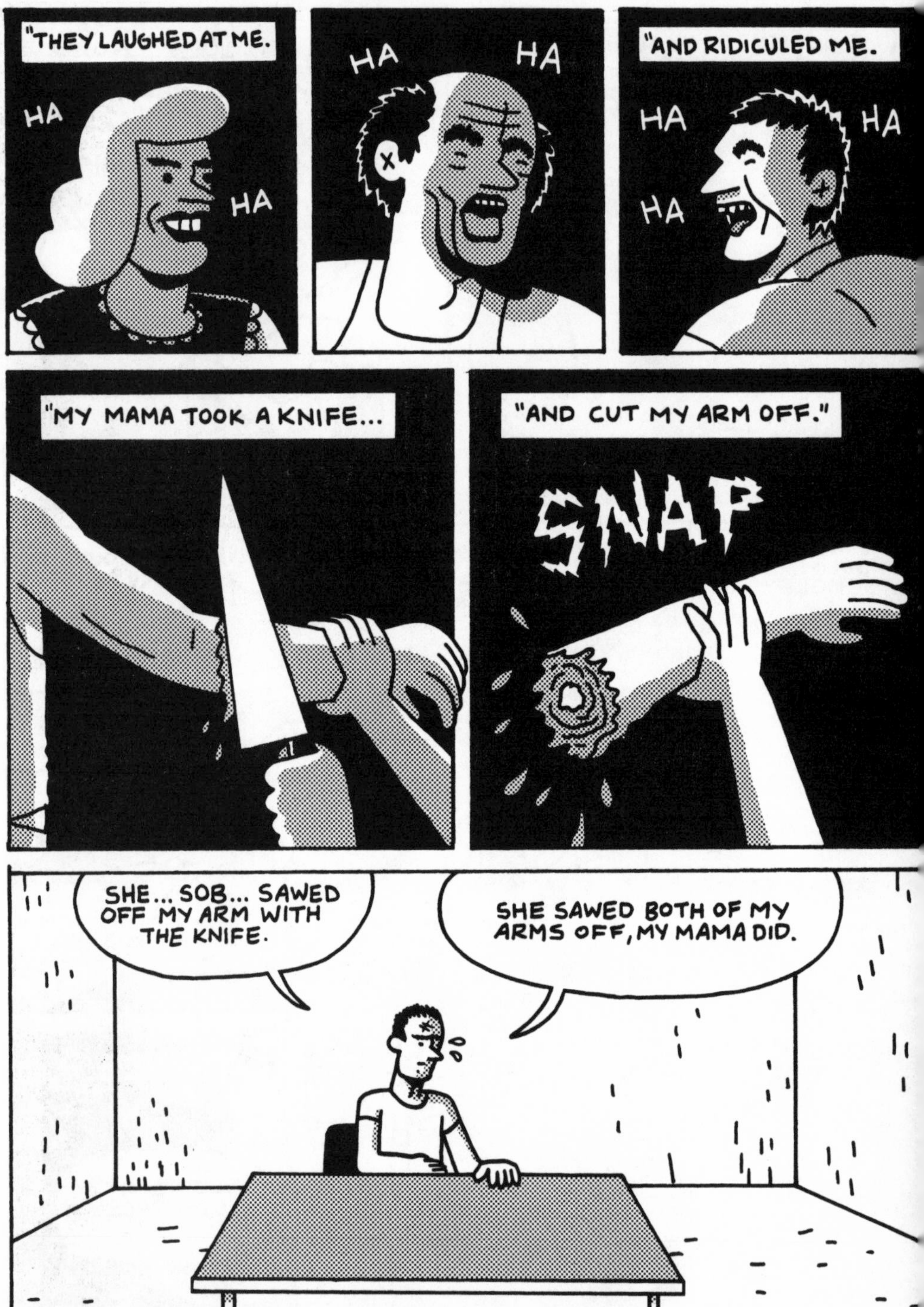
"THEY LAUGHED AT ME.
HA
HA
HA
HA
"AND RIDICULED ME.
HA
HA
HA
"MY MAMA TOOK A KNIFE...
"AND CUT MY ARM OFF."
SNAP
SHE... SOB... SAWED OFF MY ARM WITH THE KNIFE.
SHE SAWED BOTH OF MY ARMS OFF, MY MAMA DID.

MY MAMA THEN SHOVED FAKE WOODEN ARMS INTO MY STILL-BLEEDING STUMPS.

NO...

MAMA, NO!!

"IT HURT ME."

SHOVE!!

I'M MAKING YOU BETTER.

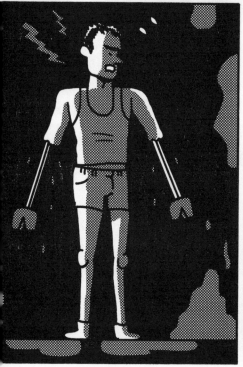

MY ARMS WERE NOW FAKE ARMS.

MY HANDS, IRON CLAWS.

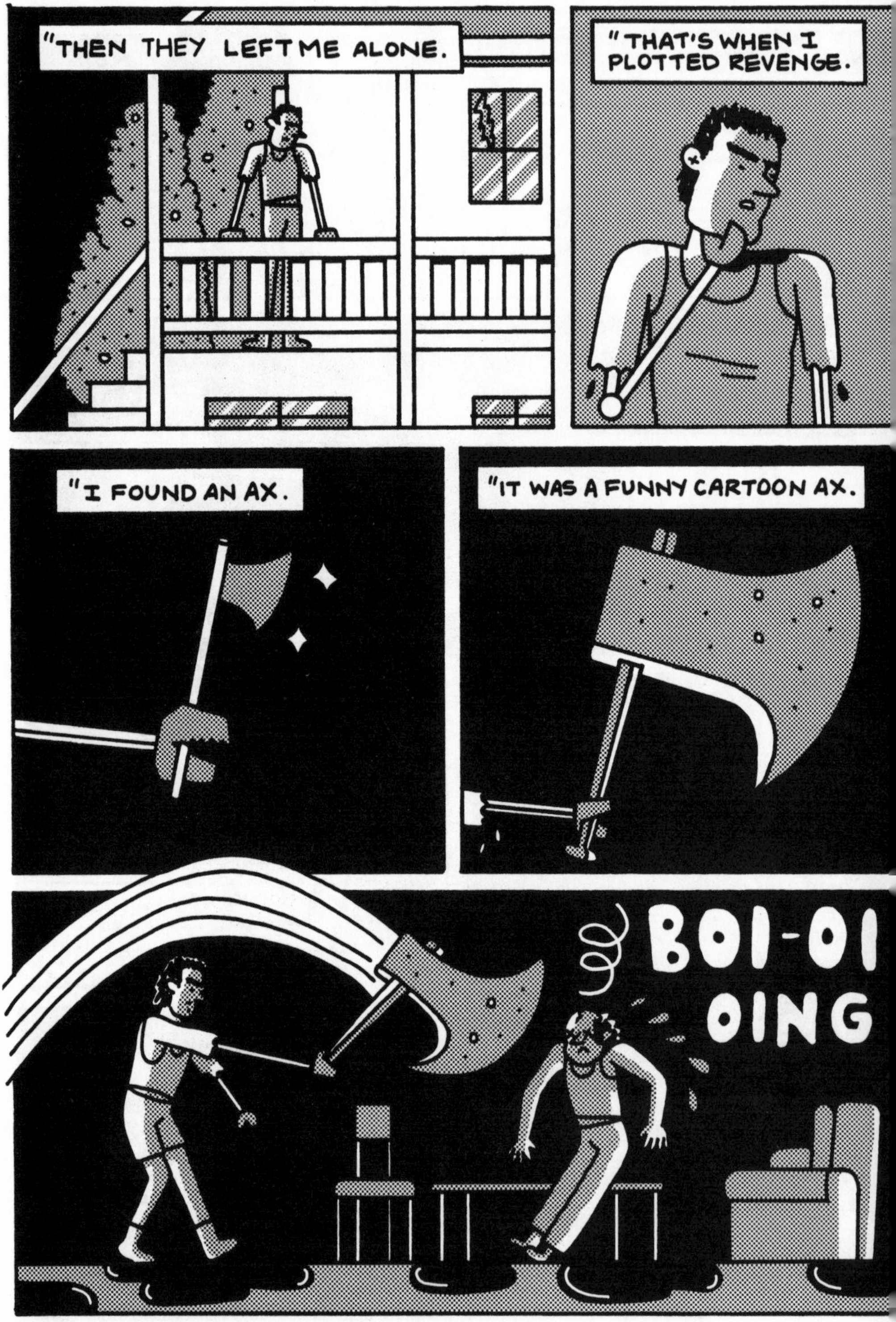
"THEN THEY LEFT ME ALONE.
"THAT'S WHEN I PLOTTED REVENGE.
"I FOUND AN AX.
"IT WAS A FUNNY CARTOON AX.
BOI-OI OING

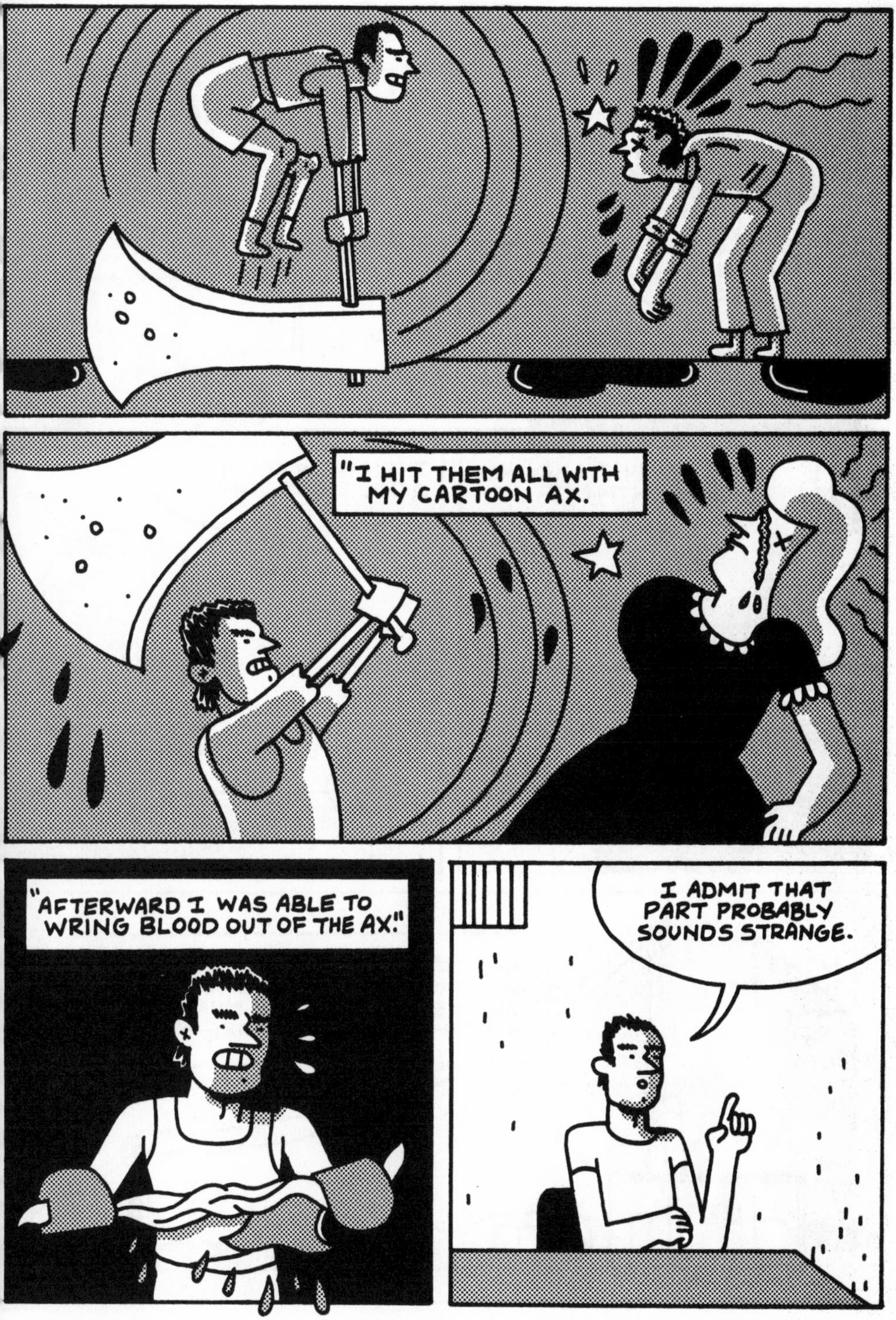
"I HIT THEM ALL WITH MY CARTOON AX.
"AFTERWARD I WAS ABLE TO WRING BLOOD OUT OF THE AX."
I ADMIT THAT PART PROBABLY SOUNDS STRANGE.

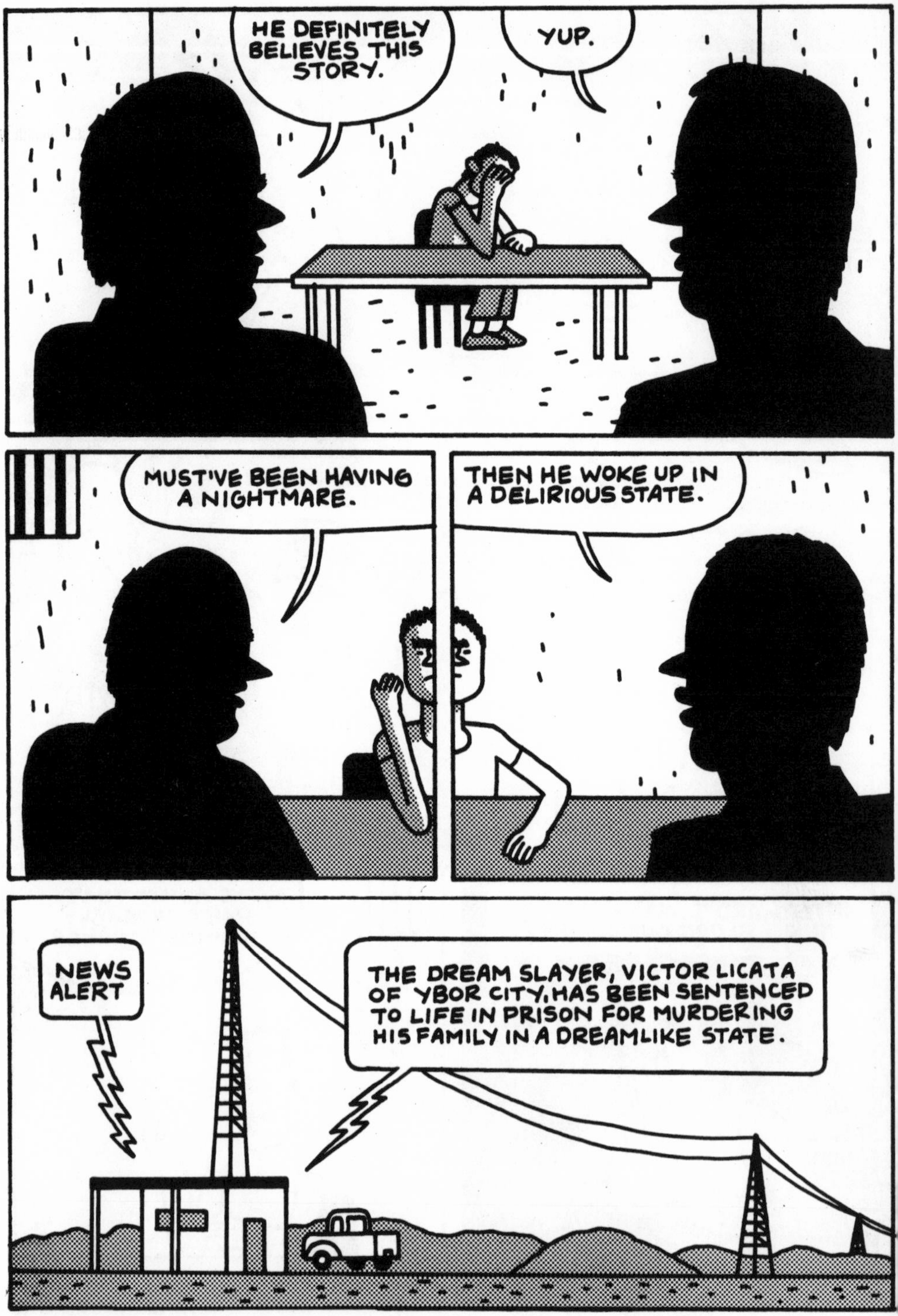
HE DEFINITELY BELIEVES THIS STORY.
YUP.
MUST'VE BEEN HAVING A NIGHTMARE.
THEN HE WOKE UP IN A DELIRIOUS STATE.
NEWS ALERT
THE DREAM SLAYER, VICTOR LICATA OF YBOR CITY, HAS BEEN SENTENCED TO LIFE IN PRISON FOR MURDERING HIS FAMILY IN A DREAMLIKE STATE.

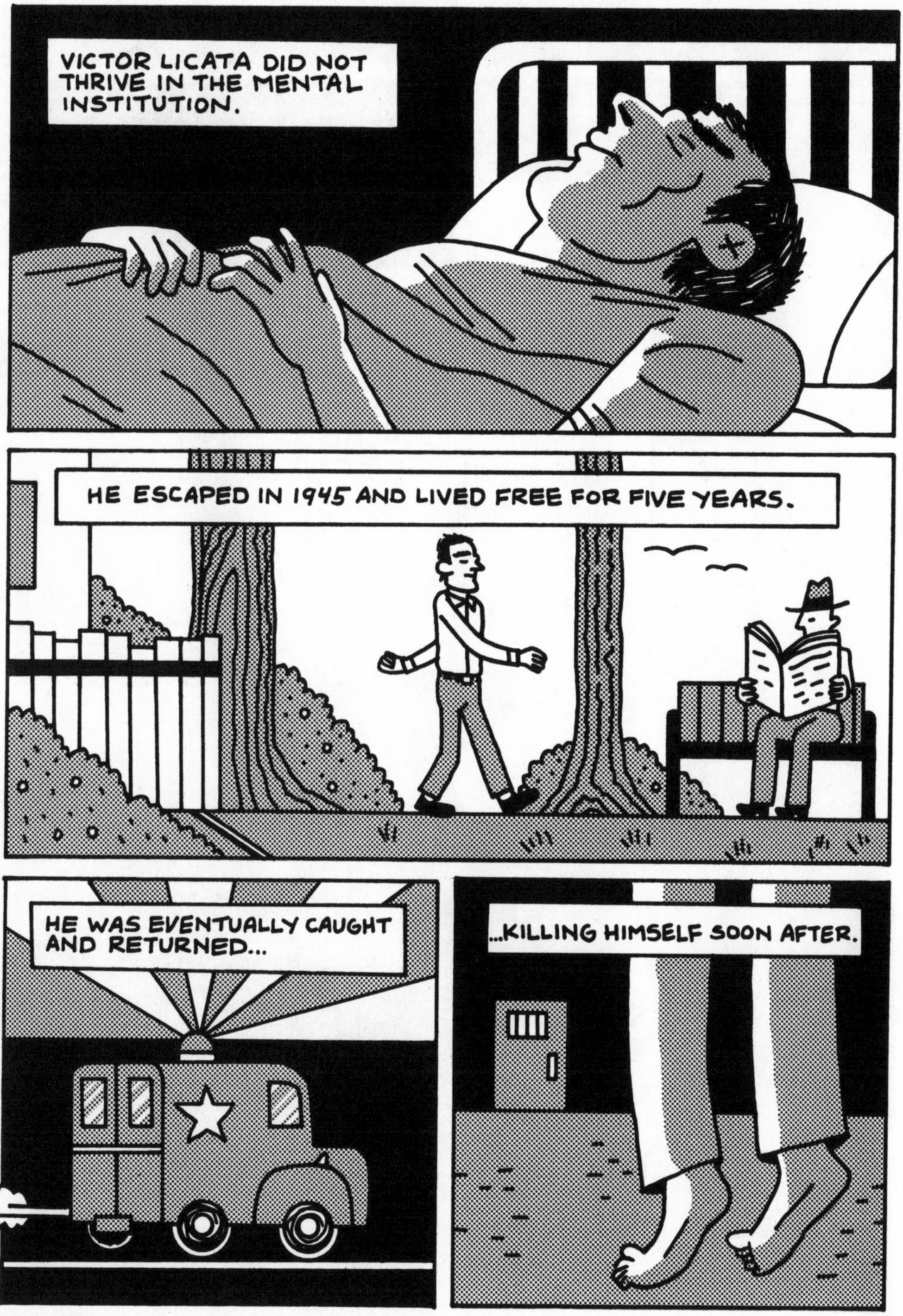
VICTOR LICATA DID NOT THRIVE IN THE MENTAL INSTITUTION.
HE ESCAPED IN 1945 AND LIVED FREE FOR FIVE YEARS.
HE WAS EVENTUALLY CAUGHT AND RETURNED...
...KILLING HIMSELF SOON AFTER.

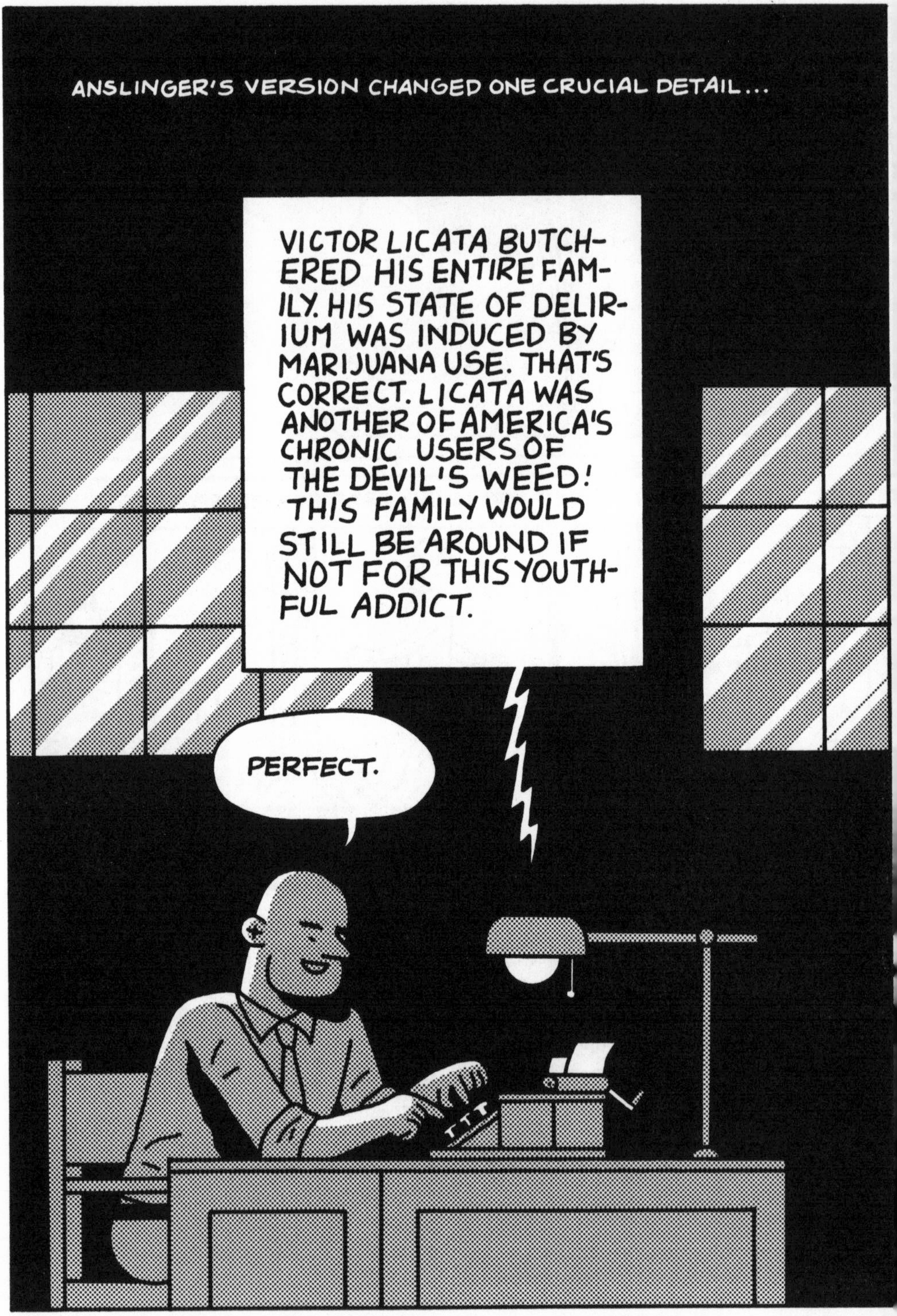
ANSLINGER'S VERSION CHANGED ONE CRUCIAL DETAIL...
VICTOR LICATA BUTCHERED HIS ENTIRE FAMILY. HIS STATE OF DELIRIUM WAS INDUCED BY MARIJUANA USE. THAT'S CORRECT. LICATA WAS ANOTHER OF AMERICA'S CHRONIC USERS OF THE DEVIL'S WEED! THIS FAMILY WOULD STILL BE AROUND IF NOT FOR THIS YOUTHFUL ADDICT.
PERFECT.

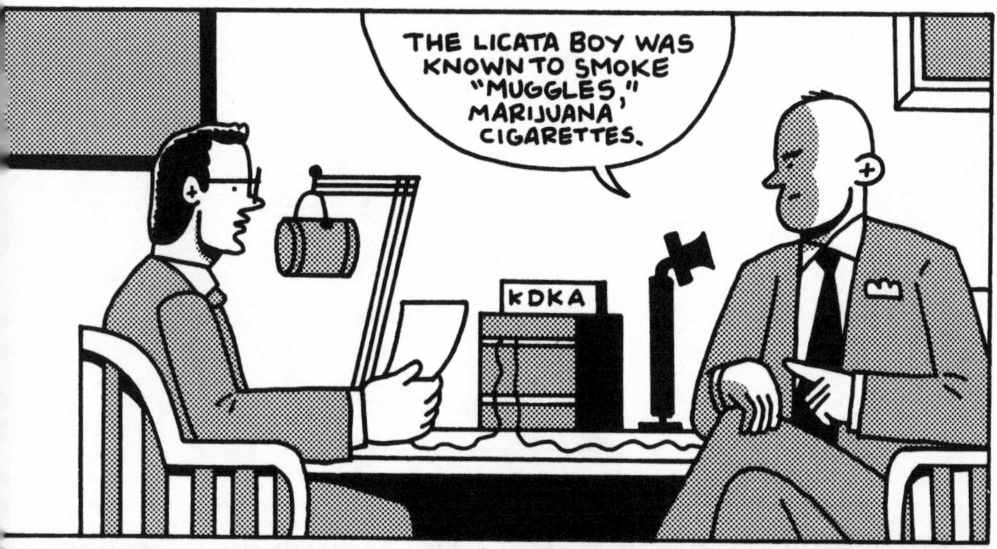
THE LICATA BOY WAS KNOWN TO SMOKE "MUGGLES," MARIJUANA CIGARETTES.
KDKA

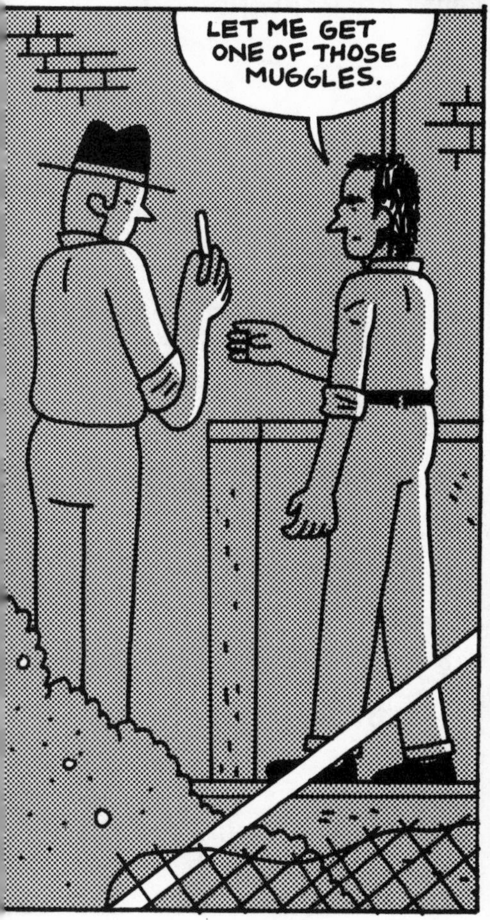
LET ME GET ONE OF THOSE MUGGLES.

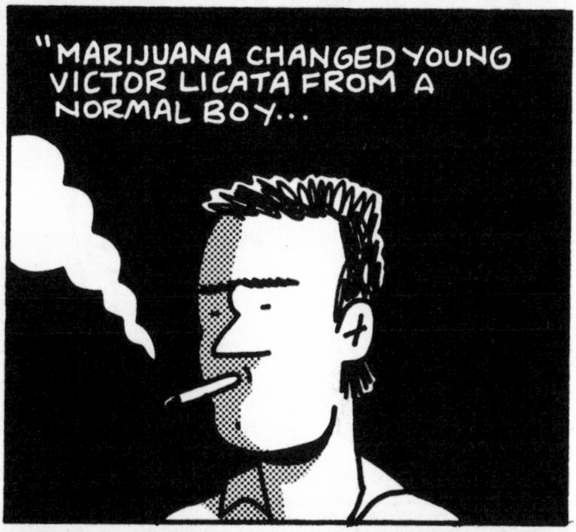
"MARIJUANA CHANGED YOUNG VICTOR LICATA FROM A NORMAL BOY...

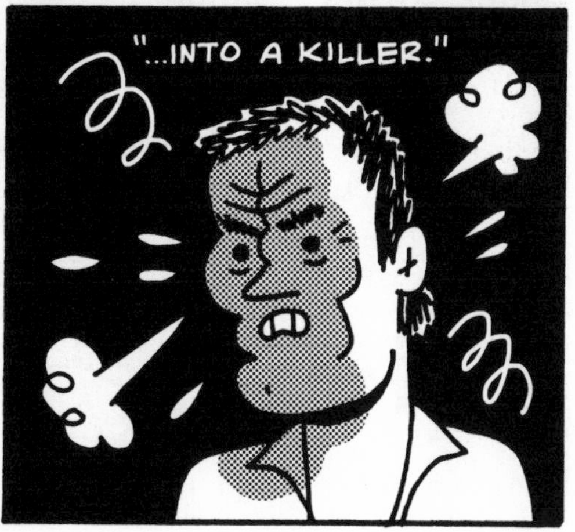
"...INTO A KILLER."

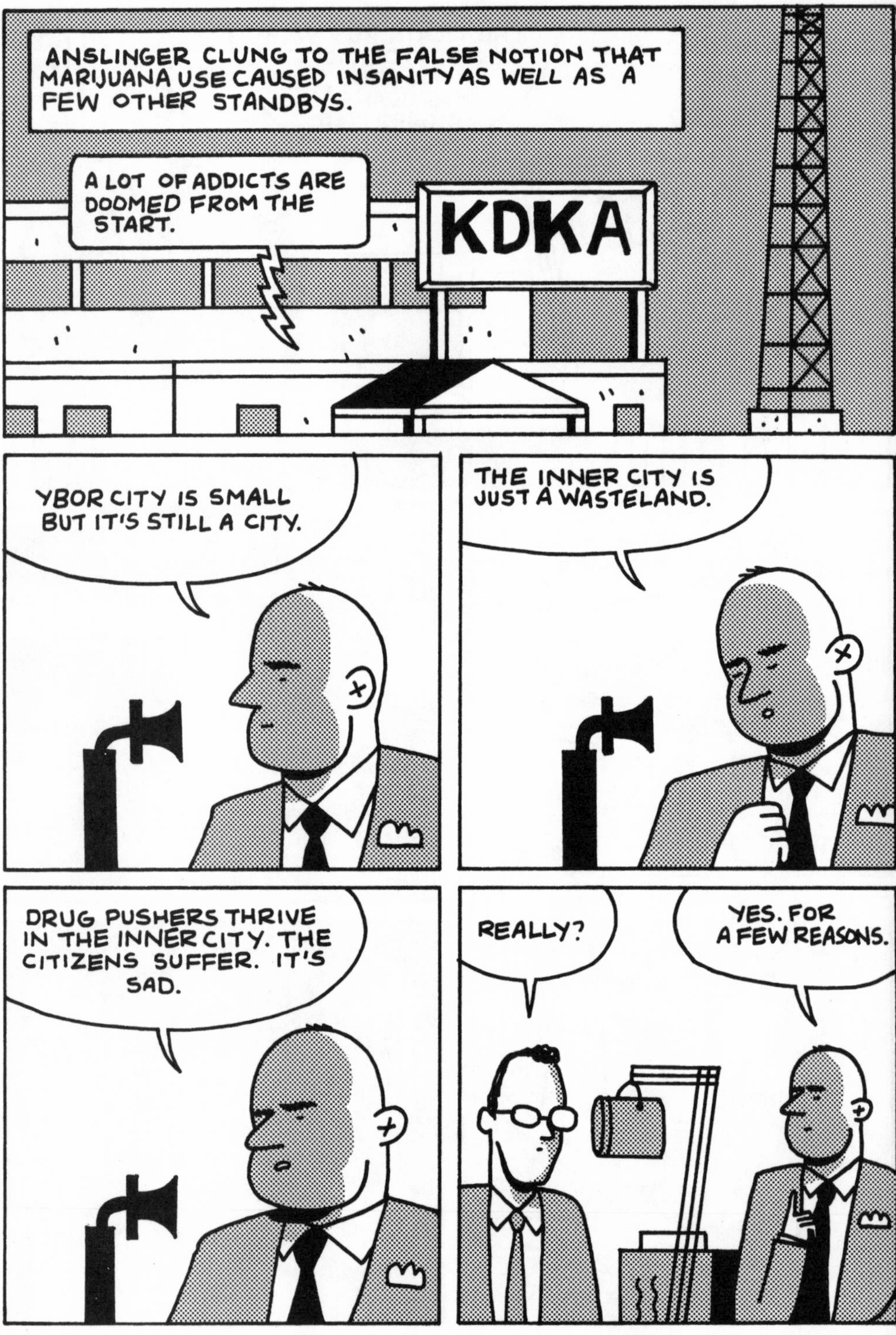
ANSLINGER CLUNG TO THE FALSE NOTION THAT MARIJUANA USE CAUSED INSANITY AS WELL AS A FEW OTHER STANDBYS.
A LOT OF ADDICTS ARE DOOMED FROM THE START.
KDKA
YBOR CITY IS SMALL BUT IT'S STILL A CITY.
THE INNER CITY IS JUST A WASTELAND.
DRUG PUSHERS THRIVE IN THE INNER CITY. THE CITIZENS SUFFER. IT'S SAD.
REALLY?
YES. FOR A FEW REASONS.

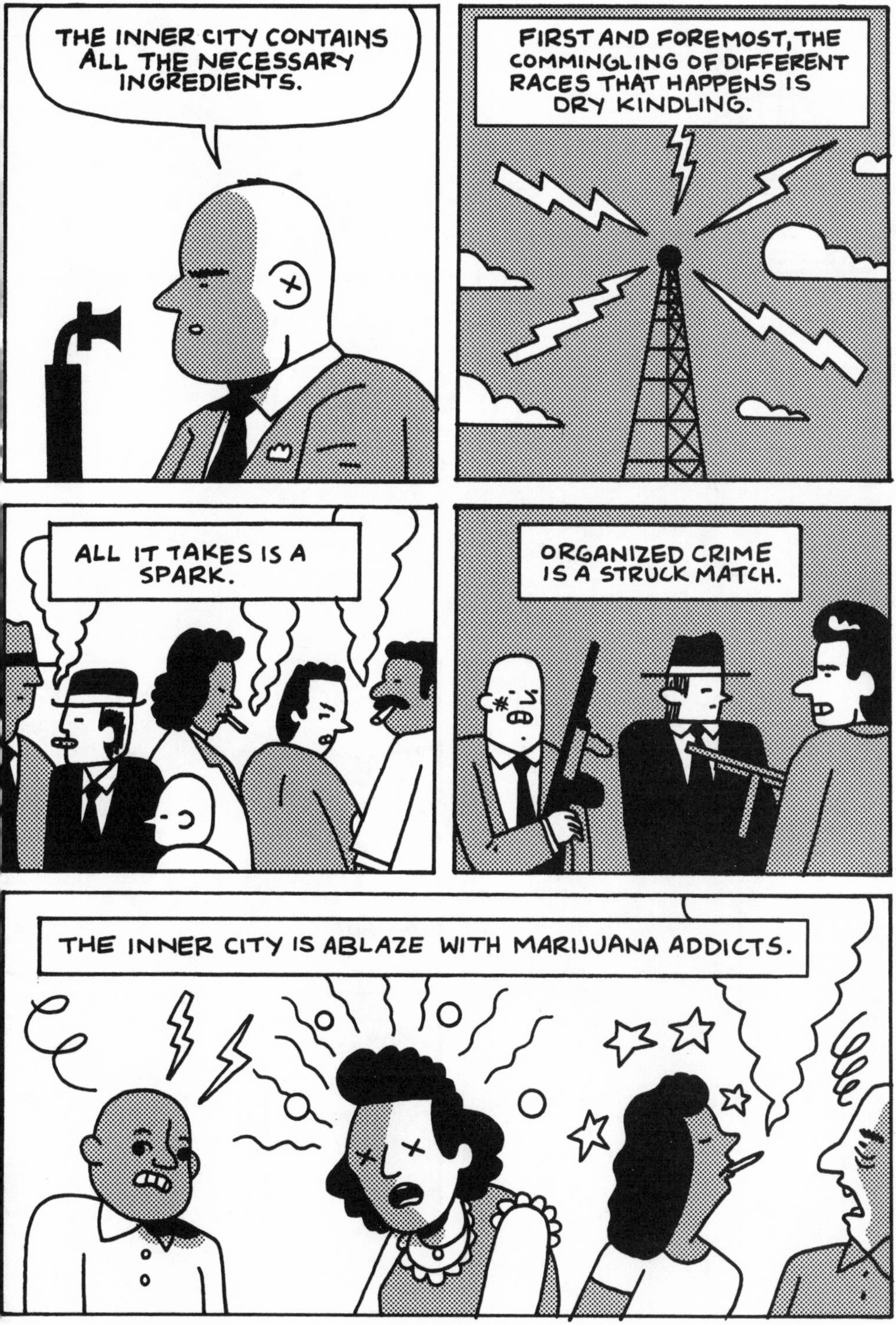
THE INNER CITY CONTAINS ALL THE NECESSARY INGREDIENTS.
FIRST AND FOREMOST, THE COMMINGLING OF DIFFERENT RACES THAT HAPPENS IS DRY KINDLING.
ALL IT TAKES IS A SPARK.
ORGANIZED CRIME IS A STRUCK MATCH.
THE INNER CITY IS ABLAZE WITH MARIJUANA ADDICTS.

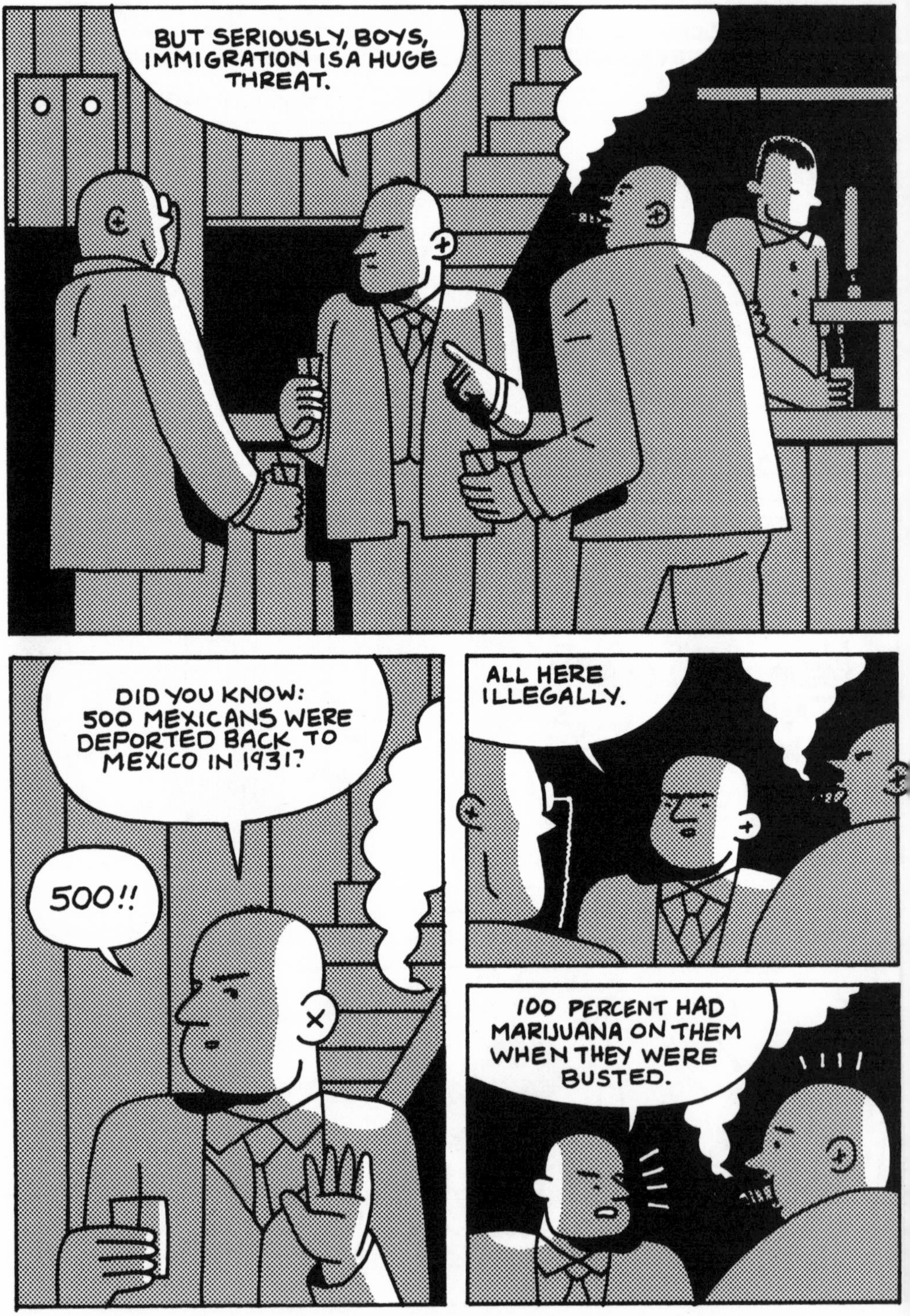

BUT SERIOUSLY, BOYS, IMMIGRATION IS A HUGE THREAT.
DID YOU KNOW: 500 MEXICANS WERE DEPORTED BACK TO MEXICO IN 1931?
500!!
ALL HERE ILLEGALLY.
100 PERCENT HAD MARIJUANA ON THEM WHEN THEY WERE BUSTED.

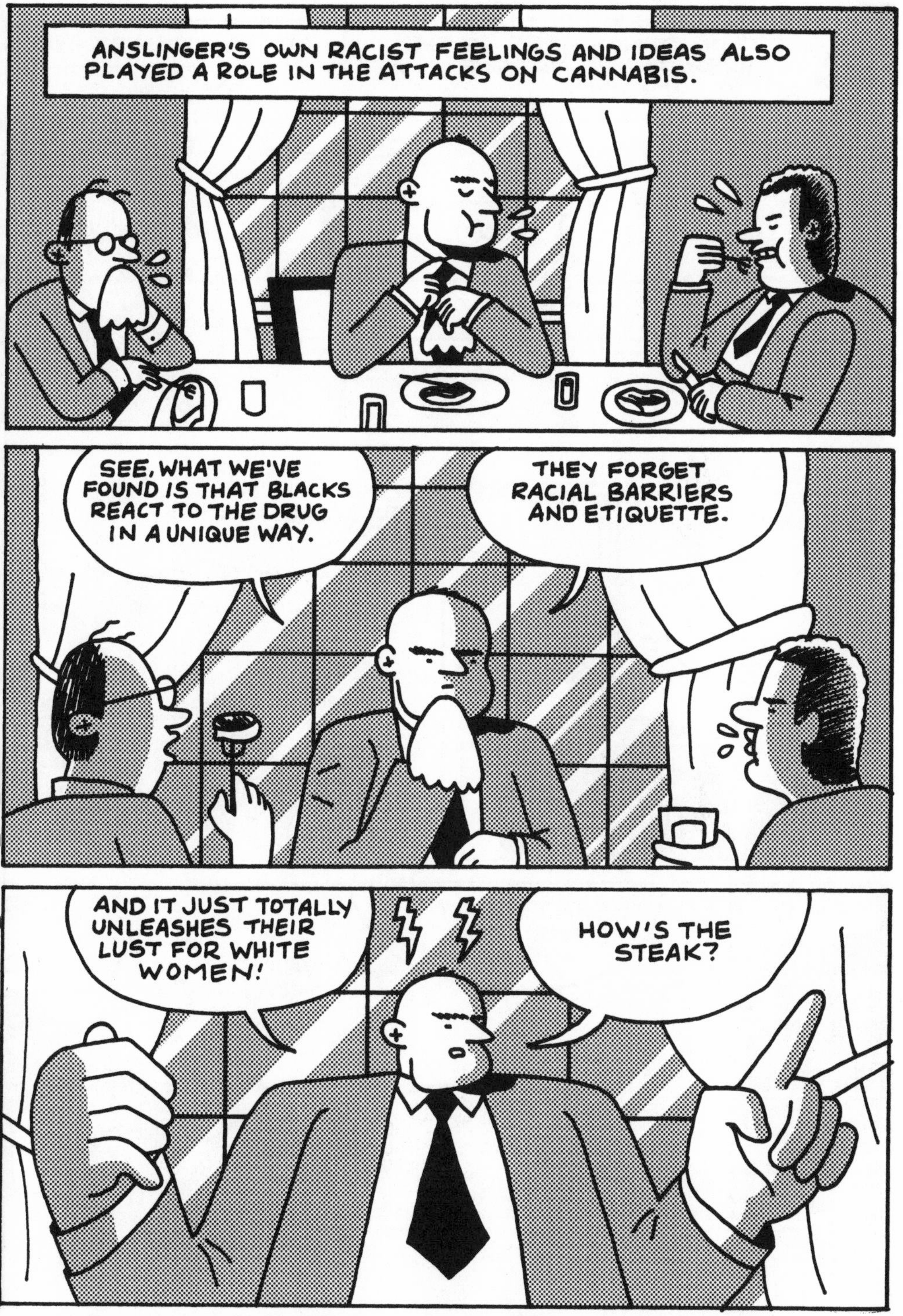
ANSLINGER'S OWN RACIST FEELINGS AND IDEAS ALSO PLAYED A ROLE IN THE ATTACKS ON CANNABIS.
SEE, WHAT WE'VE FOUND IS THAT BLACKS REACT TO THE DRUG IN A UNIQUE WAY.
THEY FORGET RACIAL BARRIERS AND ETIQUETTE.
AND IT JUST TOTALLY UNLEASHES THEIR LUST FOR WHITE WOMEN!
HOW'S THE STEAK?

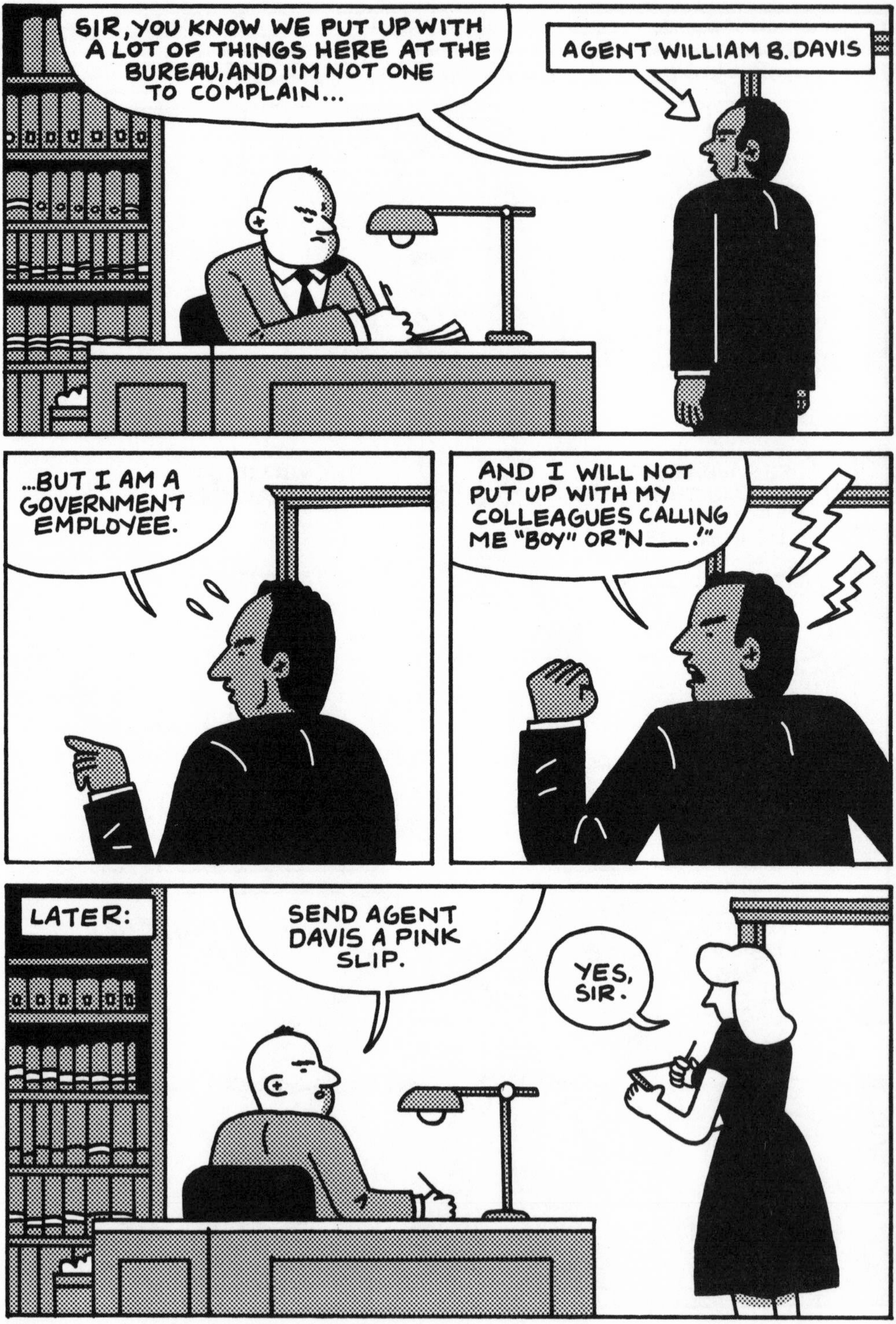

SIR, YOU KNOW WE PUT UP WITH A LOT OF THINGS HERE AT THE BUREAU, AND I'M NOT ONE TO COMPLAIN...
AGENT WILLIAM B. DAVIS
...BUT I AM A GOVERNMENT EMPLOYEE.
AND I WILL NOT PUT UP WITH MY COLLEAGUES CALLING ME "BOY" OR "N___!"
LATER:
SEND AGENT DAVIS A PINK SLIP.
YES, SIR.

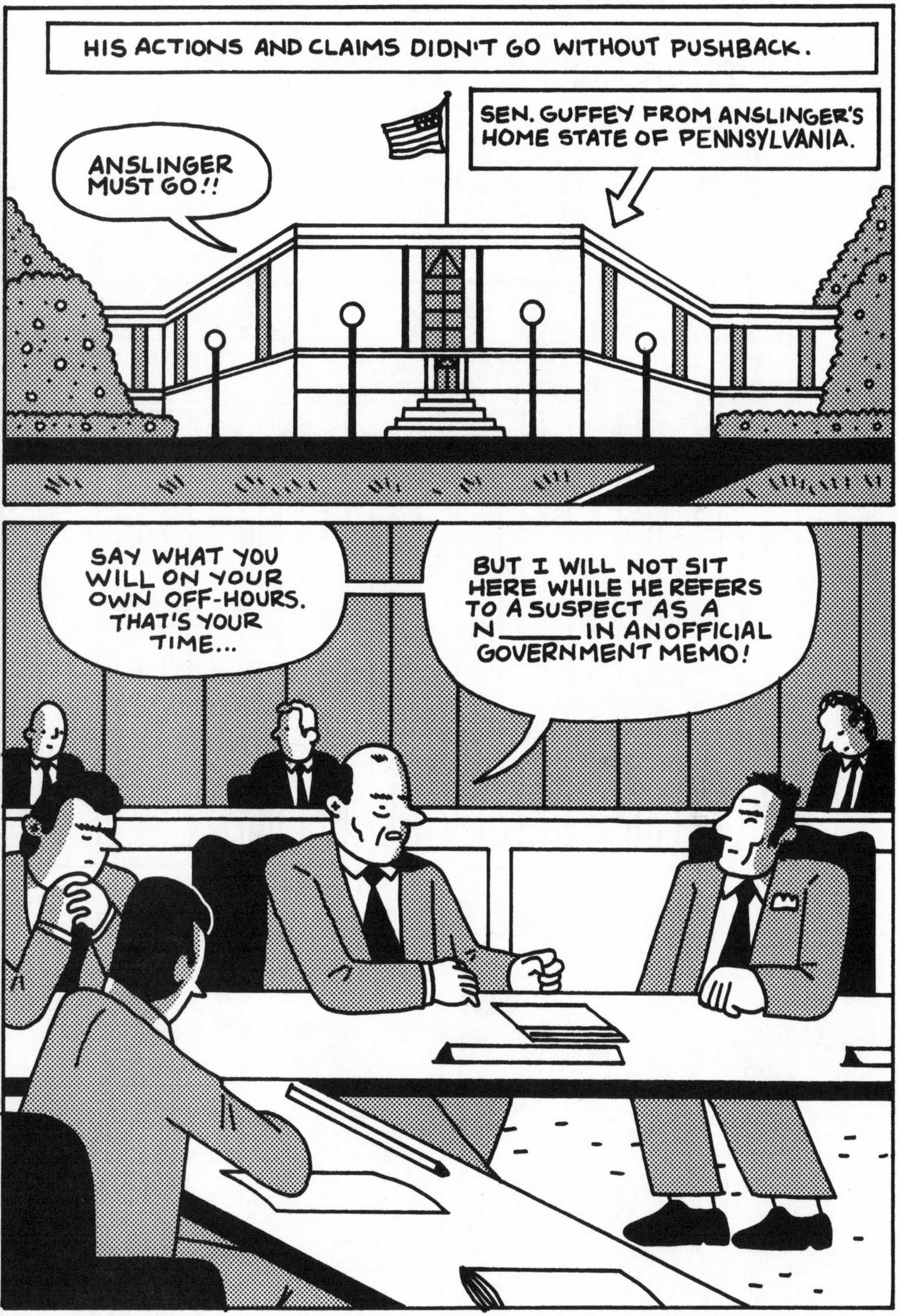
HIS ACTIONS AND CLAIMS DIDN'T GO WITHOUT PUSHBACK.
ANSLINGER MUST GO!!
SEN. GUFFEY FROM ANSLINGER'S HOME STATE OF PENNSYLVANIA.
SAY WHAT YOU WILL ON YOUR OWN OFF-HOURS. THAT'S YOUR TIME...
BUT I WILL NOT SIT HERE WHILE HE REFERS TO A SUSPECT AS A N_____ IN AN OFFICIAL GOVERNMENT MEMO!

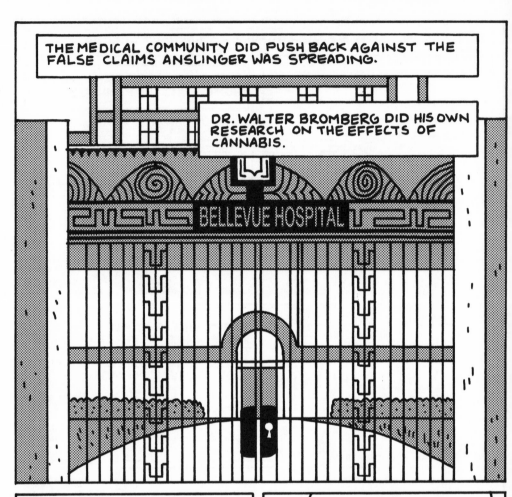

THE MEDICAL COMMUNITY DID PUSH BACK AGAINST THE FALSE CLAIMS ANSLINGER WAS SPREADING.

DR. WALTER BROMBERG DID HIS OWN RESEARCH ON THE EFFECTS OF CANNABIS.

BELLEVUE HOSPITAL

THE STUDY WAS FLAWED BUT HIS FINDINGS CONTRADICTED ANSLINGER'S.

OKAY, SUBJECT NUMBER ONE: ILLITERATE LABORER; NEGRO.

SUBJECT ONE: TWO MARIJUANA CIGARETTES SMOKED WITHIN 40 MINUTES.

YES; FINISH BOTH.

MY HEAD IS GETTING BIGGER.

AND MY HANDS ARE ROUNDER. DEFINITELY.

MY HEAD IS UP HERE. MY SKULL IS OVER HERE.

NOW I SEE SKULLS.

OH, MY GOD! A PAIR OF LEGS WALKED BY!!

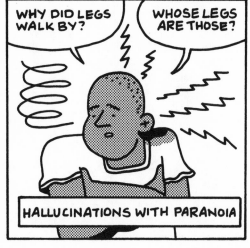
WHY DID LEGS WALK BY?

WHOSE LEGS ARE THOSE?

HALLUCINATIONS WITH PARANOIA

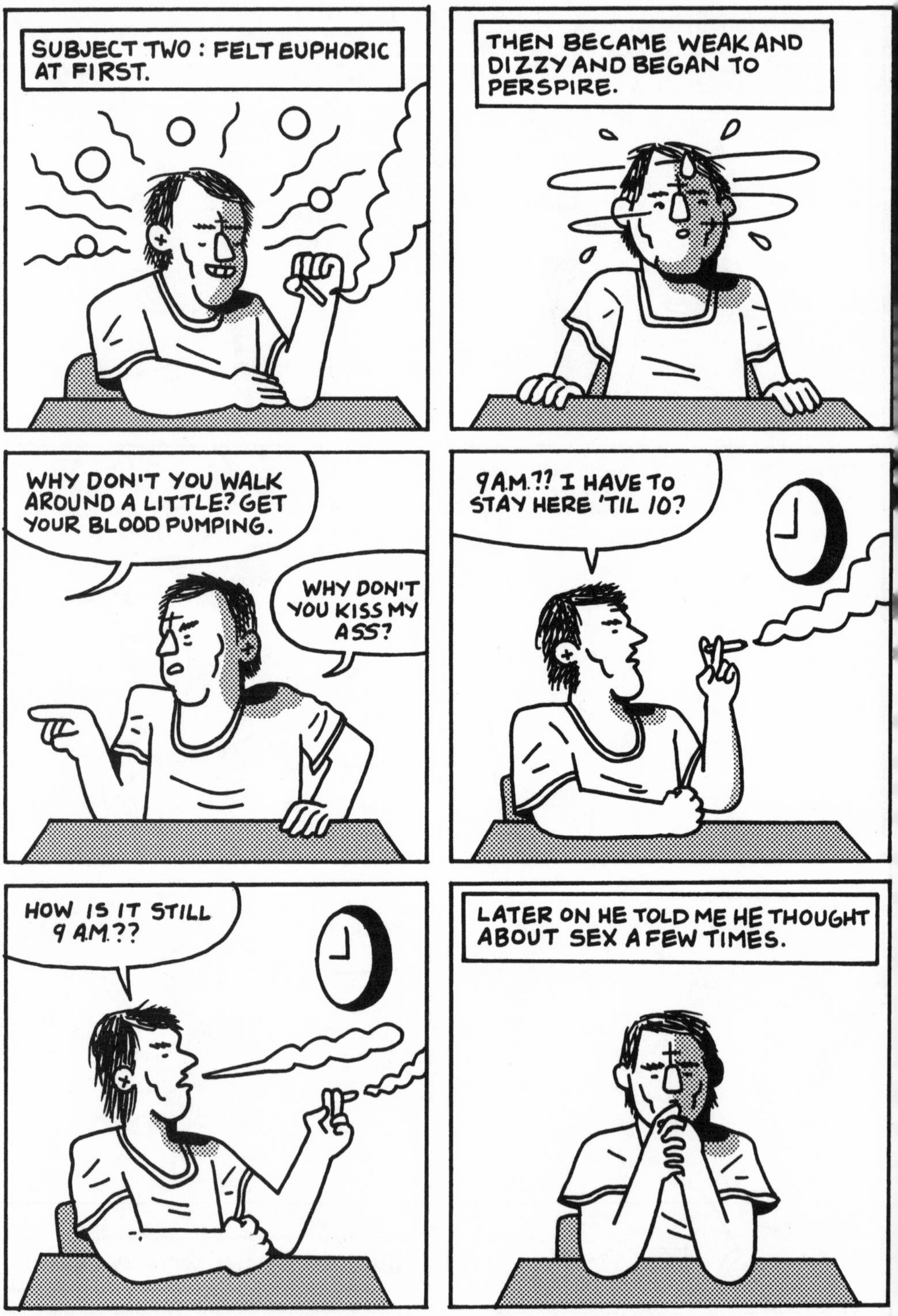

SUBJECT TWO : FELT EUPHORIC AT FIRST.
THEN BECAME WEAK AND DIZZY AND BEGAN TO PERSPIRE.
WHY DON'T YOU WALK AROUND A LITTLE? GET YOUR BLOOD PUMPING.
WHY DON'T YOU KISS MY ASS?
9 A.M.?? I HAVE TO STAY HERE 'TIL 10?
HOW IS IT STILL 9 A.M.??
LATER ON HE TOLD ME HE THOUGHT ABOUT SEX A FEW TIMES.

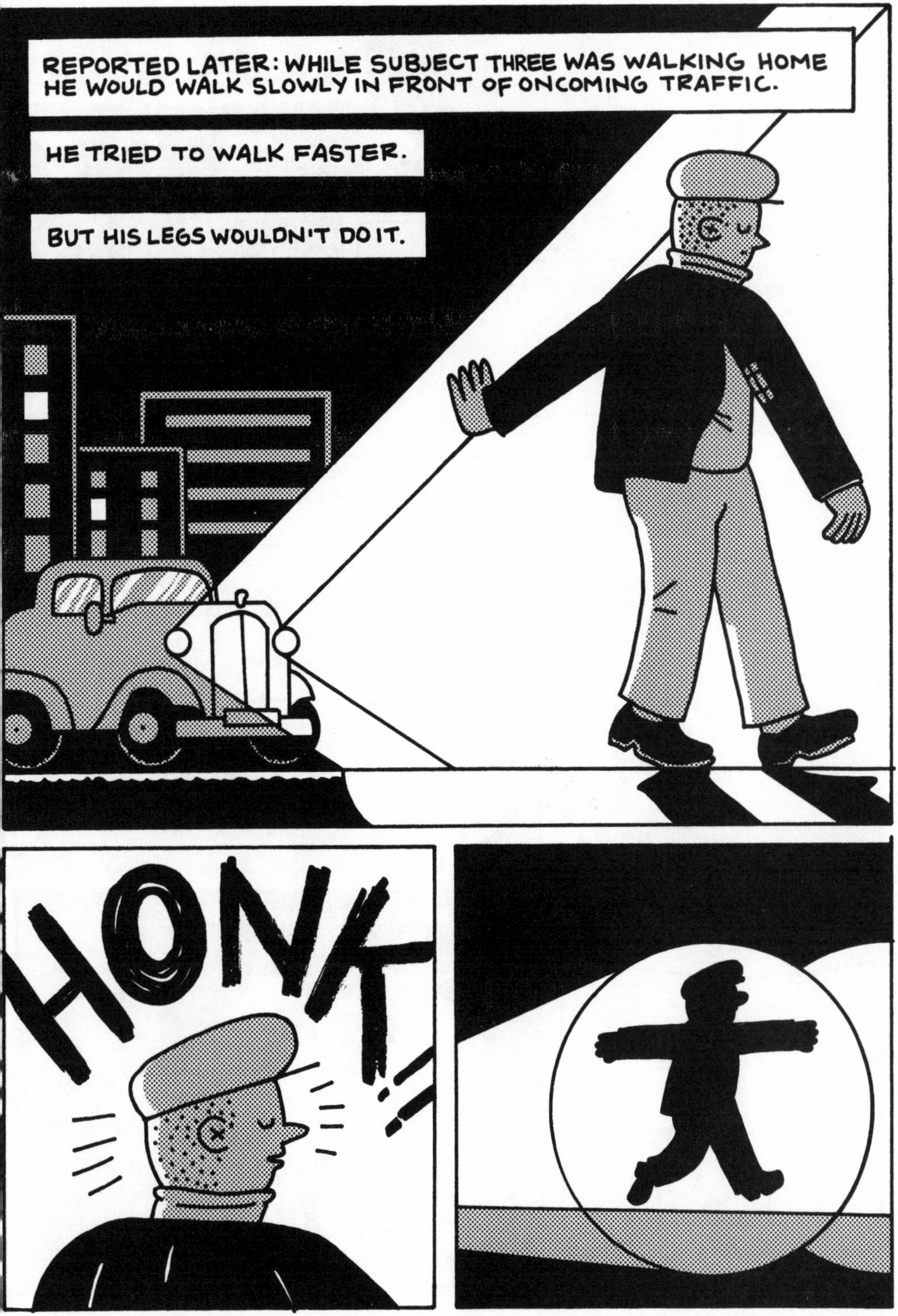
REPORTED LATER: WHILE SUBJECT THREE WAS WALKING HOME HE WOULD WALK SLOWLY IN FRONT OF ONCOMING TRAFFIC.
HE TRIED TO WALK FASTER.
BUT HIS LEGS WOULDN'T DO IT.
HONK

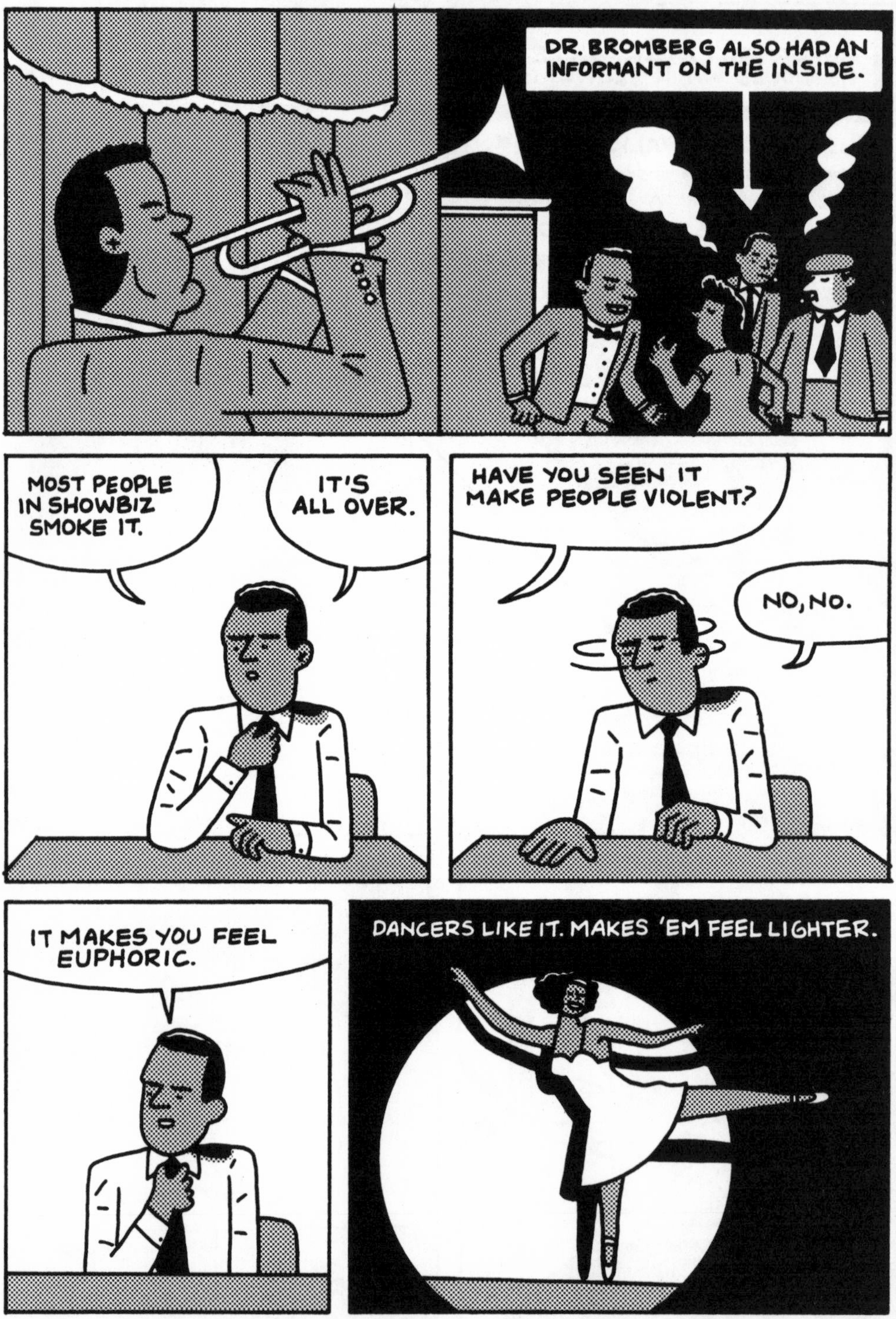
DR. BROMBERG ALSO HAD AN INFORMANT ON THE INSIDE.
MOST PEOPLE IN SHOWBIZ SMOKE IT.
IT'S ALL OVER.
HAVE YOU SEEN IT MAKE PEOPLE VIOLENT?
NO, NO.
IT MAKES YOU FEEL EUPHORIC.
DANCERS LIKE IT. MAKES 'EM FEEL LIGHTER.

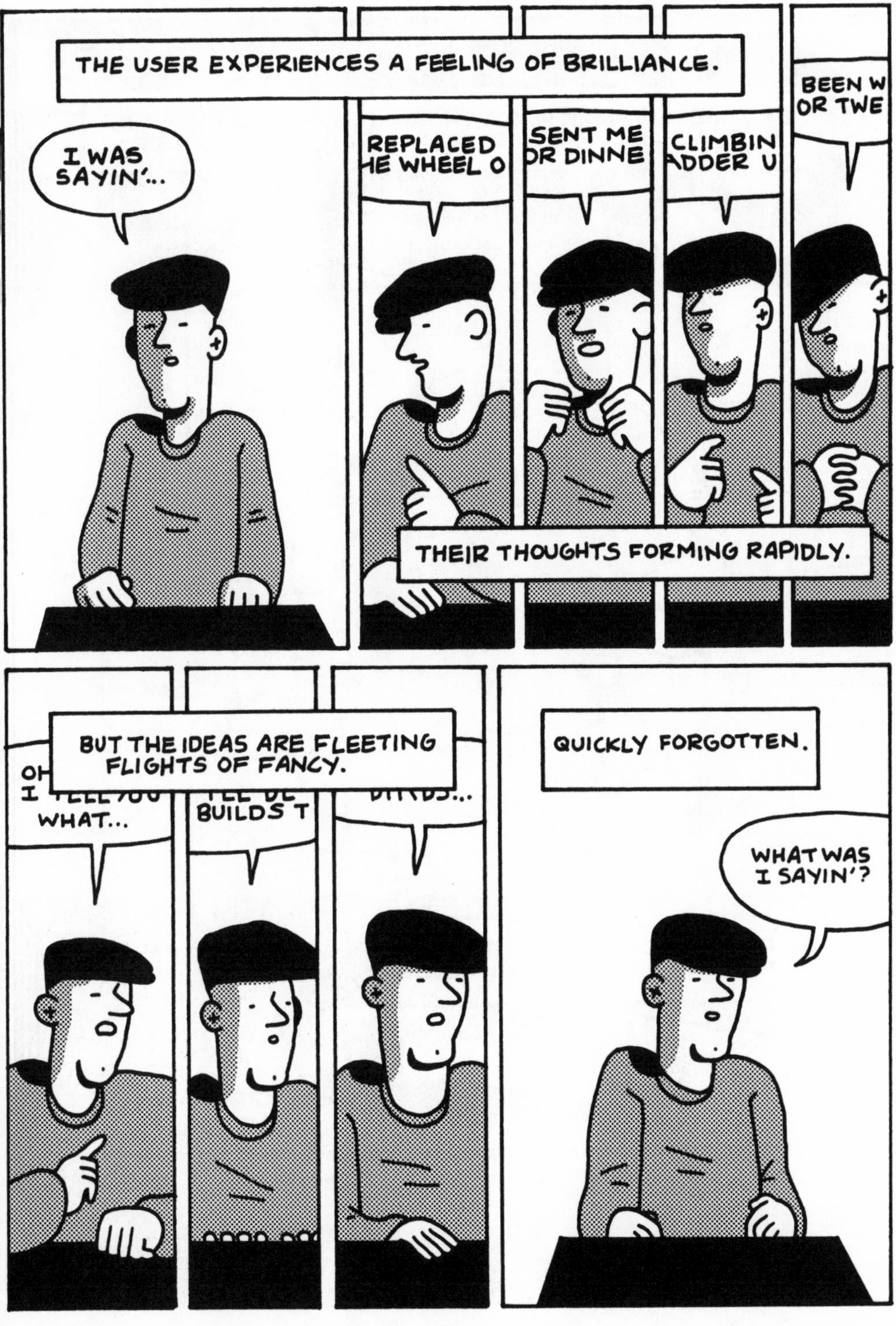

THE USER EXPERIENCES A FEELING OF BRILLIANCE.
I WAS SAYIN'...
REPLACED
HE WHEEL O
SENT ME
OR DINNE
CLIMBIN
ADDER U
BEEN W
OR TWE
THEIR THOUGHTS FORMING RAPIDLY.
BUT THE IDEAS ARE FLEETING FLIGHTS OF FANCY.
WHAT...
BUILDS T
QUICKLY FORGOTTEN.
WHAT WAS I SAYIN'?

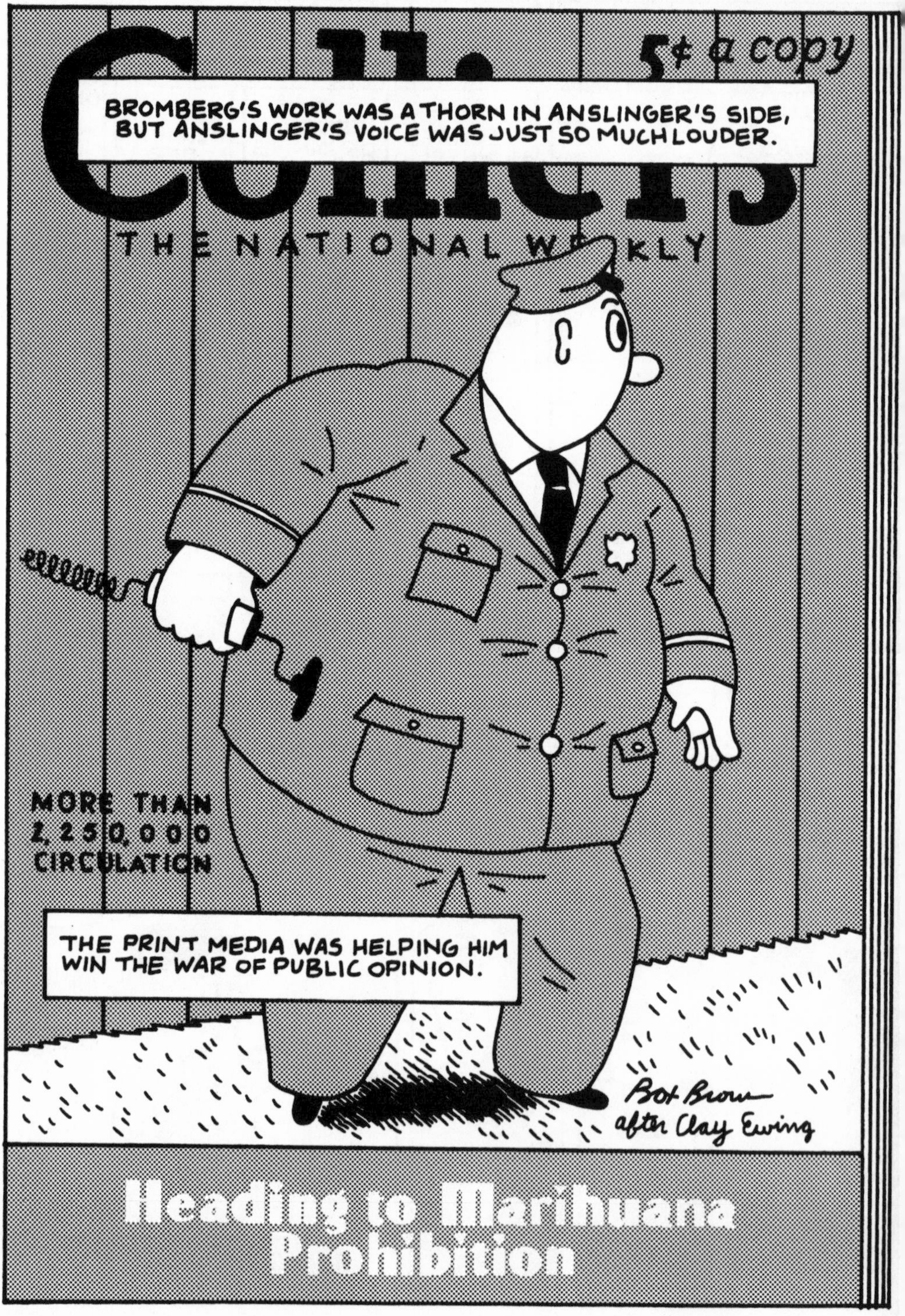
Collier's
5¢ a copy
BROMBERG'S WORK WAS A THORN IN ANSLINGER'S SIDE, BUT ANSLINGER'S VOICE WAS JUST SO MUCH LOUDER.
THE NATIONAL WEEKLY
MORE THAN 2,250,000 CIRCULATION
THE PRINT MEDIA WAS HELPING HIM WIN THE WAR OF PUBLIC OPINION.
Bob Brown after Clay Ewing
Heading to Marihuana Prohibition

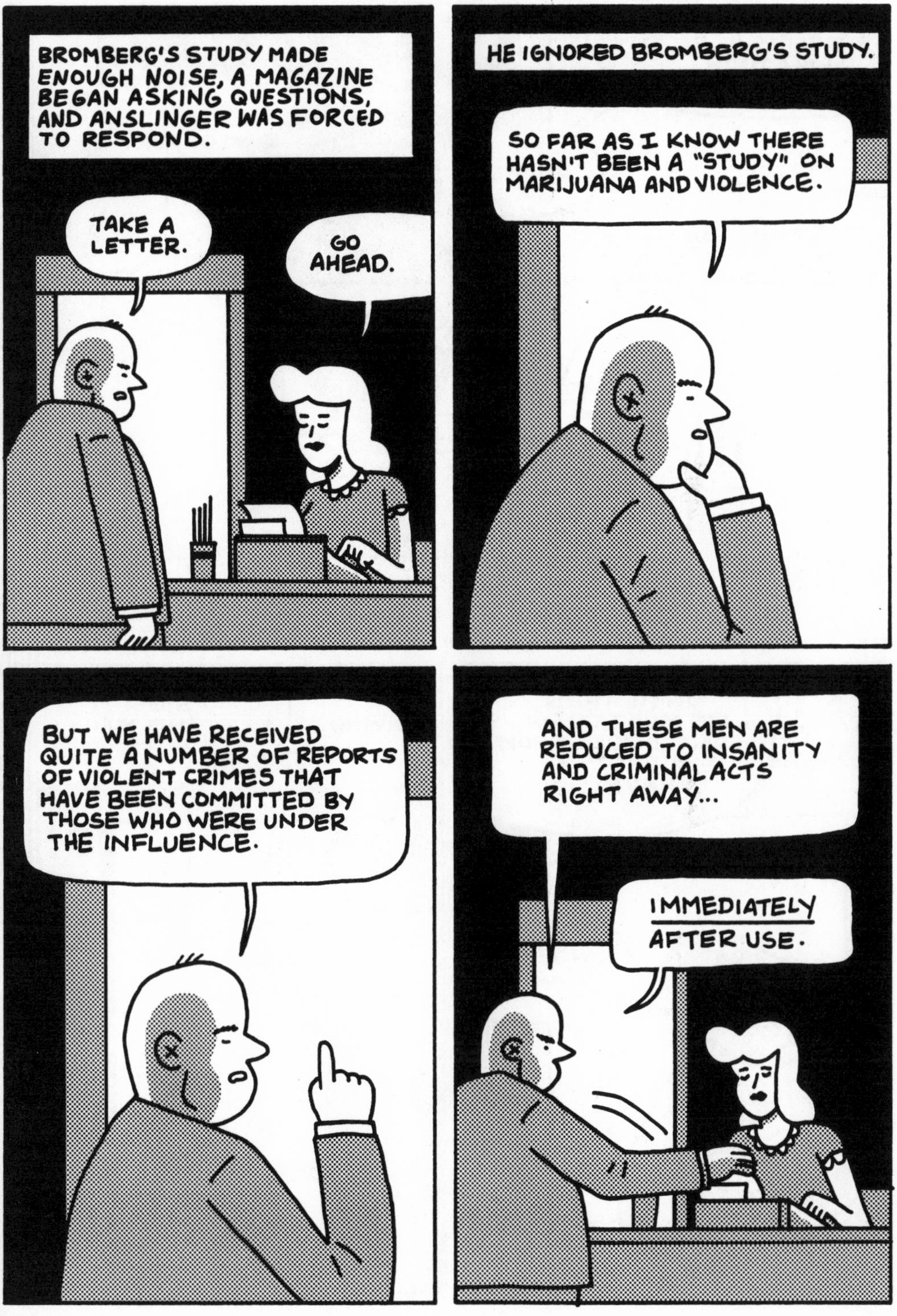
BROMBERG'S STUDY MADE ENOUGH NOISE, A MAGAZINE BEGAN ASKING QUESTIONS, AND ANSLINGER WAS FORCED TO RESPOND.
TAKE A LETTER.
GO AHEAD.
HE IGNORED BROMBERG'S STUDY.
SO FAR AS I KNOW THERE HASN'T BEEN A "STUDY" ON MARIJUANA AND VIOLENCE.
BUT WE HAVE RECEIVED QUITE A NUMBER OF REPORTS OF VIOLENT CRIMES THAT HAVE BEEN COMMITTED BY THOSE WHO WERE UNDER THE INFLUENCE.
AND THESE MEN ARE REDUCED TO INSANITY AND CRIMINAL ACTS RIGHT AWAY...
IMMEDIATELY AFTER USE.

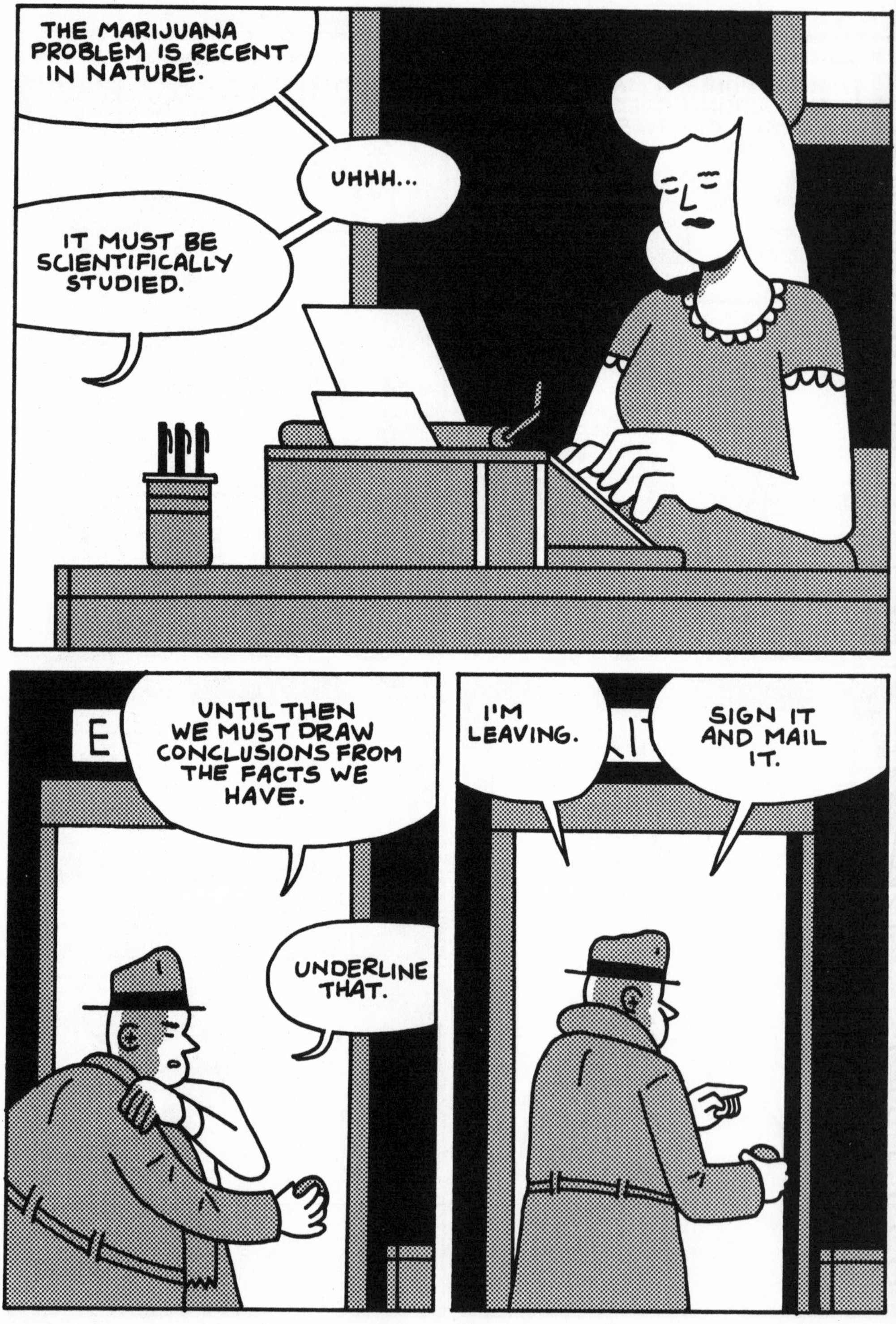
THE MARIJUANA PROBLEM IS RECENT IN NATURE.
UHHH...
IT MUST BE SCIENTIFICALLY STUDIED.
UNTIL THEN WE MUST DRAW CONCLUSIONS FROM THE FACTS WE HAVE.
UNDERLINE THAT.
I'M LEAVING.
SIGN IT AND MAIL IT.

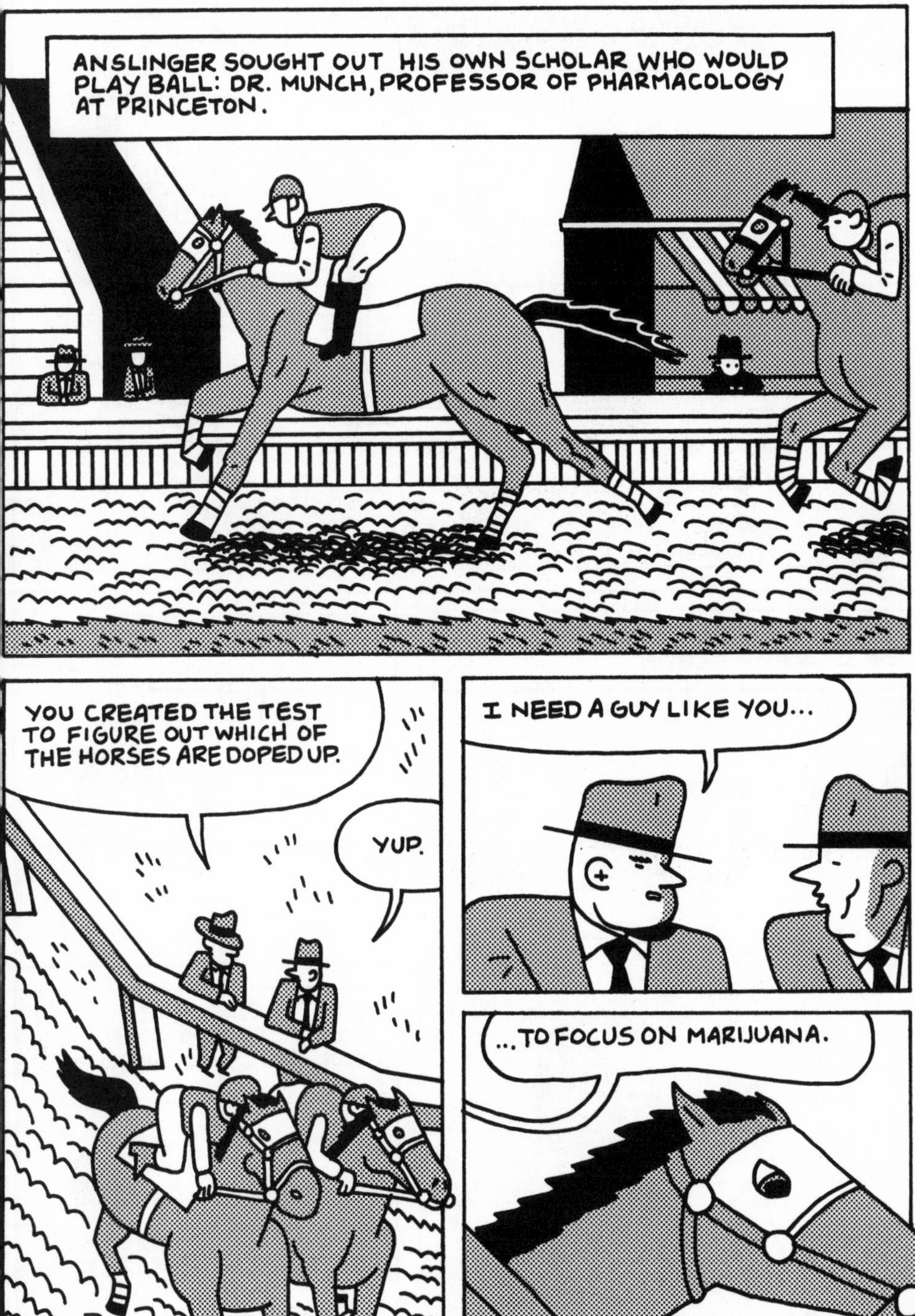
ANSLINGER SOUGHT OUT HIS OWN SCHOLAR WHO WOULD PLAY BALL: DR. MUNCH, PROFESSOR OF PHARMACOLOGY AT PRINCETON.
YOU CREATED THE TEST TO FIGURE OUT WHICH OF THE HORSES ARE DOPED UP.
YUP.
I NEED A GUY LIKE YOU...
...TO FOCUS ON MARIJUANA.

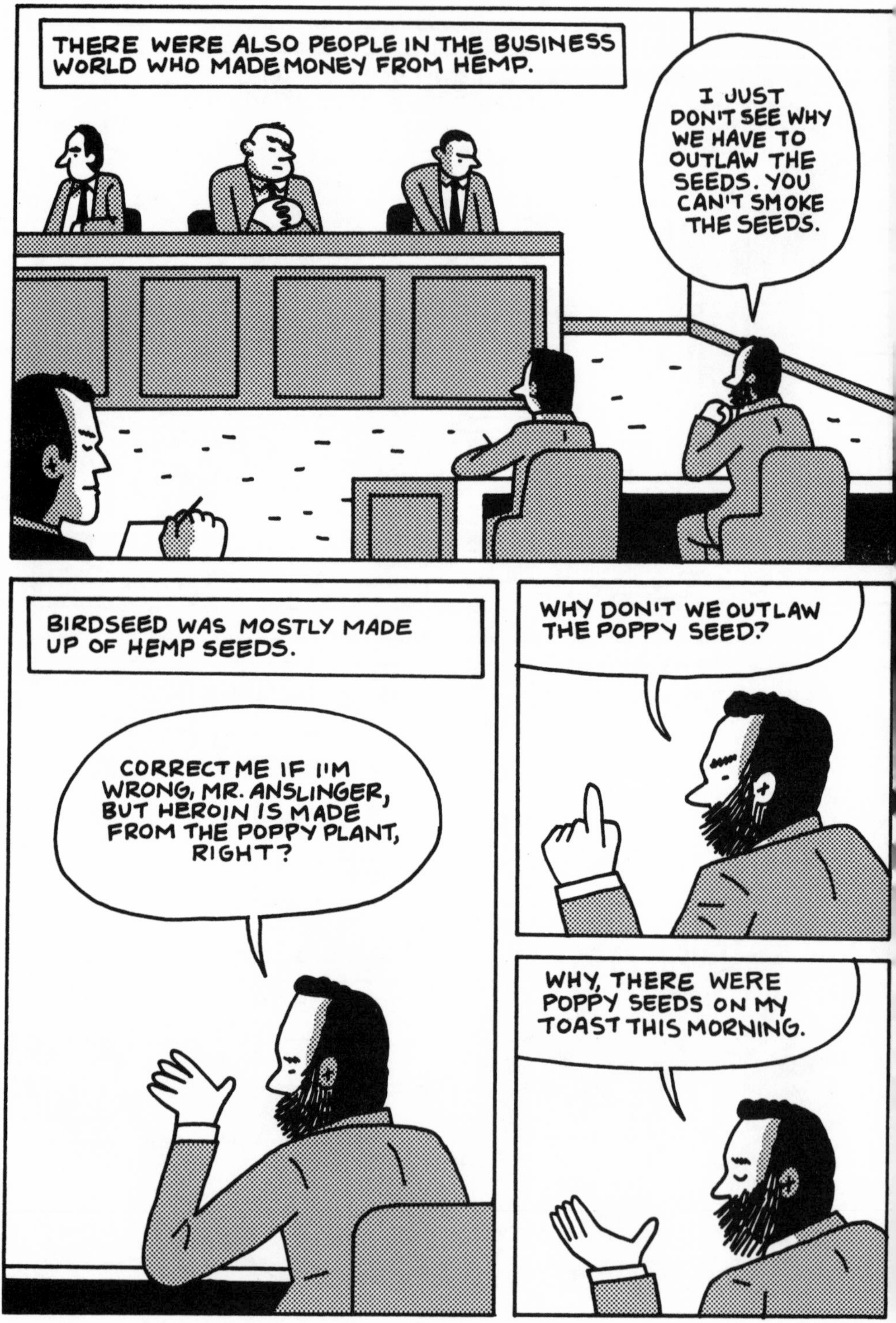
THERE WERE ALSO PEOPLE IN THE BUSINESS WORLD WHO MADE MONEY FROM HEMP.
I JUST DON'T SEE WHY WE HAVE TO OUTLAW THE SEEDS. YOU CAN'T SMOKE THE SEEDS.
BIRDSEED WAS MOSTLY MADE UP OF HEMP SEEDS.
CORRECT ME IF I'M WRONG, MR. ANSLINGER, BUT HEROIN IS MADE FROM THE POPPY PLANT, RIGHT?
WHY DON'T WE OUTLAW THE POPPY SEED?
WHY, THERE WERE POPPY SEEDS ON MY TOAST THIS MORNING.

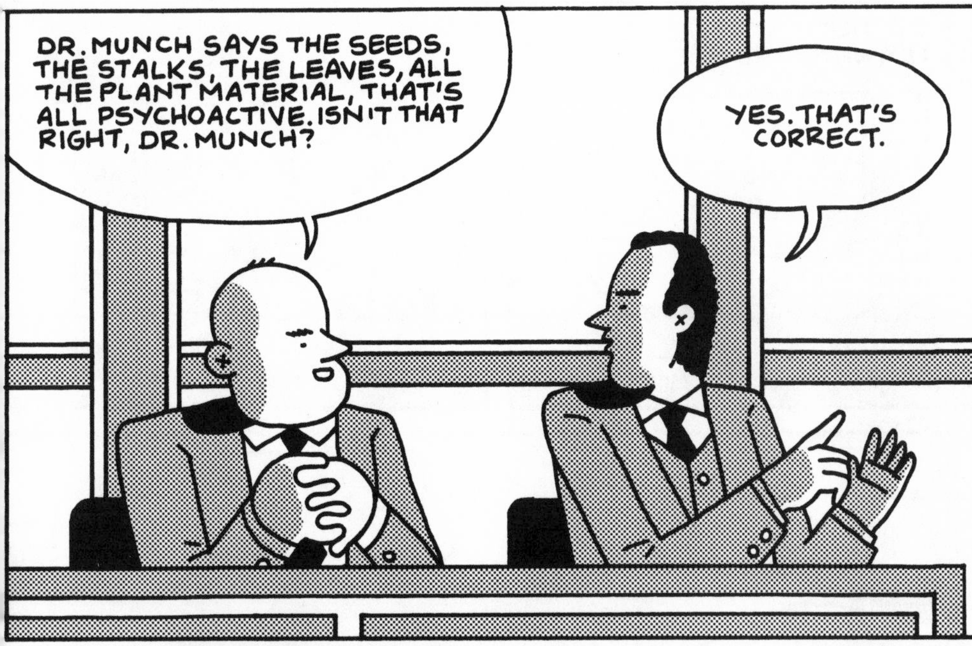
DR. MUNCH SAYS THE SEEDS, THE STALKS, THE LEAVES, ALL THE PLANT MATERIAL, THAT'S ALL PSYCHOACTIVE. ISN'T THAT RIGHT, DR. MUNCH?
YES. THAT'S CORRECT.

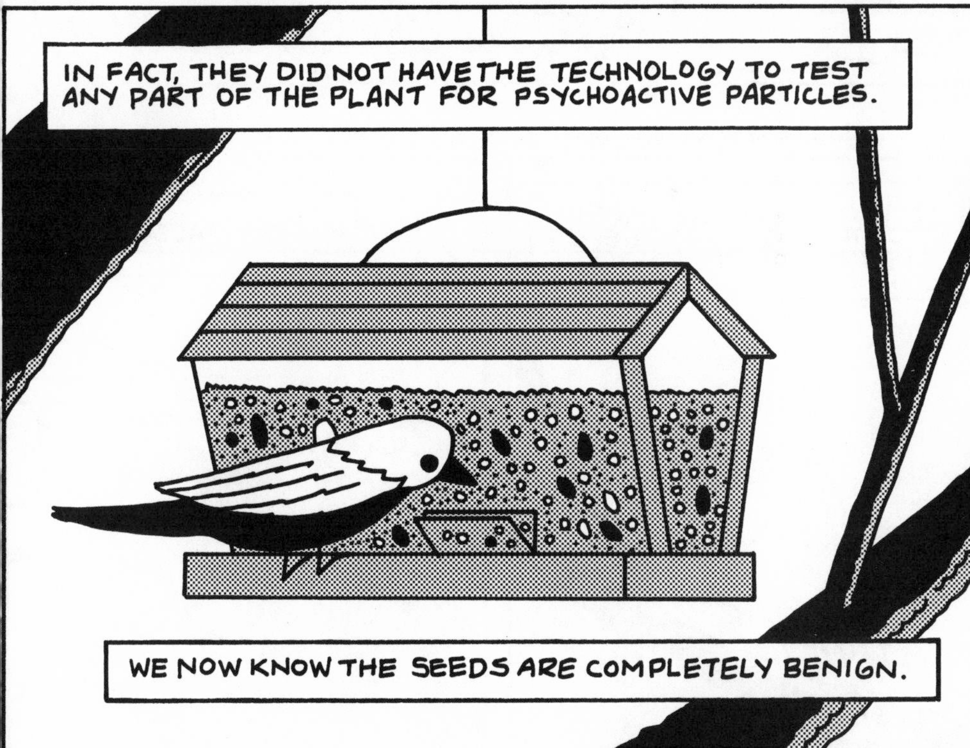
IN FACT, THEY DID NOT HAVE THE TECHNOLOGY TO TEST ANY PART OF THE PLANT FOR PSYCHOACTIVE PARTICLES.
WE NOW KNOW THE SEEDS ARE COMPLETELY BENIGN.

IT'S A PREVENTATIVE MEASURE, OUTLAWING THE SEEDS.

DON'T YOU SEE?

IF WE OUTLAW THE SEED, SOON OUR PROBLEM WILL BE GONE.

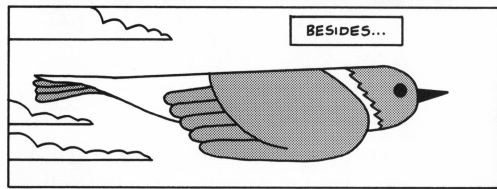

BESIDES...

DR. MUNCH TELLS ME THAT IF BIRDS ATE ONLY HEMP SEEDS THEY'D CEASE TO SING!

(COMPLETELY FALSE.)

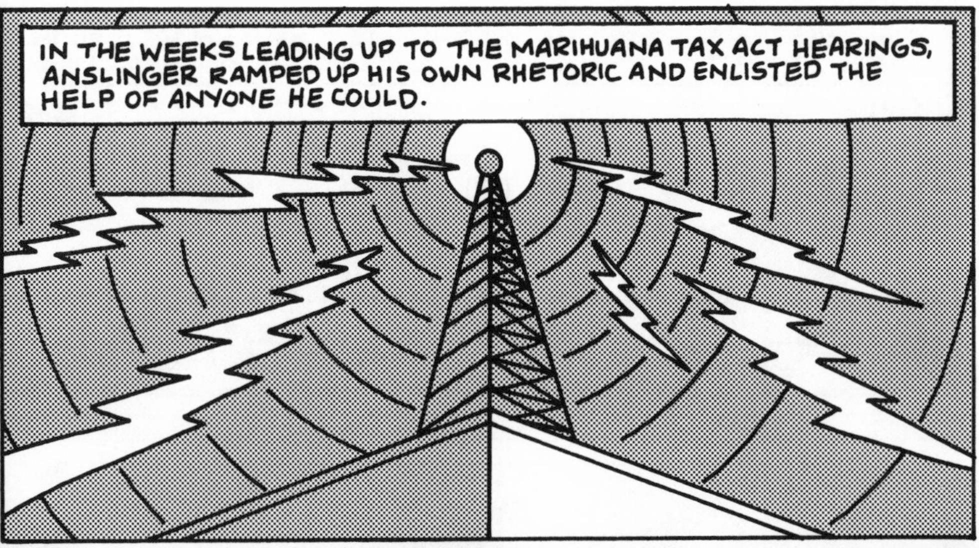
IN THE WEEKS LEADING UP TO THE MARIHUANA TAX ACT HEARINGS, ANSLINGER RAMPED UP HIS OWN RHETORIC AND ENLISTED THE HELP OF ANYONE HE COULD.

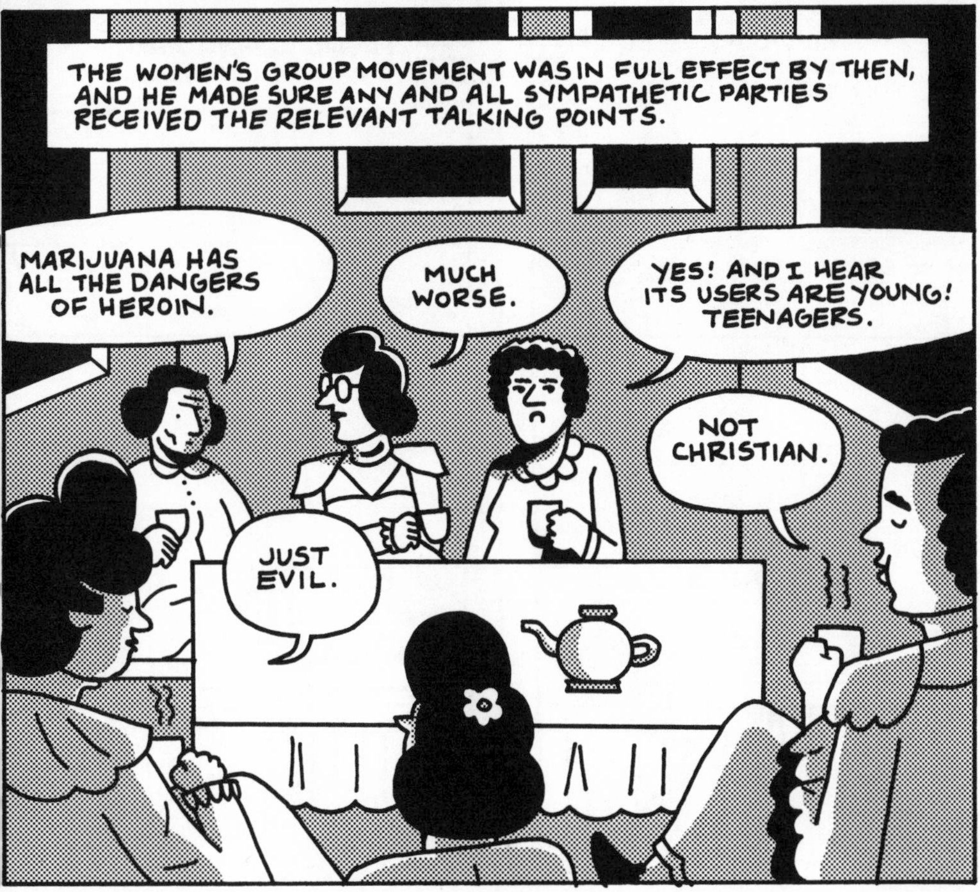
THE WOMEN'S GROUP MOVEMENT WAS IN FULL EFFECT BY THEN, AND HE MADE SURE ANY AND ALL SYMPATHETIC PARTIES RECEIVED THE RELEVANT TALKING POINTS.
MARIJUANA HAS ALL THE DANGERS OF HEROIN.
MUCH WORSE.
YES! AND I HEAR ITS USERS ARE YOUNG! TEENAGERS.
NOT CHRISTIAN.
JUST EVIL.

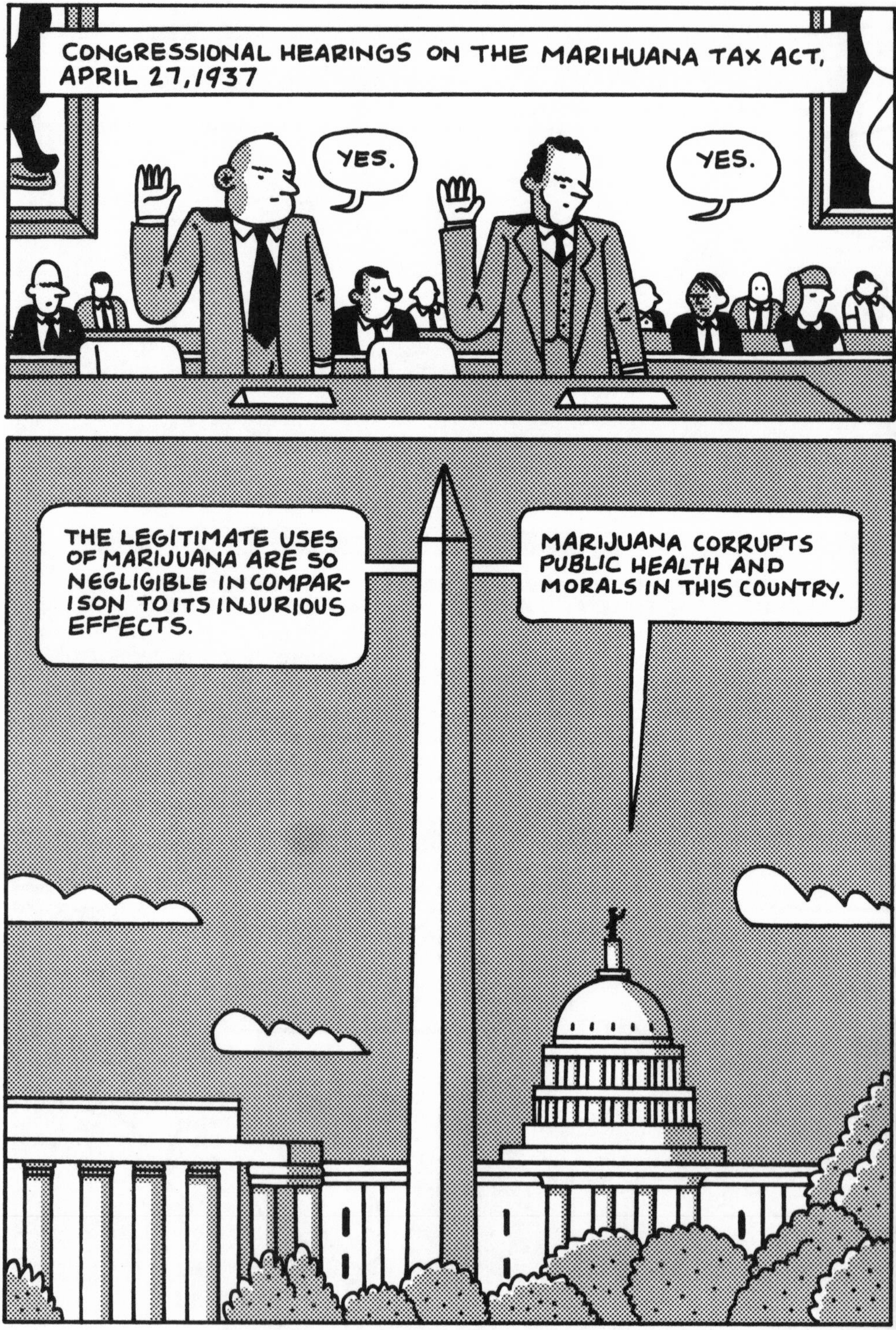
CONGRESSIONAL HEARINGS ON THE MARIHUANA TAX ACT, APRIL 27, 1937
YES.
YES.
THE LEGITIMATE USES OF MARIJUANA ARE SO NEGLIGIBLE IN COMPARISON TO ITS INJURIOUS EFFECTS.
MARIJUANA CORRUPTS PUBLIC HEALTH AND MORALS IN THIS COUNTRY.

THEREFORE WE WILL IMPOSE A TAX ON THE PRODUCTION, MANUFACTURING, AND TRANSFER OF...

AHEM.

...MARIJUANA.

THE TAX ON ILLEGITIMATE TRANSFERS WOULD BE:

$ 100 PER OUNCE

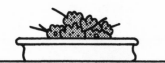

THE COST OF CANNABIS IN 1937 WAS 38¢ PER POUND!

IT IS OUR HOPE THAT THIS TAX IS EXORBITANT ENOUGH...

...TO MAKE THIS DRUG PROHIBITIVELY EXPENSIVE.

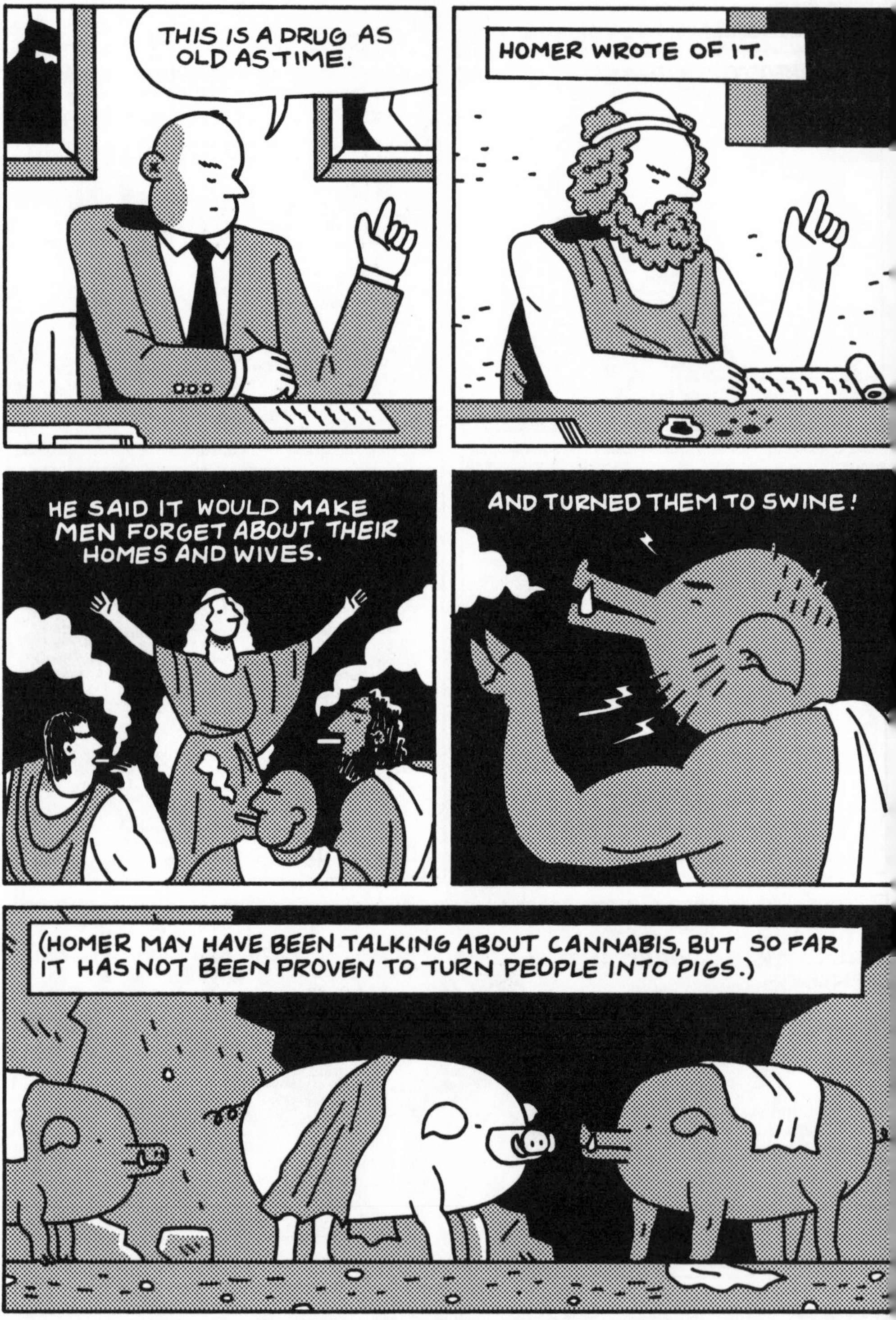

THIS IS A DRUG AS OLD AS TIME.
HOMER WROTE OF IT.
HE SAID IT WOULD MAKE MEN FORGET ABOUT THEIR HOMES AND WIVES.
AND TURNED THEM TO SWINE!
(HOMER MAY HAVE BEEN TALKING ABOUT CANNABIS, BUT SO FAR IT HAS NOT BEEN PROVEN TO TURN PEOPLE INTO PIGS.)

HE TROTTED OUT ALL THE OLD ARGUMENTS.

HE PLAYED ALL THE HITS.

YOU KNOW, HASHISH COMES FROM "ASSASSIN," AND IT MAKES YOU PERFORM ACTS OF CRUELTY...

...AND VIOLENCE.

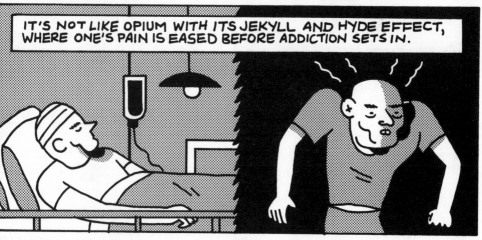

IT'S NOT LIKE OPIUM WITH ITS JEKYLL AND HYDE EFFECT, WHERE ONE'S PAIN IS EASED BEFORE ADDICTION SETS IN.

BUT WITH MARIJUANA IT'S ENTIRELY MR. HYDE.

PURE MONSTER.

NO!

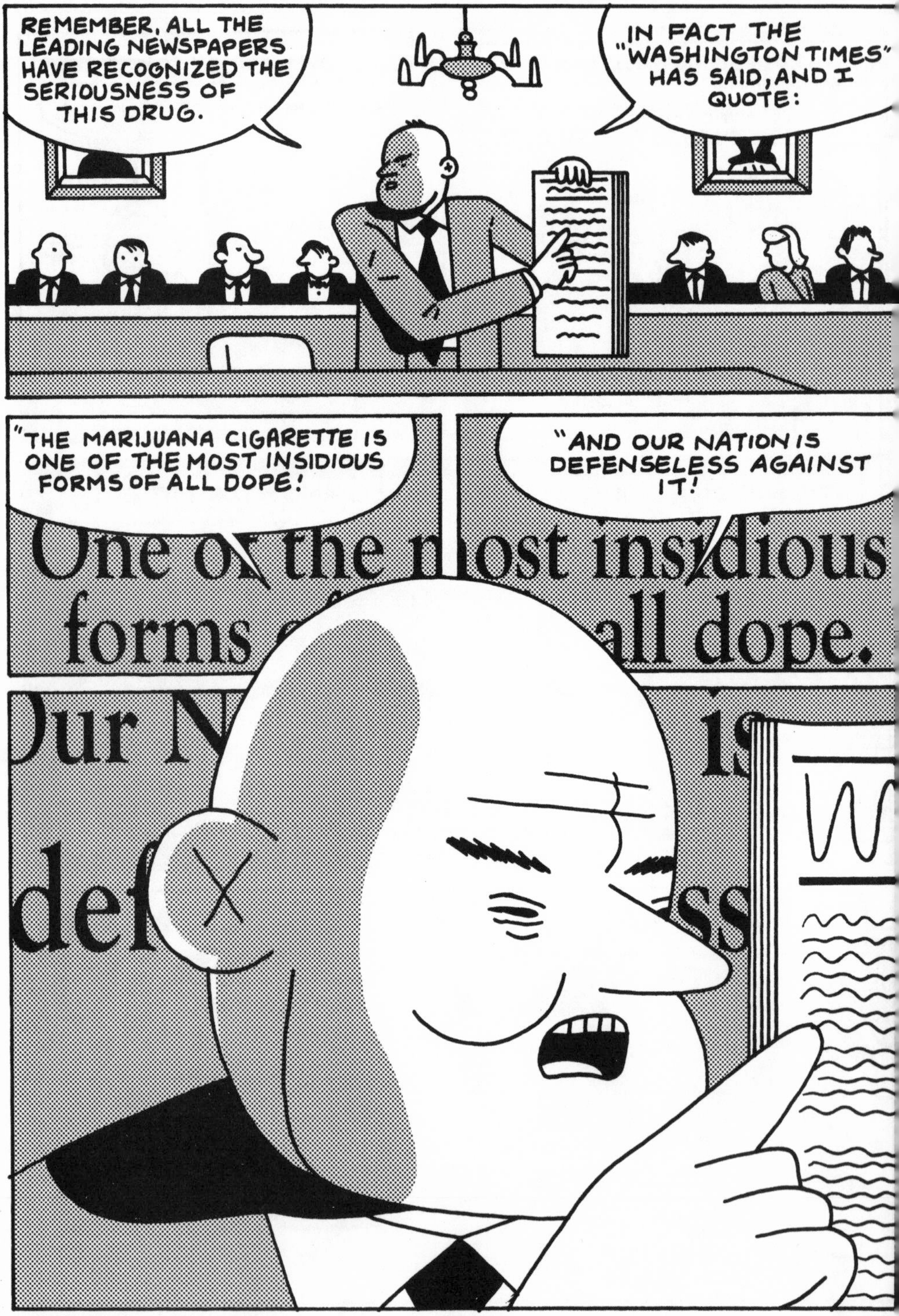
REMEMBER, ALL THE LEADING NEWSPAPERS HAVE RECOGNIZED THE SERIOUSNESS OF THIS DRUG.
IN FACT THE "WASHINGTON TIMES" HAS SAID, AND I QUOTE:
"THE MARIJUANA CIGARETTE IS ONE OF THE MOST INSIDIOUS FORMS OF ALL DOPE!
"AND OUR NATION IS DEFENSELESS AGAINST IT!
One of the most insidious
forms of all dope.

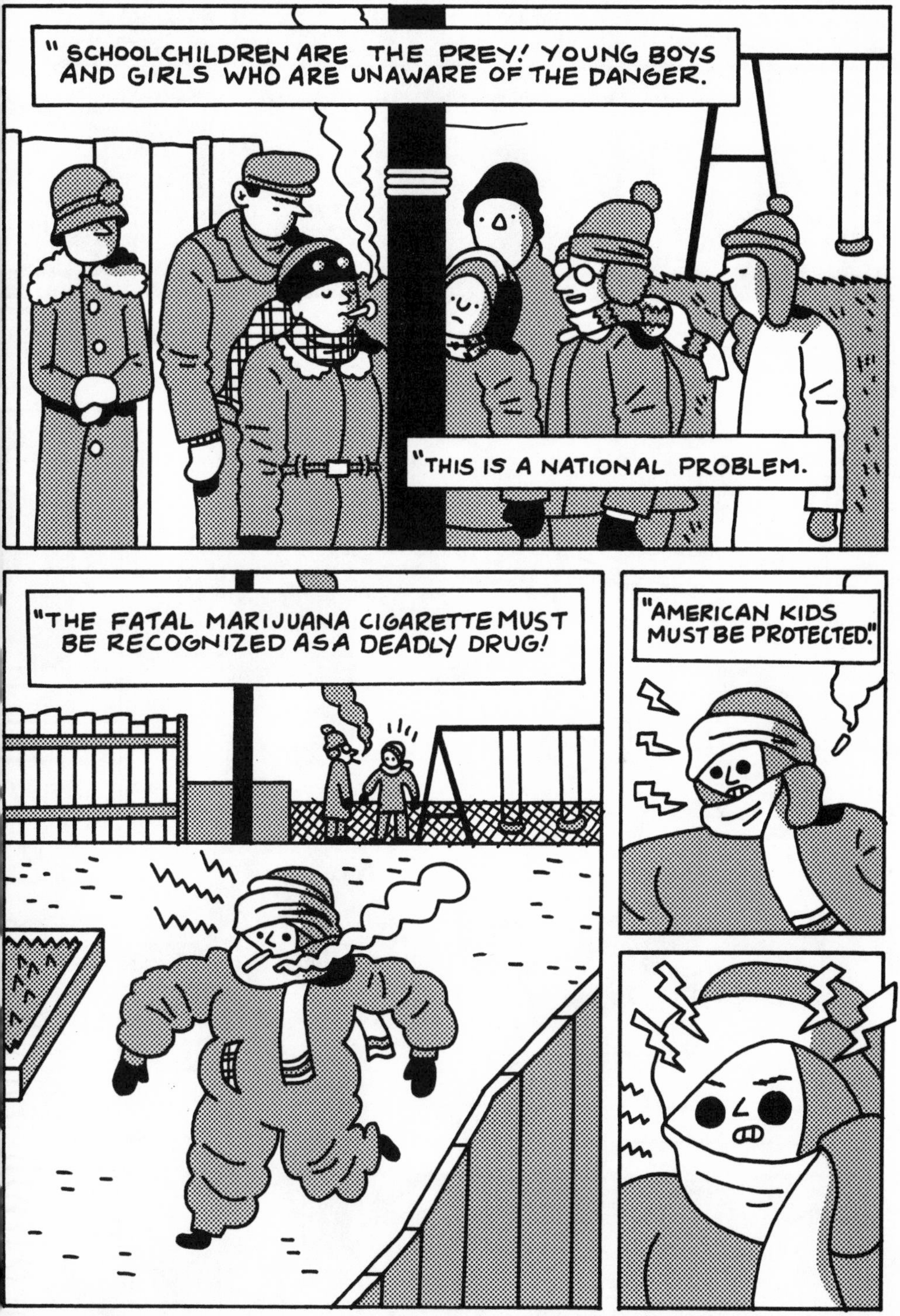
"SCHOOLCHILDREN ARE THE PREY! YOUNG BOYS AND GIRLS WHO ARE UNAWARE OF THE DANGER.
"THIS IS A NATIONAL PROBLEM.
"THE FATAL MARIJUANA CIGARETTE MUST BE RECOGNIZED AS A DEADLY DRUG!
"AMERICAN KIDS MUST BE PROTECTED."

"THIS APPEARED IN THE *WASHINGTON HERALD* AS RECENTLY AS APRIL OF THIS YEAR."

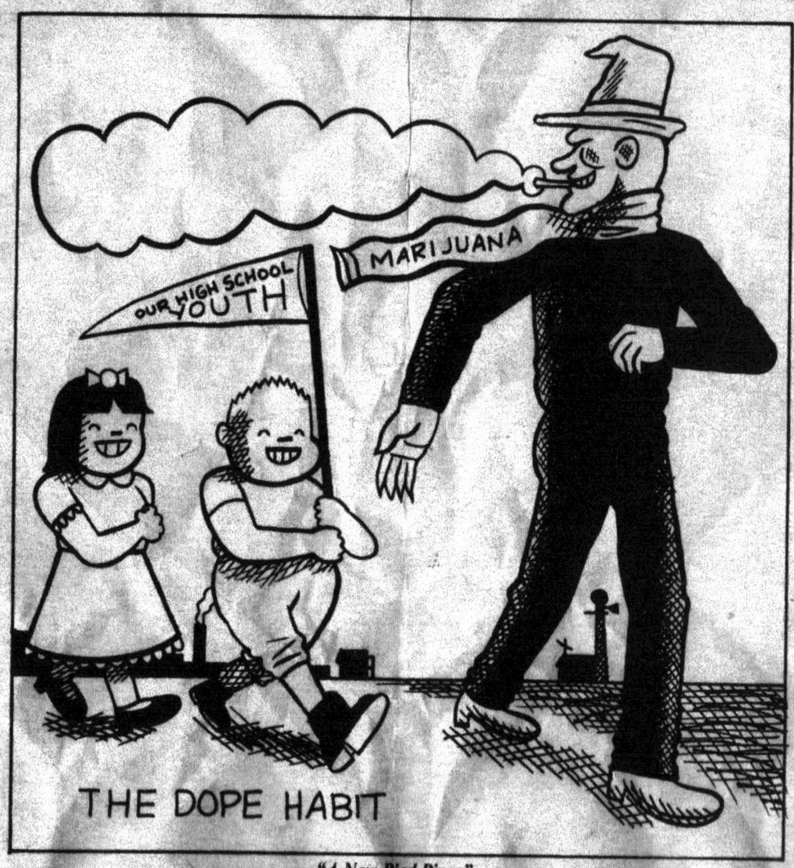
MARIJUANA
OUR HIGH SCHOOL YOUTH
THE DOPE HABIT

"A New Pied Piper"

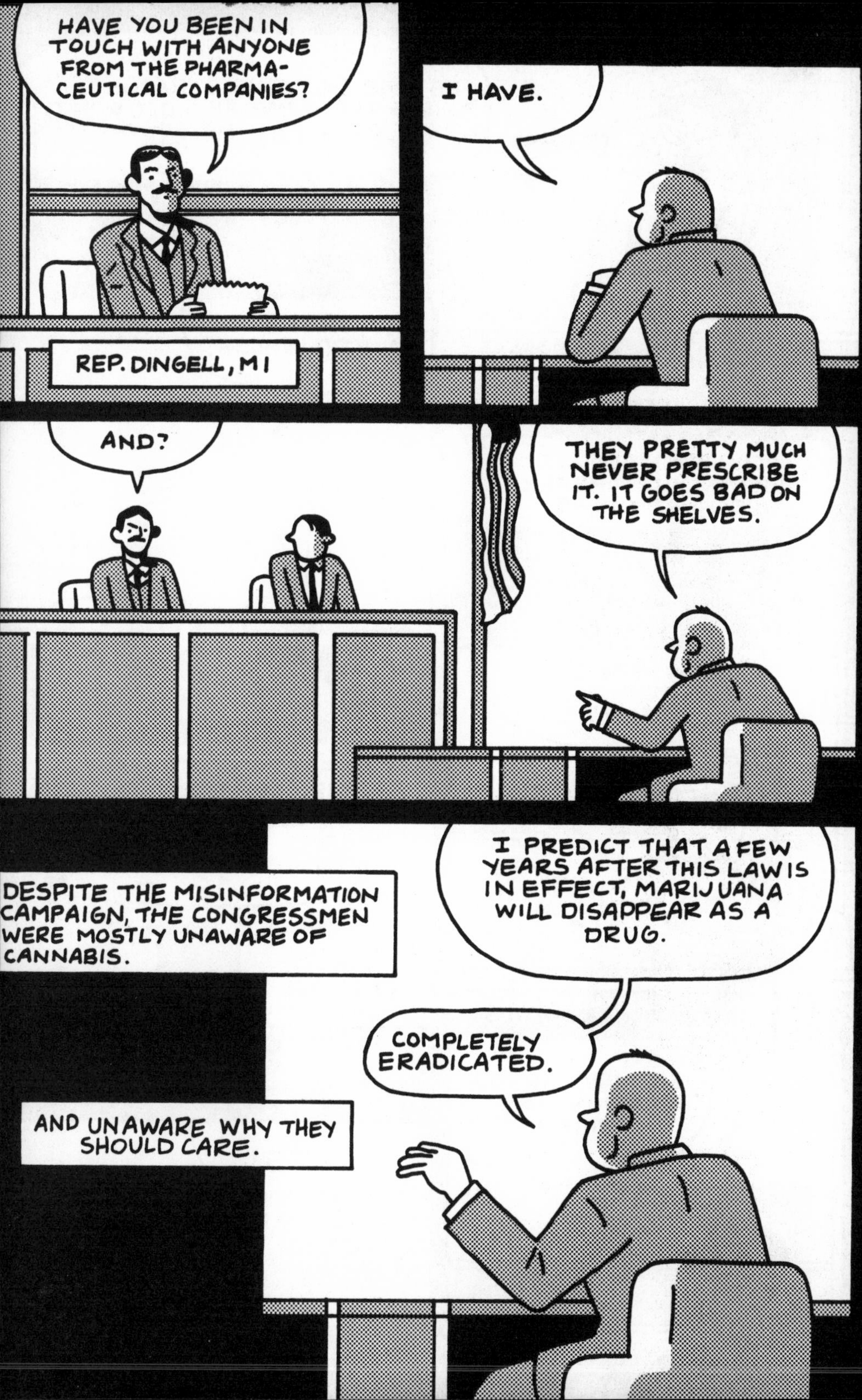
HAVE YOU BEEN IN TOUCH WITH ANYONE FROM THE PHARMA-CEUTICAL COMPANIES?
REP. DINGELL, MI
I HAVE.
AND?
THEY PRETTY MUCH NEVER PRESCRIBE IT. IT GOES BAD ON THE SHELVES.
DESPITE THE MISINFORMATION CAMPAIGN, THE CONGRESSMEN WERE MOSTLY UNAWARE OF CANNABIS.
I PREDICT THAT A FEW YEARS AFTER THIS LAW IS IN EFFECT, MARIJUANA WILL DISAPPEAR AS A DRUG.
COMPLETELY ERADICATED.
AND UNAWARE WHY THEY SHOULD CARE.

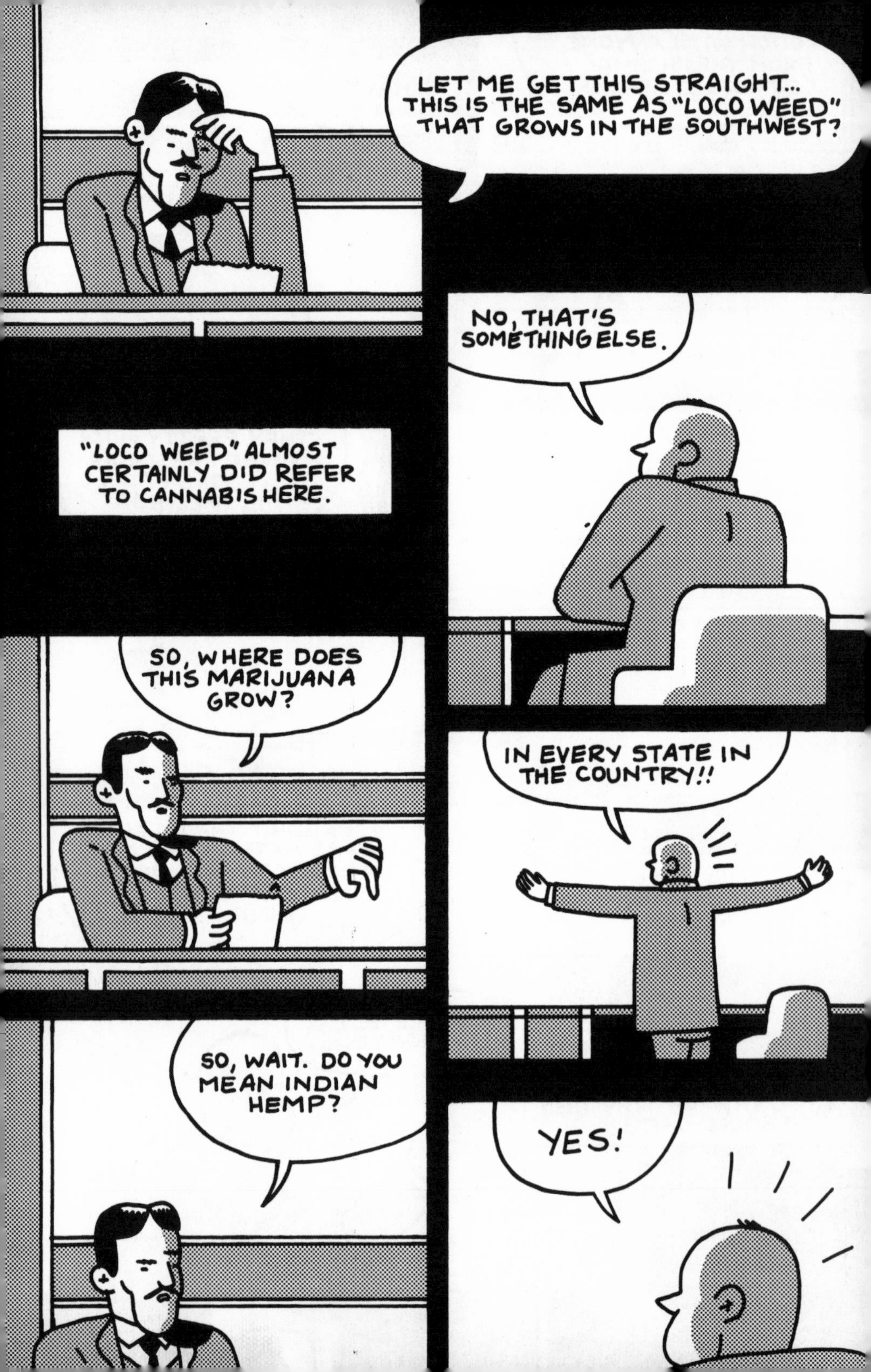
LET ME GET THIS STRAIGHT... THIS IS THE SAME AS "LOCO WEED" THAT GROWS IN THE SOUTHWEST?
NO, THAT'S SOMETHING ELSE.
"LOCO WEED" ALMOST CERTAINLY DID REFER TO CANNABIS HERE.
SO, WHERE DOES THIS MARIJUANA GROW?
IN EVERY STATE IN THE COUNTRY!!
SO, WAIT. DO YOU MEAN INDIAN HEMP?
YES!

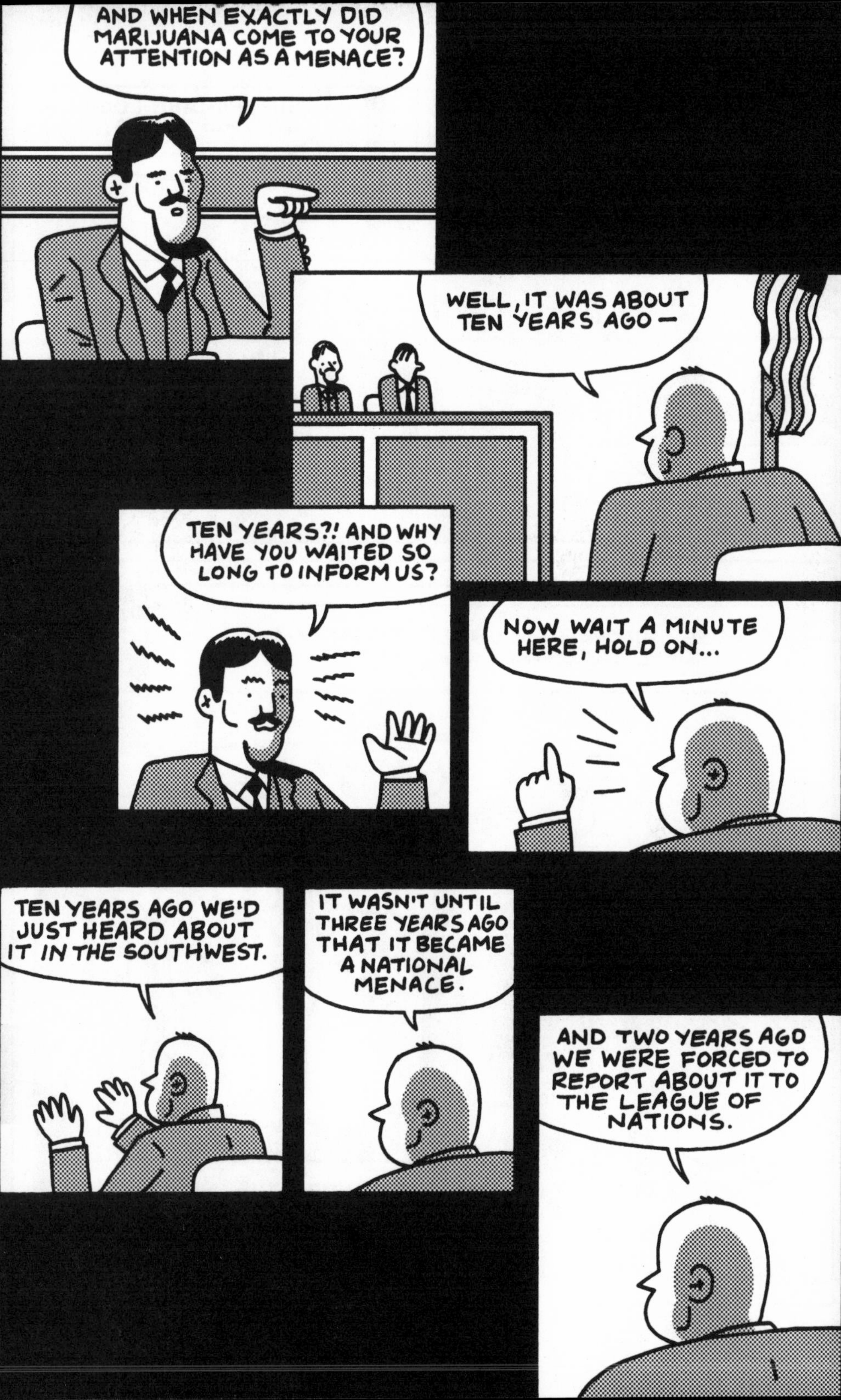
AND WHEN EXACTLY DID MARIJUANA COME TO YOUR ATTENTION AS A MENACE?
WELL, IT WAS ABOUT TEN YEARS AGO—
TEN YEARS?! AND WHY HAVE YOU WAITED SO LONG TO INFORM US?
NOW WAIT A MINUTE HERE, HOLD ON...
TEN YEARS AGO WE'D JUST HEARD ABOUT IT IN THE SOUTHWEST.
IT WASN'T UNTIL THREE YEARS AGO THAT IT BECAME A NATIONAL MENACE.
AND TWO YEARS AGO WE WERE FORCED TO REPORT ABOUT IT TO THE LEAGUE OF NATIONS.

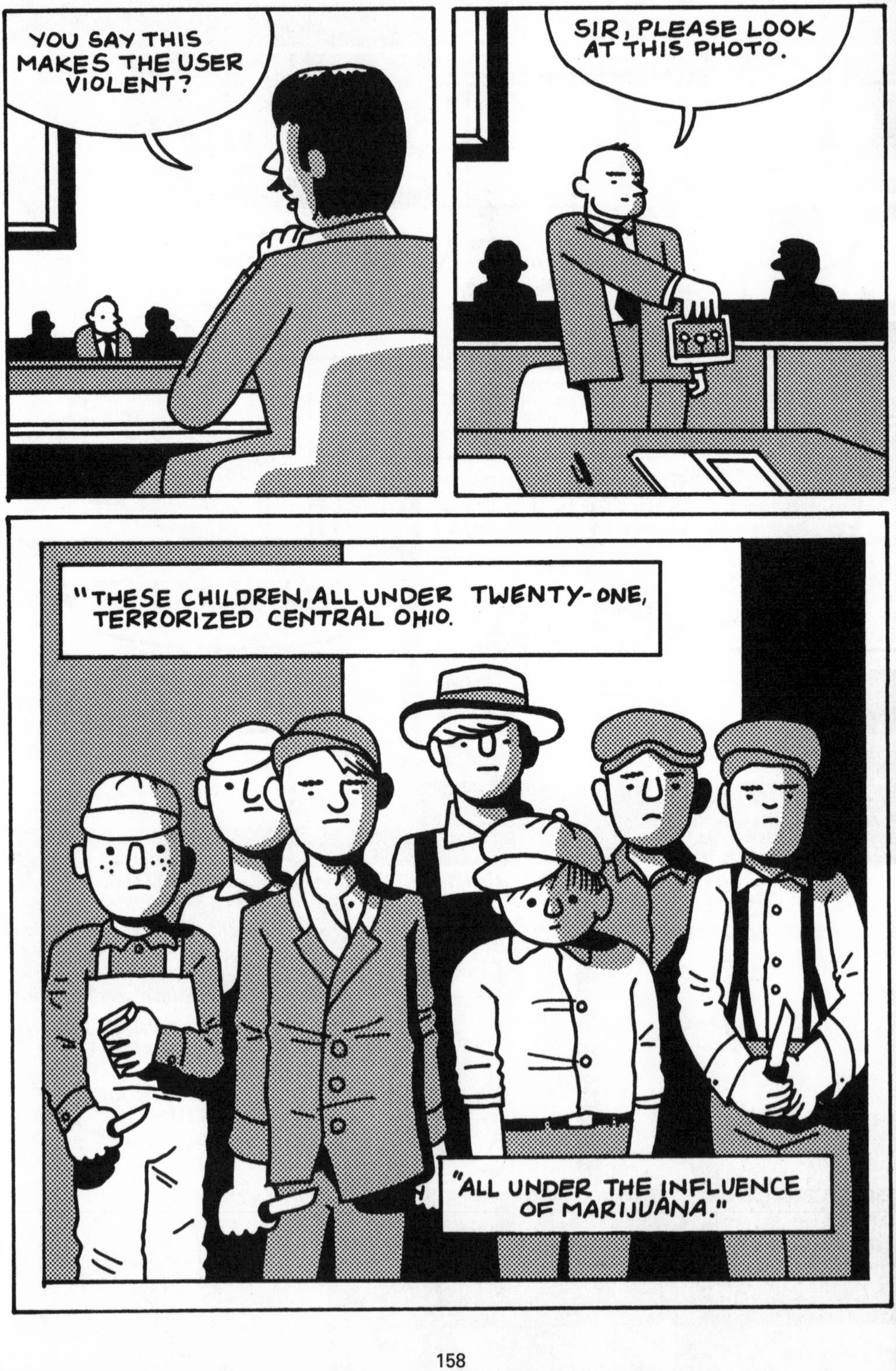
YOU SAY THIS MAKES THE USER VIOLENT?
SIR, PLEASE LOOK AT THIS PHOTO.
"THESE CHILDREN, ALL UNDER TWENTY-ONE, TERRORIZED CENTRAL OHIO.
"ALL UNDER THE INFLUENCE OF MARIJUANA."

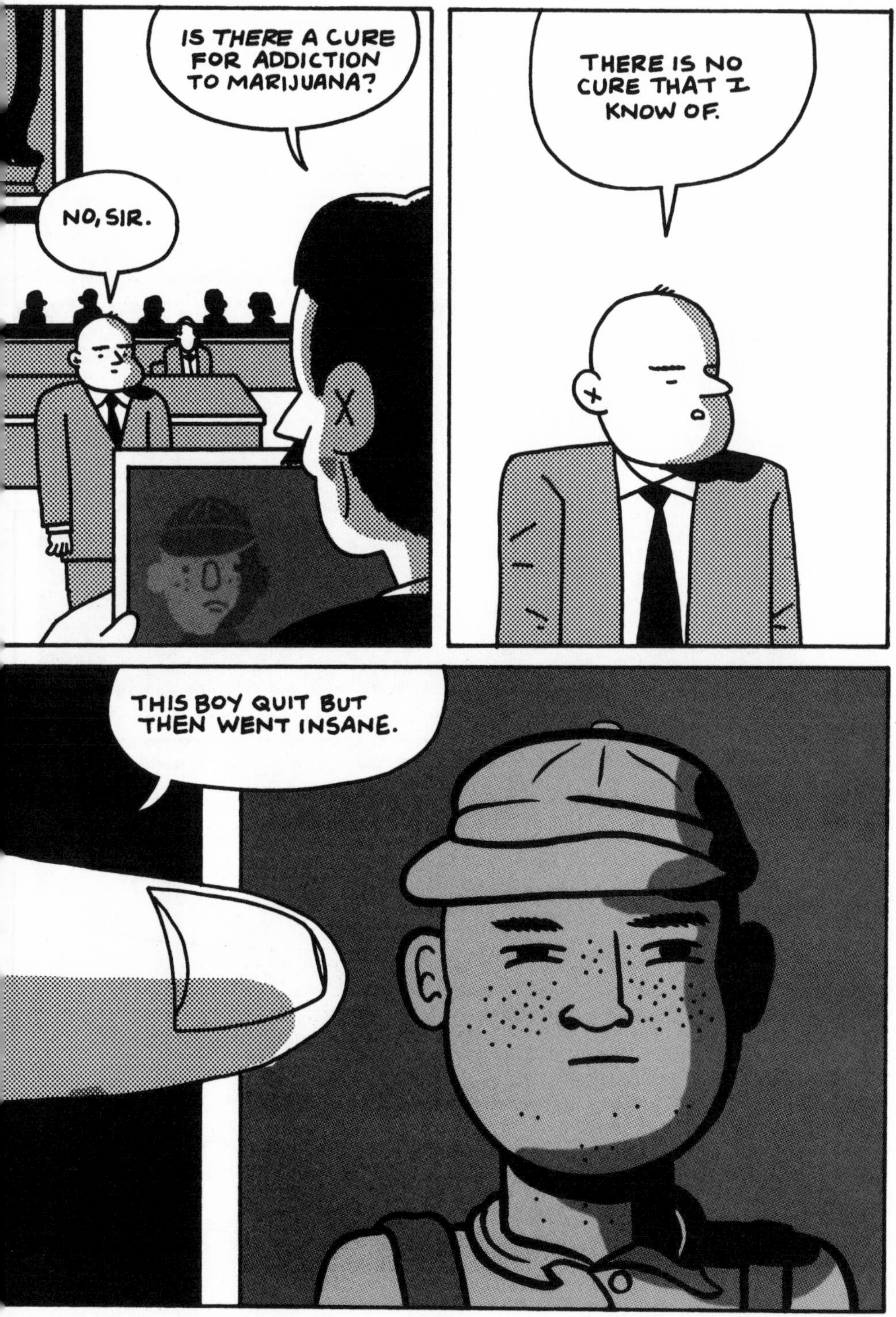
IS THERE A CURE FOR ADDICTION TO MARIJUANA?
NO, SIR.
THERE IS NO CURE THAT I KNOW OF.
THIS BOY QUIT BUT THEN WENT INSANE.

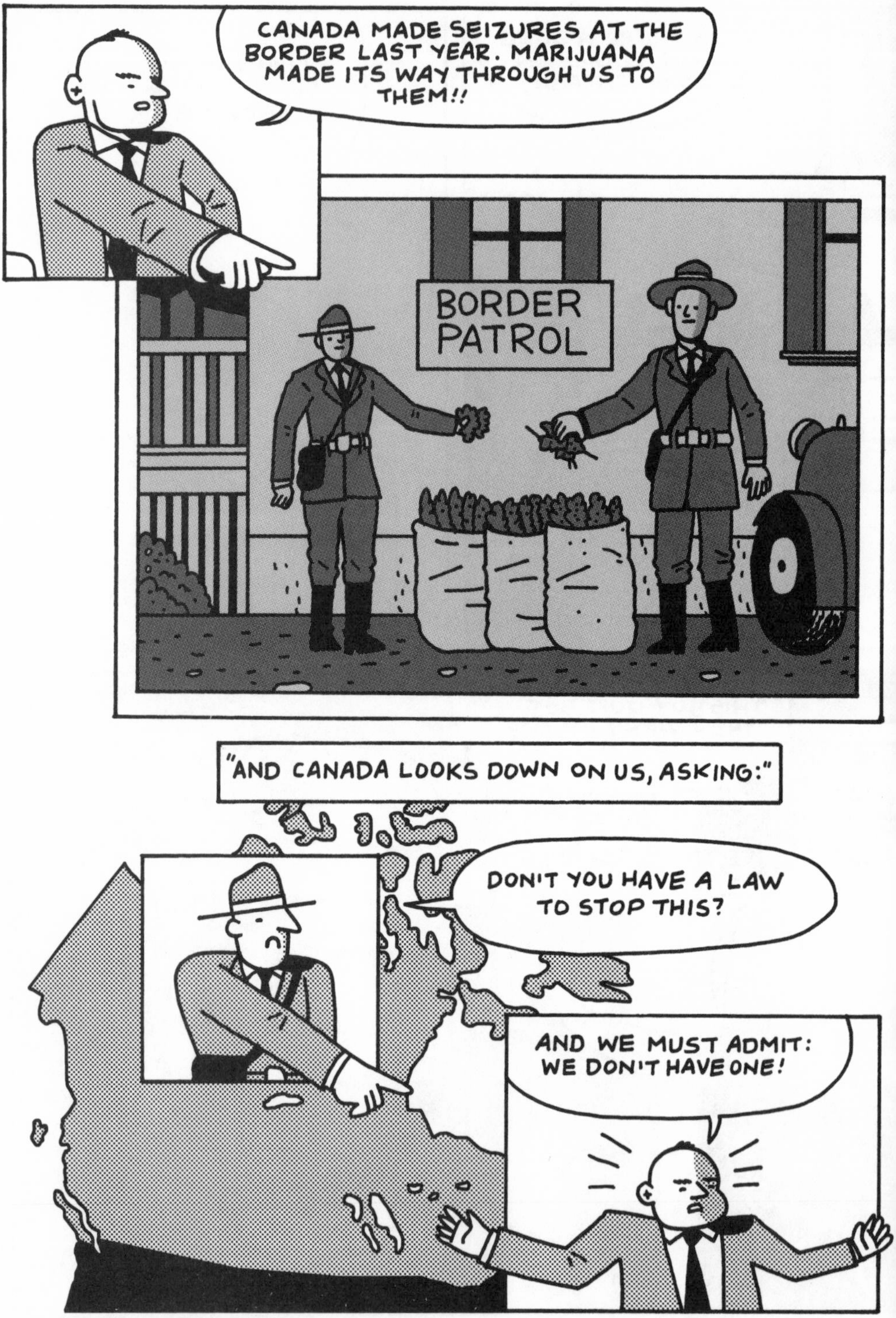
CANADA MADE SEIZURES AT THE BORDER LAST YEAR. MARIJUANA MADE ITS WAY THROUGH US TO THEM!!
BORDER PATROL
"AND CANADA LOOKS DOWN ON US, ASKING:"
DON'T YOU HAVE A LAW TO STOP THIS?
AND WE MUST ADMIT: WE DON'T HAVE ONE!

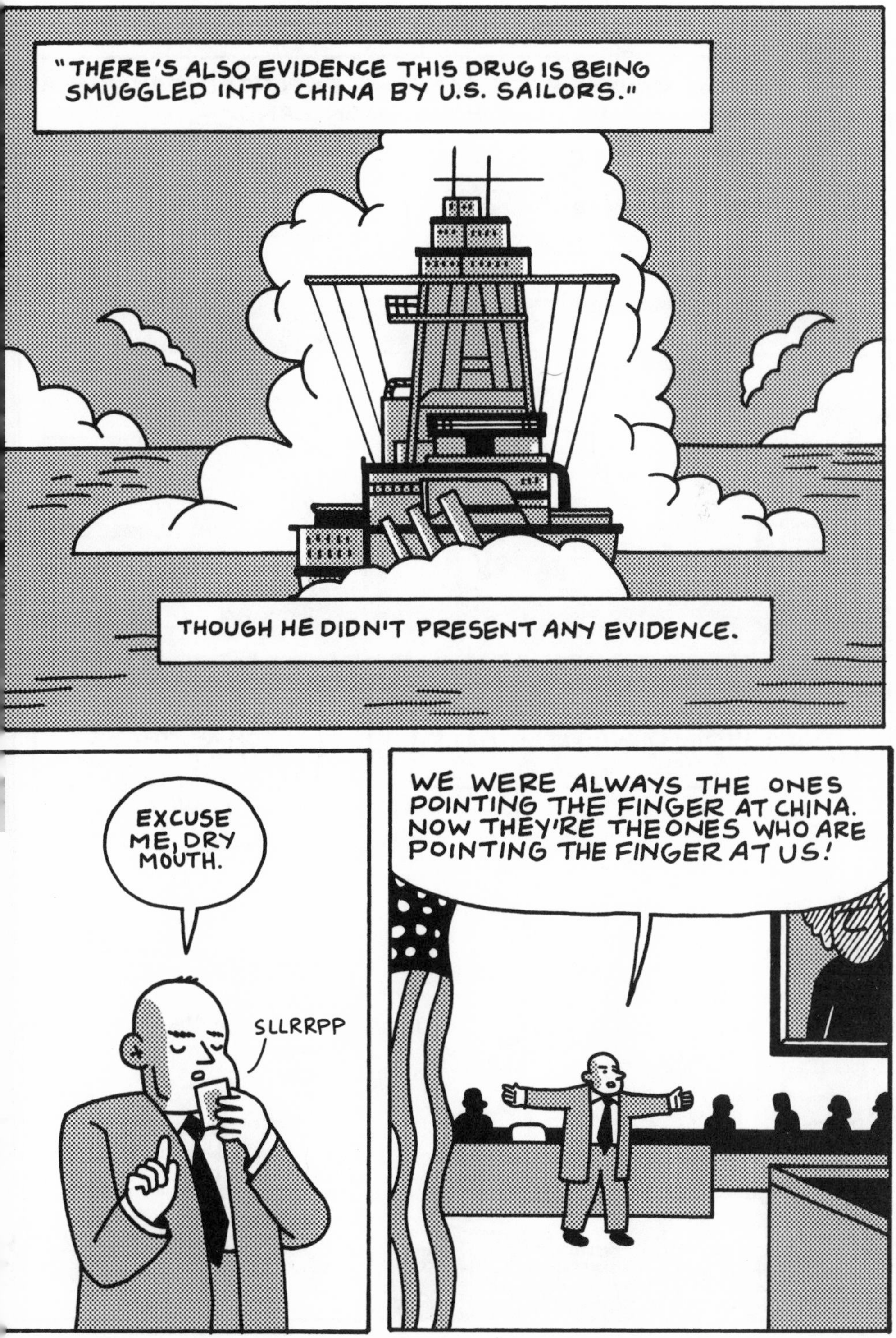
"THERE'S ALSO EVIDENCE THIS DRUG IS BEING SMUGGLED INTO CHINA BY U.S. SAILORS."
THOUGH HE DIDN'T PRESENT ANY EVIDENCE.
EXCUSE ME, DRY MOUTH.
SLLRRPP
WE WERE ALWAYS THE ONES POINTING THE FINGER AT CHINA. NOW THEY'RE THE ONES WHO ARE POINTING THE FINGER AT US!

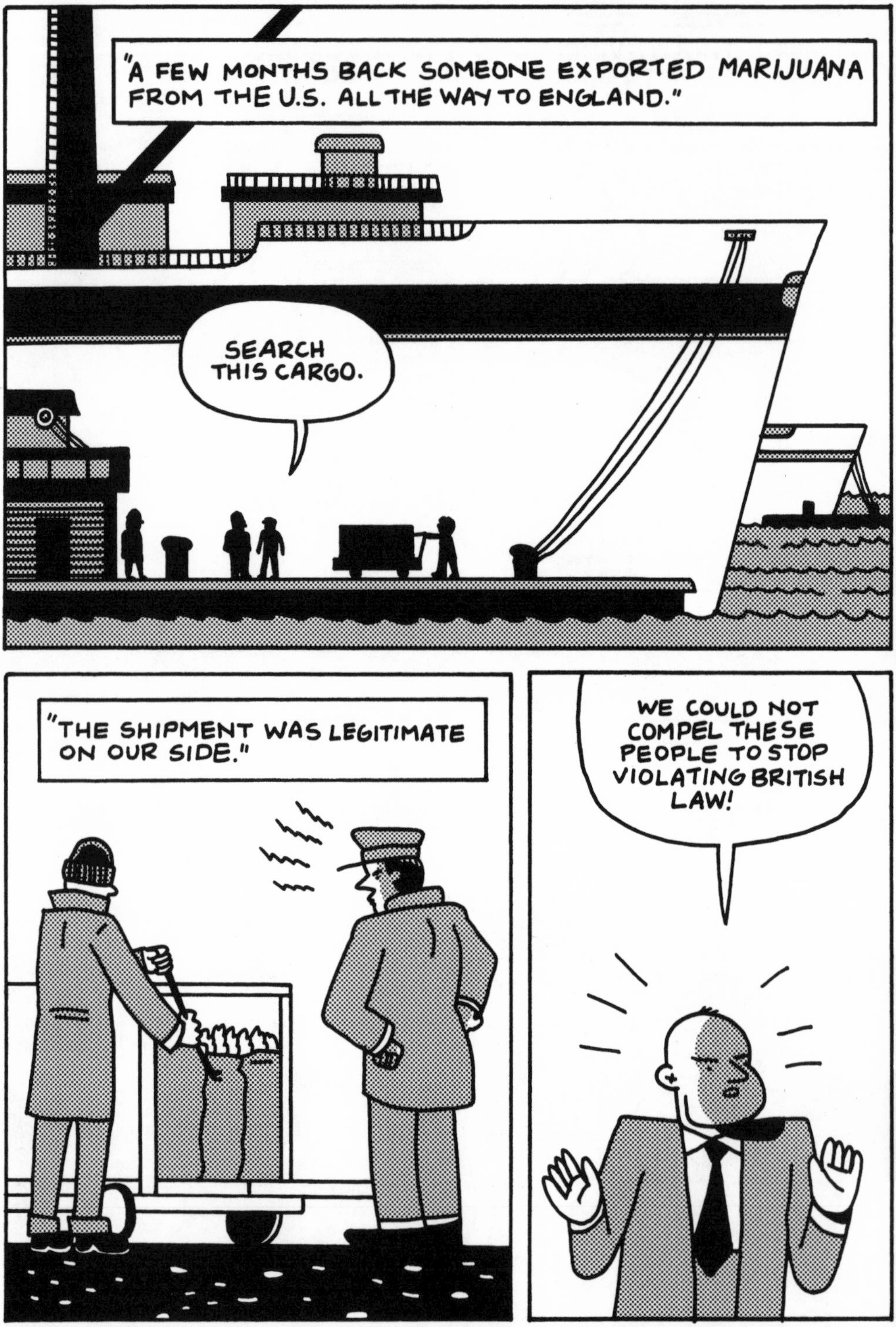
"A FEW MONTHS BACK SOMEONE EXPORTED MARIJUANA FROM THE U.S. ALL THE WAY TO ENGLAND."
SEARCH THIS CARGO.
"THE SHIPMENT WAS LEGITIMATE ON OUR SIDE."
WE COULD NOT COMPEL THESE PEOPLE TO STOP VIOLATING BRITISH LAW!

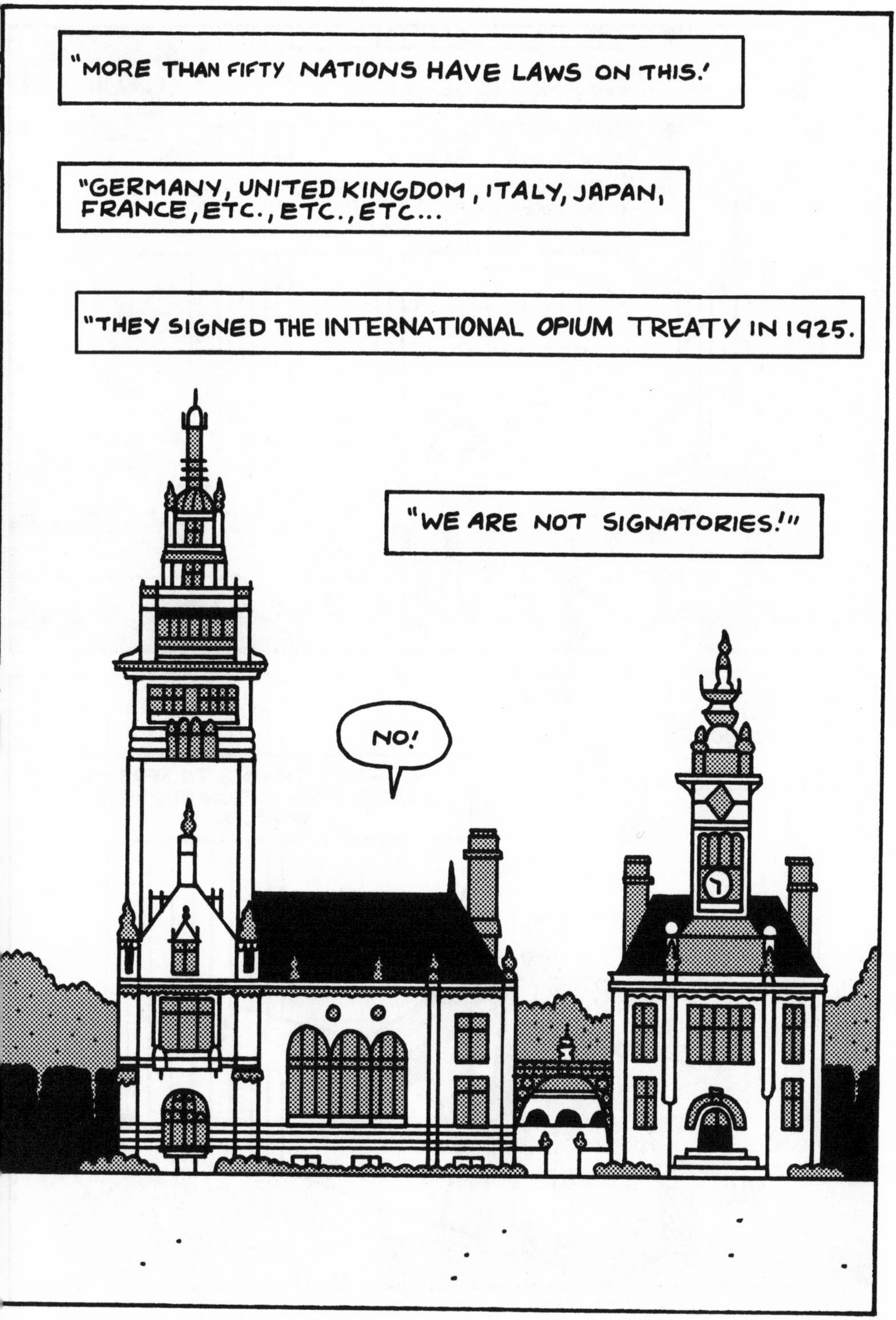
"MORE THAN FIFTY NATIONS HAVE LAWS ON THIS.'
"GERMANY, UNITED KINGDOM, ITALY, JAPAN, FRANCE, ETC., ETC., ETC...
"THEY SIGNED THE INTERNATIONAL OPIUM TREATY IN 1925.
"WE ARE NOT SIGNATORIES!"
NO!

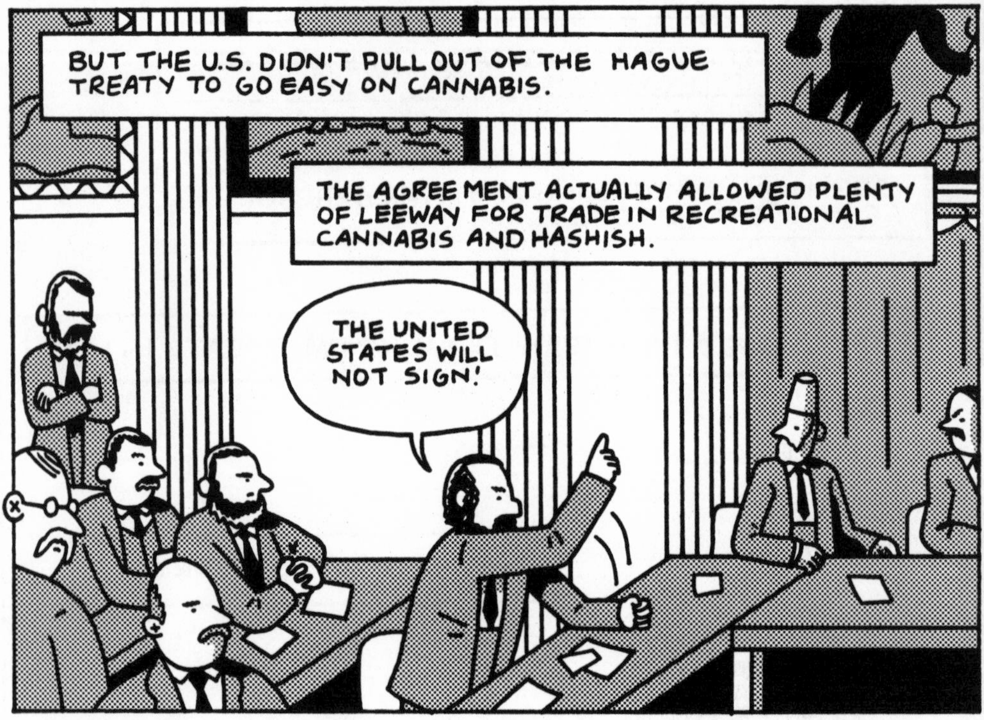
BUT THE U.S. DIDN'T PULL OUT OF THE HAGUE TREATY TO GO EASY ON CANNABIS.
THE AGREEMENT ACTUALLY ALLOWED PLENTY OF LEEWAY FOR TRADE IN RECREATIONAL CANNABIS AND HASHISH.
THE UNITED STATES WILL NOT SIGN!

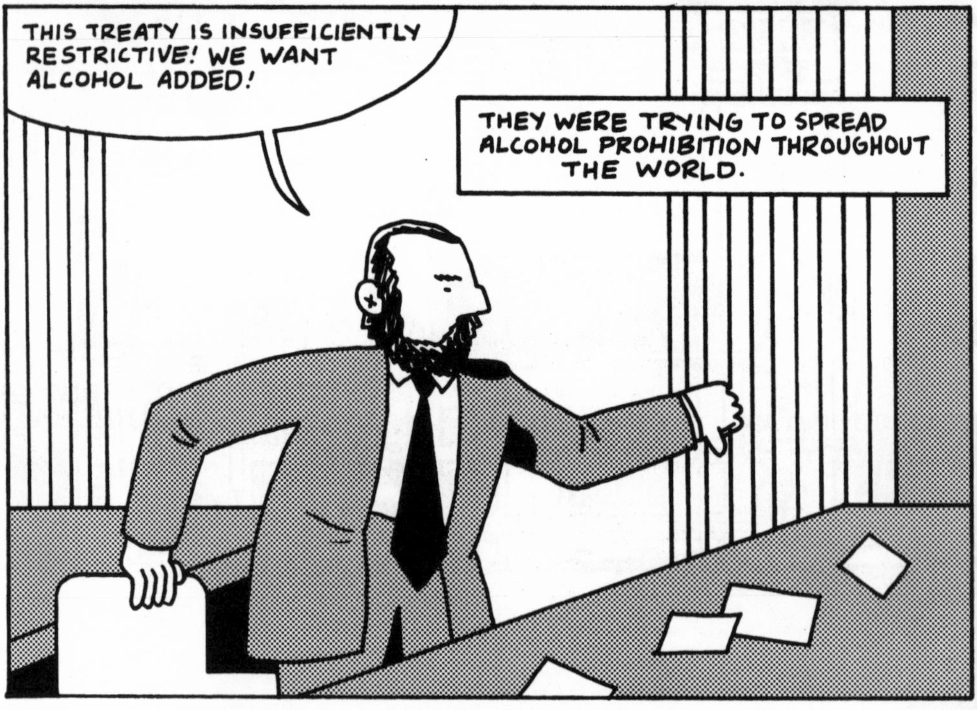
THIS TREATY IS INSUFFICIENTLY RESTRICTIVE! WE WANT ALCOHOL ADDED!
THEY WERE TRYING TO SPREAD ALCOHOL PROHIBITION THROUGHOUT THE WORLD.

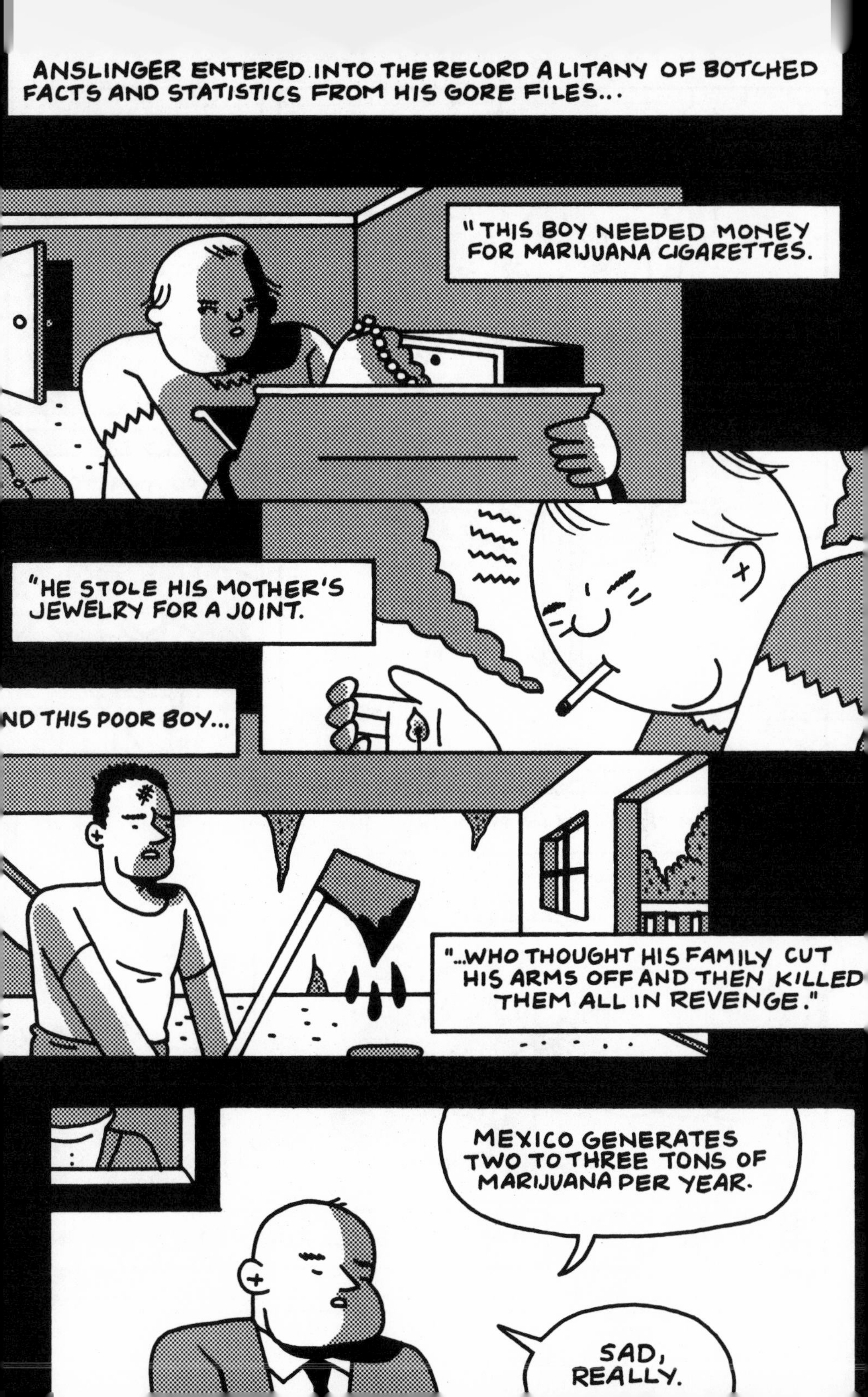
ANSLINGER ENTERED INTO THE RECORD A LITANY OF BOTCHED FACTS AND STATISTICS FROM HIS GORE FILES...
"THIS BOY NEEDED MONEY FOR MARIJUANA CIGARETTES.
"HE STOLE HIS MOTHER'S JEWELRY FOR A JOINT.
ND THIS POOR BOY...
"...WHO THOUGHT HIS FAMILY CUT HIS ARMS OFF AND THEN KILLED THEM ALL IN REVENGE."
MEXICO GENERATES TWO TO THREE TONS OF MARIJUANA PER YEAR.
SAD, REALLY.

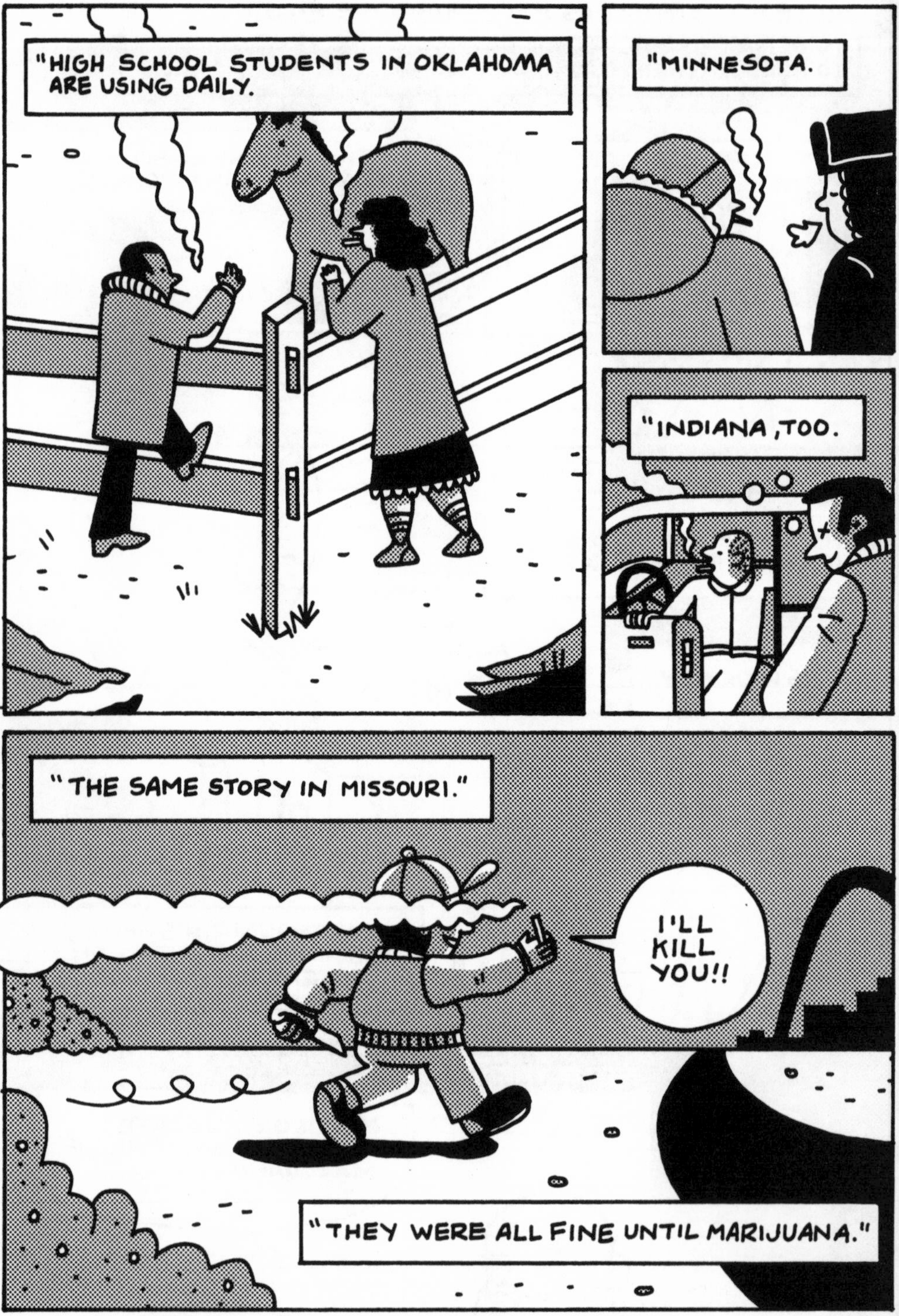
"HIGH SCHOOL STUDENTS IN OKLAHOMA ARE USING DAILY.
"MINNESOTA.
"INDIANA, TOO.
"THE SAME STORY IN MISSOURI."
I'LL KILL YOU!!
"THEY WERE ALL FINE UNTIL MARIJUANA."

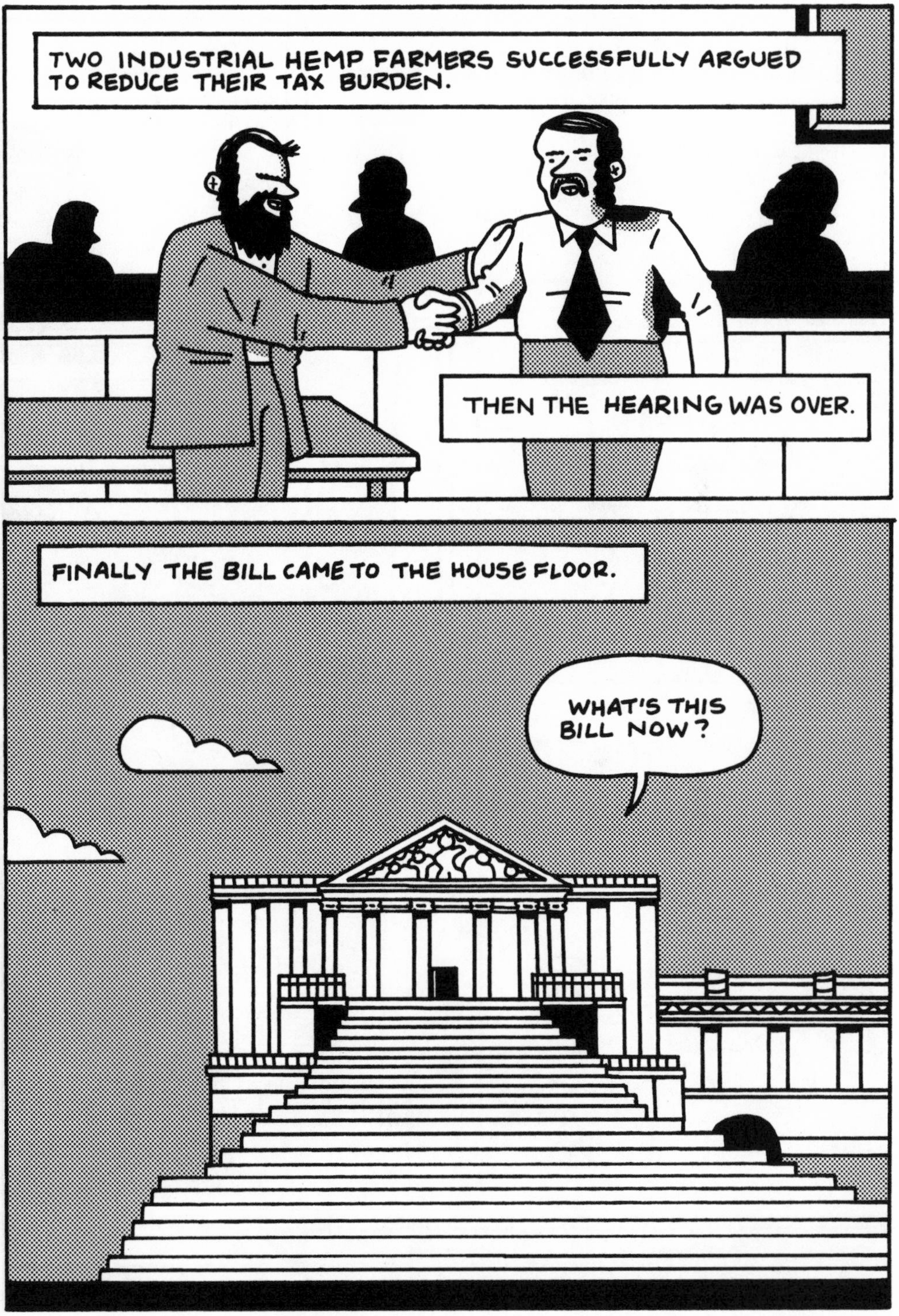
TWO INDUSTRIAL HEMP FARMERS SUCCESSFULLY ARGUED TO REDUCE THEIR TAX BURDEN.
THEN THE HEARING WAS OVER.
FINALLY THE BILL CAME TO THE HOUSE FLOOR.
WHAT'S THIS BILL NOW?

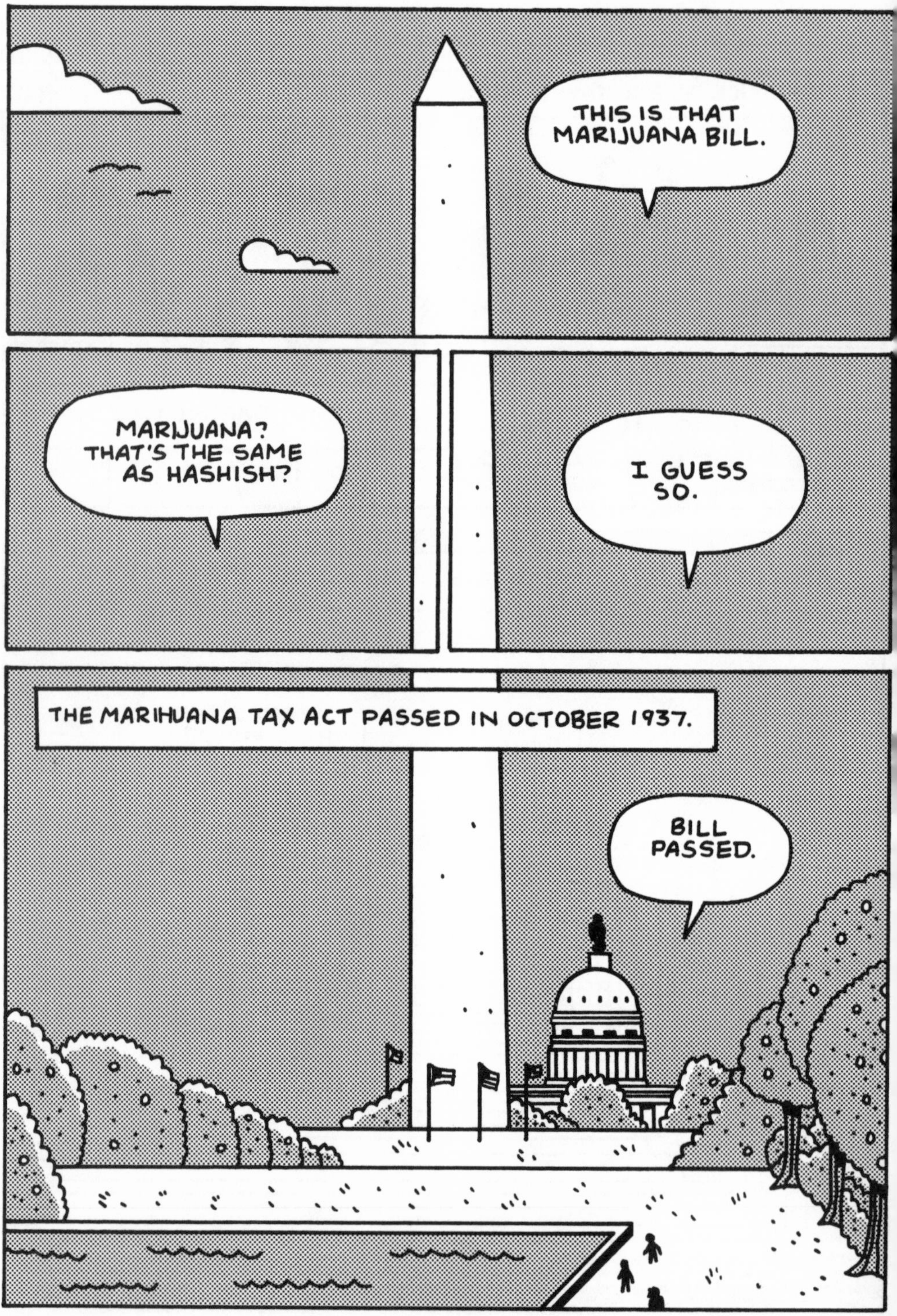
THIS IS THAT MARIJUANA BILL.
MARIJUANA? THAT'S THE SAME AS HASHISH?
I GUESS SO.
THE MARIHUANA TAX ACT PASSED IN OCTOBER 1937.
BILL PASSED.

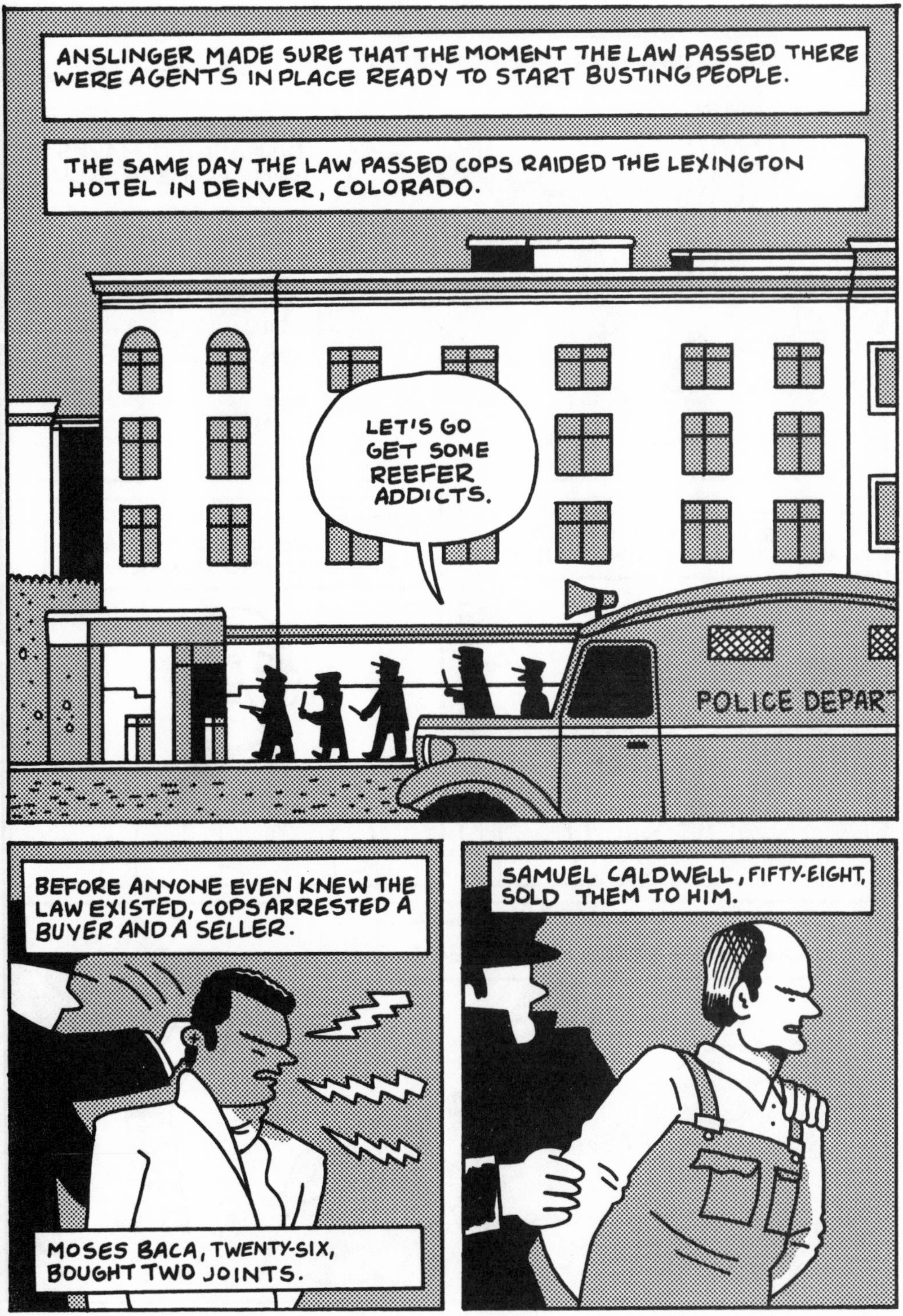
ANSLINGER MADE SURE THAT THE MOMENT THE LAW PASSED THERE WERE AGENTS IN PLACE READY TO START BUSTING PEOPLE.
THE SAME DAY THE LAW PASSED COPS RAIDED THE LEXINGTON HOTEL IN DENVER, COLORADO.
LET'S GO GET SOME REEFER ADDICTS.
POLICE DEPART
BEFORE ANYONE EVEN KNEW THE LAW EXISTED, COPS ARRESTED A BUYER AND A SELLER.
MOSES BACA, TWENTY-SIX, BOUGHT TWO JOINTS.
SAMUEL CALDWELL, FIFTY-EIGHT, SOLD THEM TO HIM.

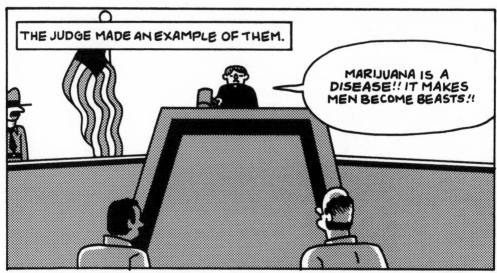

THE JUDGE MADE AN EXAMPLE OF THEM.

MARIJUANA IS A DISEASE!! IT MAKES MEN BECOME BEASTS!!

BACA RECEIVED 18 MONTHS IN JAIL FOR BUYING TWO JOINTS.

CALDWELL RECEIVED A ONE THOUSAND DOLLAR FINE...

...AND FOUR YEARS HARD LABOR.

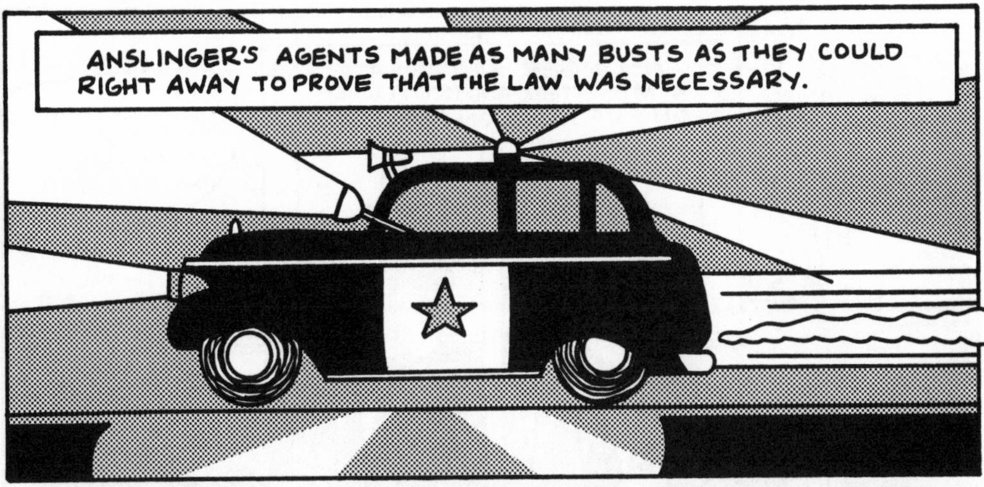
ANSLINGER'S AGENTS MADE AS MANY BUSTS AS THEY COULD RIGHT AWAY TO PROVE THAT THE LAW WAS NECESSARY.

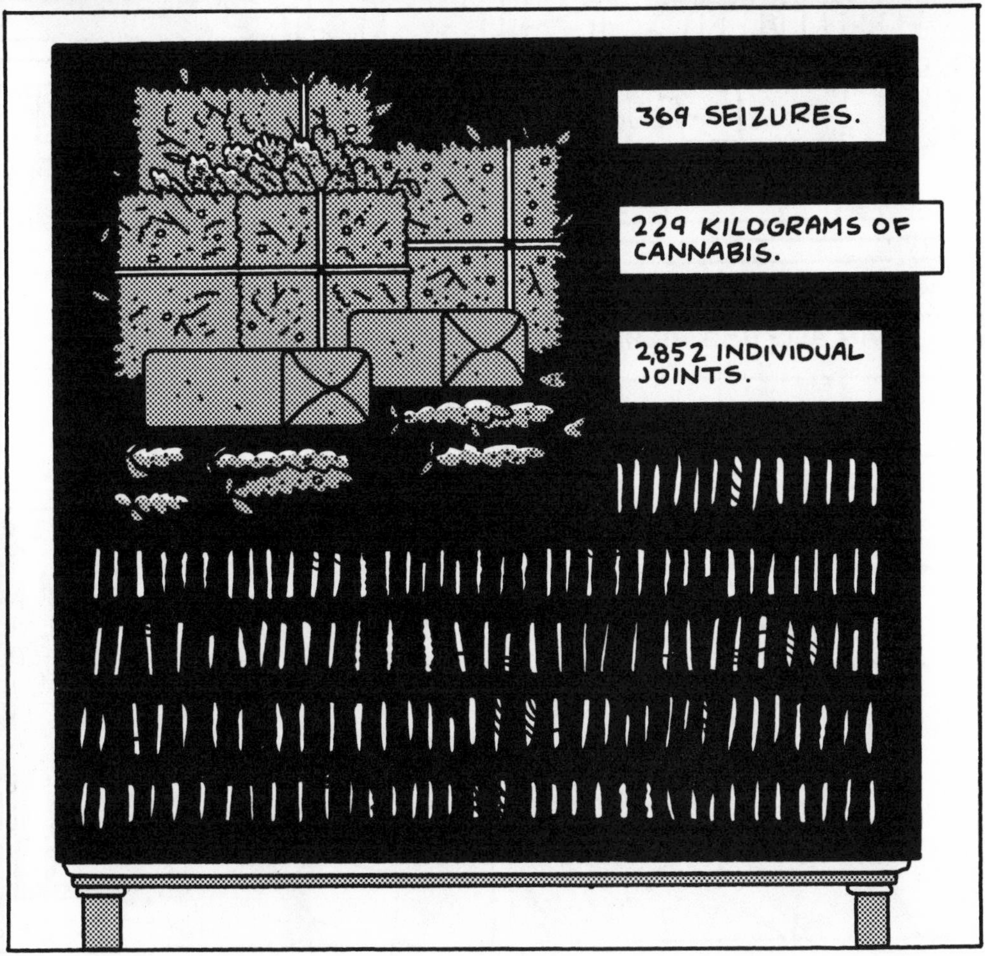
369 SEIZURES.
229 KILOGRAMS OF CANNABIS.
2,852 INDIVIDUAL JOINTS.

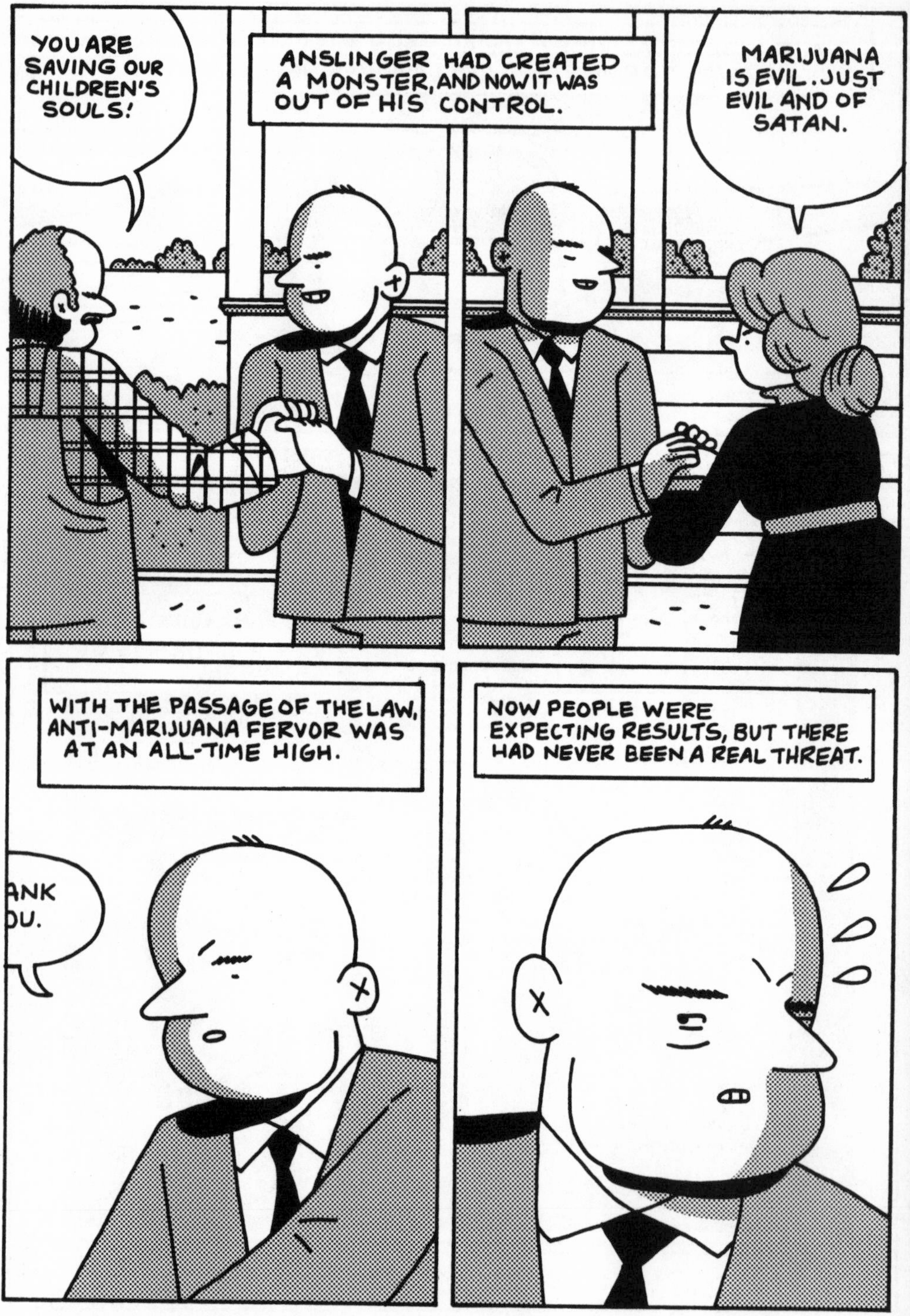
YOU ARE SAVING OUR CHILDREN'S SOULS!
ANSLINGER HAD CREATED A MONSTER, AND NOW IT WAS OUT OF HIS CONTROL.
MARIJUANA IS EVIL. JUST EVIL AND OF SATAN.
WITH THE PASSAGE OF THE LAW, ANTI-MARIJUANA FERVOR WAS AT AN ALL-TIME HIGH.
ANK
OU.
NOW PEOPLE WERE EXPECTING RESULTS, BUT THERE HAD NEVER BEEN A REAL THREAT.

RELIGIOUS GROUPS BEGAN CREATING THEIR OWN ANTI-CANNABIS LITERATURE AT A RAPID PACE, DESPITE ANSLINGER'S WISHES TO NOW COOL THE PUBLIC'S FEARS OF THE MARIJUANA MENACE.

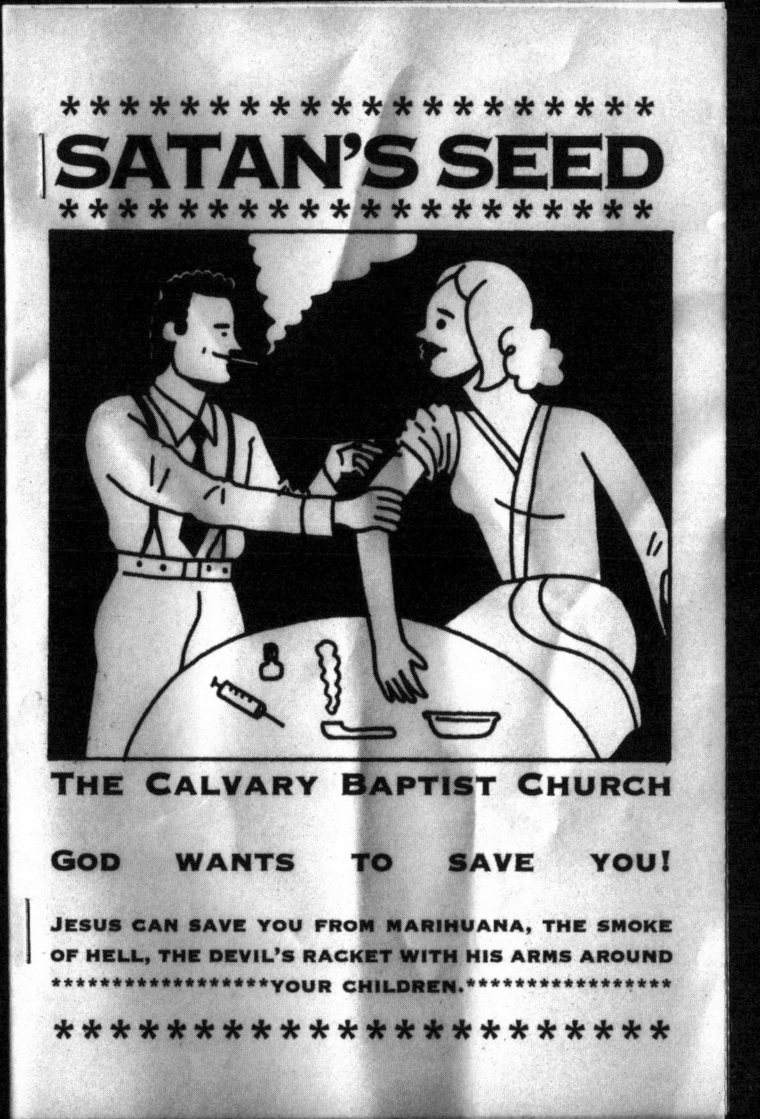

SATAN'S SEED
THE CALVARY BAPTIST CHURCH
GOD WANTS TO SAVE YOU!
JESUS CAN SAVE YOU FROM MARIHUANA, THE SMOKE OF HELL, THE DEVIL'S RACKET WITH HIS ARMS AROUND YOUR CHILDREN.

ONE CHURCH GROUP FINANCED A FILM FOR PARENTS THAT PORTRAYED THE TERRIBLE ILLS OF MARIJUANA.

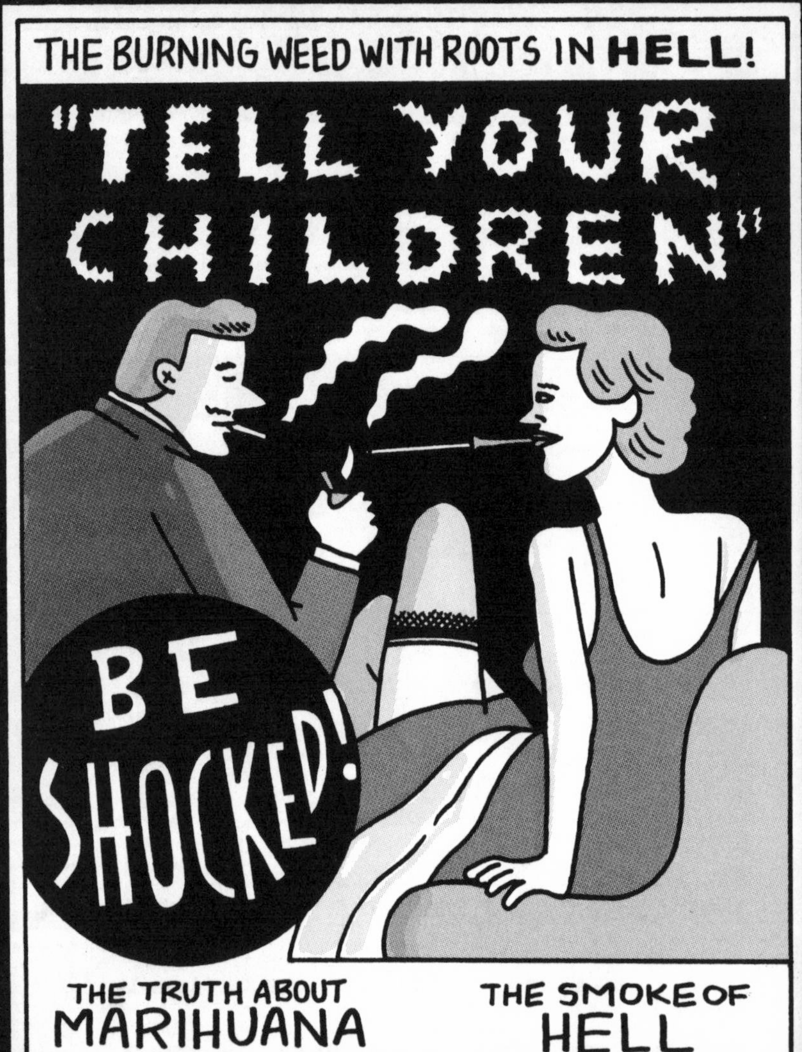
THE BURNING WEED WITH ROOTS IN HELL!
"TELL YOUR CHILDREN"
BE SHOCKED!
THE TRUTH ABOUT MARIHUANA
THE SMOKE OF HELL

IT WAS SHOWN UNDER MANY DIFFERENT TITLES, INCLUDING "THE BURNING QUESTION," "DOPED YOUTH," AND "REEFER MADNESS."

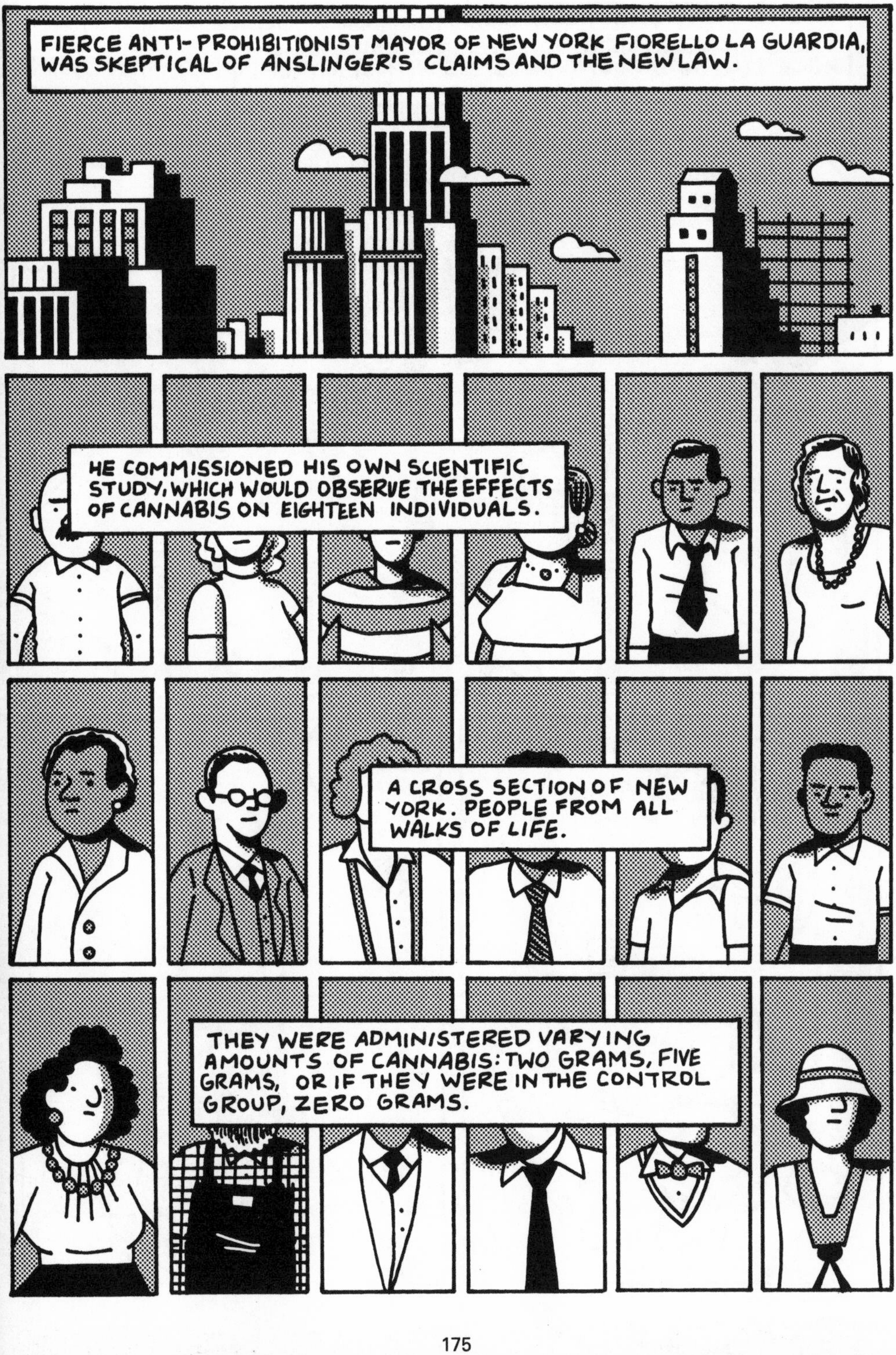

FIERCE ANTI-PROHIBITIONIST MAYOR OF NEW YORK FIORELLO LA GUARDIA, WAS SKEPTICAL OF ANSLINGER'S CLAIMS AND THE NEW LAW.
HE COMMISSIONED HIS OWN SCIENTIFIC STUDY, WHICH WOULD OBSERVE THE EFFECTS OF CANNABIS ON EIGHTEEN INDIVIDUALS.
A CROSS SECTION OF NEW YORK. PEOPLE FROM ALL WALKS OF LIFE.
THEY WERE ADMINISTERED VARYING AMOUNTS OF CANNABIS: TWO GRAMS, FIVE GRAMS, OR IF THEY WERE IN THE CONTROL GROUP, ZERO GRAMS.

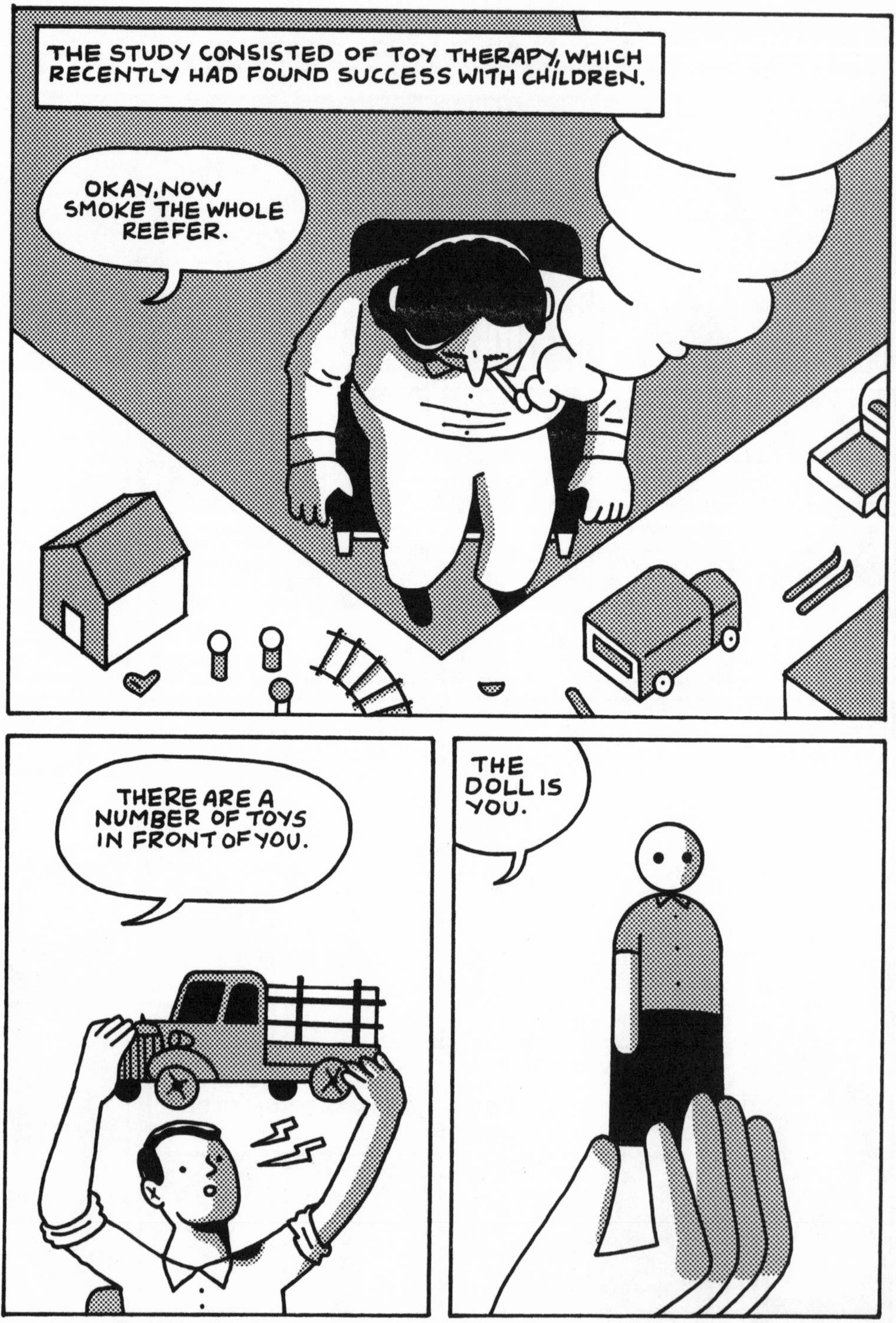
THE STUDY CONSISTED OF TOY THERAPY, WHICH RECENTLY HAD FOUND SUCCESS WITH CHILDREN.
OKAY, NOW SMOKE THE WHOLE REEFER.
THERE ARE A NUMBER OF TOYS IN FRONT OF YOU.
THE DOLL IS YOU.

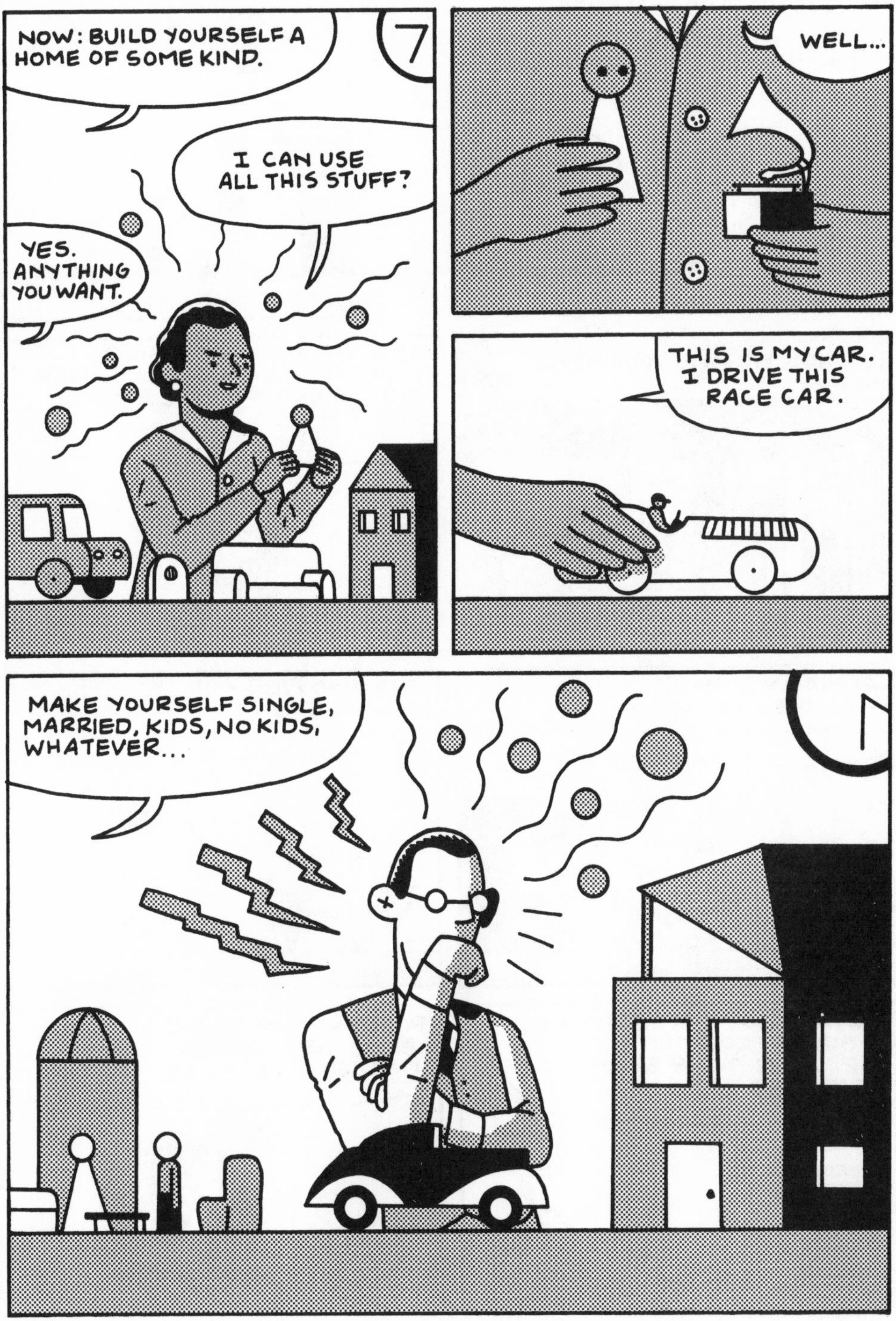
NOW: BUILD YOURSELF A HOME OF SOME KIND.
7
I CAN USE ALL THIS STUFF?
YES. ANYTHING YOU WANT.
WELL...
THIS IS MY CAR. I DRIVE THIS RACE CAR.
MAKE YOURSELF SINGLE, MARRIED, KIDS, NO KIDS, WHATEVER...

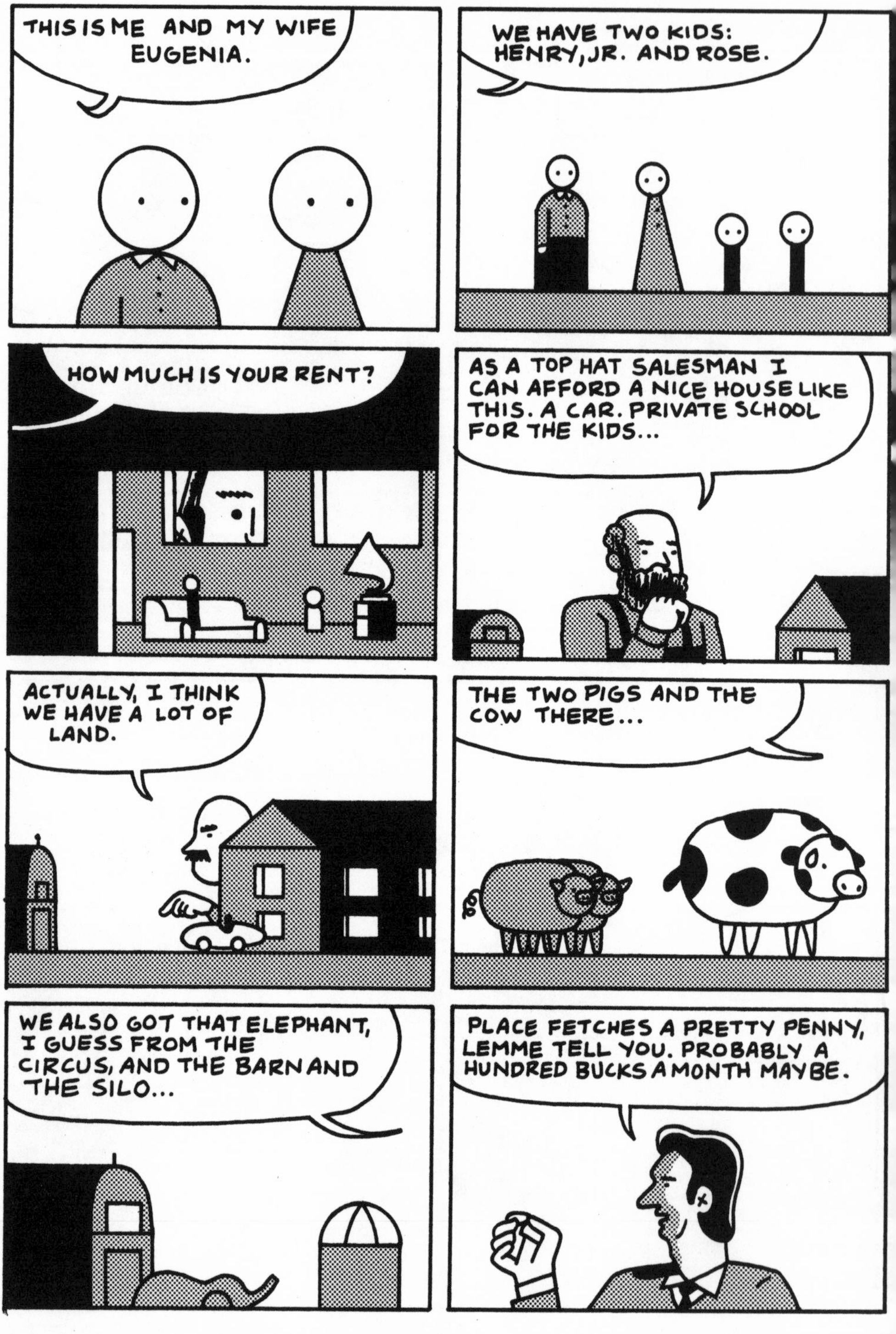
THIS IS ME AND MY WIFE EUGENIA.
WE HAVE TWO KIDS: HENRY, JR. AND ROSE.
HOW MUCH IS YOUR RENT?
AS A TOP HAT SALESMAN I CAN AFFORD A NICE HOUSE LIKE THIS. A CAR. PRIVATE SCHOOL FOR THE KIDS...
ACTUALLY, I THINK WE HAVE A LOT OF LAND.
THE TWO PIGS AND THE COW THERE...
WE ALSO GOT THAT ELEPHANT, I GUESS FROM THE CIRCUS, AND THE BARN AND THE SILO...
PLACE FETCHES A PRETTY PENNY, LEMME TELL YOU. PROBABLY A HUNDRED BUCKS A MONTH MAYBE.

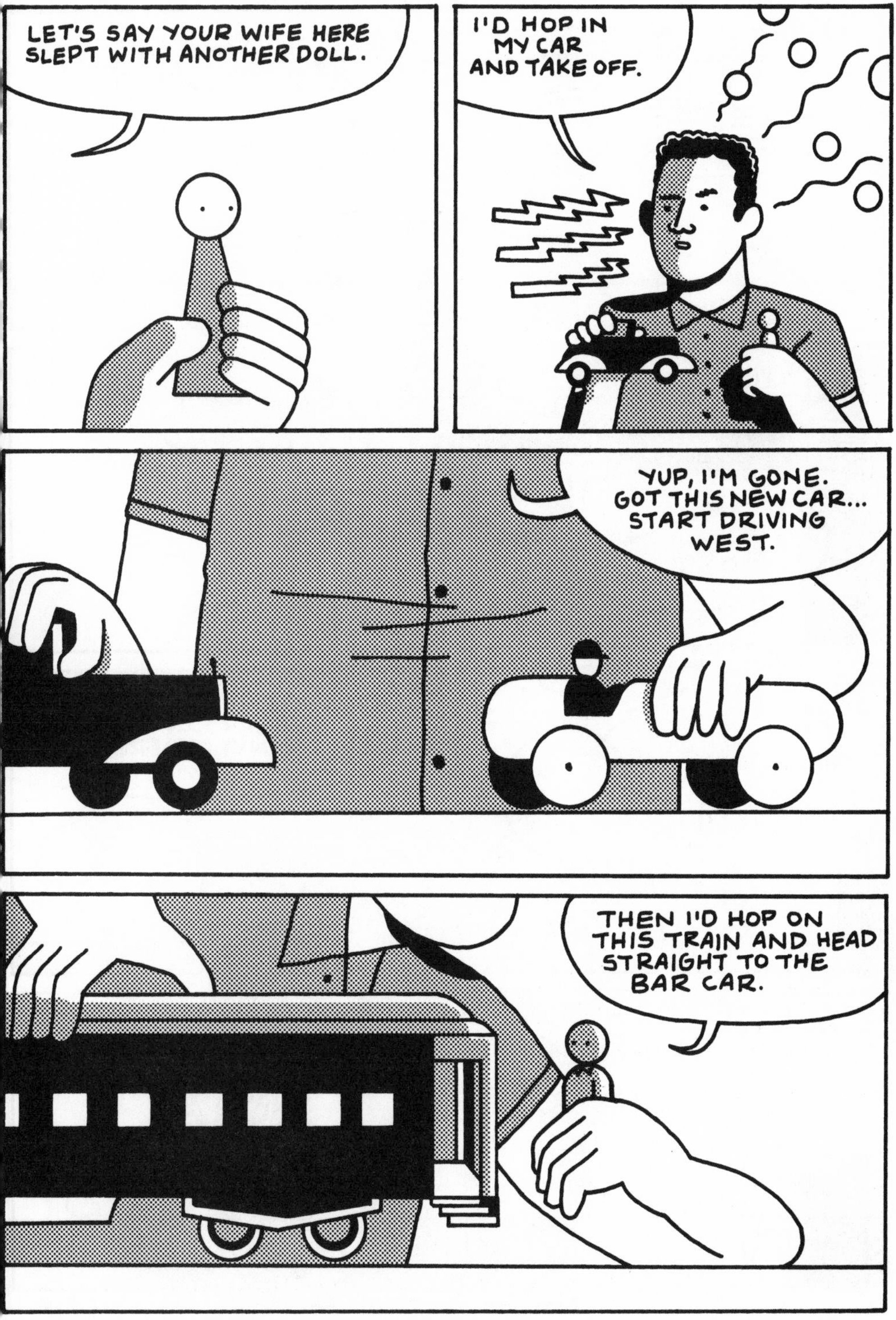
LET'S SAY YOUR WIFE HERE SLEPT WITH ANOTHER DOLL.
I'D HOP IN MY CAR AND TAKE OFF.
YUP, I'M GONE. GOT THIS NEW CAR... START DRIVING WEST.
THEN I'D HOP ON THIS TRAIN AND HEAD STRAIGHT TO THE BAR CAR.

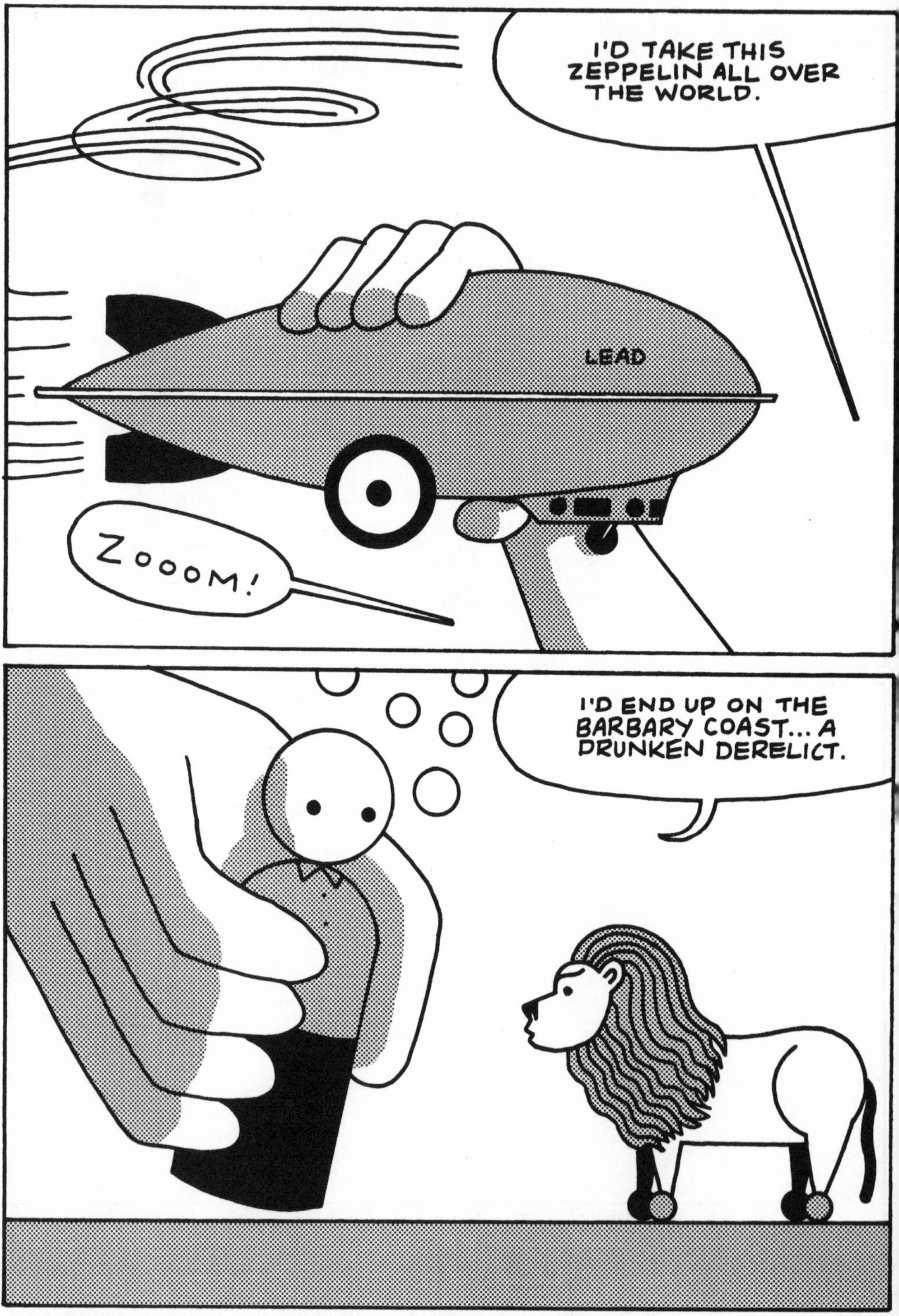
I'D TAKE THIS ZEPPELIN ALL OVER THE WORLD.
LEAD
ZOOOM!
I'D END UP ON THE BARBARY COAST... A DRUNKEN DERELICT.

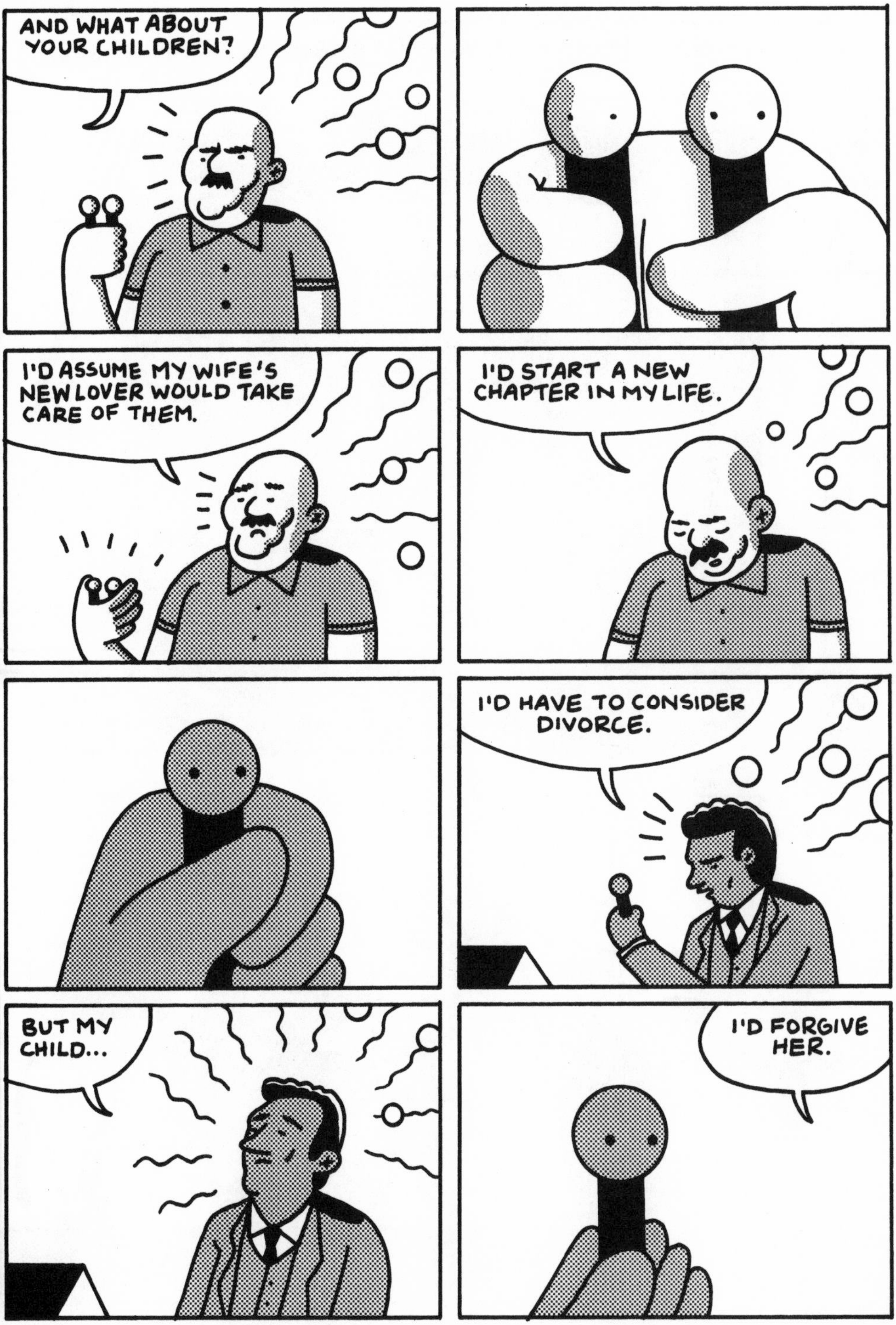
AND WHAT ABOUT YOUR CHILDREN?
I'D ASSUME MY WIFE'S NEW LOVER WOULD TAKE CARE OF THEM.
I'D START A NEW CHAPTER IN MY LIFE.
I'D HAVE TO CONSIDER DIVORCE.
BUT MY CHILD...
I'D FORGIVE HER.

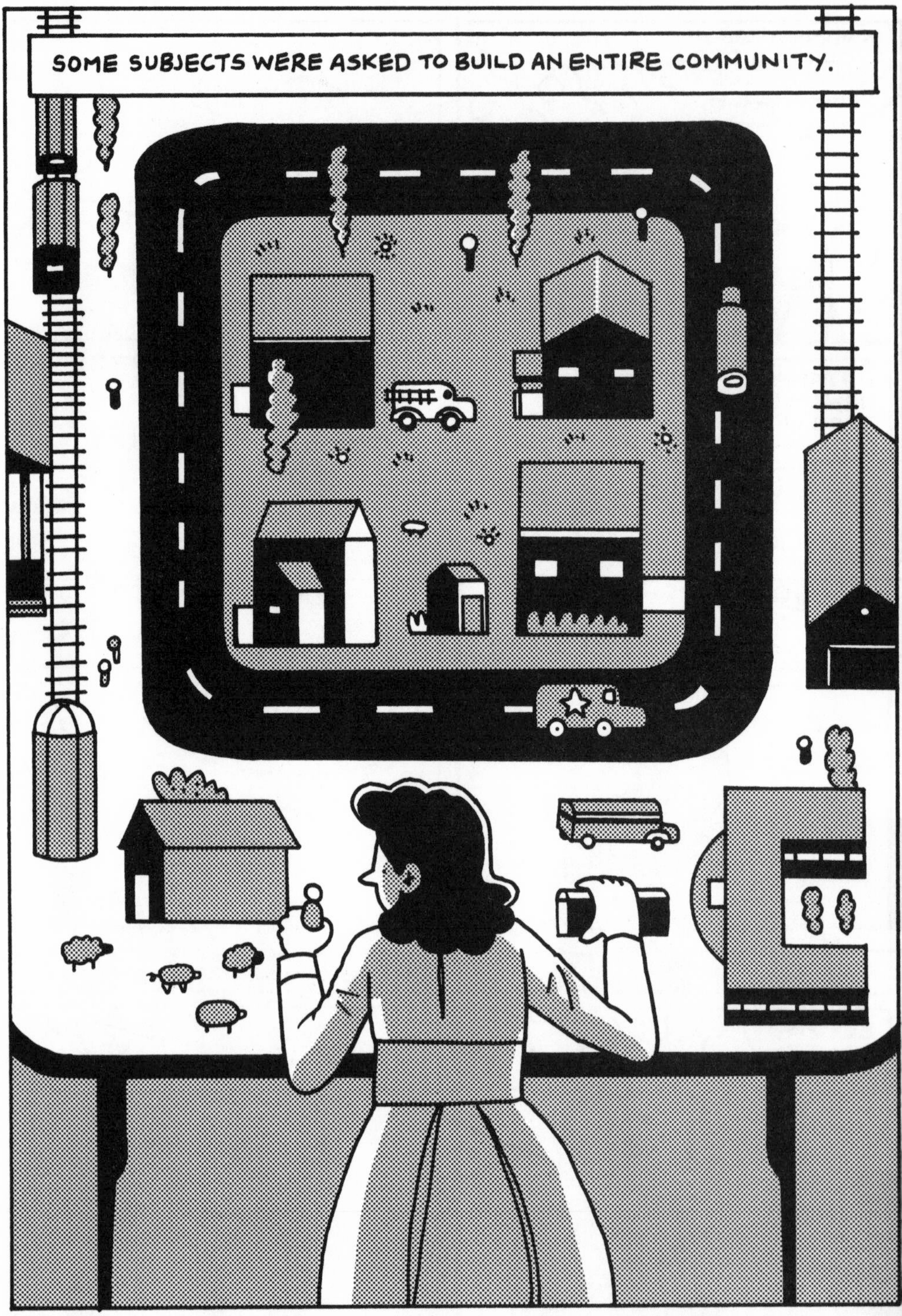
SOME SUBJECTS WERE ASKED TO BUILD AN ENTIRE COMMUNITY.

NOW PICTURE THIS: SOMEONE IN THIS HOUSE NEEDS THE AMBULANCE.

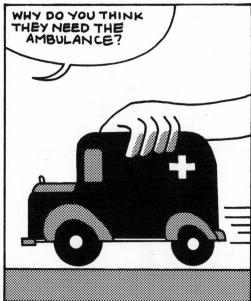

WHY DO YOU THINK THEY NEED THE AMBULANCE?

PROBABLY AN ACCIDENT.

SOMEONE WAS FAKING IT.

JUST A HYPOCHONDRIAC.

JUST SOMEONE PRETENDING TO BE SICK AGAIN.

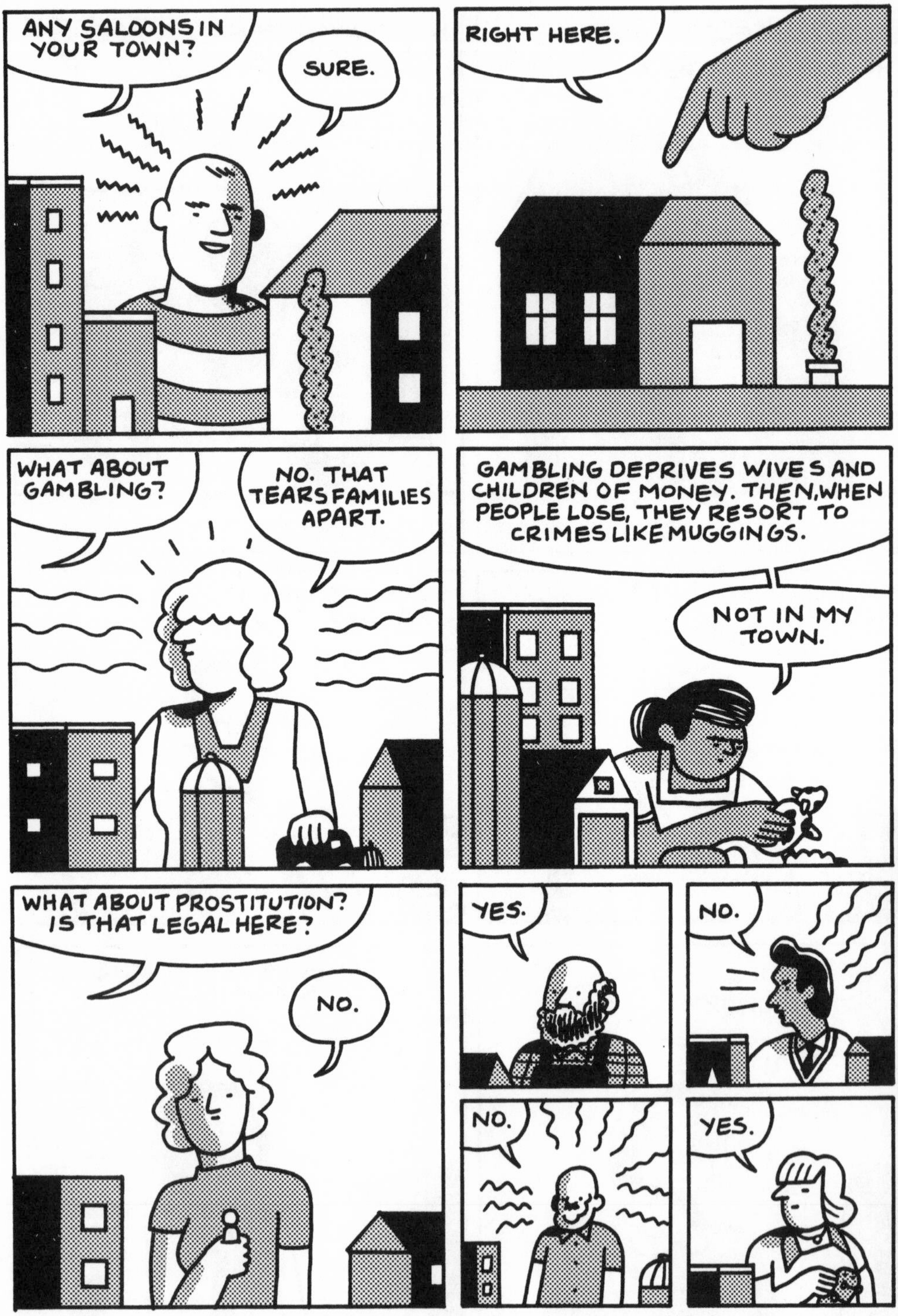
ANY SALOONS IN YOUR TOWN?
SURE.
RIGHT HERE.
WHAT ABOUT GAMBLING?
NO. THAT TEARS FAMILIES APART.
GAMBLING DEPRIVES WIVES AND CHILDREN OF MONEY. THEN, WHEN PEOPLE LOSE, THEY RESORT TO CRIMES LIKE MUGGINGS.
NOT IN MY TOWN.
WHAT ABOUT PROSTITUTION? IS THAT LEGAL HERE?
NO.
YES.
NO.
NO.
YES.

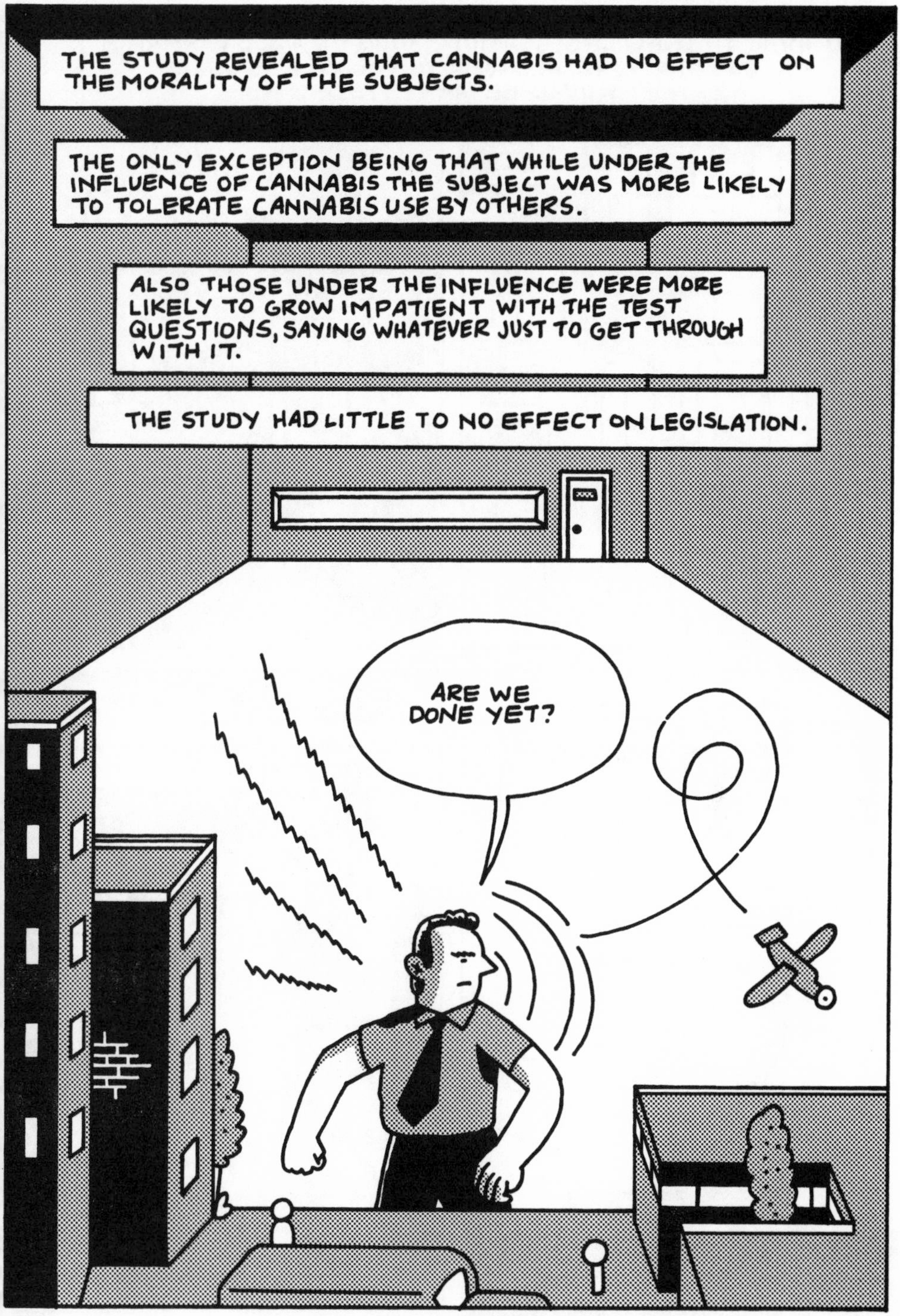
THE STUDY REVEALED THAT CANNABIS HAD NO EFFECT ON THE MORALITY OF THE SUBJECTS.
THE ONLY EXCEPTION BEING THAT WHILE UNDER THE INFLUENCE OF CANNABIS THE SUBJECT WAS MORE LIKELY TO TOLERATE CANNABIS USE BY OTHERS.
ALSO THOSE UNDER THE INFLUENCE WERE MORE LIKELY TO GROW IMPATIENT WITH THE TEST QUESTIONS, SAYING WHATEVER JUST TO GET THROUGH WITH IT.
THE STUDY HAD LITTLE TO NO EFFECT ON LEGISLATION.
ARE WE DONE YET?

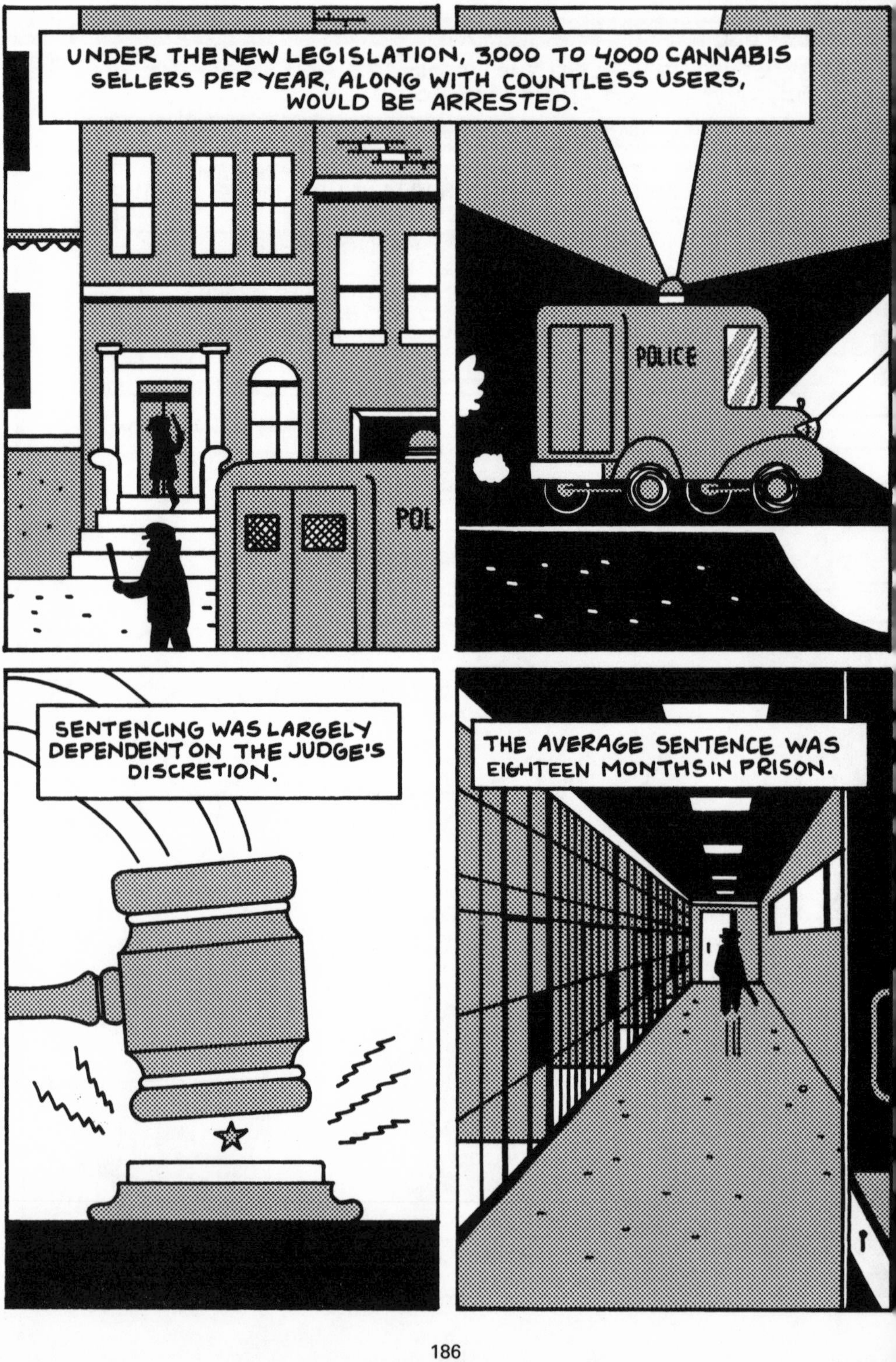
UNDER THE NEW LEGISLATION, 3,000 TO 4,000 CANNABIS SELLERS PER YEAR, ALONG WITH COUNTLESS USERS, WOULD BE ARRESTED.
POL
POLICE
SENTENCING WAS LARGELY DEPENDENT ON THE JUDGE'S DISCRETION.
THE AVERAGE SENTENCE WAS EIGHTEEN MONTHS IN PRISON.

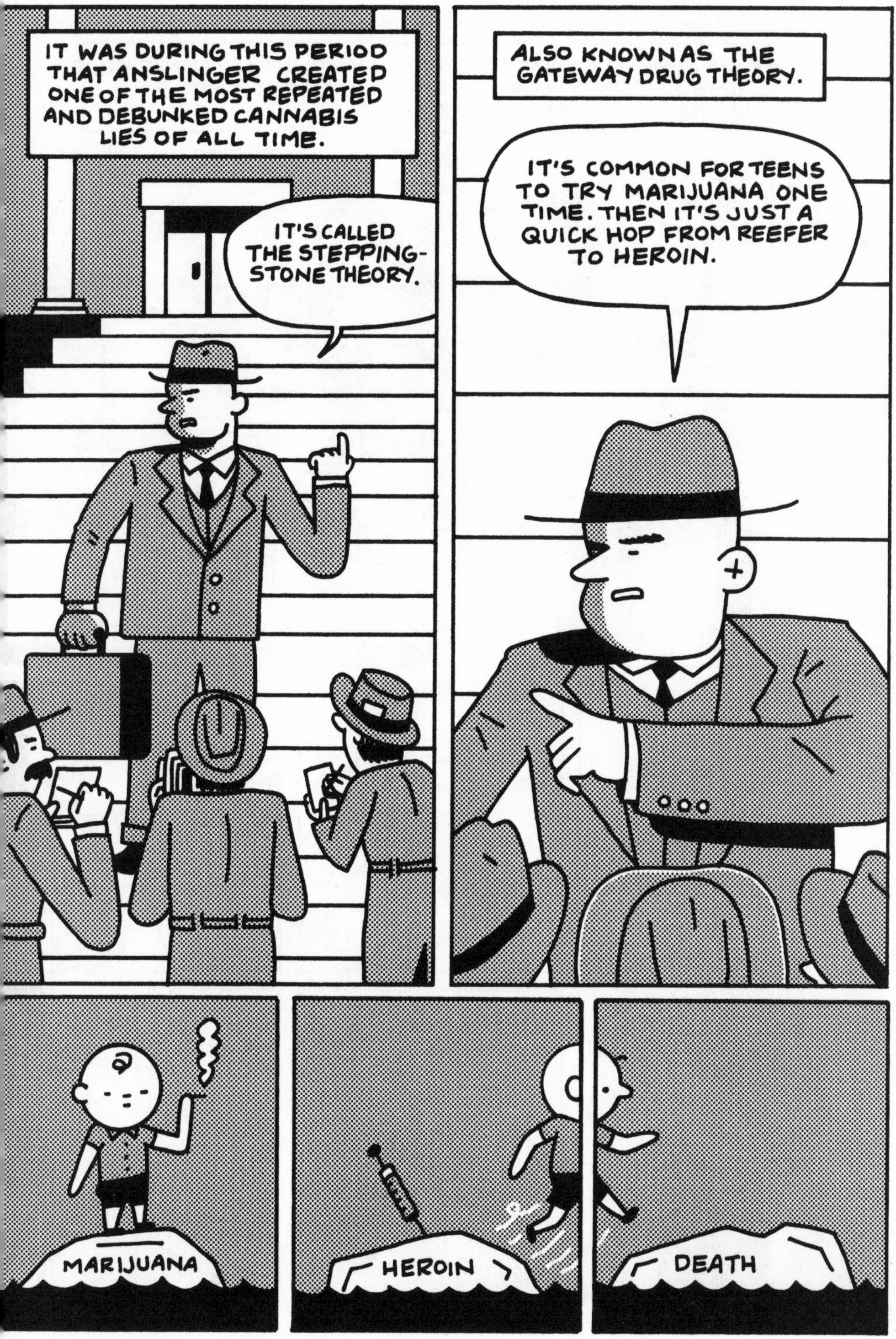
IT WAS DURING THIS PERIOD THAT ANSLINGER CREATED ONE OF THE MOST REPEATED AND DEBUNKED CANNABIS LIES OF ALL TIME.
IT'S CALLED THE STEPPING-STONE THEORY.
ALSO KNOWN AS THE GATEWAY DRUG THEORY.
IT'S COMMON FOR TEENS TO TRY MARIJUANA ONE TIME. THEN IT'S JUST A QUICK HOP FROM REEFER TO HEROIN.
MARIJUANA
HEROIN
DEATH

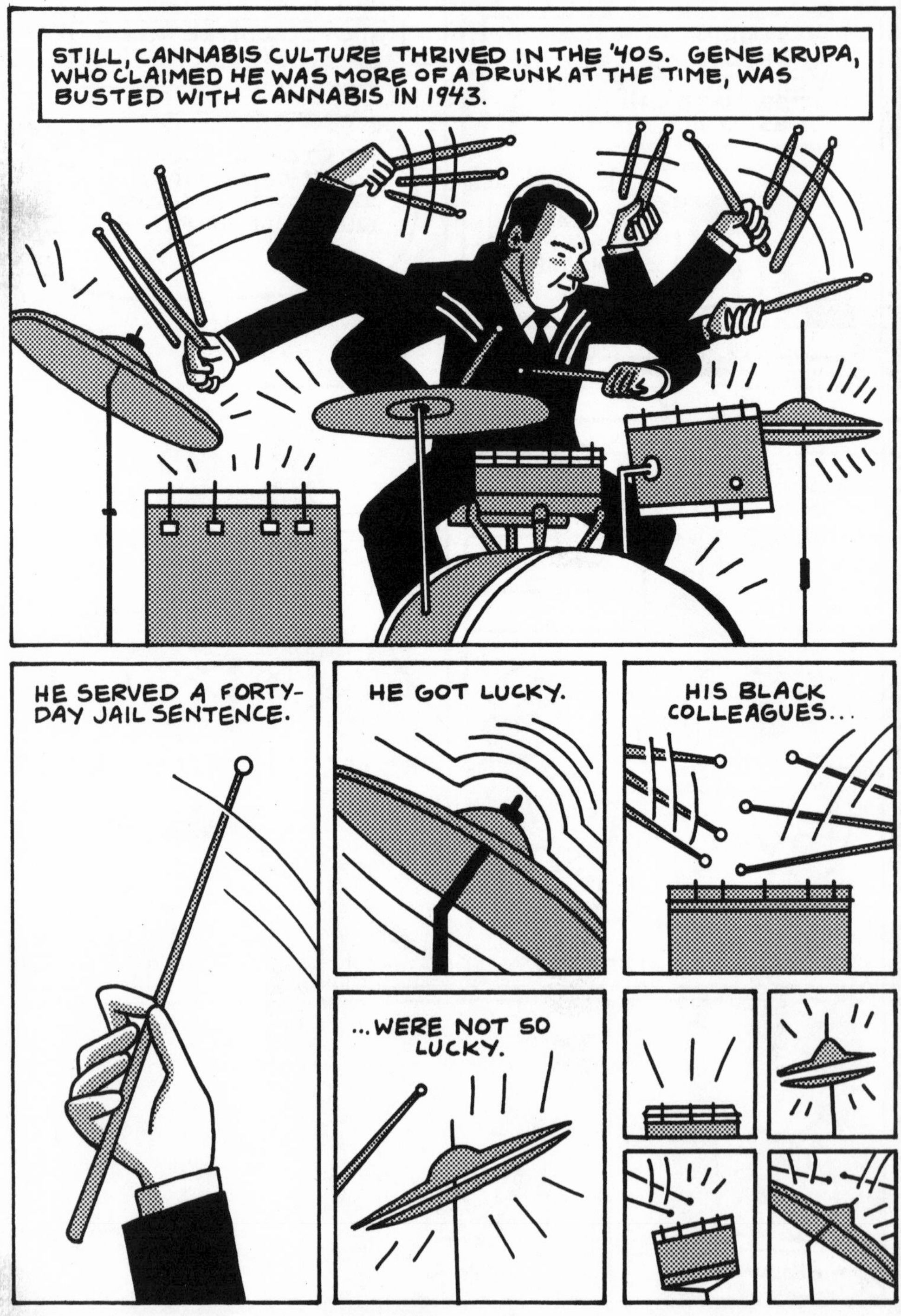
STILL, CANNABIS CULTURE THRIVED IN THE '40S. GENE KRUPA, WHO CLAIMED HE WAS MORE OF A DRUNK AT THE TIME, WAS BUSTED WITH CANNABIS IN 1943.
HE SERVED A FORTY-DAY JAIL SENTENCE.
HE GOT LUCKY.
HIS BLACK COLLEAGUES...
...WERE NOT SO LUCKY.

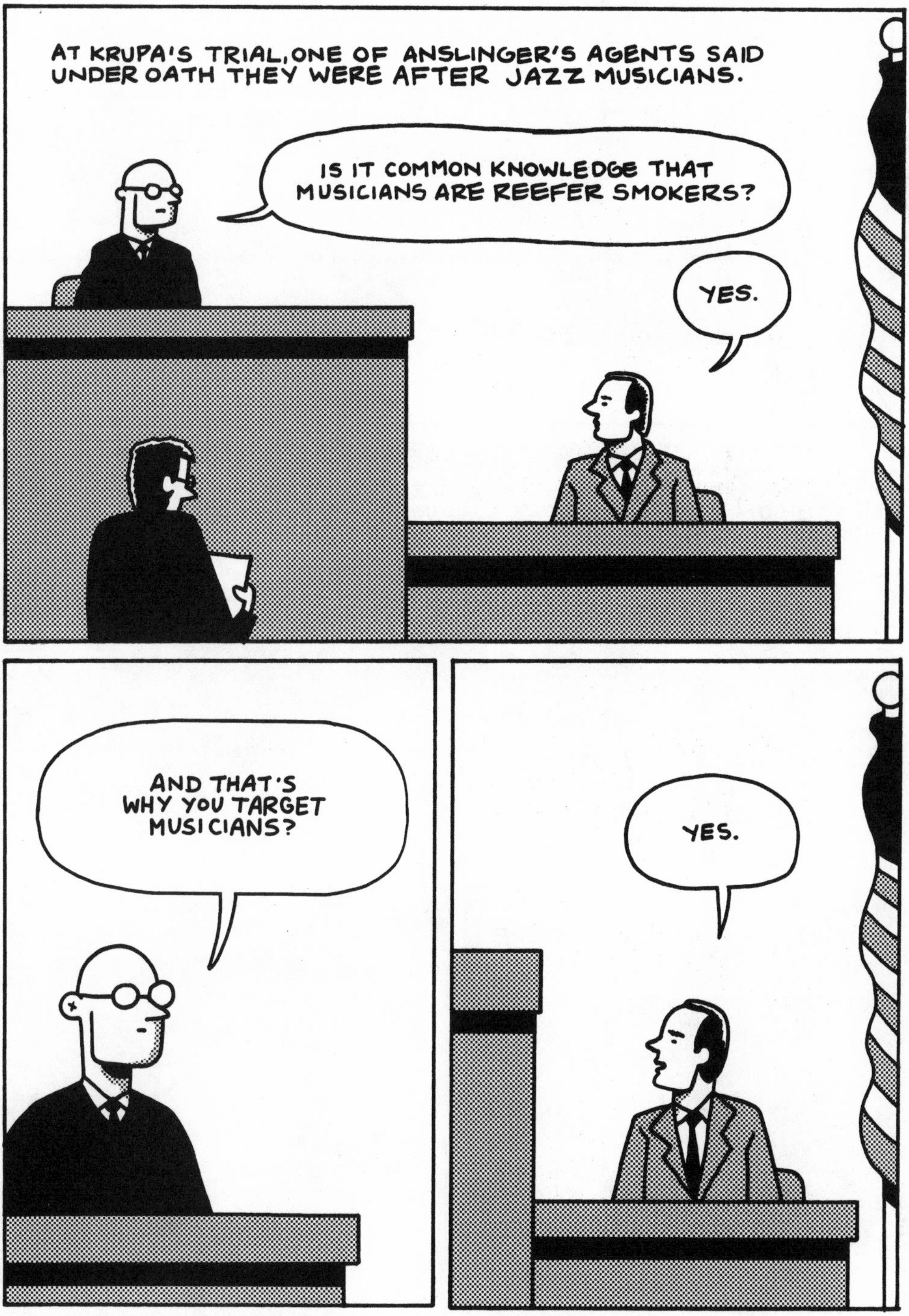
AT KRUPA'S TRIAL, ONE OF ANSLINGER'S AGENTS SAID UNDER OATH THEY WERE AFTER JAZZ MUSICIANS.
IS IT COMMON KNOWLEDGE THAT MUSICIANS ARE REEFER SMOKERS?
YES.
AND THAT'S WHY YOU TARGET MUSICIANS?
YES.

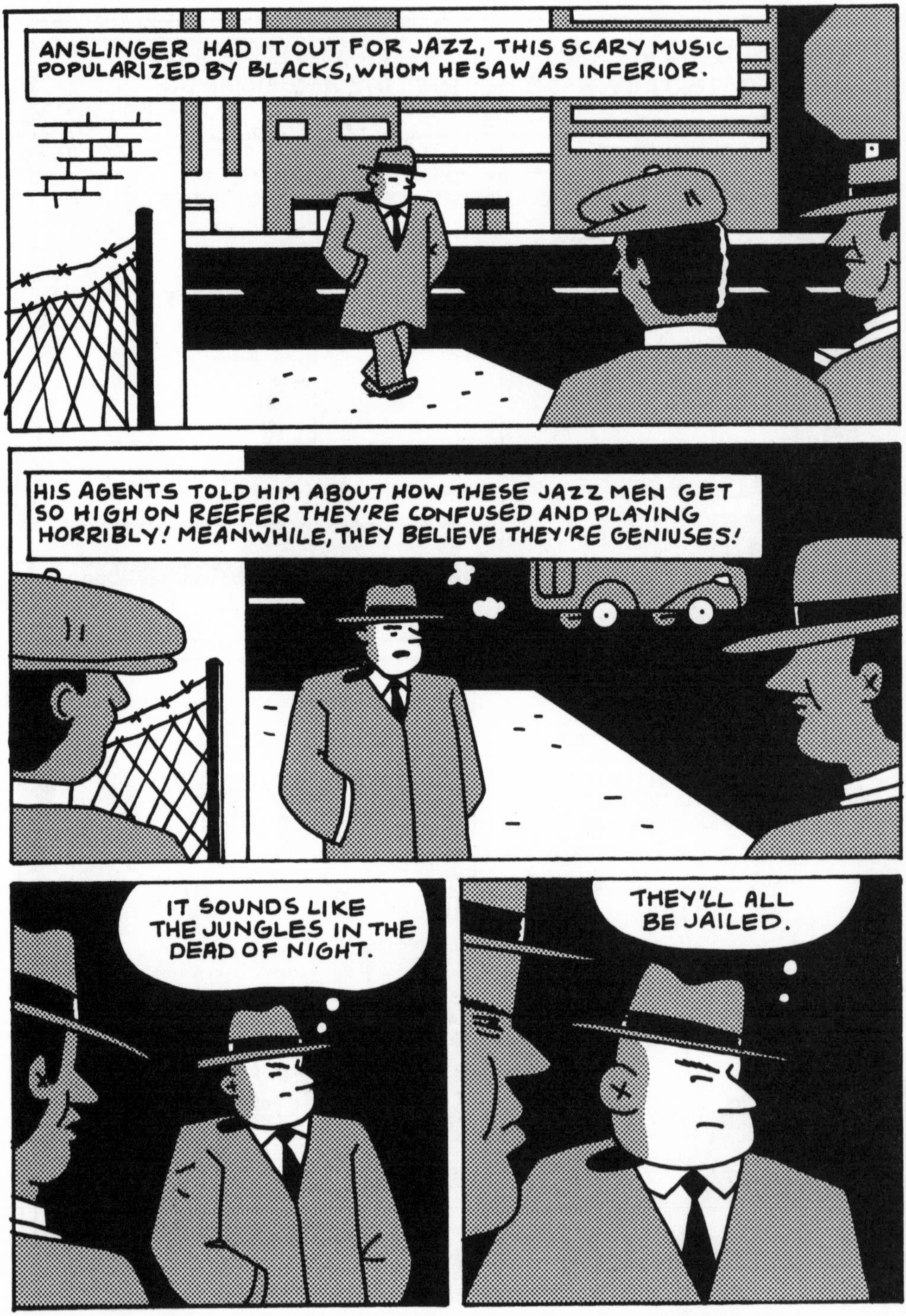

ANSLINGER HAD IT OUT FOR JAZZ, THIS SCARY MUSIC POPULARIZED BY BLACKS, WHOM HE SAW AS INFERIOR.
HIS AGENTS TOLD HIM ABOUT HOW THESE JAZZ MEN GET SO HIGH ON REEFER THEY'RE CONFUSED AND PLAYING HORRIBLY! MEANWHILE, THEY BELIEVE THEY'RE GENIUSES!
IT SOUNDS LIKE THE JUNGLES IN THE DEAD OF NIGHT.
THEY'LL ALL BE JAILED.

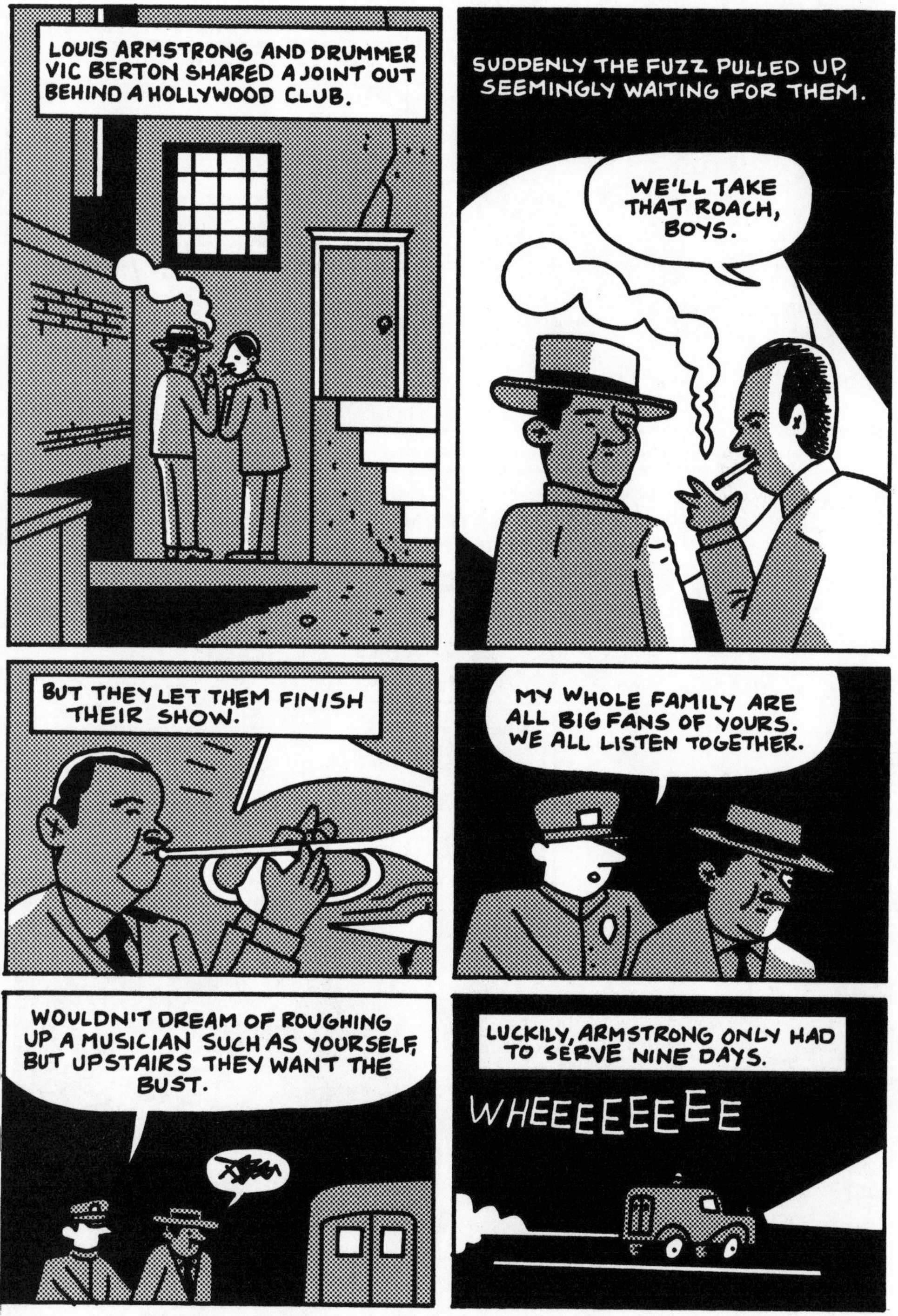
LOUIS ARMSTRONG AND DRUMMER VIC BERTON SHARED A JOINT OUT BEHIND A HOLLYWOOD CLUB.
SUDDENLY THE FUZZ PULLED UP, SEEMINGLY WAITING FOR THEM.
WE'LL TAKE THAT ROACH, BOYS.
BUT THEY LET THEM FINISH THEIR SHOW.
MY WHOLE FAMILY ARE ALL BIG FANS OF YOURS. WE ALL LISTEN TOGETHER.
WOULDN'T DREAM OF ROUGHING UP A MUSICIAN SUCH AS YOURSELF, BUT UPSTAIRS THEY WANT THE BUST.
LUCKILY, ARMSTRONG ONLY HAD TO SERVE NINE DAYS.
WHEEEEEEEE

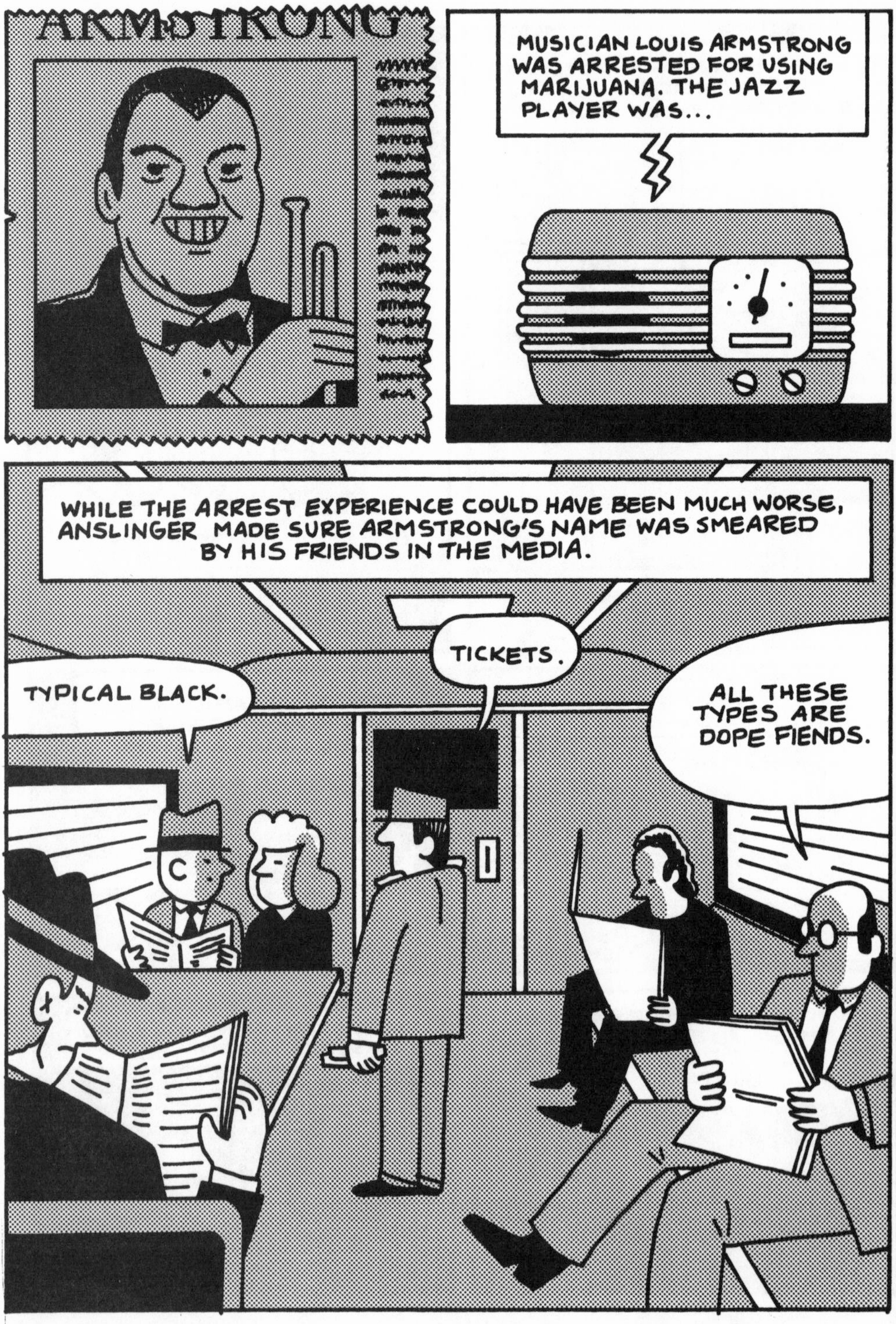
ARMSTRONG
MUSICIAN LOUIS ARMSTRONG WAS ARRESTED FOR USING MARIJUANA. THE JAZZ PLAYER WAS...
WHILE THE ARREST EXPERIENCE COULD HAVE BEEN MUCH WORSE, ANSLINGER MADE SURE ARMSTRONG'S NAME WAS SMEARED BY HIS FRIENDS IN THE MEDIA.
TYPICAL BLACK.
TICKETS.
ALL THESE TYPES ARE DOPE FIENDS.

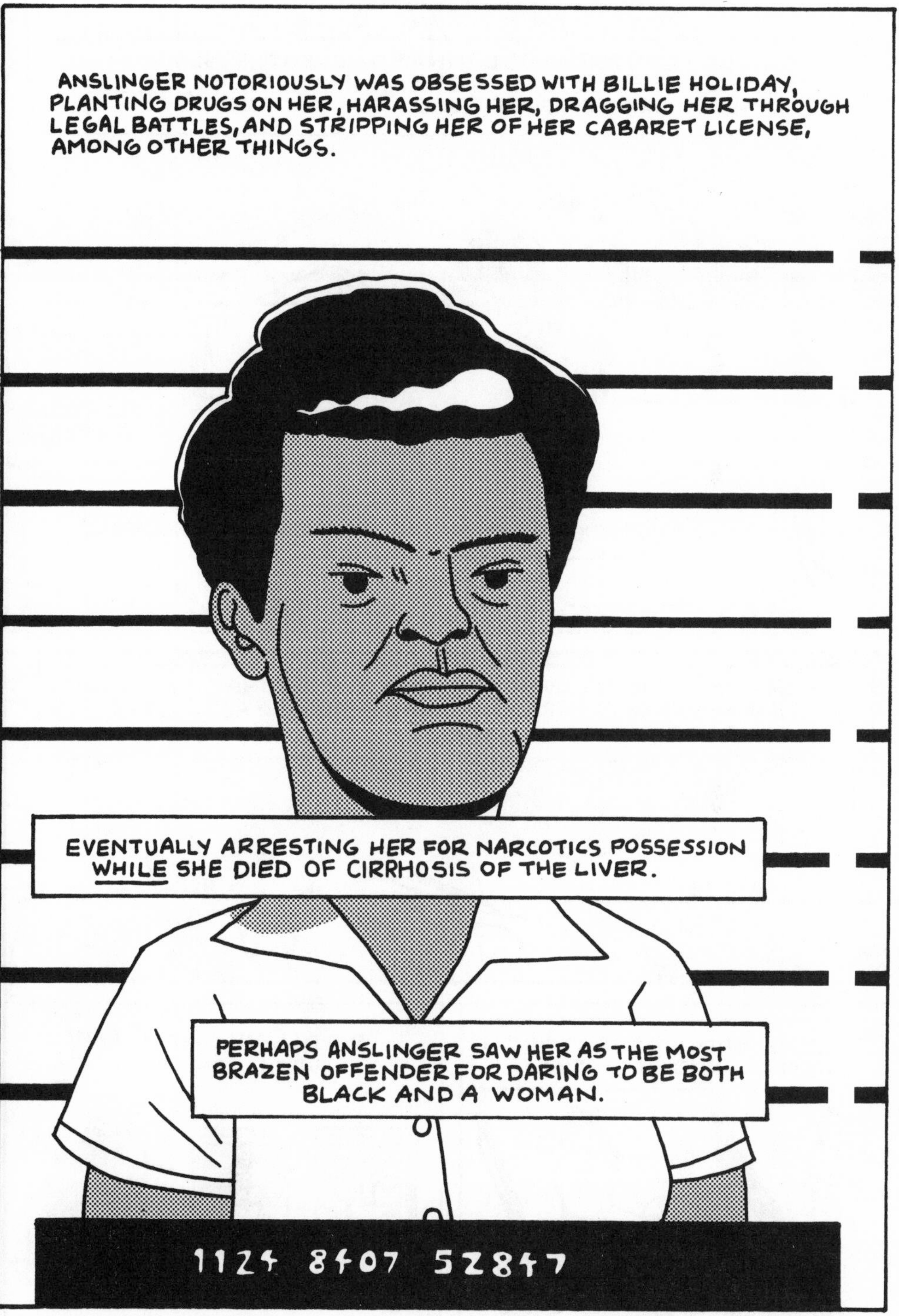
ANSLINGER NOTORIOUSLY WAS OBSESSED WITH BILLIE HOLIDAY, PLANTING DRUGS ON HER, HARASSING HER, DRAGGING HER THROUGH LEGAL BATTLES, AND STRIPPING HER OF HER CABARET LICENSE, AMONG OTHER THINGS.
EVENTUALLY ARRESTING HER FOR NARCOTICS POSSESSION WHILE SHE DIED OF CIRRHOSIS OF THE LIVER.
PERHAPS ANSLINGER SAW HER AS THE MOST BRAZEN OFFENDER FOR DARING TO BE BOTH BLACK AND A WOMAN.
1124 8407 52847

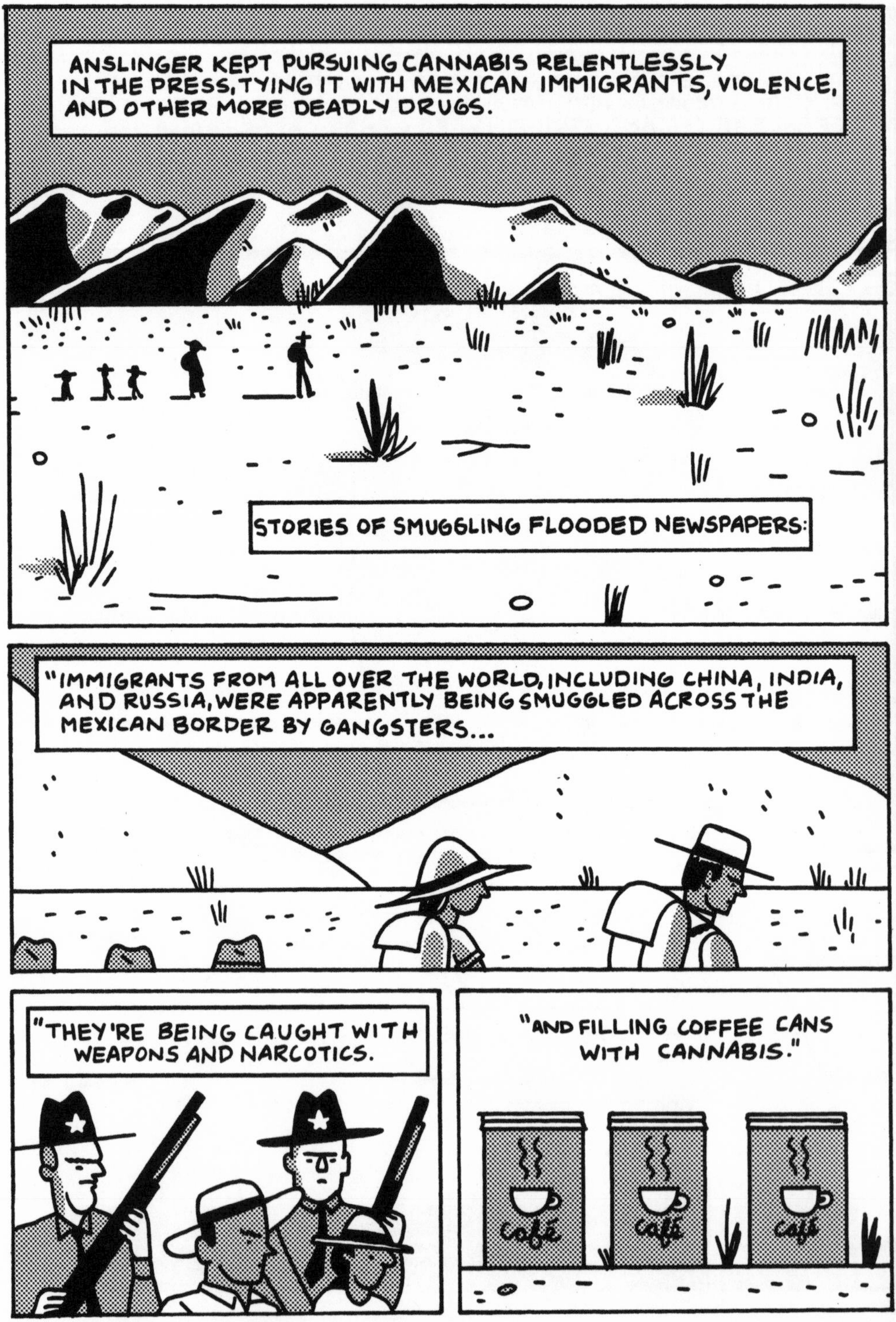
ANSLINGER KEPT PURSUING CANNABIS RELENTLESSLY IN THE PRESS, TYING IT WITH MEXICAN IMMIGRANTS, VIOLENCE, AND OTHER MORE DEADLY DRUGS.
STORIES OF SMUGGLING FLOODED NEWSPAPERS:
"IMMIGRANTS FROM ALL OVER THE WORLD, INCLUDING CHINA, INDIA, AND RUSSIA, WERE APPARENTLY BEING SMUGGLED ACROSS THE MEXICAN BORDER BY GANGSTERS...
"THEY'RE BEING CAUGHT WITH WEAPONS AND NARCOTICS.
"AND FILLING COFFEE CANS WITH CANNABIS."
Café
Café
Café

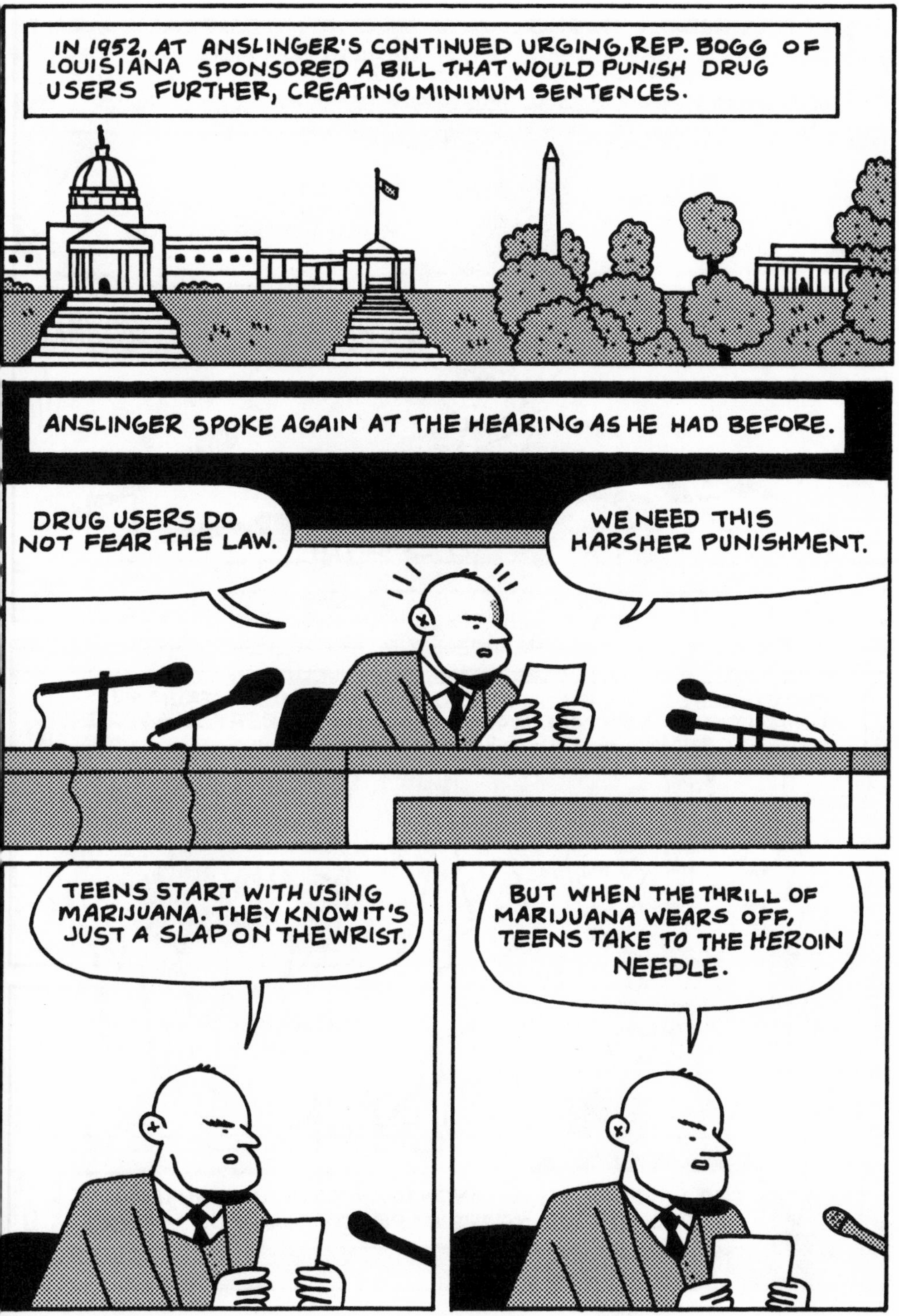
IN 1952, AT ANSLINGER'S CONTINUED URGING, REP. BOGG OF LOUISIANA SPONSORED A BILL THAT WOULD PUNISH DRUG USERS FURTHER, CREATING MINIMUM SENTENCES.
ANSLINGER SPOKE AGAIN AT THE HEARING AS HE HAD BEFORE.
DRUG USERS DO NOT FEAR THE LAW.
WE NEED THIS HARSHER PUNISHMENT.
TEENS START WITH USING MARIJUANA. THEY KNOW IT'S JUST A SLAP ON THE WRIST.
BUT WHEN THE THRILL OF MARIJUANA WEARS OFF, TEENS TAKE TO THE HEROIN NEEDLE.

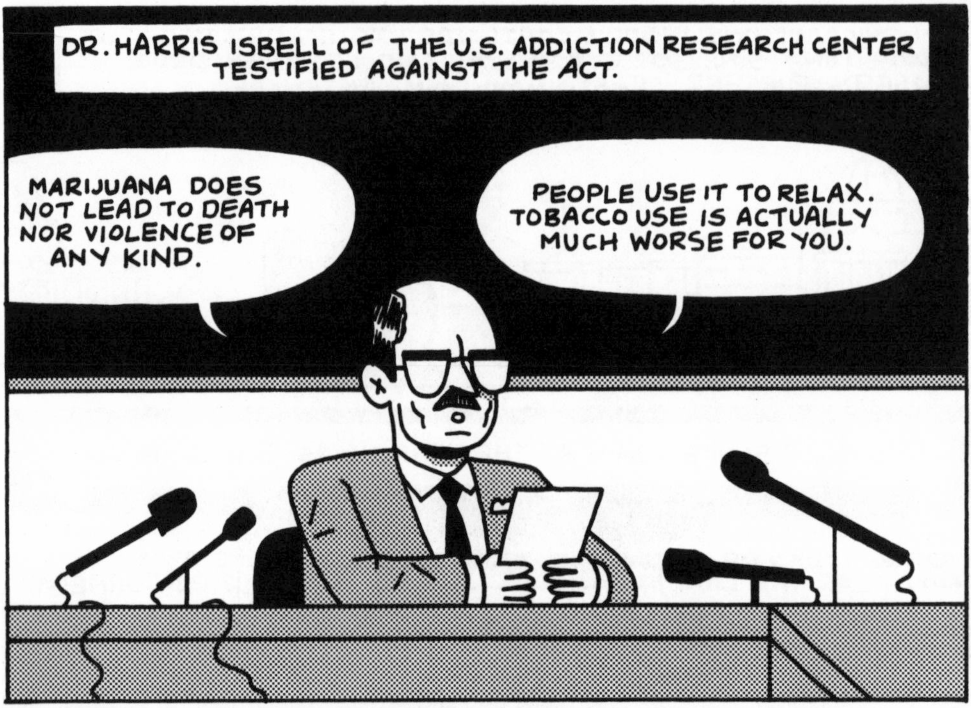
DR. HARRIS ISBELL OF THE U.S. ADDICTION RESEARCH CENTER TESTIFIED AGAINST THE ACT.
MARIJUANA DOES NOT LEAD TO DEATH NOR VIOLENCE OF ANY KIND.
PEOPLE USE IT TO RELAX. TOBACCO USE IS ACTUALLY MUCH WORSE FOR YOU.

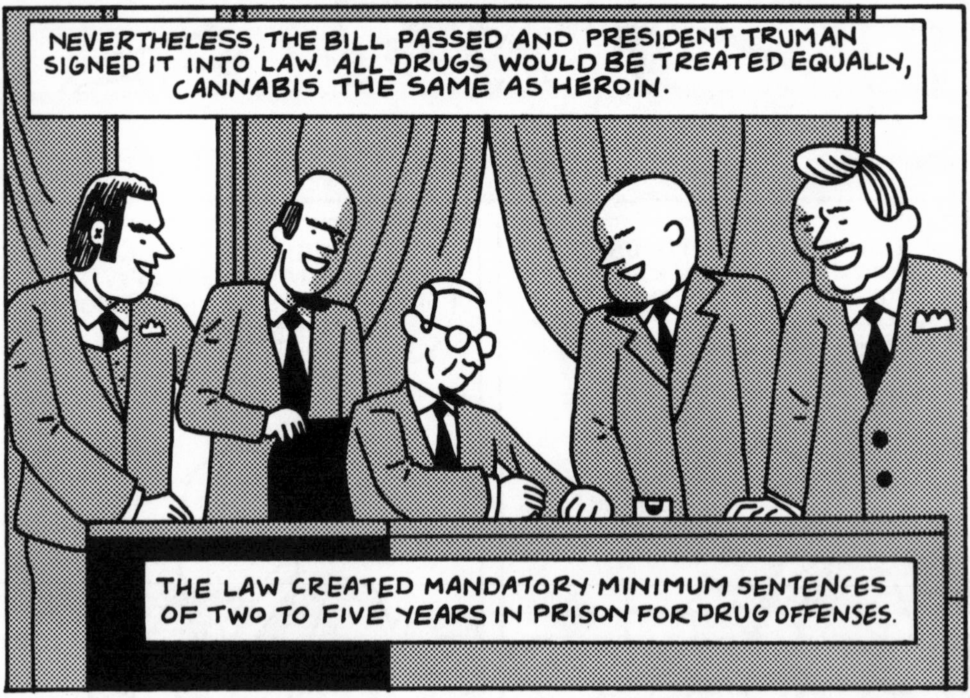
NEVERTHELESS, THE BILL PASSED AND PRESIDENT TRUMAN SIGNED IT INTO LAW. ALL DRUGS WOULD BE TREATED EQUALLY, CANNABIS THE SAME AS HEROIN.
THE LAW CREATED MANDATORY MINIMUM SENTENCES OF TWO TO FIVE YEARS IN PRISON FOR DRUG OFFENSES.

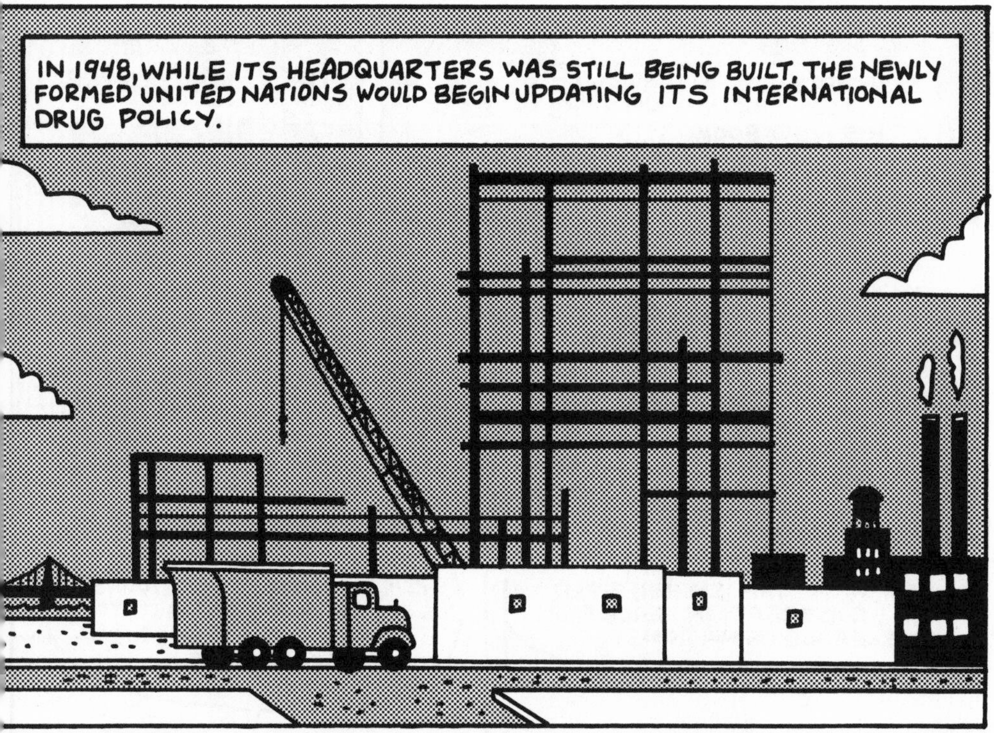
IN 1948, WHILE ITS HEADQUARTERS WAS STILL BEING BUILT, THE NEWLY FORMED UNITED NATIONS WOULD BEGIN UPDATING ITS INTERNATIONAL DRUG POLICY.

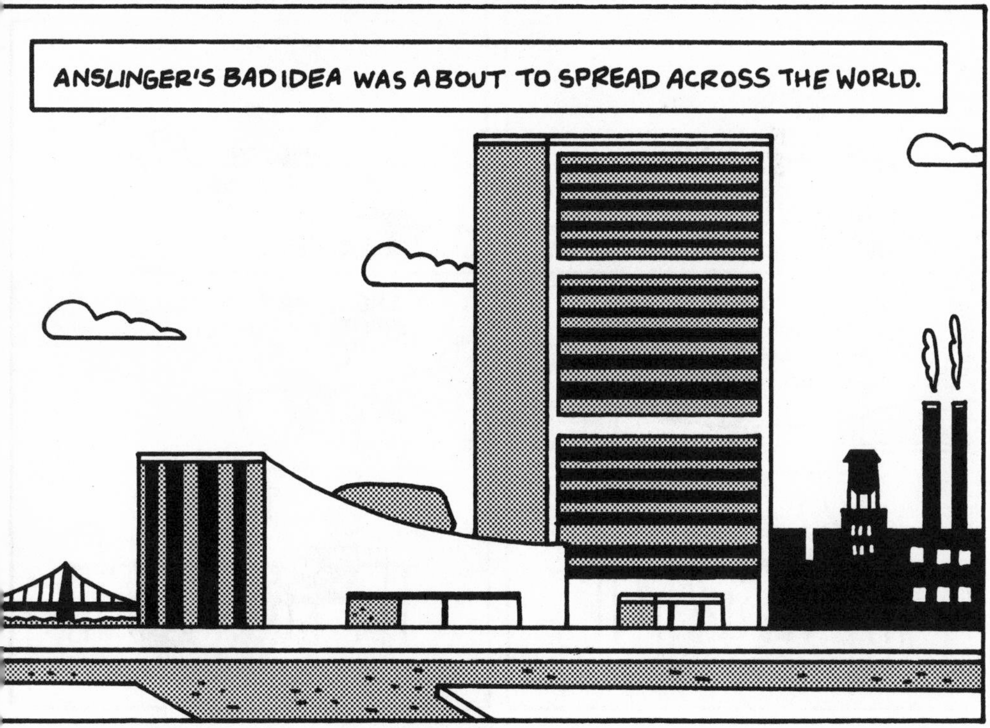
ANSLINGER'S BAD IDEA WAS ABOUT TO SPREAD ACROSS THE WORLD.

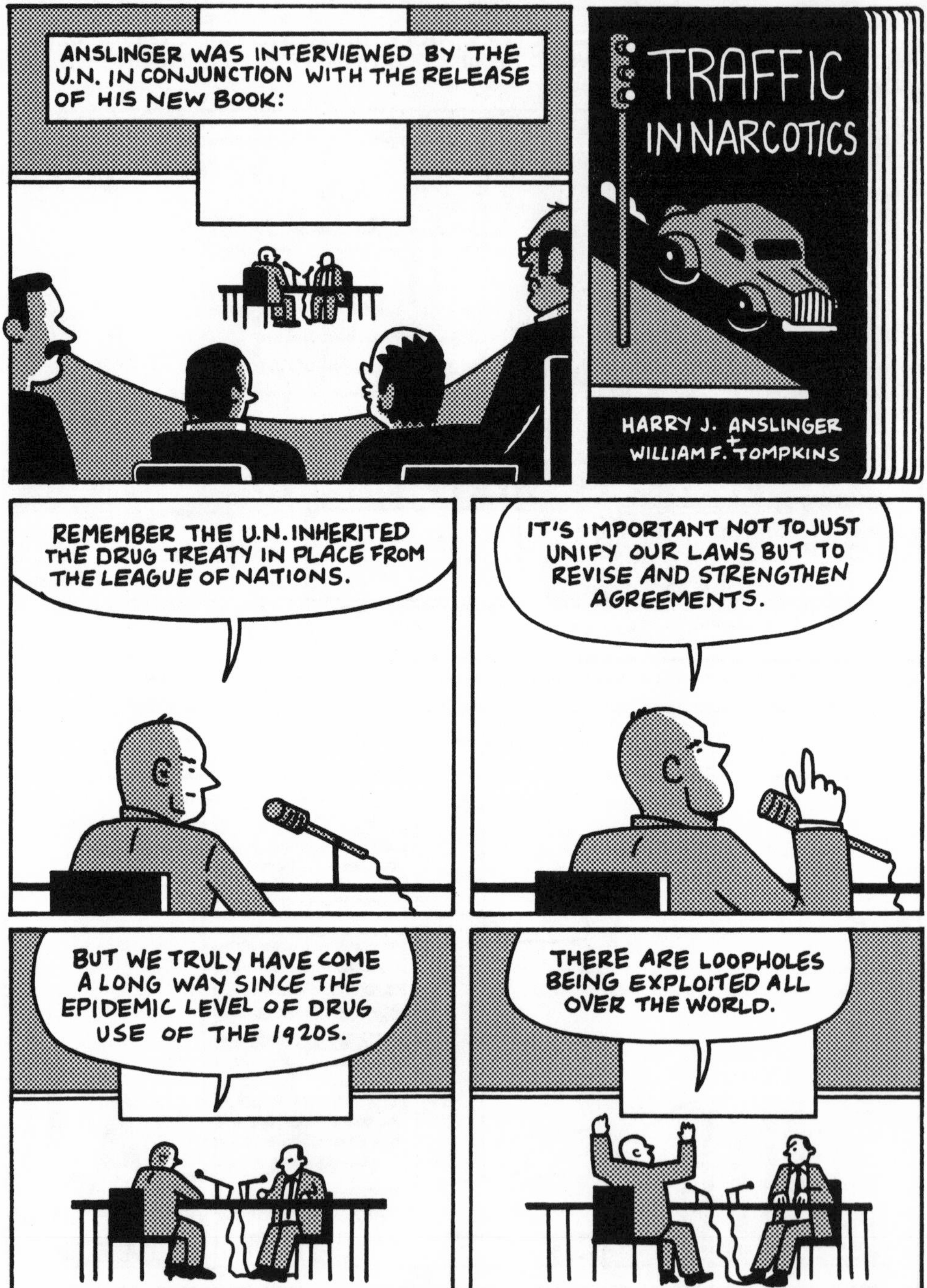
ANSLINGER WAS INTERVIEWED BY THE U.N. IN CONJUNCTION WITH THE RELEASE OF HIS NEW BOOK:
TRAFFIC IN NARCOTICS
HARRY J. ANSLINGER + WILLIAM F. TOMPKINS
REMEMBER THE U.N. INHERITED THE DRUG TREATY IN PLACE FROM THE LEAGUE OF NATIONS.
IT'S IMPORTANT NOT TO JUST UNIFY OUR LAWS BUT TO REVISE AND STRENGTHEN AGREEMENTS.
BUT WE TRULY HAVE COME A LONG WAY SINCE THE EPIDEMIC LEVEL OF DRUG USE OF THE 1920S.
THERE ARE LOOPHOLES BEING EXPLOITED ALL OVER THE WORLD.

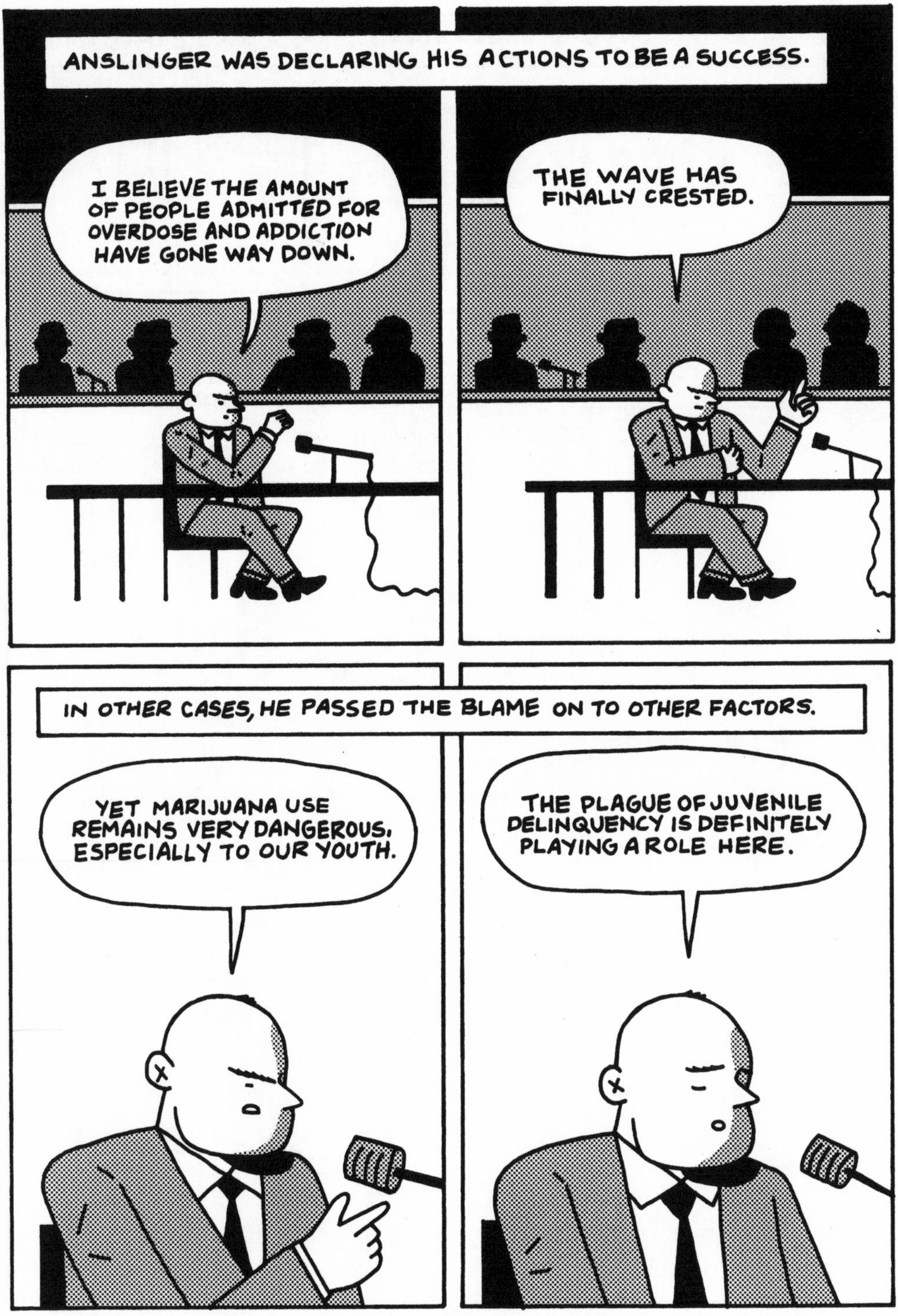
ANSLINGER WAS DECLARING HIS ACTIONS TO BE A SUCCESS.
I BELIEVE THE AMOUNT OF PEOPLE ADMITTED FOR OVERDOSE AND ADDICTION HAVE GONE WAY DOWN.
THE WAVE HAS FINALLY CRESTED.
IN OTHER CASES, HE PASSED THE BLAME ON TO OTHER FACTORS.
YET MARIJUANA USE REMAINS VERY DANGEROUS, ESPECIALLY TO OUR YOUTH.
THE PLAGUE OF JUVENILE DELINQUENCY IS DEFINITELY PLAYING A ROLE HERE.

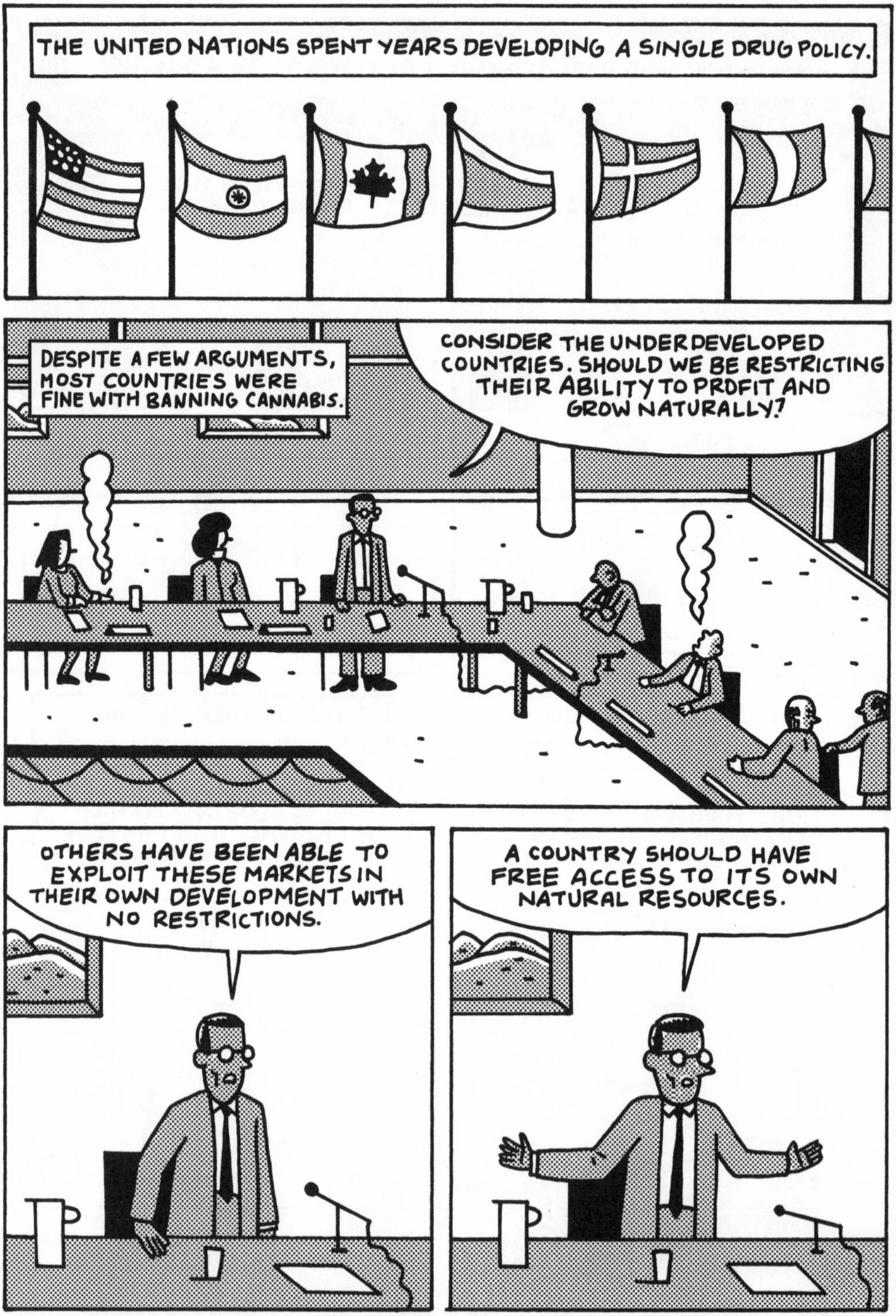
THE UNITED NATIONS SPENT YEARS DEVELOPING A SINGLE DRUG POLICY.
DESPITE A FEW ARGUMENTS, MOST COUNTRIES WERE FINE WITH BANNING CANNABIS.
CONSIDER THE UNDERDEVELOPED COUNTRIES. SHOULD WE BE RESTRICTING THEIR ABILITY TO PROFIT AND GROW NATURALLY?
OTHERS HAVE BEEN ABLE TO EXPLOIT THESE MARKETS IN THEIR OWN DEVELOPMENT WITH NO RESTRICTIONS.
A COUNTRY SHOULD HAVE FREE ACCESS TO ITS OWN NATURAL RESOURCES.

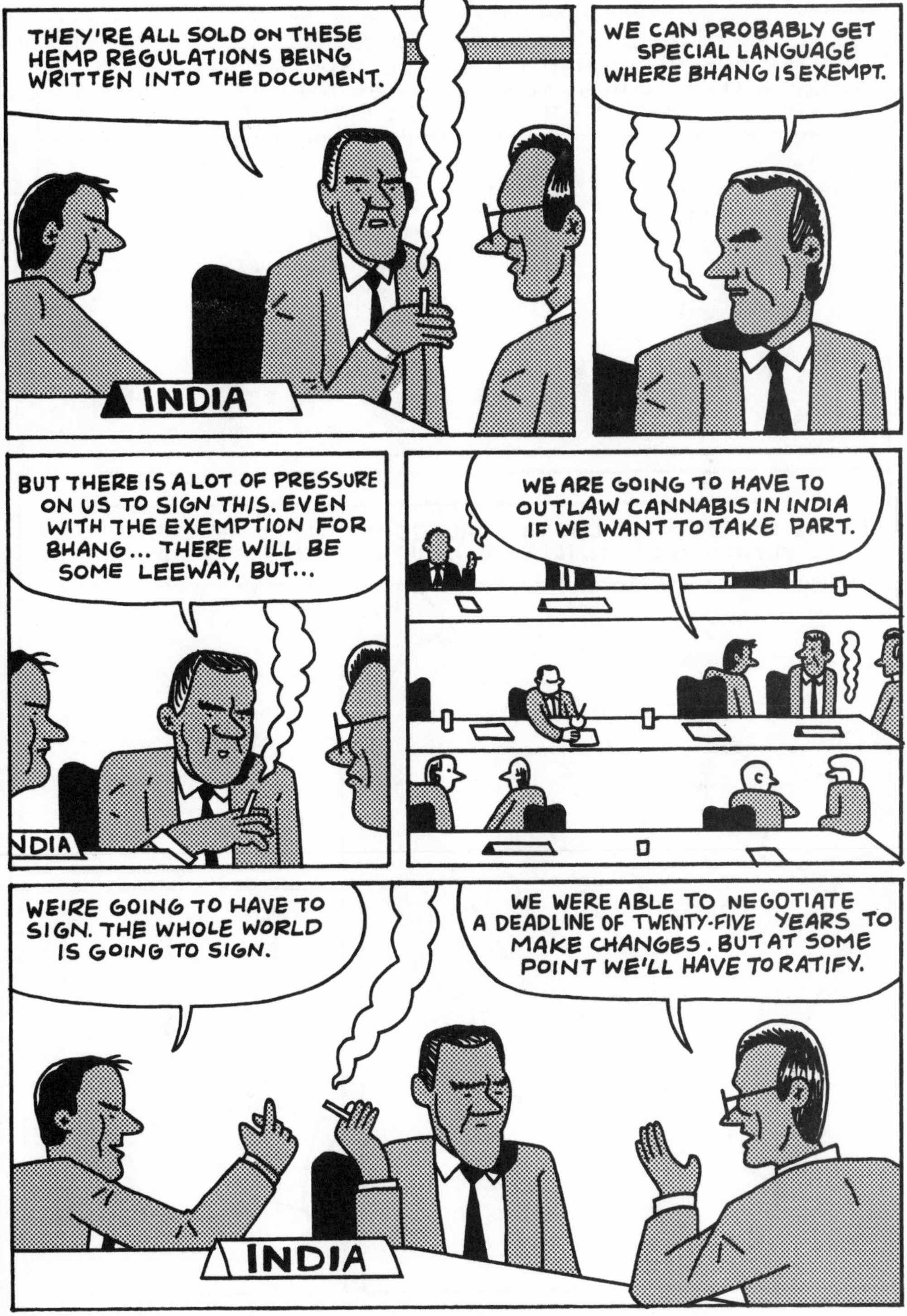
THEY'RE ALL SOLD ON THESE HEMP REGULATIONS BEING WRITTEN INTO THE DOCUMENT.
INDIA
WE CAN PROBABLY GET SPECIAL LANGUAGE WHERE BHANG IS EXEMPT.
BUT THERE IS A LOT OF PRESSURE ON US TO SIGN THIS. EVEN WITH THE EXEMPTION FOR BHANG... THERE WILL BE SOME LEEWAY, BUT...
NDIA
WE ARE GOING TO HAVE TO OUTLAW CANNABIS IN INDIA IF WE WANT TO TAKE PART.
WE'RE GOING TO HAVE TO SIGN. THE WHOLE WORLD IS GOING TO SIGN.
WE WERE ABLE TO NEGOTIATE A DEADLINE OF TWENTY-FIVE YEARS TO MAKE CHANGES. BUT AT SOME POINT WE'LL HAVE TO RATIFY.
INDIA

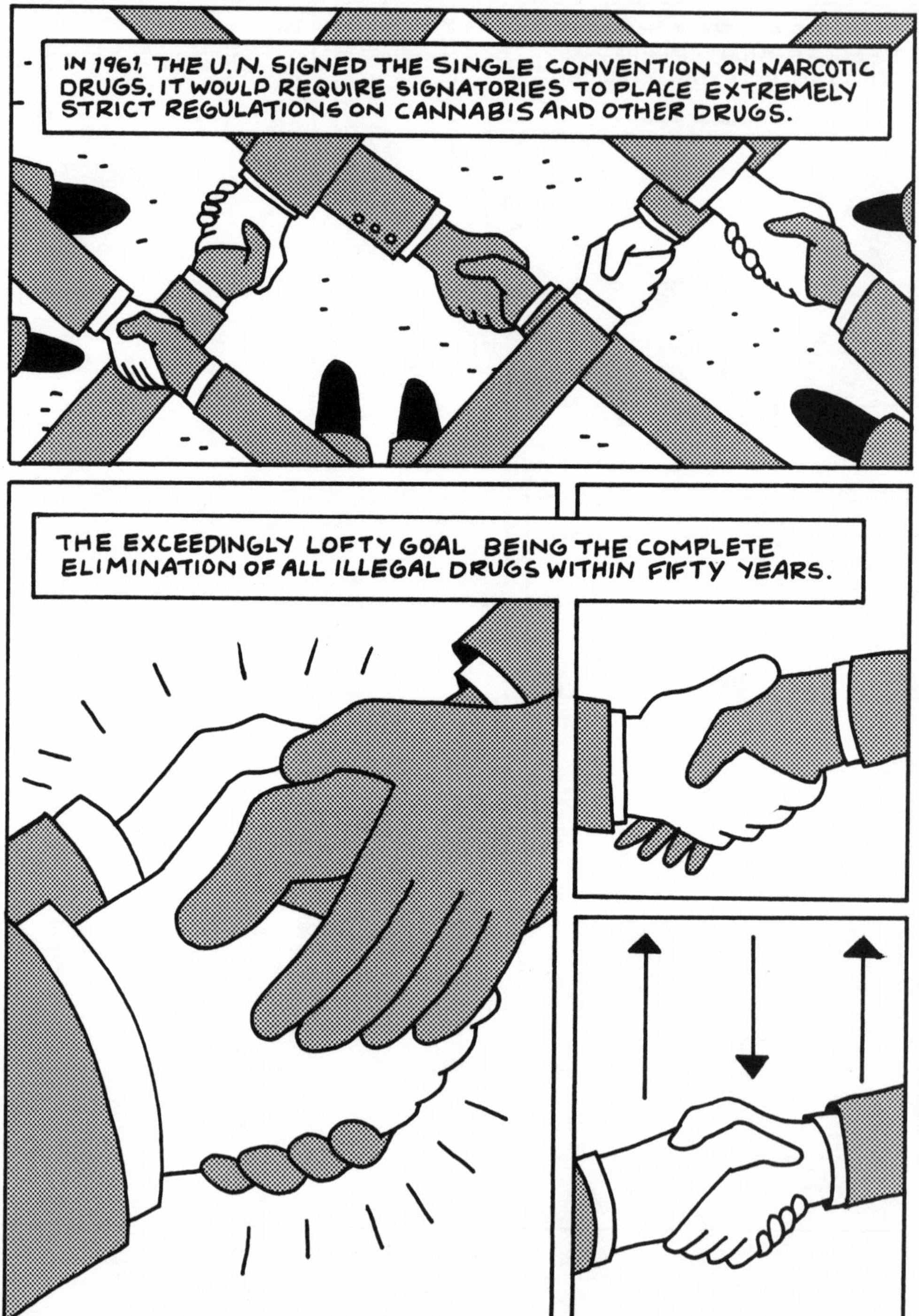
IN 1961, THE U.N. SIGNED THE SINGLE CONVENTION ON NARCOTIC DRUGS. IT WOULD REQUIRE SIGNATORIES TO PLACE EXTREMELY STRICT REGULATIONS ON CANNABIS AND OTHER DRUGS.
THE EXCEEDINGLY LOFTY GOAL BEING THE COMPLETE ELIMINATION OF ALL ILLEGAL DRUGS WITHIN FIFTY YEARS.

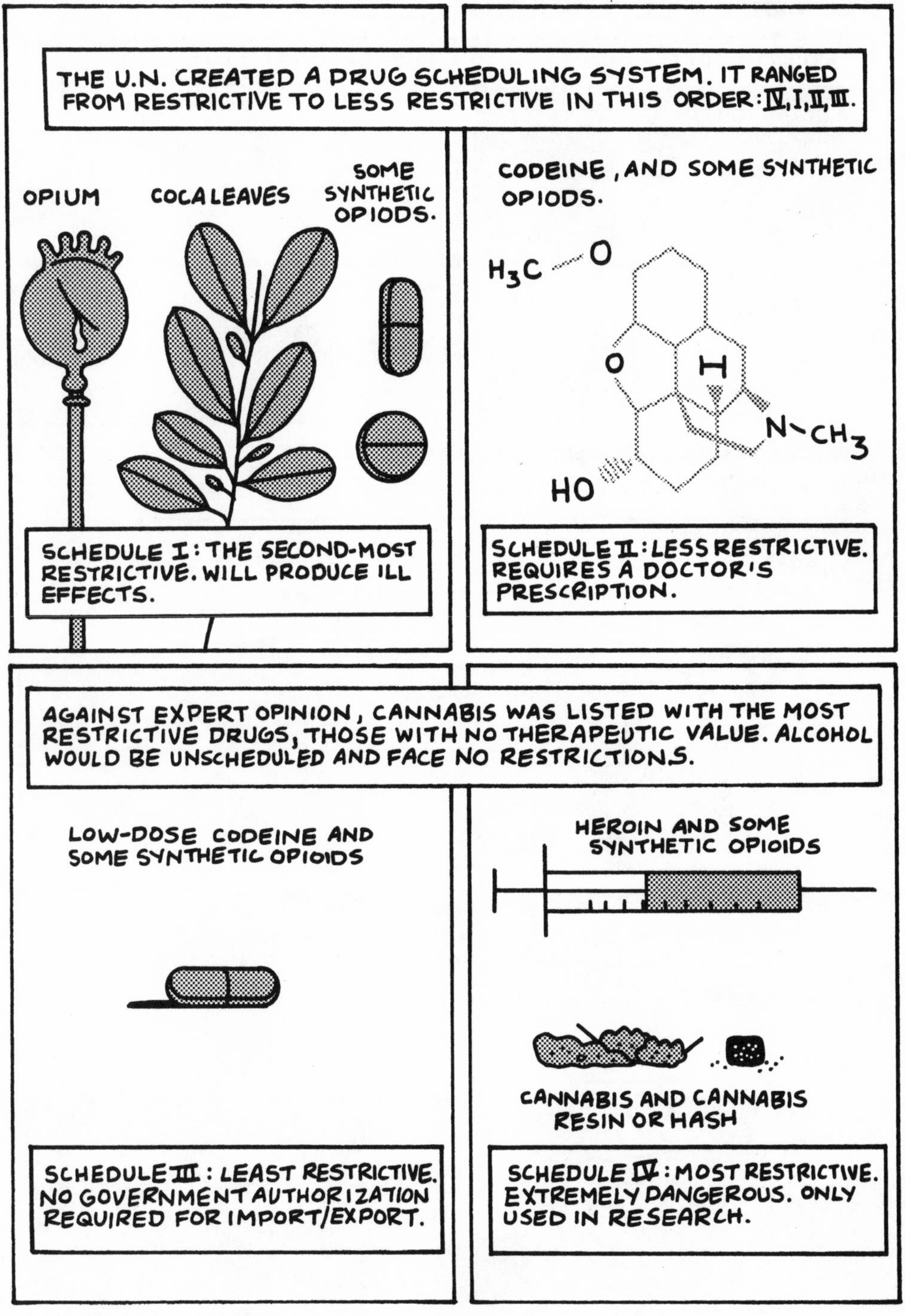

THE U.N. CREATED A DRUG SCHEDULING SYSTEM. IT RANGED FROM RESTRICTIVE TO LESS RESTRICTIVE IN THIS ORDER: IV, I, II, III.

OPIUM   COCA LEAVES   SOME SYNTHETIC OPIODS.

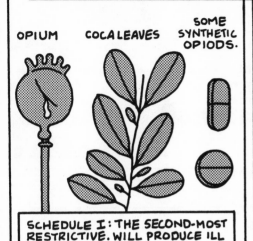

SCHEDULE I: THE SECOND-MOST RESTRICTIVE. WILL PRODUCE ILL EFFECTS.

CODEINE, AND SOME SYNTHETIC OPIODS.

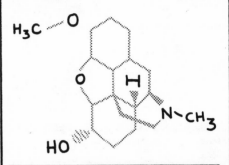

SCHEDULE II: LESS RESTRICTIVE. REQUIRES A DOCTOR'S PRESCRIPTION.

AGAINST EXPERT OPINION, CANNABIS WAS LISTED WITH THE MOST RESTRICTIVE DRUGS, THOSE WITH NO THERAPEUTIC VALUE. ALCOHOL WOULD BE UNSCHEDULED AND FACE NO RESTRICTIONS.

LOW-DOSE CODEINE AND SOME SYNTHETIC OPIOIDS

SCHEDULE III: LEAST RESTRICTIVE. NO GOVERNMENT AUTHORIZATION REQUIRED FOR IMPORT/EXPORT.

HEROIN AND SOME SYNTHETIC OPIOIDS

CANNABIS AND CANNABIS RESIN OR HASH

SCHEDULE IV: MOST RESTRICTIVE. EXTREMELY DANGEROUS. ONLY USED IN RESEARCH.

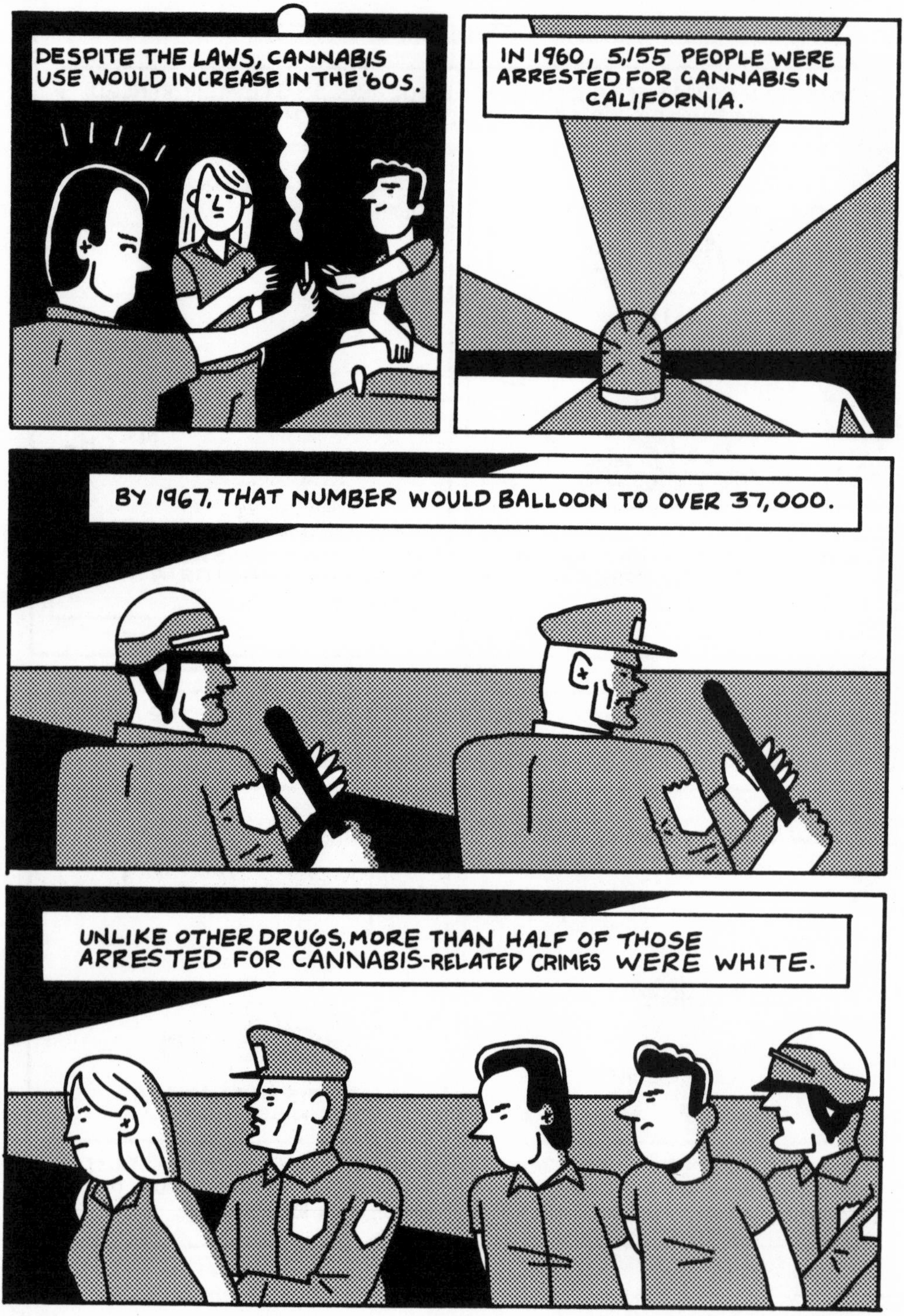
DESPITE THE LAWS, CANNABIS USE WOULD INCREASE IN THE '60S.
IN 1960, 5,155 PEOPLE WERE ARRESTED FOR CANNABIS IN CALIFORNIA.
BY 1967, THAT NUMBER WOULD BALLOON TO OVER 37,000.
UNLIKE OTHER DRUGS, MORE THAN HALF OF THOSE ARRESTED FOR CANNABIS-RELATED CRIMES WERE WHITE.

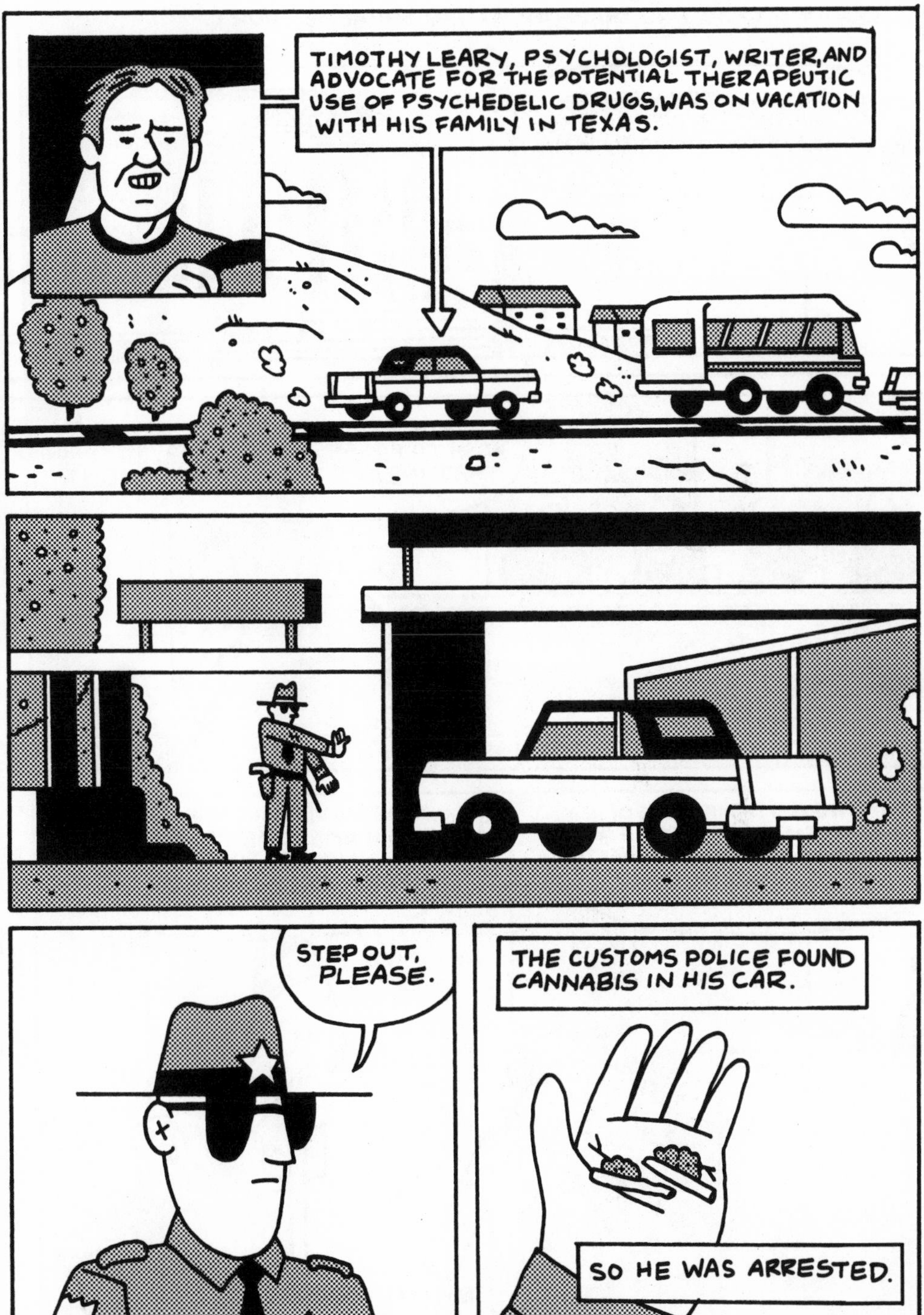
TIMOTHY LEARY, PSYCHOLOGIST, WRITER, AND ADVOCATE FOR THE POTENTIAL THERAPEUTIC USE OF PSYCHEDELIC DRUGS, WAS ON VACATION WITH HIS FAMILY IN TEXAS.
STEP OUT, PLEASE.
THE CUSTOMS POLICE FOUND CANNABIS IN HIS CAR.
SO HE WAS ARRESTED.

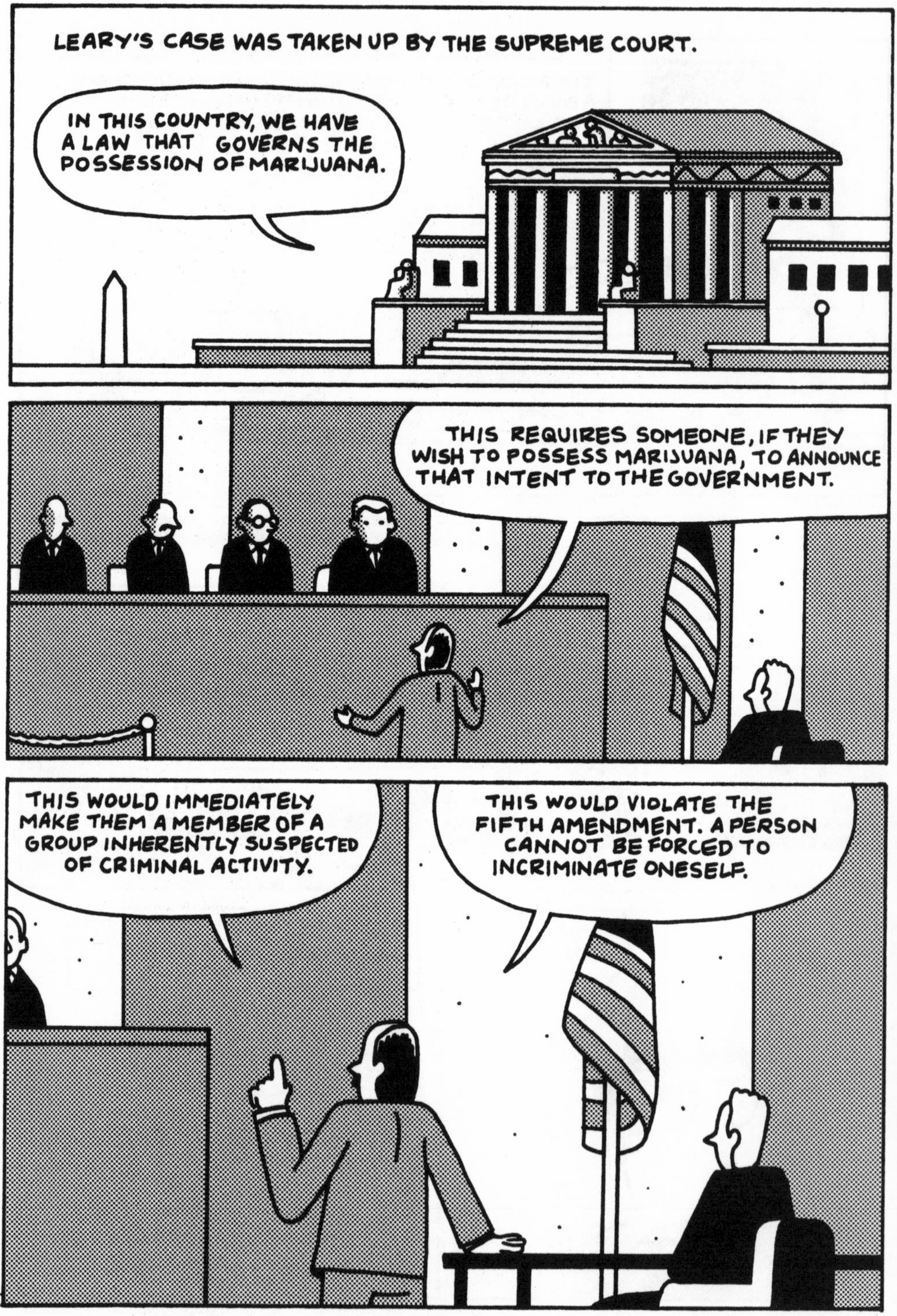
LEARY'S CASE WAS TAKEN UP BY THE SUPREME COURT.
IN THIS COUNTRY, WE HAVE A LAW THAT GOVERNS THE POSSESSION OF MARIJUANA.
THIS REQUIRES SOMEONE, IF THEY WISH TO POSSESS MARIJUANA, TO ANNOUNCE THAT INTENT TO THE GOVERNMENT.
THIS WOULD IMMEDIATELY MAKE THEM A MEMBER OF A GROUP INHERENTLY SUSPECTED OF CRIMINAL ACTIVITY.
THIS WOULD VIOLATE THE FIFTH AMENDMENT. A PERSON CANNOT BE FORCED TO INCRIMINATE ONESELF.

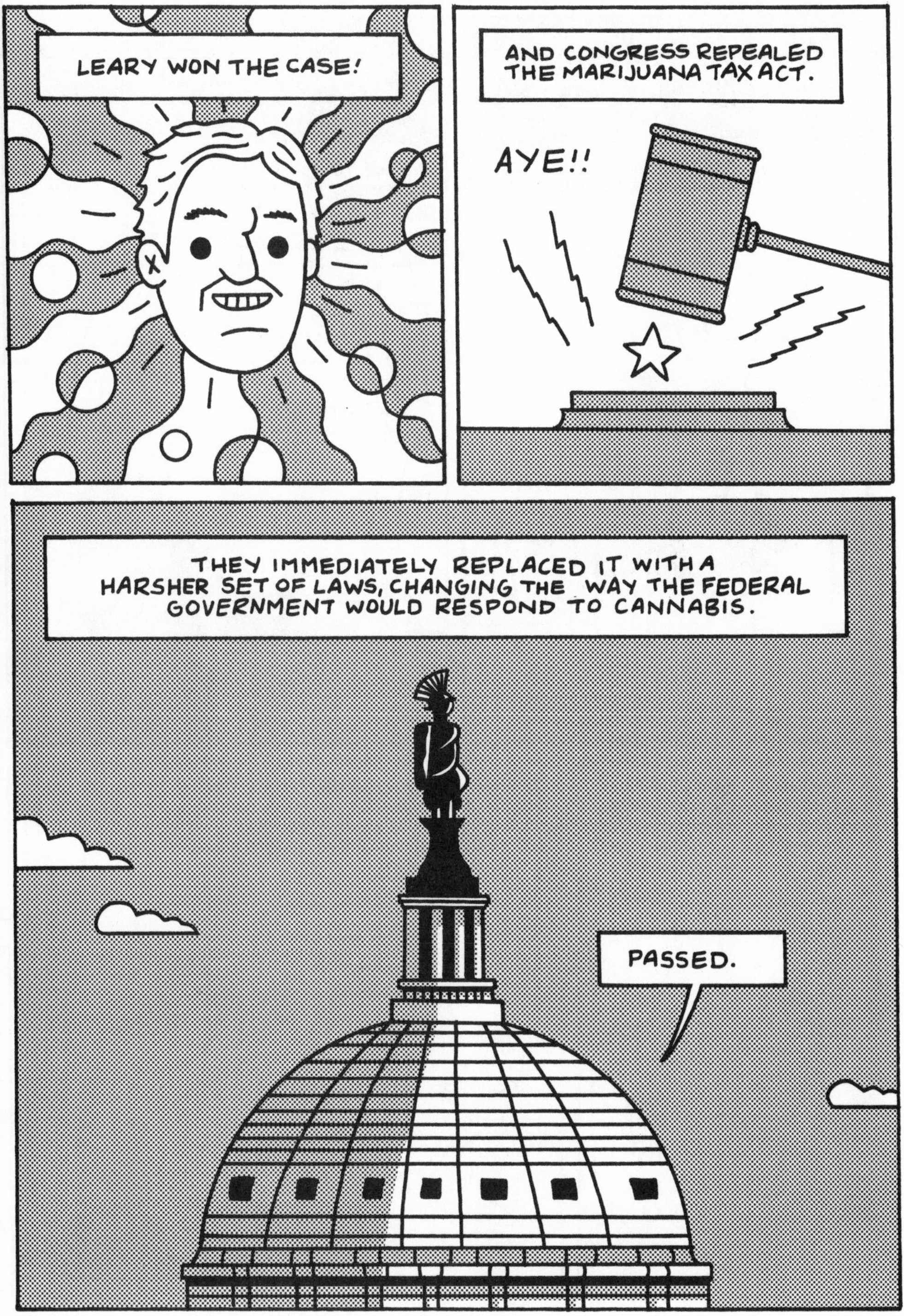
LEARY WON THE CASE!
AND CONGRESS REPEALED THE MARIJUANA TAX ACT.
AYE!!
THEY IMMEDIATELY REPLACED IT WITH A HARSHER SET OF LAWS, CHANGING THE WAY THE FEDERAL GOVERNMENT WOULD RESPOND TO CANNABIS.
PASSED.

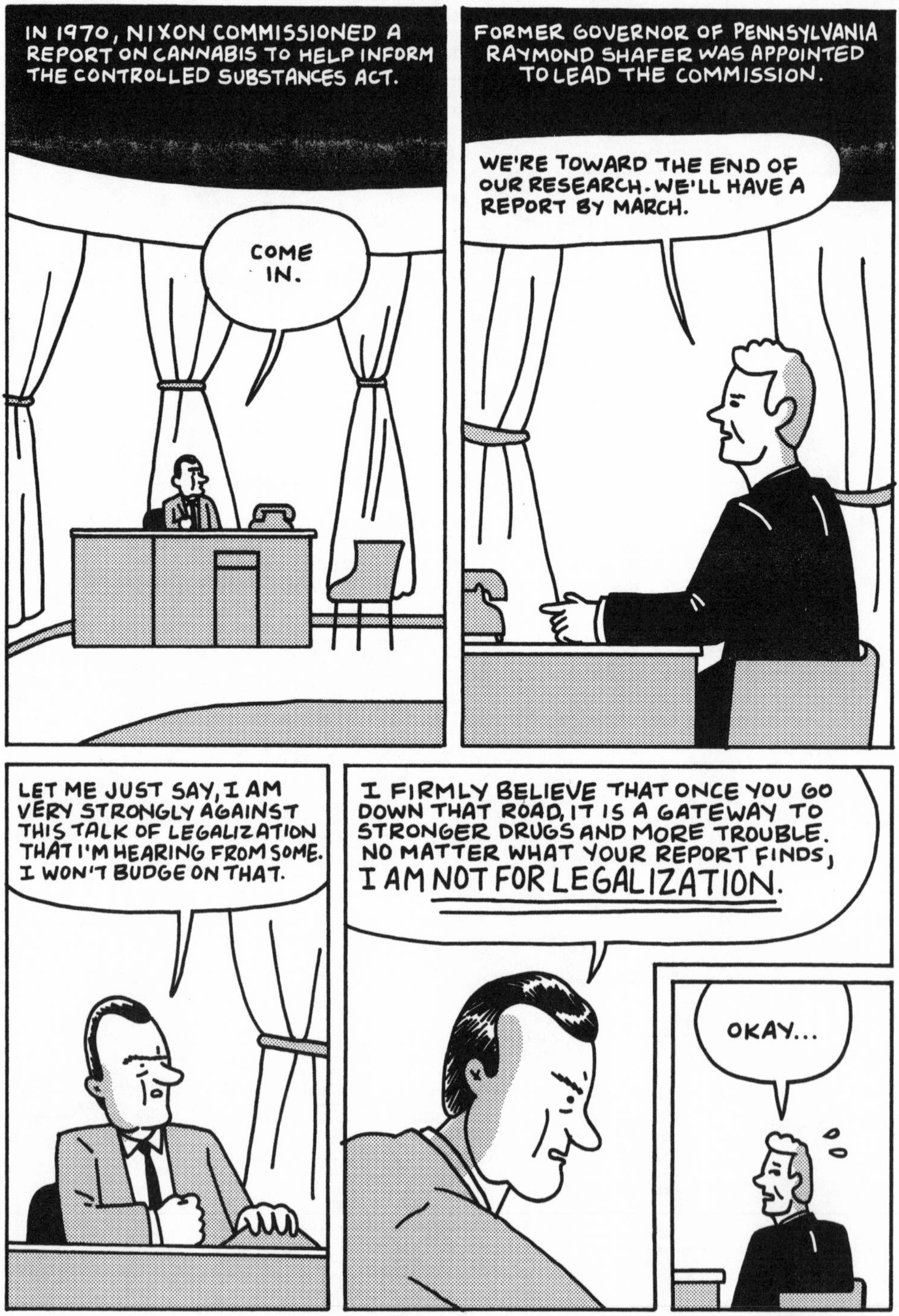
IN 1970, NIXON COMMISSIONED A REPORT ON CANNABIS TO HELP INFORM THE CONTROLLED SUBSTANCES ACT.
COME IN.
FORMER GOVERNOR OF PENNSYLVANIA RAYMOND SHAFER WAS APPOINTED TO LEAD THE COMMISSION.
WE'RE TOWARD THE END OF OUR RESEARCH. WE'LL HAVE A REPORT BY MARCH.
LET ME JUST SAY, I AM VERY STRONGLY AGAINST THIS TALK OF LEGALIZATION THAT I'M HEARING FROM SOME. I WON'T BUDGE ON THAT.
I FIRMLY BELIEVE THAT ONCE YOU GO DOWN THAT ROAD, IT IS A GATEWAY TO STRONGER DRUGS AND MORE TROUBLE. NO MATTER WHAT YOUR REPORT FINDS, I AM NOT FOR LEGALIZATION.
OKAY...

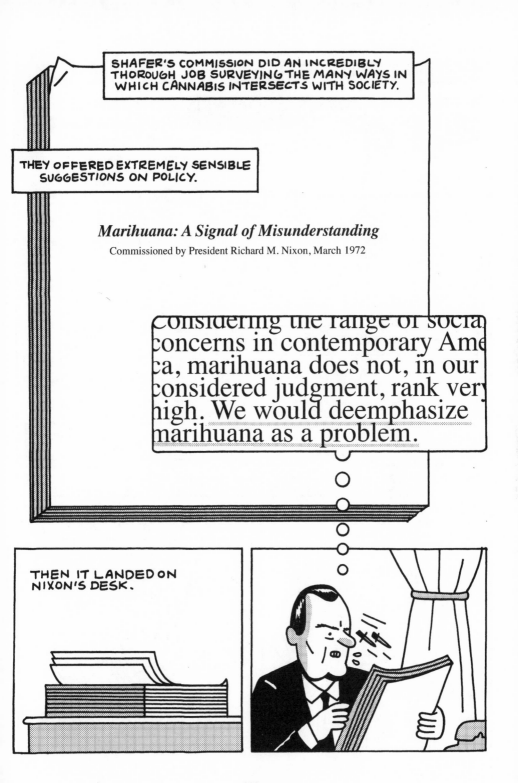

SHAFER'S COMMISSION DID AN INCREDIBLY THOROUGH JOB SURVEYING THE MANY WAYS IN WHICH CANNABIS INTERSECTS WITH SOCIETY.

THEY OFFERED EXTREMELY SENSIBLE SUGGESTIONS ON POLICY.

Marihuana: A Signal of Misunderstanding

Commissioned by President Richard M. Nixon, March 1972

Considering the range of social concerns in contemporary America, marihuana does not, in our considered judgment, rank very high. We would deemphasize marihuana as a problem.

THEN IT LANDED ON NIXON'S DESK.

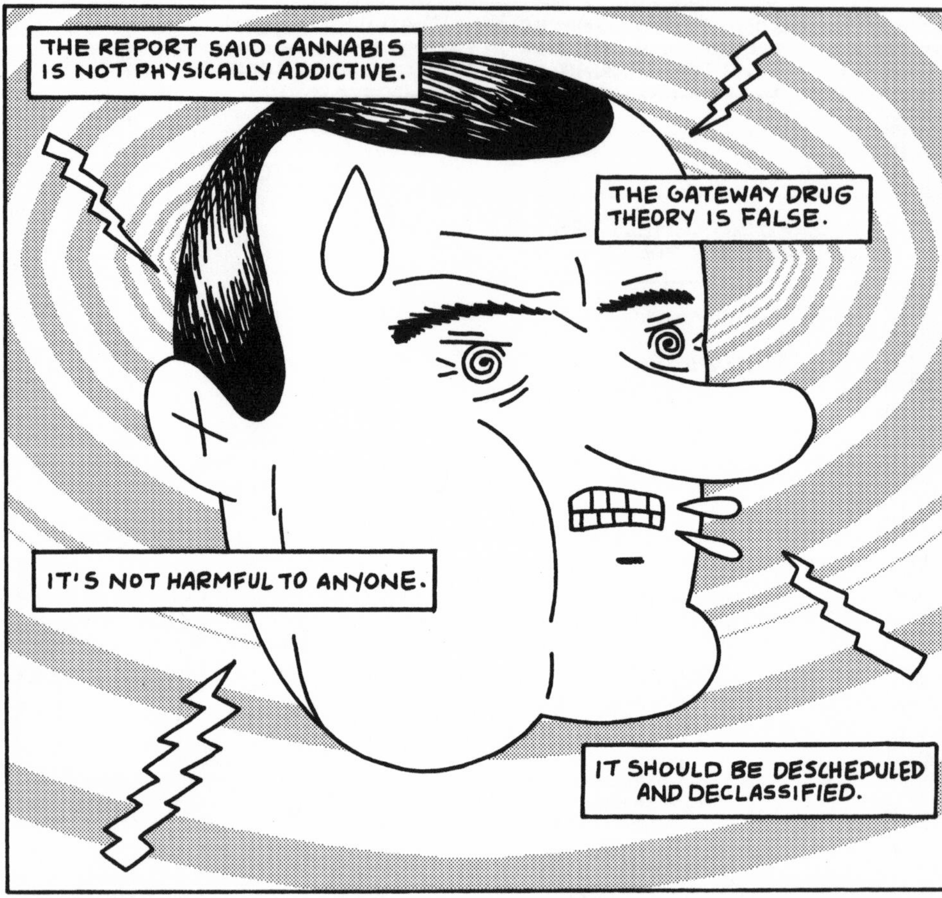
THE REPORT SAID CANNABIS IS NOT PHYSICALLY ADDICTIVE.
THE GATEWAY DRUG THEORY IS FALSE.
IT'S NOT HARMFUL TO ANYONE.
IT SHOULD BE DESCHEDULED AND DECLASSIFIED.

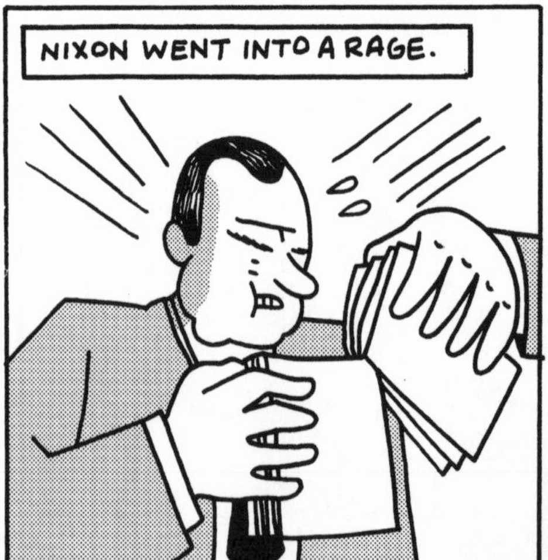
NIXON WENT INTO A RAGE.

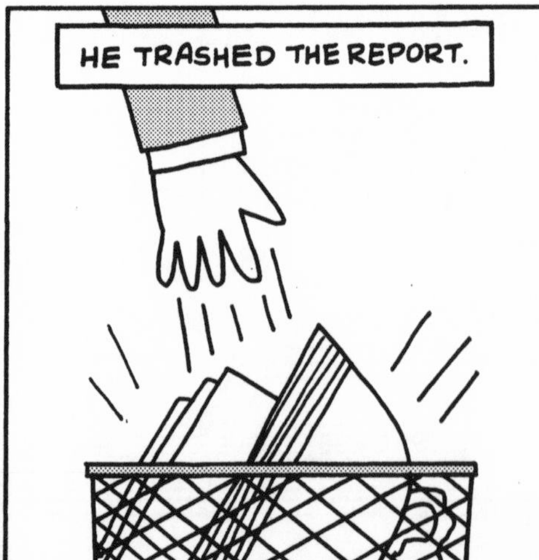
HE TRASHED THE REPORT.

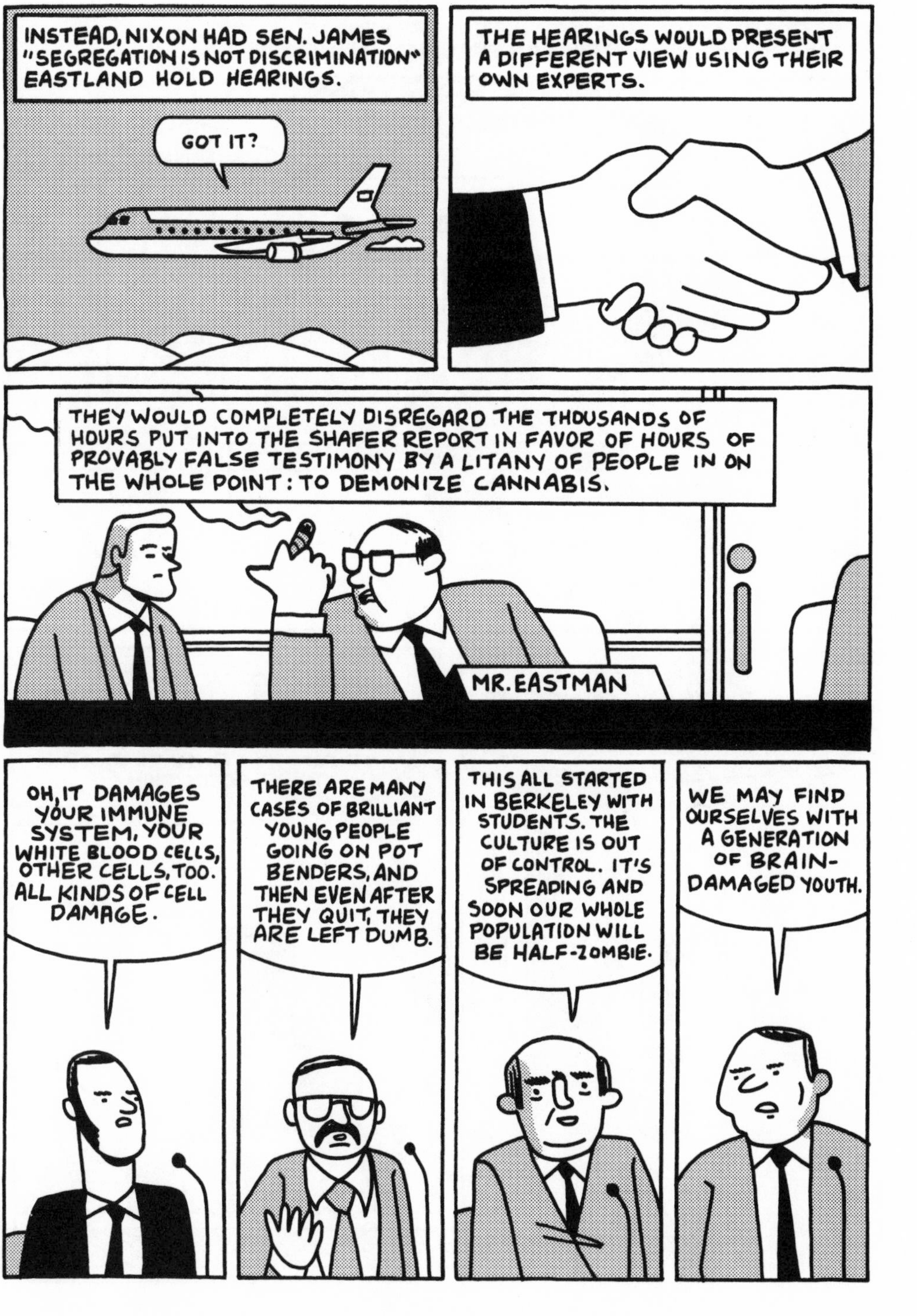

INSTEAD, NIXON HAD SEN. JAMES "SEGREGATION IS NOT DISCRIMINATION" EASTLAND HOLD HEARINGS.
GOT IT?
THE HEARINGS WOULD PRESENT A DIFFERENT VIEW USING THEIR OWN EXPERTS.
THEY WOULD COMPLETELY DISREGARD THE THOUSANDS OF HOURS PUT INTO THE SHAFER REPORT IN FAVOR OF HOURS OF PROVABLY FALSE TESTIMONY BY A LITANY OF PEOPLE IN ON THE WHOLE POINT: TO DEMONIZE CANNABIS.
MR. EASTMAN
OH, IT DAMAGES YOUR IMMUNE SYSTEM, YOUR WHITE BLOOD CELLS, OTHER CELLS, TOO. ALL KINDS OF CELL DAMAGE.
THERE ARE MANY CASES OF BRILLIANT YOUNG PEOPLE GOING ON POT BENDERS, AND THEN EVEN AFTER THEY QUIT, THEY ARE LEFT DUMB.
THIS ALL STARTED IN BERKELEY WITH STUDENTS. THE CULTURE IS OUT OF CONTROL. IT'S SPREADING AND SOON OUR WHOLE POPULATION WILL BE HALF-ZOMBIE.
WE MAY FIND OURSELVES WITH A GENERATION OF BRAIN-DAMAGED YOUTH.

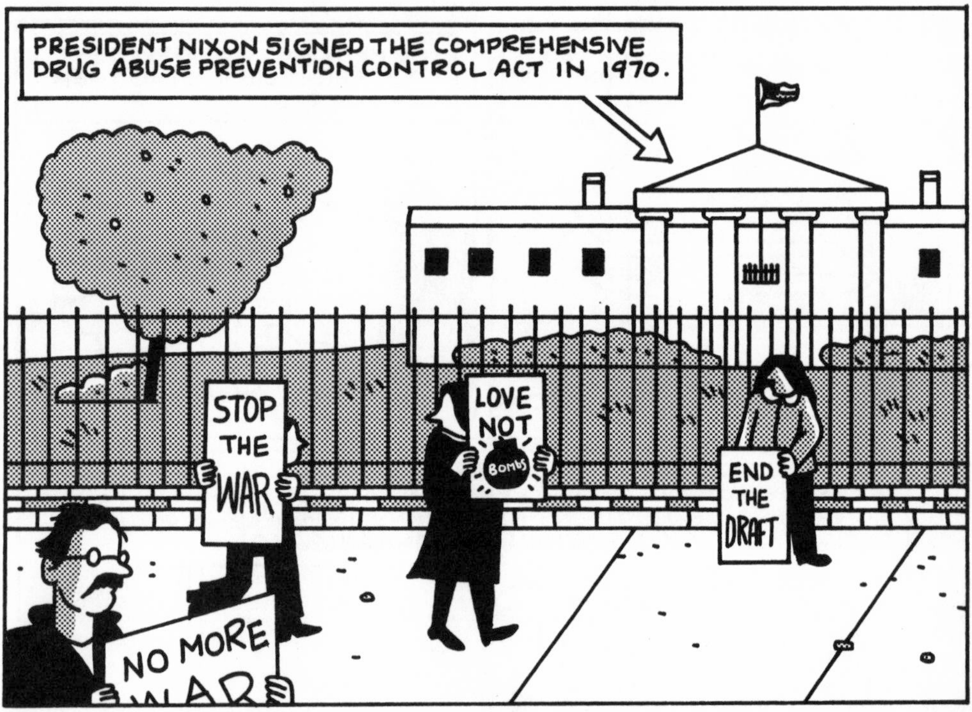
PRESIDENT NIXON SIGNED THE COMPREHENSIVE DRUG ABUSE PREVENTION CONTROL ACT IN 1970.
STOP THE WAR
LOVE NOT BOMBS
END THE DRAFT
NO MORE WAR

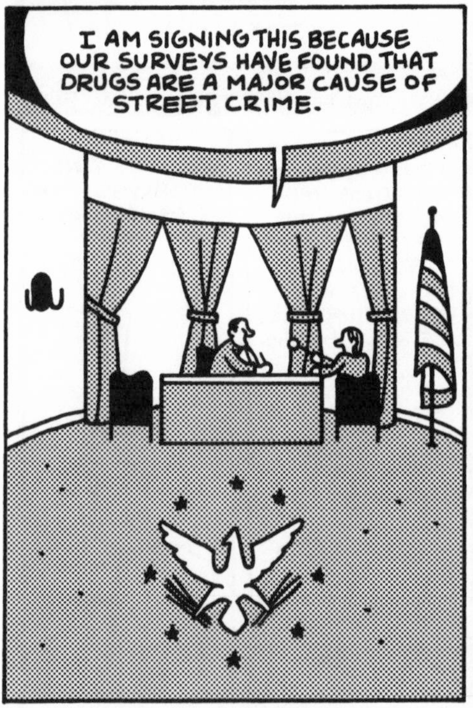
I AM SIGNING THIS BECAUSE OUR SURVEYS HAVE FOUND THAT DRUGS ARE A MAJOR CAUSE OF STREET CRIME.

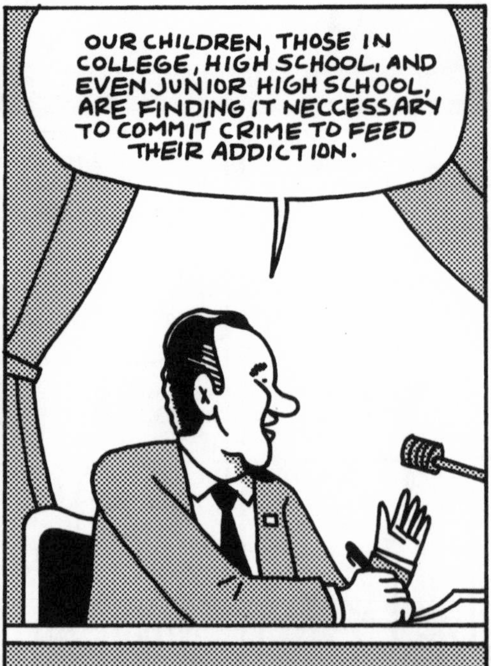
OUR CHILDREN, THOSE IN COLLEGE, HIGH SCHOOL, AND EVEN JUNIOR HIGH SCHOOL, ARE FINDING IT NECCESSARY TO COMMIT CRIME TO FEED THEIR ADDICTION.

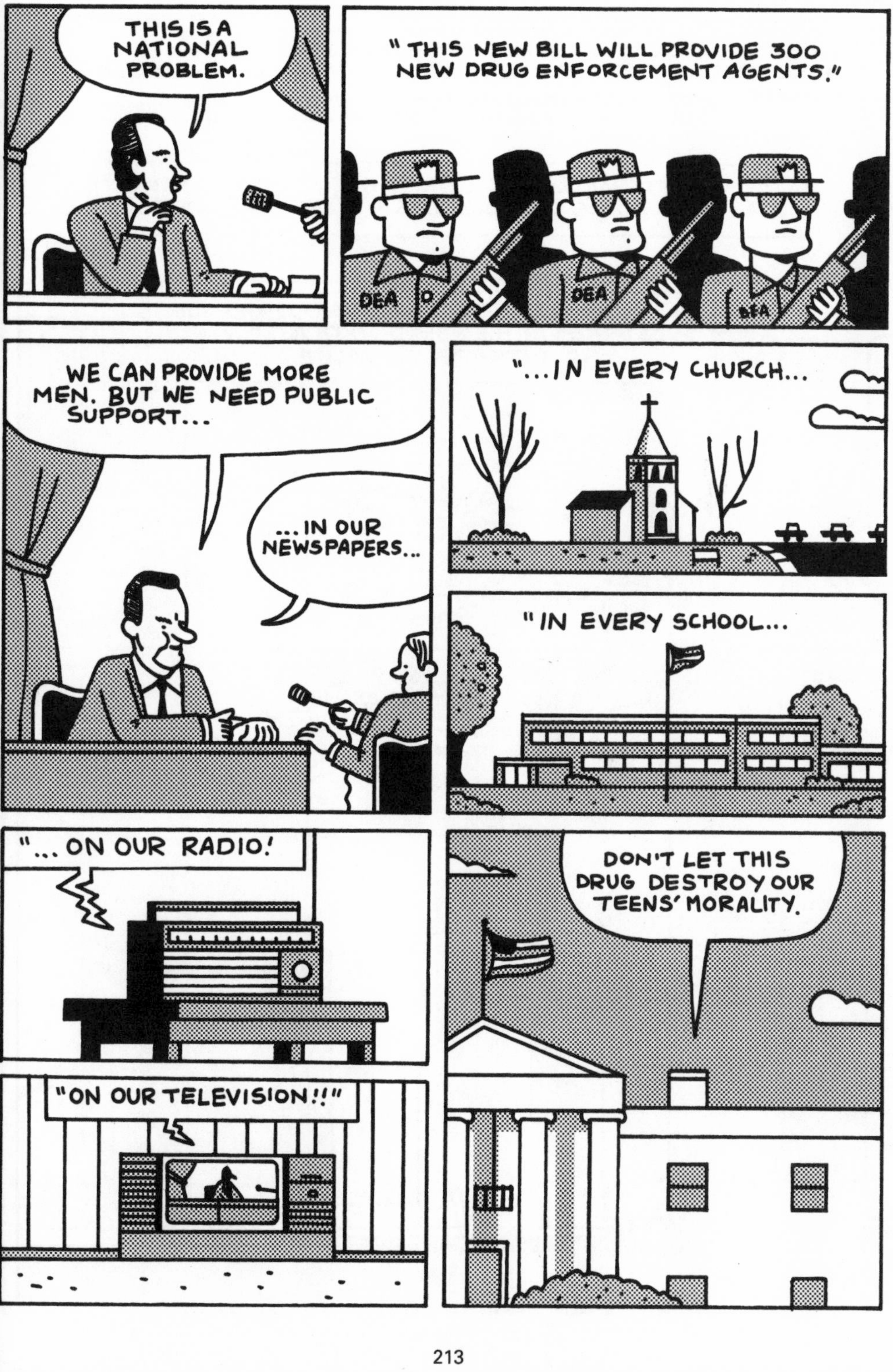
THIS IS A NATIONAL PROBLEM.
"THIS NEW BILL WILL PROVIDE 300 NEW DRUG ENFORCEMENT AGENTS."
DEA
DEA
DEA
WE CAN PROVIDE MORE MEN. BUT WE NEED PUBLIC SUPPORT...
...IN OUR NEWSPAPERS...
"...IN EVERY CHURCH...
"IN EVERY SCHOOL...
"...ON OUR RADIO!
"ON OUR TELEVISION!!"
DON'T LET THIS DRUG DESTROY OUR TEENS' MORALITY.

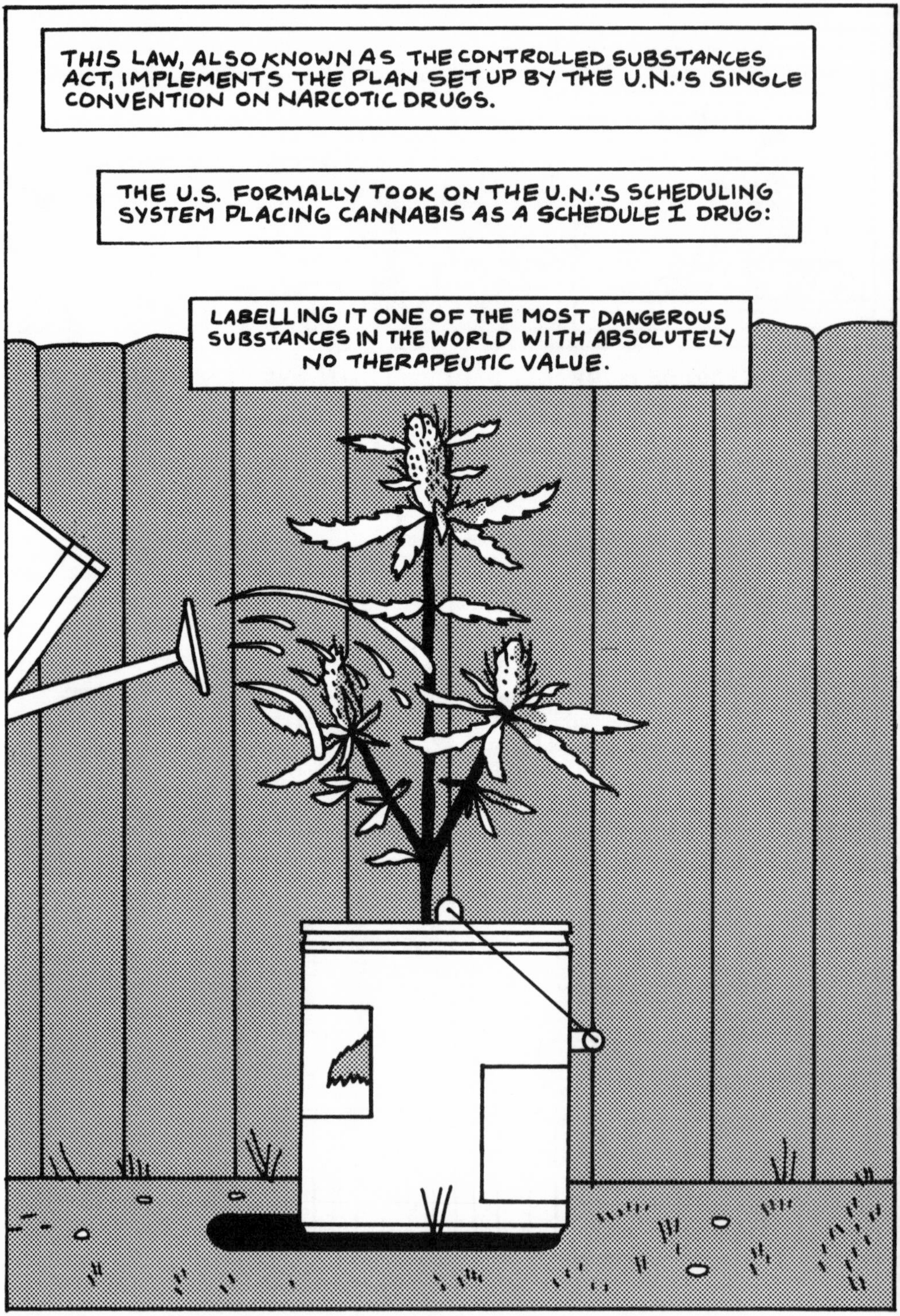
THIS LAW, ALSO KNOWN AS THE CONTROLLED SUBSTANCES ACT, IMPLEMENTS THE PLAN SET UP BY THE U.N.'S SINGLE CONVENTION ON NARCOTIC DRUGS.
THE U.S. FORMALLY TOOK ON THE U.N.'S SCHEDULING SYSTEM PLACING CANNABIS AS A SCHEDULE I DRUG:
LABELLING IT ONE OF THE MOST DANGEROUS SUBSTANCES IN THE WORLD WITH ABSOLUTELY NO THERAPEUTIC VALUE.

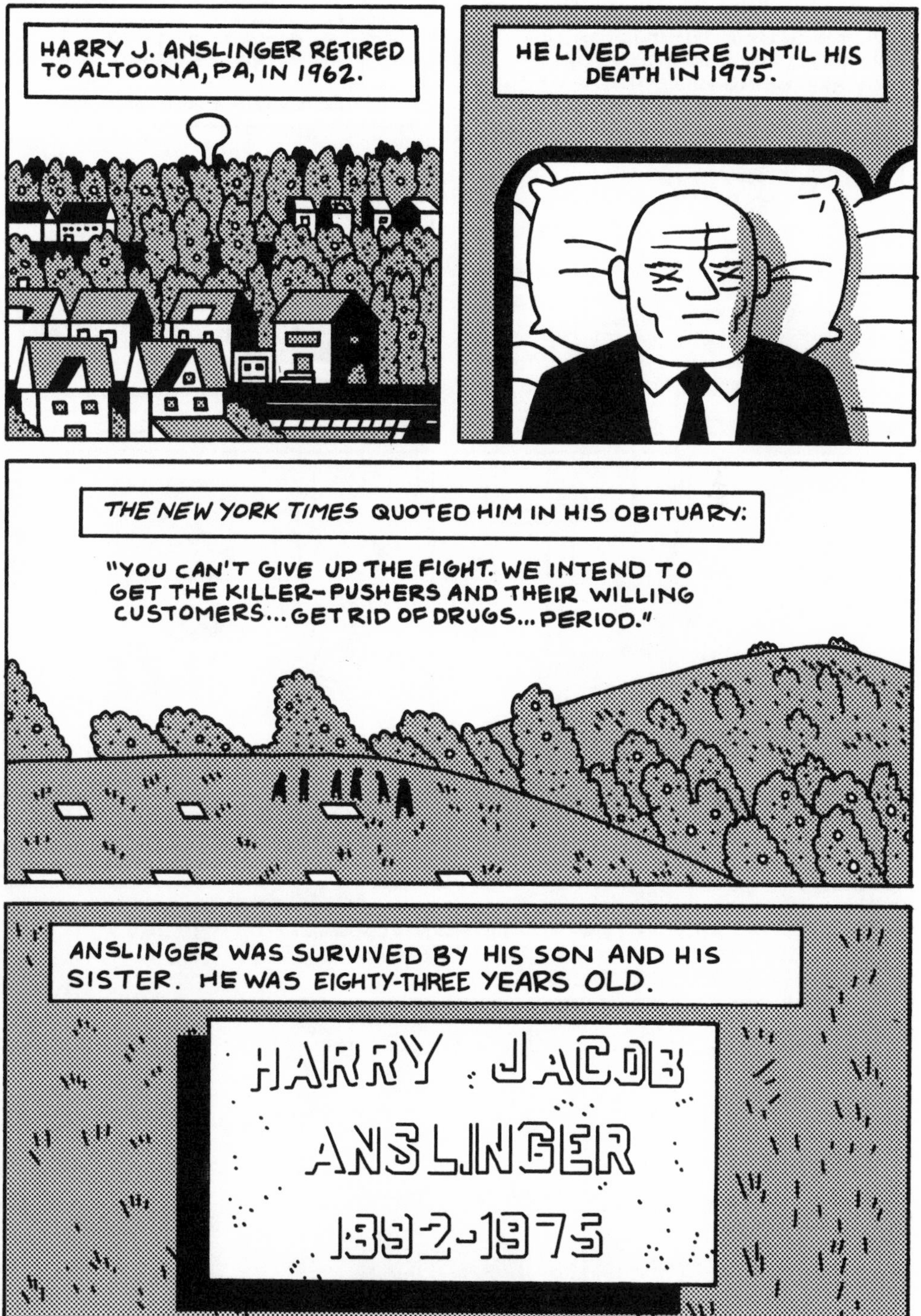
HARRY J. ANSLINGER RETIRED TO ALTOONA, PA, IN 1962.
HE LIVED THERE UNTIL HIS DEATH IN 1975.
THE NEW YORK TIMES QUOTED HIM IN HIS OBITUARY:
"YOU CAN'T GIVE UP THE FIGHT. WE INTEND TO GET THE KILLER-PUSHERS AND THEIR WILLING CUSTOMERS... GET RID OF DRUGS... PERIOD."
ANSLINGER WAS SURVIVED BY HIS SON AND HIS SISTER. HE WAS EIGHTY-THREE YEARS OLD.
HARRY JACOB
ANSLINGER
1892-1975

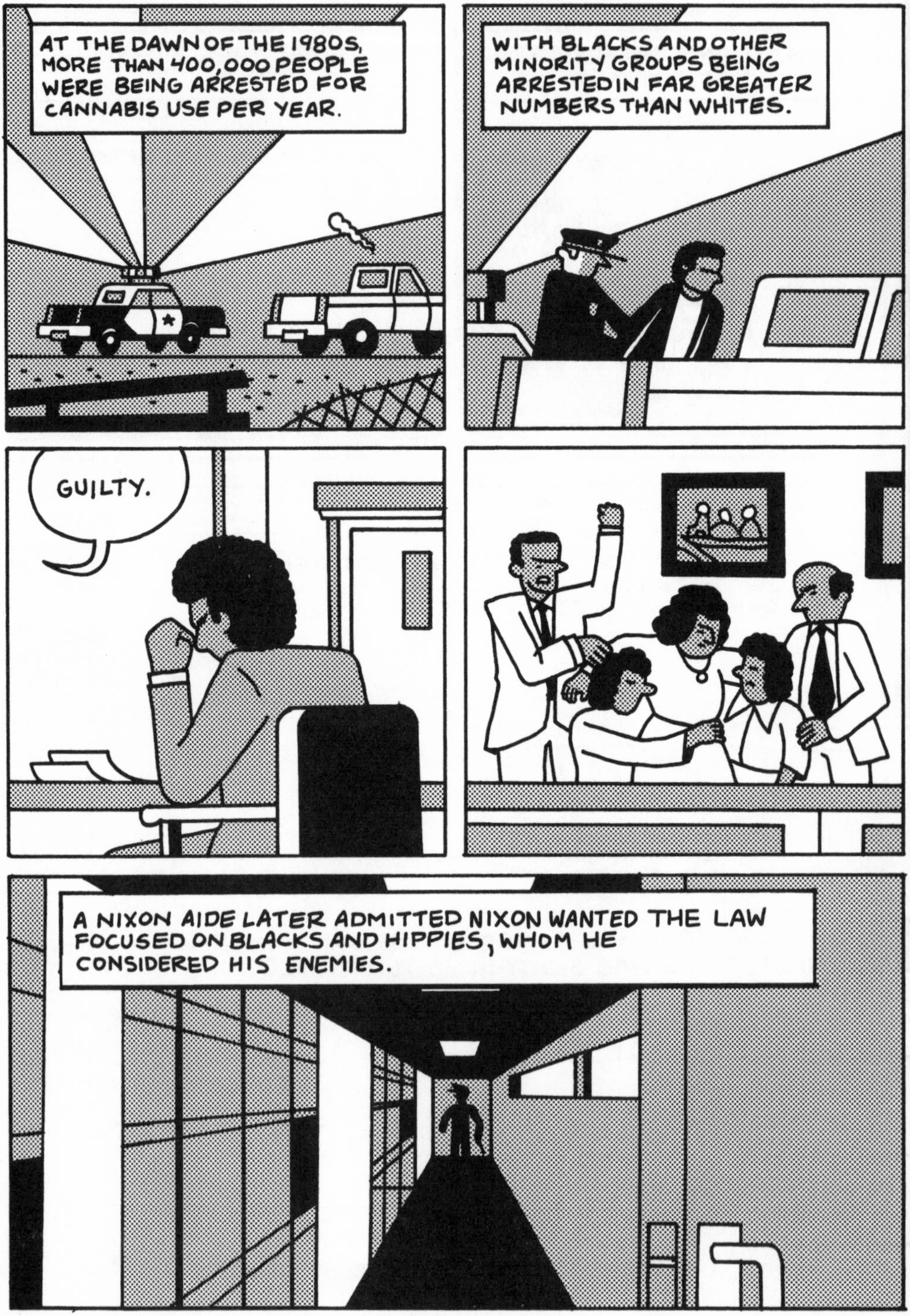
AT THE DAWN OF THE 1980S, MORE THAN 400,000 PEOPLE WERE BEING ARRESTED FOR CANNABIS USE PER YEAR.
WITH BLACKS AND OTHER MINORITY GROUPS BEING ARRESTED IN FAR GREATER NUMBERS THAN WHITES.
GUILTY.
A NIXON AIDE LATER ADMITTED NIXON WANTED THE LAW FOCUSED ON BLACKS AND HIPPIES, WHOM HE CONSIDERED HIS ENEMIES.

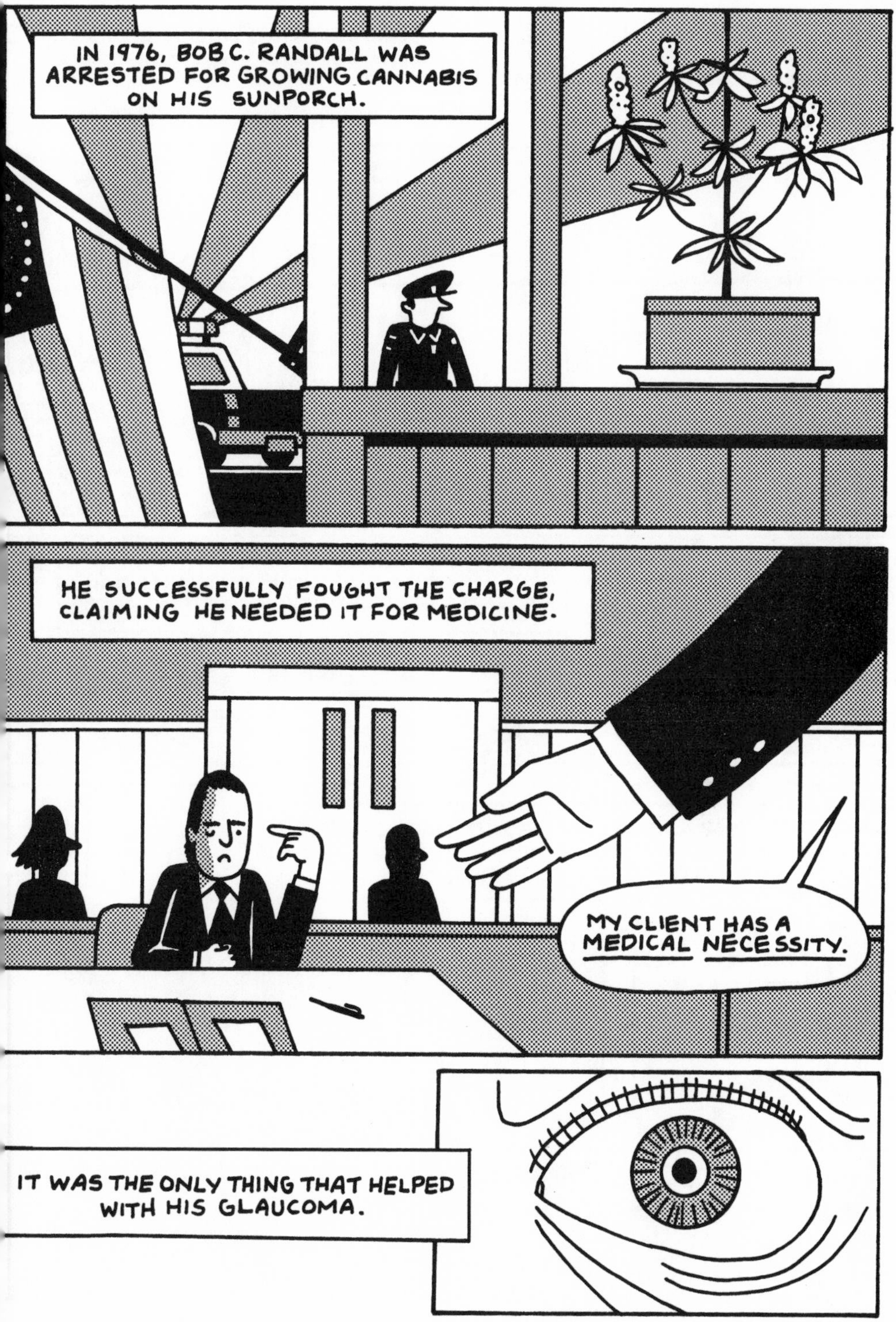
IN 1976, BOB C. RANDALL WAS ARRESTED FOR GROWING CANNABIS ON HIS SUNPORCH.
HE SUCCESSFULLY FOUGHT THE CHARGE, CLAIMING HE NEEDED IT FOR MEDICINE.
MY CLIENT HAS A MEDICAL NECESSITY.
IT WAS THE ONLY THING THAT HELPED WITH HIS GLAUCOMA.

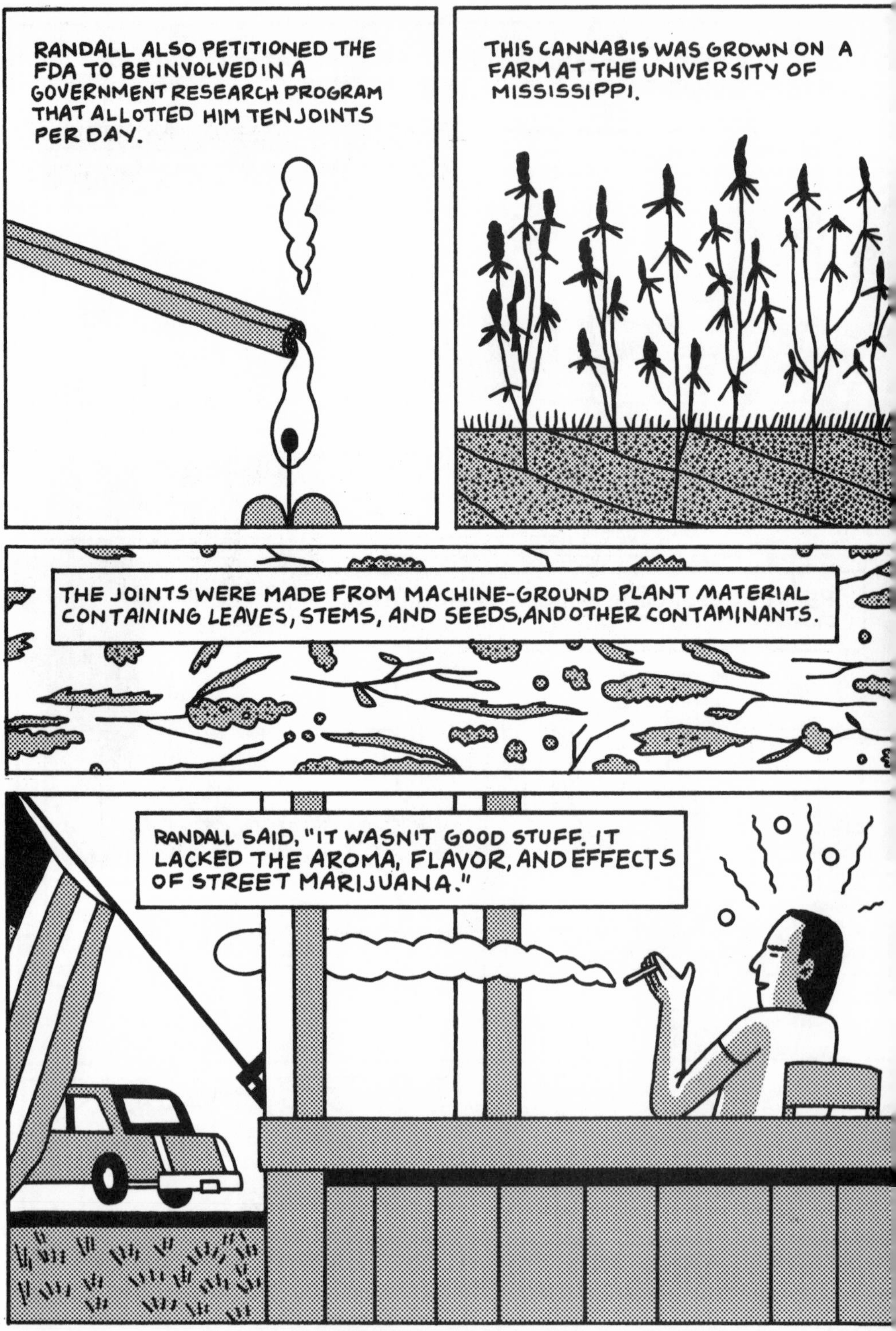

RANDALL ALSO PETITIONED THE FDA TO BE INVOLVED IN A GOVERNMENT RESEARCH PROGRAM THAT ALLOTTED HIM TEN JOINTS PER DAY.
THIS CANNABIS WAS GROWN ON A FARM AT THE UNIVERSITY OF MISSISSIPPI.
THE JOINTS WERE MADE FROM MACHINE-GROUND PLANT MATERIAL CONTAINING LEAVES, STEMS, AND SEEDS, AND OTHER CONTAMINANTS.
RANDALL SAID, "IT WASN'T GOOD STUFF. IT LACKED THE AROMA, FLAVOR, AND EFFECTS OF STREET MARIJUANA."

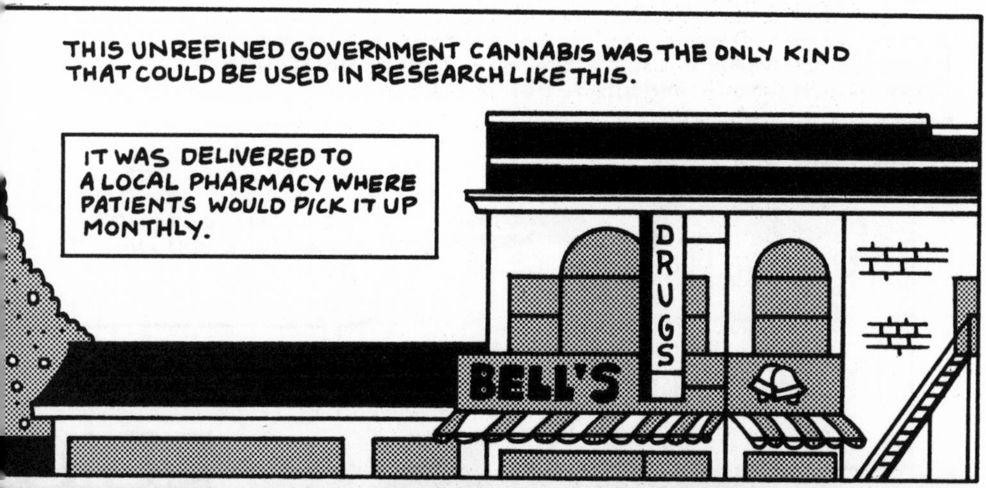
THIS UNREFINED GOVERNMENT CANNABIS WAS THE ONLY KIND THAT COULD BE USED IN RESEARCH LIKE THIS.
IT WAS DELIVERED TO A LOCAL PHARMACY WHERE PATIENTS WOULD PICK IT UP MONTHLY.
DRUGS
BELL'S

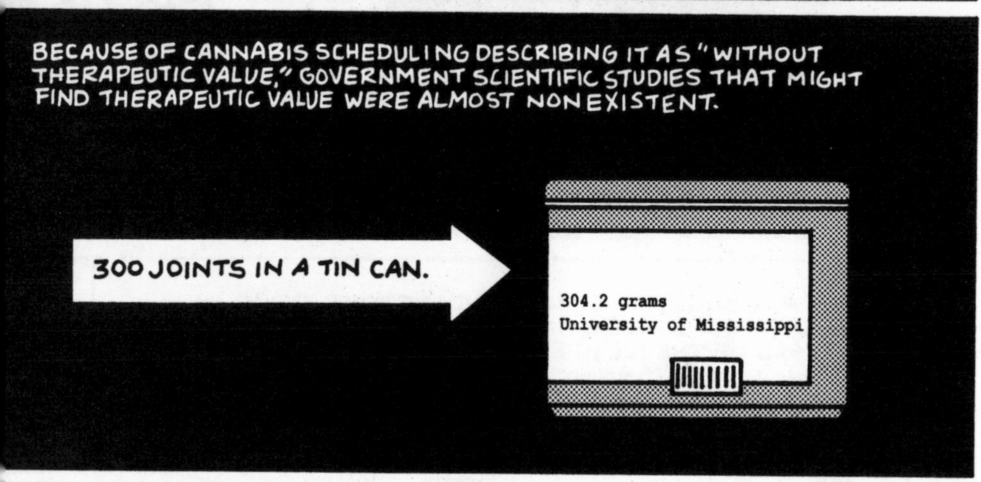
BECAUSE OF CANNABIS SCHEDULING DESCRIBING IT AS "WITHOUT THERAPEUTIC VALUE," GOVERNMENT SCIENTIFIC STUDIES THAT MIGHT FIND THERAPEUTIC VALUE WERE ALMOST NONEXISTENT.
300 JOINTS IN A TIN CAN.
304.2 grams
University of Mississippi

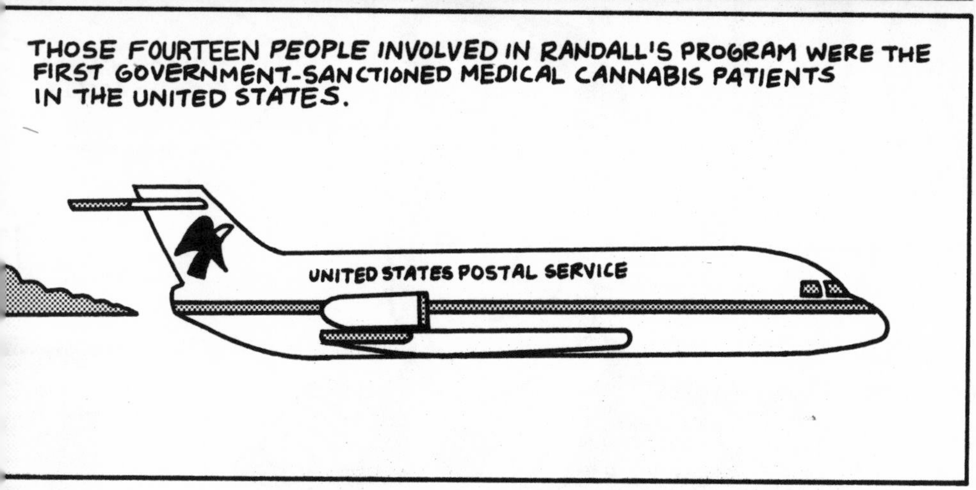
THOSE FOURTEEN PEOPLE INVOLVED IN RANDALL'S PROGRAM WERE THE FIRST GOVERNMENT-SANCTIONED MEDICAL CANNABIS PATIENTS IN THE UNITED STATES.
UNITED STATES POSTAL SERVICE

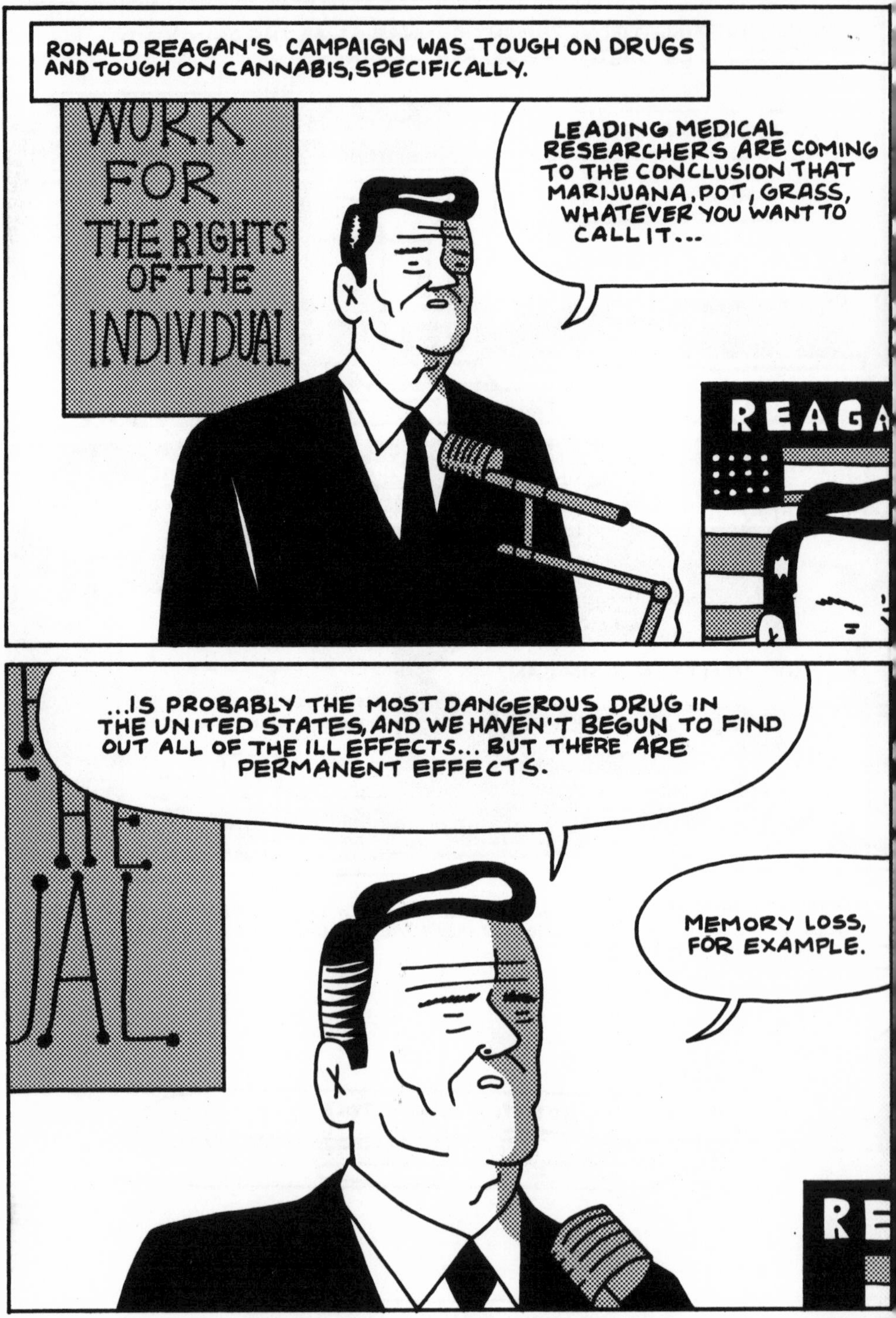
RONALD REAGAN'S CAMPAIGN WAS TOUGH ON DRUGS AND TOUGH ON CANNABIS, SPECIFICALLY.
WORK FOR THE RIGHTS OF THE INDIVIDUAL
LEADING MEDICAL RESEARCHERS ARE COMING TO THE CONCLUSION THAT MARIJUANA, POT, GRASS, WHATEVER YOU WANT TO CALL IT...
REAGA
...IS PROBABLY THE MOST DANGEROUS DRUG IN THE UNITED STATES, AND WE HAVEN'T BEGUN TO FIND OUT ALL OF THE ILL EFFECTS... BUT THERE ARE PERMANENT EFFECTS.
MEMORY LOSS, FOR EXAMPLE.
RE

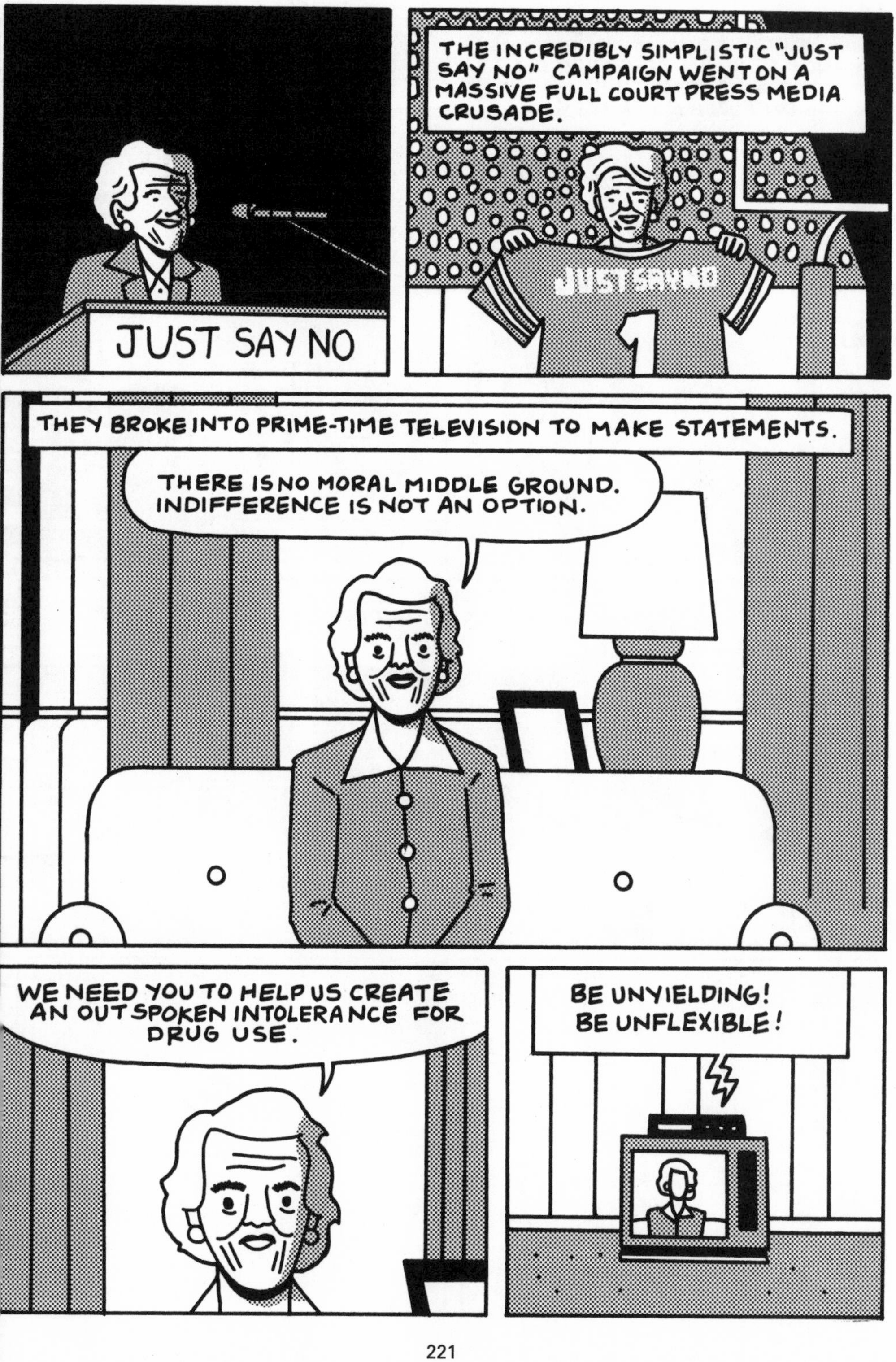
JUST SAY NO
THE INCREDIBLY SIMPLISTIC "JUST SAY NO" CAMPAIGN WENT ON A MASSIVE FULL COURT PRESS MEDIA CRUSADE.
JUST SAY NO
1
THEY BROKE INTO PRIME-TIME TELEVISION TO MAKE STATEMENTS.
THERE IS NO MORAL MIDDLE GROUND. INDIFFERENCE IS NOT AN OPTION.
WE NEED YOU TO HELP US CREATE AN OUTSPOKEN INTOLERANCE FOR DRUG USE.
BE UNYIELDING! BE UNFLEXIBLE!

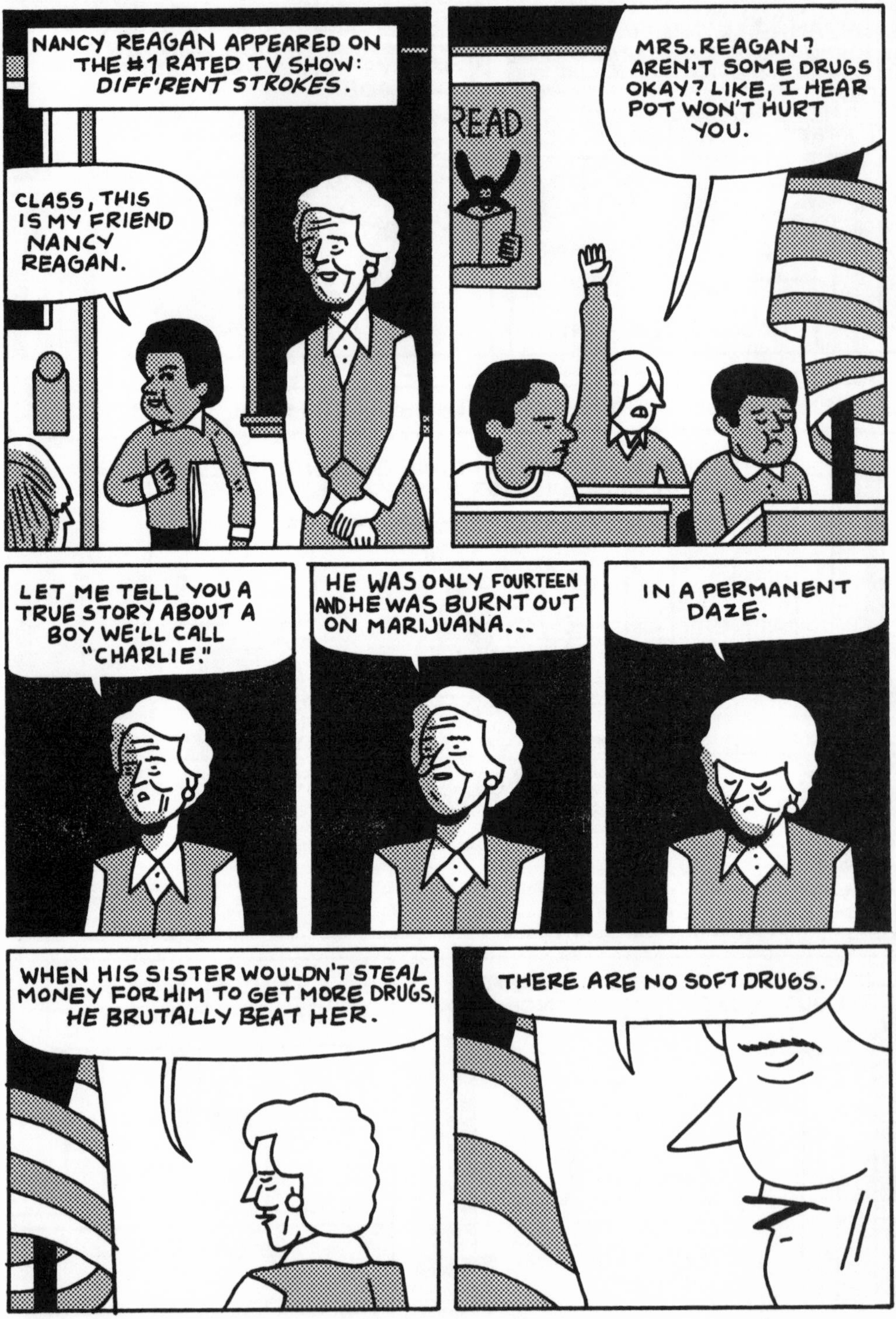
NANCY REAGAN APPEARED ON THE #1 RATED TV SHOW: *DIFF'RENT STROKES*.
CLASS, THIS IS MY FRIEND NANCY REAGAN.
READ
MRS. REAGAN? AREN'T SOME DRUGS OKAY? LIKE, I HEAR POT WON'T HURT YOU.
LET ME TELL YOU A TRUE STORY ABOUT A BOY WE'LL CALL "CHARLIE."
HE WAS ONLY FOURTEEN AND HE WAS BURNT OUT ON MARIJUANA...
IN A PERMANENT DAZE.
WHEN HIS SISTER WOULDN'T STEAL MONEY FOR HIM TO GET MORE DRUGS, HE BRUTALLY BEAT HER.
THERE ARE NO SOFT DRUGS.

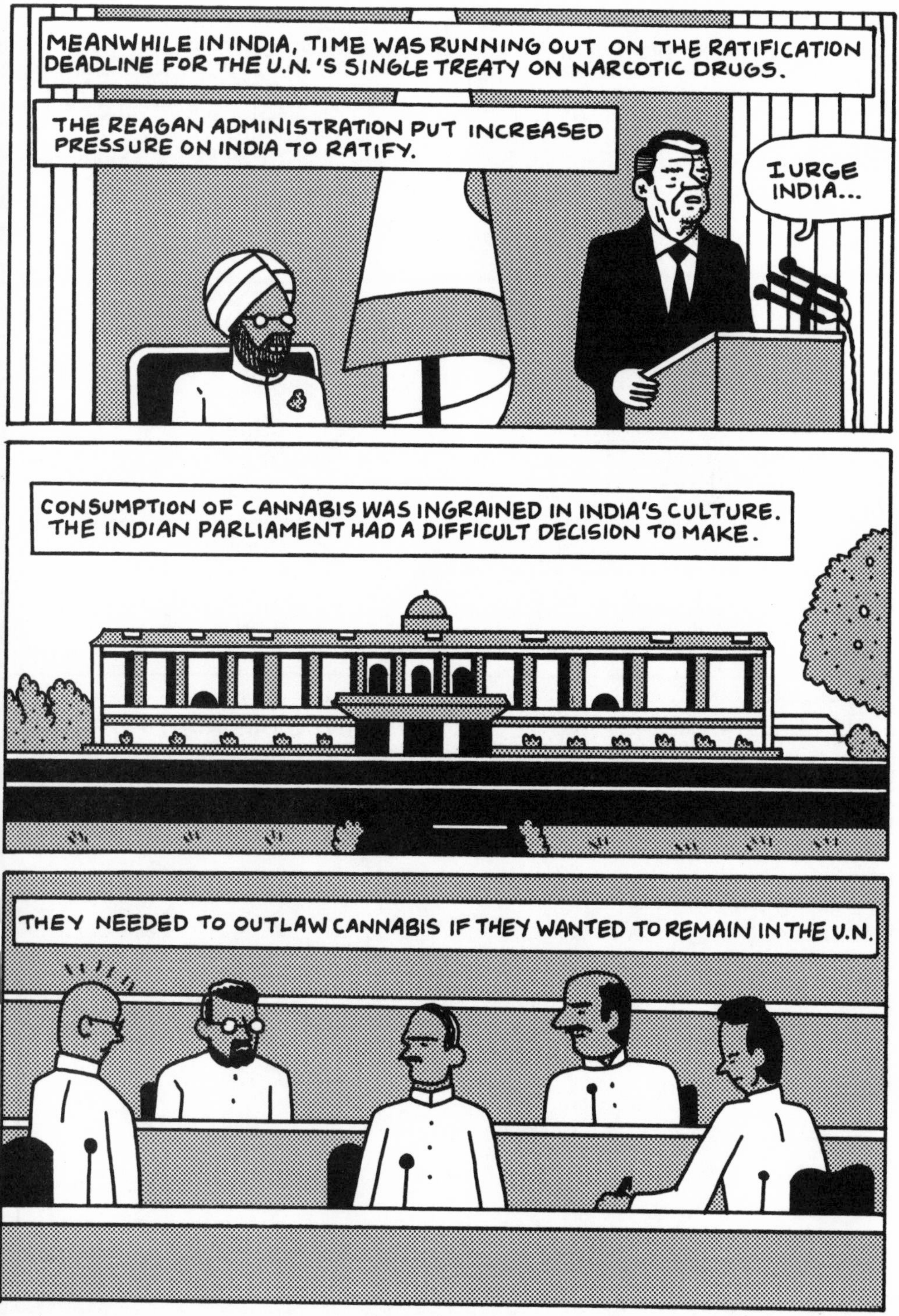
MEANWHILE IN INDIA, TIME WAS RUNNING OUT ON THE RATIFICATION DEADLINE FOR THE U.N.'S SINGLE TREATY ON NARCOTIC DRUGS.
THE REAGAN ADMINISTRATION PUT INCREASED PRESSURE ON INDIA TO RATIFY.
I URGE INDIA...
CONSUMPTION OF CANNABIS WAS INGRAINED IN INDIA'S CULTURE. THE INDIAN PARLIAMENT HAD A DIFFICULT DECISION TO MAKE.
THEY NEEDED TO OUTLAW CANNABIS IF THEY WANTED TO REMAIN IN THE U.N.

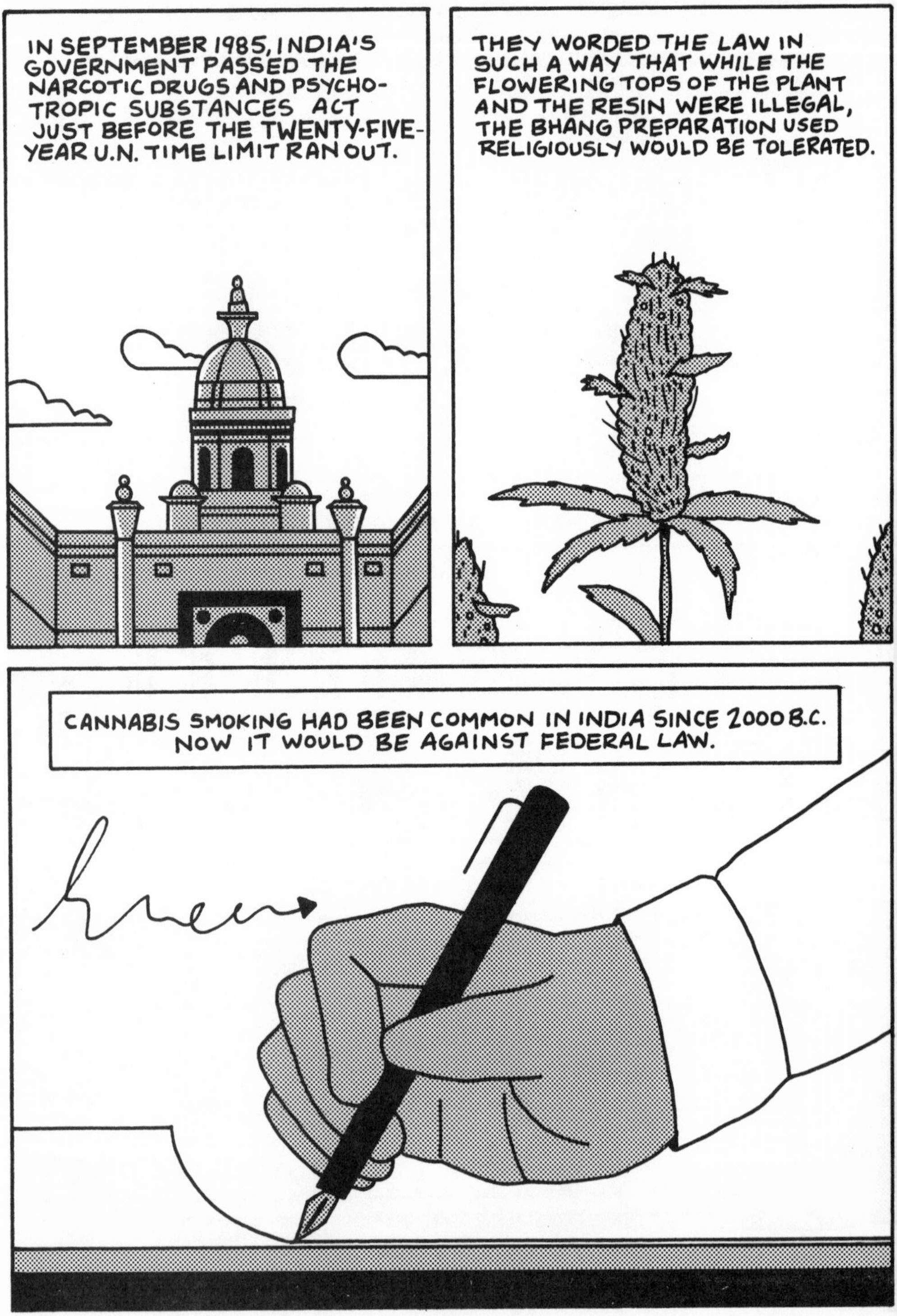
IN SEPTEMBER 1985, INDIA'S GOVERNMENT PASSED THE NARCOTIC DRUGS AND PSYCHOTROPIC SUBSTANCES ACT JUST BEFORE THE TWENTY-FIVE-YEAR U.N. TIME LIMIT RAN OUT.
THEY WORDED THE LAW IN SUCH A WAY THAT WHILE THE FLOWERING TOPS OF THE PLANT AND THE RESIN WERE ILLEGAL, THE BHANG PREPARATION USED RELIGIOUSLY WOULD BE TOLERATED.
CANNABIS SMOKING HAD BEEN COMMON IN INDIA SINCE 2000 B.C. NOW IT WOULD BE AGAINST FEDERAL LAW.

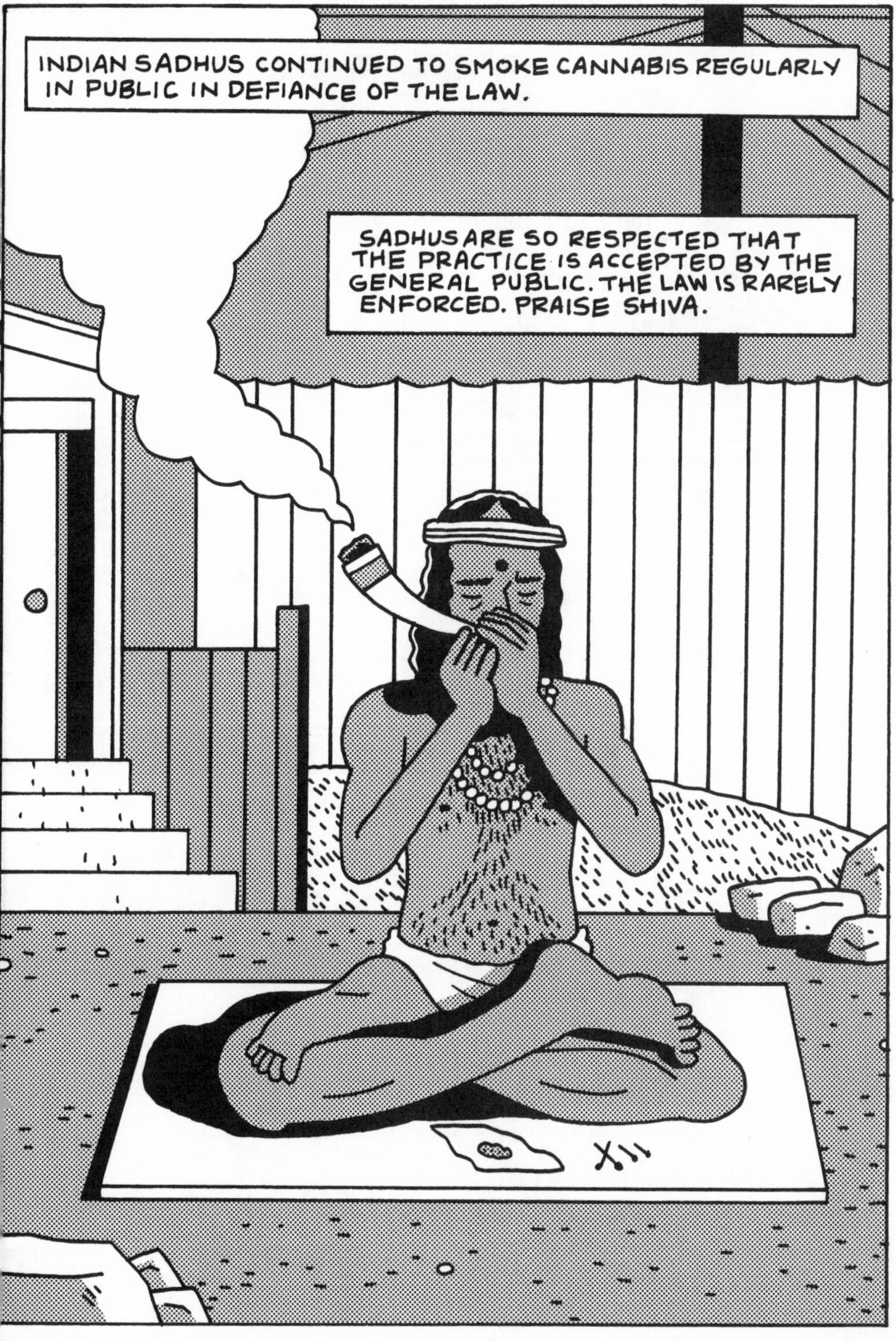
INDIAN SADHUS CONTINUED TO SMOKE CANNABIS REGULARLY IN PUBLIC IN DEFIANCE OF THE LAW.
SADHUS ARE SO RESPECTED THAT THE PRACTICE IS ACCEPTED BY THE GENERAL PUBLIC. THE LAW IS RARELY ENFORCED. PRAISE SHIVA.

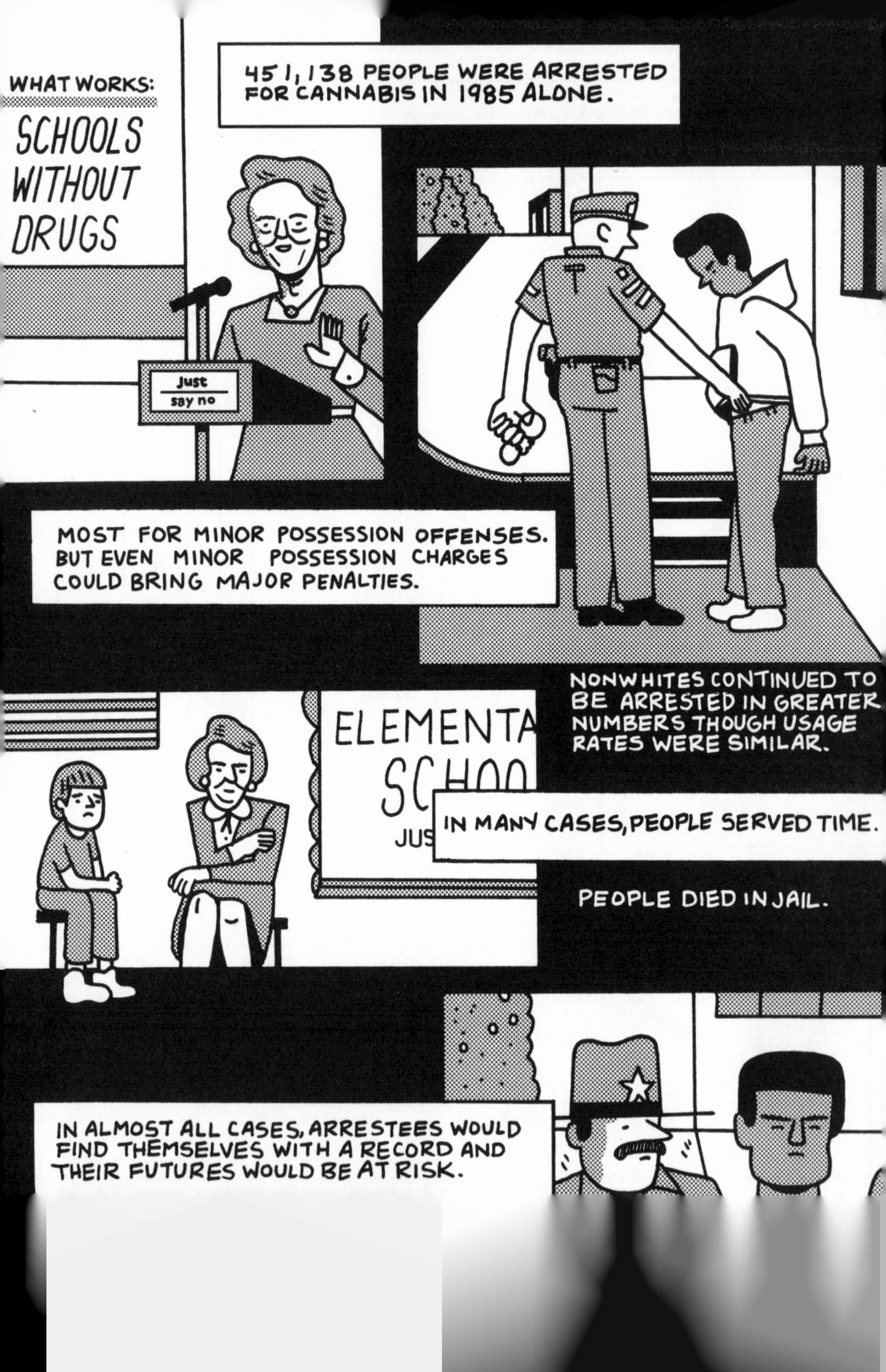
WHAT WORKS:
SCHOOLS WITHOUT DRUGS
451,138 PEOPLE WERE ARRESTED FOR CANNABIS IN 1985 ALONE.
Just say no
MOST FOR MINOR POSSESSION OFFENSES. BUT EVEN MINOR POSSESSION CHARGES COULD BRING MAJOR PENALTIES.
NONWHITES CONTINUED TO BE ARRESTED IN GREATER NUMBERS THOUGH USAGE RATES WERE SIMILAR.
ELEMENTA
SCHOO
JUS
IN MANY CASES, PEOPLE SERVED TIME.
PEOPLE DIED IN JAIL.
IN ALMOST ALL CASES, ARRESTEES WOULD FIND THEMSELVES WITH A RECORD AND THEIR FUTURES WOULD BE AT RISK.

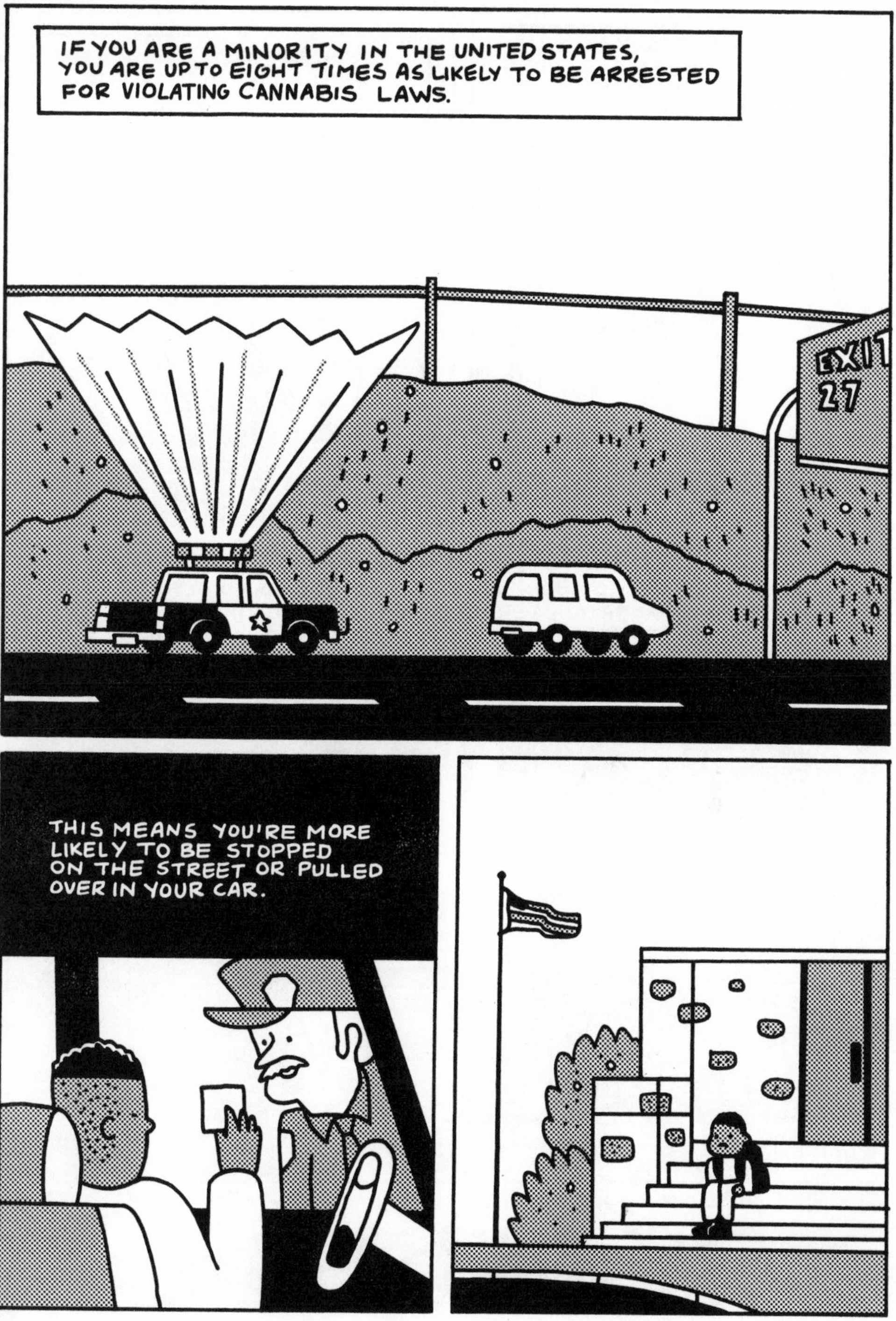
IF YOU ARE A MINORITY IN THE UNITED STATES, YOU ARE UP TO EIGHT TIMES AS LIKELY TO BE ARRESTED FOR VIOLATING CANNABIS LAWS.
EXIT 27
THIS MEANS YOU'RE MORE LIKELY TO BE STOPPED ON THE STREET OR PULLED OVER IN YOUR CAR.

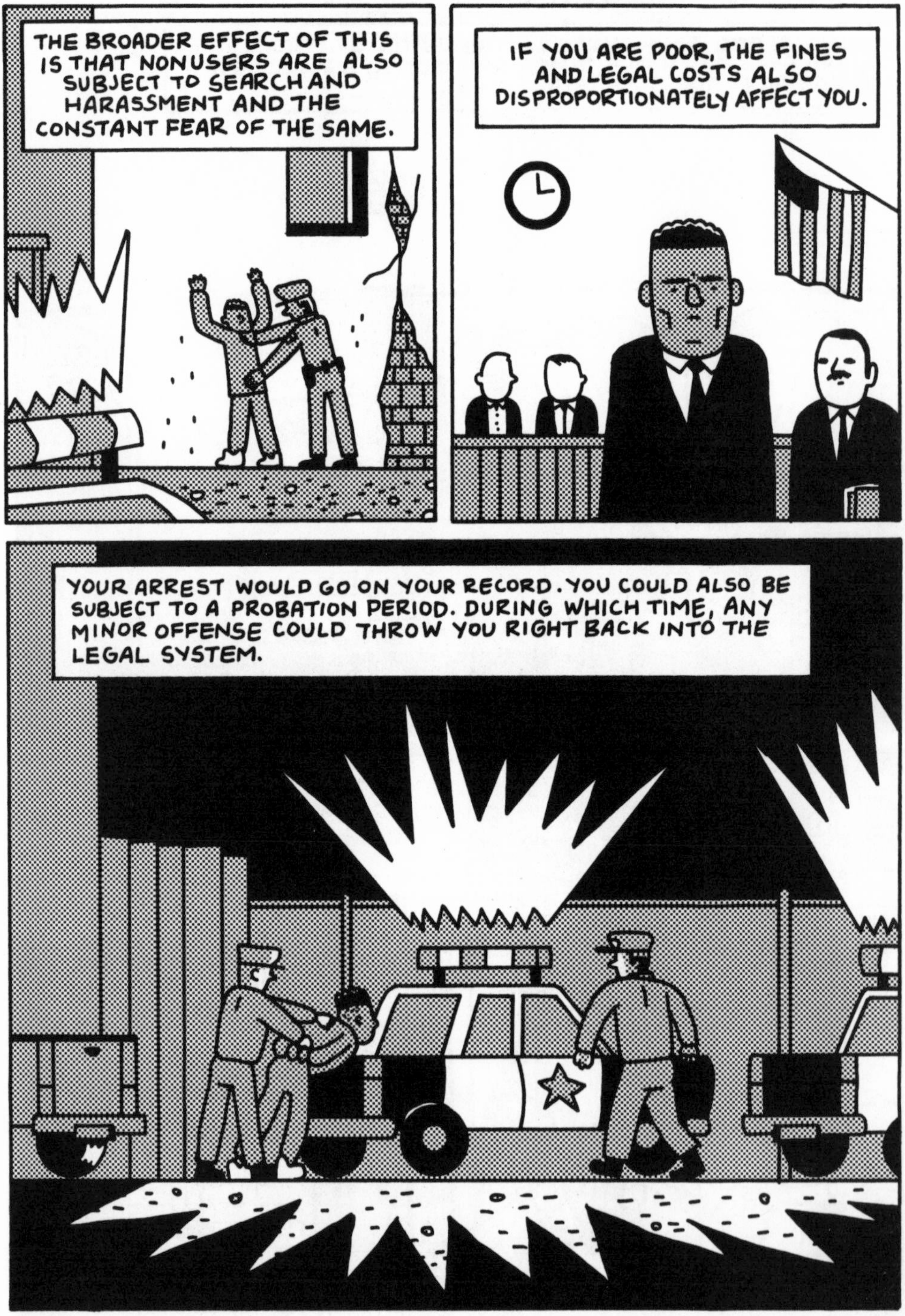
THE BROADER EFFECT OF THIS IS THAT NONUSERS ARE ALSO SUBJECT TO SEARCH AND HARASSMENT AND THE CONSTANT FEAR OF THE SAME.
IF YOU ARE POOR, THE FINES AND LEGAL COSTS ALSO DISPROPORTIONATELY AFFECT YOU.
YOUR ARREST WOULD GO ON YOUR RECORD. YOU COULD ALSO BE SUBJECT TO A PROBATION PERIOD. DURING WHICH TIME, ANY MINOR OFFENSE COULD THROW YOU RIGHT BACK INTO THE LEGAL SYSTEM.

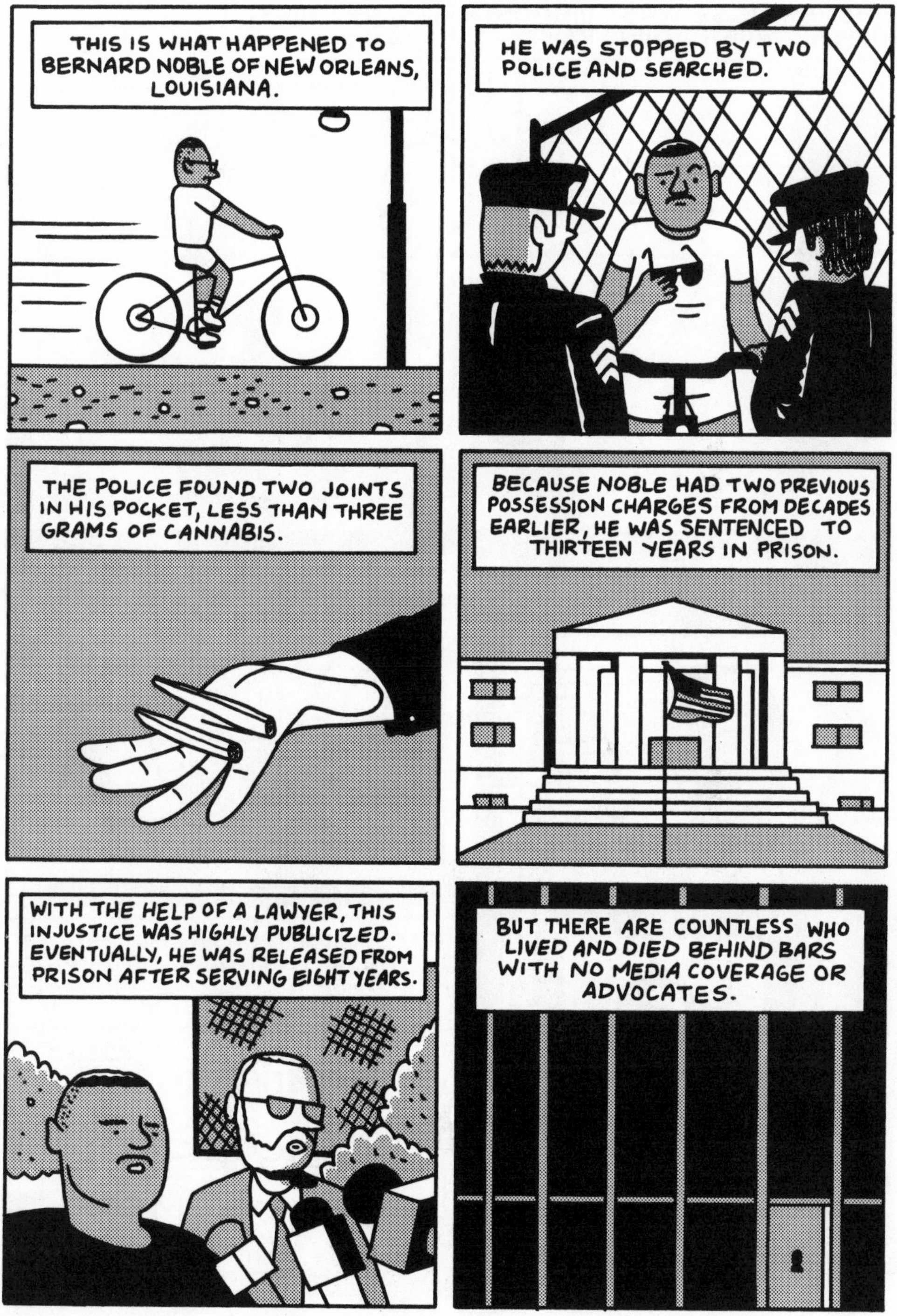
THIS IS WHAT HAPPENED TO BERNARD NOBLE OF NEW ORLEANS, LOUISIANA.
HE WAS STOPPED BY TWO POLICE AND SEARCHED.
THE POLICE FOUND TWO JOINTS IN HIS POCKET, LESS THAN THREE GRAMS OF CANNABIS.
BECAUSE NOBLE HAD TWO PREVIOUS POSSESSION CHARGES FROM DECADES EARLIER, HE WAS SENTENCED TO THIRTEEN YEARS IN PRISON.
WITH THE HELP OF A LAWYER, THIS INJUSTICE WAS HIGHLY PUBLICIZED. EVENTUALLY, HE WAS RELEASED FROM PRISON AFTER SERVING EIGHT YEARS.
BUT THERE ARE COUNTLESS WHO LIVED AND DIED BEHIND BARS WITH NO MEDIA COVERAGE OR ADVOCATES.

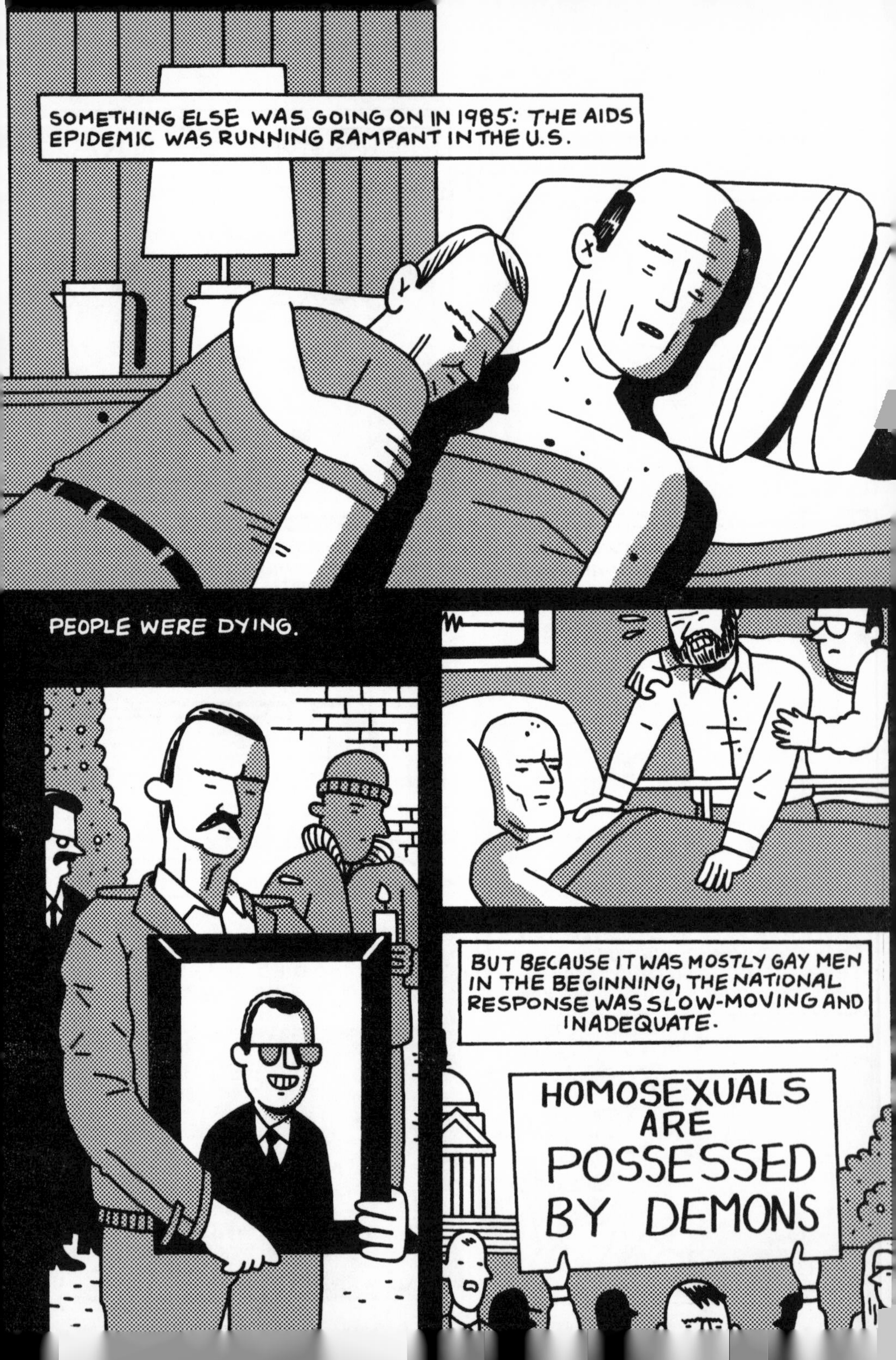
SOMETHING ELSE WAS GOING ON IN 1985: THE AIDS EPIDEMIC WAS RUNNING RAMPANT IN THE U.S.
PEOPLE WERE DYING.
BUT BECAUSE IT WAS MOSTLY GAY MEN IN THE BEGINNING, THE NATIONAL RESPONSE WAS SLOW-MOVING AND INADEQUATE.
HOMOSEXUALS ARE POSSESSED BY DEMONS

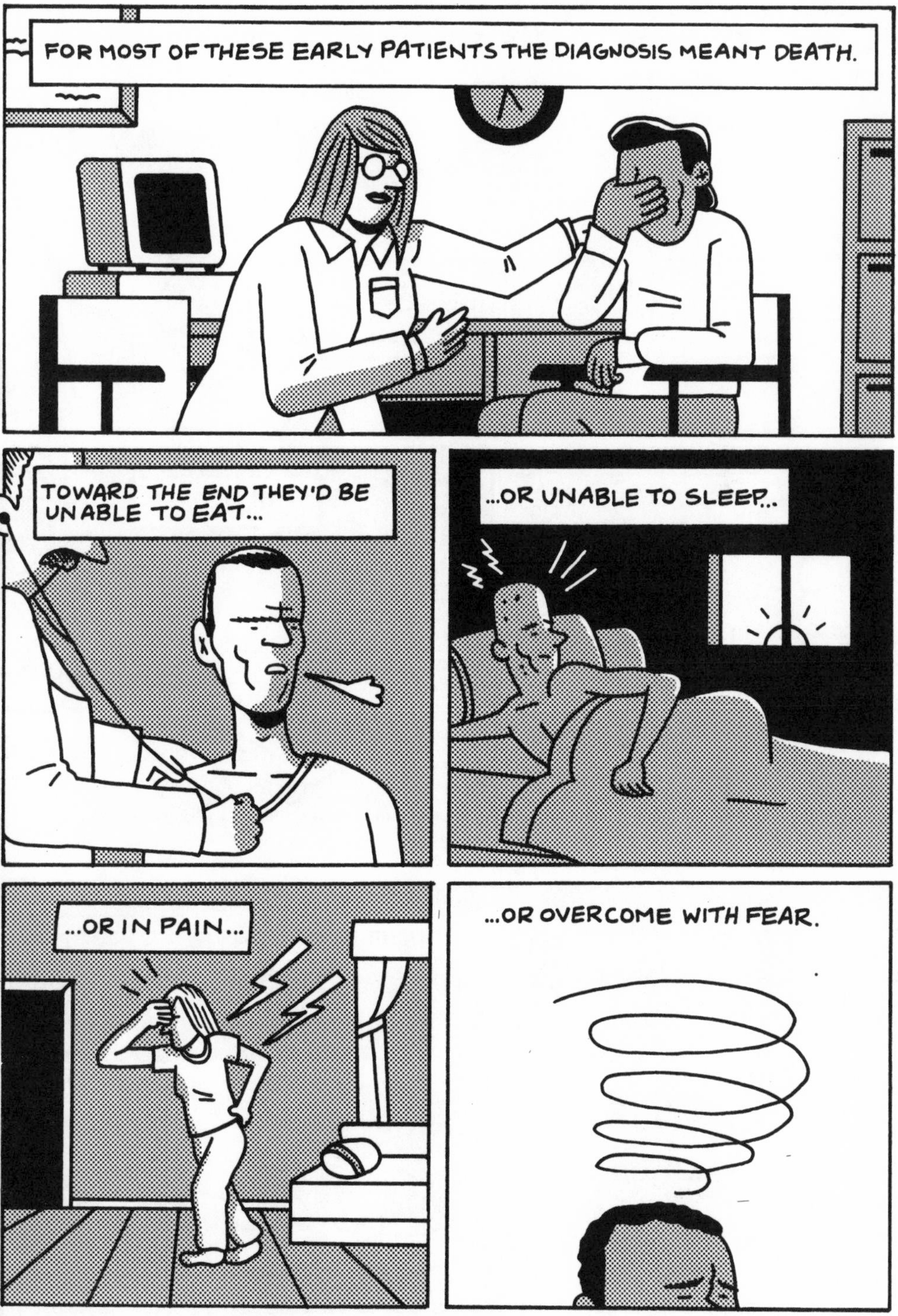
FOR MOST OF THESE EARLY PATIENTS THE DIAGNOSIS MEANT DEATH.
TOWARD THE END THEY'D BE UNABLE TO EAT...
...OR UNABLE TO SLEEP...
...OR IN PAIN...
...OR OVERCOME WITH FEAR.

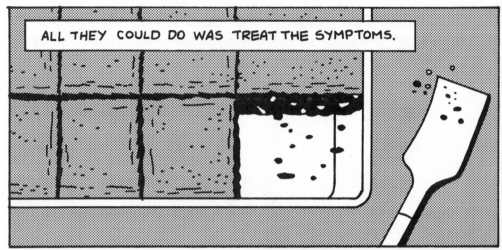

ALL THEY COULD DO WAS TREAT THE SYMPTOMS.

CANNABIS HELPED PEOPLE EAT.

AND SLEEP.

AND TO EXPERIENCE LIFE IN THEIR FINAL DAYS.

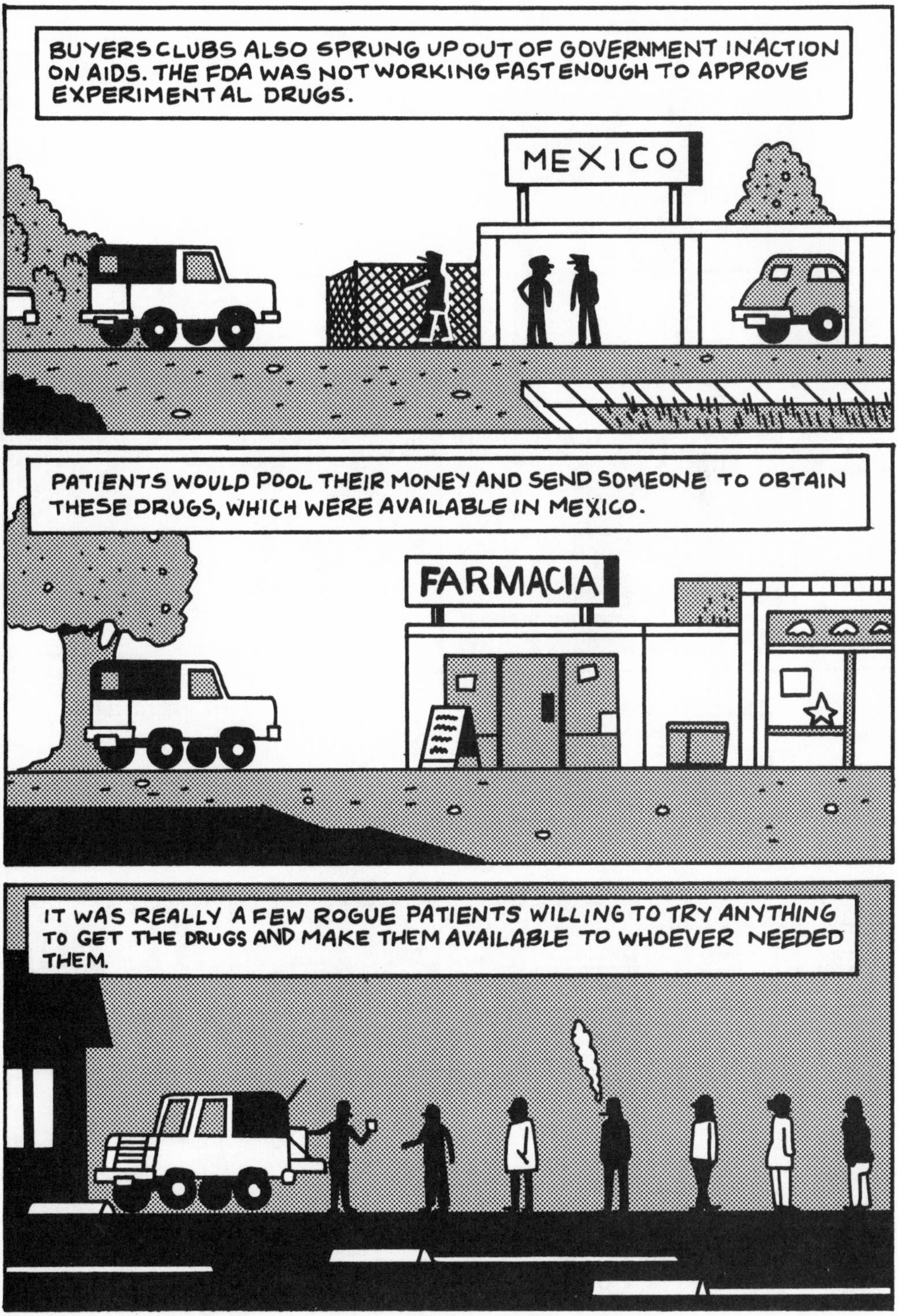
BUYERS CLUBS ALSO SPRUNG UP OUT OF GOVERNMENT INACTION ON AIDS. THE FDA WAS NOT WORKING FAST ENOUGH TO APPROVE EXPERIMENTAL DRUGS.
MEXICO
PATIENTS WOULD POOL THEIR MONEY AND SEND SOMEONE TO OBTAIN THESE DRUGS, WHICH WERE AVAILABLE IN MEXICO.
FARMACIA
IT WAS REALLY A FEW ROGUE PATIENTS WILLING TO TRY ANYTHING TO GET THE DRUGS AND MAKE THEM AVAILABLE TO WHOEVER NEEDED THEM.

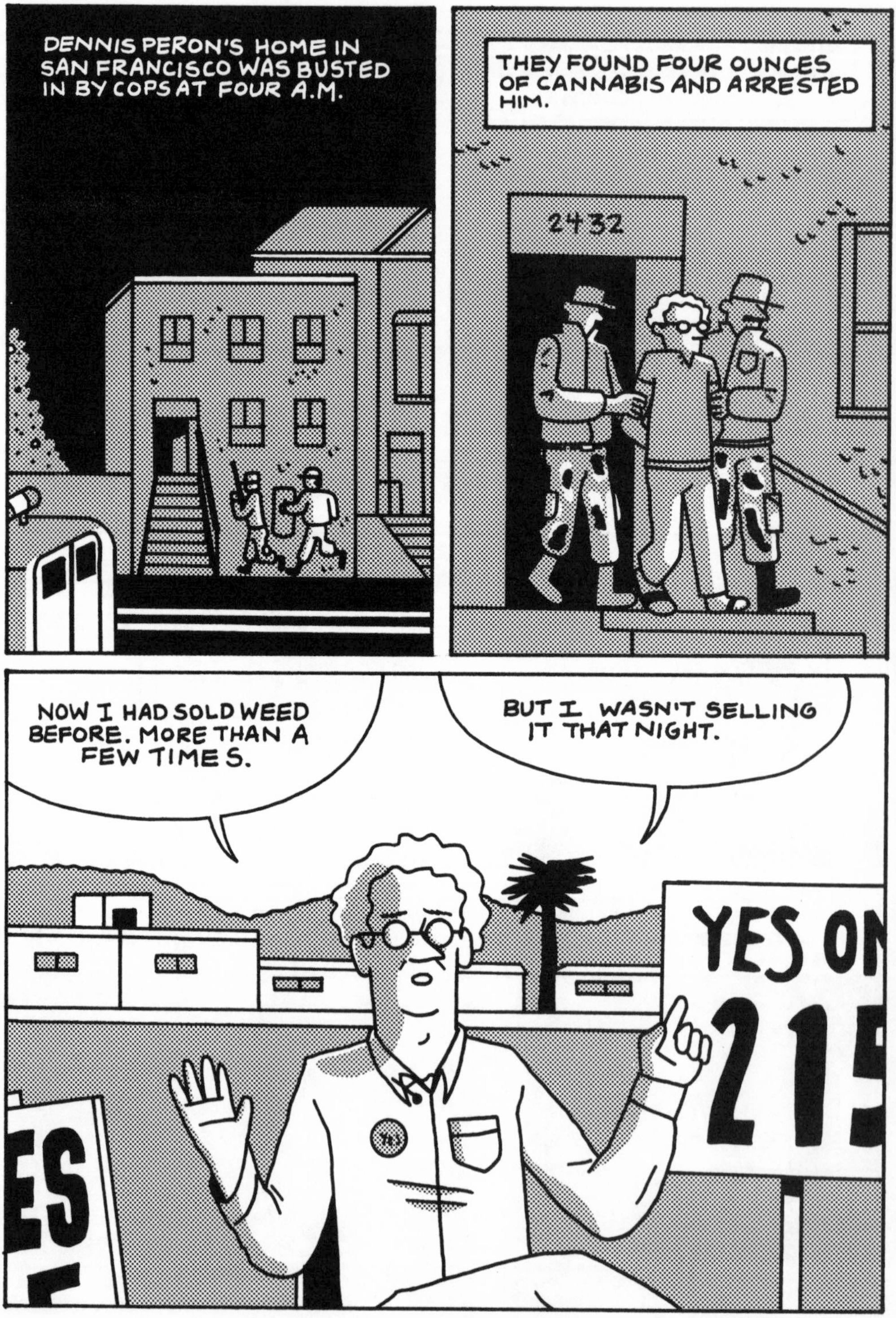
DENNIS PERON'S HOME IN SAN FRANCISCO WAS BUSTED IN BY COPS AT FOUR A.M.
THEY FOUND FOUR OUNCES OF CANNABIS AND ARRESTED HIM.
2432
NOW I HAD SOLD WEED BEFORE. MORE THAN A FEW TIMES.
BUT I WASN'T SELLING IT THAT NIGHT.
YES ON 215

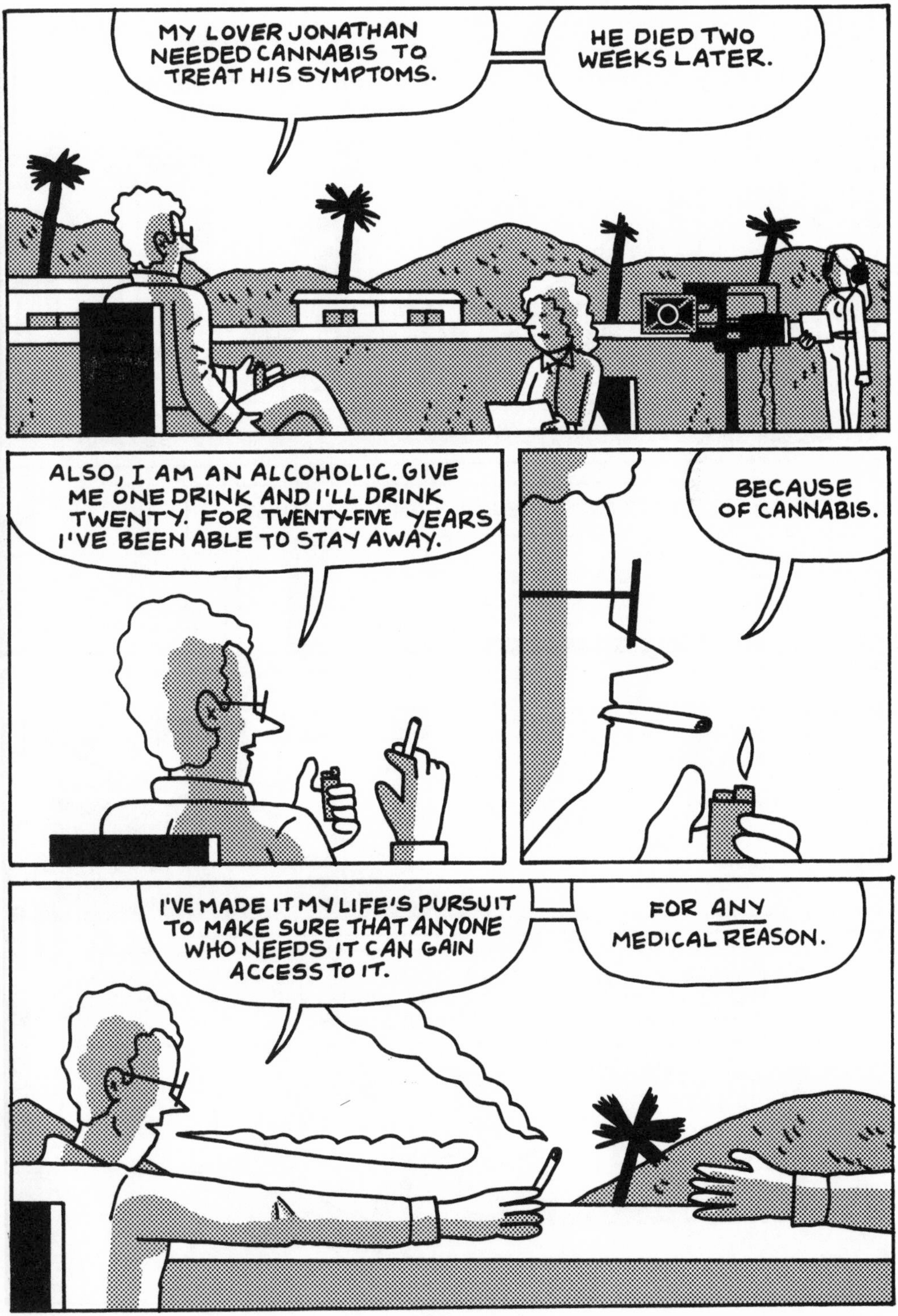
MY LOVER JONATHAN NEEDED CANNABIS TO TREAT HIS SYMPTOMS.
HE DIED TWO WEEKS LATER.
ALSO, I AM AN ALCOHOLIC. GIVE ME ONE DRINK AND I'LL DRINK TWENTY. FOR TWENTY-FIVE YEARS I'VE BEEN ABLE TO STAY AWAY.
BECAUSE OF CANNABIS.
I'VE MADE IT MY LIFE'S PURSUIT TO MAKE SURE THAT ANYONE WHO NEEDS IT CAN GAIN ACCESS TO IT.
FOR ANY MEDICAL REASON.

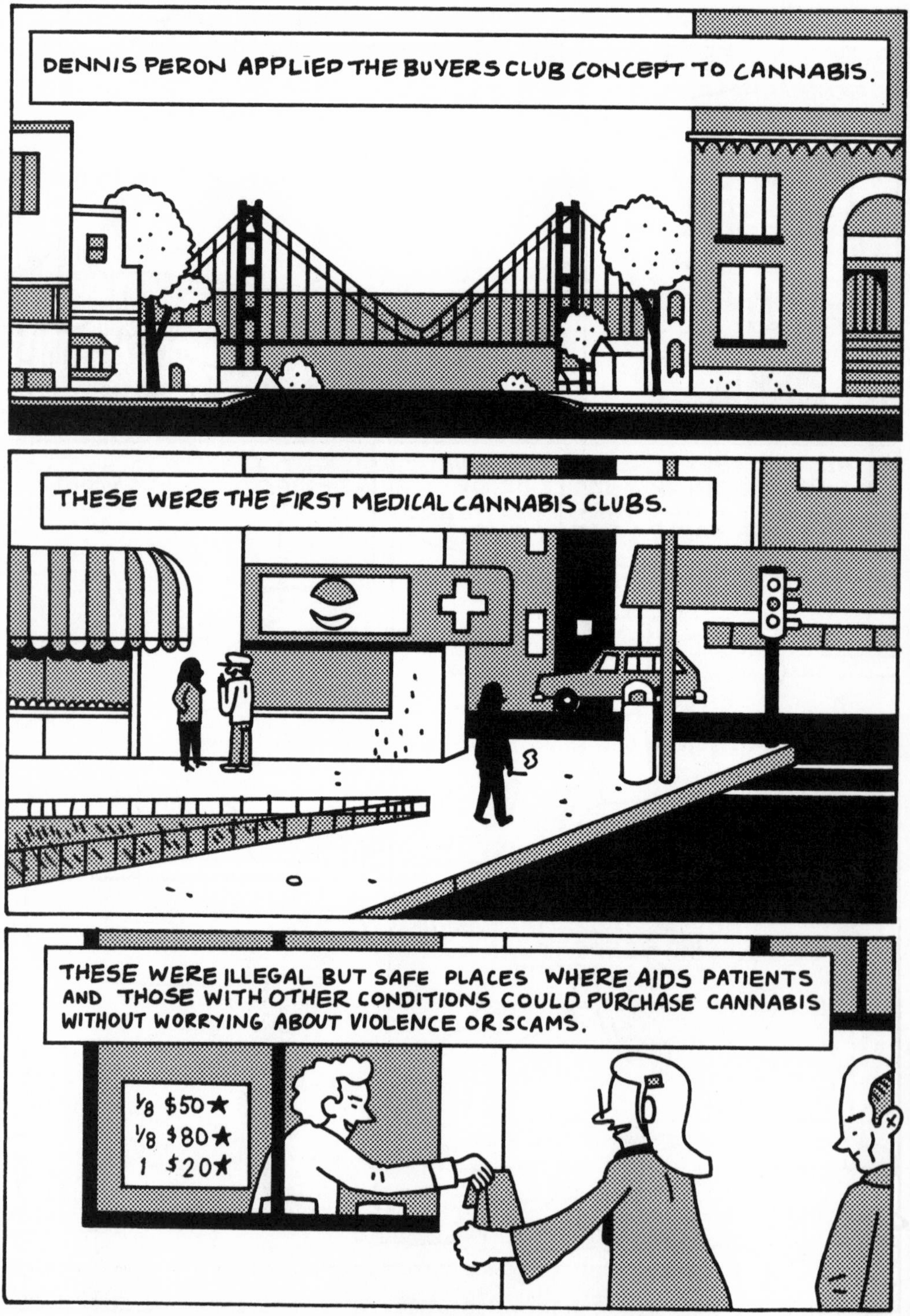
DENNIS PERON APPLIED THE BUYERS CLUB CONCEPT TO CANNABIS.
THESE WERE THE FIRST MEDICAL CANNABIS CLUBS.
THESE WERE ILLEGAL BUT SAFE PLACES WHERE AIDS PATIENTS AND THOSE WITH OTHER CONDITIONS COULD PURCHASE CANNABIS WITHOUT WORRYING ABOUT VIOLENCE OR SCAMS.
1/8 $50★
1/8 $80★
1 $20★

AT SAN FRANCISCO GENERAL HOSPITAL, A VOLUNTEER NAMED MARY JANE RATHBUN EARNED THE NAME "BROWNIE MARY" BY BAKING CANNABIS BROWNIES FOR PATIENTS.

SHE WAS ARRESTED THREE TIMES FOR DOING SO.

EACH TIME SHE GAINED GREATER ATTENTION FOR CANNABIS AS MEDICINE.

MEDICAL CANNABIS BECAME A NATIONAL MOVEMENT, THANKS TO ACTIVISTS LIKE DENNIS PERON AND BROWNIE MARY.

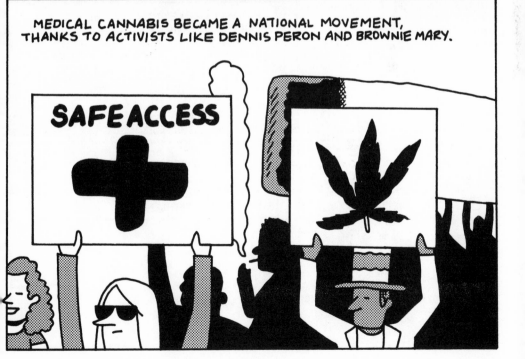

SAFE ACCESS

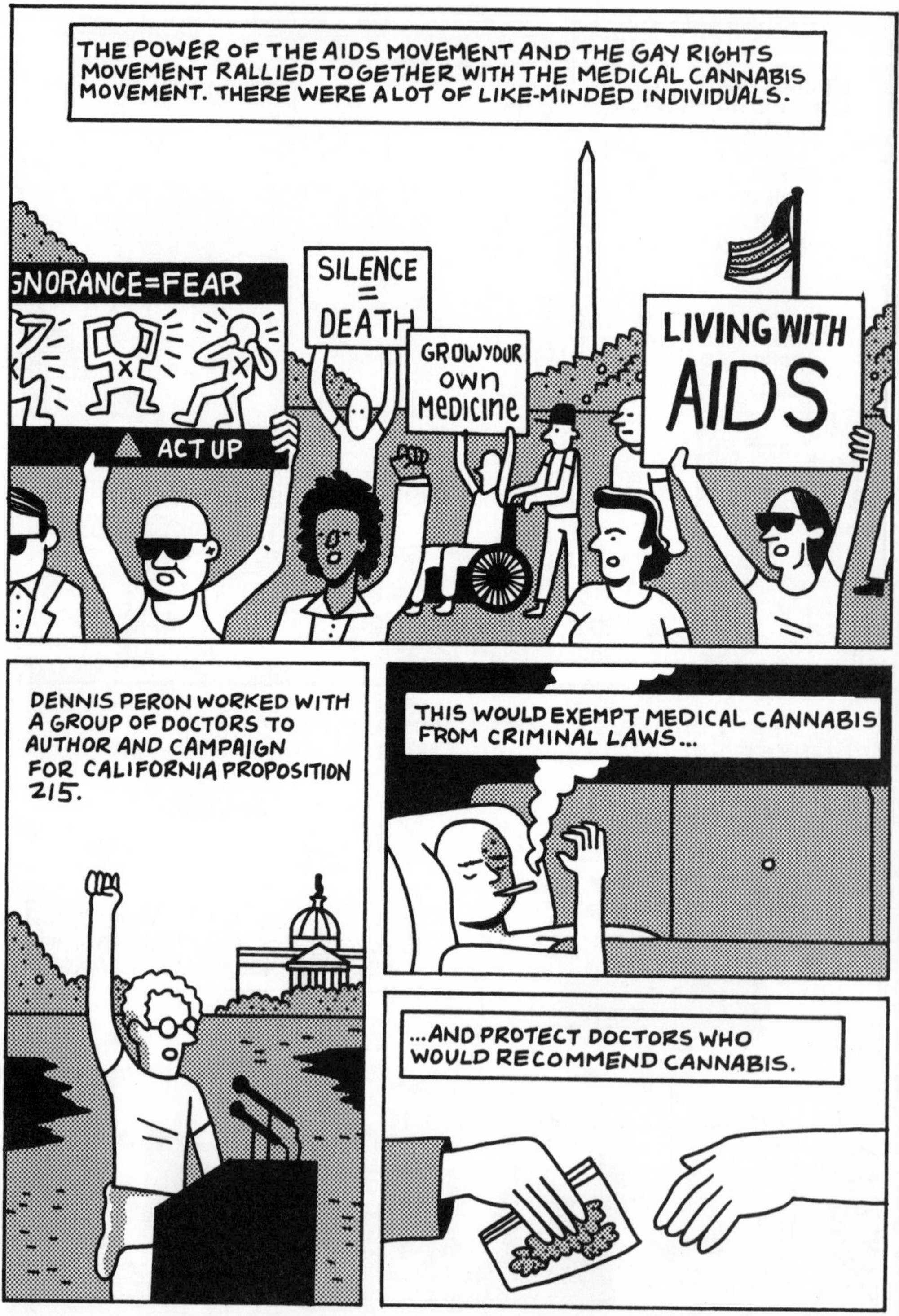
THE POWER OF THE AIDS MOVEMENT AND THE GAY RIGHTS MOVEMENT RALLIED TOGETHER WITH THE MEDICAL CANNABIS MOVEMENT. THERE WERE A LOT OF LIKE-MINDED INDIVIDUALS.
GNORANCE=FEAR
ACT UP
SILENCE = DEATH
GROW YOUR OWN MEDICINE
LIVING WITH AIDS
DENNIS PERON WORKED WITH A GROUP OF DOCTORS TO AUTHOR AND CAMPAIGN FOR CALIFORNIA PROPOSITION 215.
THIS WOULD EXEMPT MEDICAL CANNABIS FROM CRIMINAL LAWS...
...AND PROTECT DOCTORS WHO WOULD RECOMMEND CANNABIS.

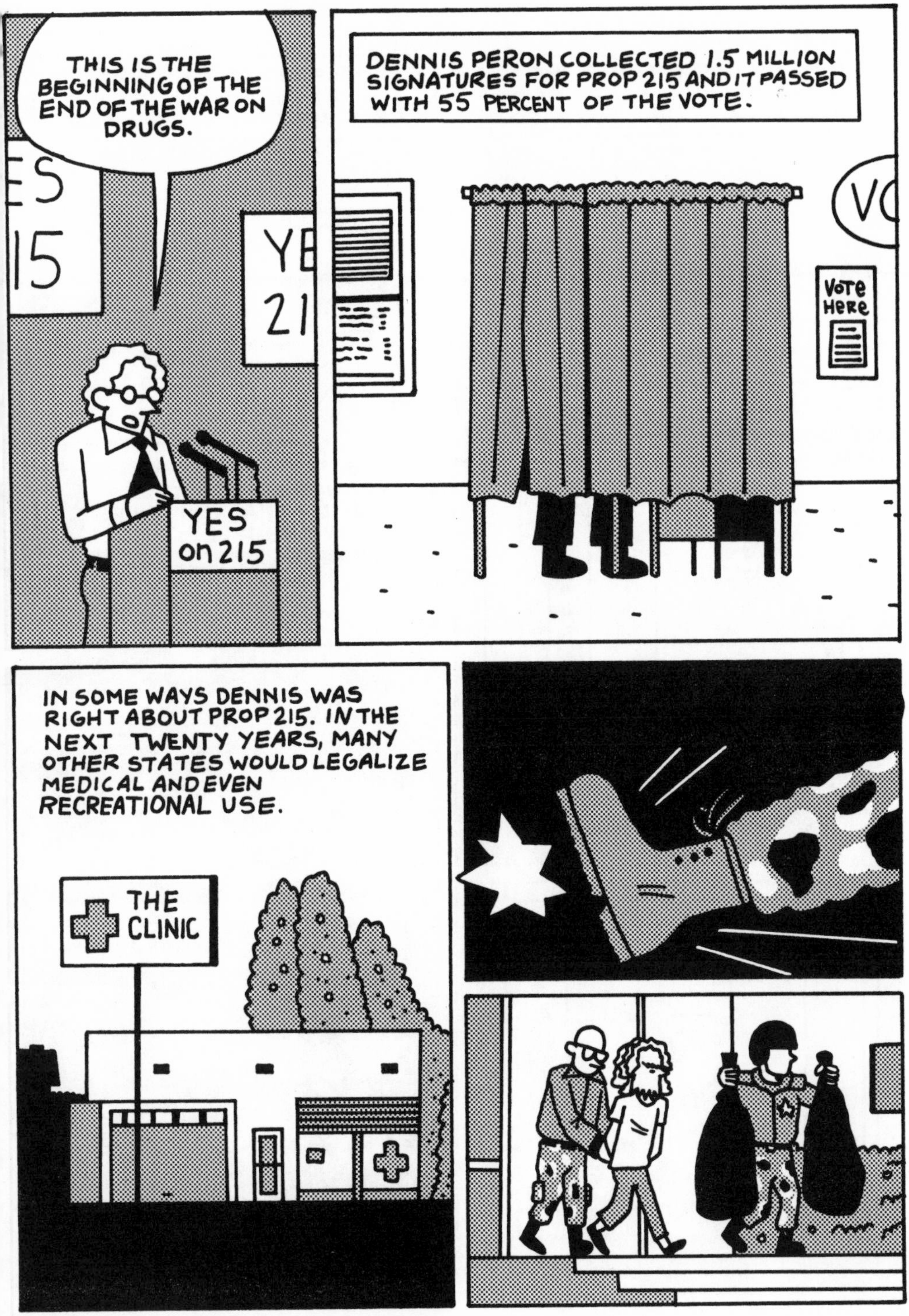
THIS IS THE BEGINNING OF THE END OF THE WAR ON DRUGS.
YES 215
YE 21
YES on 215
DENNIS PERON COLLECTED 1.5 MILLION SIGNATURES FOR PROP 215 AND IT PASSED WITH 55 PERCENT OF THE VOTE.
VO
Vote Here
IN SOME WAYS DENNIS WAS RIGHT ABOUT PROP 215. IN THE NEXT TWENTY YEARS, MANY OTHER STATES WOULD LEGALIZE MEDICAL AND EVEN RECREATIONAL USE.
THE CLINIC

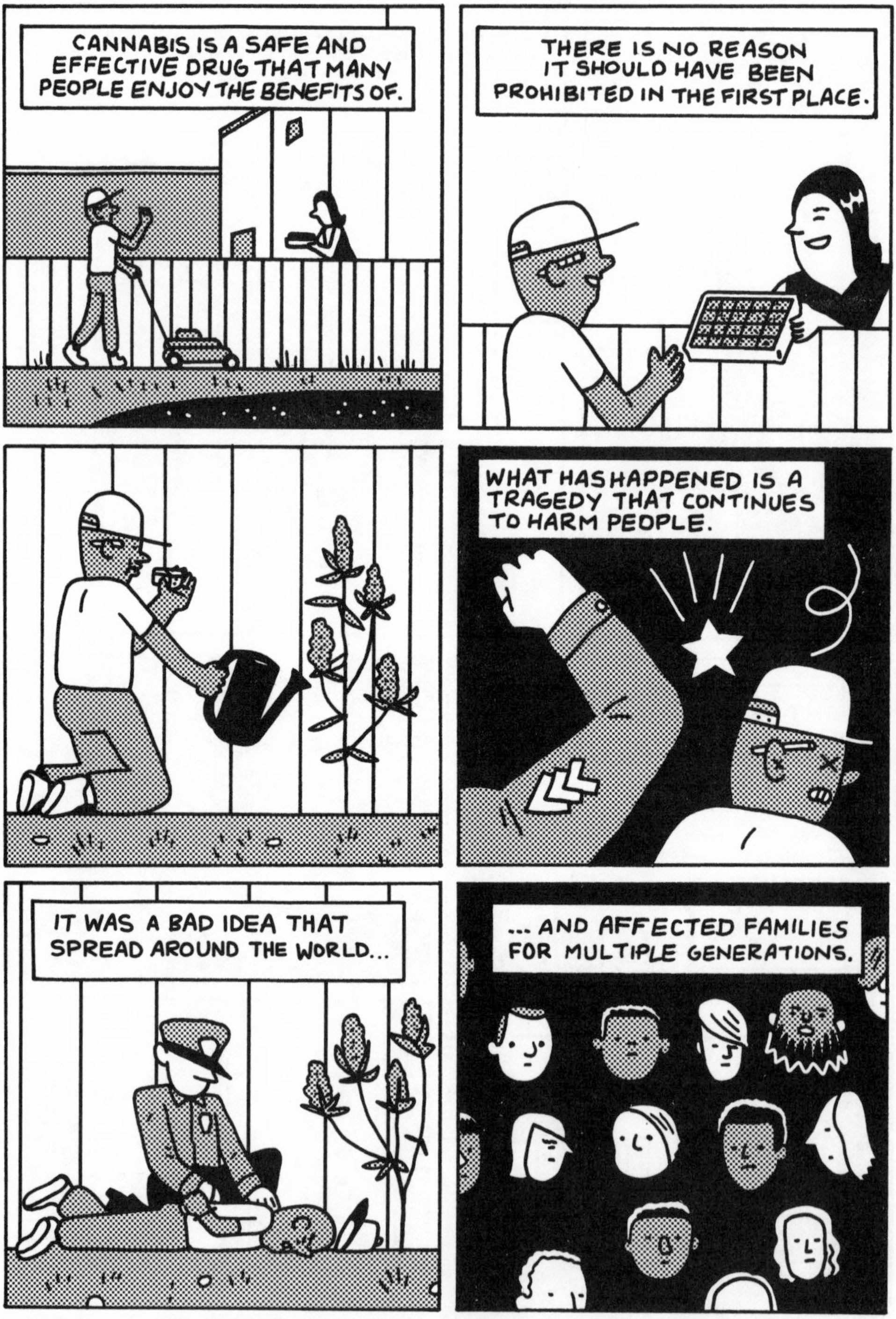
CANNABIS IS A SAFE AND EFFECTIVE DRUG THAT MANY PEOPLE ENJOY THE BENEFITS OF.
THERE IS NO REASON IT SHOULD HAVE BEEN PROHIBITED IN THE FIRST PLACE.
WHAT HAS HAPPENED IS A TRAGEDY THAT CONTINUES TO HARM PEOPLE.
IT WAS A BAD IDEA THAT SPREAD AROUND THE WORLD...
... AND AFFECTED FAMILIES FOR MULTIPLE GENERATIONS.

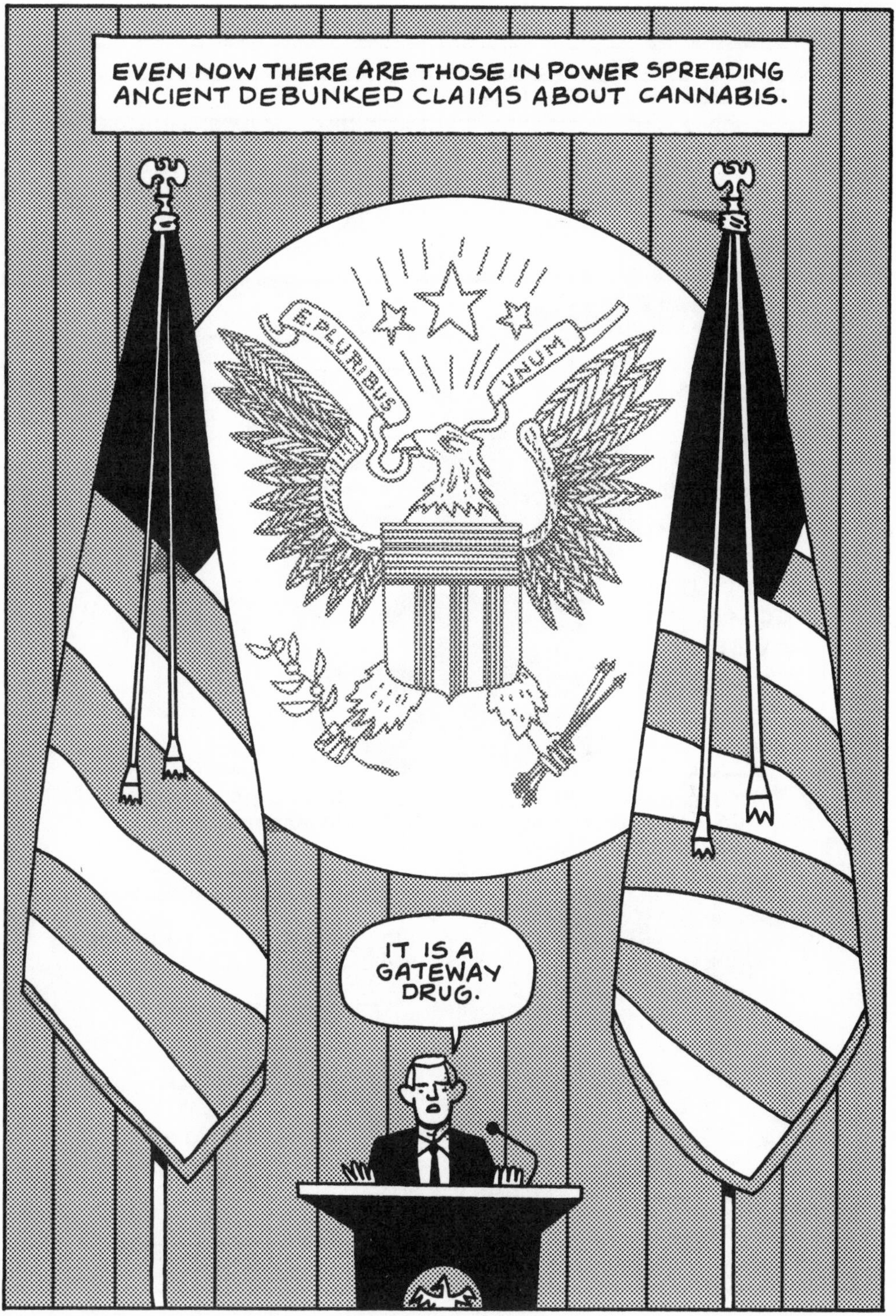
EVEN NOW THERE ARE THOSE IN POWER SPREADING ANCIENT DEBUNKED CLAIMS ABOUT CANNABIS.
E PLURIBUS UNUM
IT IS A GATEWAY DRUG.

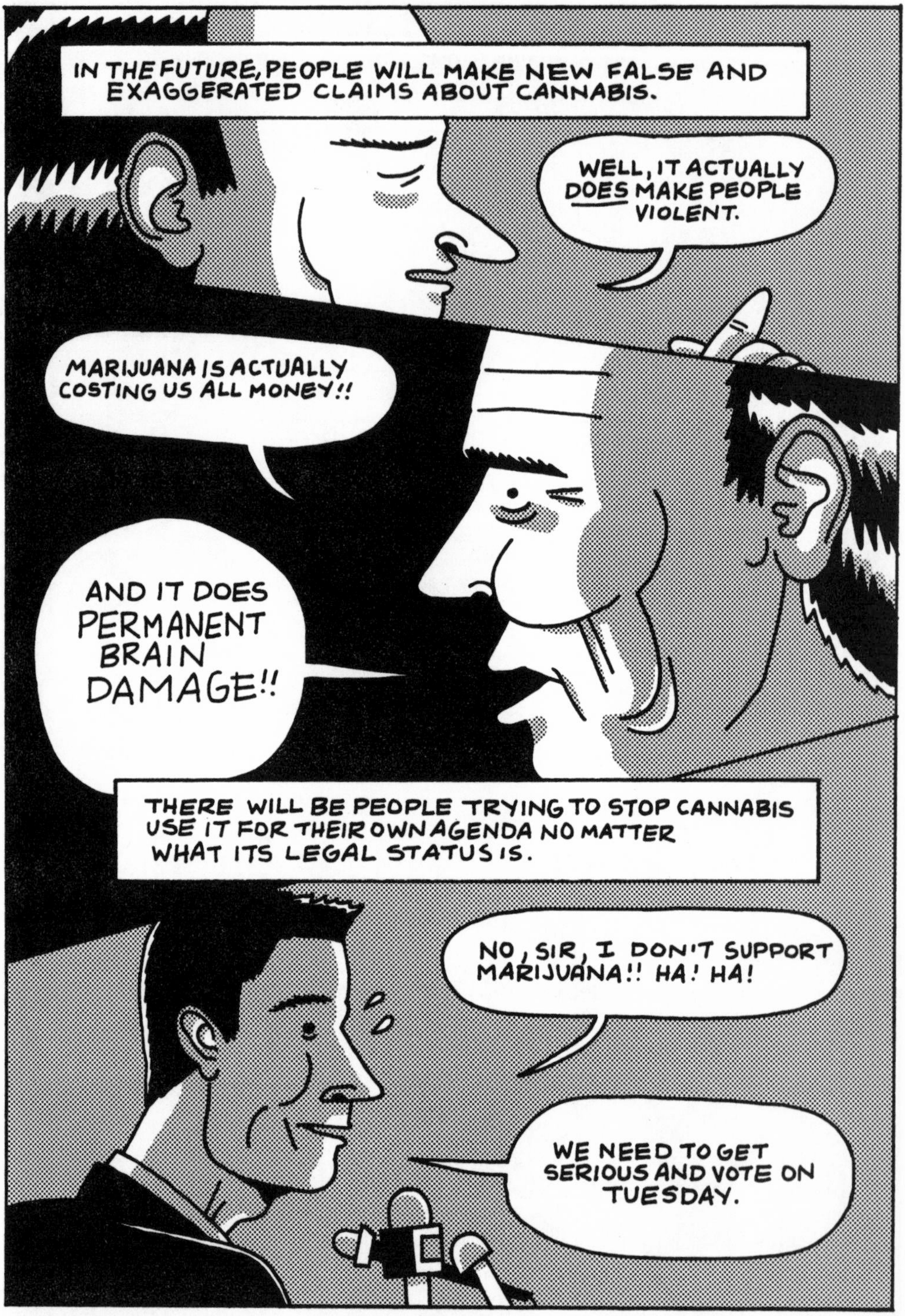
IN THE FUTURE, PEOPLE WILL MAKE NEW FALSE AND EXAGGERATED CLAIMS ABOUT CANNABIS.
WELL, IT ACTUALLY DOES MAKE PEOPLE VIOLENT.
MARIJUANA IS ACTUALLY COSTING US ALL MONEY!!
AND IT DOES PERMANENT BRAIN DAMAGE!!
THERE WILL BE PEOPLE TRYING TO STOP CANNABIS USE IT FOR THEIR OWN AGENDA NO MATTER WHAT ITS LEGAL STATUS IS.
NO, SIR, I DON'T SUPPORT MARIJUANA!! HA! HA!
WE NEED TO GET SERIOUS AND VOTE ON TUESDAY.

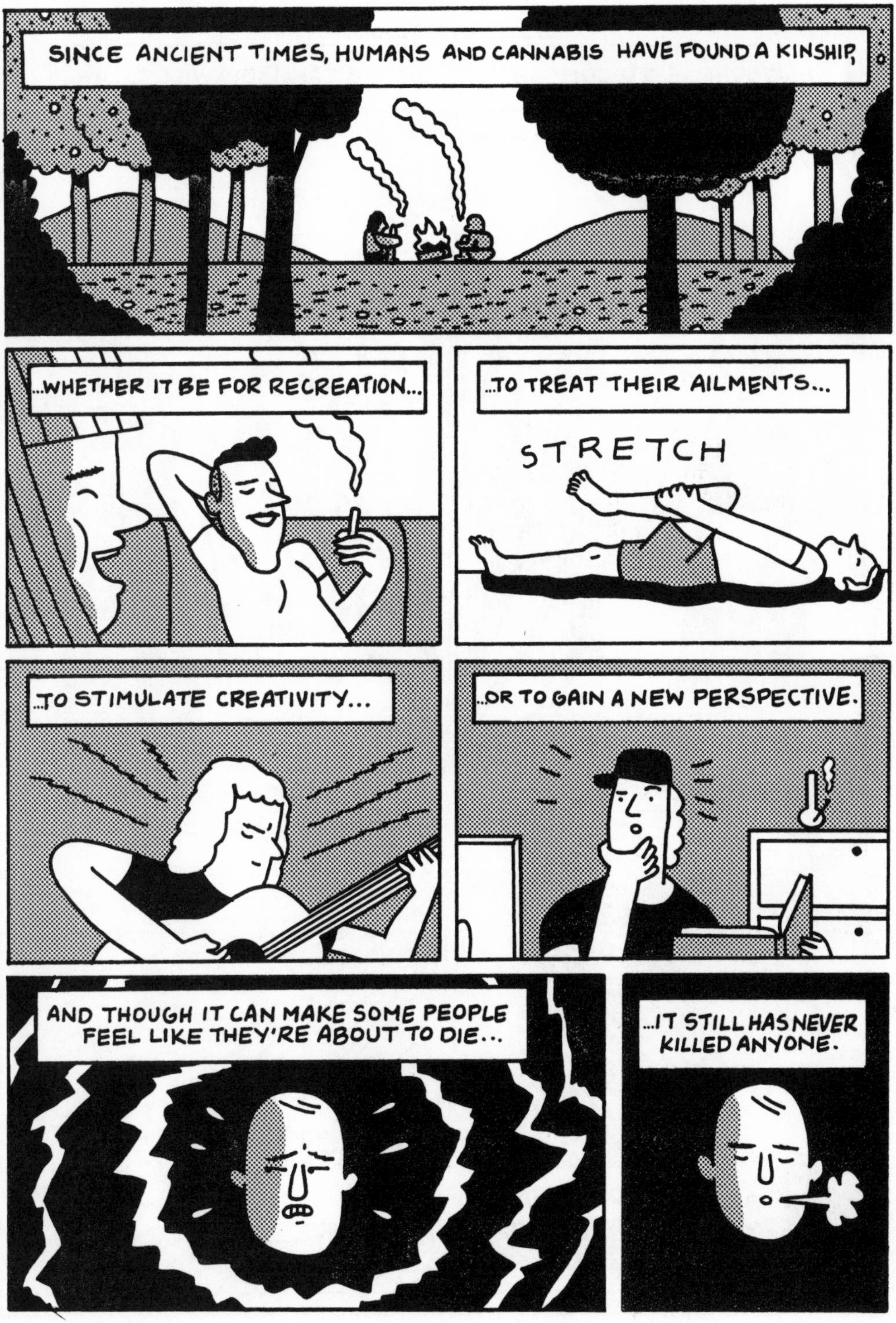
SINCE ANCIENT TIMES, HUMANS AND CANNABIS HAVE FOUND A KINSHIP,
...WHETHER IT BE FOR RECREATION...
...TO TREAT THEIR AILMENTS...
STRETCH
...TO STIMULATE CREATIVITY...
...OR TO GAIN A NEW PERSPECTIVE.
AND THOUGH IT CAN MAKE SOME PEOPLE FEEL LIKE THEY'RE ABOUT TO DIE...
...IT STILL HAS NEVER KILLED ANYONE.

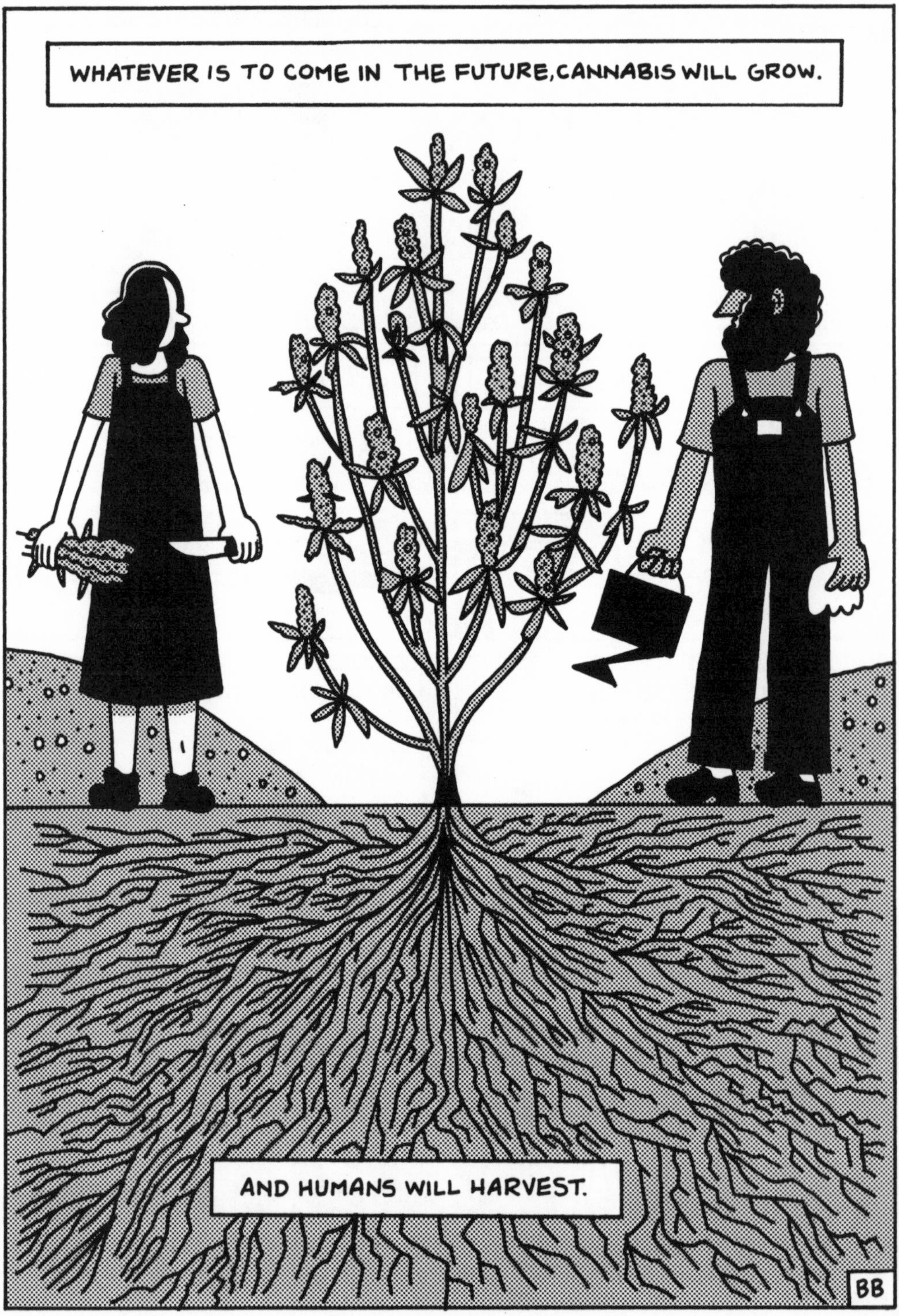
WHATEVER IS TO COME IN THE FUTURE, CANNABIS WILL GROW.
AND HUMANS WILL HARVEST.
BB

BIBLIOGRAPHY

Print

Barker, Joseph. "British India: Empire, Ideology & Race." *Sonder Magazine*, October 20, 2015.

Campos, Isaac. *Home Grown: Marijuana and the Origins of Mexico's War on Drugs*. Chapel Hill, NC: University of North Carolina Press, 2014.

Chanock, Martin. *The Making of South African Legal Culture 1902–1936: Fear, Favour and Prejudice*. Cambridge, United Kingdom: Cambridge University Press, 2007.

Chasin, Alexandra. *Assassin of Youth: A Kaleidoscopic History of Harry J. Anslinger's War on Drugs*. Chicago, IL: University of Chicago Press, 2016.

Chasteen, John Charles. *Getting High: Marijuana Through the Ages*. Lanham, MD: Rowman & Littlefield Publishers, 2016.

Cramp, Arthur Joseph, ed. *Nostrums and Quackery. Vol. 2*. Chicago, IL: Press of American Medical Association, 1921.

Hari, Johann. *Chasing the Scream: The Opposite of Addiction Is Connection*. New York, NY: Bloomsbury, 2016.

Holwell, John Zephaniah. *India Tracts*. London, United Kingdom: T. Becket and PA de Hondt, 1764.

Musto, David F. *The American Disease: Origins of Narcotic Control*. New York, NY: Oxford University Press, 1999.

Sloman, Larry. *Reefer Madness: A History of Marijuana*. New York, NY: St. Martin's Griffin, 1998.

Web Resources

Aldritch, Michael, Dr. "Cannabis Roots: The Hidden History of Marijuana." PotTVNetwork, YouTube. November 21, 2012. Accessed July 5, 2018. youtube.com/watch?v=5389jBtf-yQ&list=WL&index=13

Alsop, Julia. "Without Early AIDS Patients, the Medical Marijuana Movement Wouldn't Exist." Vice. October 2, 2016. Accessed July 5, 2018. vice.com/en_us/article/nnke57/without-early-aids-patients-the-medical-marijuana-movement-wouldnt-exist

"American Medical Association (AMA) Biography." Should Marijuana Be a Medical Option? Accessed July 5, 2018. medicalmarijuana.procon.org/view.source.php?sourceID=000134

"Balm of America: Patent Medicine Collection." National Museum of American History. Accessed July 5, 2018. americanhistory.si.edu/collections/object-groups/balm-of-america-patent-medicine-collection?ogmt_page=balm-of-america-history

Barkan, Ilyse D. "Industry Invites Regulation: The Passage of the Pure Food and Drug Act of 1906." *American Journal of Public Health* 75, no. 1 (1985): 18–26.

Beach, Bob. "Highlighting Race, Ignoring Motive: Science, Subjectivity, and Walter Bromberg at Bellevue." Points: The Blog of the Alcohol & Drugs History Society. August 11, 2016. Accessed July 5, 2018. pointsadhsblog.wordpress.com/2016/08/11/highlighting-race-ignoring-motive-science-subjectivity-and-walter-bromberg-at-bellevue

Berman, Eliza. "What the Panic Over Pot Looked Like in 1967." *Time*. Accessed July 5, 2018. time.com/3825484/pot-panic-1960s/

Blackwell, Fritz. "The British Impact on India, 1700–1900." *Education About Asia* 13, no. 2 (2008). Accessed July 5, 2018. aas2.asian-studies.org/EAA/EAA-Archives/13/2/800.pdf

Cannabis Culture. Accessed July 5, 2018. cannabisculture.com

Chasteen, John Charles. "How Mexican 'Herbolarias' Transformed Hemp into Psychoactive Marijuana." Leafly. February 7, 2016. Accessed July 5, 2018. leafly.com/news/cannabis-101/how-hemp-became-psychoactive-marijuana-in-mexico

CNN. "CNN: 1986: Nancy Reagan's 'Just Say No' Campaign." YouTube. February 28, 2011. Accessed July 5, 2018. youtube.com/watch?v=IQXgVM30mlY

DRCNet Online Library of Drug Policy. Accessed July 5, 2018. druglibrary.net

Eastland, James O. "Marihuana-Hashish Epidemic and Its Impact on United States Security: Hearings Before the Subcommittee to Investigate the Administration of the Internal Security Act and Other Internal Security Laws of the Committee on the Judiciary, United States Senate, Ninety-third Congress, Second Session." The Internet Archive. Accessed July 5, 2018. archive.org/stream/marihuanahashish00unit/marihuanahashish00unit_djvu.txt

Glass, Andrew. "Pure Food and Drug Act Passes." June 23, 2014. Accessed July 5, 2018. politico.com/story/2014/06/fda-theodore-roosevelt-108164

"Gold Artifacts Tell Tale of Drug-Fueled Rituals and 'Bastard Wars.'" National Geographic. May 22, 2015. Accessed July 5, 2018. news.nationalgeographic.com/2015/05/150522-scythians-marijuana-bastard-wars-kurgan-archaeology

Guzzo, Paul. "Gruesome Ybor Murder Was Backbone for Anti-Marijuana Campaign." TBO. August 17, 2013. Accessed July 5, 2018. tbo.com/news/gruesome-ybor-murder-was-backbone-for-anti-marijuana-campaign-20130817/

Hanson, Hilary. "Nixon Aide Reportedly Admitted Drug War Was Meant to Target Black People." The Huffington Post. January 3, 2017. Accessed July 5, 2018. huffingtonpost.com/entry/nixon-drug-war-racist_us_56f16a0ae4b03a640a6bbda1

Hari, Johann, Jeff Greenfield, John McKay, Joyce Vance, Norman Eisen, and Ben Schreckinger. "The Hunting of Billie Holiday." About Us. January 17, 2015. Accessed July 5, 2018. politico.com/magazine/story/2015/01/drug-war-the-hunting-of-billie-holiday-114298

"Harry S. Truman: Executive Order 10302—Interdepartmental Committee on Narcotics, November 2, 1951." The American Presidency Project. Accessed July 5, 2018. presidency.ucsb.edu/ws/?pid=78436

"History of Cannabis in India." *Psychology Today*. Accessed July 5, 2018. psychologytoday. com/us/blog/the-teenage-mind/201106/history-cannabis-in-india

"How Did Marijuana Become Illegal in the First Place?" Drug Policy Alliance. Accessed July 5, 2018. drugpolicy.org/blog/how-did-marijuana-become-illegal-first-place

Kaul, Chandrika, Dr. "From Empire to Independence: The British Raj in India 1858–1947." BBC. March 3, 2011. Accessed July 5, 2018. bbc.co.uk/history/british/modern/independence1947_01.shtml

Kennedy, Paul P. "Nearly 500 Seized in Narcotics Raids Across the Nation." *New York Times*. January 5, 1952. Accessed July 5, 2018. nytimes.com/1952/01/05/archives/nearly-500-seized-in-narcotics-raids-across-the-nation-arrests-here.html

"LaGuardia Committee Report on Marihuana (1944) Biography." Accessed July 5, 2018. medicalmarijuana.procon.org/view.source.php?sourceID=005934

"Leary v. United States." Supreme Court of the United States, 1969. Google Scholar. Accessed July 5, 2018. scholar.google.com/scholar_case?case=2456490274118138895&hl=en&as_sdt=6&as_vis=1&oi=scholarr

Malmo-Levine, David. "Human and Cannabis Coevolution." Cannabis Culture. May 2, 2009. Accessed July 5, 2018. cannabisculture.com/content/2009/04/24/human-and-cannabis-coevolution

"Marijuana: Medical Papers (1839–1972)." Research Findings on Medicinal Properties of Marijuana. Accessed July 5, 2018. marijuanalibrary.org/Dr_Mikuriya.html

"Mayor Fiorello La Guardia Slams Federal Drug War (1939–1944)." Janos.nyc. April 21, 2015. Accessed July 5, 2018. janos.nyc/2015/04/20/mayor-fiorello-la-guardia-first-american-politician-to-study-marijuana

McDonald, David. "The Racist Roots of Marijuana Prohibition | David McDonald." Foundation for Economic Education. April 11, 2017. Accessed July 5, 2018. fee.org/articles/the-racist-roots-of-marijuana-prohibition/

"Music: The Weed." Time. July 19, 1943. Accessed July 5, 2018. content.time.com/time/subscriber/article/0,33009,777874,00.html

Musto, David F., Dr. Interview. PBS, Frontline. Accessed July 5, 2018. pbs.org/wgbh/pages/frontline/shows/dope/interviews/musto.html

"Nancy Reagan On Diff'rent Strokes." NBC. Internet Archive. April 30, 1983. Accessed July 5, 2018. archive.org/details/nancyreagandiffrentstrokes

Nelson, Shasta. "I'm a Friend of Dennis." *DOPE Magazine*. June 16, 2017. Accessed July 5, 2018. dopemagazine.com/im-friend-dennis-patron-saint-peron

Schlosser, Eric. "Reefer Madness." *The Atlantic*. August, 1994. Accessed July 5, 2018. theatlantic.com/magazine/archive/1994/08/reefer-madness/303476

"Timeline: The Use of Cannabis." Panorama, BBC News. June 16, 2005. Accessed July 5, 2018. news.bbc.co.uk/2/hi/programmes/panorama/4079668.stm

PRØHBTD. Accessed July 5, 2018. prohbtd.com

"Prohibition '37: Anslinger's Testimony." Anderson Valley Advertiser. May 1, 2013. Accessed July 5, 2018. theava.com/archives/21703

"Richard Nixon: Remarks on Signing the Comprehensive Drug Abuse Prevention and Control Act of 1970." October 27, 1970. The American Presidency Project. Accessed July 5, 2018. presidency.ucsb.edu/ws/?pid=2767

"Samudra Manthan." All About Hinduism. February 27, 2013. Accessed July 5, 2018. allabouthinduism.info/2013/02/27/samudra-manthan

"The Churning of the Ocean." Sanatan Society. Accessed July 5, 2018. sanatansociety. org/indian_epics_and_stories/the_churning_of_the_ocean.htm#.w0oml1zkjuj

"The Illegalization of Marijuana: A Brief History." Origins: Current Events in Historical Perspective. Accessed July 5, 2018. origins.osu.edu/article/illegalization-marijuana-brief-history.

The National Organization for the Reform of Marijuana Laws. Accessed July 5, 2018. norml.org

"The UN Drug Control Conventions." Transnational Institute. October 8, 2015. Accessed July 5, 2018. tni.org/en/publication/the-un-drug-control-conventions#box1

Thompson, Matt. "The Mysterious History of 'Marijuana.'" NPR. July 22, 2013. Accessed July 5, 2018. npr.org/sections/codeswitch/2013/07/14/201981025/the-mysterious-history-of-marijuana

"Understanding the Differences Between Hemp and Cannabis." Health Benefits of Medical Marijuana, Cannabis 101. July 13, 2017. Accessed July 5, 2018. medicaljane. com/2015/01/14/the-differences-between-hemp-and-cannabis

United Nations Office on Drugs and Crime. Accessed July 5, 2018. unodc.org

Wishnia, Steven. "Debunking the Hemp Conspiracy Theory." Alternet. Accessed July 5, 2018. alternet.org/story/77339/debunking_the_hemp_conspiracy_theory

Wood, Michael. "The Story of the Conquistadors." BBC. March 29, 2011. Accessed July 5, 2018. bbc.co.uk/history/british/tudors/conquistadors_01.shtml

Zielinski, Graeme. "Activist Robert C. Randall Dies." Washington Post. June 8, 2001. Accessed July 5, 2018. washingtonpost.com/archive/local/2001/06/08/activist-robert-c-randall-dies/c6e832a4-55e2-47fc-a3c8-5e011da66e04/?noredirect=on&utm_term=.1851e826e67e

Zutshi, Chitralekha. "Debating the Past: Academic and Popular Histories in India." Perspectives on History, American Historical Association. Accessed July 5, 2018. historians.org/publications-and-directories/perspectives-on-history/december-2009/debating-the-past-academic-and-popular-histories-in-india